Cult places and cultural change in Republican Italy

A CONTEXTUAL APPROACH TO RELIGIOUS ASPECTS OF RURAL SOCIETY AFTER THE ROMAN CONQUEST

TESSE D. STEK

AMSTERDAM UNIVERSITY PRESS

This book meets the requirements of ISO 9706: 1994, Information and documentation – Paper for documents – Requirements for permanence.

Cover illustration: courtesy of the Archivio Fotografico della Scuola di Specializzazione in Archeologia di Matera.
Cover design: Kok Korpershoek, Amsterdam
Lay-out: Bert Brouwenstijn, Grafisch Ontwerp Almere

ISBN   978 90 8964 177 9
e-ISBN   978 90 4851 143 3
NUR   682

© Tesse Stek / Amsterdam University Press, Amsterdam, 2009

All rights reserved. Without limiting the rights under copyright reserved above, no part of this book may be reproduced, stored in or introduced into a retrieval system, or transmitted, in any form or by any means (electronic, mechanical, photocopying, recording, or otherwise), without the written permission of both the copyright owner and the editors of this book.

CONTENTS

ACKNOWLEDGEMENTS IX

INTRODUCTION 1

1   ROME AND ITALY: IDEAS ON CULTURAL CHANGE 9
1.1   Early Roman cultural dominance 10
1.2   Two objections: historiographical constructs and the mechanism of self-romanisation 11
1.3   Conclusion: deconstruction and new perspectives 15

2   'RELIGIOUS ROMANISATION' AND THE FATE OF ITALIC RURAL SANCTUARIES 17
2.1   Rome in Italy: modes of intervention and the role of colonies 18
    2.1.1   Non-intervention as a policy and its exceptions 18
    2.1.2   The *senatusconsultum de Bacchanalibus* 19
    2.1.3   Colonies and cults 21
2.2   The fate of Italic sanctuaries: destruction, desolation and colonisation 28
    2.2.1   Did Rome close sanctuaries? 28
    2.2.2   Sanctuary, cult and community in warfare 29
    2.2.3   The decline and incorporation of rural sanctuaries after the Social War 32
2.3   Conclusion: urbanity and the unaffected countryside 33

3   SAMNIUM: THE SACRED CONSTRUCTION OF COMMUNITY AND ARCHITECTURAL FORMS 35
3.1   Samnium: research history 35
    3.1.1   Modern and ancient views 36
    3.1.2   Economy and patterns of settlement 37
3.2   Samnite sanctuaries: new forms and tradition 39
3.3   Monumentalisation: wealth, politics and architectural forms 44
    3.3.1   Wealth 44
    3.3.2   Politics 46
    3.3.3   Style: 'external' cultural elements and models 48
    3.3.4   Traditionalism in Samnite sanctuaries? 51
3.4   Conclusion: the construction of community 52

4   LOCATION AND FUNCTION OF ITALIC SANCTUARIES IN SOCIETY: THREE MODELS 53
4.1   Transhumance: sanctuaries, Hercules and '*tratturi*' 55
4.2   Sanctuaries as territorial markers 58
4.3   Sanctuaries and the so-called *pagus-vicus* system 65
    4.3.1   Samnite settlement and the *pagus-vicus* system: an 'immemorial Italic institution' 66
    4.3.2   The role of sanctuaries within the *pagus-vicus* system 68
    4.3.3   The rise and fall of rural sanctuaries between *pagus-vicus* system and municipalisation 74
4.4   Conclusion: between images and evidence 76

5	**LANDSCAPES OF THE SACRED: CONTEXTUALISING THE SAMNITE SANCTUARY OF S. GIOVANNI IN GALDO, COLLE RIMONTATO (CB)**	79
5.1	Research approach and methodology	80
	5.1.1 Choosing the sanctuary of S. Giovanni in Galdo and previous research	80
5.2	Problem-oriented field survey: the sacred landscape project survey (2004, 2005)	82
	5.2.1 Survey methodology	83
	5.2.2 Results	86
5.3	The excavation data (*Soprintendenza per i Beni Archeologici del Molise*, 1974-1976)	96
	5.3.1 Black gloss	97
	5.3.2 Italian terra sigillata	100
	5.3.3 African Red Slip	102
	5.3.4 Other finds	102
5.4	Conclusion: a rural community around the sanctuary	104
6	**ROMAN SACRED LANDSCAPES? THE PAGUS-VICUS SYSTEM REVISED**	107
6.1	The *pagus*: "*die uritalische siedlungsform*"?	108
	6.1.1 Rome	109
	6.1.2 Capua	110
	6.1.3 Pre-Roman names of *pagi*	110
6.2	The *pagus*: a Roman invention?	111
6.3	The pre-Roman or Roman *vicus*	112
	6.3.1 Archaeology	113
	6.3.2 Literary sources: Festus 502-508L	113
	6.3.3 The *vicus* as an 'anti-urban' and non-Roman institution (Capogrossi Colognesi)	115
	6.3.4 The *vicus* as a Roman, urban feature (Tarpin)	116
	6.3.5 Evaluation I: The *vicus* as a Roman, urban feature	118
	6.3.6 Evaluation II: The *vicus* as an 'anti-urban' and non-Roman institution	118
6.4	The relationship between *pagus* and *vicus*	120
6.5	Conclusion: new perspectives on *pagus* and *vicus*	120
7	**CULT AND COLONISATION: PAGI, VICI AND SANCTUARIES**	123
7.1	*Pagi* and *vici* in sanctuaries and cults	125
7.2	*Pagus* and temple at Castel di Ieri: Capitoline aspirations?	129
7.3	Colonies, *pagi* and *vici* and the example of Ariminum	133
	7.3.1 Roman urban 'mimic': the Roman urban model copied in colonial urban centres?	133
	7.3.2 The possibility of early rural Roman *vici* near Latin colonies	135
	7.3.3 A hypothetical example: *pocola deorum* and the Ariminate *vici* and *pagi*	138
7.4	Rural *vici* and sanctuaries in the *ager Praetutianus*	146
	Località Piano Vomano – Colle del Vento	147
	Località Case Lanciotti-Masseria Nisii (Comune di Montorio al Vomano)	147
	Pagliaroli (Comune di Cortino)	148
	Collina di S. Berardino	148
	The *vicus Strament(arius)* or *Strament(icius)*	148
	Contrada S. Rustico (Comune di Basciano)	148
	Cellino Vecchio, loc. Valviano, Case Carnevale (Comune di Cellino Attanasio)	151
	Vico-Ornano (Comune di Colledara)	151
	Colle S. Giorgio (Comune di Castiglione Messer Raimondo)	151
7.5	The rural *vici* near the Fucine lake	154

		The *Aninus vecus* or *vicus Aninus*	154
		The *vicus Petinus*	155
		The *vicus F(i)staniensis*	156
		The '*vicus*' of Spineto, Colle Mariano	157
		The *vecos supinas* or *vicus Supinum* and its sanctuaries	158
7.6		Conclusion: *vici*, *pagi*, sanctuaries and 'new communities'	168

8 ROMAN RITUAL IN THE ITALIAN COUNTRYSIDE? THE PAGANALIA AND THE LUSTRATIO PAGI — 171

8.1	*Pagus* and *Paganalia*: between rusticity and administrative control	171
	8.1.1 *Paganalia*, *Sementivae*, and *lustratio pagi*	173
	8.1.2 The *Paganalia* according to Dionysius of Halicarnassus	175
	8.1.3 Rustic images of administrative control	177
8.2	*Lustratio pagi* and *Paganalia* in Italy outside Rome	177
	8.2.1 The location of the festival	178
	8.2.2 *Lustratio pagi*	178
	8.2.3 The payment for the rituals and *thesauri*	180
8.3	Conclusion: the ritual definition of new communities	184

9 ROMAN RITUAL IN THE ITALIAN COUNTRYSIDE? THE COMPITALIA AND THE SHRINES OF THE LARES COMPITALES — 187

9.1	The *Compitalia*: a paradoxical picture	187
	9.1.1 The festival of the *Compitalia*	188
9.2	Private and public: an integrative cult	190
	9.2.1 'Private': a family affair?	190
	9.2.2 'Public': the origin of the *Compitalia* according to Dionysius of Halicarnassus	191
	9.2.3 *Vicus* and *compitum*	194
	9.2.4 'Private' and 'public' in city and countryside	194
	9.2.5 'Public' and 'private', or integration of both?	197
9.3	The development of the *Compitalia*: from the countryside to the city or vice versa?	200
9.4	The *compitum* shrines: form and location in city and countryside	203
	9.4.1 Crossroads and shrines	203
9.5	Conclusion: Roman institutions and ritual in the Italian countryside	212

10 CONCLUSIONS — 213

ABBREVIATIONS — 223

BIBLIOGRAPHY — 227

INDEX — 257

Acknowledgements

This study is based on my PhD thesis which was accepted in 2008 at the University of Amsterdam. Only minor changes have been made to the original texts and illustrations. I should like to express my gratitude to all those who have contributed to my research and this study. First of all I wish to thank my promotores prof. Marijke Gnade and prof. Eric Moormann. I also thank prof. Peter Attema, prof. Gianfranco de Benedittis, prof. Herman Brijder, prof. Emmanuele Curti, prof. Massimo Osanna, prof. Harm Pinkster, prof. Maria Josè Strazzulla, prof. Gianluca Tagliamonte, prof. Henk Versnel and prof. Douwe Yntema who contributed in various ways to aspects of this study.

Much of this research was carried out in Italy. The *Soprintendenza per i Beni Archeologici del Molise* has always shown the greatest interest and willingness to cooperate and has facilitated both the field work and the re-study of their excavation finds in all possible ways. I thank therefore dott.ssa Stefania Capini and dott. Mario Pagano, who have been responsible as *Soprintendente* for our permissions, as well as dott.ssa Valeria Ceglia and dott.ssa Cristiana Terzani. In particular, I am thankful to dott.ssa Angela di Niro, responsible for the excavations of the sanctuary of S. Giovanni in Galdo, Colle Rimontato and our principal contact person at the *Soprintendenza*, for her continuous support and assistance. Moreover, this fieldwork could not have been done without the support of the *Comune* of S. Giovanni in Galdo, and I am greatly indebted to the mayor Mr. Eugenio Fiorilli for providing housing for our research groups on several occasions. Furthermore, I wish to express my gratitude to all inhabitants of S. Giovanni in Galdo and especially the owners of the fields we investigated, who have remained surprisingly friendly, welcoming and informative when confronted with groups of students trampling their fields, heartily giving us oil, wine and fruits from their lands.

The Royal Dutch Institute in Rome (*KNIR; Istituto Olandese*) has facilitated my research project greatly; several grants from the Institute enabled me to work over longer periods in the libraries of Rome and to present the results to an international audience on various occasions, and I am especially grateful to the respective directors of Ancient Studies, dr. Nathalie de Haan and dr. Gert-Jan Burgers. I also wish to express my appreciation to the staff of the *Deutsches Archäologisches Institut Rom*, the British School at Rome, the *École française de Rome* and the *Istituto Regionale per gli Studi del Molise* at Campobasso.

In the field surveys many people have been involved. Special thanks are due to my friend and colleague Jeremia Pelgrom; we planned and directed the field survey campaigns around the sanctuary of S. Giovanni in Galdo together and he has been a prime intellectual sparring partner throughout my research. Also Ellen Thiermann and Jitte Waagen have been invaluable for the project. Moreover, the cooperation of Michele Roccia in the initial phase of the project has been very important. The teams we have worked with were wonderful; I thank Antonio Bruscella, Vanessa D'Orazio, Sandra Fatica, Miko Flohr, Michele Fratino, Marie-Catherine Houkes, Rogier Kalkers, Martijn Kalkwarf, Karel-Jan Kerckhaert, Francesca Laera, Debora Lagatta, Antonella Lepone, Muriel Louwaard, Antje van Oosten, Bruno Sardella, Laura Stek, Barbara Valiante, Jolande Vos, Heleen de Vries, Jeroen Weterings, and Neelson Witte. During the study of the excavation finds, Anneke Dekker, Laura Hoff, Francesca Laera, Alma Reijling, Ilona Steijven, and Alessandra Zaccardi made up a formidable team. I am furthermore grateful to Fulvio Coletti and Jeltsje Stobbe for their advice with regard to the black gloss ceramics. Precious comments upon parts of the texts were given by Jan Theo Bakker, Eva-Maria Lackner, Antonella Lepone, Jeremia Pelgrom, Benjamin Rous, Jamie Sewell, Jeltsje Stobbe, Ellen Thiermann, Nicola Tien, Jetze Touber and Anne Versloot.

The research itself and the publication of this book were only possible thanks to the support of several organisations. The Institute of Culture and History of the Faculty of Humanities of the University of Amsterdam (*ICG*) funded my post as PhD student, whereas the field projects were funded mainly with grants from the Netherlands Organisation for Scientific Research (*NWO*), and additionally by the *ICG*, Leiden University, the *Stichting Philologisch Studiefonds Utrecht*, and Mrs. A.M. Kalmeijer (Rijswijk). Mrs. Kalmeijer also generously contributed towards the cost of preparing the texts and illustrations for printing, along with the *Hendrik Muller's Vaderlandsch Fonds*. I thank Bert Brouwenstijn for the lay-out and illustrations, which were in part originally produced by Jitte Waagen (the GIS part in Chapter 5) and René Reijnen (line illustrations). The cover illustration was kindly provided by Prof. Massimo Osanna. The English text was revised by Heather van Tress and Isabelle Vella Gregory. Finally, thanks are due to the editorial board of Amsterdam Archaeological Studies for their willingness to include this book in their series.

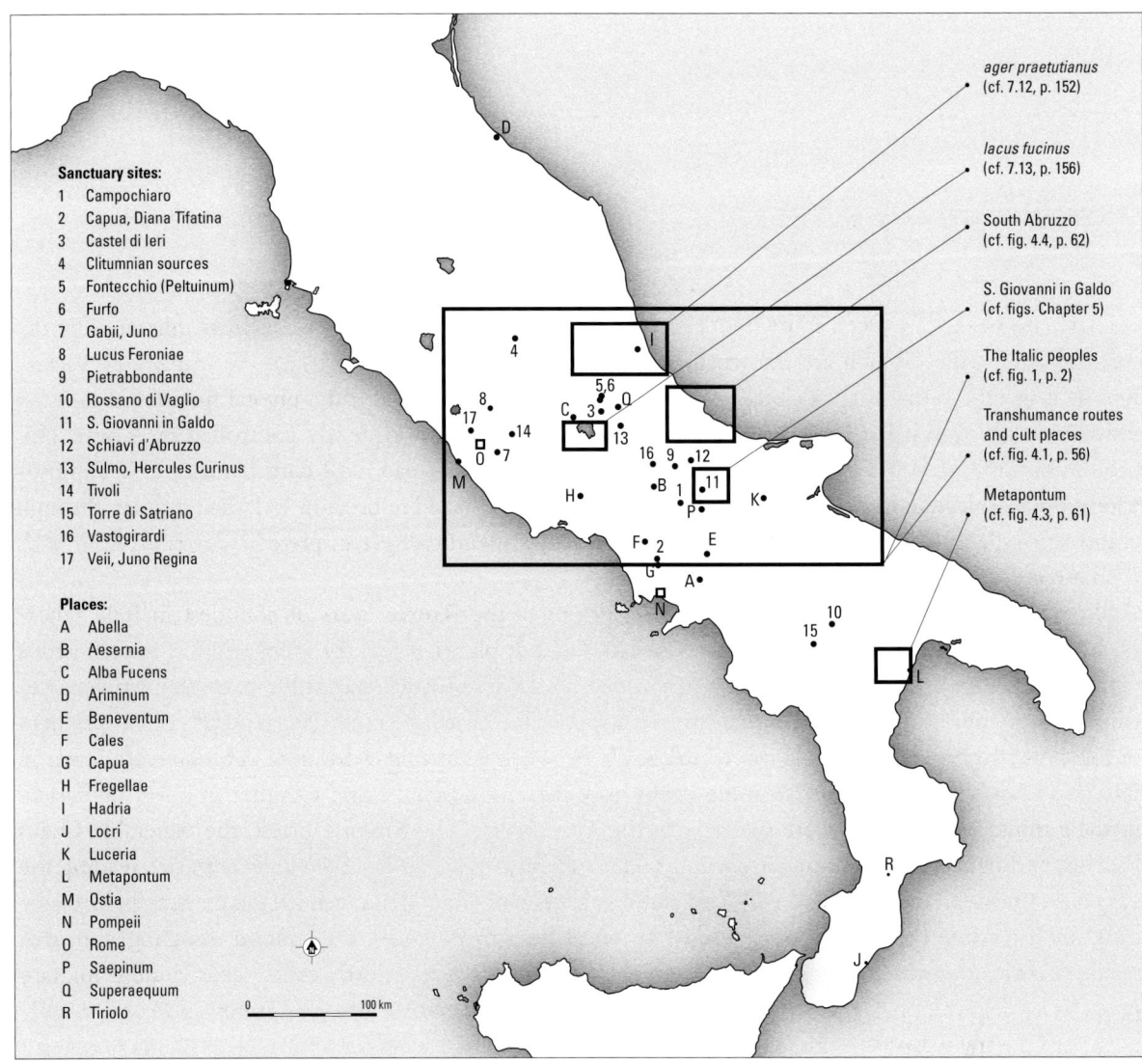

Map of Italy showing some of the major places and sanctuaries mentioned in the text.

Introduction

Central-southern Italy faced immense changes in the last four centuries BC. The areas inhabited by the various 'Italic tribes' which are known to us from the ancient sources (fig. 1), were initially characterised by a specific non-urban societal organisation, in which sanctuaries had a pivotal function. From the fourth century onwards, the area was gradually conquered and subsequently controlled by Rome. This profoundly uprooted the geopolitical make-up of Italy. Not only had local communities to accommodate Roman rule, but also new Roman communities were installed in previously Italic territory through colonisation. In this period of change and conflict, religion and cult places played a central role in both Roman and Italic communities.

This role comes clearly to the fore in descriptions of the Roman wars of conquest in Italy, where ancient Roman writers highlight religious rituals and cult places as foci for ideological as well as actual combat. Italic rituals and cult places are presented as places of resistance against Roman authority. A notorious case in point is the ritualised formation of a special legion by the most dangerous Roman opponent of the time, the Samnites, on the eve of the battle between Roman and Samnite armies at Aquilonia in 293 BC. Livy (10.38) describes in some detail how the elite soldiers came together in a *locus consaeptus* in their military camp, and were sworn into the *legio linteata*. The Samnite priest, the venerable Ovius Paccius, performed the ceremony according to an ancient rite (*ex vetusta Samnitium religione*), reading the sacred text from an old linen book. The initiated soldiers were forced to pledge allegiance to the Samnite cause by a terrible oath; those who refused lay dead next to the altars, their blood mingling with that of the sacrificed animals. This rite, so colourfully described by Livy, clearly reinforced Samnite military strength by legitimating and codifying it with a sacred rite. Furthermore, the Samnites Pentri ritually deposited enemy weapons – amongst them Roman armour – at the central sanctuary at Pietrabbondante.

Contemporaneously, in Rome temples celebrating the victories over the Samnites started to appear.[1] Besides commemorating the deeds of the victorious generals and their *gentes*, these temples boosted the morale of the Roman community in those fearful times. Some of the gods that were introduced neatly illustrate this connection to the welfare of the state, for example *Salus* (Safety) was vowed a temple by the consul C. Junius Bubulcus during the Samnite wars, and she received her home on the Quirinal in 302 BC.[2] After the battle at Aquilonia – the Samnite oath apparently did not prevent them from losing it – T. Papirius Cursor and Sp. Carvilius Maximus returned to Rome with so much Samnite booty that the new temple of Quirinus and the forum were too small to exhibit all of it.[3]

Moreover, Rome consciously destroyed or disarmed Italic cult places – or at least so it is imagined in later myth and historiography. A good example is provided by the sanctuary of Diana Tifatina near the Campanian city of Capua, which in myth and poetry was closely connected to Capys, the heroic founder of the city. Capys was said to have kept a white deer which was dedicated to Diana and lived for thousand years from the foundation of the city onwards. In 211 BC, Q. Fulvius Flaccus besieged Capua, which had defected from Rome in this critical period. Before the city was taken, the consul sacrificed the holy deer:[4] by doing so, the Roman general symbolically destroyed the Capuan community even

---

[1] Until 273 BC, at least eight temples were erected in honour of victories *de Samnitibus*.

[2] Liv. 9.43.25; Liv. 10.1.7-9.

[3] Liv. 10.46.

[4] Sil. *Pun.* 13.115-137; cf. Chapter 2.

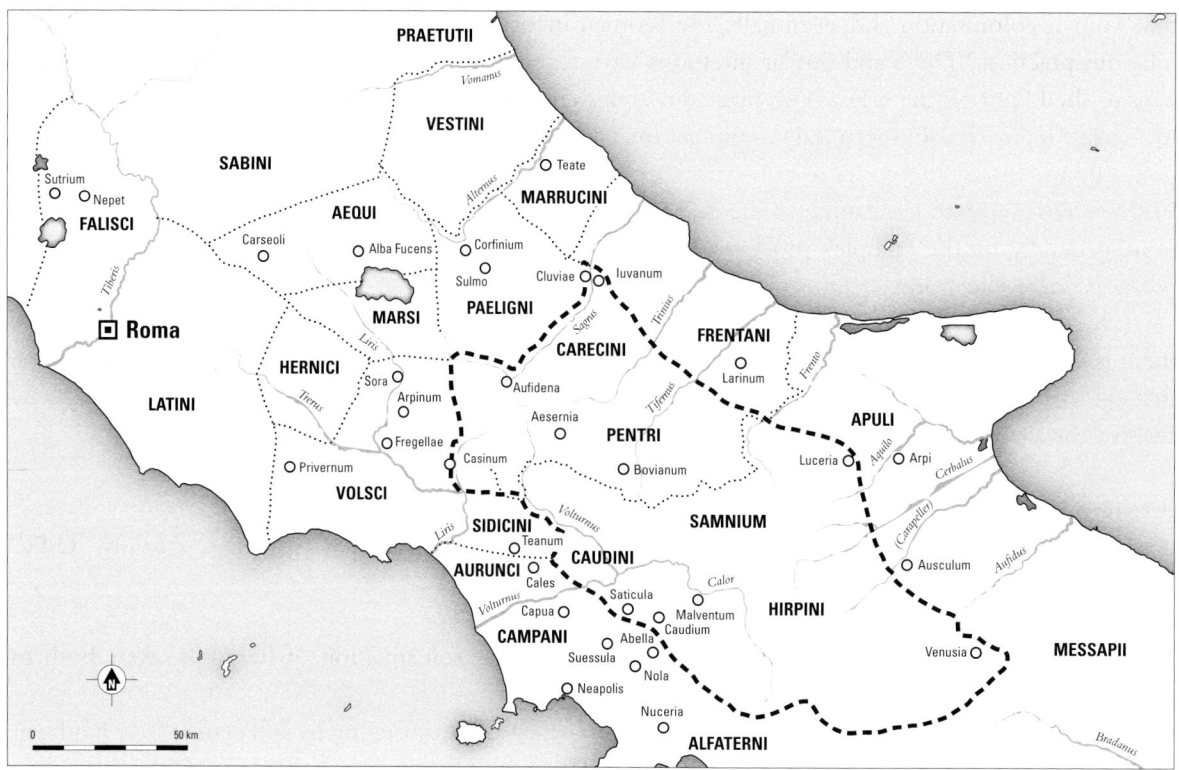

Fig. 1. The Italic peoples that according to the sources inhabited ancient Italy (adapted from Salmon 1967, 25, pl. 1).

before its actual military submission. Similarly, enemy gods could be summoned away from their cities by promising them a temple in the victorious city of Rome. Such a fate would, according to Livy (5.21–22), have befallen Juno Regina during the capture of the Etruscan city of Veii in 396 BC.

From the pacification of Italy onwards however, Italic cult and religion vanish from our sight. When Italic cults and religious practices eventually resurface in texts referring to the imperial period, the situation could not be more different: under the early empire, Italian countryside religion is exalted in poetry and art and portrayed as true and pure in its uncontaminated, traditional quality. Images of rustic and frugal Italic religion abound in wall-paintings, poems and literature, and some Italic cult places even gain in popularity under the empire: this all forms part of 'Roman religion' now. The process in between warfare and harmony, however, remains difficult to grasp with the given scarcity of literary sources.

Although the literary sources for this period are silent, the archaeological record is rich. The remains of innumerable sanctuaries lie dotted over the modern landscapes of central-southern Italy, demonstrating the importance of cult places in especially the third to early first centuries BC. As a matter of fact, sanctuaries appear to have been the prime focus of embellishment and monumentalisation in this period, leaving other public, domestic and funeral sites far behind. Even in the non- or scarcely urbanised areas of Apennine and Adriatic Italy, splendid monumental complexes with elaborate architectural decorations were erected, many of which can still be seen *in situ*, whereas others are attested by inscriptions. This raises several questions. Why was so much invested in rural cult places, far from any urban settlement?[5] And by whom? Why precisely in this period of growing Roman pressure; and how does their appearance relate to Roman political and cultural models? Did 'Rome' have anything to do with it at all? How

---

[5] For the definition of urban, cf. e.g. Osborne/Cunliffe 2005; for definitions of rural, extra-urban, non-urban etc. cult places see e.g. Edlund-Berry 1987 and here Chapter 4.

did Roman colonisation and, eventually, the Roman incorporation of these areas affect cult places and religious practices? These and similar questions have formed the point of departure of this study, which aims to shed light on the role of cult places and religion in the social, cultural and political processes that took place in central-southern Italy in the last four centuries BC. To this end, it investigates the social and political function of cult places in non-urban society and how this role changed under Roman influence. In this way, it seeks to contribute to the debate on the Roman impact on Italic religious structures, and more generally, on the complex processes of change and accommodation that Italy witnessed as a result of the Roman expansion.

In light of several provocative contributions in the last ten years to the 'romanisation' debate, I think there is also room and indeed need for a (re-)analysis of some of the sacred aspects. Indeed, I will argue that cult places and religious rituals, in their role as focal points for ancient communities, played crucial roles in the developments and discourses set off or triggered by the Roman conquest.

ROMANISATION, CULT PLACES AND THE CONSTRUCTION OF COMMUNITY

This view is inspired by the recent course the debate on the romanisation of Italy has taken, both in historical-interpretive and in theoretical respects (Chapter 1).

As to the first, in recent times scholarship on the history and historiography of Roman Italy has been revolutionised under the influence of postmodern and postcolonialist thought. Indeed, the latter half of the previous century witnessed a turn from a plainly Romanocentric and colonialist perspective to another radical position, which puts the 'indigenous' perspective at the centre. Some studies have implemented this new orthodoxy *in extremis*, and have combined postcolonial (or, perhaps, anti-colonial) theoretical assumptions with radical 'deconstruction' of the literary accounts. In the traditional framework, sovereign Italic tribes would have populated the peninsula up to the fifth or fourth centuries, until in the fourth and third centuries BC these early ethnic groups were uprooted as a consequence of Roman expansion and colonisation. During the third and second centuries BC the Italic population would have been enticed to assimilate themselves to Roman standards, or did so spontaneously. In this view, bestowing the Roman citizenship on all Italian allies after the Social War (91–88 BC) merely made official the 'Roman Italy' that was already long underway.

More recent studies in the postcolonial tradition have tried to deconstruct the idea of an already deeply romanised Italy in the third and second centuries BC. This has sometimes been successful, indeed scholars of the generation of Theodor Mommsen had been suspiciously eager to conceptualise a cultural and political convergence of Rome and Italy already from the third century BC onwards. In particular, the important work by Henrik Mouritsen has shown that these nationalist ideas persist in modern scholarship.[6] In this line of thought, revisionist studies have emphasised the cultural and political sovereignty of Italic communities prior to the definitive incorporation after the Social War. Only then would Italic communities have lost their political and cultural independence, indeed resulting in a 'Roman Italy'. There are several objections to parts of the revisionist view, especially the undervaluation of Roman impact and strategies. Indeed, in reaction to the traditional view, this line of thought might have swung a bit too far to the other extreme. Nonetheless, the critique on the modern view of a culturally 'romanised Italy' in the third and second centuries BC holds true.

The importance of this deconstruction can hardly be overestimated because it frees us from persistent frames of thought that have, for more than a century and to a considerable degree, determined the

---

[6] Mouritsen 1998.

interpretation of the historical and archaeological evidence. In my view, one of the most important points raised by this debate is indeed that we should try to abandon general interpretive frameworks that accept cultural assimilation as a logical consequence of (or prerogative for) long-term historical developments that only can be appreciated as such by hindsight.

Combined with a second development, that of the general theoretical debate on romanisation, a clear outline for an approach focused on cult places and religion presents itself. In general, recent romanisation studies have, in the wake of interpretive archaeology, recognised the pivotal role of religion and ideology in the processes of negotiation and accommodation set in motion in native societies when confronted with a new political order.[7] More specifically, numerous recent studies on the subject show that the social and cultural processes involved are primarily to be understood as active creations or 'constructions' of specific communities in specific historical circumstances and with very specific goals.[8] As a result, these processes and their outcomes may have varied considerably from place to place and from time to time. There are several ways in which the ancient communities of Italy could define or redefine themselves when faced with the changed order after the Roman conquest. As anthropological and sociological studies have amply demonstrated however, in particular cult and religion play central roles in such processes. It is in effect a common historical phenomenon that especially in times of stress or structural changes, the ritual and religious 'anchors' and boundaries of communities are enhanced, or indeed, invented.[9] In this way, cult places and religious rituals can become strong symbols for defining and legitimating the position of communities old and new. Crucially, this centrality of cult places and religion for the ancient communities of Italy is also attested by the ancient literary sources, as we have just seen for instance in the cases of Samnium, Rome and Capua, showing that this approach can reasonably resist the accusation of anachronism.

This notion of centrality, in my view, justifies trying to approach the changing attitudes and self-definitions of both Italic and Roman communities through an analysis of the sacred dimensions. It also follows from these considerations that one should refrain from trying to develop from the outset an integrated view on the 'romanisation process' in the regions under study; and such has indeed explicitly not been the aim of this study. As a matter of fact, from the perspective outlined above, 'romanisation' is not so much a *process* to be understood in a single model or theory, but could rather be seen as an interesting and, notwithstanding recent assertions to the contrary, relevant research *question* that can serve as a point of departure for further investigation in single historical instances. By adopting or developing a defined generalised theory about the course or mechanism of the process at the start of investigation, one risks answering the question prior to analysis. In this study, I have therefore opted for a contextualised 'bottom-up' approach to single and particular historical situations, in each of which the role of cult places and religion for the ancient communities involved is investigated. Admittedly, this of course presupposes a specific conception of the process too, but at least the outcome is open and dependent on every local course of events. This point of departure, moreover, enables overcoming easy dichotomies like 'Roman' vs. 'Italic', because it investigates the local and specific ways in which these and other identities could be built up.

---

[7] E.g. Metzler *et al.* 1995; Roymans 1996; Derks 1998.

[8] E.g. Terrenato 1998a; Terrenato 1998b; Terrenato 2001; Van Dommelen 2001; Van Dommelen/Terrenato 2007.

[9] Esp. Cohen 1985; cf. Graves-Brown *et al.* 1996; Hobsbawm/Ranger 1983.

IDEAS ON THE RELIGIOUS ROMANISATION OF ITALY

From this background, this study seeks to contribute to the modern debate on the 'religious romanisation' of Italy. Although the debate about the role of cult places and religion has its own momentum and is, for various historical reasons, not directly consonant with the development of general romanisation studies, parallels can be drawn (Chapter 2). The basic idea has long been that as a rule Rome did not interfere in the religious affairs of conquered territories. The only factor of some significance in the spread of Roman religious models has generally been recognised in the newly installed Roman and Latin colonies. In these colonial foundations, rituals and cults echoing those of the *Urbs* would have expressed allegiance to the mother city; the installation of *Capitolium* temples would be a prime example of this. The countryside and allied territories would have remained largely unaffected. An indirect effect has been presumed however: Roman architectural and/or religious models (or Hellenistic ones, spread through mediation by Rome) are thought to have 'irradiated' from the colonies to the Italic communities by voluntary adoption, through a process of 'self-romanisation'. In this way, for instance, specific temple plans and decorations, and also votive rituals are imagined to have spread gradually through Italy. As regards the period after the Social War, Roman influence on rural Italic sanctuaries is generally thought to have taken the form of a negative secondary effect. The cult places of old would have dwindled as a consequence of the new, Roman emphasis on urban centres. A desolate sacred countryside would therefore represent the major outcome of the 'religious romanisation' of the non-urban areas of Italy.

A central idea underlying most modern views of 'religious romanisation', both with regard to the role of colonies and the fate of rural cult places after the municipalisation, is that direct Roman influence would limit itself to cities and towns.

The view outlined above is still dominant in the scholarly discourse, and it is only recently that some critical studies have appeared that undermine elements of it. Most important in this respect is a recent development in the studies on Roman Republican colonisation, which in the wake of postcolonialism seeks to re-dimension the statist and superior character of Roman colonial foundations,[10] as well as the specific rituals that would have spread from them.[11] Since, as noted, colonies were traditionally considered as virtually the only factors of substance in the spread of Roman religion, these deconstructivist studies further reduce the Roman religious impact on the conquered areas. This tendency, therefore, at first sight appears to undermine the notion of Roman impact in the religious realm altogether.

In this study, I have tried to test, and to an extent question, some of the ideas that have been outlined above. As will become clear, I largely endorse the recent critical developments with regard to the role of colonial centres, but I will eventually offer an opposite view on the Roman impact on religious structures in the rural areas, which in my opinion was considerable.

APPROACH AND METHODS: CULT PLACES AND CONTEXTS

In light of the theoretical considerations mentioned earlier, as well as other ones I will now explain, I have approached the issue by investigating the function of sanctuaries and religious rituals in their broader societal context, rather than opting for a detailed study of sacred aspects in isolation. To this end, I have explored different ways to provide a background against which the changing function and meaning of cult places and rituals may be understood. The main focus of this study is on the spatial and functional relation of cult places to other elements in the settlement organisation. This information, I will argue, is essential for understanding their function in society at large. Chapters 3 to 7, which are devoted to this

---

[10] Esp. Bradley/Wilson 2006.   [11] Gentili 2005; Glinister 2006a.

issue and form the core of this study, present different approaches using different datasets to study the relations between cult places and the communities involved.

In Chapter 3, I start by investigating the historical and ideological contexts within which Samnite sanctuaries functioned. Besides giving an introduction on Samnite society and cult places, this chapter also illustrates the risks of narrow artefact-based analyses and demonstrates the need for broader contextualisation. Indeed, although previous studies have mainly been concerned with the material culture and especially the architectural aspects of sanctuaries, an approach based solely on architectural forms presents difficulties for answering the kinds of questions of cultural change and its meaning that I would like to approach here. This point is illustrated with the case of Pentrian Samnium, where sanctuaries such as that of Pietrabbondante, even if perhaps adopting Roman / Latial / Hellenistic architectural elements, could perfectly constitute foci of Samnite resistance against Rome. The 'resistant' function of the sanctuary complex is in this case historically and ideologically well-documented. Yet, the paradox regarding the relationship between cultural forms and ideological content is important. The point is that in the case of Pietrabbondante, for which the epigraphic and historical evidence is exceptionally eloquent, knowledge of the ideological context leads to an interpretation of the complex as a whole that stands diametrically against the interpretation that one could have given it on the basis of, for instance, the architectural plan alone.

In order to understand the function of such sanctuaries within Italic society (especially the smaller ones for which little or no literary and epigraphic evidence is at hand), the next two chapters are dedicated to the reconstruction of their spatial context, i.e. the patterns of settlement and related societal structures within which the cult places were located. Various ideas on the functioning of sanctuaries in Italic society have been put forward, and in Chapter 4 these are discussed from a historiographical perspective. I distinguish and critically examine three models, one which links cult places to transhumance routes, one which sees them as frontier markers, and one which sees them as an integral part of a specific, Italic, settlement organisation, the so-called *pagus-vicus* system (in Italian *sistema pagano-vicanico, vel sim.*). An important problem in the evaluation of these ideas is that they are mostly based on an incomplete picture of the ancient Italic landscapes. Hill-forts and sanctuaries now dominate the Apennine and Adriatic archaeological landscapes, whereas minor settlements are almost invisible. I will argue that this 'emptiness' of the landscape has significantly influenced the functional interpretation of the apparently isolated sanctuaries. In recent years, field survey research has altered the picture considerably, but in the pursuit of different research agendas, this research often took a large scale and long term perspective, which is not particularly appropriate for the functional analysis of cult places.[12] Therefore, in Chapter 5 a specific research approach for investigating the direct spatial context of sanctuaries is presented. It consists of intensive off-site field surveys (2004, 2005) around the Samnite sanctuary of S. Giovanni in Galdo, Colle Rimontato (CB) and a comparison with the finds from the excavations carried out by the *Soprintendenza per i Beni Archeologici del Molise* in the 1970s. The aim is to reconstruct the ancient landscape surrounding this Samnite temple and to provide it with a chronological depth. In this way, the ancient 'audience' of the monumental temple is tentatively reconstructed. This is directly relevant for its interpretation. As I will show, the survey permitted a reconstruction of a dense settlement pattern consisting of farms, a necropolis and a village in the environs of the small temple.

Still investigating settlement organisation, but moving from an archaeological perspective to an institutional one, in Chapter 6 I discuss the literary and epigraphic evidence for the *pagus-vicus* system. This term refers to a specific settlement organisation made up of districts and villages. Traditionally, this system is thought to have been a typical, pre-Roman Italic feature. Moreover, rural sanctuaries are thought to have occupied a prominent place in this system, because these yield inscriptions mentioning the involve-

---

[12] Esp. Barker 1995, concerned explicitly with the *longue durée*.

ment of *pagi* or *vici*. Although this system, and the role of sanctuaries in it, has been widely accepted, it needs serious rethinking. Recent studies in the institutional and juridical realm by Luigi Capogrossi Colognesi and Michel Tarpin have questioned – in different ways – both the validity of the hierarchical relation laid between *pagus* and *vicus*, and even their pre-Roman origin.[13] As a matter of fact, the institutions of *pagus* and *vicus* rather appear to have been introduced by Rome and functioned as part of the Roman administration of the territory. I will contend that this re-interpretation potentially has a significant impact on current ideas on Roman influence in rural cult places. As I will argue, it may indeed provide evidence for direct Roman religious impact outside colonial centres and other urban contexts, and provide an explanatory framework for understanding these local 'romanising' processes. In Chapter 7, the possible consequences for the interpretation of sanctuaries and cults are explored by discussing several cases for which epigraphic and archaeological evidence is most readily available. In this discussion I will draw special attention to the relation of *pagi* and *vici* and their cult places to Roman colonisation, and I will tentatively demonstrate how rural communities and colonial centres interacted on a religious level. In addition, the rural communities of *pagi* and *vici* had their own festivals, respectively the *Paganalia* and the *Compitalia*, which I discuss in Chapters 8 and 9. I suggest that these Roman festivals, which were closely related to Roman administrative control, were celebrated in the Italian countryside, possibly even re-using old Italic sanctuaries. As a result, the investigation in Chapters 6 to 9 of the institutional context leads to a significantly different understanding of rural cult places related to *pagi* and *vici*. A summary of the results and a general conclusion are offered in Chapter 10.

In this way, this study aims to bring together different methods and types of evidence in order to analyse the role of cult places within settlement organisation and institutional structures. From a methodological point of view, it demonstrates that looking at the ways in which sanctuaries were embedded in the societal organisation is indispensable for a meaningful interpretation of sanctuaries and cults and, consequently, their significance for different communities. With this approach, it is hoped that the crucial role of sanctuaries and cults in the variegated developments which followed the Roman conquest of Italy, which involved the re-formulation or establishment of both different 'Italic' and new 'Roman' communities, will be demonstrated.

[13] Capogrossi Colognesi 2002; Tarpin 2002.

1 Rome and Italy: Ideas on Cultural Change

It is under the heading of 'romanisation' that the cultural, socio-political and economic changes in Italy from, say the fourth century BC, are often discussed. This concept of romanisation, which was first developed in the 19th and early 20th centuries, has in turn shaped modern ways of thinking about ancient Italy and has also structured the interpretation of the historical and archaeological data. Clearly, this situation runs the risk of falling prey to circular reasoning. Romanisation has been discussed more than extensively in the last decades,[1] and only aspects that are directly relevant to the next chapters are briefly presented here.[2] Rather than seeking to adopt or develop an a priori, specific theoretical model of romanisation, this short chapter serves mainly to provide a historical background against which the position adopted in this study, in which the active role of communities in constructing and defining themselves stands central, should be understood.

When discussing ideas on the Roman impact on Italy, it is in the first place important to note that the romanisation debate has been strongly dominated by an Anglo-Saxon oriented community of researchers working especially in the north-western provinces and that the debate on the romanisation of Italy has taken a specific course due to different academic traditions, with differing research questions and approaches. In the debate on the north-western provinces, a clear development of theoretical stances can be recognised and directly be related to contemporaneous political and academic developments and theories. Firmly embedded in colonialist ideology, the term romanisation was first used in a positive sense and was indeed thought to lead to the 'betterment and happiness' of the conquered peoples, which of course closely aligns with contemporary ideas about colonialism and the European civilising mission.[3] Although this basic notion lasted for a long period during the 20th century, from the 1970s onwards, under the influence of New Archaeology, theoretical and methodological models such as acculturation theory, world-systems theory, and various others were sought to provide more 'scientific' explanations for the adoption of Roman material culture by natives. Pretty soon, however, this paradigm was overturned by interpretive or postprocessual approaches, emphasing the role of ideology and symbolism in the process of adoption.[4] By contrast, the debate on and in Italy has been characterised from the outset by a strong idealist and humanistic tradition and only recently found some common ground with the more theoretically oriented studies developed in the Anglo-Saxon world.[5] Indeed, whereas New Archaeology has had little impact on classical archaeology in Italy, postprocessualism has been embraced more warmly, perhaps because – at least superficially – it fits better into the established Italian tradition emphasising ideological and culture specific aspects.[6] Nonetheless, in the romanisation debate one of the

---

[1] The bibliography on the debate in a provincial context is immense; see e.g. Woolf 1996-97; Derks 1998, 2-8; Webster 2001, 210-217; Mattingly 2002 for overviews, e.g. Hingley 2005 for a recent in-depth study.

[2] See the excellent overview in Mouritsen 1998, 59-86, esp. for the historiographical part; also discussed below.

[3] Most notably Haverfield 1912, who first developed the term, and who was himself very well aware of the parallel with the British Empire; cf. Hingley 2000, esp. 111-155; Freeman 2007.

[4] Notably Metzler et al. 1995; Roymans 1996; Derks 1998.

[5] Esp. contributions in Keay/Terrenato 2001; contributions in *MEFRA* 118 (2006).

[6] Cf. D'Agostino 1991; Barbanera 1998; Terrenato 2005. Terrenato (p. 41) warns that "post-processualism became a convenient new label to stick on the same old idealist historicism".

[7] Most explicitly Torelli, cf. *infra*.

most influential models had already been adopted earlier in both Anglo-Saxon and Italian studies: the so-called 'emulation model' or 'self-romanisation paradigm'. This theoretical explanation for the mechanism of romanisation has been developed in the latter decades of the 20th century and has often remained implicit in studies on Italy.[7] A rather precise view of the cultural changes in Italy following the Roman conquest had already taken root earlier. The idea of a gradual cultural and political unification of Italy under Roman guidance was first established in the 19th century.[8] The mechanism of self-romanisation can therefore be seen as the later theoretical underpinning of a pre-existing view of cultural developments in Italy in the Republican period. I will therefore turn first to this idea of cultural unification and Roman cultural dominance before discussing the later theoretical explanation for it.

1.1 EARLY ROMAN CULTURAL DOMINANCE

In his *Römische Geschichte* and thus as part of his general historical framework, Theodor Mommsen postulated that an Italic-Roman cultural fusion began as early as the third century BC.[9] This view persisted, albeit modified, long into the 20th century. Explicit ideas on the how and why of the spread of cultural models were of minor relevance to this idealist tradition; cultural convergence was presumed rather than explained.[10] Since Italy was conceptualised as a unified whole, 'Romans' and 'Italic people' were by a certain time held to be interchangeable. A change or transition from 'Italic' to 'Roman' is presupposed but the process itself was hardly questioned. Something that goes into the direction of an explanation is the idea of decline or 'crisis' of the Italic peoples. In this view, the 'crisis' would have cleared the way for the adoption of a Roman identity.[11] The culturally weakened Italic peoples would have forsaken their Italic identities and become Romans. In an often cited passage, Strabo (6.1.2–3) seems to say as much on the Samnites and affiliated peoples, albeit in a later period:

> *"But the [Leucani], and the Brettii, and the Samnites themselves (the progenitors of these peoples) have so utterly deteriorated that it is difficult even to distinguish their several settlements; and the reason is that no common organisation longer endures in any one of the separate tribes; and their characteristic differences in language, armour, dress, and the like, have completely disappeared; and, besides, their settlements, severally and in detail, are wholly without repute ... The Leucani are Samnite in race ... But now they are Romans."*[12]

In one line preceding these, Strabo states in similar fashion that the Campani had in the meantime become interchangeable with Romans. The coming of Rome was thus at the cost of local traditions, to the extent that these could not even be recognised anymore. This view seems to underpin modern studies.[13] Arthur Keaveney, for example, defines romanisation as "that process whereby the different peoples of Italy put off their own peculiar identities and assumed that of Rome".[14] Likewise, Edward Togo Salmon presents romanisation in his otherwise rather 'pro-Samnite' standard work on the Samnites straightforwardly in terms of an inescapable process.[15]

---

8   Cf. already in 1845 Adolf Kiene, speaking of the "*Annäherung ... in der gesamten Denk- und Anschauungsweise*" of Italic people and Romans (Kiene 1845, 120); see Mouritsen 1998, 59.

9   Mommsen [1976] 1854-1855, vol. 1-3. On the reasons for this early date, cf. *infra*.

10 Mouritsen 1998, cf. *infra*.

11 E.g. De Juliis 1994, 44 on "*la crisi delle culture indigeni e la conquista romana*". Cf. in general Massa-Pairault 1990.

12 Transl. Loeb.

13 E.g. Torelli/Lachenal 1992, xxvii.

14 Keaveney 1987, 21.

15 Salmon 1967, 316.

16 Amongst other approaches there is e.g. the *clientela*

In this framework, empirical evidence is largely subsidiary to views on Roman supremacy. One popular view of Roman rule that resonates clearly with ideas on romanisation is the centre-periphery model, in which Rome would have formed the centre within a constellation of centripetal oriented communities.[16] In particular, Mario Torelli has applied this model,[17] putting forward an image of peninsular Italy which is made up of different cultural bands. These represent zones with different settlement patterns, accordingly presenting different cultural developments. These cultural zones are supposed to have interacted differently with Roman influence. Thus, the relative prosperity of the first zone, Oscan Campania, is explained as the consequence of a "profound social, economic and political interaction",[18] whereas the second zone, formed by the "peri-urban" territories, is characterised as "a peripheral and dependent area" oriented on colonies and other cities.[19] The third zone is the Apennine area, inhabited by the 'Sabellian' or Samnite peoples.[20] In this "world of non-cities"[21] Rome would have had an "*evidentissima funzione di guida*" in the introduction of new architectonic forms and construction techniques.[22] In short, Rome would have had a crucial role in the trend towards urbanisation[23] and cultural development in general, and especially the urban colonies founded by Rome in the early and mid-Republican period would have been a key factor in this process.[24]

1.2 TWO OBJECTIONS: HISTORIOGRAPHICAL CONSTRUCTS AND THE MECHANISM OF SELF-ROMANISATION

There are at least two fundamental problems with the standard hypothesis positing early Roman cultural dominance in the peninsula. First, this view can be shown to rely heavily on idealist notions of the Roman empire. Second, the mechanism of cultural change which is generally presupposed has serious weaknesses. The first point has been especially elaborated by Mouritsen in his provocative book on 'Italian unification' in relation to the Social War.[25] Analysing the ideological frameworks within which both ancient and modern authors constructed a Romanocentric view of the Social War, he exposes the idea of a linear development aimed at one goal, the supremacy of Rome. In this teleological model Italy was subservient to Rome's development.

In the traditional view, endorsed by the ancient sources and followed by modern historians, the main reason for the allies to revolt in 91 BC was their supposed eagerness to become official Roman citizens.[26] Though it has been acknowledged that other aims may have played a role,[27] Mouritsen casts doubts on

---

model, in which power relations between Rome and her Italic 'allies' are paralleled with patron-client relationships; see Badian 1958. For the centre-periphery model cf. Champion 1989.

[17] E.g. Torelli 1982; Torelli 1995.

[18] Torelli 1995, 3-4; thus allowing for reciprocal influences, forming "the foundation of the *koiné* Romano-Italic culture of the third and second centuries BC".

[19] Torelli 1995, 9.

[20] On 'Sabelli' and Samnites cf. Dench 1995; see also Chapter 3, this volume.

[21] Torelli 1995, 10.

[22] Torelli 1982, 243, with reference to the first half of the second century BC.

[23] The emphasis on urbanisation as a result of romanisation is particularly strong in Italian scholarship. Cf. e.g. Desideri 1991, 583.

[24] E.g. Salmon 1969, 54, calling Latin colonies "the real instrument in the romanization of Italy" and Torelli 1995, 12: "the prevailing cultural models and the artistic production are those presented by the Roman world, sometimes directly by Rome and sometimes indirectly through the Latin and Roman colonies"; cf. Chapter 2 for the elaboration of this idea in the discussion on the spread of Roman religious models.

[25] Mouritsen 1998; cf. also Mouritsen 2006.

[26] The classic is Brunt 1965.

[27] E.g. Brunt 1965, esp. 91; Walbank 1972, 152; see discussion of various strands in Mouritsen 1998.

[28] Mouritsen 1998, 59: "The idea of Italian romanisation

the Roman narrative in a comprehensive alternative framework in which Italic peoples fought the Social War for sovereignty, rather than citizenship. Mouritsen traces the modern 'making of' the Romanocentric integrative model of Roman-Italic relations back to 19th century German scholarship. Idealist and nationalist notions, suggested by the contemporaneous formation of the German nation, were projected onto the Roman Republic. This view was supported by the most detailed ancient account on the Social War, the version by Appianus, who presents it as a preparatory phase to the following *bellum civile*. Within the logic of this model, the cultural and political diversity of Italy formed an obstacle in the creation of a unified Italy. Moreover, it could cast doubts on the goals pursued by the Italic allies. Consequently, in order not to undermine the Romanocentric version of the Italian unification, the cultural unity of Italy before the Social War had to be emphasised. Cultural unity, on the other hand, did not seem self-evident at a time of political rivalry between Rome and the Italic peoples in the period directly preceding the Social War. Paradoxically, therefore, the idea was put forward that this cultural romanisation must have predated the Hannibalic War.[28] According to Mouritsen however, the actual cultural unification occurred only after the political one had been enforced by military power and bloodshed more than a century later, i.e. after the Social War.[29]

Several objections can be made to Mouritsen's alternative historical reconstruction, especially with regard to the undervaluation of the profits of the Roman citizenship[30] and Roman influence in general.[31] However, his excellent analysis of the 'idealist' construction of an early 'cultural convergence' of Italy under Rome still stands.[32]

The second objection is the mechanism of cultural change which is often presumed in the 'unification' model. This mechanism refers to the concept of 'self-romanisation' or *autoromanizzazione* in Italian.[33] As I have noted, to some extent this model can be seen as the later theoretical footing for the already existing idea of Roman cultural leadership, although emphasis is put on local initiatives and strategies. According to this concept, Italic peoples would have actively adopted Roman cultural models. Motives for doing so relate to a wish to gain profit from the new power balances (e.g. the joining in trade networks or the pursuit of a political career). Italic elites would also have sought the direct support of their Roman confrères. These aims are thus directed at Rome or the Roman empire at large. Alternatively, adopting the Roman way of life would have secured status within the local community, i.e. an 'internal' incentive. The most explicit study on self-romanisation positing an 'internal' logic is Martin Millett's work on the romanisation of Britain.[34] Native British elites would have actively adopted symbols of 'Romanitas' to reinforce their social position within local society. As a result of restrictions on the use and display of weapons imposed by the Roman rulers, the native social hierarchy would have been endan-

was thus both derived from and used to explain the Social War. Therefore, as a historical fact implied by the political events, the existence of cultural romanisation was not itself dependent on evidential demonstration; the sources merely served as illustrations of this phenomenon. The main problem outstanding was how to date this unity – and here the theory of a mounting antagonism between Rome and her allies in the second century suggested that it predated the Hannibalic War."

[29] The periodisation of the major cultural change in the late Republic has also been proposed by various other authors, a.o. Gabba 1972; Torelli 1983; Torelli 1995, 14; Torelli 1999, 89.

[30] Cf. e.g. Bradley 2007, 302-306.

[31] Pobjoy 2000; Bradley 2002; Adams 2003, esp. 150-155 and 751-755 on linguistic aspects. Also Mouritsen's view of the "rapid 'provincial' process of romanisation" (p. 86) which he sees as "more or less spontaneous acculturation" (p. 74) which would have followed the Social War needs explanation, because here he seems to accept a direct relation between power and culture which he otherwise explicitly dismisses (e.g. p. 70).

[32] Cf. Bradley 2002.

[33] Esp. Torelli 1995; Torelli 1999, but cf. also, more implicitly, e.g. contributions in Zanker 1976 and Coarelli/La Regina 1984.

[34] Millett 1990a; Millett 1990b.

[35] Millett 1990b, 38.

gered. The weapons, important symbols of authority, were now replaced by power symbols from Rome. Material culture, new beliefs, language and attitudes passed down the social hierarchy through a process of emulation. In Millett's words, "the motor for romanisation can be seen as internally driven, rather than externally imposed".[35] Local elites could maintain power and thereby identified their interests with those of Rome, enabling Rome to keep control with minimal effort. Romanisation is understood as the outcome of internal social processes rather than a planned Roman 'civilising mission'.

In studies on Italy, which traditionally place more emphasis on institutional structures, this mechanism would not only account for cultural but also for politico-institutional change. In the view of Emilio Gabba "the assimilation of the behaviour of the Italic elites to Roman norms, which had forged ahead at ever greater speed over the previous century, had gone beyond language and culture to affect the political systems and magistracies of the allied cities", and indeed speaks of the "assimilation of the political structures of the allies to those of Rome".[36] The fundamental assumption in the self-romanisation concept is that Roman models were sought after, even if no direct political rule had been yet established. Even political structures would have been 'affected' by Roman influence, but without Roman force.

It is exactly against the self-romanisation paradigm, that from the 1990s onwards much criticism has been uttered, at least in the archaeological debate in the Anglo-Saxon world as a response to Millett's 1990 work. First, the model places crucial emphasis on elites, whereas the rest of the population is not regarded, or is assumed to have followed suit.[37] The 'trickle-down effect' leaves no room for the possibility that some groups may react differently to similar circumstances than others do.[38] Diversity in responses to Roman dominion is also an important possibility for entire communities. It does not necessarily follow that the new order was always accepted and was possibly even resisted. Indeed, 'self-romanisation' still seems to operate within a 'directional' framework of thought;[39] it offers an alternative explanation for *how* romanisation worked but still seems to take its actual occurrence for granted. In many postcolonial studies emphasis has been put on resistance, often in reaction to the earlier colonial situation and sometimes merely inverting the old colonial discourse.[40] At least in academia, the militant variant of this approach has not found much support in Italy.[41] The notion of plurality and diversity in response is, however, certainly important.

A second point of critique levelled at the self-romanisation model is its use of a naïve view of 'Roman material culture', which is not dissimilar from the culture-historical model it seeks to replace. It is assumed that local elites adopted Roman goods to consolidate their position within local society. These goods were, according to Millett, seen as "symbols of Romanitas", and, for this reason, mediated power to the owner.[42] However, were cultural elements present and produced all over the Roman empire perceived as 'Roman' by their beholders? Perhaps they were just part of convenient newly available materials and structures. Meaning is given to artefacts and models; they do not carry an intrinsic 'Romanness' in

---

[36] Gabba 1994b, 109, writing on the period on the eve of the Social War. Similarly, on Bantia, Torelli 1995, 137-138 speaks of "a process of spontaneous Romanization, already under way in the full second century BC" and "a Romanization which assumes the form of an economic as well as an institutional homologation". Cf. the discussion on the *lex Osca Bantina*, possibly predating the Social War; Crawford 1996, 271-292.

[37] Freeman 1993.

[38] Cf. Hingley 1996.

[39] Freeman 1993; Hingley 1996; Woolf 1996-97.

[40] Most notably, Bénabou 1976; Pippidi 1976; cf. Mattingly 1997a; for a general critique of resistance as a model, see Brown 1996.

[41] In contrast to popular culture, e.g. in Molise, where Samnite resistance against Rome is often exalted. Cf. in some respects Salmon 1967, in which romanisation was, however, always clearly the end stage.

[42] On the misapplication of the term *Romanitas*, first attested in Tert. *Pall.* 4.1.1., see Dench 2005, 31 with n. 84.

[43] Freeman 1993, esp. 444; cf. Woolf 1996-97.

them. Therefore, by itself, the adoption of what we now define as 'Roman' elements does not prove a desire to be (seen as) 'Roman'.[43] Indeed, in Anglo-Saxon theoretically driven studies there is a whole spectrum of different approaches to the adoption of material culture and cultural models, ranging from 'silent' or 'symbolic' resistance to 'hybridisation', 'creolisation', 'métissage', and so on.[44] The possible conflictual aspect of these processes has been pointed out: what appears to be a submissive attitude of the 'subjugated', may in fact reflect "a complex mix of fear and desire, resistance and adaptation".[45] Of course, the main problem with these comparative conceptualisations is anachronism. Notwithstanding assertions to the contrary,[46] one may ask if it is legitimate to discern a similar 'discourse' between 'Romans' and 'natives' on the one hand and a slave driver and his slaves on the other,[47] or (early) modern colonial powers in Africa and the East and the local population.[48] Crucially, in many of these approaches[49] more or less separate cultures before colonial contact are presupposed, which in the case of the highly interconnected Mediterranean world is absolutely untenable.[50]

A third, more subtle point is the emphasis on ideology in a constructive, rather than oppositional sense. Partly as a reaction to processualist archaeology, especially in the Anglo-Saxon debate from the 1990s onwards, several studies have explored the importance of ideological frameworks. Studies have concentrated on the local ('native') embedding of new cultural forms and have tried to explain regional diversity in this respect.[51] For example, local communities could sometimes use new material culture to similar ends within the societal structures of old through a process of 'cultural bricolage',[52] but also new communities could be formed as a consequence of a changed socio-political order.[53] Cognitive aspects and ideologies are thus of central importance for the way in which people experience and order the (material) world, and thus in the way newly available elements or ideas are adopted. The 'construction' of communities evades the simplistic dichotomy between 'Roman' and 'native'.[54]

Importantly, however, all this does not mean that Rome was insignificant in the process. It has convincingly been argued that a common reaction of communities to threat entails enhancing its symbolic 'boundaries'. Historians and social anthropologists alike have demonstrated this process of symbolic enhancement in which sometimes 'ancestral' traditions are evoked or invented, but also 'new' elements are used to model the own distinctiveness and pride.[55] Often, religious or ritual institutions, such as festivals, processions and sacred meetings play an important role in this process.[56] Sanctuaries, the material part

---

[44] See Mattingly 2002.

[45] Webster 1996-97, 327.

[46] E.g. Webster 1996-97, 330: "there is a point beyond which the 'fact' of colonialism cannot be deconstructed, but within which the discourses of colonialism maybe subject to comparative analysis."

[47] E.g. Fincham 2002, drawing on Scott 1990.

[48] Cf. Dench 2005, 10: "to counter images of Roman cosmopolitanism and 'do-it-yourself' 'Romanization' with images of domination and discrimination, creating a nightmare world, is still to place modern dreams too much at the centre."

[49] Or at least their theoretical grounding borrowed from the social sciences.

[50] See Horden/Purcell 2000. In this sense, the term "mediterranization" (Yntema 2006, 126) would be more appropriate; cf. Curti *et al.* 1996, 188 for other "-isations" as different perspectives on cultural change than 'romanisation'. Cf. however *infra* on the undeniable importance of Roman agency in these processes.

[51] E.g. Metzler *et al.* 1995. N. Roymans, for example, holds "different regimes of ideas and values" (most notably "high social esteem for military virtues and animal husbandry") responsible for macro-regional diversity in romanisation processes in the Lower Rhine populations: Roymans 1995; Roymans 1996, 8 (quote). On ritual and religion: Derks 1998.

[52] Terrenato 1998a; Terrenato 1998b; Terrenato 2001.

[53] E.g. Van Dommelen 1998; Van Dommelen 2001; Van Dommelen/Terrenato 2007.

[54] Yet another solution is to speak of cultural 'bilingualism', as has recently been proposed, indicating the parallel existence of different Roman, native and other cultural traditions: Wallace-Hadrill 2008.

[55] E.g. Barth 1969; Hobsbawm/Ranger 1983; Cohen 1985.

[56] Esp. Cohen 1985.

of some of these activities, are therefore suitable locales for investigating the processes of enhancement, or formulation, of communities.[57]

Along with the rehabilitation of the impact of Roman strategies, it is important to stress that these strategies should not be seen as a constant factor. Changing Roman attitudes will have had major implications for local and regional developments.[58] The re-emphasising of Roman agency is in part a reaction to the native-oriented postcolonial approaches with a tendency to neglect Roman impact. In Italy, the importance of Roman strategies and intervention has almost never been doubted; the literary sources list colonisation, forced migration, and even genocide. Roman impact on itself has therefore hardly been underestimated in studies on the romanisation of Italy, but at the same time there has been a tendency to understand this impact as a rather constant factor and especially to retroject it to earlier periods for which evidence is scarce or non-existent. It is important to acknowledge that Roman impact and strategies will have varied considerably over time. Thus, aside from a discussion on material culture and its limits, one should also ask to what extent 'Rome' itself was a solid and continuous entity and changes in self-perceptions over time and place should be taken into account.[59] Recently the suggestion to speak of the 'romanisation of Rome' when considering the Republican period has been raised,[60] and perhaps this also offers some clues for the variegated character of the 'romanisation' of other parts of Italy.

1.3 CONCLUSION: DECONSTRUCTION AND NEW PERSPECTIVES

In summary, the recent objections against the view which posits early cultural convergence under Roman guidance should be taken seriously. Later views on the mechanism of cultural change, i.e. self-romanisation, have also proven to be problematic. The common ground in both the cultural convergence and self-romanisation concept is readily discerned: its origin lies in an 'idealist' notion which presupposes Roman superiority and consequently the superiority of Roman cultural models. Indeed, generally in the discourse on the romanisation of Italy less attention has been paid to material culture, and more to ideological, political and institutional issues. Somewhat paradoxically, empirical research has traditionally occupied an important place, but the interpretation of material culture has often been subservient to idealist notions.[61] In romanisation studies this becomes apparent with the emphasis on political and ideological aspects, often distilled from (later) literary accounts, whereas the cultural consequences are often seen as mere illustrations or 'proof' of these phenomena. The role of early and mid-Republican colonisation is a good example; little hard proof is fitted into (mostly literary) models of later fabrication (cf. the discussion on the religious aspects of Latin colonies treated in Chapter 2 and their urban organisation in Chapter 7). A remark made by Torelli concerning this evidential situation is illustrative of this approach; he states that romanisation would often only be "detectable in its terminal stages, when productive, cultural, and political integration appears to be complete".[62] Apparently, the early stages exist only in the *idea*.

Another clear example is the way 'hellenisation' has been fitted into the idealist model of Roman cultural supremacy. In the course of the 20th century, the view of Rome as the centre of cultural influence radiating new 'Roman' cultural forms proved to be untenable, and it became clear that instead 'Hellen-

---

[57] On the 'sacred landscape' as a "socio-ideological document": Alcock 1993, 173; Pelgrom 2004; Stek 2004; Stek 2005a; Stek 2005b.

[58] E.g. Hanson 1997; Whittaker 1997; Häussler 1998; Williams 2001.

[59] See Dench 2005.

[60] Curti 2000, 90-91.

[61] Cf. in general Barbanera 1998; Terrenato 2005.

[62] Torelli 1999, 89.

istic' culture accounted for most of the change. Within the idealist framework, an attractive alternative could thus arise: the image of Rome as propagator of Hellenistic culture.[63] Since evidence for this guiding role is scarce (cf. e.g. Chapter 3), material evidence is rendered subservient to an aprioristic model of Roman superiority.[64]

What may be concluded is that the image of an already culturally homogeneous or strongly 'romanising' Italy in the third and second centuries BC, so strongly attacked by Mouritsen, can indeed be questioned since the basis of this view proves to be weak. It is important, however, to emphasise that these objections do not necessarily prove the contrary, i.e. that during this period Rome was only of minor importance in cultural terms: the above discussion has shown that such a role is not *self-evident*, not that it is *non-existent*. This is in itself an important conclusion, as will be seen throughout this study. Furthermore, the definition of specific cultural elements as signalling 'Romanness' is not self-evident, as postprocessual archaeologists have shown. Neither is the existence of a coherent, culturally distinctive and identifiable 'Roman' Rome from the early Republic to the imperial period. However, even if this 'Rome' was perhaps more varied, capricious and contradictory than often is supposed in regional studies, and was clearly undergoing an important transformation process itself, the impact of this same Rome was fundamental, even solely measured by its military and political actions. In any case, we cannot afford to underestimate it. This means that the processes following the Roman conquest should not necessarily be conceptualised merely in neutral or positive terms such as, for example, 'self-romanisation', or more recent, 'negotiation' or 'becoming Roman'.[65]

This discussion leaves us therefore with a big question mark regarding the cultural developments in the third and especially the second centuries BC. Cultural convergence cannot be taken for granted, but neither should Rome be eliminated from these developments by overstating a *laissez-faire* policy. Rather than as a *non liquet*, this question mark should, in my view, be seen as a useful point of departure. Indeed, it frees us from top-down perspectives of cultural and political developments in the long-term and opens up an interesting field of research into the dynamic interplay, including clashes, of various groups and currents in this period. Moreover, the above discussion offers some clear outlines for possible approaches. In particular, the active ideological construction and reformulation of communities seems a promising avenue, which fortunately can have a material dimension. The crux is therefore to identify the locations where these ideological discourses are expressed and to contextualise them as fully as possible. As has been seen, 'religion', in the communal sense, and sanctuaries as their material focus, present appropriate locations. In Chapter 3, this approach will indeed be proposed for Samnite sanctuaries in the second to early first centuries BC. Given that romanisation or 'being Roman' cannot be understood as a self-evident and natural process, this approach accounts also for 'Roman' communities and this point will be developed in more detail in Chapters 7, 8 and 9. First, however, the idea of 'religious romanisation' will be discussed in the following chapter.

---

[63] Mouritsen 1998, 59-86; esp. 82-83. In the words of Salmon 1982, 100: "Hellenistic sculpture, painting and architectural details, Hellenistic writing and modes of thought came to be quickly noted and eclectically imitated at Rome, and Rome's hegemony ensured their rapid transmission into other parts of Italy."

[64] Cf. similar observations by Gallini 1973, on hellenisation and '*romanità*'.

[65] Cf. Curti 2001, 24 on the political correctness of recent conceptions of romanisation as 'negotiation' or 'debate', "sanitizing our perception of the Roman empire", cf. also Cecconi 2006; Dench 2005, 32: "Despite modern nervousness about Romanocentric perspectives, it is hard to deny that sometimes empire was experienced or exercised as, primarily, power and domination ..."

2 'Religious Romanisation' and the Fate of Italic Rural Sanctuaries

Opinions on the religious aspects of the romanisation of Italy have not developed analogously to ideas on the 'general' romanisation of Italy. Admittedly, there are some parallels, but the subject has not by far been discussed as explicitly and vehemently as 'general' romanisation, and sometimes the discussion has even developed into the opposite direction. This is at least in part due to the fact that the 'romanisation' discussion often implicitly encompasses material culture, which is the realm of archaeologists, whereas Italic and Roman religion have traditionally been the field of *Religionswissenschaftler*, ancient historians and especially linguists, who have been less preoccupied with the predominantly Anglo-Saxon archaeologically oriented romanisation debate. In any case, if the discrepancy in the development of the research agendas between studies on Italy and the provinces is already evident for the general romanisation discussion, it is unmistakable in the religious realm.[1]

One might discern three tendencies in modern scholarship which have influenced ideas on the religious aspects of the romanisation of Italy. First, Italic religion has usually been studied separately from discussions on the Roman conquest and romanisation. It is seen a distinctive aspect of Italic culture and is discussed in chapters or books in which the coming of Rome figures mainly as an endpoint.[2] Indeed, with the general waning of pre-Roman cultures (cf. Strabo 6.1.2), the related religions would have faded as well. This notion fits well into the traditional notion of crisis and subsequent cultural assimilation to Rome in the fourth to third centuries BC (Chapter 1).

Second, many studies on Italic religion have focused on the similarities, and not the differences and interactions between Roman and Italic religions.[3] Departing from the concept of a basic 'Italic religion', Roman religion would be analogous to or part of it. Since direct literary evidence for Italic religion is virtually absent and it is primarily known from the material record, the literary evidence for Rome has been combined with the Italic evidence to construct a meaningful framework. In particular, in studies on religion influenced by Indo-European theory[4] there is a tendency to fit all evidence into one model, with the result that no meaningful difference can be made between Roman and other Italic religions even before the 'arrival of Rome' in Italy. It is important, however, to acknowledge regional diversity within Italic religions which may be largely hidden by a lack of evidence, and indeed this very tendency in scholarship to merge evidence from different contexts into one model. It seems right therefore to underscore, with Olivier de Cazanove, that the religions of different Italic peoples are "in fact homologous religious cultures, but they do not coincide exactly",[5] and to also account for incompatibilities. Moreover, even if the religious systems may have been similar, this of course does not imply that Roman and other Italic religions were interchangeable, or indeed 'open' to everyone (cf. *infra*).

Third, a similar 'merging' of evidence becomes apparent with regard to a later period in time. General studies on Roman Italy, i.e. Italy after its incorporation into the Roman state, have almost without

---

[1] In contrast to studies on the situation in Italy, the bibliography for explicit studies on the religious aspects of the romanisation of the provinces is huge. Cf. e.g. Henig 1984; Metzler *et al.* 1995; Webster 1995; Derks 1998; Frankfurter 1998; Scheid 1999; Van Andringa 2002; Häussler 2005; Häussler/King 2007.

[2] E.g. Bottini 1994.

[3] For an overview of ideas on continuity from prehistorical (Mycenaean) times onwards, cf. Cancik 2008, esp. 8-13. Cf. also Rüpke 2007, 2.

[4] Cf. esp. the works by G. Dumézil.

[5] De Cazanove 2007, 46. Cf. Campanile 1991.

exception assumed that religious practices in 'Roman Italy' were basically identical to those known from the city of Rome. In this way, the cults, festivals and calendar from Rome have been extrapolated to the whole of Italy.[6] These assumptions on religion in Roman Italy prove to be problematic,[7] but more disturbing in this discussion is that the developments between the *floruit* of 'Italic religions' and the presence of an apparently entirely 'Roman' religion a few centuries later disappear in the gap between disciplines. It is fair to ask what has happened in the meantime. My concern here is not so much about changing religious ideas and belief systems at large, which is outside the scope of this discussion, but rather about the relationship between Roman political dominance and Roman and Italic religious practices and, in particular, cult places.

2.1 ROME IN ITALY: MODES OF INTERVENTION AND THE ROLE OF COLONIES

2.1.1 NON-INTERVENTION AS A POLICY AND ITS EXCEPTIONS

What was the Roman attitude to Italic religious life? With some exceptions, the general scenario seems to be that Rome fostered a minimum intervention policy with regard to religious affairs in Italy outside its territory. Rome would have been generally uninterested in what happened outside Roman territory on a religious level and this would have changed only after the municipalisation. This idea follows from the view of Roman religion as basically a state religion which only had relevance for its subjects,[8] and as De Cazanove has rightly argued, conversion or proselytism has no role to play in such a model.[9] The civic model of Roman religion means that Rome could only actively influence religious matters in the areas whose inhabitants had citizenship, i.e. *municipia* and colonies.[10] This would mean that we can only meaningfully speak of the 'religious romanisation' of the *socii* after the Social War if we define romanisation here in an active sense as incorporation into the Roman state. Even then this process should not be seen as the rude imposition of totally new cults, but rather as a reorganisation of existing cults according to Roman standards. In the incorporated communities, pre-existing cults could be perpetuated as part of the *municipalia sacra*, which are defined by Festus as those cults "which the peoples concerned had always observed, before receiving Roman citizenship, and which the pontiffs wanted them to continue to observe and perform in the traditional forms of old".[11] John Scheid has emphasised the fundamental importance of the local authorities and traditions in the formation of a new religious system in colonies and *municipia* in the Roman western provinces and it could be argued that the situation was not very different in Italy.[12]

---

[6] E.g. Lomas 1996, esp. 166: "Rome itself is the best-documented city in Italy in terms of religious ritual, but the pattern of religious behaviour seems to be broadly similar elsewhere in Italy."

[7] See e.g. Cooley 2006 for nuanced cases of Roman religious aspects outside Rome; for calendars, see Rüpke 1995.

[8] Scheid 1985a; Scheid 1985b, 47-76. Cf. on prodigies William Rasmussen 2003; Rosenberger 2005.

[9] De Cazanove 2000c, 71. On the civic model cf. Woolf 1997; Bendlin 2000.

[10] For a strong statement of this view: De Cazanove 2000c. On Latin colonies, with the Latin right, cf. *infra*.

[11] Fest. 146 L.: *municipalia sacra vocantur, quae ab initio habuerunt ante civitatem Romanam acceptam, quae observare eos voluerunt pontifices, et eo more facere, quo adsuessent antiquitus.*

[12] Even if the difference between Italian and provincial municipalities should be acknowledged. Scheid 1997, esp. 55-56; cf. also Scheid 1999; De Cazanove 2000c, 73; Frateantonio 2003, 70-73.

Briefly put, from the moment that a given area became part of the Roman state, local representatives of Roman authority probably had something to say about the official cults that were celebrated and how they were to be organised and it is in this controlling mechanism that 'religious romanisation' could perhaps be recognised.[13] The civic model does not, of course, preclude the possibility that Italic people adopted aspects or elements that appear to belong to what we define Roman religious culture of their own free will, in other words, self-romanisation on a religious level. As I show, such a process has indeed been conceptualised by some scholars. However, on the whole there is a consensus on the general *laissez-faire* attitude by Rome with regard to religious matters outside its territory before the Social War. To this general rule of non-intervention before the Social War, two important exceptions are often highlighted. First, there is the attempted suppression of the Bacchanalia in 186 BC by a *senatusconsultum*, and secondly the colonies and their cults and rituals. Another, related topic which could be added is the (supposed) treatment of Italic sanctuaries by Rome, which will be discussed separately.

2.1.2 THE SENATUSCONSULTUM DE BACCHANALIBUS

According to Livy (book 39, 8-19), the Senate wished to curtail the cult of Bacchus in 186 BC. The basic content of Livy's vivid account seems to be confirmed by an inscription with, apparently, a copy of the edict, which was found in 1640 in the Calabrian locality of Tiriolo.[14] It does not seem necessary to discuss the nature of the evidence and the debate on the Bacchanalia itself, which has an immense bibliography,[15] but I would like to highlight here some relevant points for the discussion on Roman interference within allied territory.

Livy writes on several occasions that the Bacchanalia were suppressed not only in Rome but *per totam Italiam*.[16] Thus, at first sight it seems that Rome did, in fact, intervene in the religious affairs of its allies. A complicating factor, however, is that the concept of *Italia* has changed over time and it is not to be excluded that it referred in the first place only to Roman territory within the Italian peninsula, a situation which may have been misunderstood by imperial authors (such as Livy) writing in a by then unified Italy.[17] At Tiriolo, in ancient Bruttium, a small settlement of the third and second century BC has been excavated,[18] and the inscription mentions explicitly the *ager Teuranus*, which probably coincides with

---

[13] In the words of Rüpke: "If the Romans did not export their religion, they certainly exported their concept of religion." Rüpke 2007, 5.

[14] *CIL* I², 581. Cf. Pailler 1986, 61-122.

[15] Cf. with further bibliographical references Pailler 1986; Gruen 1990; Cancik-Lindemaier 1996; Nippel 1997; Linke 2000; Takács 2000; Briscoe 2003. For resonances of drama in Livy's account cf. Walsh 1996; Flower 2000.

[16] Liv. 39.14.7; 17.4; 18.7. Livy writes (39.14.7) that the priests and priestesses of the Bacchanalia should be looked for "not only in Rome, but also in all the *fora* and *conciliabula*" and continues that edicts should be dispatched *et in urbe et per totam Italiam*. It has been argued that *Italia* is used here as a stylistic variation on *fora et conciliabula*, and in this context would be synonymous with 'Roman Italy'; i.e. those parts of Italy that held the citizenship, and therefore does not include allied territory (Mouritsen 1998, 50-52). Liv. 39.17.4 does refer to the Italian allies, but does not mention Roman intervention, whereas 39.18.7-8 repeats the general *Roma / Italia* distinction; cf. De Cazanove 2000b.

[17] Galsterer 1976, 37-41 (38 on the Bacchanalian affair) proposed that *Italia* as a legal term refers only to *ager Romanus* in the second century BC, cf. Mouritsen 1998, 45 n. 25 who criticises, however, the notion of a common terminology in all sources, with further references. For a clear overview of the evidence (esp. Polyb. 6.13.4-6 and Livy 39) and the ideas on the meaning of *Italia* see Mouritsen 1998, 45-58. Cf. Pailler's reaction to Galsterer, Pailler 1986, 330-332.

[18] Kahrstedt 1959, 191; Spadea 1977; Spadea 1988, the site seems to have been abandoned at the beginning of the second century BC (connected by De Cazanove 2000b, 63 to the installation of the colony of Vibo).

modern Tiriolo. This area was confiscated from the indigenous Bruttians and presumably *ager publicus populi Romani* at least from the Second Punic War onwards.[19] Both the locations mentioned by Livy in the context of the Bacchanalian affair and the place of recovery of the inscription could thus possibly relate to Roman territory, not to *socii*, which has suggested to some that the suppression of the Bacchanalia was restricted to Roman territory.[20]

The opening lines of the inscription suggest something else however. The edict regards explicitly 'the Bacchanalia of the *foideratei*' (lines 2-3: *de bacanalibus quei foideratei esent*). It seems that the Bacchanalia (which can indicate both the rituals and the cult places involved) of a *civitas foederata* are meant rather than those on Roman territory. Mommsen has tried to resolve the discrepancy between the place and the target group by suggesting that *foideratei* indicates not a political status, but rather the sworn members of the cult.[21] However, since *foederatus* is not used in this sense elsewhere, this solution remains highly doubtful.[22] Jean-Marie Pailler has proposed that *foideratei* generally refers to the inhabitants of the confiscated territory who did not have the Latin or Roman rights,[23] and De Cazanove has recently suggested that the 'Latin allies' are intended, i.e. the inhabitants of a Latin colony, perhaps Vibo Valentia, installed in 192 BC, but neither this solution seems very plausible.[24]

Lines 7-8 of the inscription state that neither *cives Romani, nomen latinum* nor *socii* can participate in the Bacchanalia unless special authorisation is granted by the *praetor urbanus* and the Senate. Allies are thus banned from the cult. Admittedly, it is not explicitly stated that this also applies to allied *territory*, and it is, as Mouritsen argues, possible that line 7 is only an explication of the reach of the edict within Roman territory, affecting people of all legal statuses.[25]

The archaeological evidence for the repression of the Bacchanalia is, to say the least, ambiguous. Disagreement exists about the only *Bacchanal* outside Roman territory that would have been demolished as a consequence of the *senatusconsultum*, at Bolsena (Volsinii). De Cazanove has argued that it was not a cultic place but a cistern, thus eliminating this possible archaeological attestation of the repression,[26] but the archaeological evidence seems to point indeed to a Bacchic cult place.[27] Another example of a *Bacchanal* outside Roman territory apparently survived the edict. The Bacchic sanctuary of S. Abbondio near Pompeii, originating in the third century BC and still in use in 79 AD, would, according to the excavators, have survived the *senatusconsultum* because it was one of the ancient and respectable cult places exempted from persecution (Liv. 39.18.7).[28] It is true that this reasoning strips the archaeological evidence of the

[19] Dion. Hal. *Ant. Rom.* 20.15. Cf. Pailler 1986, 285-297 (on 288: "*un de ces conciliabula et fora*", or rather a *praefectura*: Kahrstedt 1959, 176, 191); Mouritsen 1998, 52; De Cazanove 2000b, 59. Ando 2007, 437, states that the inscription was found "outside Roman territory", but it is unclear on what grounds.

[20] Recently, Mouritsen 1998; De Cazanove 2000c; De Cazanove 2000b (arguing for Latin territory, however, cf. *infra*).

[21] Mommsen 1877 1, 249, n. 3; Mommsen 1899, 875, followed by many others, amongst whom Galsterer 1976, 169 and more recently Mouritsen 1998.

[22] Pailler 1986, 290 dismisses this interpretation. In defense of Mommsen's thesis, Mouritsen 1998, 54 considers this counterargument "hardly cogent", since "the source is very early and deals with an otherwise unique situation".

[23] Pailler 1986, 290-291.

[24] De Cazanove 2000b, esp. 61-62, cf. Dahlheim 1968, 118 n. 19 for the consideration that relations between Latin colonies and Rome were regulated by a *foedus*; cf. Mouritsen 1998, 53 n. 46. Perhaps the *ager Teuranus* was part of the colony of Vibo; cf. Costabile 1984, 96, who suggests that it represents one of the *fora et conciliabula* mentioned by Livy, but depended on the colony. De Cazanove's thesis is dismissed by Pfeilschifter 2006, 120 n. 26, in light of the distance between Vibo and Tiriolo, and the, ultimately, curious use of *foederati* for 'Latin allies'. Cf. now also Briscoe 2008, 246.

[25] Mouritsen 1998, 55. This would thus constitute a useless repetition of what was actually self-evident.

[26] De Cazanove 2000a.

[27] Jolivet/Marchand 2003.

[28] Elia/Pugliese Carratelli 1975, 146-153; Elia/Pugliese Carratelli 1979.

possibility to test the thesis of Roman intervention outside Roman territory, but I doubt whether this evidence can be used as 'a strong argument' to the contrary, i.e. that the legislative reach of the edict included only *ager Romanus*.[29] For example, this Dionysiac cult place could have been closed temporarily, invisible in the archaeological record, or did not have an orgiastic, 'dangerous' character, the main point of Roman concern, as the excavators suggest.[30] What is more, we do not know the relationship between the intentions of the Roman authorities and their practical effectiveness.[31] In order to employ archaeological data meaningfully in this discussion a larger sample size than one or two is needed.

As a whole, it seems most reasonable to assume that the Roman authorities indeed sought to interfere in allied territory; the various alternative solutions are ultimately unconvincing.[32] It seems more logical that *foideratei* indeed refers to the most obvious meaning of the word, i.e. citizens of *civitates foederatae*; *socii*, although the addressees of the edict under consideration might have been indeed Roman / Latin citizens. This 'inconsistency' could perhaps be explained if we understood better the particular process by which the inscription was constituted.[33]

Although it thus seems that in the case of the Bacchanalia, Rome indeed aspired to intervene in religious affairs outside its territory, I would refrain from considering it as proof for the existence of a Roman 'policy' of religious intervention; not only because of the still somewhat dubious evidence, but because of the clearly limited and exceptional character of the episode. Another argument to separate the extraordinary Bacchanalian affair from the discussion on religious romanisation is that the repression was apparently prompted by concerns on a political level, not by the cult itself. The measures described in the *senatusconsultum* regard especially the organisation of the cult, which must be placed under Roman control.[34]

2.1.3 COLONIES AND CULTS

Perhaps the Bacchanalian affair can be, at most, described as a negative form of Roman influence in the religious sphere; repression and control, not the active spread of Roman forms of religion seem to have been the objective.[35] An active spread of Roman religious ideas has been recognised relatively unequivocally, however, in relation to Roman colonisation. Not only are these newly installed communities thought to have performed rituals according to Roman customs themselves, but they are also conceptu-

[29] Thus Mouritsen 1998, 56.
[30] G. Pugliese Carratelli in Elia/Pugliese Carratelli 1979, 473-474. "*Si dovrà piuttosto ritenere che nell'ambito del thíasos pompeiano non si sia sospettata o riscontrata nessuna di quelle violenze della normale tradizione sacrale che giustificavano la severità del senatus consultum de Bacchanalibus*"; cf. G. Pugliese Carratelli in Elia/Pugliese Carratelli 1975, 151-152.
[31] Cf. the surprise of the Roman authorities at the discovery by Sp. Postumius, whilst engaged in his enquiries, that the Roman colonies of Sipontum and Buxentum, founded only 9 years before, were left by its inhabitants (Liv. 39.23.3-4).
[32] See now Bispham 2007, 116-123; Briscoe 2008, 246.
[33] Discussion on the formation and composition of the inscription, by Roman or local authorities, or both: e.g. Bernard 1908; Fraenkel 1932; Keil 1934; Krause 1936; MacDonald 1944, esp. 28-31; on the importance of the public declamation of the text cf. Martina 1998.
[34] But cf. North 1979, 91, on the inseparability of religious and political issues: "It is obviously a relevant and important fact that the Senate should be so interested in controlling the external form and property of the Bacchic group. But it would be quite wrong to argue that this interest in organization shows that they were indifferent about the religious issue"; cf. also Nippel 1997 for the social / psychological motives; 72: "*Eine Erklärung für das massive Zuschlagen dürfte in einem tief in der römischen politischen Kultur verwurzelten Verschwörungssyndrom liegen*," and Linke 2000, esp. 272-273.
[35] On the important mechanism of control as a factor of change, cf. *infra*.

Fig. 2.1 The tracing of the *sulcus primigenius*. This sestertius of 106 AD shows the emperor Trajan in the role of founder (Kent 1978, pl. 76 no 266).

alised as strategic centres for the consequent spread of Roman culture and religion in Italy outside the colonial settlements. Indeed, colonies have been described as the "greatest tool of social and military control, and afterwards of Romanization",[36] and even as "religious staging posts of Roman expansion".[37]

In this perspective, the foundation ritual of colonies is thought to have been 'Roman', including the ploughing of the *sulcus primigenius*, thereby marking the *pomerium* (see fig. 2.1), and the offering of the first fruits of the earth in a ritual pit.[38]

Furthermore, Roman foundation myths would have been used to consolidate the Roman efforts.[39] Indeed, in this view, the installation of the new colonial *oppidum* was accompanied by the establishment of a political and ideological set of elements which more or less copied the urban organisation of the mother city in synthetic form. Colonies were actually 'small copies' of Rome, as Aulus Gellius argued as late as AD 169.[40] Amongst these elements are the *auguraculum*, the forum, and, perhaps most important of all, the typical *Capitolium*-temple. These temples with three *cellae* on a high podium are thought to have expressed proud urbanity and Romanness, to the effect that others in the area came to admire and eventually imitate the model (see fig. 2.2).

The Etrusco-Italic temple model would thus have spread as a superior symbol of Romanness and urbanity.[41] A similar case has been made for the terracotta decoration of the temples and the ideological programme behind the depicted figures and scenes.[42] Architecture and decoration forged a firm relationship with the metropolis.

Similarly, the ties between the colonies were strengthened by rituals, some of which were performed in the same way as at the shrine of Diana on the Aventine; in various colonies reference is made to this sacred law set up in Rome for the regulation of the colonial cults.[43] Further, the dedication of black gloss cups to the gods, so-called *pocola deorum*, has been interpreted as a typically colonial ritual which would have established a link between the colonies and Rome (see fig. 2.3).

---

[36] Torelli 1999, 3. Cf. Salmon 1969, 54: "the Latin colonies ... were the real instrument in the romanization of Italy", similarly Salmon 1982, 166.

[37] De Cazanove 2000c, 75.

[38] Cf. e.g. the vivid accounts in Brown 1980, 16-17 and Salmon 1969, 24; cf. also Gargola 1995.

[39] For instance in the case of the Latin colony of Luceria: Torelli 1999, 93-97 (= Torelli 1992). Cf. also Torelli 1999, esp. 31-32 (= Torelli 1988a).

[40] Gell. *NA* 16.13.9. Cf. Salmon 1969, 18: "... although Gellius was referring to colonies of his own day (AD 169), his description is valid to a great extent also for those of the Republic."

[41] Torelli 1999, 127.

[42] E.g. Strazzulla 1981; Torelli 1993a; cf. Guidobaldi 1995 for the *ager Praetutianus*. Cf. e.g. the map in Torelli 1999, 123 fig. 54, with the legend: "Map of distribution of architectural terracottas of Etrusco-Italic type: hachured the original area; in grey the second-century BC diffusion as a consequence of imitation (Umbrian area) or of the influence of Roman colonization (Picene and Samnite areas)".

[43] At Salona (AD 137), Narbo (AD 11) and Ariminum (first century AD). Cf. Beard *et al*. 1998, 330.

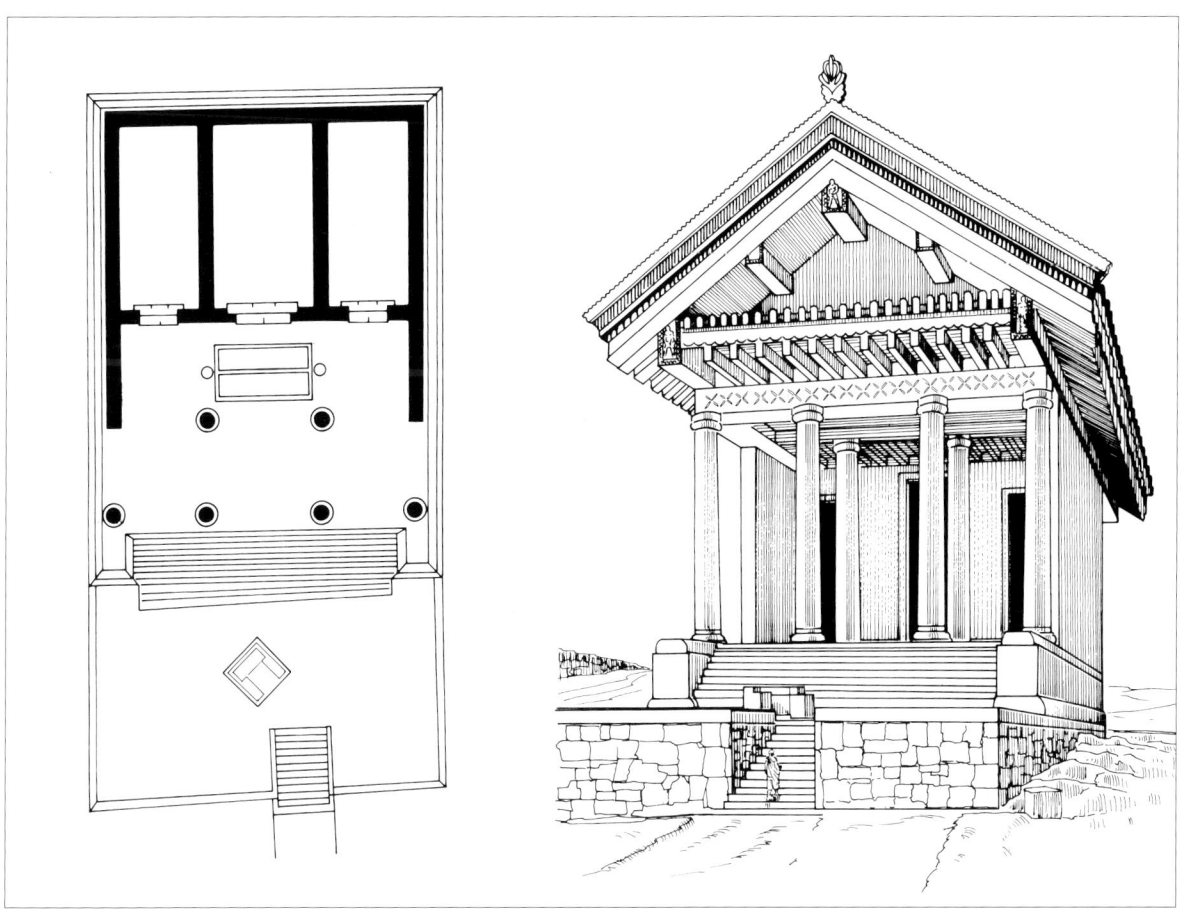

Fig. 2.2. The 'Capitolium' of Cosa (adapted from Brown et al. 1960, 95 fig. 71 and 109 fig. 82.

Not only are the black gloss cups themselves regarded as 'Roman / Latin' or 'romanised',[44] but their use, and especially the gods that are inscribed on them would also specifically relate to Roman or Latin religious ideas (cf. Chapter 7).[45] Other types of black gloss ceramics have similarly been related to Roman influence in colonial contexts.[46]

Another typical colonial practice would have been the dedication of anatomical ex-votos of the so-called Etrusco-Latial-Campanian group of votive materials. The appearance of this specific type of terracotta dedications in the form of human body parts, probably offered in thanks or as requests for a cure, fertility or general well-being, has been geographically linked to Roman colonisation.[47] The phenomenon

---

[44] Morel/Coarelli 1973. Cf. Franchi De Bellis 1995, 370 who states, on the relation between colonists and material culture (after citing Gellius) that in particular the evidence of ceramics "*delinea, nei primi anni della colonia … una continuità di gusti e stili tipicamente 'romani'*", also with regard to the preferred forms. She links these preferences to the Latial origin of the colonists. Nonnis in Cifarelli et al. 2002-2003 sees the spread of the *pocola* also as indicative of romanisation, just as the so-called '*Heraklesschalen*'.

[45] Cf. Ortalli 2000, 503 and Franchi De Bellis 1995, 371. In Chapter 7 the so-called *pocola* of Ariminum are discussed in more detail.

[46] Esp. in relation to Hercules: Morel 1988; cf. Bispham 2006, 108.

[47] Briefly in Torelli 1973; cf. also Fenelli 1975; full documentation in Comella 1981, esp. p. 775 on the relationship with colonisation; Torelli 1999, 121-122; De Cazanove 2000c. Cf. also, polemically, Sisani 2002 and Sisani 2007.

Fig. 2.3. A *pocolom deorum* (Degrassi 1986 pl. 14, fig. 3).

would have been introduced from Greece[48] to Latium, and from there the practice would have followed closely the stages of the Roman conquest of Italy, in particular in the areas occupied by Latin colonies. They would have been "*véritables indicateurs de la conquête*".[49] In this way, the appearance of votives of this type in the southern Latin colonies of Luceria (314 BC) and Paestum (273 BC) has been interpreted as indicative of the link between colonisation and the spread of the model. Often a very direct connection between the ethnic or legal status of people and material culture is made. Torelli argues for example that regional differences in the content of deposits reflect differences in the make-up of the population, full Roman citizens being responsible for 'standard' votive deposits, and *cives sine suffragio* for anomalies.[50] Similarly, ex-votos of this type are seen as direct indicators of the presence of Roman colonists outside the area of origin.[51] In any case, the anatomical votives are charged with ideological weight: according to Torelli "Latin colonisation was responsible for propagating, well beyond the original borders of central Etruria, Latium, and Campania, the use of anatomic ex-votos, with all the possible implications of such use – a striking sign of Roman superiority both in the ideological and material sphere."[52]

---

[48] Sometimes connected, incorrectly, with the introduction of Aesculapius in Rome in 293 BC: e.g. Comella 1982-1983; De Cazanove 2000c with the critique by Schultz in her review of De Cazanove 2000c in *BMCR* (2002.06.30) and Glinister 2006a, 21-23.

[49] De Cazanove 2001, 153, cf. *infra* n. 51.

[50] The diversity would reflect "the difference in treatment of the areas after the Roman conquest and the consequences of different types of population mix. Trebula and Corvaro [where votive deposits of the Latin type were found], with their more distinctly Roman cultural and religious characteristics, suggest that their territories were included in the *agri quaestorii* and were therefore lands primarily, if not exclusively inhabited by Roman citizens, while the votive deposits of Nursia and Plestia, with their mixed character, perfectly reflect the situation of the *praefecturae* ... where, for time at least, *cives optimo iure* cohabited with *cives sine suffragio*". (Torelli 1999, 122).

[51] Torelli 1983, 241 on "*le tangibili prove di questa presenza coloniale rispetto alle aree circostanti appartenenti a socii*" and "*l'impatto 'romanizzatore'*" in relation to, amongst other things, the votive deposits of Trebula Mutuesca and Carseoli. Cf. also Coarelli 2000, 200, on the votives in Pisaurum: "*questo tipo di ex-voto è caratteristica esclusiva della cultura laziale: esso costituisce in effetti uno dei più sicuri fossili-guida per identificare la presenza, al di fuori dell'area di origine, di coloni provenienti da Roma o dal Lazio. La presenza di tali oggetti nel lucus pesarese attesta, senza possibilità di dubbio, la frequentazione di esso da parte di coloni viritani ...*"

[52] Torelli 1999, 41-42.

It is important to point out that, in the common view, the material reflections of these typical Roman colonial religious models are not restricted to the colonies and the colonists themselves. Rather, these symbols of *urbanitas* and Romanness would have irradiated from the colonies and affected the surrounding areas. The colonies were in every respect, in Cicero's words, *propugnacula imperii* (*Leg. agr.* 2.73), strongholds of Roman control, and spreading Roman religion outside Rome.[53] Temple architecture, terracotta decoration, and anatomical ex-votos have been assigned key roles in ideological-religious aspects of Roman colonisation, but at the same time these ideological-religious aspects are seen as the agents and markers of 'religious romanisation' *beyond* the colonies. They would have functioned as catalysts, and their beneficiary influence would have spread into the 'indigenous' Italic areas. In particular, the *Capitolium* model would have expressed urbanity and Roman ideals, an abstraction of imperial power and sophistication, and its prestige was the reason Italic neighbours adopted the model. Indeed, according to Torelli, "the superiority of the [*scil.* urban] model ... rendered easy and consequential the exportation of the cultural forms ingrained in that model. Amongst these cultural forms Etrusco-Italic temple building ... took first place".[54] This reasoning therefore posits a development from centre to periphery, with colonies as intermediary points. In this way, architectural or artistic developments in the 'remote' Italic areas can all be ultimately linked to Rome. The Samnite three *cellae* temple at Pietrabbondante located deep in the Apennine mountains, for instance, is generally thought to have been inspired by Roman models (cf. Chapter 3). This view on Roman influence on Italic temple building is, for example, present in Salmon's work. While describing the general influence of Hellenistic culture through mediation by Rome, he states that "the inspiration clearly came from Rome. The many new temples, for instance, owed much to her example," and further on, on Pentrian Samnium, "the temples were not necessarily built to Roman measurements, but in style, lay-out and decoration they owed much to Rome."[55]

This view of the romanising role of colonies is, however, for several reasons problematic. It draws heavily on both a rather unilinear conception of cultural communication (cf. Chapter 1) and a narrow and specific concept of Roman colonisation, which in the last years has been convincingly challenged. As to the latter, in recent studies the uniform and stable, and indeed 'Roman' character of colonies in especially the mid-Republican period has been problematised and to an extent undermined. Especially Michael Crawford, Elizabeth Fentress, and, in more detail, Edward Bispham have shown that much of what we thought we knew about mid-Republican colonisation is actually reconstructed on the basis of late Republican and imperial evidence, reflecting to a large measure anachronistic historical and ideological frameworks.[56] These scholars have shown how the whole edifice rests to a large extent on the Gellian conception of colonies as 'small Romes', whereas contemporary evidence, especially archaeological, to sustain this thesis is lacking. The idea that the founding of colonies was, in the mid-Republican period, the result of a well-planned effort organised by the state authorities which entailed the implantation of a premeditated set of Roman cultural elements has been particularly well debated. Questions have been posed as to the ethnicity of the colonists and especially the influence or persistence of local elements on the formation of the colonies, including their religious dimension.[57]

It goes without saying that with the deconstruction of the "Romanness" of Roman colonisation, the argument that precisely these colonies formed the key factors in the romanisation of Italy is seriously

---

[53] Cf. Cancik 2008, 3-4: "*Die Capitolia in Italien und den Provinzen zeigten auch architektonisch die sakrale Bindung der Kolonie an die Mutterstadt. So diffundierte römische Religion in nicht-römische Gebiete.*"

[54] Torelli 1999, 127. Cf. preceding note.

[55] Salmon 1982, 100, 117.

[56] Crawford 1995; Fentress 2000a, esp. Fentress 2000b; Bispham 2000b; Bispham 2006; cf. also Bradley 2006 on ethnicity and cultural identity, and Mouritsen 2004 on *fora*.

[57] Torelli 1999, 3-5, 14-42, 43-88 and *passim*; Bradley 2006; Bispham 2006.

weakened. This line of reasoning can be developed even further if we take into account the debatable urban character of mid-Republican colonies (an issue which will be discussed in more detail in Chapter 7) but in this chapter the discussion will be limited to the religious aspects that are traditionally associated with ('urban') Roman colonisation.

Recent research into some of these aspects tends to undermine the religious impact of colonies. First, *Capitolium*-temples are actually less ubiquitous than has often been assumed.[58] Neither were they all installed directly or even soon after the foundation of the colony.[59] Whereas for the Republican period, *Capitolia* have been documented in the second and the first centuries BC[60] the situation is quite different in earlier periods. By far most *Capitolia* date to the triumviral and imperial period[61] and in particular Augustan (re-)colonisation seems to have had a crucial role. This has led Bispham to conclude that the Capitoline model, together with the 'Gellian simulacrity' cannot be applied before the second century BC,[62] and Clifford Ando goes so far as to state that it was indeed especially in late Republican and imperial times that the model is to be expected to have worked and, by inference, not earlier.[63] Interestingly, it has been pointed out that the Gellian image of colonies as 'small Romes' is untenable even during the imperial period, including on a religious level. As Mary Beard, John North and Simon Price contend, the "imitation of the religion of the capital must in practice always have been a creative process, involving adaptation and change".[64] Using as an example two altars of Augustan date, where elements of Roman monuments are adapted, it is shown how the *colonia* of Carthage was "expressing its own version of Roman identity", and indeed that "different *coloniae* were Roman in very different ways".[65]

Likewise, the foundation rites of the colonies, with the ritual marking of the *pomerium* are likely to have been especially important in the late Republican and Augustan periods. Ando argues that it is no coincidence that evidence for the use of ploughs in colonial foundations dates to the times of Caesar (Capua, Urso) and Augustus (Asia Minor).[66] If, according to him, the practice of ploughing the primordial furrow in these late colonies was "notionally modelled on that at Rome, we should probably regard it as modelled on a self-understanding achieved in light of antiquarian research and no small amount of invention".[67] Thus, both the *pomerium* and the proliferation of *Capitolia* are to be understood within the creation of a particular ideology situated in the late Republican and Augustan period.[68]

[58] Bispham 2006.

[59] Capua, colonised several times, apparently only received a *Capitolium*-temple under Tiberius (Suet. *Tib.* 40).

[60] Second century: Luna, 177 BC; possibly Liternum 194 BC. The *Capitolium* identified by Johnson (Johnson 1935, 18-41) at Minturnae built "soon after 191 BC" might not have been one: Coarelli 1989, 51-52, since it was located outside the original Roman *oppidum*. First century, especially under Sulla: e.g. the conversion of the temple of Jupiter into a *Capitolium* at Pompeii and perhaps Faesulae (*CIL* XI, 1545) as well. Barton 1982, 262-266. See Bispham 2006, 93 n. 111 with other references, and esp. 99-100 for the weak evidence for the earlier period.

[61] Standard works on *Capitolia* in Italy are Cagiano De Azevedo 1940; Bianchi 1950; Barton 1982, 259-266 (cf. also Todd 1985), see now Lackner in press. Cf. also the considerations in Cifarelli 2003. For Spain, cf. Keay 1988, 117-118, 145-146: (late) second century BC.

[62] Bispham 2006, esp. 93.

[63] Ando 2007, 431-436. Ando questions the importance of *Capitolia* prior to imperial times, arguing that it is "by no means obvious that the tutelary deities of all colonies were – or could be – the same. Not surprisingly, then, *Capitolia* are rather less well attested in early and mid-Republican colonies, but proliferated in the western provinces in the imperial period."

[64] Beard *et al.* 1998, 331.

[65] Beard *et al.* 1998, 333, 334.

[66] Capua: Dessau, *ILS* 6308; Urso: *lex Ursonensis* c. 73; Asia Minor: Levick 1967, 35-37.

[67] Ando 2007, 433.

[68] Bispham 2006, esp. 74-75; Ando 2007, 434, on religious institutions in colonies: "As with the *pomerium*, so with *Capitolia*, it may be that practice homogenized around a particular ideal in response to cultural changes at work in Rome in the late Republic and early Principate."

This deconstruction of the traditional model of continuity in ideology and physical layout of colonies is extremely important. It might not be necessary to relegate these colonial religious and ideological elements solely to late Republican and early imperial invention. The fact that most of the evidence comes from later periods is in itself no proof that similar ideologies did not exist in previous times, and in some cases this is indeed documented. But it is important to re-dimension our views on the 'Romanness' of Republican colonies, and not to fill in the blanks uncritically with later evidence. Furthermore, the periodisation is crucial for the general model. As has been seen, the importance of the *Capitolium* type temple as a firm symbol of Romanness for the early and mid-Republican periods (fifth-third centuries BC) is hard to document, and therefore also the notion of a far-reaching 'romanising' effect of these on the surrounding non-urban areas. From the second century BC onwards there is evidence for the installation of *Capitolia* however, and it seems quite probable that these indeed formed symbols of Romanness and *urbanitas*, or at least expressed allegiance to Roman ideologies, by then. It should be borne in mind however, that Italy had changed profoundly in the meantime and that the gap between the Italic "world of non-cities" and Roman cities that is often conceptualised was in most areas less impressive by then. If the temples could well represent civic or urban pride and express a certain identity for the own urban community, their 'irradiating' effect on the hinterland was therefore perhaps rather limited.

Furthermore, the idea that the spread of Roman religious ideas and superiority were documented by way of the distribution of anatomical votives has been particularly criticised. Maria Donatella Gentili and Fay Glinister have recently pointed out several weaknesses in the idea that anatomical votives closely reflect Roman influence.[69] In the first place, the concept that the distribution pattern of this type coincides neatly with Latin colonisation has been partly formed by a research bias in favour of Latin / Roman areas. The correlation has therefore to be nuanced, since several other less 'Roman' areas also yielded this type of ex-votos,[70] while other areas of Latin colonisation did not yield any at all.[71] Another problem regards the dating of the votives, which is difficult. In any case, Etruscan votives of this type predate Roman colonisation in that area. Moreover, although Greek influence is clear, this cannot be equated with Roman influence (especially since the phenomenon predates the official introduction of Aesculapius in Rome, with which it erroneously has been connected)[72] and local traditions may have played an important role in the development of the type.[73] Thus, both in temporal and in geographical terms, the practice of dedicating anatomical terracottas seems to have been a wider phenomenon.

More fundamentally, Glinister criticises the conceptualisation of the mechanism responsible for the spread of anatomical votives in the traditional 'colonialist' vein. She argues that it is hard to see a deliberate Roman strategy in this regard and points out that their appearance can be better understood as the result of various, local processes by which people chose to adopt these elements as part of the Hellenistic cultural *koiné*.[74] Therefore, anatomical terracottas appear in Roman and Latin communities but "this would represent neither a conscious Roman policy, nor the spread of a distinctively Roman religious form".[75] In other words, even if the relationship between colonisation and this type of votives cannot be entirely downplayed, it seems at least fair to ask whether anatomical votives constituted "quintessentially Roman"[76] rituals, or

[69] Gentili 2005, esp. 372-373; Glinister 2006a; cf. also Glinister 2006b.

[70] Esp. from the Apennines and the Adriatic coast: Gentili 2005, 372 and Glinister 2006a, 18-19, with references. One could add, e.g. Schiavi d'Abruzzo (Campanelli/Faustoferri 1997) and the sanctuary at Casalbore, for which Bonifacio 2000, 34 argues that the appearance of anatomicals found here "*riconduce al discorso degli influssi diversi subíti in questa zona per la presenza di mercenari e la notata posizione dell'area sacra in rapporto con un'importante direttrice di traffico*". Guidobaldi 2005, 397 explains the presence of the type in the 'ethnic' sanctuary of the Marrucini by the romanising influence of colonists.

[71] Gentili 2005, 372.

[72] Cf. *supra* n. 48.

[73] Turfa 2004.

[74] Glinister 2006a, 23-27.

[75] Glinister 2006a, 25, cf. 32.

[76] Torelli 1999, 96.

were perceived as such. Glinister effectively deconstructs the ideological, 'romanising' aspect of anatomical terracottas, and with it their possible role in the 'religious romanisation' of Italy.

The argument is of course basically identical to the discussion on the role of the three *cellae* temple or '*Capitolium*'. It all comes down to the inherent impossibility to read fixed meanings in certain expressions of material culture. These material expressions only gain their possible 'Roman', 'urban' or 'superior' quality within an ideological framework or discourse constructed for that purpose. Whereas a case can surely be made for the interplay with such a discourse in the context of *Capitolia* (in particular in later periods, and much less for three *cellae* temples in general), a similar framework does not seem to exist in the case of the anatomical votives (or at least not in antiquity!). In sum, the image of colonies as key elements in the religious romanisation of Italy in the Republican period needs to be more nuanced, especially regarding the 'irradiation' of Roman religious culture outside the colony. This is not to say that religion and ritual were not important in the colonies; on the contrary, it does seem justified to believe that they were fundamental to the constitution of the new community. Amongst the scanty archaeological evidence for the earliest phases of colonies, cult sites take first place – especially when compared to domestic architecture, for instance. However, whether these rituals were in any way (conceived to be) Roman, or even meant to be spread beyond Roman territory, is an entirely different matter.

2.2 THE FATE OF ITALIC SANCTUARIES: DESTRUCTION, DESOLATION AND COLONISATION

2.2.1 DID ROME CLOSE SANCTUARIES?

It has been noted that the general attitude of Rome towards religious affairs outside its territory is thought to have been one of tolerance, or simply lack of interest. Along with the possible exception of the *Bacchanalia*, one might discern another exception, which in itself is, interesting enough, largely a modern construction, i.e. the idea that Rome closed down or 'abolished' sanctuaries.

Sanctuaries could, as will be discussed in more detail in Chapter 3, become important political foci of the Italic peoples, especially in the non-urbanised areas. As a logical consequence of this political function, it is often assumed that sanctuaries were destroyed or closed after the incorporation in the Roman state. Especially federal or tribal sanctuaries are often thought to have been closed down, such as Pietrabbondante and the Etruscan *fanum Voltumnae*.[77] The idea is present in many studies, especially with regard to Samnite sanctuaries.[78] The sanctuary of Pietrabbondante has even been described as having undergone a proper *damnatio memoriae*,[79] or alternatively a "*profanatio dei sacra publica*", and it has in this context also been assumed that the cult at the sanctuary of Campochiaro was suppressed and transferred to the *municipium* of Bovianum.[80]

---

[77] Gabba 1994a (= Gabba 1972), 97. Cf. p. 98 "*Sembra naturale supporre che si volesse eliminare un centro di autonomismo politico-religioso*". Torelli 1968, 74.

[78] Cf. e.g. Dyson 2003, 79-80: "Since the sanctuaries were the focus of elite resistance to Rome, they were attacked by the Romans, especially during the Social War in the early first century BC. Most were destroyed, but a few did remain in use under the Empire," and recently Zaccardi 2007. Cf. also the reversal of this idea: the fact that sanctuaries had an important function would be proved by the consequent abandonment after the loss of independence: Dench 1995, 139; Lomas 1996, 171.

[79] Scheid 2006b, 78: "*Son abandon traduit la damnatio memoriae définitive du lieu de culte qui servit un temps de centre politique aux insurgés, ainsi que les inscriptions l'attestent. Mais il s'agit là d'un cas extrême.*"

[80] Coarelli/La Regina 1984, 204. Cf. also La Regina 1976, 237 on "*la cancellazione giuridica e la soppressione delle attività ufficiali*". More carefully on Pietrabbondante e.g. Capini 1991b, 114.

Although it is true that the boom in architectural refinement and construction seems to come to an end after the Social War, it is important to emphasise that there is not really evidence for the closure or destruction of Samnite sanctuaries. Archaeologically, at least, it seems hard to find evidence for the official shutting down or destruction of sanctuaries. In fact, post-Social War activity is registered on virtually all of the Samnite cult sites. This applies to not only the most important 'political' sanctuary of Pietrabbondante, but also to Schiavi d'Abruzzo and S. Giovanni in Galdo, the finds from which are discussed in Chapter 5.[81] It is of course possible that these archaeological remains represent 'private' actions, whereas the 'public' aspect of the cult was abolished. A total closing or destruction can be excluded however, and since there is no positive evidence that sanctuaries underwent this kind of official restrictive measures, judgment is perhaps best suspended.[82]

There is, of course, no doubt that sanctuaries were often the target of plunder and destruction, especially during wars and numerous instances are listed in the literary sources.[83] A famous example is the Proserpina sanctuary in Locri which was plundered in 205 BC by Roman soldiers after the city had defected to Hannibal (Liv. 29.8.1). In peace time, the temple of Hera Lacinia near Croton was stripped of its marble tiles by the censor Q. Fulvius Flaccus in 173 BC (Liv. 42.3) and, in a provincial context, the greed of C. Verres between 73 and 70 BC is telling. However, plunder for economic reasons or conscious destruction for ideological reasons in the heat of battle is different from an official restrictive policy banning the use of these sanctuaries once the war was over. Moreover, although the above mentioned cases may represent the tip of the iceberg, it should be emphasised that in each case action was undertaken to protect the affected parties.[84] Before returning to the position of Italic sanctuaries after the Roman conquest, it is of some interest to briefly consider the role of sanctuaries and cult in warfare.

2.2.2 SANCTUARY, CULT AND COMMUNITY IN WARFARE

The sanctuary of Diana Tifatina, on the Mons Tifata some three and a half miles north of Capua, was of central importance for the Capuan community. It may already have occupied a central place in the organisation of the settlement in the ninth century BC.[85] In myth and poetry, the sanctuary is closely connected to the heroic founder of Capua, Capys. Although the genealogical position of this figure remains unclear (he is, in the sources, variously great-grandfather of Rhomos, a relative of Aeneas, one of the Alban kings, or a Samnite hero), the myth may have existed as early as the fourth century BC.[86] The story goes that from the moment that he drew the *sulcus primigenius* of the city, Capys had a white deer that was dedicated to Diana. Since the foundation of the city, the deer had become the *numen loci*, and lived for thousand years (Sil. *Pun.* 13.115-137). Q. Fulvius Flaccus sacrificed the holy deer before taking Capua, which had defected from Rome in 211 BC.[87] As I noted in the introductory chapter, the Roman general thus symbolically destroyed the Capuan community.

[81] Pietrabbondante: cf. esp. Crawford 2006; Vastogirardi: Morel 1984; Schiavi d'Abruzzo: La Regina 1976, 237; cf. for the Roman phase of Campochiaro: Cappelletti 1991 (although perhaps destroyed during the siege of Bovianum in 89 BC, there are materials from the first century BC as well).

[82] Cf. Chapters 7, 8 and esp. 9 on the problem of archaeological 'continuity' at sanctuaries, which may hide re-use under rather different conditions.

[83] Interesting is the example of the rich sanctuary of the *lucus Feroniae*, plundered by Hannibal; apparently the soldiers would have been too scrupulous to take everything out of *religio* (Liv. 26.11.8-10).

[84] Frateantonio 2003.

[85] Frederiksen 1984, 118.

[86] Frederiksen 1984, 118 n. 11 for sources; cf. Heurgon 1942, 325.

[87] Cf. Heurgon 1942, 321-324 and De Franciscis 1956, 45-46 for the sources and the connection to the sanctuary.

In Rome itself, sanctuaries were the symbol *par excellence* for the whole community. In a society whose temples were almost by default the result of military successes,[88] it is perhaps not surprising that conversely great fear existed that the community's gods might fall into the hands of the enemy. During the preparations for the Gallic war in 390 BC, the hierarchy of the Roman values that were to be defended was as follows: *fana deum et coniuges et liberos* (Liv. 5.49.3); first the sanctuaries, then the family.[89] Equally, after the Gauls had left, purifying the temples was given priority (Liv. 5.50). Furthermore, in the highly rhetorical speech by Sp. Postumius Albinus after the defeat in the Caudine Forks, it appears that the greatest fear was the possibility that *hanc urbem templa delubra fines aquas Samnitium esse* (Liv. 9.9.5), again emphasising sanctuaries by giving them the utmost importance, directly after the city itself.[90] It is clear that at least in Livy's text, which was published in a period of religious restoration by Augustus, sanctuary and community were closely bound together.[91]

Another recurring element in descriptions of war is the deportation of cult statues to Rome,[92] again symbolically taking the conquered community into captivity. Often reference is made to the so-called ritual of *evocatio*, i.e. the summoning of the gods of the hostile city to leave the city and come to Rome. However, the historical cases of *evocatio* are few and suspiciously they are especially mentioned in relation to the most imminent and critical moments in Roman history, such as the conflicts during the early Roman expansion into Italy, notably with Veii, and Carthage. Indeed, the capture of Veii in 396 BC with the *evocatio* of Juno Regina has been generally recognised as the prime example.[93] Other cases have been recognised in Volsinii (264), where Vertumnus would have been 'evoked' (and a relation with the *fanum Voltumnae* has been suggested here; cf. *infra*), in Falerii (Minerva Capta and Juno Curitis), and in Carthage (in 146 BC, Juno Caelestis). However, all these cases are quite dubious, reconstructed as they are on rather late and seldom explicit historical evidence (especially Livy, Servius and Macrobius).[94] An inscription found at Isaura Vetus in Turkey, dating to 75 BC, has also been interpreted as evidence for an *evocatio*, but this cannot be inferred from the actual text.[95]

In a critical study, Gabriella Gustafsson has shown that the idea of the existence of a fixed practice or rite of *evocatio* is highly problematic and that later mythography and historiography, and especially the intertwining of these, have (in)formed our scarce sources to such a degree that the concept of *evocatio* is hard to use for historical analysis.[96] It might seem therefore that accounts on the ritual of the *evocatio* can be highly interesting in the context of the ideological and theological frameworks at the time that these accounts were written,[97] but are to be used with great caution in the discussion on the religious romanisation of Italy in the Republican period.

Even if some of these episodes have a historical basis, it should not be excluded that stories of *evocationes* were especially or even exclusively important to (a certain group of leading) citizens of Rome and did

---

[88] Cf. Ziolkowski 1992; Aberson 1994; Orlin 1997.

[89] *in conspectu habentes fana deum et coniuges et liberos et solum patriae deforme belli malis et omnia quae defendi repetique et ulcisci fas sit*: "They must keep before their eyes the temples of the gods, their wives and children, and their country's soil, disfigured by the ravages of war-everything, in a word, which it was their duty to defend, to recover or to avenge."

[90] For these examples, Stek 2004, 32-33.

[91] For religion in Livy cf. Levene 1993, on the relation with Augustan ideology esp. 245-248.

[92] E.g. the statue of Jupiter Imperator from Praeneste in 380 BC: Liv. 6.29.8.

[93] Liv. 5.21-22. On *evocatio* see esp.: Basanoff 1945; Le Gall 1976; Blomart 1997; Gustafsson 2000; Ferri 2006.

[94] See Gustafsson 2000, 46-62 for discussion.

[95] Le Gall 1976 followed by Beard *et al.* 1998, 133, dismissed by Gustafsson 2000, 60-62.

[96] Gustafsson 2000. Cf. the attempt by Blomart 1997 to opt for a wider definition of *evocatio* – including e.g. the introduction of Magna Mater (204 BC) and Aesculapius (292 BC), which however only leads to the devaluation of the term.

[97] Cf. e.g. Feeney 1998.

not affect the communities that were 'deprived' of their gods. In any case, it remains doubtful whether the conquered communities believed that their gods had left to Rome of their own will. In this context, it is interesting to ask what happened to the cult places after they had been robbed of their gods. Answering this perhaps somewhat naïve question is of course difficult in light of the nature of the evidence, but it is nevertheless important, especially with regard to the possible intentions from the Roman side.

The *evocatio* of Juno Regina from Veii is often accepted as more or less historical.[98] The discussion on the location of the temple of Juno Regina has perhaps not yet been satisfactorily concluded and still awaits firm proof, but present evidence seems to support Torelli's thesis that the temple is to be identified on the edge of the Piano di Comunità, and not, as previously thought, in the Piazza d'Armi temple.[99] It follows that the 'break' in the cult that has been recognised in the Piazza d'Armi temple[100] has nothing to do with the *evocatio* of Juno Regina. Moreover, the cult place on the Piano di Comunità presents a rather different scenario, with materials varying from bucchero through black gloss to Roman wares apparently documenting continuity from the fifth century BC to the Roman imperial period.[101] Nearby, a deposit with votives dating from the fourth to second centuries BC has been revealed. Thus, as Torelli demonstrates, the cult seems to have continued after the alleged transfer of the cult statue in 396 BC.[102]

One could argue therefore, that this case of *evocatio* reveals the existence of discrepant experiences in Roman and local traditions. No mention is made of the duplication or continuation on the place of origin of cults in *evocatio* contexts, but it might be suggested that this is not accidental because to the Roman audience for which the *evocatio* was 'evoked', it was of no importance whether the cult continued in the place of origin or not.

A thorough analysis of the relevant passages on the destruction of sanctuaries during warfare is outside the scope of this discussion,[103] but one gets the impression that the above posited nature of the *evocatio* accounts could apply as well to the more general descriptions of sanctuaries that are being destroyed. This is of course not to say that Roman soldiers did not ransack sanctuaries, but it seems quite probable that the rhetorical and ideological frameworks within which the Roman historians worked highly influenced these accounts and the factual destruction of a sanctuary could have been given a specific and differing meaning according to the different groups involved.

---

[98] E.g. Rüpke 1990, 162-163; Beard *et al.* 1998, 34-35 and even the very critical Gustafsson 2000, 52 admits that "it is reasonable to assume that there is at least a core of historical truth in it".

[99] Torelli 1982, arguing that Piazza d'Armi cannot be the *arx*, whereas Livy 6.21.10 explicitly states that the *aedes Junonis* was located *in Veientana arce*. Followed also by Colonna 2004. (Somewhat curiously, Gustafsson 2000, 46-47 seems to suggest that the Portonaccio temple is also a candidate).

[100] Ward-Perkins 1961, 55, followed by Gustafsson 2000, 47 (apparently unaware of Torelli 1982).

[101] Torelli 1982, 125. There might have been as well an Augustan reconstruction phase: 128. Excavations have been prompted by Torelli's hypothesis: cf. Colonna 2004. Interesting to note, in Livy 5.22, before the transfer, the statue of Juno is asked to come to Rome again after the *evocatio* proper (although it should be remembered that the word *evocatio* does not appear once in the whole passage).

[102] Torelli extrapolates this situation, interpreting it as a typical feature of *evocationes*. He argues that the rite "*consisteva in effetti nella sola traslazione del signum*" and adduces Falerii and *lucus Feroniae* as further examples of *evocationes* where cult continued (Torelli 1982, 128). In these last two cases no *evocatio* is documented however. (On Falerii see Gustafsson 2000, 56-59. No sources exist for Feronia's alleged *evocatio*, but it has been proposed to connect her cult in Rome with M.' Curius Dentatus' campaign in 290 BC in the Sabine area, or the capture of the *lucus Feroniae* near Capena in 395 BC. Cf. Torelli 1982, 128 n. 53; Coarelli 1980, 284; Coarelli 1981b, 40-42; Coarelli 1997, 198).

[103] Cf. e.g. Frateantonio 2003, 88-95; on the relation between sanctuaries and warfare in esp. the Greek / Hellenistic world cf. the contributions in Sordi 1984.

2.2.3 THE DECLINE AND INCORPORATION OF RURAL SANCTUARIES AFTER THE SOCIAL WAR

Whether or not Rome violently or legally suppressed Italic sanctuaries, there is general consensus that rural sanctuaries declined after the Social War. This is most often seen as a result of the urbanisation that was a feature of Roman municipalisation. Attention was focused on the new urban centres and it is there that most monumental buildings arise. The survival of Italic cult places would have depended on the extent of their integration in the new municipal structures.[104] In this sense, Kathryn Lomas, voicing a widely held view, argues that the decline of rural sanctuaries after the Social War "was symbolic of increasing Romanization" and that "emphasis shifted towards temples and shrines in the growing (and Romanized) cities".[105] Similarly, Stephen Dyson states that "in areas like Samnium this [legal restructuring] meant the development of new urban entities designed to replace the old system of *pagi*, *vici* and tribal sanctuaries. Some of the great sanctuaries like Pietrabbondante were sacked … Others continued in use, but they were subordinated to the local *municipia*".[106]

The elaboration of this view will be treated in greater detail in Chapter 4. It is however important to note here that the development of rural sanctuaries is thus seen as *antagonistic* to Roman impact. In equating romanisation with urbanisation, rural sanctuaries are associated with traditional Italic patterns of settlement. In this view, Roman religious models would have spread in the new urban centres but would have left rural religious structures untouched.[107] In cases where rural sanctuaries continue to exist, these are explained in terms of the 'survival' of obsolete countryside traditions or as chance integration into Roman structures. An often quoted example of the latter is the sanctuary of Hercules Curinus in Abruzzo. This cult place is thought to have originated as an Italic *pagus* sanctuary but would have developed into a municipal sanctuary after the installation of a *municipium* at Sulmo (cf. Chapter 4).[108] The general idea, however, is that chances for survival of rural Italic sanctuaries into Roman times were small and this is an important undercurrent in modern conceptions of the changing role of non-urban cult places in Italy during the last centuries BC.

Yet, in at least some cases Rome betrayed a special interest in ancient Italic sanctuaries, as can be seen in the legal statuses that were assigned to them after the Roman conquest. As has recently been pointed out by Scheid, at least in the latter half of the first century BC and in the early empire, and not surprisingly in particular under Augustus, a strategy of incorporation of cult places can be discerned.[109] Examples are the *lucus Feroniae*, which was transformed into a colony, and at Hispellum, where Octavian apparently installed the new colony on the site of an ancient Umbrian federal or 'ethnic' sanctuary. A similar case may be made for the ancient sanctuary of Cupra maritima[110] and the sanctuary of Angitia, in

---

[104] Curti *et al.* 1996, 179. Cf. e.g. also Lomas 1996, 171.

[105] Lomas 1996, 172.

[106] Dyson 1992, 67.

[107] Cf. esp. Letta 1992.

[108] Cf. Guarducci 1981, 226 and *infra*. The link with the *municipium* would be demonstrated by an inscription of a *miles e municipio Sulmone* and an inscription referring to an *auguratus*, "probabilmente municipale" (Letta 1992, 116). As for the sanctuary of Hercules at S. Agata in Campo Macrano, near Castelvecchio Subequo, which would have started as a *pagus* sanctuary and was later incorporated in the centre of the *municipium* of Superaequum (Van Wonterghem 1984, 78, site 1, 5c), the epigraphic evidence does not seem to justify such an interpretation.

[109] Scheid 2006b, 80 (quote). Cf. e.g. also Basanoff's interpretation of the appropriation of the *fanum Voltumnae* (Basanoff 1945, 59-63); Gabba 1994a, 97 on *lucus Angitiae*; Whittaker 1997, 143, who points out, in relation to the *evocatio* of Juno from Carthage in 146 BC, that "local cults were to be colonised"; the first Roman Carthage was called *colonia Junonia*.

[110] Scheid 2006b, 80-84; Coarelli 2001b. The evidence for Fanum Fortunae seems too meagre to argue for a similar case however. Cf. also the case of Monte Giove in Picenum, Chapter 7.

Marsic territory was made *municipium*, perhaps already before the mid-first century BC.[111] According to Scheid, this policy was not exclusive to the Augustan period, with its well-known program of religious restoration. Augustus would rather have continued an earlier tradition in the treatment of symbolically important sanctuaries.[112] Although the evidence for earlier periods is often somewhat fragile, early examples of incorporation could be recognised in the usurpation of the Latin sanctuary at Monte Cavo after the dissolving of the Latin league, or the sanctuary of Juno Sospita at Lanuvium, which was now common to both Romans and Lanuvians, and at Lavinium rites were also celebrated in common.[113] Perhaps also the sanctuary of Clitumnus, famous in imperial literature, could have already been colonised in an early stage, together with the installation of the Latin colony of Spoletium in 241 BC.[114] The already mentioned sanctuary of Diana Tifatina was to have, in later times, a similar fate. After his victory on Norbanus at Mons Tifata, Sulla gave lands and salubrious sources to this sanctuary, a situation which was reaffirmed under Augustus and Vespasian.[115] Moreover, the sanctuary held, at least in the imperial period, an independent status comparable to a *municipium* or a *praefectura*. It appears that Sulla and his successors transformed the cult place into an autonomous district, thereby retracting the sanctuary from other influences and appropriating it for Roman purposes.[116] The precise significance of the granting of these legal statuses (especially in the case of imperial colonisation) must in most cases remain unclear. But it is certainly appealing to discern, with Scheid, a Roman habit of consciously appropriating some famous Italic cult places, by which these cult places, full of symbolic power, acquired an autonomous and by consequence Roman status. Interestingly, in this way the cult places are often transformed into Roman 'urban' or semi-urban structures. One could add that the rationale behind this policy might have also had an economic dimension since many of the sanctuaries involved, such as the *lucus Feroniae*, were important market places.

2.3 CONCLUSION: URBANITY AND THE UNAFFECTED COUNTRYSIDE

This brief survey of ideas on the 'religious romanisation' of Italy in relation to the development of Italic sanctuaries seems to indicate that the influence of Roman religious models on other Italic peoples is much harder to trace than has often been assumed, or at least occurred in different forms than often assumed. Indeed, the basic notion is that Rome would have fostered a non-intervention policy. Equally, the most generally accepted idea on the development of rural Italic cult places after the Roman conquest and/or the Social War is that they slowly declined as a result of the Roman emphasis on urban centres, not through active intervention by Rome.

In addition, all the identified 'exceptions' to this general framework appear to be rather problematic or marginal. As regards active restriction, the standard example of the *senatusconsultum de Bacchanalibus* remains problematic because the addressees of the ban are unclear. Even if it seems more reasonable to accept that Rome also wanted to intervene outside Roman territory, this must indeed have been an exceptional case. Evidence for the active destruction or closing down of sanctuaries is moreover practi-

---

[111] Cf. Gabba 1994a, 97; Scheid 2006b, 84: "*et sans doute encore par Sylla.*" This is on the basis of the idea that the IIIIvir of *CIL* IX, 3894 is actually from *lucus Angitiae*, and not from Alba Fucens (as argued by Letta 1972).

[112] Scheid 2006b, esp. 77, 80, 86.

[113] Liv. 8.14.2; Macrob. *Sat.* 3.4.11. Scheid 2006b, 79.

[114] Plin. *Ep.* 8.8. Scheid 2006b, 80.

[115] Vell. Pat. 2.25.4; *CIL* X, 3828; Dessau, *ILS* 3240 = *AE* 1894, 146.

[116] Scheid 2006b, 79: "*le principe de l'initiative est transparent: il s'agissait de soustraire ce fameux sanctuaire et site à toute influence extérieure, pour le rendre autonome, autrement dit dépendant de Rome seule.*"

cally non-existent. Surely, sanctuaries were pillaged during conflicts (and also in peace time), but there is no evidence for the systematic suppression of Italic cult places.

Urban centres have been seen as the key feature in the process of the spread of Roman religious ideas in Italy. Latin and Roman colonies would have displayed urbanity and 'Romanitas' by means of cults, rituals or other religious representations. In particular two elements are often highlighted in this context, namely the Capitoline cult and associated temples, and votives of the Etrusco-Latial-Campanian type. Yet, it is precisely the role of colonies that has been seriously undermined by a recent development in studies on Roman Republican colonisation, which following postcolonialist insights seeks to re-dimension the 'Roman' and rigidly state-organised character of Roman colonisation. As to the specific case of the anatomical votives, it has been shown by Gentili and Glinister that the idea that this type of votives would map the level of religious romanisation of different parts of Italy is highly problematic. They can certainly not simply be used as an 'indicator' of Roman or 'romanised' people. Furthermore, *Capitolia* are less well attested than one would perhaps expect for the mid-Republican period, although in the late Republican period they apparently could convey an urban, 'Roman' ideology. The supposed 'irradiation' of this model and the conception of the architectural model as 'Roman' outside the colonial territories remains however a moot point. These recent developments might seem, therefore, to further diminish the Roman religious impact on Italy.

It therefore might appear that the influence of Rome in the sacred realm was on the whole fairly limited. Moreover, this influence can be recognised almost exclusively in urban contexts. Although it sometimes has been proposed that religious forms 'irradiated' from there to the countryside, this aspect has been particularly hard to prove. Rather, the countryside seems to have remained largely untouched and developments there are seen as antithetic to the Roman urban forms. In this way, for the Apennine region, Cesare Letta has indeed argued that "*nei santuari rurali della regio IV la romanizzazione praticamente non tocca le tradizioni religiose locali, formatesi nei secoli precedenti ... I culti propriamente romani che vengono trapiantati nella regio IV sono introdotti nelle città, non nell'ambiente rurale.*"[117] In the few cases that Roman influence can be documented in Italic cult places, this involves a strategy of incorporation in the Roman state, often by 'autonomisation', and indeed 'urbanising' them.

What in any case comes clearly to the fore is that when discussing 'religious romanisation' there is a strong tendency in modern scholarship to make a sharp distinction between urban and rural contexts. Rural patterns of settlement, and the sanctuaries and cults within them, are commonly seen as persistent and uninterrupted features of Italic life, untouched or only remotely affected by new developments. But was the Italic countryside indeed left behind, and did change only occur in the new urban centres? Such an idea must be carefully tested in light of the changing roles of Italic sanctuaries before and after growing Roman influence and authority.

---

[117] Letta 1992, 122.

3 Samnium: The Sacred Construction of Community and Architectural Forms

In the preceding chapters I questioned the developments in central-southern Italy after the Roman conquest from the perspective of cultural change and noted difficulties with the interpretation of material culture as an indicator of romanisation (Chapter 1). The central importance of religion and cult places for the expression of communal identities has become clear, for example in Capua with Diana's deer, or with the late Republican Roman *Capitolia* in urban centres (Chapter 2). Many of these themes of cultural change, material culture, and the role of religious places can be tested, or illustrated in the case of Pentrian Samnium. The role that sanctuaries assumed in this mountainous area during and after the Roman conquest is conspicuous, as is their material aspect. As shown here, Pentrian Samnium offers a solid example of the role that sanctuaries could assume in the reinforcement of specific identities in relation to the changed situation after the Roman conquest. Moreover, it will be argued that the adoption of different cultural elements or architectural 'styles' can be seen as a corollary to this specific process, rather than as an autonomous 'spread' of these models because of their presumed intrinsic cultural values. In order to contextualise this case study on the sacred landscape of Samnium, I present a short review of the research history and ideas on Samnite society.

3.1 SAMNIUM: RESEARCH HISTORY

Amongst Italy's inland regions, Samnium has long held a privileged position in modern research, interest being stimulated early on by Livy's vivid account of the Samnite Wars. The territory inhabited in antiquity by the Samnites Pentri, one of five subgroups considered to have made up the "Samnites", forms the heartland of ancient Samnium. The area largely occupies modern upland Molise and part of southern Abruzzo. In antiquity the mountainous landscape formed one of the most impervious and (at least from a central-Tyrrhenian perspective) remote areas of central Italy, hard to access by land and with none of the limited advantages of the Adriatic coastal area,[1] which was occupied by the Frentani. The historical sources on the Samnites Pentri are relatively abundant. In Greek and Roman sources the belligerent Pentri are depicted as the major obstacle on Rome's route to absolute power over the Italian peninsula, from the fourth century to the Social War. Their geographical position and historical role have helped to create an image of the area as the 'core-region' of Samnite culture and resistance to the spread of Roman dominion. The Pentri are also relatively well known through the material record.

The ubiquitous hill-forts and sanctuaries have always constituted the most visible elements of the Samnite landscape and have therefore attracted – and dominated – scholarly interest. The ample archaeological knowledge of Samnium is due to a remarkable interest from Italian, regional and Anglo-Saxon scholarship.[2] The *Soprintendenze* of Abruzzo and Molise have, starting with the pioneering studies, espe-

---

[1] Cf. D'Ercole 2002.

[2] Samnium, occupying a central place in central-Italian research, is well represented in general studies on central and south Italy: cf. Crawford 1981 for literature up to 1981, and up to 1996 Curti *et al.* 1996.

cially those by Adriano La Regina in the 1960s and 1970s, brought to light much of the archaeological material. The results have been published in various contributions and especially in a series of exhibition catalogues.[3] Furthermore, various predominantly British field survey projects have added invaluable information about ancient settlement patterns.[4] Most famous is the Biferno Valley project directed by Graeme Barker through the 1970s, a benchmark project in Mediterranean archaeological research and especially renowned for its application of a long term perspective.[5] Scholarly research on Samnite culture has met modern interest in the construction of a local or regional identity for the relatively underdeveloped and depopulated region of Molise, for which purpose Samnite 'resistance' to the Roman hegemony has been paralleled with (desired) local attitudes to politics in Italy and the European Union.[6] Local interest resulted in research by archaeological clubs and other amateurs mainly published privately or in regional journals.

The classical work *Samnium and the Samnites* by the Canadian Edward Togo Salmon[7] is fundamental but is to a considerable extent outmoded by recent archaeological data as well as developments in historical and historiographical research. With regard to the historical framework, the works of Marta Sordi and more recently Tim Cornell are important, since they have questioned the traditional chronologies and character of the Samnite wars.[8] Indeed, it could be asked whether the military actions actually deserve the name 'Samnite Wars'. The usual subdivision into three or four Samnite wars is a modern invention, dating back to Niebuhr's *Römische Geschichte* (1833), whereas ancient authors refer to one 'Great Samnite War' from 343 to 290 BC. Cornell suggests that the actions referred to may rather have consisted of a series of independent military actions.[9]

More importantly, archaeological knowledge has expanded tremendously since 1967. If the first systematic research starting in the 1960s did not at first permit an integrated narrative to complement Salmon's more historical approach, the situation has changed in recent years due to data coming from the *Soprintendenze*'s long-term and rescue excavations, as well as other projects in the wake of the general reappraisal of Italic archaeology. The most recent and comprehensive general study on Samnite history, culture and socio-political organisation is the work by Gianluca Tagliamonte entitled *I Sanniti: Caudini, Irpini, Pentri, Carricini, Frentani*, carefully integrating historical, epigraphic, numismatic and archaeological material.[10]

3.1.1 MODERN AND ANCIENT VIEWS

The prevailing Graeco- or Romanocentric views of both ancient and modern historiographic traditions have certainly helped to establish an image of a backward Samnite culture. Salmon tends to depict Samnites as a fierce, stubborn and valiant mountain tribe and sympathises with their struggle against the Romans.[11] Notwithstanding this partisan element, one may find that Salmon did not break free from the historical framework and preconceptions provided by Livy. He stresses the opposition between Romans

---

[3] La Regina 1976; Cianfarani *et al.* 1978; *Sannio* 1980; *Sannio* 1984; Capini/Di Niro 1991; *Romanisation* 1991; *Sanniti* 2000; cf. Jones 2004.

[4] See the overview in Patterson 2006a, 80-82.

[5] Barker 1995.

[6] Dench 1995, 4-10; see the introduction in Sirago 2000.

[7] Salmon 1967.

[8] Esp. Sordi 1969; Cornell 2004.

[9] Cornell 2004.

[10] Tagliamonte 1997.

[11] As Martin Frederiksen stated in a review in 1968 (Frederiksen 1968, 224): "indeed, Professor Salmon has almost changed into a Samnite himself. His heart clearly warms to the majestic landscape of the Apennines; and when he turns to write of the long struggle between Samnium and Rome, he becomes frankly and engagingly partisan."

and Samnites quite heavily and in the end his Samnites are not very dissimilar from the Livian *montani atque agrestes*.[12] It has been noted that a fatalistic element seems present in Salmon's work, which sees the final Roman conquest as an inescapable and perhaps not undesirable event,[13] a conception that fits well into the unification paradigm outlined in Chapter 1.[14]

In her groundbreaking work *From Barbarians to New Men* Emma Dench highlights and deconstructs these conceptualisations of the peoples of the central Apennines and Samnium proper.[15] She shows how certain preoccupations have influenced the depiction of these peoples in antiquity. The importance of portraying the enemy negatively, for instance, accounts for Livy's somewhat contradictory assertions on both Samnite primitivism and *luxuria*. Even more interesting are the changes in the Roman perception of the Italic peoples as they, once under Roman rule, were invaluable for the supply of manpower. In the late Republic and Augustan age, the 'foreignness' of Samnite culture is even instrumentalised to enhance the moral excellence attributed to the Sabines by conflating both Samnites and Sabines in the neologism 'Sabelli'.[16] In this way, an 'Italic' ideal is invented by combining Sabine piety and Samnite bravery.

With regard to modern views, Dench has more recently shown how various factors have contributed to the 'anti-classical' image of Samnium.[17] Livy's account of the Samnite Wars and the archaeologically most visible mid-Republican period were most important in the evocation of an anti-Roman and anti-classical image. This view was enhanced by the disciplinary divide between archaeology and history. The lack of discussion and cross-fertilisation between Barker's landscape research and more classical studies can, for example, be explained by this disciplinary divide.

3.1.2 ECONOMY AND PATTERNS OF SETTLEMENT

The general image of 'backwardness' discussed above has influenced ideas on economy and settlement patterns in Samnium. Modern studies may have over-emphasised the importance of pastoralism for Samnite economies.[18] Recent studies tend to balance this pastoralist vision with evidence for risk-spreading mixed farming.[19] Research on the Iron Age communities that apparently participated in Italic networks on a larger scale than formerly assumed, combined with an increasing interest in Greek-Hellenistic elements in Samnite culture, have contested the alleged isolation of Samnium.[20] From the third century BC onwards, many Italic people appear to have participated in the Mediterranean trade networks and it is thought that Samnium benefited from these enterprises. Yet, there can be no question about the distinctive character of ancient Samnium. Its particularly late urban development firmly deviates from Graeco-Roman ideas of civilisation. We must not overestimate the relatively poor material culture of the Iron Age. After all, it cannot seriously compete with the Tyrrhenian or even neighbouring 'peripheral' Samnite regions such as internal Campania, if not understood within different societal frameworks.

---

[12] Dench 1995, 5.

[13] Dench 2004.

[14] Interestingly, we may distinguish a certain development in Salmon's view of Roman domination since, after adopting a 'partisan' position in his 1967 work, via his *Nemesis of Empire* lectures, he ends up with his strongly pro-Roman *The making of Roman Italy* of 1982 (Salmon 1982).

[15] Dench 1995.

[16] Dench 1995.

[17] Dench 2004.

[18] In particular, the scale and forms of transhumance (the seasonal moving of the herds) have been discussed at length. Central to this discussion is the applicability of evidence of later periods (mostly Roman imperial or even early modern) to earlier times (cf. Chapter 4 for discussion).

[19] Contributions in Barker/Lloyd 1991; Barker 1995.

[20] E.g. La Regina 1989; Barker 1995; Tagliamonte 1997; Lloyd *et al.* 1997.

The standard view of the Samnite landscape can be summarised as 'dispersed villages and farms around hill-forts and rural sanctuaries'. The Samnites have often been described as a tribal society, based on a *pagus-vicus* pattern of settlement, in which *pagi* (territorial districts) would include one or more *vici* (villages or hamlets).[21] From an archaeological point of view the still visible hill-forts and sanctuaries have attracted the most attention. Hill-forts, mostly built up in polygonal walling, are spread throughout the whole central Apennines. Due to a lack of excavation data, their date and function within the ancient settlement pattern often remain problematic. It is not clear whether they were permanently inhabited or served only as temporary refuges for the people living in the valleys.[22] The small sample of excavated hill-forts yielded evidence for at least semi-permanent habitation in all cases.[23] The west-Lucanian hill-fort of Roccagloriosa has been thoroughly investigated using a combination of excavation and field survey in the territory.[24] Roccagloriosa is often evoked as a model for hill-forts within Samnite society.[25] According to this model, local elites from within the walls controlled a community living dispersed in the direct territory of the hill-fort.[26] Hill-forts would thus have assumed a centralising role in the formulation of institutional and political structures.[27] To give weight to this central role, Maurizio Gualtieri has argued for a '*vicus-pagus-oppidum* system', a variant of the *pagus-vicus* system with more emphasis on the hill-fort or *oppidum*.[28]

The question remains, however, whether this west-Lucanian model may be used to complement our knowledge of the more internal zones of Samnium. Regional differences remain essential and interpretations must in the first instance depend on the actual local data. Settlement patterns in Lucania and Samnium differ substantially in archaeological and chronological terms. The well-documented site of Roccagloriosa risks overshadowing other less investigated sites in inland Samnium, dominating the interpretation of the latter. Arguably, for other Samnite hill-forts we should adopt the admirable *methodology* applied at Roccagloriosa, rather than the actual model of settlement organisation encountered there.[29]

---

[21] Cf. Chapter 4 for a description and Chapter 6 for detailed critique of the *pagus-vicus* system.

[22] Cf. Oakley 1995 for discussion.

[23] Oakley 1995, 142. All eight (partially) excavated hill-forts yielded evidence for habitation, six of which are located in the Samnite heartland: Curino (Alfedena): Mariani 1901; La Regina 1976, 219-223; Coarelli/La Regina 1984, 260-265; Terravecchia (Saepinum): Colonna 1962; Matteini Chiari 1997; Rocca d'Oratino: Oakley 1995, 116-117; Monte Pallano: Lloyd *et al.* 1997, 47-48; Monte Vairano: a.o. De Benedittis 1980; De Benedittis 1990a; De Benedittis 1991; De Benedittis 2004; Bovianum: De Benedittis 1977; De Benedittis 2004. Outside the direct Samnite territory: Conta Haller 1978; the Marsic centre of Collelongo (Amplero): a.o. Letta 1991; Paoletti 1988, and the Paelignian Colle delle Fate (Roccacasale): O. Zanco in: Mattiocco 1981, 83-92; Roccagloriosa in Lucania: Gualtieri/Fracchia 1990; Gualtieri/Fracchia 2001; Gualtieri 2004.

[24] Gualtieri/Fracchia 1990; Gualtieri/Fracchia 2001.

[25] E.g. Oakley 1995, 142; Lloyd *et al.* 1997, 48; Gualtieri 2004.

[26] The inclusion of hill-forts within *pagi* is, however, firmly part of the traditional concept of the *pagus-vicus* system, cf. e.g. Kornemann 1942b, 2321: "*Jeder p[agus] enthielt auch ein oder mehrere oppida. Zum offenen Gau gehörte als Zufluchtsort die Gauburg.*" Cf. Kornemann 1942a, 710: "*Wie pagus der Gau, so ist o[ppidum] in der kleinsten Form die Gauburg, in grösseren Dimensionen dagegen die Stammes- oder Volksburg. Pagus und o[ppidum], Gau und Gauburg, sind die beiden wichtigsten Glieder altitalischen Siedelns.*"

[27] In this regard a fragment of a bronze plaque with an inscribed *lex*, thought to derive from a public building near the central gate at Roccagloriosa, is relevant because it mentions magistrates and other formulae seem reminiscent of Latin *leges*. Gualtieri dates it to the first half of the third century BC (the late date around 130 BC initially proposed by Tocco 2000, 224 must be erroneous; see Gualtieri 2000).

[28] This system would have formed an "embryonic form of territorial 'city-state'": Gualtieri 2004, 46.

[29] Stek 2006, 405-406.

If the evidence for Samnite hill-forts is already meagre, other types of settlements have unfortunately been even less investigated. Although as noted the general image of Samnite society is one of dispersed villages and farms, and field surveys have revealed relatively high densities of rural settlements, only very few of them have been excavated. Amongst them are the farmsteads at Matrice and Cercemaggiore, dating to the third century BC onwards.[30] The excavation and complete publication of a small Samnite village or hamlet at Capracotta by Ivan Rainini as yet stand alone.[31]

More attention has been paid to the sanctuaries,[32] and the available evidence allows creating a general picture of their development in relation to developments in Samnite history and society. In the overview I give in the following, the sanctuaries of Pietrabbondante and S. Giovanni in Galdo are discussed in more detail because of their status as the most 'typical' Samnite sanctuaries in modern literature. Whereas the first would represent the Samnite 'federal' or 'state' sanctuary, the latter allegedly represents a typical small Samnite sanctuary.

3.2 SAMNITE SANCTUARIES: NEW FORMS AND TRADITION

The remains of monumental sanctuaries form the most conspicuous part of the archaeology of the Hellenistic period in Samnium and have therefore attracted much of the scholarly attention devoted to this region. Our modern view of Samnium is certainly biased in favour of sanctuaries because of scholarly traditions, disproportionably preoccupied with monumental architecture. However, this situation also reflects at least in part an ancient preoccupation with sacred places. The few well excavated remains of domestic and funeral contexts from the same period appear rather poor when compared to the relatively opulent temples. It appears that in this period the ancient inhabitants of Samnium invested more readily in their sacred places than in, for instance, sumptuous funerals, houses, or secular public buildings.

A diachronical perspective is useful to gauge this importance. Before the fifth century BC there is no evidence for cult places of any substance but rich graves occupy a prominent position. Cult places become visible in the archaeological record from about the fourth century BC and their heyday is after the Samnite Wars in the late third and second centuries BC. Graves almost disappear from sight and reveal a standardisation in grave gifts unfamiliar to the earlier period. In sum, a shift of focus away from graves to sanctuaries is evident.[33]

Generally, sanctuaries do not yet appear in monumentalised form until the third century. Votive objects and weapons are deposited at some cult places. Weapons of foreign origin have been found at the sanctuary at Pietrabbondante. Some of the weaponry can be dated as early as the late fifth century BC. They have been interpreted as a communal dedication, booty being offered and displayed in the sanctuary after battle (*spolia hostium*, perhaps even a proper *congeries armorum*)[34] but probably also reflect different rituals on an individual level.[35] In light of these finds, Pietrabbondante may have already been serving as a symbolic central place in this period.[36]

---

[30] Matrice: Lloyd/Rathbone 1984; Lloyd 1991b; Barker 1995, 224-226. Cercemaggiore: Di Niro/Petrone 1993.

[31] Rainini 1996.

[32] Although the publication of the excavation data is often rather brief, primarily available as short contributions in catalogues or guides. For research on Samnite sanctuaries see *infra* and Chapter 4.

[33] E.g. Tagliamonte 2004, 104-105; cf. similar ideas on the shift of focus from different contexts in D'Ercole 2000.

[34] La Regina 1976, 226; La Regina 1984, 24-25.

[35] For the weapons, cf. Coarelli/La Regina 1984, 236-238, with Tagliamonte 2002-2003 and Tagliamonte 2006 for a careful reinterpretation.

[36] Cf. *infra* n. 70.

The Samnite Wars ended in 290 BC with an unequal treaty for the Samnites. After the Roman victory, the pattern of settlement changed dramatically. In 263 BC the Romans placed the Latin colony Aesernia in the middle of Pentrian territory and later a *praefectura* was established at Venafrum, the important passage to Campania. A three *cellae* temple was apparently built at Aesernia in this time, perhaps indeed a *Capitolium*, symbolising and propagating an urban way of life and 'Romanness' (cf. Chapter 2).[37] It is also during this period that Samnite cult places are structured more solidly. Cult buildings were erected in locations which presumably had formerly been open-air cult places. The best example of this development is the sanctuary at Pietrabbondante.

Excavations at Pietrabbondante began in 1857 under the Bourbons. In the 1960s and 1970s systematic research was carried out by La Regina and this has been resumed recently. The results have been published in various contributions.[38] In the course of the second half of the third century BC this sanctuary assumed monumental forms. The so-called 'Ionic temple' can be dated to this time. The surviving architectural remains suggest that it consisted of a temple and some smaller structures.[39] This temple probably occupied the space later taken by the theatre-temple complex.[40] La Regina suggests that the form of this earliest sanctuary[41] reflected the *locus consaeptus* mentioned by Livy when describing a Samnite military rite performed at Aquilonia in 293 BC, in the course of the Third Samnite War (Livy 10.38; cf. Introduction). This time-honoured Samnite ritual, which was central to the formation of the *legio linteata* (the elite soldiers of the Samnite army), took place in a square sacred area of 200 by 200 feet which was boarded off and covered all over with linen cloth. According to La Regina this would match the dimensions of the theatre and the frontal alignment of the later Temple B.[42] At the end of the third century BC the 'Ionic temple' was destroyed.[43]

A new temple (Temple A) was built in the second quarter of the second century BC. It was set on a podium (17.70 x 12.20 x 1.65 m) and was probably prostyle and tetrastyle, with a single *cella*. Several Oscan inscriptions mentioning magistrates indicate that this temple was the focus of Samnite political life during the second century BC. Parts of the building were dedicated by magistrates and the *gens Staia* appears to have been especially active here.[44] The most intriguing inscription is however Vetter 149, dated to the second century BC, which mentions *safinim sak*, referring to a *sak[araklum]* or in any case a sacred

---

[37] E.g. Uytterhoeven 1998-99, 244-246, interprets the building as the *Capitolium* of the colony; indeed it forms a crucial argument in her location of the forum. For the three *cellae*: Valente 1982, 250-251. See Coarelli/La Regina 1984, 167 ("*Capitolium?*"); Terzani 1991 (cautiously, on p. 112: "il principale luogo di culto della colonia latina") and Terzani 1996, 149-151 with previous bibliography. Cf. now Pagano 2005, 76 on the location of the 'arx' in this area, rather than the forum.

[38] E.g. Strazzulla 1971; La Regina 1976; *Sannio* 1980, 131-196; La Regina 1984; Coarelli/La Regina 1984, 230-256.

[39] La Regina 1976, 246; Coarelli/La Regina 1984, 234-239.

[40] La Regina 1976 suggests that the 'Ionic temple' replaced an earlier sanctuary, of which, apart from some material found *ex situ*, no trace remains, p. 226: "*uno più antico [santuario], documentato della presenza di materiali, tra cui ricorderò un frammento di lamina bronzea della fine del IV secolo*"; later however, La Regina sees the 'Ionic temple' as the earliest sanctuary, and the area sacra would consequently relate to this phase: Coarelli/La Regina 1984, 234-239, esp. 234: "*questo primo santuario [scil. 'tempio ionico'], comunque il più antico tra quelli accertati ...*"

[41] That is, the sanctuary preceding the 'Ionic temple' (La Regina 1976), or the phase of the 'Ionic temple' itself (Coarelli/La Regina 1984), cf. the preceding note.

[42] Liv. 10.38.5. La Regina 1976, 226: "*E in effetti lo spazio occupato dal teatro, ed esteso fino all'allineamento frontale dei due basamenti adiacenti al tempio B, corrisponde nella forma e nelle dimensioni alla descrizione liviana.*" [55 m = 200 Oscan feet (0.275 m)].

[43] La Regina 1976, 226-229; Coarelli/La Regina 1984, 234-239: according to La Regina by Hannibal.

[44] Ve. 152; La Regina 1976, 233; La Regina 1989, 361.

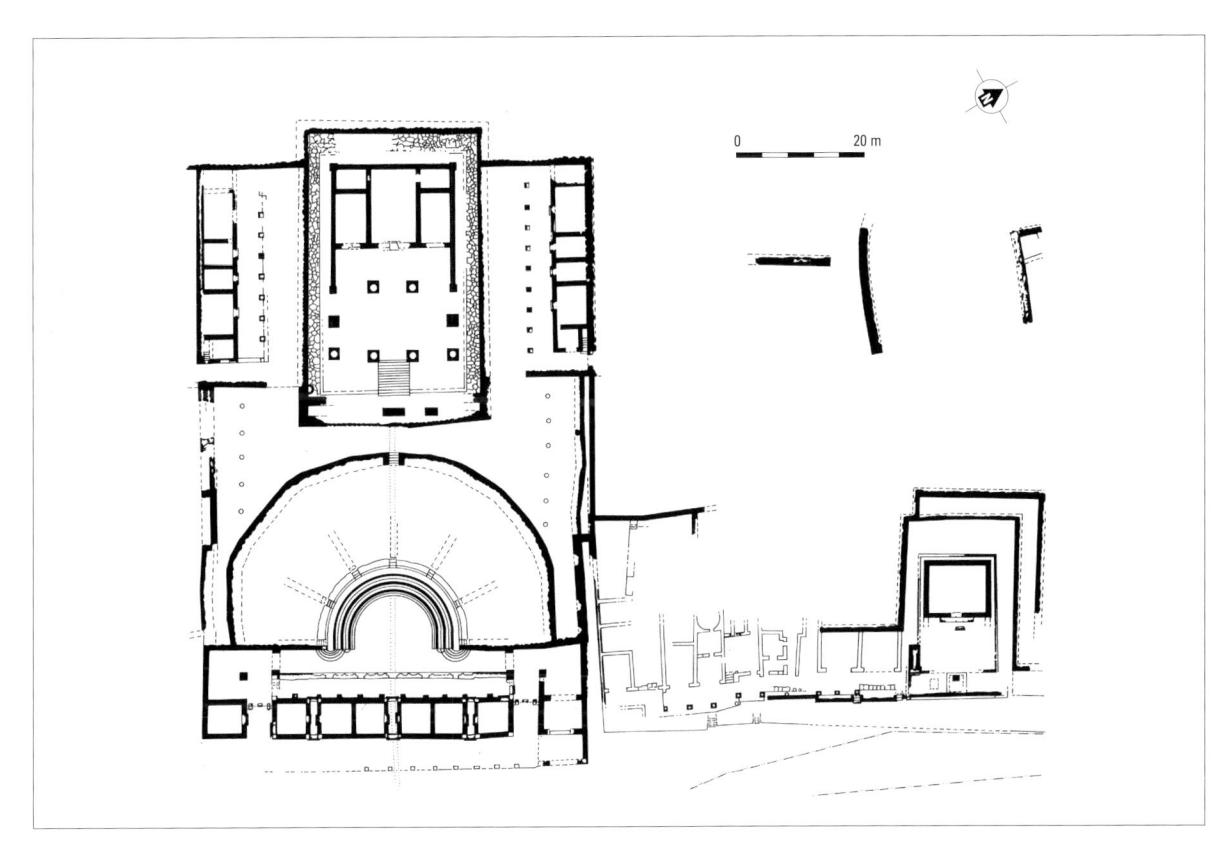

Fig. 3.1. Pietrabbondante, Temple B with theatre and Temple A (adapted from *Sannio* 1980, 166 fig. 32).

dedication[45] and thus apparently defining the sanctuary as that of the Samnites as an ethnic group (cf. *infra*).[46]

The most grandiose architectural enterprise was the theatre-temple complex known as Temple B, which must have been built shortly before the outbreak of the Social War (fig. 3.1). G. Staatis L. Klar, member of an important Samnite family, seems to have been responsible for the construction of part of the podium.[47] The tetrastyle temple, with a podium measuring 35.75 x 23.10 x 3.57 m, presents a plan with three *cellae* (rather than a single one with *alae*). The building has a long pronaos and in the middle

---

[45] *Sak/araklum* or *sak/arat* has been read; Rix 2002, 83 prefers *sak/arat*. Cf. e.g. Ve. 150. Cf. also bibliography in the following note.

[46] Untermann 2000, s.v. ; cf. Vetter 1953 no. 149, on p. 109: "*Das Wort safinim scheint auf die Tätigkeit des Stifters als Bundesbeamter hinzuweisen*," criticised by Lejeune 1972 who argues for an interpretation as federal Samnite sanctuary, interpreting *safinim* as an ethnic: "*C'est donc le temple A qui, à la date de notre texte, est qualifié de safinim (*sabhnyom) 'samnite'. Cet ethnique, on le sait, fournit (concurremment avec víteliú) la légende figurant au revers des émissions monétaires fédérales osques au temps de la Guerre Sociale (Ve. 200 G2)*" (100-101). La Regina interprets the inscription as a testimony to the 'state' character of the sanctuary: Coarelli/La Regina 1984, 241: "*Vi compare infatti menzionato il nome del Sannio (Safinim), che rivela esplicitamente la funzione politica e religiosa che il tempio, e quindi l'intero santuario di Pietrabbondante, svolgeva per lo stato sannitico.*" Cf. pp. 171-172: "*Soprattutto sull'incomprensione di questo modello (scil. the "nomen tribale dei Pentri") si fondano ricostruzioni ingiustificate, come ad esempio una lega di città sannitiche o il carattere federale di un santuario.*" On the question of 'state' or federal organisation, cf. n. 68 and discussion *infra*. The important point here is that in any case a connection is made between the sanctuary and the notion of a 'Samnite' identity.

[47] Ve. 154; Pocc. 18. Cf. La Regina 1976, 233 with discussion in 244; Coarelli/La Regina 1984, 253-254; La Regina 1989, 338.

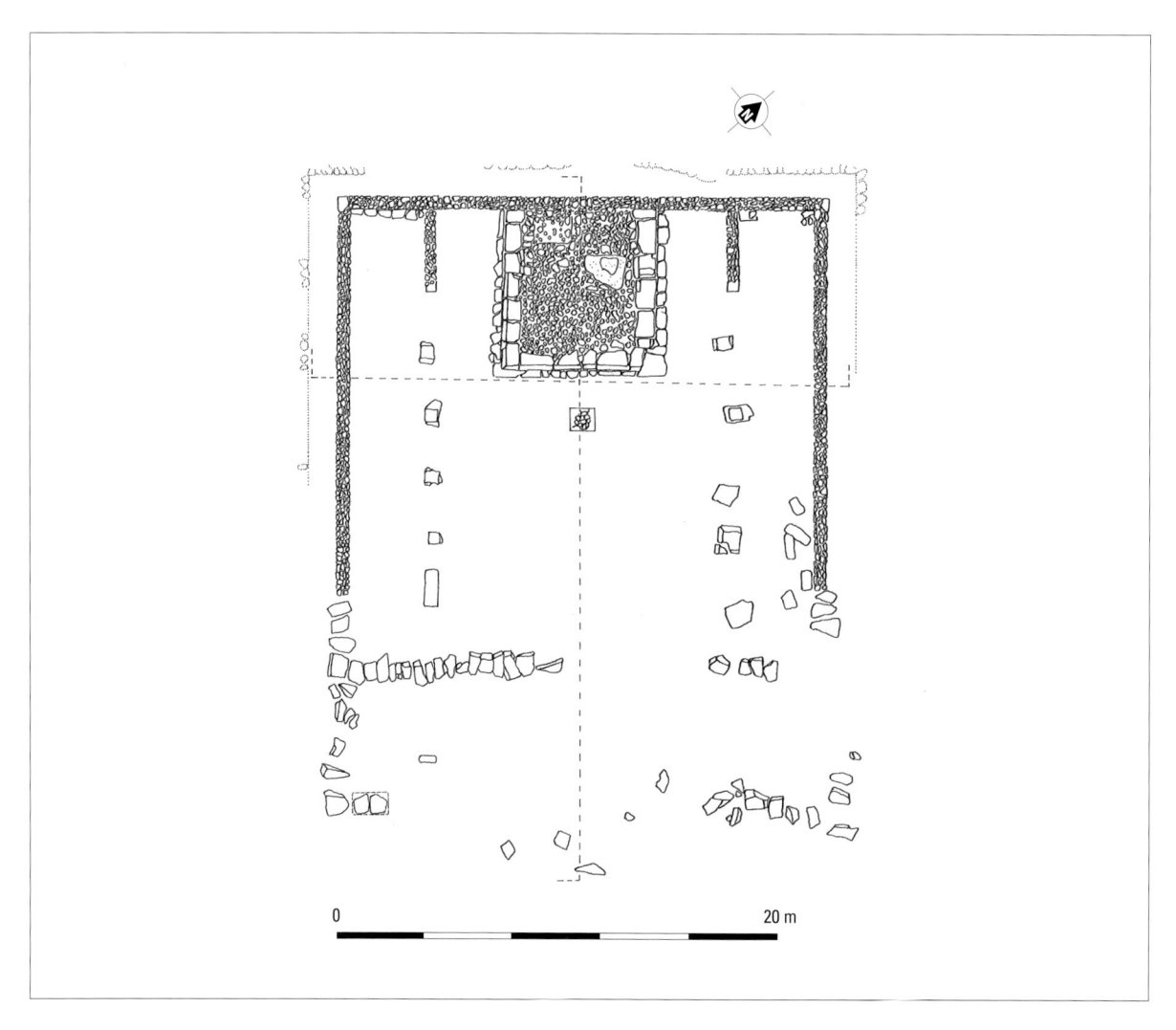

Fig. 3.2. The sanctuary of S. Giovanni in Galdo, Colle Rimontato (adapted from Zaccardi 2007, 63 pl. 1).

of the front of the podium there is a flight of stairs leading to the podium. Two altars stand in front of the podium aligned with the central and eastern *cellae* and it seems legitimate to reconstruct a third one aligned with the western *cella*. The temple building was flanked by two lateral porticoes. The theatre, with impressive polygonal walls on the outside and elegantly decorated with amongst other things *telamones* on the inside, was built shortly before the temple and occupies the space in front of it.[48]

In sum, this sanctuary, where weapons were already deposited from the fifth to fourth centuries BC onwards, flourished in the period after the Roman victory in the Samnite Wars, from the third century BC right up to the Social War. It was located away from the colony at Aesernia and apparently constituted a 'traditional Pentrian' cult place. Pietrabbondante represents by far the most imposing complex in Samnium. Other cult places appear to have been frequented from the fourth or third centuries BC onwards, with a subsequent phase of monumentality mostly dated to the second or early first centuries BC (and

[48] La Regina 1976, 233-234; Coarelli/La Regina 1984, 243-247.

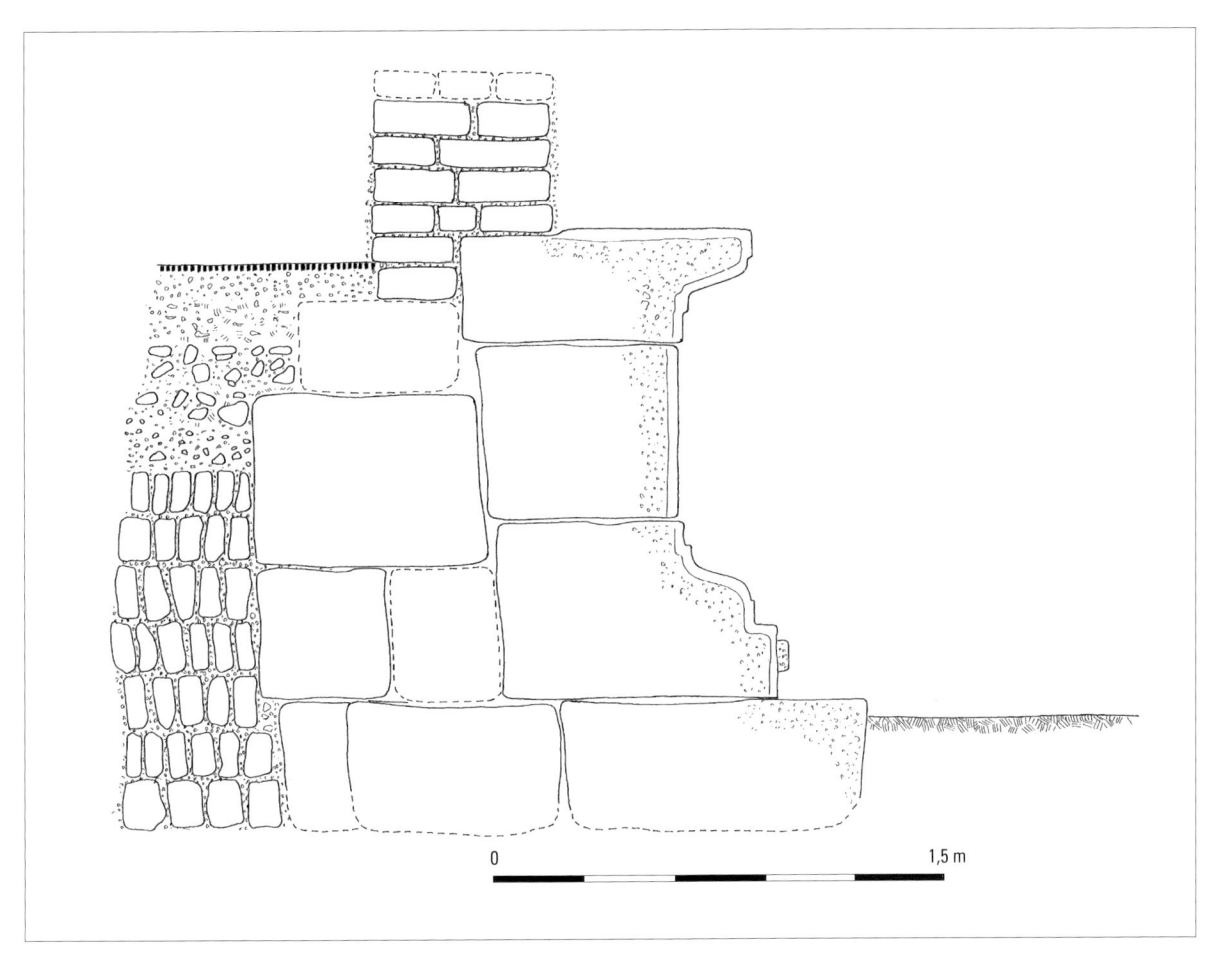

Fig. 3.3. Podium of the *sacellum* (adapted from Di Niro 1980, 273 fig. 46).

sometimes earlier). The best known examples are Schiavi d'Abruzzo,[49] Vastogirardi,[50] Campochiaro,[51] S. Pietro in Cantoni,[52] Quadri,[53] Atessa,[54] and S. Giovanni in Galdo.

The sanctuary at S. Giovanni in Galdo, Colle Rimontato, was frequented from the late fourth century or early third centuries BC onwards (cf. Chapter 5) but only monumentalised at the very end of the second or the beginning of the first century BC. A terminus post quem of 104 BC is provided by coins under the pavement of the central *sacellum*. This *sacellum* was located within a square precinct (ca. 22 x 22 m; cf. fig. 3.2).

This area is protected on three sides by a retaining wall and the space between this wall and the precinct walls is about one metre at the back of the sanctuary and 1.30 m at the sides. Within the precinct, two lateral porticoes were located at the west and east sides, each 4 m wide. Columns supported the porticoes whereas the back part of the porticoes may have been closed off.[55] A *sacellum* was placed against the centre of the precinct's back wall. It stood on a high podium (7 x 7.50 x 1.54 m) which is rather well

[49] La Regina 1976, 230, 237; Coarelli/La Regina 1984, 269-273; La Penna 1997b; La Penna 1997c; *Schiavi* 2001; La Penna 2006.
[50] Morel 1976; Morel 1984; Coarelli/La Regina 1984, 257-259; Pagano *et al.* 2005.
[51] *Campochiaro* 1982; Coarelli/La Regina 1984, 202-209; Capini 1991a; Capini 2000; Capini 2003.
[52] Matteini Chiari 1994; Matteini Chiari 2000; Matteini Chiari 2004.
[53] La Penna 1997a.
[54] Fabbricotti 1982-83; Fabbricotti 1997.
[55] Coarelli/La Regina 1984, 295; cf. Zaccardi 2007, 95-96 proposing six columns on each side.

preserved, presenting a profile typical of many Samnite sanctuaries (fig. 3.3), see for example Temple A of Pietrabbondante. The plan of the *sacellum* can no longer be delineated, but a tetrastyle reconstruction has been suggested.[56] The *sacellum* was paved with a red *signinum* floor decorated with white mosaic *tesserae*, the mosaic is currently exhibited in the *Questura* of Campobasso. Apparently no permanent stairs were foreseen for the *sacellum* as the podium continues on all three sides. This feature has led La Regina to suppose that it was not a real *sacellum*, but rather a *thesaurus* perhaps containing a statue.[57]

3.3 MONUMENTALISATION: WEALTH, POLITICS AND ARCHITECTURAL FORMS

As noted, the sanctuary of S. Giovanni in Galdo is part of a larger phenomenon of monumentalisation of cult places in especially the second century BC. In a period during which both private and secular public buildings appear to be unostentatious or non-existent, these grand temples must have had a strong visual impact. Why was so much invested in the Samnite cult places?

3.3.1 WEALTH

Different ideas have been proposed to explain the widespread construction of sanctuaries in the late third and second centuries BC. Most popular (and at the same time the most generic) is the thesis that connects the construction of sanctuaries to the economic profits made by Italians within the Roman imperial system. In particular, the opening of the eastern Mediterranean markets is considered to have been of great importance. Citing the Italic *negotiatores* or *mercatores* active on Delos has almost become a *topos*.[58] The possibility of the Samnites participating in the Mediterranean trade network has been seen as a favour granted by the Romans, who punished the Italic groups that defected during the Hannibalic War but rewarded those who had remained loyal.[59] Indeed, some members possibly from the same families that were active in the construction works of the sanctuaries are attested epigraphically on Delos, although the identification remains uncertain.[60] The economic prosperity of Italians abroad is often presented as an 'explanation' for the appearance of the lavish Samnite sanctuaries.[61] Characteristi-

[56] See Zaccardi 2007, 95.

[57] Coarelli/La Regina 1984, 296-297: "*probabilmente una statua o un donario importante ivi dedicato per intervento dello stato o per munificenza di qualche magistrato.*" Coarelli 1996 suggests that the precinct was destined for some sacred initiation rites, and presumes that the precinct wall continued also at the front, closing off the sacred area. Here, only foundation walls on a lower level have been found however and this reconstruction has been recently dismissed by Zaccardi 2007, 70.

[58] On the role of Italic *negotiatores*, cf. Hatzfeld 1912; Hatzfeld 1919; Càssola 1970-71; Gabba 1976, 74-77.

[59] According to La Regina, "*Tale notevole fioritura edilizia ... deve collegarsi all'aiuto offerto a Roma dai Samnites Pentri durante la guerra annibalica, ed ai conseguenti benefici che dovettero derivare loro, a differenza di altre popolazioni che subirono un trattamento punitivo. Sotto tale prospettiva si giustifica anche la partecipazione di Sanniti alle lucrose attività commerciali e finanziarie aperte da Roma nel Mediterraneo orientale, così ben attestato a Delo*". La Regina 1976, 229. See also e.g. La Penna 1997a, 68. However, see Torelli 1988c, 60 on building activities in general, with the idea that these in central Italy received a "*forte battuta d'arresto*" by the Roman conquest in the third century, "*fino alla ripresa generale dell'economia italica nella seconda metà del II secolo a.C.*".

[60] Staii are for example attested at Delos; La Regina 1976, 229-230. See Gaggiotti 1983, esp. 138 and 146-147 fig. 2a.

[61] On the relationship with temple building Crawford 1985, 178-181. Cf. Torelli 1983, 242; *Campochiaro* 1982, 26-27; Lomas 1996, 171.

cally, in this view the architectural form of the temples would have been shipped together with riches to Italy.[62] It should be stressed, however, that the accumulation of wealth does not automatically lead to the erection of a temple and a direct architectural influence from the eastern Mediterranean is much more complicated.[63]

Other economic factors have also been considered, for example another hypothesis connects the construction of sanctuaries in Samnium to the economic profits made by large-scale transhumance instead of trade in the East.[64] However, in my view wealth should first be seen as a *conditio sine qua non*. In the process from wealth to temple there were active choices to be made. Moreover, it is seldom specified how the acquired wealth would have been funnelled into the construction works, i.e. through direct private investments or rather through communal funding. It is certain that the names of a small group of families recur in the inscriptions found in the sanctuaries but it is often unclear whether they acted on their own behalf or on behalf of the community as a whole in an official capacity.[65] In any case, this scarcity of evidence precludes all too direct comparisons with the situation in Rome, where most mid-Republican temples can be linked to competing *gentes*, apparently without much state intervention.[66] It should also be pointed out that in Rome a variety of public buildings for diverse political and social functions were close at hand, whereas in Samnium sanctuaries virtually form the exclusive focus of attention. Even if a decisive role for elite individuals would be accepted, the basic question remains why they chose to construct or embellish sanctuaries and not other structures. Why was it – to retain the economic vocabulary – profitable to invest in sanctuaries? If status is achieved by the grace of an audience the inevitable answer is that sanctuaries apparently had an important function within society. In this way, even considering the argument that wealth was the 'reason' for the monumental building of sanctuaries, we end up with questions about the *audience* envisioned by the rich *negotiatores* and therefore with questions about the role of the sacred place in society also before its monumentalisation.

[62] E.g. Gaggiotti 1983, 138, on '*il Sannio pentro*': "*In seguito all'apertura dei ricchi mercati orientali, in particolare Delos, cui parteciparono largamente mercatores, soprattutto laziali e campani, confluirono nelle regioni di origine ingenti capitali, parte dei quali furono impiegati nella ristrutturazione di vecchi santuari o nella costruzione di nuovi, per i quali si adottarono soluzioni architettoniche e planimetriche <u>importate anch'esse</u> dalle zone di tradizione culturale ellenistica nelle quali i mercatores stessi si erano trovati ad operare.*" (added emphasis). This idea is echoed in Patterson 2006b, 611-612: "Italian communities benefited from this influx of wealth collectively … exploiting the commercial openings made possible by the Roman conquest of the Aegean. Indeed, the building of monumental sanctuaries seems to have been particularly characteristic of this period in Latium and the adjacent territories … modeled on Hellenistic sanctuaries such as those at Kos, Lindos, and Delos itself. Even the Samnite sanctuaries of the central Apennines – Pietrabbondante, S. Giovanni in Galdo, Vastogirardi and others – were rebuilt in Hellenistic style in the same period … both the resources needed to build the sanctuaries and the architectural inspiration for their design came from the East"; cf. also e.g. La Torre 1989a, 145 and esp. Caliò 2003.

[63] Cf. also *infra*.

[64] Lloyd 1991a, 184-185 and Dench 1995, 121 for this suggestion. Cf. Chapter 4 on the relation between transhumance and sanctuaries.

[65] Evidence is rich for Pietrabbondante, cf. e.g. Ve. 151 mentioning the dedication of Temple A by a *meddix tuticus* but also many dedications by persons without mentioning their official capacity are found. Less abundant is the evidence for other, smaller sanctuaries, especially when brick stamps mentioning state officials are dismissed as evidence for their direct intervention in the construction (corpus in Rix 2002, 83-91). Cf. Dench 1995, 121: "it is as well to admit that we simply do not have good epigraphic evidence to answer conclusively questions about the extent to which building was actually funded by individuals or by communities as a whole," with n. 37: "It is worth emphasizing the fact that there is little positive evidence for the funding of parts of the rural sanctuaries in Samnium by individuals."

[66] Esp. Ziolkowski 1992 for this view; but cf. Orlin 1997.

3.3.2 POLITICS

A more specific interpretation of the monumentalisation of sanctuaries can be found in the socio-political realm. A political function has been posited for several large sanctuaries in Italy, similar to the Latial Jupiter Albanus sanctuary and the Etruscan *fanum Voltumnae*.[67] Sanctuaries have been directly linked to the presumed political organisation of the Italic peoples, resulting in the widely used term 'federal' (or even 'state') sanctuary.[68] For example, the sanctuaries of Mefitis at Rossano di Vaglio for the Lucani and in the Val d'Ansanto for the Hirpini, as well as the sanctuary of Marica at the mouth of the Garigliano for the Aurunci, have been considered as such.[69] That the sanctuary of Pietrabbondante also functioned as an important sanctuary for the Samnites (Pentri) has long been acknowledged.[70] It would have constituted the political centre of the Samnites in their particular political configuration (as 'tribal *nomen*', *populus*, or *touto*; cf. Chapter 4). Here, the Samnites would have held their political meetings, the sanctuary being the focus of the people under arms.[71]

This military and political function seems to be supported by the only deity documented at the site with certainty. *Víkturraí* or Victoria appears on a late second century or early first century BC dedication on a bronze sheet, which perhaps can be connected to Temple B.[72] She is actually a very 'Roman' goddess and makes her first appearance here in Oscan territory,[73] although she possibly reflects an Aphrodite Nikèphoros of earlier times (who, however, is not directly attested).[74] The abundant finds of weapons from the late fifth and fourth centuries BC, as has been noted, might attest to the political and military importance of the sanctuary already in earlier periods.

Moreover, the socio-political dimension of the sanctuary is explicitly documented by the already mentioned inscription which seems to identify the sanctuary as belonging to (the) *safinim*; a sanctuary of 'the Samnites', perhaps here restricted to the Pentri and reflecting a conscious appeal to their Samnite / Sabine tradition.[75] If the earlier socio-political role of Pietrabbondante must remain somewhat hypothetical, at least in the course of the second century BC the sanctuary could adopt a strong political and perhaps even ethnic connotation.

In general, one should be careful with the application of ethnicity in archaeological and historical research and in fact many examples of so-called 'ethnic' or 'tribal' sanctuaries are exclusively defined as such by outsiders (mostly modern and sometimes ancient writers). The recognition of an ethnic role for the sanctuary of Pietrabbondante can, however, withstand criticism. In theoretical literature, the fundamental importance of the ethnic definition by the involved group itself (emic) in this process, rather than assertions by others (etic) has been highlighted.[76] This is exactly what the *safinim* inscription seems

---

[67] Cf. e.g. Ampolo 1993; Zevi 1995; Briquel 2003.

[68] For discussion of the political organisation ('federal' or 'statal') of the Samnites, see Letta 1994 and the contributions by La Regina, e.g. La Regina 1989.

[69] See Lejeune 1990; Rainini 1985; Mingazzini 1938. Cf. Chapter 4.

[70] La Regina 1970, 196; Lejeune 1972; La Regina 1976, 233; La Regina 1984, 21-22; Coarelli/La Regina 1984, 204, 238; La Regina 1989, 303, 422; Tagliamonte 1997, 180. Cf. e.g. Lomas 2004, 203 for Pietrabbondante as "possible headquarters of the Samnite League". Cf. on the deposition of weapons *supra* nn. 34 and 35.

[71] "*esso è il santuario del popolo in armi*": La Regina 1989, 422.

[72] Pocc. 16; Sa. 24. La Regina 1966, 275.

[73] Cf. Chapter 7 on the *vicus Supinum*, with discussion on her 'Romanness'.

[74] On the cults, cf. Colonna 1996, 121-128. The identification (cf. *infra* n. 90) with *Cominium Tuticum* = *Touxion* is decisive here since from this place Q. Fabius Maximus Gurges would have transferred a statue of this goddess to Rome during the third Samnite War (Ps.-Plut. *Parallela minora*, 37b).

[75] Dench 1995, 139 and 175-217; Tagliamonte 1997, esp. 128-136 and 235-261. Cf. n. 46.

[76] E.g., for archaeological applications, Jones 1997; and esp. Hall 2002 on the distinction between cultural and ethnic identity.

Fig. 3.4. Coin struck by the Italian allies, showing the Samnite bull goring the Roman she-wolf (Kent 1978, pl. 14 no. 46).

to be: a reference to the perceived old Samnite / Sabine roots by the Pentri themselves. The historical framework within which this development has to be understood can be reconstructed fairly well. It is tempting to see this process of self-assertion in relation to the antagonism between Romans and Samnites on the eve of the Social War.[77]

This antagonism is best illustrated by the well-known parallel / opposition between the Roman she-wolf and the Italian calf (*viteliu* − *Italia*),[78] to which, in the case of the Pentri, the association with the Samnite bull, the leading animal during the *ver sacrum* that would have led the Samnites from the Sabines to their new homeland, seems to have been added. On coins from the Italian allies minted in the period of the Social War, the Italian or Samnite bull is depicted as trampling or even raping the Roman she-wolf (fig. 3.4).[79] Interestingly, an analysis of the animal bones from the sanctuary revealed a preponderance of cattle in the animal sacrifices performed at Pietrabbondante.[80]

This development, in which a community strengthens its symbolic boundaries at a time when the structural base of the community is threatened, is in line with the social anthropological theories referred to in the first two chapters. Moreover, in this process religion and cult places are symbolic markers *par excellence*.[81] In sum, there arguably hardly exists a better documented case of cultural, political and military resistance to Roman power in Italy. Supported by ample historical, epigraphic and iconographical evidence, we can discard the reservations that one may have against 'resistant' interpretations in general,

---

[77] Esp. Coarelli/La Regina 1984, 254; Dench 1995, 139 (with 212-217 on the ideology of the Social War); Torelli 1996, 41-42; Tagliamonte 1997, 188-190. Cf. Barth 1969; Cohen 1985, 69: "people become aware of their culture when they stand at its boundaries."

[78] Hellanicus *FGrH* 4, F111 = Dion. Hal. *Ant. Rom.* 1.35.

[79] Campana 1987 6c/103. Dench 1995, esp. 213-215; Dench 1997; Pobjoy 2000.

[80] Barker 1989, also in relation to other sanctuaries such as Campochiaro and Colle Sparanise.

[81] Cohen 1985; cf. also e.g. Graves-Brown *et al.* 1996.

perhaps indeed over-popular in postcolonialist theory.[82] Once this specific connotation of the sanctuary at Pietrabbondante is accepted, as seems legitimate at least for the period leading up to and during the Social War, questions of style and substance can be posed.

3.3.3 STYLE: 'EXTERNAL' CULTURAL ELEMENTS AND MODELS

Is there a correlation between the cultural elements or models adopted in the monumental sanctuary of Pietrabbondante and the specific function of the sanctuary within Samnite society? Different provenances of the architectural elements in the sanctuary have been suggested, and its 'eclecticism' has often been stressed.[83] As noted earlier, there exists the general (and not merely metaphorical) idea that cultural models were shipped from Delos and other places in the East together with the resources for constructing temples.[84] Others have emphasised the influence from Latium and especially Campania[85] (and thereby 'indirect' eastern influence).[86] The closest parallels come from Campania, the cornice of the podium of Temple B has an almost exact parallel in the sanctuary of Fondo Patturelli near Capua[87] and the theatre and its decorations have parallels at Pompeii and Sarno.[88] According to Hans Lauter, these theatres clearly belong to Great Greek theatre architecture and this formal similarity would indicate that the Samnite theatrical performances were of Greek tradition rather than Latial.[89] The axiality and planimetrical layout of the temple-theatre complex, on the other hand, recalls similar combinations of half round stairways in front of the actual temple buildings in Latial sanctuaries such as Gabii and Tivoli (fig. 3.5).

This resemblance has even been thought to recall the so-called (and in itself rather problematic) *curia-comitium* model (fig. 3.6), which remains a moot point however, as Tagliamonte has demonstrated.[90] Perhaps most striking however, is the presence of a three *cellae* plan in Temple B. This feature has been gen-

---

[82] Cf. Brown 1996; see Chapter 1.

[83] E.g. La Regina 1976; Tagliamonte 1997, 189. Cf. for a case study on 'eclecticism' and its possible meaning Naerebout 2007.

[84] E.g. Gaggiotti 1983, 138; Patterson 2006b, 611-612 (both quoted *supra* n. 62); cf. also Caliò 2003.

[85] La Regina (La Regina 1976 and La Regina 1989) points to Campanian parallels, but also emphasises the originality of Temple B; Torelli 1983, 242: "*Nelle aree meno evolute, i secoli IV e III coincidono con una definitiva urbanizzazione (area umbro-picena) o con la prima monumentalizzazione delle strutture centrali – i santuari –, dell'habitat paganico (area sannitica): anche qui non si mettono in evidenza tipi edilizi particolari, dal momento che le forme archittetoniche sono tutte senz'eccezione derivate dalle zone etrusco-laziali e campane.*"

[86] This is not the place to enter the debate but the date of the monumental phase of the sanctuary at Kos, for example, is important in respect to the alleged influence on the construction of several Latial sanctuaries.

[87] See La Regina 1976, 225 fig. VI. It is generally dated to the later second century BC, but without hard evidence. At the sanctuary a building inscription has been found which dates to 108 BC, but its relationship to the podium is unclear (cf. Coarelli 1995a, 379).

[88] Lauter 1976, with discussion (esp. the contribution of Coarelli on pp. 422-423); La Regina 1976, 233; cf. in general Nielsen 2002.

[89] Lauter 1976, 418: "*Diese formale Übereinstimmung dürfte aber auch implizieren, dass die Aufführungen der Samniten nach der Art der griechischen Aufführungen ausgelegt waren, und im Gegensatz zum latinischen Brauch das Nebeneinander skenischer und thymelischer Darbietungen aufwiesen.*"

[90] Coarelli/La Regina 1984, 254; La Regina 1989, 303-304, 421-422; Coarelli 1996, 4-7. Related is the proposal to recognise the place *Cominum* or *Cominium Tuticum* in Pietrabbondante (La Regina 1989, 420-422; Colonna 1996, 128; Tagliamonte 2002-2003, 119). On the 'Roman theatre-temple' or 'cultic theatre' in general cf. Hanson 1959; Nielsen 2002, esp. 180-196. Tagliamonte 2007, esp. 56-57, for dismissal of the connection with the *curia-comitium* model.

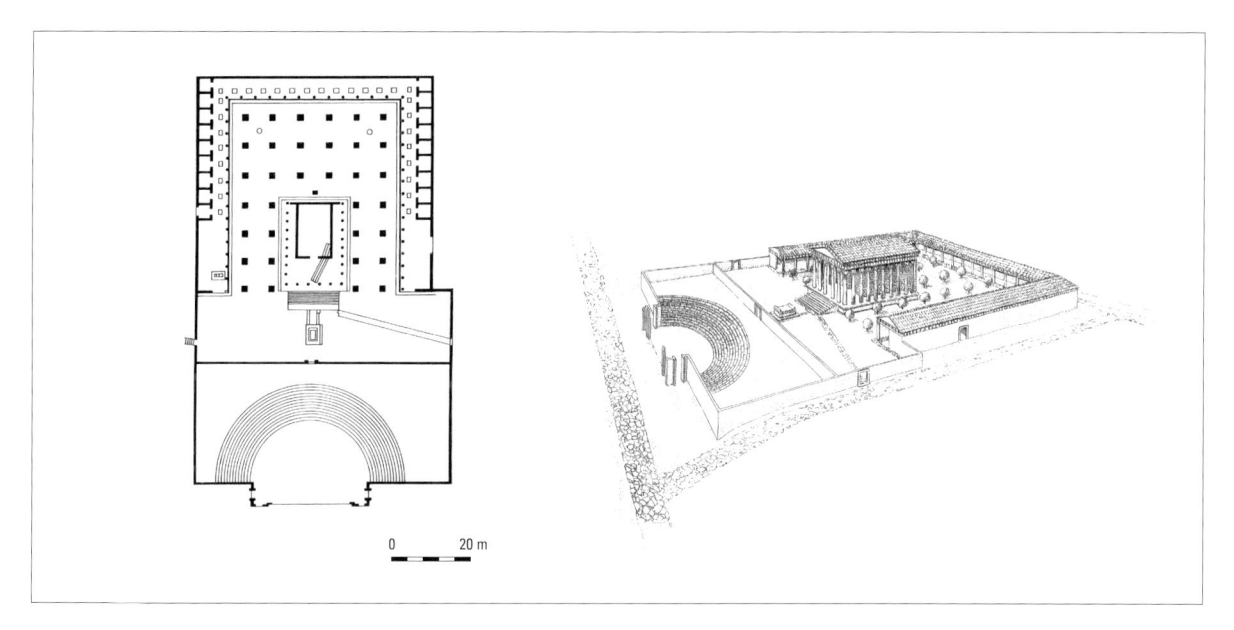

Fig. 3.5. Sanctuary of Juno, Gabii (mid second century BC), plan and reconstruction (adapted from Almagro Gorbea 1982, 584-585 figs. 1 and 2).

erally interpreted as the result of 'Roman' or 'Latin' influence;[91] the importance attributed to the model of the Capitoline temple has been discussed in Chapter 2. It was noted there that the model is thought to have spread by way of the Roman urban centres, especially colonies, which proudly boasted *Capitolia* within their city walls. As noted, a three *cellae* temple dating to the third century BC has been found in the Latin colony of Aesernia, installed in the Pentrian territory in 263 BC, and was perhaps the *Capitolium* of the colony.[92] It is, in sum, not to be excluded that the three *cellae* model in Pietrabbondante was indeed inspired by the Roman / Latin model.[93] Unfortunately, the deity or deities venerated at Pietrabbondante remain unknown, apart from the already mentioned dedication to *Víkturraí*, who need not have been one of the principal deities. In any case, no triad to fit the three *cellae* has been documented.

The question is what the adoption of a design scheme, such as (perhaps) the *curia-comitium* model, or the 'Capitoline' Etrusco-Italic temple with high podium and three *cellae*, actually entailed. Regrettably, too little is known about Samnite society to establish whether these features would have been regarded as typically 'Latial' or 'Roman'. If that were indeed the case, it would suggest the conscious appropriation or reinterpretation of elements perhaps perceived as 'hostile'. Somewhat differently, the adoption of these models can be seen as an emulation strategy, as has been argued by La Regina, Coarelli and Tagliamonte.[94]

---

[91] La Regina 1976, 233; Coarelli/La Regina 1984, 252: "*il modello a cui si dovette ispirare la scelta di erigere un tempio a cella tripartita fu certamente la aedes capitolina*"; Tagliamonte 1997, 190-193. Cf. Salmon 1982, 100, 117. Coarelli 1996, 15 even speaks of a "*perfetta simmetria con il culto capitolino di Roma*".

[92] See n. 37.

[93] Although it should be emphasised that little is known about 'traditional' Samnite cult places. The sanctuary at Casalbore, loc. Macchia Porcara might be an example, but seems rather to consist of a central *cella* with *alae* and the architecture and planimetry do not reflect the 'Tuscanic' model.

[94] Emulation of the Roman model is advocated by La Regina (Coarelli/La Regina 1984, 252, 254); cf. Coarelli 1996, 16: "*Non è certo un caso se, nella sua ricostruzione immediatamente precedente la guerra sociale, il tempio principale di Pietrabbondante, ricostruito a tre celle e con tre altari, si ispirò al modello del tempio capitolino*"; cf. also Tagliamonte 1997, 189: "*evidentemente [come] esito di processi di acculturazione e di emulazione competitiva*" and Tagliamonte 2007, 68.

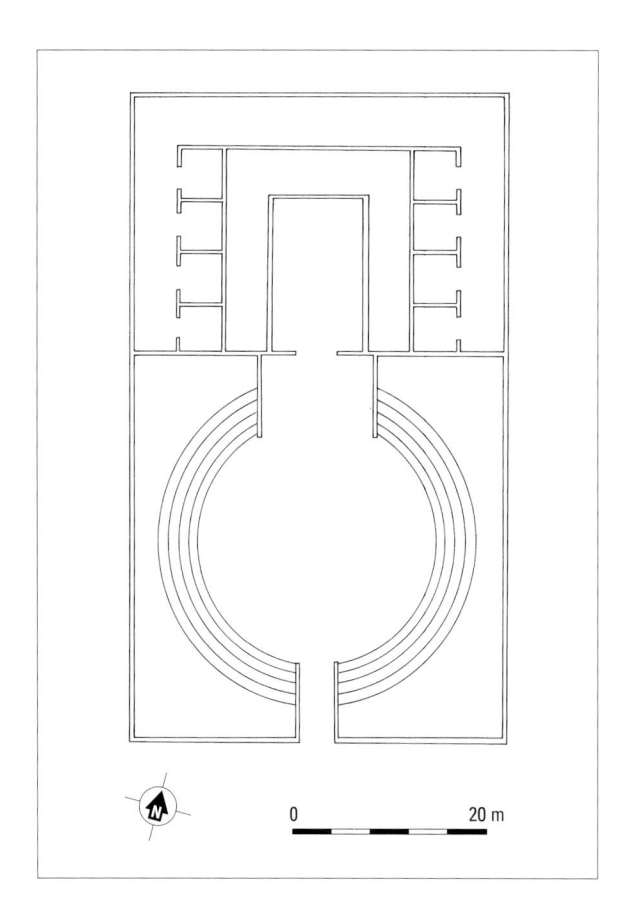

Fig. 3.6. The *comitum-curia* complex in Fregellae (adapted from Coarelli 1981a, 123 pl. III).

In this way, a symbolic language similar to that of Latium, including Rome, was constructed and put to use to convey a proper message. The result is in any case an original creation, not a slavish copy or clumsy hybrid.[95]

Both explanations, which are complementary rather than mutually exclusive, can find support in the use of other images in different contexts in this period.[96] I have already mentioned the well-known antagonism between Rome and Samnium expressed by the emblems of the she-wolf and the bull, the Roman imagery of the she-wolf is effectively distorted by the concurrent image of the Samnite bull goring the Roman animal.[97] This interaction in symbolic language can also be discerned on other occasions. The insurgence of the allies resulting in the Social War is described in the sources as a pernicious conspiracy and an interplay with the famous Samnite oath of 293 BC seems probable.[98] That the Italic allies indeed swore an oath is documented on a coin struck at Corfinium – in the course of the revolt renamed 'Italica' – where soldiers are depicted taking the oath.[99]

The interesting point here is that the image recalls the oath sworn by Aeneas and Latinus, depicted on golden staters at the moment that the (Trojan) Romans most needed their Latin allies during the Hannibalic invasion.[100] On the Social War coin the Roman model is appropriated and used against Rome. In this context the adoption of the Roman goddess Victoria – in Oscan *Víkturraí* – evoked at Pietrabbondante most probably in hope of a victory over the Romans,[101] suggests the same process. Although the architectural aspects of the sanctuary are perhaps less explicit and therefore more difficult to interpret, there is no reason *per se* to think that the underlying processes leading to the adoption of these models was fundamentally different from that of the images just evoked. The models adopted had no intrinsic significance but acquired it in the process. The only way to try to understand what significance could have been attributed to them is by trying to reconstruct the ideological frameworks within which the building was conceived. No explicit evidence survives that informs us about Pentrian views of the three *cellae* temple or the *comitium* model, but from the ideological framework reconstructed from other sources it appears that the adoption of what modern authors have called 'Roman' or 'Latial' cultural models can, in the case of

---

[95] Cf. La Regina 1976, 234: "*il grande tempio di Pietrabbondante ... è l'unico esempio di architettura templare nel Sannio in cui, oltre a motivi formali riconducibili all'uno o all'altro ambiente da cui derivano, sia possibile riconoscere la personalità e la fantasia di un architetto nella originale elaborazione dello schema di tradizione italica.*"

[96] Cf. Stek 2004.

[97] Sydenham 1952 no. 628.

[98] Rouveret 1986.

[99] By Q. Pompadeius Silo; Felletti Maj 1977, 129-130.

[100] Sydenham 1952 nos. 69, 70; Felletti Maj 1977, 129-130, 159 n. 3; Burnett 1998, 169.

[101] Thus Prosdocimi 1989, 540.

Pietrabbondante, demonstrably *not* be equated with acceptance of Roman rule or ways of life.[102] A situation that with less contextual evidence (e.g. only the planimetry) could perhaps have appeared as rather 'romanised' actually hides an entirely different reality than that qualification seems to imply.

3.3.4 TRADITIONALISM IN SAMNITE SANCTUARIES?

Apart from these various influences from 'outside', elements of traditionalism have also been recognised. As noted, La Regina has pointed out that the area occupied by the earliest sanctuary at Pietrabbondante measures probably 200 by 200 feet, thereby recalling the Samnite *locus consaeptus* where the *legio linteata* was formed according to Livy (10.38).[103] The area later occupied by the theatre and the foremost part of the temple apparently retained these measurements, although the temple itself did not fall within this precinct. That the *legio linteata* is probably more than just legend[104] seems to be supported by the discovery of a fragment of mural decoration showing the linen legion found in the area of Cumae.[105] The painting dates to around 300 BC. Although this does not, of course, prove the reliability of the size of the sacred area Livy gives, it seems at least that he was informed. Even if it is not entirely sure that Livy actually refers to a sanctuary proper, it suggests that indeed ancient traditions existed (*ex vetusta Samnitium religione, ex libro vetere linteo*) which prescribed the form of places where rituals were performed. The size and form of the sanctuary of Pietrabbondante may in this case represent more than just an analogy. In a recent study, Pietrabbondante has, on other grounds, been identified with Livy's Aquilonia.[106] If correct (which remains difficult to prove), this means that the traditional sanctuary at Aquilonia / Pietrabbondante was to some extent respected by the later construction phases.

At any rate, the appearance of the early sanctuary at Pietrabbondante would have been that of a *sacellum* in the centre with lateral porticoes and set within a precinct. This is basically the same scheme that is found in the sanctuary of S. Giovanni in Galdo. Here, a rectangular precinct encloses a small *sacellum* with two lateral porticoes. Apparently, this is the same model that is applied in the last construction phase at Pietrabbondante with Temple B, the temple representing the *sacellum* flanked by two lateral porticoes. This would thus represent, as La Regina puts it, "*una sicura memoria degli originari santuari sannitici*" of the type known from Livy, whereas the buildings and decoration would constitute "*l'evoluzione del modello originario, arricchito con elementi introdotti dalla diffusione dell'ellenismo in ambiente italico*".[107] Admittedly, this hypothetical reconstruction of a traditional scheme in Samnite sanctuaries, although suggestive, rests at present on little evidence and elaborations of this thesis should consequently be treated with caution.[108] However, if this interpretation

---

[102] Cf. Stek 2004; Stek 2005a; Stek 2005b and on 'emulation' supra n. 94.

[103] La Regina 1976, 226.

[104] Cf. Coarelli 1996, who believes Livy's description to be, in the end, a trustworthy ethnographic description.

[105] Valenza Mele 1996; Caputo 2000; Moormann *in prep*.

[106] Sisani 2001a, but cf. La Regina 1989, 421.

[107] Coarelli/La Regina 1984, 298. Cf. Coarelli 1996, 8: "*Esiste comunque almeno un altro santuario che corrisponde perfettamente alla fase più antica del complesso di Pietrabbondante: il santuario di S. Giovanni in Galdo*," and p. 16 calling it a "*probabile replica ridotta di un modello più antico in cui non è difficile identificare quello di Pietrabbondante*"; cf. also Capini 1996, 63: "*Lo stesso schema [scil. dell'area sacra originaria di Pietrabbon-dante] si conserva invece con grande chiarezza nel santuario in loc. Colle Rimontato a S. Giovanni in Galdo*," and she thinks that "*l'impianto di I secolo non fa che ricalcare lo schema della fase precedente*" (p. 64; cf. Tagliamonte 1997, 185). See Torelli 1996, 41-42 on the general notion of the monumentalisation of sanctuaries as part of a "*fenomeno panitalico*" in both urban (the Latial sanctuaries) and more rural (Samnite, Lucanian) contexts, which he interprets in a "*prospettiva di natura controacculturativa*" and as "*manifestazioni di resistenza alla romanizzazione*", followed by Tagliamonte 1997, 188.

[108] And I have to make a retraction here with regard to a paper in 2003 (Stek 2005a) in which I may have over-schematised and extrapolated the developments discussed here.

is correct, it would help explain the reasons for the development of small monumental sanctuaries in the second century BC such as S. Giovanni in Galdo. Although in every single situation local circumstances will have been important, the apparent harking back to ancient 'Samnite' traditions may suggest that at least one of the sentiments at play was indeed the affirmation of a Samnite consciousness on the eve of the Social War, just as is documented for Pietrabbondante at this time. However, it is important to acknowledge that this possible 'harking back' to ancient customs is no simple traditionalism but rather the eclectic use of traditional elements for contemporary purposes. In the words of the social anthropologist Anthony Cohen, "it is a selective construction of the past which resonates with contemporary influences".[109]

3.4 CONCLUSION: THE CONSTRUCTION OF COMMUNITY

The example of the Samnites Pentri presents an interesting illustration of the problems involved in the interpretation of material culture as well as the role of sanctuaries within ancient society. In Samnium, a largely non-urbanised area, sanctuaries occupied a privileged position in society. The Samnites fought dire wars against Rome. Only after their surrender in the third century BC were sanctuaries embellished in monumental forms. This has been explained as a result of economic prosperity but instead this seems to be a precondition. At least for the central sanctuary at Pietrabbondante a connection with the political and military organisation of the Samnites can be demonstrated. Widely-spread Hellenistic cultural forms, and perhaps even elements that could have been regarded as 'Roman' or 'Latin' in this context, are apparently employed to serve *proper* purposes and were given a new meaning, which is at direct variance with any straightforward notion of 'romanisation' or 'hellenisation'.

Although one should be cautious in using terms such as cultural resistance, sometimes applied too readily, there are strong indications in the case of the Pentri to support such an approach. The ideological framework as it appears in legends and images indicates an antagonism between Rome and Samnium, communicated in a common imagery. Indeed, the adoption of what moderns call 'Hellenistic', 'Latin' and 'Roman' elements at Pietrabbondante are not to be interpreted as 'self-romanisation', but rather as the choosing of building materials for the construction of a Samnite Pentrian identity in specific historical circumstances. In other words, there was cultural change but without loss of local distinctiveness.

The monumentalisation of the sanctuary of Pietrabbondante on the eve of the last insurrection against Rome can be seen to represent the symbolic expression of a community that defines itself as 'Samnite' at the very moment that this sovereign identity is threatened by outsiders. Perhaps similar incentives played a role in the development of smaller Samnite monumental sanctuaries. Supposed 'traditional Samnite' elements in some sanctuaries could support such an interpretation. The enhancement of the 'sacred landscape' of Pentrian Samnium could thus perhaps be seen at least in part as a reaction to the changes that Roman dominance brought with it; a case of 'constructing' the community, strengthened by the harking back to perceived ancient proper traditions in which cult places and religion play key roles.

This ideological aspect of sanctuaries as reconstructed from epigraphic, historical and, to a lesser extent, archaeological evidence constitutes only one side of the coin however. The impact and meaning of these cult places cannot be ascertained without knowledge of the communities that actually interacted with them. Indeed, to understand the socio-political messages conveyed by the monumentalisation of these cult places – whether this should be ascribed to economic prosperity, to a growing ethnic consciousness, or something else – we must know the intended audience. Who visited these sanctuaries? For whom were they constructed or embellished? In order to further our understanding of the role that sanctuaries, large and small, fulfilled within this discourse it is essential to understand the local function of cult places. It is with these local functions that the next chapters will be concerned.

[109] Cohen 1985, 99.

4 Location and Function of Italic Sanctuaries in Society: Three Models

As has become clear, knowledge of the social and political context within which sanctuaries were constructed and functioned is crucial for understanding their role in society. In this chapter I will pursue this contextualisation further by examining the local or regional functions of sanctuaries in relation to settlement organisations in Italic society. This provides important information on the groups of people that probably installed and visited the cult places which is essential for a better understanding of their socio-political role as well as the intended impact of architectural and other aspects of the cult places themselves. In addition, it provides a model against which the changes after the Roman conquest can be assessed.

Thinking again of Pietrabbondante, we could ask to what 'Safinim' the *safinim* inscription (Vetter 149) was actually visible; who could and did visit this Samnite cult place? It seems reasonable to assume that the eloquent inscription in fact represents an initiative of one or more members of the ruling elite, dedicated in the most 'official' sanctuary of the Samnites, which was probably not meant to be visited on a regular basis by devotees as part of personal religious practice. Rather, the temple complex at Pietrabbondante seems to have been a supra-local sanctuary that was important for military and political meetings, as may be concluded from the large quantities of weapons found and the expensive sacrifices, mostly consisting of bulls, that were made there (Chapter 3). Unfortunately, it is not possible to tell in what spatial and social environment the sanctuary of Pietrabbondante was located. Apart from graves in località Troccola and the wall-structures on Monte Saraceno,[1] structures that could indicate dense settlement in this area are currently lacking, although this could be due to the lack of systematic archaeological research in the direct environment of the complex.[2] However, at this stage, there is no evidence that large numbers of average Samnite people from the area visited this non-urban sanctuary on a regular basis.

Even less is known about the possible audiences at Samnite sacred places on a local level, down the hierarchy; at the smaller sanctuaries and shrines dispersed over Samnite territory. It is however of considerable importance to understand the local functions of such Samnite cult places: arguably these form their very *raison d'être*, and determine the audience to whom cultural messages might have been directed. As has been seen, especially in the third and second centuries many smaller Samnite sanctuaries are built or reconstructed in monumental forms. Often, these sacred places are generally referred to as 'rural sanctuaries', but their supposed 'rurality' cannot simply be assumed a priori and, indeed, *ex silentio*. Moreover, the term 'rural' has to be further explained, what do we mean by stating that a sanctuary is 'rural'? I also argue that the possibility of a major bias in our view of sanctuaries within the general pattern of settlement should be taken into consideration. This bias is the result of a scholarly tradition that, as observed earlier, pays disproportionate attention to the monumental elements of the landscape, such as hill-forts and temples, at the expense of more modest forms of settlement. Before discussing this problem I will examine some current ideas regarding the local function of Italic sanctuaries in relation to the spatial

---

[1] Coarelli/La Regina 1984, 231-232.

[2] Recently, excavations directed by La Regina revealed a large structure which has been interpreted as a public building. Presented during a conference in November 2006 at Isernia.

organisation of the landscape. Although reference will often be made to 'Samnite' sanctuaries proper, this analysis regards sanctuaries in central-southern Italy in general, including the central Apennines and Adriatic areas (i.e. the so-called 'Sabellian' and 'Samnite' areas).

Until a few decades ago, few studies explicitly tried to understand why and for what specific purposes sanctuaries were actually built in antiquity. Within a culture-historical paradigm, most attention has been directed to the architecture and the aesthetic (as well as economic) value of the votive objects and adornment of temples. In the last two decades, however, interest has grown immensely, influenced by the postprocessual focus on symbolism, cognition and experience, the realm of religion *par excellence*. This development can be best seen in studies on Greek religion and sanctuaries, for example the influential studies of Colin Renfrew, François de Polignac, Madeleine Jost, Albert Schachter, Susan Alcock, to name but few and numerous collections of studies.[3] Not surprisingly, Magna Graecia is also relatively well covered, especially as regards the Great-Greek temples themselves, but sanctuaries have also played a special role in the discussion about the relationship and interaction between indigenous Italians and Greek colonists.[4] The Tyrrhenic coast is well served with studies as varied as Giovanni Colonna's *Santuari d'Etruria* and Filippo Coarelli's *Santuari del Lazio*, as well as Ingrid Edlund-Berry's *The gods and the place*, on both Etruria and Magna Graecia.[5]

For inland Italic sanctuaries, the situation is rather different and only few attempts have been made to explain, problematise or theorise the function of sanctuaries. There are good reasons for this situation. The first is related to the advance of archaeological research, a lot of sanctuaries have only been excavated relatively recently and there is no firm archaeological framework within which the new discoveries can be interpreted. Second, the absence of written sources relating to sanctuaries (apart from a few exceptions, cf. Introduction and Chapter 2) and the scarcity of epigraphic material have not invited to venture into historical interpretations. Most studies on Italic sanctuaries have focused primarily on the publication of the architecture, rather than the roles these sacred places assumed in Italic society.

In Samnium proper the situation is rather awkward: together with the remains of hill-fort walls, the landscape of ancient Samnium appears to have existed almost exclusively in the presence of sanctuaries, the most visible remains of the Samnites (Chapter 3). It therefore does not come as a surprise that the cult places of Samnium are, within the Italic world, relatively well-known and are often cited as examples of architecture outside urban centres. However, detailed studies lag behind. After Valerio Cianfarani's publication of a small booklet entitled *Santuari del Sannio*,[6] the most influential study regarding Samnite sanctuaries has been La Regina's contribution on Samnium in general to the seminal Göttingen congress on *Hellenismus in Mittelitalien* (1974), in which La Regina presented the evidence from several new (and at the time ongoing) excavations, fitting it into an integral narrative on the development of Samnium.[7] In this and later contributions, La Regina examined the architectural features as well as the epigraphy and the narrow ties between a few families and the fate of the sanctuaries.[8] Studies that focus entirely on Samnite sanctuaries in general (as opposed to studies on single sanctuaries) are almost non-existent after Cianfarani's essay, although Samnite sanctuaries figure prominently in handbooks and standard works on classical archaeology.[9]

Nonetheless, several ideas regarding the function of these sanctuaries in society have been formulated. In this chapter, I identify some current approaches and frame them within their different scholarly traditions. For central-southern Italy, it seems possible to discern three main strands of thought on the general function

---

[3] E.g. Renfrew 1985; de Polignac 1984; Jost 1985; Schachter 1992; Alcock 1993; contributions in Alcock/Osborne 1994 and in Marinatos/Hägg 1995.
[4] Cf. *infra* on cult places as territorial markers.
[5] Colonna 1985; Coarelli 1987; Edlund-Berry 1987.
[6] Cianfarani 1960.
[7] La Regina 1976.
[8] La Regina 1976, and esp. La Regina 1989.
[9] E.g. Gros/Torelli 1988; Flower 2004; Alcock/Osborne 2007.

of sanctuaries. These are mostly implicit and different authors attach different values to various factors in the location and construction of sanctuaries.[10] Thus, although the distinction between these models should not be applied too rigidly, I present these models under different headings for the sake of clarity.

4.1 TRANSHUMANCE: SANCTUARIES, HERCULES AND 'TRATTURI'

"*la struttura tradizionale è appunto quella del santuario di campagna, in relazione stretta con un grande tratturo*" (Torelli 1996, 36).

It has often been argued or assumed that there is a direct relationship between the location of sanctuaries and the long transhumance routes that cut through central and southern Italy. Along these so-called *tratturi* flocks moved seasonally from the lower plains to the higher pastures, e.g. from Apulia to the Abruzzi and back. Different branches of *tratturi* intersected, forming a network of communication routes (cf. fig. 4.1).[11] For example, the sanctuary of S. Giovanni in Galdo has been interpreted in light of a nearby branch of a *tratturo*.[12]

The cult places would have provided a safe place for trade along the *tratturi* and would also be suitable locations for cattle and sheep markets. The location of sanctuaries along or in the vicinity of transhumance routes has usually been connected to the deity venerated in these sanctuaries. In some important instances, Hercules is known to have been worshipped in sanctuaries along major transport routes, most famously in Tivoli, Rome, and Alba Fucens, in his role as patron deity of herdsmen and trade, especially of salt.[13] Combined with the fact that the cult of Hercules was popular in Italic territory, the argument for a correlation seems to be strengthened. The connection between Hercules and pastoralism is often seen as very direct,[14] and it is thus assumed that herdsmen made up an important part of the audience of the sanctuaries.[15] Also, the accumulation of wealth through transhumance has

---

[10] Cf. e.g. Menozzi 1998, where a sanctuary near a '*vicus*' is interpreted as a frontier sanctuary, but later connected as well to transhumance.

[11] Cf. Salmon 1967, 68-69; Gabba/Pasquinucci 1979; Whittaker 1988; Corbier 1991; Petrocelli 1999. Cf. Dench 1995, 111-125 and Crawford 2005 for a critical overview.

[12] Di Niro 1980, 269; De Benedittis 1990b, 26.

[13] Esp. Van Wonterghem 1999. Cf. e.g. also Torelli 1996, 36. On salt trade cf. Coarelli/La Regina 1984, 87; Coarelli 1988b; Torelli 1993b (on Hercules Salarius in Alba Fucens in connection to the *forum pecuarium*, perhaps the sanctuary at Campochiaro can be identified with the Hercules Ranus from the Tabula Peutingeriana, where Ranus would constitute the Samnite version of Salarius; cf. however Capini 2000). For an example of the connection of Samnite sanctuaries with transhumance *without* the connection with Hercules (but rather with Mefitis) cf. Bonifacio 2000, 34.

[14] The spread of the cult of Hercules is sometimes even seen as an *indicator* of the practice of transhumance: e.g. Pasquinucci 1996, 23: "*La distribuzione del culto di Ercole e l'esistenza di fora pecuaria attestano una pratica capillare della pastorizia e delle attività economiche connesse.*" Cf. also Mancini 1998, 23: "*Nei pressi dei tratturi sorgevano frequentemente i templi dedicati ad Ercole ... La distribuzione di questi luoghi di culto lascia intravedere la loro particolare funzione di grandi mercati, anche e soprattutto in relazione alla transumanza. La maggior parte dei santuari dedicati ad Ercole ... sorgeva sempre in relazione ai punti cruciali di collegamento e di incrocio dei percorsi della transumanza e del sale ed in relazione alle sorgenti.*" Cf. e.g. also Coarelli 2001a for the Doric temple of Pompeii.

[15] Although it is admitted that other people must have also visited the sanctuaries, e.g. Van Wonterghem 1999, 415: "*Anche se i pastori transumanti potevano costituire una clientela regolare dei santuari, è pero poco probabile che siano loro i responsabili dell'espansione monumentale che alcuni di essi conobbero*" and "*... i santuari situati presso una fonte ... venivano senz'altro visitati anche da altri devoti e non solo dai pastori transumanti*".

[16] Lloyd 1991a, 184-185; Dench 1995, 121.

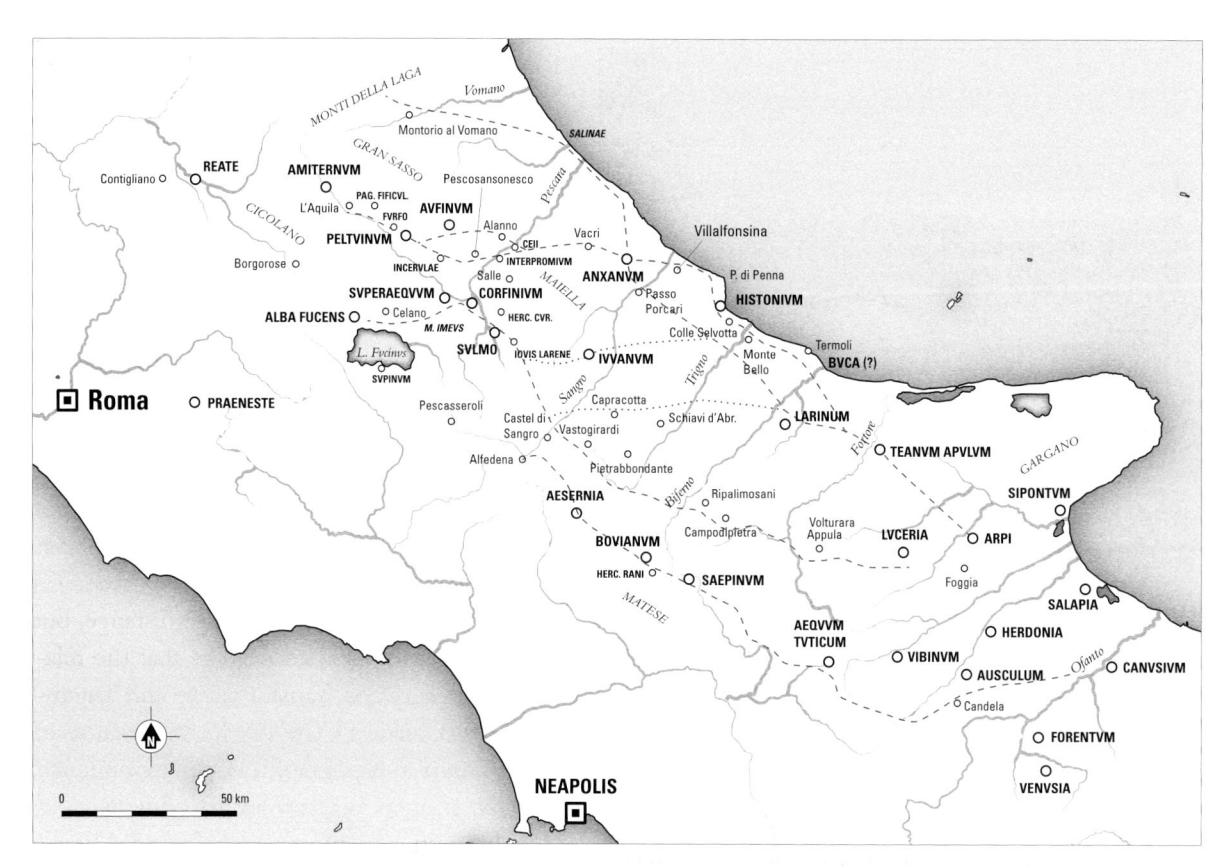

Fig. 4.1. Transhumance routes, important places and sanctuaries (Van Wonterghem 1999, 415 fig. 2)

been connected to the elaborate architecture of some cult places.[16] Although there certainly is a correlation in some instances, it must be admitted however that in many cases there is scant evidence for the veneration of one specific deity (especially if we dismiss the numerous Hercules bronzes dispersed all over Italy[17] as evidence for a proper cult place dedicated to this god).[18] Indeed caution is required, because inversely Italic sanctuaries have sometimes been assigned to Hercules precisely because of their presumed location along *tratturi*, evidently a case of circular reasoning. In fact, the cult of Hercules is attested with certainty in fewer cases than one might think and also the connection with transhumance is not always clear cut. For instance, one of the most famous sanctuaries in the Italic area is the sanctuary of Hercules Curinus in the territory of ancient Sulmo, modern Sulmona in Abruzzo. This sanctuary is especially well known because of its monumental rebuilding after the Social War and forms one of the few examples of non-urban sanctuaries that survive the changes in the settlement pattern following the municipalisation (cf. *infra*). It is perched on a steep side of Monte Morrone, with a height difference of over 200 m to the valley floor of the river Sagittario. A similar situation can be seen in the major sanctuary at Campochiaro, in Samnite territory, which has been identified with the Hercules Ranus sanctuary indicated on the Tabula Peutingeriana by Torelli.[19] This sanctuary is located on a side of the high mountain range of the Matese, at a height of ca. 800 m a.s.l., ca. 300 m above the Boiano basin, set on a plateau. Just as the Hercules Curinus sanctuary, the Campochiaro sanctuary is not easily reached from the valley floor. Because it will take at least 2 hours, following steep paths, this location does not seem particularly appropriate for a sanctuary controlling the moving of flocks with a connected market func-

[17] For these, cf. Di Niro 1977.

[18] Cf. Crawford 2003a, 63.

[19] Torelli 1993b, cf. n. 13.

[20] Following the suggestion by La Regina (La Regina 2000,

Fig. 4.2. Cattle in Saepinum, Porta Bojano, in 2005 (photo author).

tion. In any case, in both situations it is difficult to imagine a *forum pecuarium* on the steep hill with only relatively small plateaus for the cult buildings, and the same might account for the sanctuaries at Schiavi d'Abruzzo (it is unknown to which deities they were dedicated), if these indeed are to be related to a market function.[20] It is true that it might not be necessary to imagine the flocks themselves reaching the sanctuary proper since business could have been done at some distance, but it is important to acknowledge that the relationship between transhumance and sanctuaries was made in the first place because of the putative topographical correspondence, which is, as we see, not always obvious.

Interestingly, most examples of Hercules supervising market places, and especially sheep and cattle markets, seem to date to the Roman period and are found mainly in Roman urban centres such as colonies or *municipia* (e.g. Alba Fucens, Herdonia, Luceria and Saepinum; fig. 4.2), or in other urban contexts (Teanum Apulum, Larinum, Corfinium).[21] It is not to be excluded that such centres arose especially in the surroundings of ancient market / cult places (in some cases this seems indeed to be the case), but at present there is too little evidence for early phases of these sanctuaries and market places pre-dating the settlements to resolve the issue satisfactorily.

On the other hand, most evidence for the connection between the cult of Hercules proper and transhumance dates to the second century BC or later, and although continuity is often presumed, this is not self-evident. It could therefore be that this dimension of Hercules became prominent only in a later stage. Indeed, as Guy Bradley has emphasised, Hercules was venerated in different Italic regions long before large-scale transhumance can be presumed to have been an important factor.[22] This is not to say that Hercules was not important in the Italic world in his role as patron of herdsmen and merchants, but the evidence for the direct relation between Hercules and (flock) market activities for the Republican

219) that the toponym Schiavi (d'Abruzzo) could be related to the Oscan word *slaagid, slag[ím]*, which could indicate a marketplace. The sanctuaries are located on a steep hill almost 300 m above the valley floor.

[21] Cf. on marketplaces Gabba 1975 (155-156 on the relation with sanctuaries); for *macella*, appearing also from the second half of the second century BC, see de Ruyt 1983. One of the 'Italic' exceptions could perhaps be the sanctuary at Abella, known from the *cippus Abellanus*. The actual presence of a major *tratturo* is not attested here, but if *slaagid* ?= *campus* relates to a marketplace, as suggested by La Regina 2000, 219, the market place was linked to the sanctuary of Hercules. However, this would only document the presence of a generic marketplace near the sanctuary, no explicit connection with cattle markets or transhumance is attested.

[22] Bradley 2005, 139.

period is less abundant than it may sometimes appear in modern accounts on Samnite economy and sanctuaries. The question is related, of course, to the discussion to what extent long-distance transhumance was practised on a large scale before the Roman 'pacification' of the Italic areas. This debate is of course complex, but it must be noted that evidence for large-scale transhumance is late and often even derived from (early) modern parallels.[23] In any case, the image of Samnite economy as being based largely on transhumance reflects, at least to some extent, clichés on the primitiveness and pastorality of Samnite society more than hard evidence.[24]

Even if it is true that we do not normally find Samnite 'peak sanctuaries' far from the inhabited landscape as in some other Italic areas,[25] it is important to underline that very few Samnite sanctuaries are located *directly* along the long *tratturi*. In itself, it is not remarkable that sanctuaries are located not too far from important transportation and communication routes and one could wonder whether analyses of the location of sanctuaries in relation to 'normal' roads in, say, Etruria and Latium, would produce significantly different scenarios. It does not seem methodologically possible to sustain that the location (and very appearance) of sanctuaries was dictated by the presence of transhumance routes, since the latter are ubiquitous in the Samnite landscape.[26] The evidence for a convincing image of Samnite sanctuaries essentially functioning as road shrines or caravanserais along the Samnite *tratturi* and serving primarily passing herdsmen and merchants is in conclusion too sparse, and although such a dimension is certainly attested, it is not to be excluded that this was a relatively late development.

4.2 SANCTUARIES AS TERRITORIAL MARKERS

"L'ultima categoria di 'indicatori territoriali' … è quella dei santuari di confine" (D'Ercole 2000, 127)

Another quite different aspect sometimes attributed to Italic sanctuaries is their supposed function as markers of the territory of a certain community or their role as boundary marker between separate communities. Sanctuaries would thus define a border between 'in' and 'out', and they would accordingly have operated both as frontier markers and as places of exchange between the bordering communities. This idea has been developed in most detail for Greece and the Greek colonies, where relatively well-defined communities (*poleis*, colonies) have been recognised from the geometric period onwards. Most influential has been the thesis put forward by De Polignac, in his analysis of 'the birth' of the Greek city (1984). His study puts religion, ritual and thereby sanctuaries at the centre of the development of the Greek *poleis* in the eighth and seventh centuries BC.[27] The ritually created 'civic space' would moreover have a bipolar structure, *"où la société se reconnaît et s'organise à la fois en son centre et sur la périphérie géographiques"*.[28] Because the cults of the city-centre were not able to maintain control over the territory, the territorial

---

[23] Sabattini 1977 for the idea that large-scale transhumance was the result of changes after the Hannibalic War. Cf. the discussion in Dench 1995, 111-125 and Crawford 2003a; Crawford 2005, esp. 164 with n. 12.

[24] On these images, see Dench 1995.

[25] Esp. in Umbria and in the Marche, cf. e.g. Bradley 1997; D'Ercole 2000, 129.

[26] Cf. the considerations in Bradley 2005, 139-140; cf. also Crawford 2005, 162.

[27] *"C'est en termes cultuels que sont conçus et mis en oeuvre les intégrations, entrées en dépendance, conflits et exclusions par lesquels, dans le cadre territorial délimité par la guerre, s'édifie le nouvel agencement des groupes sociaux auparavant juxtaposés : la participation aux rites garantit la reconnaissance mutuelle des statuts et scelle l'appartenance en définissant une première forme de citoyenneté. Et c'est en termes cultuels, par l'essor des rites et le début d'édification des sanctuaires autour des divinités présidant à cette mise en ordre, que la société émergente manifeste sa cohésion nouvelle et prend ses premières décisions collectives, donc politiques, à long terme; l'espace cultuel qui se dessine alors constitue le premier espace civique."* de Polignac 1984, 155.

[28] de Polignac 1984, 155.

cult was located in the extra-urban sanctuary and this would therefore constitute "*le pôle de la constitution sociale de la cité*".[29] In this manner, De Polignac discerns typically structuralist binary oppositions between cultivated and natural land and argues that the borders between the two are marked by extra-urban sanctuaries. These were under direct control of the major urban centre and this control was manifested and enlivened by religious 'centrifugal' processions, for example the *pompê* from Miletus to Didyma.[30]

Although the model proposed by De Polignac has significantly changed the direction of studies on the relations between Greek politics, religion and sanctuaries, his approach has proven to be too rigid, as he himself explains in a later restatement of his central thesis.[31] In this revision, he allows for more diversity in these processes and stresses the concepts of mediation and competition as central to the development of sanctuaries. The idea is that cult places could sometimes develop from more or less neutral central places of contact between different communities into a great rural sanctuary where the sovereignty of a city is made manifest. An example would be the Argive Heraion, which from a rather isolated meeting point for different communities in the ninth century BC developed into the great monumental complex relating to the city of Argos, which regained regional hegemony in the Classical period.[32] He thus allows for a more complex development over time for the formation of the model.[33]

De Polignac discusses both mainland Greece and Greek colonies in his model of the birth of the city and in some way he sees colonies as the *prêt-à-(im)porter* versions of the mainland Greek evolutions.[34] Research on extra-urban sanctuaries as territorial markers in Greek colonies in southern Italy has a long history, indeed partly because of this 'exemplary' character of colonies.[35] In particular, Pier Giovanni Guzzo established a 'scheme' for the location and function of different sanctuaries in different liminal or 'threshold' zones.[36] Guzzo distinguishes three border zones in Greek colonial establishments; first the boundary between city and the cultivated countryside, second the boundary between cultivated and uncultivated countryside, and finally the frontier between territories belonging to different colonies or different *ethnê*. Within this system, the sanctuaries would serve primarily to formalise and normalise the contacts between different zones. In addition, in research on Magna Graecia in the last decades there has been much interest in the contacts between colonists and the indigenous population, and sometimes the role of the extra-urban sanctuaries as meeting points is emphasised.[37] This emphasis has resulted in a perspective wherein the extra-urban sanctuaries do not exclusively serve the community of the hegemonic city, but also other neighbouring communities.

A clear example of the apparently 'ideal' colonial situation is documented in the territory of the Greek colony of Metapontum by Joseph Carter.[38] This case illustrates both the wealth of the Great Greek

---

[29] de Polignac 1984, 155.

[30] de Polignac 1984. He distinguishes between sanctuaries of the city, '*sanctuaires suburbains*' directly outside the city, and extra-urban sanctuaries.

[31] de Polignac 1994.

[32] de Polignac 1994, 4-5.

[33] According to some scholars also the final, 'completed' stage, with the extra-urban sanctuary expressing a city's sovereignty over its territory, should be seen as more flexible. The distinction between cultivated land and non-cultivated land may be too rigid and would tend to regard sanctuaries as boundaries rather than as the integrative elements between hinterland and *polis* that they could have been. Cf. e.g. McInerny 2006 who stresses the economic role of extra-urban sanctuaries on the border of agricultural and pastoral economies and their consequent 'integrative' function; cf. also Polinskaya 2003 for criticism on the notion of liminality.

[34] "The peculiarity of the colonial world lies more in how speedily and systematically it develops what in the Aegean world is the outcome of an evolutionary process at work since the ninth century ..." de Polignac 1994, 15-16.

[35] Esp. Vallet 1968; Guzzo 1987. Cf. in general on the foundation of sanctuaries in relation to colonisation Malkin 1987, esp. 135-186; Veronese 2000; Carter 1994; Carter 2006.

[36] Guzzo 1987.

[37] Cf. the contributions in *Modes* 1983 and Stazio *et al.* 1999; Torelli 1977.

[38] Carter 1994; Carter 2006, 157-173.

evidence (Metapontum presenting perhaps the best studied *chora* of all Great Greek cities) and the careful elaboration of De Polignac's hypothesis, substantiated by solid data. In the *chora* belonging to the Greek urban centre of Metapontum that rose probably somewhere at the end of the seventh century BC, rural shrines dating mostly from the sixth century BC onwards are distributed regularly along the river valleys of the Basento and (to a lesser degree) the Bradano, at an interval of ca. 3 km, sometimes with smaller shrines in between. Their location seems to be the result of careful planning (cf. fig. 4.3) both in light of their symmetrical position and because of the similarity between both the rural cults themselves and between rural and urban cults. The typology of the votive figurines for instance is strikingly uniform and sometimes the same moulds seem to have been used. So far this would fit nicely into the picture of a colony manifesting authority over its territory. However, in the vicinity of the sanctuaries that are located in the area, surveyed intensively by Texas University, there seem to be significantly more individual family farms. From this observation Carter concludes that "the distribution of sanctuaries may have corresponded to a division of the *chora* made in the sixth century into a dozen or so larger units", accordingly organised and inhabited by different local communities. Ultimately, he compares the shrines to modern parish churches.[39] Thus, Carter puts the emphasis more on the local significance of these rural sanctuaries, albeit the direct result of colonial planning.

Similar ideas that link the location and function of sanctuaries with territoriality have been developed for central and central-southern Italy. In the city of Rome space was religiously defined by the location of sanctuaries at ritual boundaries, for example the *pomerium* and the sanctuaries along the roads at the first or fifth and/or sixth mile.[40] Especially revealing in this respect is the festival of the *Terminalia*, celebrated at the sixth mile of the *via Laurentina*, an institution attributed to the mythical king Numa renowned for his piety.[41]

Comparable hypotheses have been put forward for Etruria, in particular by Andrea Zifferero, who discerns clear developments in the importance of different extra-urban sanctuaries over time and links this to political developments.[42] He concludes that the border between the cities of Caere and Tarquinia became clear only after the (re-)organisation of the rural population beginning in the orientalising period. This border followed ecologically defined lines, whereas in the sixth century a mixed frontier system was in operation, "*a barriera interrotta*", but which was reinforced at critical points with extra-urban sanctuaries. In the fourth century this system would have been enhanced by the divergent political developments of Caere, now more under Roman influence, and Tarquinia expanding into internal Etruria, but was ultimately disturbed by the Roman conquest at the beginning of the third century BC.[43] Zifferero's study illustrates well the possibilities of diachronic research. The territorial character of early Etruscan colonisation in the Po basin has been similarly outlined in the religious realm by Monica Miari, who discerns "*una articolata trama di segni, che scandiva ed organizzava lo spazio delineando un 'paesaggio del culto'*",[44] and she also emphasises the expression of sovereignty through the location of cult places.

Similar approaches have been adopted with reference to Italic inland areas, explaining the existence and location of sanctuaries as frontiers within the settlement pattern. In particular Vincenzo D'Ercole has taken this perspective in his studies on the Abruzzo region (the areas inhabited in antiquity partly by the Praetutii, Vestini, Marruccini, Frentani, Carricini, Pentri, Paeligni, Marsi and Aequi), analysing the function and significance of Italic sanctuaries (and, for that matter, cave sites, habitation centres and necropoleis) within the general pattern of settlement.[45]

---

[39] Carter 1994, 181. Cf. Leone 1998, 15.
[40] Scheid 1987; Rüpke 1990, 30-41; Colonna 1991. Cf. also Cancik 1985-1986.
[41] Piccaluga 1974.
[42] Zifferero 1995; cf. also Zifferero 1998; Zifferero 2002.
[43] Zifferero 1995, 348.
[44] Miari 2000b, 57.
[45] D'Ercole *et al.* 1997; D'Ercole 2000. For Campania, cf. Carafa 1998.

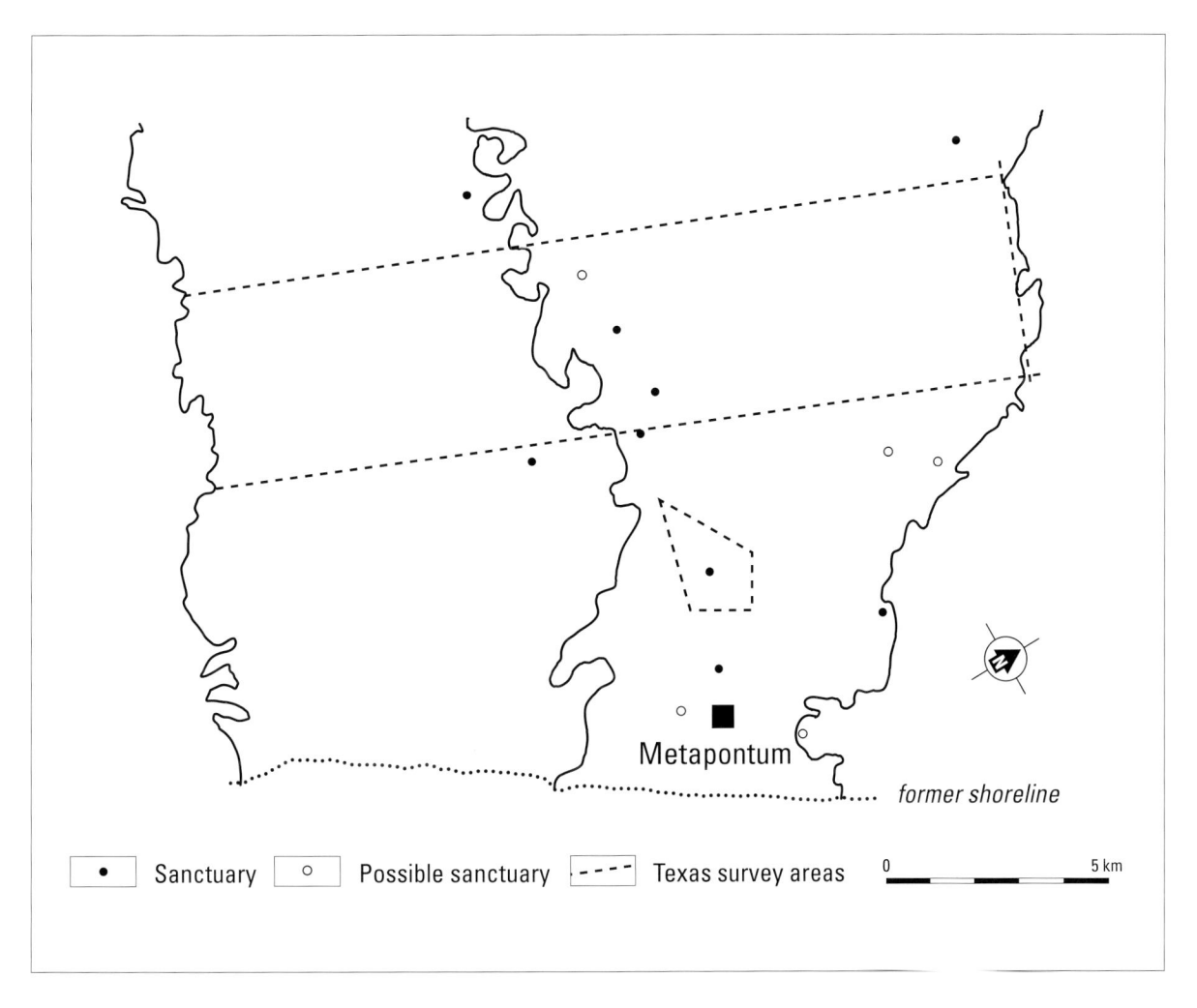

Fig. 4.3. Metapontum with *chora* (adapted from Carter 1994, 163 fig. 7.1).

Taking a long term perspective, D'Ercole puts forward the thesis that in different eras different 'markers' in the landscape were predominant. Put simply, whereas caves were of central importance in the Bronze Age, this position would have been taken up by the necropoleis with conspicuous tumulus graves dating to the late Bronze Age to the early Iron Age, and this privilege would then, in the Hellenistic period, be passed on to sanctuaries.[46] According to D'Ercole, these sanctuaries would have marked the territories of different tribes, suggesting that this would have been reflected in the choice of the venerated deities, every tribe ('*popolo*') worshipping different (characteristics of) gods.[47] In his contribution to *Paesaggi di potere*, the proceedings of a conference held in 1996 explicitly dealing with spatial analysis, D'Ercole studies the whole modern region Abruzzo. He concludes that sanctuaries reflect the intention

---

[46] D'Ercole 2000, 121-127. On p. 146 n. 65, D'Ercole sees a 'paradigmatic' situation in the area of the river Raiale (west of Gran Sasso) where a cave site ("*il marker territoriale della preistoria*"), necropoleis ("*i markers della protostoria*") and the "*caratteristico santuario di confine d'epoca storica*" of Feronia at Civita di Bagno, are situated within a range of 10 km.

[47] D'Ercole 2000, 127: "*L'ultima categoria di 'indicatori territoriali' ... è quella dei santuari di confine. Essi sembrano rivestire in Abruzzo quel ruolo precedentemente svolto dalle sepolture a tumulo (e, forse, ancora prima dalle grotte), di marcare cioè un territorio non più attraverso il ricordo di antenati mitizzati ed eroizzati ma mediante il culto di vere e proprie divinità, formalmente definite, con caratteristiche e forse nomi, diversi a seconda dei vari popoli.*"

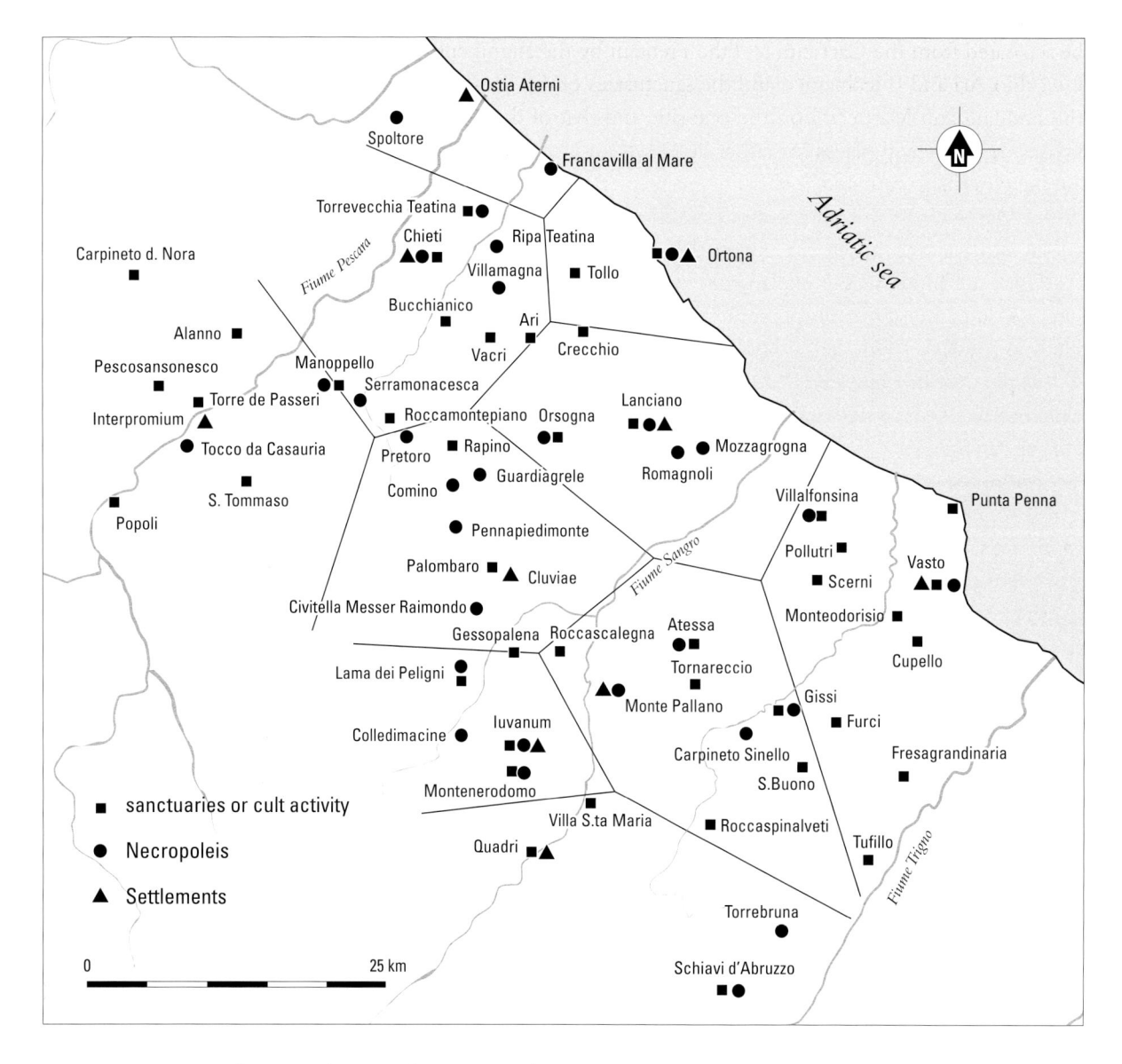

Fig. 4.4. Sanctuaries as frontiermarkers according to D'Ercole *et al.* 1997, fig. on p. 23.

to express territoriality by different communities. For comparative reasons, this discussion will focus on work on the 'Samnite' region of southern Abruzzo.[48] Here, the location of sanctuaries in relation to habitation centres and necropoleis was analysed by D'Ercole, together with Vincenza Orfanelli and Paola Riccitelli. Figure 4.4 reproduces the resulting proposal for a territorial division in southern Abruzzo in the 'Samnite' period. Thiessen polygons were used to establish the dimensions of the different centres in the region.[49]

Their analysis included all indicators of cultic activity, namely sanctuaries with structural remains, finds of bronze statuettes and inscriptions relating to cults. According to their reconstruction, several cult places are located along borders of ethnic groups and cities. For instance, the territory of the Marruccini would

[48] D'Ercole *et al.* 1997.

[49] Unfortunately nothing is said about the decision to use this model and its exact application especially with regard to included sites. This approach to the reconstruction of borders in antiquity forms part of a long tradition, cf. e.g. Renfrew 1975; Hodder/Orton 1976.

be separated from the Carricini and the Frentani by the alignment of the finds of bronze statuettes at Tollo, Crecchio, Ari and Bucchianico and the sanctuaries of Vacri and Rapino. In the same way, the territories of the Frentani and Maruccini on the one side and that of the Carricini and the Pentri on the other would be drawn by the cult places (or rather dispersed finds of statuettes) of Orsogna, Palombaro, the sanctuary of Atessa, Furci, S. Buono and Tufillo. Furthermore, the 'hegemonic' centres of Teate (modern Chieti, territory of the Marruccini), Histonium (modern Vasto, territory of the Frentani) and perhaps that of Iuvanum (territory of the Carricini) would express their territorial boundaries with extra-urban sanctuaries.[50]

There are limits to the explanatory power of this spatial approach to sanctuaries. In the first place, it remains difficult to postulate a geopolitical organisation on the basis of the archaeological record because it relies so heavily on the very completeness of that record; if we happen to 'miss' one important centre, the whole picture with Thiessen polygons changes considerably. The other way around, if one wants to include evidence like bronze statuettes and other haphazardly found objects possibly (but not certainly) indicating cult places, there is a risk to read too much into the material, which is after all not the result of systematic archaeological research. The suggestion that there is a strong relation between the location of necropoleis and sanctuaries is highly interesting.[51] The combination of funeral and religious contexts with no corresponding settlements would strengthen the idea of territorial limitation by means of these kinds of markers. Also here caution is required however, especially since it is precisely sanctuaries and necropoleis that are overrepresented in the archaeological record of central Italy, due to the poorer visibility of (and attention to) habitation sites. Only systematic archaeological research, such as intensive field survey, can establish whether the correspondence is a historical one or rather the result of an observer's bias.

As to the groups under consideration in this model, another question regards the possibility of tracing ethnic boundaries in the archaeological record. Ethnic identities will certainly have been important at some places and some specific moments in time (cf. Chapter 3), but it does not necessarily follow that these ethnic distinctions translated into fixed territorial 'states'. The imposing character of ethnicity should not be overstated, and the possible discontinuity in its importance, or even existence, should be taken into account. Ethnicity is a social construct and depends on specific socio-historical situations and is therefore very sensitive to historical changes.[52] In other words, it can be seriously questioned whether there were stable ethnic boundaries during the whole Hellenistic period,[53] precisely because this does not correspond to the very nature of ethnic groups. Methodologically, there is the problem that we cannot easily check or falsify the proposed ethnic boundaries as signalled by cult places. There is, apart from very scarce epigraphic evidence, no possibility to establish these ethnic boundaries by other archaeological evidence and historical evidence is problematic because of its etic character, later date and lack of precise descriptions. Even in the arguably 'exemplary' Greek world, recent studies have increasingly emphasised that the borders between the territories of different communities both in the Greek mainland and colonies were less clear-cut than has been envisioned before.[54] Moreover, a devil's advocate could connect

---

[50] D'Ercole et al. 1997, 22-23.

[51] D'Ercole et al. 1997, 23, n. 21: especially for the Paeligni, at Corfinio; cf. D'Ercole 2000, *passim*.

[52] Cf. in general Jones 1997; and esp. Dench 1995 for central Italy.

[53] This accounts a fortiori for possible precursors of ethnically defined territories in the pre-and protohistorical periods, see D'Ercole 2000, on the link between south-Picene inscriptions and the distribution of tumulus graves, and 124-125, n. 15 on the existence of 'proto'-peoples. Cf. in this respect also Faustoferri 2003.

[54] Cf. the recently concluded project *Regional pathways to complexity* by the Free University Amsterdam and the Groningen Institute of Archaeology (see e.g. Burgers 2002). Cf. the discussion on the sanctuary of Timpone della Motta, the identification of which as a Greek frontier sanctuary is dismissed by Kleibrink 2001, 39-42, cf. however Guzzo 2003. See Leone 1998, esp. 11-18 and 31-35 on theories on extra-urban sanctuaries in Archaic Magna Graecia). Cf. e.g. Burgers/Crielaard 2007 on Greek colonial-indigenous interactions.

the dots on the map just as well in a different manner and create different patterns, especially if one is not looking exclusively for large ethnic groups and takes also into account the existence of smaller local communities, or other not necessarily ethnically defined groups.

Even if it therefore seems imprudent to interpret non-urban sanctuaries generally as part of a geopolitical constellation formulated along ethnic lines, it is certainly likely that some sanctuaries functioned in and as a border zone between different communities (some evidence will be discussed below). We could ask however what their precise function was. Where they, to the like of perhaps the (Great) Greek extra-urban sanctuaries, primarily related to the expression of territorial sovereignty? There is reason to doubt that the situation in Apennine central Italy was similar to the Tyrrhenian and Greek world. In many areas of Greece a strong territorial claim would have already existed from the early Iron Age onwards, simultaneous with the rise of the *poleis*.[55] In a highly centralised and hierarchically organised society, the fixity of boundaries perhaps makes more sense, as do the extra-urban sanctuaries at the fringes of the city's territory. The same goes for the Etruscan (and early Roman) forms of political organisation.[56] However, I would argue that at this stage we should be cautious in presuming a rigid territorial organisation with clear boundaries coinciding with cult places in the non-urban Italic world.

Even if we accept the interpretation of certain sanctuaries as boundary markers (for different types of group), the question remains what exactly happened in these border sanctuaries; were they only visual territorial markers or do we have to imagine processions and specific border rites, or should we perhaps think of them as places of contact between the neighbouring peoples? For Abruzzo, it has been argued that different gods appealing to different peoples would have been venerated in different sanctuaries, which would have underlined ethnic difference.[57] This view suggests that these cult places had an *exclusive* quality; that the border sanctuaries were intended for the own group, excluding others and at the same time enhancing (ethnic) group identities. Unfortunately, in most cases in the Italic world the names (let alone the specific characteristics or epithets) of the venerated deities are unknown and any analysis on a grand scale therefore seems impossible at present. Although there certainly were exclusive cults in Italy, as for example the rather xenophobic ritual documented in the Iguvine tablets where 'outsiders' are formally banished might indicate, it is much less clear if this attitude corresponded to an exclusive character of territorial sanctuaries. As a matter of fact, the 'urban' case of Gubbio does not necessarily represent religious behaviour in the rest of Italy.[58] For now, it

[55] But cf. De Polignac's reservations with regard to the application of a conceptualisation of the city based on the classical Greek city for the Geometric and early Archaic periods, de Polignac 1994, 4. Without entering the debate on the Greek situation, it should be pointed out that further deconstruction of this fixed territorial idea for Greece would only strengthen my argument for the situation in Italy.

[56] However, this is not to say of course that it is easy to establish the location of these boundaries: cf. the remarks in Zifferero 1995, 335-336. Incidentally, it is good to keep in mind that we know from several sources that boundaries or frontiers were considered sacred in the Etruscan and Roman societies: cf. for Rome e.g. the necessity for magistrates to retake the auspices after crossing the *amnis Petronia* in the *campus Martius*. For Etruria cf. Zifferero 1995, 333 n. 4; cf. for the linguistic evidence Lambrechts 1970, and Colonna 1988. Apart from the intriguing example of the Iguvine Tablets, which in the end refers to an 'urban' reality, there is to my knowledge no evidence for the non-urbanised Italic regions that this kind of territorial view was formulated this rigidly. Most evidence in this realm derives from (semi / proto etc.) urban contexts, with a strong emphasis on the importance of the city walls, not territorial boundaries. For the Iguvine Tablets, cf. Poultney 1959; Prosdocimi 1984; Prosdocimi 1989; Malone/Stoddart 1994; Sisani 2001b; Porzio Gernia 2004. Cf. *infra* on the *cippus Abellanus*.

[57] D'Ercole 2000, 127: "... di marcare cioè un territorio ... mediante il culto di vere e proprie divinità, formalmente definite, con caratteristiche e forse nomi, diversi a seconda dei vari popoli." (see longer quote at n. 47).

[58] See Chapter 2 on the problem, and n. 56 on the Iguvine tablets.

seems unwise to transpose the specific ideas developed for differently organised areas in Greece and Magna Graecia to the Apennines.

Whatever the nature of contact may be, there is evidence that sanctuaries were sometimes located in border zones between different ethnic groups or other communities. The most famous example is the *lucus Feroniae*, near Capena, which according to Dionysius of Halicarnassus (*Ant. Rom.* 3.32.1) was frequented by Sabines and Latins alike, especially for markets and fairs.[59] Apparently, the sanctuary profited from its location between different cultures. The *cippus Abellanus*, from Abella in Campania and dating to the end of the second century BC,[60] may be the most explicit evidence for an 'Italic border sanctuary'. The rules regarding the use of a sanctuary dedicated to Hercules are laid down in the Oscan text. It is explicitly stated that the sanctuary served the inhabitants of the towns of Nola and the inhabitants of Abella and in order to resolve problems of property, it seems that the terrain of the sanctuary itself was extra-territorial, in a 'no-man's-land' between the two communities. However, this is not an ethnic border.

In the strict sense, these cases seem to offer evidence for sanctuaries at the borders of different communities. However, the apparent function of the sanctuaries is precisely *not* to signal closed boundaries, demarcating one group. On the contrary, if anything, these sanctuaries seem to have served as meeting places, as places of social contact in a religious sense and possibly even more so in a commercial one (note that both epigraphic texts mention financial arrangements and that trade is highlighted by Dionysius). Such an interpretation, which sees sanctuaries as a central functional element in the organisation of settlement and communication, rather than as a merely demarcating and confining one, sets the scene for another line of interpretation that is discussed in the following section.

4.3 SANCTUARIES AND THE SO-CALLED PAGUS-VICUS SYSTEM

"*I santuari sono di solito di pertinenza paganico-vicana*" (La Regina 1980, 39).

"*A shrine normally belonged to a single pagus, but the shrine at Pietrabbondante was clearly supported by many pagi*" (Salmon 1982, 117 n. 345).

So far, I have discussed different conceptualisations of the role or functions of sanctuaries that directly relate to ideas on territorial organisation, economy and infrastructure. The theory on sanctuaries as frontier-markers discussed above has the drawback that it has to rely on presumed fixed territorial boundaries of different tribes. Since independent proof for such boundaries is scant, a risk of circular reasoning exists. This model also has the serious drawback that it has been developed for a specific type of society, specifically urbanised areas, such as Greek *poleis* and colonies and to a lesser degree Etruria. The interpretation of sanctuaries as road shrines along the long distance transhumance routes, on the other hand, does take into account a (at least perceived) particular feature of Italic society. As has been pointed out however, this interpretation seems to be rather one-sided and cannot be used as a generalised explanatory model.

---

[59] "There is a sanctuary, honoured in common by the Sabines and the Latins, that is held in the greatest reverence and is dedicated to a goddess named Feronia ... To this sanctuary people used to resort from the neighbouring cities on the appointed days of festival, many of them performing vows and offering sacrifice to the goddess and many with the purpose of trafficking during the festive gathering as merchants, artisans and husbandmen; and here were held fairs more celebrated than in any other places in Italy" (transl. Loeb). Cf. also Livy 26.12.

[60] According to La Regina 2000 ca. 120-110 BC.

It seems attractive, however, to try to understand the place and function of sanctuaries in relation to a specific Italic pattern of settlement, rather than using Greek or other models.

A third line of interpretation discernable in modern studies is indeed more directly linked to particular ideas on the organisation of Italic society. In this model, sanctuaries are an integral part of a distinct pattern of settlement. This model could be called the *pagus-vicus* system, a translation of *il sistema pagano-vicanico* or *paganico-vicano vel sim.* often found in Italian literature, and indicating the two most important elements making up this model of settlement. The *vicus* is understood as a village, and the *pagus* is (mostly) understood as a territorial district containing one or more *vici*. The model has been tremendously popular in both Italian and other mainland European research, as well as in Anglo-Saxon studies.

The discussion on this conception of Italic settlement patterns is complex, not least because recently the very premises of this model have been shown to be rooted in poor evidence. Because sanctuaries in central-southern Italy are often understood to have functioned within this *pagus-vicus* system, both implicitly and explicitly, it is important to address the model itself at least briefly. For a more detailed discussion on the development of the model one is redirected to the thorough and recent works by Capogrossi Colognesi and Tarpin.[61] Their studies, although not in all respects unanimous, are the basis for the critical reconsideration of the *pagus-vicus* model and the role of sanctuaries within it, which will be returned to in more detail in Chapters 6 and 7. First, I will discuss the traditional view of the *pagus-vicus* system in relation to general ideas on Italic settlement patterns. This will be followed by a discussion of the supposed role of sanctuaries within it.

4.3.1 SAMNITE SETTLEMENT AND THE PAGUS-VICUS SYSTEM: AN 'IMMEMORIAL ITALIC INSTITUTION'

General accounts, handbooks and specialised studies alike depict Italic or Samnite peoples as living in small villages and hill-forts and some dispersed settlements which are mostly small farms. This image *per se* is well-supported by the archaeological evidence. Hill-forts are virtually the only imposing remnants in the Samnite landscape and a lack of urban centres would, together with the idea that the population density was relatively high,[62] indeed sustain such an idea. This scenario also seems to fit literary evidence which describes the Samnite settlement pattern as consisting of small villages rather than towns. Livy 9.13.7 is classic,[63] *Samnites ... in montibus vicatim habitantes* – as is Strabo 5.4.12, κωμηδόν ζώσιν. These modern and ancient observations on the settlement pattern have been interpreted as representing a specific settlement organisation. In the chapter on the Roman conquest of Italy in the *Cambridge Ancient History* for example, Tim Cornell proposes the following ideas on the nature and organisation of Samnite society:

"... it still remains true in general that before the Roman conquest the region was poor and relatively backward, with few, if any, urban centres, no coinage and little trade. The inhabitants supplemented their livelihood by warfare and raiding ... The political organization of the Samnites was correspondingly simple and unsophisticated. The basic local unit was the pagus, a canton comprising one or more villages (vici), which was economically self-sufficient and possessed a large measure of political autonomy. Each pagus was probably governed by an elected magistrate called a mediss (Latin meddix – Festus 110L). A group of such pagi would together form a larger tribal unit, for which the Oscan term was touto (Latin populus). The chief magistrate of the touto had the title mediss tovtiks (meddix tuticus)."[64]

---

[61] Capogrossi Colognesi 2002; Tarpin 2002. Esp. Capogrossi Colognesi treats the history of research in detail.

[62] Esp. on the basis of Polybius 2.24. Cf. discussion in Dench 1995, 142.

[63] Also 10.17.2. is often, improperly, cited in this context.

[64] Cornell 1989, 353-356.

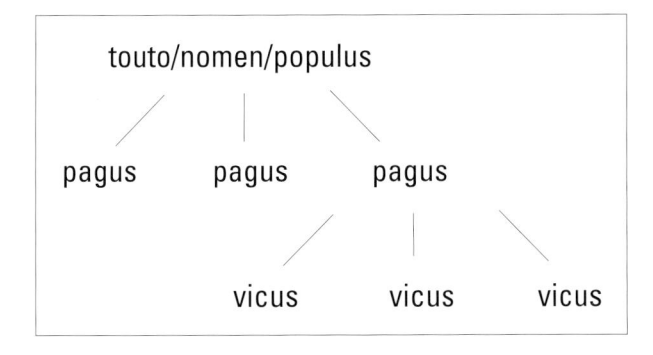

```
         touto/nomen/populus
            /     |      \
        pagus   pagus   pagus
              /    |     \
            vicus  vicus  vicus
```

Fig. 4.5. Scheme showing the traditional view of the *pagus-vicus* system as an Italic feature.

Cornell's text neatly illustrates some general ideas on Italic, in this case more specifically Samnite patterns of settlement. An institutional hierarchy between *vicus* (village), *pagus* (here as a territorial district or canton) and *touto* ('tribe': Latin *populus, civitas* or *nomen*) is indicated.[65] In the traditional view, Italic tribes would thus have been subdivided into *pagi*,[66] whereas within these *pagi* people lived in small villages (*vici*), hill-forts (Latin: *oppida*) or dispersed over the territory. (cf. fig. 4.5).

The *oppida* are sometimes considered to be merely defensive structures of the *pagus* as a whole because few habitation structures have been found in the hill-forts, but this may to a certain degree represent the status quo of archaeological research rather than the ancient reality (cf. Chapter 3).[67] La Regina has developed the model further with reference to the central Apennines and Samnium proper and has also investigated a possible relation between the surface area of the respective territories of different tribes and the number of *pagi* in which it was divided.[68]

It is generally assumed that this organisation stems from very ancient times (on the argumentation and reasons for this see the discussion in Chapter 6). Edward Togo Salmon for example calls the *pagus* "the immemorial Italic institution", and sees it as the Samnites' "sub-tribal entity", and this forms part of a longer tradition going back to late 19th century German scholarship.[69] Until recently little attention has been paid to the chronological development of the *pagus-vicus* system,[70] and for a long time there has been a general consensus on the pre-Roman date and nature of the system.

After the Roman conquest, the *pagus-vicus* system would however have endured in some cases, if it was not supplanted by the new municipal system. The *pagus-vicus* system is then regarded as a persistent 'tribal' survival, which continued to exist despite of, and parallel to, the new Roman organisation of the territory. In a study on the interference of the municipal system with the pre-existing *pagus-vicus* system, Umberto Laffi thus sketches a scenario in which after the Social War the Romans found regions organised according to the *pagus-vicus* system, which would have been much more difficult to re-organise within

---

[65] The 'translation' of *touto* is unclear, and depends on different conceptions of the evolution of Samnite society organisation as well (e.g. the remarks in Letta 1994, esp. 395). Cf. thus here Cornell 1989, 356: *populus*; Torelli 1988b, 72: *civitas*; La Regina 1980: 'tribal' *nomen*, also followed by Dench 1995, 136-137 and Tagliamonte 1997, 180, 258. Cf. e.g. also Torelli 1988c, 55-56 for the same hierarchical order tribe-*pagus-vicus*.

[66] Salmon 1967, 79-81 (p. 80: "each *touto* contained a number of *pagi* ... When, however, a number of *pagi* agreed to cooperate closely a *touto* was born"); see also in particular La Regina 1970; La Regina 1980; La Regina 1989 and La Regina 1991; cf. also Torelli 1988c.

[67] e.g. Laffi 1974, 336: "*Ogni pagus si articolava in uno o più vici, che rappresentavano nuclei di stanziamento compatti, subordinati al pagus, nei quali si raccoglieva stabilmente parte della populazione rurale del pagus stesso. Oppida e castella, ubicati per solito in posizioni elevate, assicuravano la difesa dell'intera comunità territoriale paganica.*"

[68] La Regina 1970-1971, 444-6; the average area occupied by a *pagus* would have amounted to 34-36 km² and by an average *vicus* 11-12 km². Criticised by Capogrossi Colognesi 2002, 175 with n. 37.

[69] Salmon 1967, 79-80. On p. 79: "Their sub-tribal entity was the immemorial Italic institution, the *pagus*; and traces of their *pagus*-arrangements survived into Roman times." Cf. discussion in Chapter 6.

[70] But cf. e.g. Letta 1988; Letta 1991.

the Roman system of municipalisation than the areas which already included urban structures.[71] Laffi generally envisages a persistence of the *pagus-vicus* system alongside the Roman municipal system. *Vici* and *pagi* would have preserved their religious and administrative functions and every *pagus* and every *vicus* would have continued to constitute an autonomous '*respublica*', the only infringement on their autonomy being jurisdiction, to be dispensed by the *municipia*.[72] A general Roman policy of non-intervention in the tribal structures would have been the reason for the continued existence of the *pagus-vicus* system in the first century BC.[73] Moreover, Laffi discerns different developments in the Roman organisation before the Social War with regard to the independence of the Italic *pagi* and *vici*. The Roman *praefecturae*, representing only juridical power, would have had little influence on the traditional Italic structures. On the other hand, the relatively autonomous *municipia* would have gradually controlled the whole territory and therefore altered the Italic patterns of settlement much more profoundly. However, *vici* and *pagi* also maintained their organisational roles during the empire, even if their powers were diminished and partly transferred to the city authorities.

This view of Italic or Samnite settlement organisation and its persistence has been widely assumed in studies on pre-Roman central-southern Italy, although different nuances have been made. Others for example see the *pagus-vicus* system rather as a 'substrate' for the later Roman institutions.[74] In general, therefore, the *pagus-vicus* system in Roman times is described in terms of 'persistence' or continuity, despite the Roman conquest, and its remarkable vitality in Roman times has often been emphasised.[75] This persistence is sometimes formulated in almost romantic wording, contrasting the traditions of the unchanged countryside with the new, Roman, urban developments.[76] It is within this system that the rural sanctuaries of central-southern Italy are often thought to have functioned, and I shall now discuss this idea in more detail.

4.3.2 THE ROLE OF SANCTUARIES WITHIN THE PAGUS-VICUS SYSTEM

> *"The Samnites ... maintained a separation between their settlements and the various forms of communal or state activity they engaged in. They lived in villages or on farms dispersed throughout the territory (Livy 9.13.7), but each locality (pagus) had a hill fort for defensive purposes and a religious sanctuary that acted as a focus not just for sacrifices and festivals but also for markets, legal hearings, and assemblies of the local people. These assemblies seem to have chosen magistrates to govern them in much the same way as a city was*

---

[71] Laffi 1974, e.g. 336: "*l'imposizione dello schema del municipium esigeva in via preliminare un'ampia opera di ristrutturazione del contesto politico-amministrativo.*"

[72] Laffi 1974, 337.

[73] Laffi 1974, 338.

[74] E.g. Rainini 2000, 238; cf. on this antagonism – substrate paradox e.g. Gabba 1994a: 74: "*Il processo di municipalizzazione dopo la Guerra Sociale è in stretto collegamento con il ricordato fenomeno dell'urbanizzazione dell'Italia nel corso del I sec. a.C. Credo, anzi, che il passaggio dalla fase degli insediamenti tribali, caratteristica di larga parte dell'Italia centrale e meridionale (nonché, ovviamente, della cisalpina), alla fase urbana rappresenti l'aspetto più imponente della municipalizzazione dell'Italia dopo l'89 a.C.*" and on p. 97: "*... i nuovi impianti urbani (scil. municipi), costruiti secondo lo schema ortogonale, cercarono di sostituire gli antichi insediamenti basati sui pagi e i vici. In molti casi, il vicus più importante in un gruppo di pagi sarà stato scelto per divenire il centro urbano del municipium.*"

[75] Besides Laffi, cf. e.g. La Regina 1970-1971; Frederiksen 1976, 350; Gaggiotti 1983; Letta 1992; on the idea of a 're-emergence' of the system in the late antique period, see e.g. Volpe 1996, 146.

[76] Cf. e.g. Buonocore 2002, 43-45, ending his article on the subject as follows: "*Dalla fase di insediamento paganico-vicano si passò ad una fase urbano-cittadina la quale, sebbene si sia sovrapposto alla precedente, non credo mai, almeno in certe aree sabelliche, che sia riuscita ad annullarla.*" Cf. also Letta 1992, 124, on a "*sorta di fedeltà alle radici*".

governed and to have banded together into larger political units, each known as a touto. These in turn seem to have formed a federation, known to modern historians as the Samnite League, which had the power of declaring peace and war. A number of larger and more elaborate sanctuaries probably served as the meeting points of the touto, and a particularly large and imposing example at Pietrabbondante has been identified as a possible headquarters of the Samnite League." (Lomas 2004, 201-203)

This passage from a recent handbook, the *Cambridge Companion to the Roman Republic* published in 2004, well illustrates both the general consensus on the relationship between Samnite settlement patterns and sanctuaries, and, at the same time, the very ambiguity of this model. Indeed, Italic sanctuaries are so often attributed a specific role within the so-called *pagus-vicus* system that it has become commonplace. One recurring feature in discussions of the *pagus-vicus* system is the alleged spatial separation of functions.[77] In this respect, the hill-forts would serve defensive purposes, separated from the *vici* and necropoleis.[78] Sanctuaries would have occupied a specialised position. In the above quoted passage, this boils down to the idea that different types of sanctuaries served different levels of the Samnite societal organisation; from small to large, different cult places would have formed the meeting places on the level of respectively the *pagus*, the *touto*, and the 'Samnite League'.[79] In this way, rural sanctuaries are seen as constituents of a specific Italic pattern of settlement, which is characterised by spatial differentiation. In fact, the *pagus* is conceptualised as an 'exploded' city, with the societal functions concentrated in an urban context here dispersed over the territory.[80] The principal function of sanctuaries would consequently have included political, religious and economic aspects, just as the forum in urban societies. Thus, broadly speaking within the *pagus-vicus* system sanctuaries are seen as a pole of aggregation. As will be obvious, to see sanctuaries as central places within the general and directly local settlement pattern is substantially different from viewing them as frontier markers or road shrines.[81] Within this broad view, subdivisions have subsequently been made, discerning different types of sanctuaries with different appeals. Such divisions are reminiscent of other, more general typologies of sanctuaries. For example Helena Fracchia and Maurizio Gualtieri distinguish three types of sanctuaries in late fifth to fourth century Lucania: large 'cantonal', extra-urban sanctuaries such as Rossano di Vaglio, small rural sanctuaries "at crossroads" and cult places in aristocratic houses.[82] Furthermore, the divisions made by Colonna for Etruria and by Edlund for Etruria and Magna Graecia,[83] illustrate this idea of a hierarchy between

---

[77] Cf. also Cornell 1989, 356. Interestingly, many authors are at the same time depreciatory about the functional 'merging' as would be apparent in the magistratures, combining sacral, juridical and military functions in one person.

[78] Cf. Tagliamonte 1994, 37 (on the seventh to mid-sixth centuries BC) "*La forma insediativa propria di queste genti è costituita da un ambito territoriale (pagus) pertinente a una comunità, provvisto di strutture diffuse con funzioni differenziati (vici, oppida, castella),*" including structures that would sometimes have been provisional or seasonal, which Tagliamonte links to Varro's *casae repentinae* (*Rust.* 2.10.6).

[79] Another example of a differential approach to the function of sanctuaries can be found in the section by Mario Torelli on the Apennines ("*l'antico cuore del sottosviluppo*") in *Storia di Roma*. Torelli 1988c, 55-56: "*Di fatto perciò, i territori di queste tribù sono articolati in aree paganiche … nelle quali gravitano più vici, le cui arces sono da identificare con le cinte fortificate, e uno o più santuari gestiti tanto da uno o più vici quanto da uno o più pagi … Il pagus dunque vive e «funziona» come una città, il santuario principale del pagus ne costituisce in buona sostanza il forum, con tempio e mercato, sia pur periodico o stagionale, mentre gli oppida sulle vette montane fungono da rocche per la necessità di difesa*". Cf. Torelli 1983, 242, where sanctuaries are seen as the "*strutture centrali dell'habitat paganico (area sannitica)*".

[80] See preceding note.

[81] Even if, as said, none of these functions are exclusive of course, cf. *supra*.

[82] Fracchia/Gualtieri 1989. Cf. also Greco 2000; Horsnaes 2002.

[83] Colonna 1985; Edlund-Berry 1987.

different sanctuaries, whereas the idea that the different Italic tribes each had a central 'tribal' sanctuary is also well-established.[84]

The particularity with the case of the *pagus-vicus* system is, however, that these differing roles of sanctuaries are attached to different *institutional* entities: *vicus*, *pagus*, and *touto / populus / nomen*. In this way, the large rural sanctuaries would constitute the gathering places on the level of the *civitas* or *touto*, for example Pietrabbondante, whereas the smaller ones, connected with springs and communication routes, would have formed the meeting places for the *pagi*.[85] For example, Samnite sanctuaries such as Schiavi d'Abruzzo, Vastogirardi and S. Giovanni in Galdo have been described as having a *pagus*-wide reach.[86] Sanctuaries that relate to *vici* could be seen as a category further down the hierarchy.

By far the most elaborate study on the function of sanctuaries in relation to the *pagus-vicus* system, and especially its persistence into the first century BC, is the 1992 article by Letta on the central Apennines.[87] Indeed, Letta explicitly departs from the idea that the *pagus-vicus* system has to form the basis for further interpretation.[88] Therefore, the rural sanctuaries he focuses on in this article are placed by default within this 'grid'. Using the inscriptions of the Augustan *regio IV* which indicate cult places outside the municipal centres, he classifies the rural sanctuaries according to their function in relation to settlements.

Letta discerns four types. The first is a type of sanctuary located outside settlements, *municipia* as well as *vici*, that would relate primarily to the whole *pagus* ("*tipo A*"). He suggests that most sanctuaries in the areas with *pagi* can be classified as such. The best example of this type would be the temple at Fontecchio, in the Vestine territory of Peltuinum. The podium of a temple dating to the first century AD has been recognised under the modern church of S. M. della Vittoria.[89] This represents a restoration phase and the date of the original building is unfortunately unknown.[90] The sanctuary was dedicated to *Quirinus* (perhaps *Juppiter Quirinus*).[91] There is an inscription mentioning magistrates but it is unclear whether they belong to a *vicus* or a *pagus* (or yet another institution).[92] An additional inscription re-used in the same church however mentions the settlement of Aufenginum, the actual Fagnano Alto.[93] The influence of a *vicus* from elsewhere

---

[84] E.g. the *fanum Voltumnae* for the Etruscans, Pietrabbondante for the Samnites Pentri, Rapino for the Marruccini. Cf. Chapter 3 n. 69.

[85] E.g. Torelli 1988b, 72: "*Alcuni grandi santuari di aperta campagna ne [il territorio di un segmento tribale; la touta] rappresentano il centro naturale e tradizionale di riunione religiosa e politica, con ovvio richiamo per fiere e mercati periodici, mentre i santuari minori, di norma connessi con sorgenti (e percorsi naturali), al pari dei maggiori, costituiscono i punti di raccolta per i pagi, articolazioni geografiche e politiche della civitas, così come i vici (e gli oppida) sono a loro volta articolazioni di un pagus.*"

[86] E.g. Coarelli/La Regina 1984, 168 = La Regina 1980, 39: "*La distribuzione dei luoghi di culto, noti attraverso i resti monumentali o il rinvenimento di oggetti votivi, riproduce e talvolta integra il quadro complessivo della densità e ubicazione degli insediamenti. I santuari sono di solito di pertinenza paganico-vicana. La 'aedes Furfensis', nei Vestini, era amministrata da un edile di Furfo, vico, ma avevano competenza su di essa in sede di giudizio popolare i Furfensi, i Fificulani, e i Taresuni, ossia probabilmente l'intero 'pagus'. Condizione non diversa doveva avere la maggior parte dei luoghi di culto che conosciamo del Sannio e, tra quelli già esplorati, Schiavi d'Abruzzo, Vastogirardi, S. Giovanni in Galdo. Rilevanza maggiore, perchè afferente a più comunità, doveva avere il santuario di Campochiaro. Preminenza su tutti, ossia santuario dell'intera nazione dei 'Samnites Pentri', del 'touta', era sicuramente Pietrabbondante.*" Cf. however Torelli 1983, 248 where the sanctuaries of Pietrabbondante, Schiavi d'Abruzzo, Vastogirardi are characterised as "*federali*". Cf. also Salmon 1982, 117 n. 345 (quoted *supra*).

[87] Letta 1992.

[88] Letta 1992, 110: "*è necessario sforzarsi ... di utilizzare la distinzione pagus / vicus come griglia per l'inquadramento e l'interpretazione dei dati.*"

[89] La Regina 1967-68, 387-392; Coarelli/La Regina 1984, 30-31.

[90] Letta 1992, 110 argues that it dates to the second half of the second century BC, referring to La Regina 1967-68, but here (p. 392) it is only said that the type of cornice is spread "*a partire dalla metà del II secolo a.C*".

[91] If related to *AE* 1968, 154 found in another church nearby.

[92] *CIL* IX, 3440 (= *CIL* I², 3265).

[93] *AE* 1968, 153.

would document the *pagus*-wide reach of this sanctuary.[94] Another example of a *pagus* sanctuary would be provided by an inscription dating to the period of Sulla found near Fiamignano at S. Angelo in Cacumine, in the territory of the Aequicoli.[95] At least two people dedicated different sacred objects to an unnamed deity, these were paid for by four different groups which would correspond to four *vici*.[96]

A second type of sanctuary ("*tipo B*") would be characterised by its relevance to the whole *pagus*, whereas it was located within one of its *vici*. An example of this type would be the temple of Jupiter Liber known from the so-called *lex aedis Furfensis*, dating to 58 BC.[97] Here, apart from the *vicus Furfensis* where the temple apparently stood, possibly also the communities of the *Fif[iculani]* and *Tares[uni]* are mentioned, thus representing three *vici*, which would be part of one and the same *pagus*.[98]

The third type ("*tipo C*") could be recognised in sanctuaries in or in the direct neighbourhood of the *vicus*, and which, differing from the "*tipo B*", would exclusively serve the population of the *vicus* itself. For example, in Marsic territory there is the sanctuary of *Victoria* at Trasacco which presents a late third or early second century BC dedication on behalf of the *vecos Supna[s]* or *vicus Supinum*.[99] *Juppiter Trebulanus*, venerated at the sanctuary of Quadri in Samnite territory, would have taken its name from a *vicus* of the same name, thus attesting to another *vicus* sanctuary.[100] Sanctuaries in the territory of the Marsi can according to Letta all be assigned to the *vicus* "C" type as *pagi* do not seem to have existed in Marsic territory.[101]

The last type (in late Republican sanctuaries; "*tipo D*") could be distinguished in sanctuaries that are located outside the municipal urban area but relate firmly to the *municipium*. An example would be the sanctuary of Hercules Curinus 5 km north of the ancient city of Sulmo, modern Sulmona in Abruzzo, that would have developed from a *pagus* sanctuary to a municipal one.[102] The sanctuary of Jupiter Stator at Alba Fucens, attested by three inscriptions, would have related to the colony of Alba from the very beginning.[103] One of these inscriptions, with a consular date of 168 AD, was found outside the colonial urban centre in Antrosano and apparently mentions the erection of a honorific statue in a public place to a certain C. Amaredius, who was amongst other things, *curator aput Iovem Statorem*.[104] Letta identifies this public place with the sanctuary which would therefore be extra-urban.[105]

A typology of sanctuaries with different ambits on different organisational levels has thus been established. It is however important to point out that in modern scholarship the *pagus-vicus* system and the role of sanctuaries within it have become such fixed preconceptions, that rural Italic sanctuaries are almost by definition assigned to one or another level, irrespective of the actual evidence at hand. In this way, even sanctuaries that do not yield epigraphical evidence for *vici* or *pagi* are routinely classified as *vicus* or *pagus* sanctuaries. However, since the *pagus-vicus* system regards specific institutional entities, which are by definition not recognisable from archaeology alone (cf. Chapter 6), it must be admitted that only explicit epigraphical or literary evidence can be used to ascertain the relation between *pagi* or *vici* and sanctuaries. In fact, this hard evidence is surprisingly scarce. For instance, the Samnite sanctuaries of Schiavi d'Abruzzo, Vastogirardi, Campochiaro and S. Giovanni in Galdo have not yielded evidence for the involvement of *pagi* or *vici*, and the precise competence of Pietrabbondante remains, despite its rich epigraphical record, unclear – in any case no *pagi* (or *vici*) are documented.[106] Also, the evidence for Letta's typology is not always as strong as one would like it to be.

[94] Letta 1992, 111.
[95] *AE* 1984, 274.
[96] Letta 1992, 112 with previous bibliography.
[97] *CIL* IX 3513 (= *CIL* I², 756).
[98] La Regina 1967-68, 393-396; Letta 1992, 112; Laffi 1978, 142.
[99] *CIL* IX, 3849 (= *CIL* I², 388); Letta 1992, 115.
[100] *CIL* IX, 2823 of Hadrianic date; Letta 1992, 115.
[101] Letta 1992, 115-116.
[102] Cf. Chapter 2 n. 108 and *infra*.
[103] *CIL* IX, 3923; 3949; 3950.
[104] *CIL* IX, 3950.
[105] Letta 1992, 117.
[106] Cf. Chapter 3 for discussion of the role of Pietrabbondante on a larger organisational level.

Fig. 4.6. The *lex aedis Furfensis* (Degrassi 1986, pl. 29)

For instance, the best example of a *pagus* sanctuary ("*tipo A*") would be constituted by the Fontecchio sanctuary, dedicated to (*Juppiter*) *Quirinus*. Since it is unknown what roles the mentioned *magistri* actually had, it is on the basis of this inscription not possible to tell whether or not this sanctuary functioned in the context of a *pagus* (and neither is a *vicus* or a *pagus* mentioned in the other possibly relevant inscriptions: Aufenginum is not defined as *vicus*). The evidence for another suggested *pagus* sanctuary in the area of the Marruccini is also inconclusive.[107] Regarding the other alleged *pagus* sanctuary, at S. Angelo in Cacumine near Fiamignano in the territory of the Aequicoli, an inscription dating to the period of Sulla tells us that at least two people dedicated different sacred objects which were paid for by four different *iuventutes*: the *Subocr[ina]*, *Aserea*, *Suparfaia*, and *Farfina*.[108] Letta supposes that the names of these *collegia iuvenum* reflect four different communities that would have been in charge of this sanctuary. However, it is not said that these communities were *vici*, and neither is their relation to a *pagus* attested.[109] The evidence for *pagus* sanctuaries located outside nucleated settlements might thus disappoint (cf. however Chapters 7 and 8).

---

[107] This *pagus* sanctuary would be attested by the first-century AD dedication to the deified river Aternus, found in the bed of the river (now called Pescara). Letta 1992, 111 links this inscription to another one found in 1850 and now lost, mentioning a *pagi Ceiani aqua*. This inscription was found at a source (Fonte Almone-Limone), albeit not far from the river (La Torre 1989b, 133). The architectural remains of a fountain or *perhaps* a temple have been seen at the end of the 19th century on the other side of Scafa, at località Fosse (De Petra/Calore 1900, 177-179). With the present data it seems difficult to combine the presence of a *pagus*-aqueduct at a natural source with a river cult in another place and architectural remains in yet another (albeit within a short range) in order to propose the existence of a *pagus* sanctuary, especially since the presence of tombs and funeral monuments in the neighbourhood seems to point to a nearby settlement (La Torre 1989b, 133).

[108] *AE* 1984, 274.

[109] Letta 1992, 112: "*evidentemente si tratta di quattro vici compresi in un unico pagus, e il santuario comune a tutti e quattro era appunto il santuario del pagus.*"

With regard to the second type of sanctuary ("tipo B") that would be characterised by its relevance to the whole *pagus*, being located however in one of its *vici*, the example of Furfo remains intriguing. The *lex aedis Furfensis*[110] from 58 BC would attest to the existence of three *vici* within one *pagus* which had a common sanctuary at the *vicus* of Furfo (fig. 4.6).

The *lex* is a dedication of a temple to Jupiter Liber, made by a magistrate and a priest of Furfo. It is dedicated *Furfone*, which can be interpreted as "in the *vicus Furfensis*", actually mentioned some lines further. The *lex* concerns the definition of the temple area and regulations regarding alterations of the temple and the handling of objects that are donated to the sanctuary. In this context, it is stated that if someone would steal a sacred object, the aedile could determine the amount of the fine. Then a rather problematic expression follows: *idque veicus Furf[ensis] mai[or] pars, FIFELTARES sei apsolvere volent sive condemnare*. The incomprehensible *FIFELTARES* has been amended into *Fif[iculani] e[t] Tares[uni]*, on the basis of other inscriptions in the region (ignoring the *L* and accepting that the interpunction, otherwise present, was forgotten here).[111] In this interpretation, the *vicus* of Furfo had apparently a privileged position in the juridical procedure, but other parties, the *Fif[iculani]* and the *Tares[uni]* are also concerned.

Working within the framework of the *pagus-vicus* system, many scholars have interpreted these *Fif[iculani]* and *Tares[uni]* as representing two other settlements which would have been *vici* comprised in the same *pagus*.[112] In this way, the sanctuary of Furfo would represent a sanctuary that served the whole *pagus*, consisting of at least three *vici*. The sanctuary would have been dominated however by the *vicus* of Furfo, in whose territory it was located.[113] Notwithstanding the fact that there is indeed mention of a *vicus*, that of Furfo, there is no direct evidence of a *pagus*[114] and the other two communities are actually known as *iuvenes* elsewhere, not as *vici*.[115] It seems therefore that the preconception of the *pagus-vicus* system as a 'given' structure has determined the interpretation. This is of course not to say that *pagi* had no influence in sanctuaries. There are other epigraphically known sanctuaries where *pagi* had at least some sort of control, as is attested by inscriptions like *de pagi sententia* or *ex pagi decreto*, or the cult of *Juppiter Victor decem pagorum*.[116] Their relationship to corresponding *vici* is however uncertain.

---

[110] *CIL* IX, 3513 (= *CIL* I², 756).

[111] La Regina 1967-68, 393-396; followed by, e.g., Laffi 1978; Coarelli/La Regina 1984, 16. Adamik 2003, 81 argues in his new reading of the inscription to interpret *fifeltares* as 'fiduciaries' or 'trustees'. Scheid 2006a, 25 reads *fifeltares* without further comment as "likely the local authority".

[112] Letta 1992, 112. La Regina 1967-68, 393-396; cf. Laffi 1978, 142 ("*evidentemente due comunità vicane*"); Coarelli/La Regina 1984, 16: "*Si tratta infatti della dedica di un tempio a Juppiter Liber, fatta dal magistrato e dal sacerdote di Furfo, ma nella quale vengono citate, come parti contraenti, anche gli abitanti degli altri due vici del pagus, i Fificulani e i Taresuni.*"

[113] According to Coarelli/La Regina 1984, 16: "*Siamo cioè di fronte a un caso perfettamente ricostruibile di organizzazione paganico-vicana, con un 'pagus' diviso in tre 'vici'*". Letta 1992, 112-113 goes further, and ingeniously proposes to recognise the *pagus Frentanus* in the *pagus* relating to the temple at Furfo. The reasoning is as follows: the *Fificulani* are also found in the form of *iuvenes Fificulani Herculis cultores*, found at Paganica. Now, near Paganica, at Ponte di Grotta, a sanctuary to Hercules has been identified, "*evidentemente*" guided by these *iuvenes Fificulani Herculis cultores*. A funerary inscription from elsewhere (S. Martino di Picenze) mentions a *collegium Herculaneu[m] Frenetium*, which Letta links to the other inscriptions which in turn would lead to the identification of the *pagus* comprising Furfo as the *pagus Frentanus*. One may or may not feel inclined to follow this reasoning, depending as it does on the conflation of different inscriptions found in different places. It seems however far from certain that from this would follow that the sanctuary at Ponte di Grotta was a *pagus* sanctuary of the "B or A type", only because the *collegium Herculaneum Frenetium* may be connected to it.

[114] The relation with the *pagus* mentioned in *CIL* IX, 3521 (= *CIL* I², 1804), which was found near Barisciano cannot be established securely.

[115] *AE* 1968, 152 and *CIL* IX, 3578.

[116] *CIL* I², 3269; for *pagi* active in sanctuaries, cf. Chapters 7 and 8.

There are clear examples of sanctuaries that have yielded inscriptions mentioning only one *vicus* ("*tipo C*"). Therefore, these could be recognised as sanctuaries in or in the direct neighbourhood of the *vicus*. Different from the "*tipo B*" sanctuaries, they would have exclusively served the population of the *vicus* itself. The sanctuary of *Victoria* at Trasacco with a late third or early second century BC dedication on behalf of the *vicus Supinum* is a beautiful example.[117] At the end of the second or beginnings of the first century BC, also the nearby *vicus Aninus* dedicated to a goddess, in this case Valetudo.[118]

For now, two conclusions may be drawn. First, the actual evidence for the involvement of *pagi* and *vici* in sanctuaries is much more limited than usually suggested in modern scholarship, and in some areas, such as Pentrian Samnium, even non-existent. Second, even if there are instances of cult places related to *pagi* or *vici*, there is no epigraphical evidence from the sanctuaries themselves attesting to a hierarchical relation between them that would correspond to the supposed *touto / nomen* – *pagus* – *vicus* distinction. Crucially, there is no valid example of Letta's B type sanctuary (located in a *vicus*, but pertaining to the entire *pagus*), an indispensable chain in the hierarchical model. Since there is no additional evidence to suggest such a hierarchy, this means that the hierarchical model rests entirely on the acceptance of the validity, and omnipresence, of the *pagus-vicus* system. Needless to say, the general attribution of all sanctuaries in certain areas to the *vicus* or *pagus* type also solely rests on this acceptance.[119] This conclusion stands to a certain degree apart from the discussion on the pre-Roman origin of *pagi* and *vici*, discussed in Chapter 6.

4.3.3 THE RISE AND FALL OF RURAL SANCTUARIES BETWEEN PAGUS-VICUS SYSTEM AND MUNICIPALISATION

"The fate of rural sanctuaries ... seems to have varied from place to place, depending on the extent of their integration in the municipal structures of the area. ... similarly most of the vici, which had formed the core of the traditional settlement pattern seem to have lost their political importance" (Curti et al. 1996, 179).

In accordance with the view of rural sanctuaries functioning within the *pagus-vicus* system, the idea has been developed that Roman influence in the Italic territories can be seen in the abandonment of these sanctuaries in the Roman period. Because the Italic settlement structures were ruptured, and building activities would have concentrated on the new municipal centres, the sanctuaries became obsolete. In the words of Lomas, "the close association between these [Samnite] cult places and non-Roman culture and forms of government is demonstrated by their later history ... The background to this is the breakup of the indigenous Samnite states and the imposition of a Romanized system of *municipia*". This view is

---

[117] *CIL* IX, 3849 (= *CIL* I², 388). As regards the *Juppiter Trebulanus* venerated at Quadri; this god may have taken its name from a nearby settlement, but this settlement is never qualified epigraphically as a *vicus*: *CIL* IX, 2823; the relevant part of this Hadrianic inscription reads: [..] *consc[ripti]/trebui ob [merita]/Iovi Tre[bulano]*.

[118] *CIL* IX, 3813 (= *CIL* I², 391). See for detailed discussion of the *vicus Aninus* and the *vicus Supinum* Chapter 7.

[119] As noted, for the territory of the Marsi, where *pagi* seem to have never existed at all, Letta would assign all sanctuaries to *vici*, whether inscriptions mentioning a *vicus* were present or not. Letta 1992, 115-116: "*santuari marsi ... tutti di tipo C, cioè esclusivamente vicani, sia che nelle iscrizioni relative il vicus sia espressamente menzionato, sia che non compaia.*" As to *pagus* sanctuaries, referring to the Paelignian area Van Wonterghem 1984, 42, generally considers sanctuaries as "*nuclei religiosi di pagi*", and therefore sees the presence of sanctuaries as proof of the persistence of the *pagus* as principal core of the tribe down to the first century BC. In his n. 311 various sanctuaries are listed that would belong to a *pagus*. Of the nine sanctuaries mentioned, however, only one is directly linked with a *pagus* (Prezza), another one (Secinaro) possibly indirectly.

illustrated in this quote on Samnium proper, but the idea that Rome had to 'overcome' the traditional settlement pattern of *pagus* and *vicus*, with negative consequences for the non-urban sanctuaries, has been developed also for other areas of central Italy.[120] The only way for sanctuaries to 'survive' would be to happen to be favourably located within the new municipal order.[121] Most studies refer to one example, which has become paradigmatic, that of the sanctuary of Hercules Curinus in Paelignian territory.

One of the earliest expressions of the view that the survival of sanctuaries depends upon the integration in the new municipal system is to be found in the 1971 article on the 'Sabellian and Samnite territories' by La Regina and it seems that this study has considerably influenced subsequent research. Three important ideas are developed in this article. First the idea *per se* of the *pagus-vicus* system as central organisation form, second the idea that sanctuaries served different *vicus*-type settlements, and third the idea that the fate of these sanctuaries in Roman times would depend directly on their fitting in the new Roman municipal settlement organisation. Therefore, it seems worthwhile to consider the argument briefly.

Connecting the spread of rural settlement to the rise of non-urban sanctuaries, La Regina discerns one of the most important examples of the latter in the temple of Hercules Curinus.[122] The monumental phase seen today, reminiscent of Latial terrace sanctuaries, is dated after the Social War[123] but there are the remnants of an earlier phase. According to La Regina, the sanctuary in this earlier phase did not belong to the city of Sulmo alone but to the whole territory and therefore to the rural *vicus*-type of settlement.[124] Sulmo apparently did not develop enough territorial power in the period before the municipalisation to be able to exert control over the sanctuary. As to the supposed function within the *vicus*-type settlement of the early sanctuary, La Regina does not discuss material evidence, apart from a comparison with the Vestine territory.[125] There, the constellation of a *pagus-vicus* system would be proved by the cult of Jupiter Victor *decem pagorum*.[126] In a rather rhetorical way, it is argued that the Vestine case would demonstrate "*un rapporto identico, tra insediamenti e santuario, a quello già visto per i Peligni*", a relationship which, however, was not substantiated by evidence in the sanctuary of Hercules Curinus. Moreover, the cult practised or organised by ten Vestine *pagi* would point to a specific "*momento del processo sinecistico*" which would eventually lead to the formation of a municipality.[127]

---

[120] Quote: Lomas 1996, 171. For the general shift of focus in the first century BC, see the classic works of Torelli 1983; Gabba 1972 (= Gabba 1994a, 63-103). For the idea that the *pagus-vicus* system had to be broken by Roman administration: Coarelli/La Regina 1984, 13-14, on the Sabelli: "*Una grave difficoltà dovette rappresentare per lo stato romano la situazione socio-politica dei territori conquistati, privi di città e organizzati, come tutta l'area sabellica, in 'pagi' (aree territoriali) entro i quali gravitavano uno o più villaggi ('vici'). Il sistema seguito fu quello della prefettura ... Anche l'urbanizzazione di età augustea rappresentò del resto un fenomeno quasi del tutto artificiale, che modificò solo superficialmente l'organizzazione precedente, e che si dissolse quasi subito per dar luogo alla situazione originaria. Tipico ... il caso di Amiternum, ... dove permane la vecchia organizzazione per 'vici'*". Sanctuaries in decline: e.g. La Regina 1970, 196; Capini 1991a, 119 (on Campochiaro); Lomas 1996, 171; Dench 1995, 139-140. Along similar lines Van Wonterghem 1984, 45, "*il pagus, che fino alla fine della Repubblica aveva costituito il più importante nucleo religioso ed amministrativo, a partire dall'età imperiale, sembra aver perduto ogni significato ufficiale.*"

[121] E.g. La Regina 1970, 196; Dench 1995, 140, Curti *et al.* 1996, 139 (cf. quote *supra*).

[122] La Regina 1970-1971, 444. "*In stretta connessione con la vasta disseminazione dell'insediamento rurale prende consistenza il santuario non urbano.*"

[123] La Torre 1989a.

[124] La Regina 1970-1971, 444.

[125] La Regina 1970-1971, 444-445: "*Questa situazione è confermata dal vicino santuario di Iuppiter Victor, nei Vestini ... , con la differenza però che il santuario peligno non cade in abbandono dopo la guerra sociale ... e ciò per il semplice motivo che con l'assetto municipale esso entra nell'orbita di Sulmo.*"

[126] *CIL* I², 3269. See Chapter 8.

[127] La Regina 1970-1971, 445.

Turning to the sanctuary of Hercules Curinus near Sulmo, the only circumstance that changed its destiny and preserved it from abandonment would have been its location within the orbit of Sulmo, the new *municipium*, at a distance of 5 km. Accordingly, the monumentalisation of this sanctuary, relatively unique for extra-urban sanctuaries in the post-Social War period in central Italy, would have to be explained within this specific adaptation to the Roman system. This view is further supported by the negative evidence from the area inhabited by the Samnites (Pentri), where the abandonment of sanctuaries would correspond to the installation of *municipia* in the plains.[128]

Although this thesis may sound convincingly logical at face value, and indeed seems to suit much of the archaeological evidence, it is important to acknowledge the factual basis for what has become a firm interpretational model. In fact, for the case of Hercules Curinus, there is no evidence that points to its function within a *pagus-vicus* system before the municipalisation. In any case, the presence of a cult for Jupiter Victor *decem pagorum* from the adjacent Vestini does not prove that the sanctuary of Hercules Curinus functioned within a constellation of *vicus*-like settlements. Actually, it must be admitted that we do not know anything about the function and ambit of the sanctuary prior to the municipalisation. A last remark regards the suggestion that the cult of the ten *pagi* would reflect a specific moment in a process of synoecism. This seems to suggest that the *pagus-vicus* system had the tendency to evolve to more nucleated or perhaps even urban forms of settlement. In another contribution, La Regina develops this idea further with regard to the same sanctuary of Hercules Curinus (Quirinus) at Sulmona in combination with that of Jupiter Quirinus at the *municipium* of Superaequum, referring to the function of the Roman god Quirinus as patron of the *curiae*, the public assemblies. According to La Regina, this process of synoecism would have been "*in gran parte forzato*", and was not able to eliminate the *pagus-vicus* system entirely.[129] Thus, in this view, the *pagus-vicus* system forms on the one hand a persistent pre-Roman, Italic, mode of settlement, but on the other would have been susceptible to manipulation by the Roman administration to enforce nucleation processes.

4.4 CONCLUSION: BETWEEN IMAGES AND EVIDENCE

In this chapter, three main lines in the modern interpretation of sanctuaries in central-southern Italy have been distinguished and discussed. The idea that sanctuaries were connected to the large transhumance routes that cris-crossed central-southern Italy has the merit that it seeks to interpret the phenomenon within a specific Italic context, the pastoral economy. This pastoral image of the Italic peoples might however have been overemphasised, whereas evidence for large-scale transhumance before the Roman period is rather scarce. Furthermore, the connection between Italic sanctuaries dedicated to Hercules and the *tratturi* has clearly been overstated and there seems to be a certain circularity in the argument. Interestingly, examples of the connection between the god and marketplaces feature more often in Roman and/or urban contexts than in rural 'Italic' ones. Whereas a relation with economic activities such as tran-

---

[128] La Regina 1970-1971, 456: "... *si ha la testimonianza archeologica ed epigrafica di una eccezionale vitalità edilizia nella seconda metà del II sec. a.C., con il totale abbandono negli anni immediatamente successivi alla guerra sociale. E questi sono proprio gli anni in cui prendono vigore quegli insediamenti di pianura, come Saepinum, Bovianum, che riceveranno la costituzione municipale.*"

[129] Coarelli/La Regina 1984, 113 and 132. Actually, here the idea seems to have been changed somewhat (?); the sanctuary first would have been of local significance only and consequently would, after the municipalisation, have assumed the Roman epithet Quirinus, from then on constituting the "*santuario tutelare del sinecismo, mediante il quale i vari pagi della zona furono unificati in un unica entità amministrativa, il municipio di Sulmona*". Accordingly, the sanctuary was transformed "*da struttura puramente locale in un grandioso organismo a terrazze*" (Coarelli/La Regina 1984, 132).)

shumance surely will have existed in certain cases, there seems to be no reason to regard it as a key factor in the genesis, location or monumentalisation of rural Italic sanctuaries. The theory that sees sanctuaries as frontier markers of different ethnic territories derives from studies on Greek and other areas where urban centres held a principal position. The transposition of the model to the less or non-urbanised Italic world is problematic, especially because the supposed Italic ethnic groups, and in particular their territorial manifestations, evade us. In any case, it is interesting that the few sanctuaries for which we have evidence pointing at a border position seem to have had an integrative rather than an exclusive function. A function as a central meeting place, also for commercial ends, seems therefore reasonable. The most popular view of Italic sanctuaries is their being part of the so-called *pagus-vicus* system. In this supposedly typically Italic settlement pattern made out of small villages and farms, sanctuaries would have occupied a special position. They would have served at different levels, at that of the *vicus*, at that of the *pagus* comprising more *vici*, and at that of the *civitas* or *touto*, including several *pagi*.

'Romanisation' is seen as antithetic to this settlement pattern; municipalisation would have entailed the suppression of this Italic mode of living, although it sometimes shows a remarkable persistence. In this view, municipalisation would therefore also explain the abandonment of Italic sanctuaries after the Social War. Exceptions to this rule are the sanctuaries that fitted well into the new municipal organisation. Although this last model is by far the one best developed in modern research, it must be admitted that the evidential basis is actually rather thin. This accounts especially for the hierarchical ordering of sanctuaries according to their different roles within the *pagus-vicus* system. A more general observation on all three 'models' is that views of Italic economy and society have strongly influenced ideas on the functioning of sanctuaries, whereas factual evidence relating to the sanctuaries themselves and their environment is scarce and in most cases simply non-existent. In the next chapter, I will therefore try to offer a 'bottom-up' view starting from a sanctuary and its direct environment.

5 Landscapes of the Sacred: Contextualising the Samnite Sanctuary of S. Giovanni in Galdo, Colle Rimontato (CB)

A simple, yet fundamental aspect in interpreting the sanctuaries of central-southern Italy regards their direct spatial context. Knowing more about the local functioning of sanctuaries can help us better understand other processes, such as their monumentalisation (cf. Chapter 3) and their possible function within larger political and/or economical structures (cf. Chapter 4), as well as possible relations between them. Generically, we define the Italic sanctuaries found dotted over the landscapes of central-southern Italy as 'rural'. But what does that mean? Were sanctuaries located in isolation from domestic and other sites? Do we have to envisage long processions from the places where people lived to their sacred places? Or did the cult places rather serve the local population, and if so, where did this population actually live? In short, which groups can be reasonably expected to have visited the 'rural' sanctuaries of central-southern Italy on a regular basis?

To answer these questions, knowledge of the direct environment of these cult places is indispensable. This spatial context is also needed, in the case of Pentrian Samnium, to formulate more precisely questions as to how – if at all – the experience of these communities of worshippers relates to the construction of a larger 'Samnite' entity, as documented in the temple complex of Pietrabbondante (Chapter 3). Clearly, it makes a difference if the monumental Samnite sanctuaries of the second century BC were located in isolation, or if they were rooted in a local settlement pattern.

The 'rural' cult places of internal central-southern Italy are generally seen as isolated elements in the landscape. One could say that it is this allegedly isolated location that has inspired the various hypotheses about the specific function of cult places in Italic society discussed in the previous chapter, i.e. as transhumance shrines, frontier markers or local (political) meeting points. But on what evidence does this isolated image rest? In this chapter, I focus attention on the direct environment of Italic sanctuaries in central-southern Italy and present a research approach and case study on one such 'rural' Italic sanctuary, that of S. Giovanni in Galdo, Colle Rimontato (CB, Molise) in the Samnite Pentrian area.

Virtually all known Italic sanctuaries have been discovered and studied because of the visual impact provided by their elaborate architecture. Following discovery, research has practically without exception concentrated on the architecture. Fieldwork focused on documenting and sometimes excavating the cult places themselves, not on their relationship with the surrounding environment. Consequently, the overall picture is that we lack reasonably systematic data on the direct environment for the vast majority of known Italic sanctuaries. Nevertheless, general topographical references to the most imposing archaeological remains in the area (such as hill-fort wall circuits) or indeed ancient traffic routes (notably the *tratturi*) are available in several cases. Some detailed topographical studies exist, such as the *Forma Italiae* series for the Paelignian area and Larinum or the *carta archeologica* of the Vomano area.[1] These studies can provide important data regarding the direct environment of cult places located within their research areas. Yet, caution is required since the often unsystematic character of these studies (in the sense that no attempt is made at full coverage of the area with intensive field research) and their focus on monu-

---

[1] Van Wonterghem 1984; De Felice 1994; *Vomano* 1986; *Vomano* 1991.

mental remains means that more humble sites and archaeological remains, such as surface scatters, tend to be underrepresented. The detailed settlement pattern around sanctuaries in these areas is thus hard to reconstruct.

Fortunately, our knowledge of Italic patterns of settlement has increased considerably in recent decades as a result of systematic intensive field surveys. Obviously, such surveys would produce the best data for answering questions on the settlement pattern surrounding cult places. Only a very limited number of sanctuaries have been discovered during regular archaeological field survey research but in a few cases the areas covered by systematic field surveys include sanctuary sites that were previously known, providing contextual data. Most notable in the area under study is the large-scale survey project in Samnium directed by Graeme Barker, which filled to an extent the gaping blanks in the landscape between the highly visible remains of hill-forts and monumental sanctuaries (cf. Chapter 3). However, the issue of settlement patterns has never been specifically addressed from a wish to understand the functioning of Italic sanctuaries within it. Consequently, research strategies have not been designed to answer the more limited, but also more specific questions I would like to ask in this context, especially as a consequence of the narrow chronological range required and the need to cover a representative area directly around the cult places with high resolution investigation. An apposite strategy is therefore needed and I have attempted to develop one in a case-study on the small temple of S. Giovanni in Galdo.

5.1 RESEARCH APPROACH AND METHODOLOGY

Two elements are required to investigate the local context of sanctuaries. First, detailed knowledge of the surrounding settlement pattern can shed light on the relationship between cult places and other elements in the cultural landscape on a small scale, such as settlements, necropoleis and roads. This 'landscape of the sacred' can thus help us understand the changing functions and cultural meanings of the sanctuaries. Second, the archaeology of the settlement patterns should be related as directly as possible to the archaeology of the sanctuary itself. As has been noted, modern research has often focused on the monumental phases of sanctuaries but attention to the small finds of all periods from these sites is important as it enables a comparison with the material from the surroundings, and is of course crucial for establishing the period during which the cult site was frequented.

The research strategy for the cult place of S. Giovanni in Galdo, located in the higher part of the Tappino valley has been developed with these criteria in mind, while also taking financial and time considerations into account. The strategy consists of small-scale intensive field survey research in the area around the sanctuary, including the sanctuary site itself, combined with a study of the excavation data of the sanctuary which was explored in the 1970s by the *Soprintendenza per i Beni Archeologici del Molise* under the direction of Angela Di Niro.

5.1.1 CHOOSING THE SANCTUARY OF S. GIOVANNI IN GALDO AND PREVIOUS RESEARCH

The choice to investigate the sanctuary at località Colle Rimontato (709 m a.s.l.) near the village of S. Giovanni in Galdo (Campobasso) was made on several grounds (fig. 5.1).

In the first place, the sanctuary is generally considered as a typical small 'rural' sanctuary and is often cited as such in the modern literature. More specifically, the sanctuary of S. Giovanni in Galdo represents one of the best dated examples of cult places that were monumentalised at the end of the second century or beginning of the first century BC. Coins under the pavement of the shrine date its construction to after 104 BC. It reflects the ground plan found in Temple B of Pietrabbondante, which would be,

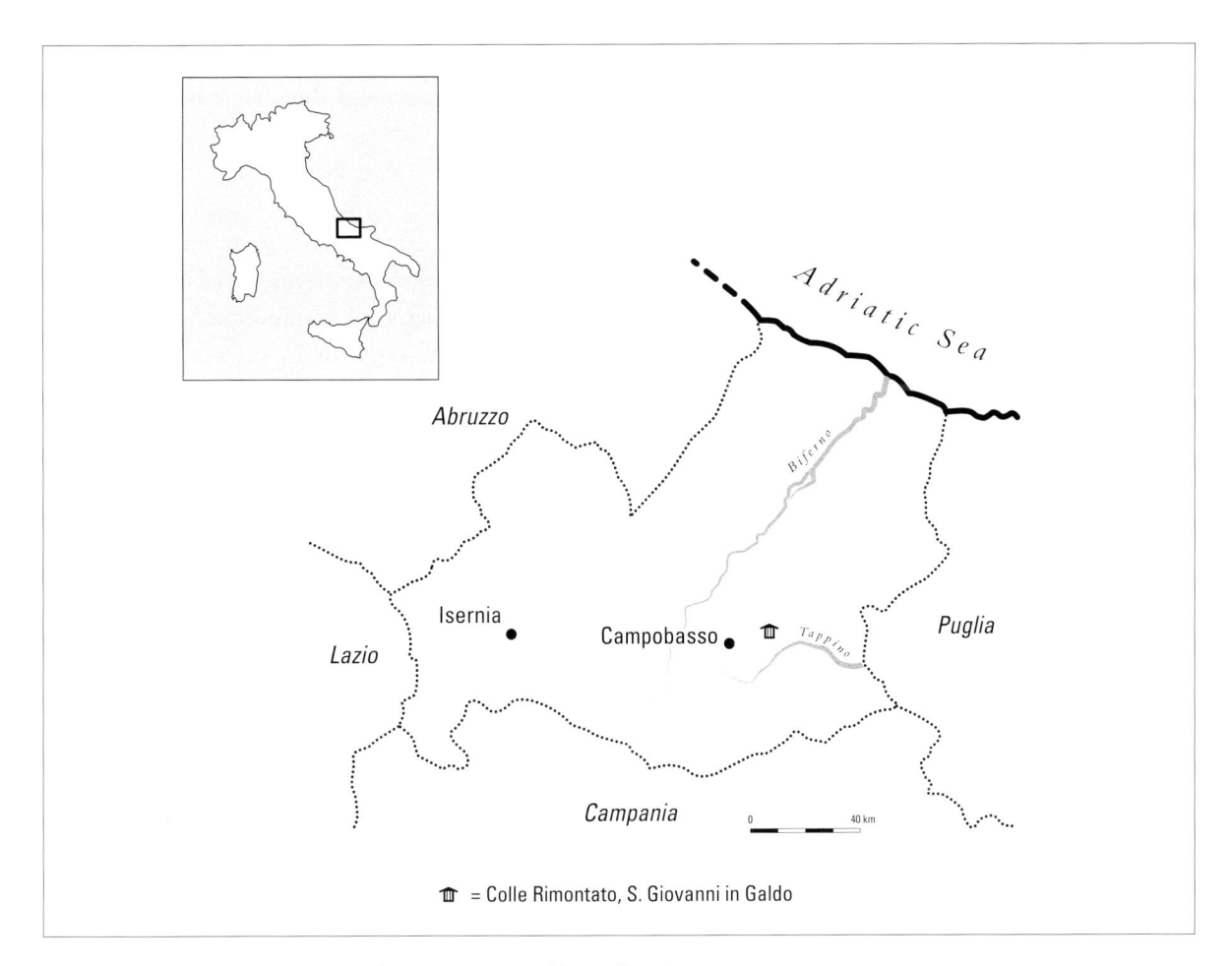

Fig. 5.1. Location of the sanctuary of S. Giovanni in Galdo, Colle Rimontato.

according to some, reminiscent of the Livian description of the place where a Samnite sacred oath was sworn in 293 BC (cf. Chapter 3). As the small counterpart of the sanctuary complex at Pietrabbondante and with its relatively well preserved remains, this sanctuary has almost come to constitute a canonical site when speaking of Italic or Samnite sanctuaries.

Additional reasons for choosing the sanctuary of S. Giovanni in Galdo had a more practical and methodological character. During initial investigations of several Italic sanctuaries from Abruzzo to Lucania together with Jeremia Pelgrom in spring 2003, this part of the Tappino valley appeared as a largely agricultural landscape with relatively many cultivated fields and few woodlands, promising relatively good field survey conditions. Moreover, at the other side of the valley, at 9 km distance, another Samnite sanctuary has been identified at località Cupa (Gildone), which seemed to allow comparison of two sanctuary sites within a small geographical distance. The area around Gildone, Cupa was also subject of the 2004 and 2005 surveys but will not be discussed here further.[2] Another attractive feature is that the Biferno Valley Project, directed and published by Barker, covers an area adjacent to the one under study here (cf. fig. 5.28).[3] Since the project presented here has a relatively limited geographical focus, the possibility of comparison with the patterns of settlement on a larger scale seemed important.

[2] The first results of the survey around the sanctuary of loc. Cupa at Gildone, pointing at relatively dense settlement in the area, are published in Stek/Pelgrom 2005; final publication of the survey data is in preparation by Michele Roccia.

[3] Barker 1995.

81

The sanctuary of S. Giovanni in Galdo had been known locally long before it was privately excavated by the proprietor of the land, Mr Marini, in the 1930s, who uncovered part of the podium and the pavement. Objects found at the site, including coins and statuettes, were sometimes taken home by inhabitants of S. Giovanni in Galdo and some of them were later apprehended by the Carabinieri.[4] The sanctuary has thus been susceptible to disturbances for a long time before systematic excavations were undertaken in 1974 (cf. *infra* on the excavation data). Previous research has concentrated on the physical remains of the sanctuary itself, the area directly surrounding it being formerly unknown except for some isolated finds.[5] A more general topographical study on the Alta Valle del Tappino provides a larger framework for both the sanctuary of S. Giovanni in Galdo and that of loc. Cupa, Gildone.[6]

5.2 PROBLEM-ORIENTED FIELD SURVEY: THE SACRED LANDSCAPE PROJECT SURVEY (2004, 2005)

In view of the relatively narrow research aim, both in chronological and spatial terms, a focused approach rather than a macroscopic view of a large part of territory seemed most appropriate. The research aims also required a relatively high resolution of data collection in order to try to reconstruct the ancient landscape in detail and minimise the risk of missing sites. The relatively short period that is directly relevant to the research question, the Hellenistic-Roman period, and the aim to understand the settlement pattern on a small scale required a relatively intensive study of the sites that were found, including revisiting sites and geophysical research at some representative sites. This problem-oriented research on a modest scale differs fundamentally from, for example, the large-scale surveys conducted by Barker, who was especially interested in the *longue durée* development of a whole valley, from prehistory to the early modern period.

Through the kind permission and collaboration by the *Soprintendenza per i Beni Archeologici del Molise*,[7] research could be carried out during two field campaigns in October – November 2004 and February-March 2005, along with several smaller campaigns directed at additional site analysis, study of the survey data and geophysical research through 2004, 2005 and 2006. The first survey results were published in 2005,[8] the final publication of all the survey data is in preparation together with co-director Jeremia Pelgrom. The aim of the 2004 and 2005 surveys was to shed light on the relationship of the sanctuaries of S. Giovanni in Galdo and loc. Cupa, Gildone with their direct environment, which was formerly virtually unknown. This has been done by trying to establish the settlement pattern into which the respective sanctuaries were inserted.

---

[4] As was discussed at the conference on the sanctuary organised by the Comune of S. Giovanni in Galdo in August 2007.

[5] Cf. Di Niro 1980, 271, Rizzi 1855. Di Niro, *loc.cit.*, assumes dispersed rural settlement and mentions a *"necropoli, coeva al primo periodo di vita del santuario"* on the eastern slope of the Colle Rimontato, but no material is presented. A Roman funeral inscription found on the Colle Rimontato, now held by the Soprintendenza (n. inv. 51412), mentions a *(C)apicius* or *Apicius*: cf. Zaccardi 2007, 66 n. 3). In general on the sanctuary: La Regina 1966, 261; La Regina 1970, 196; Strazzulla 1971, 16; La Regina 1976, 237-241; Di Niro 1977, 38-40; Di Niro 1978a; Di Niro 1978b (on the inscriptions); Di Niro 1980; Coarelli/La Regina 1984, 295-298; Zaccardi 2007. See also on the interpretation, esp. the connection to Pietrabbondante: Capini 1996; Coarelli 1996; Tagliamonte 1997, 185-187; Stek 2005a. See also Chapter 3.

[6] Di Niro/Petrone 1993.

[7] Most notably in the persons of Mario Pagano, Stefania Capini, Angela Di Niro, and Cristiana Terzani.

[8] Stek/Pelgrom 2005. Also, an internal report (*schedatura*) was compiled for the *Soprintendenza* in 2004. Cf. also Stek 2005b.

Fig. 5.2. A 3D reconstruction of the Alta valle del Tappino showing areas surveyed (left S. Giovanni in Galdo, Colle Rimontato; right Gildone, loc. Cupa).

5.2.1 SURVEY METHODOLOGY

In order to find answers to the questions posed above, an area of c. 7 square km in the form of a circle with a radius of c. 1.5 km around each sanctuary was investigated with an intensive off-site survey strategy, cutting through different geomorphological features such as hilltops, slopes, river valleys and terraces (fig. 5.2).[9]

Both sample areas were surveyed in units of approximately 50 by 100 m (0,5 ha) at 10 m intervals between participants (~20% coverage) (fig. 5.3).[10] All the archaeological material encountered was collected, washed and studied. If there were too many tiles to collect, they were counted in small sample areas of 1 m², enabling a rough estimate of the overall quantity. For each unit, the land use, noted erosion processes, tillage and various visibility factors (stones, shade, vegetation, soil humidity, presence of recent material) were recorded. These factors determined the final visibility (cf. fig. 5.4).

[9] The modern centre of S. Giovanni in Galdo, a village of medieval origin, could of course not be surveyed. Private excavations and construction works have, to my knowledge, not yielded Hellenistic and Roman archaeological remains of any importance.

[10] The applied survey methodology was originally developed within the framework of the *Regional Pathways to Complexity Project*: Burgers et al. 1998; Burgers 2002; Van Leusen 2002.

Fig. 5.3. 20% coverage survey in the S. Giovanni in Galdo area (photo J. Pelgrom).

All find concentrations of more than five artefacts per square metre (which was used as a rule of thumb in the field to initially distinguish 'sites', along with other factors such as quality and typodiversity of the finds) were subject to closer examination. After a first standard sampling as described above with a 20% coverage, all sites were re-sampled in order to quantify the density of material at various locations within a concentration (also with a 20% coverage strategy), as well as to collect more diagnostic material for dating and functional analysis (sometimes through an additional 'diagnostic sample'). A handheld GPS was used to establish the co-ordinates and contours of the encountered find concentrations. During the 2005 survey, PDA computers with a connected GPS were used in the field for both navigation and data input, with a software application that was designed for this purpose in collaboration with the SpinLAB of the VU University Amsterdam. Both survey unit boundaries and site contours were mapped on 1:10000 maps of the region.

Whereas the 20% coverage strategy appeared to work for establishing patterns of settlement, a more detailed strategy was applied at the sanctuary of S. Giovanni in Galdo and its immediate surroundings. The area directly around the sanctuary was surveyed in units of 10 by 10 m (0.1 ha) at 2 m intervals (~100% coverage; see fig. 5.5).[11] In the first place, the objective of this time-consuming strategy was to make an artefact density contour map of the area around the visible remains of the sanctuary. The detailed data thus acquired were expected to permit hypotheses on the possible existence of other structures near the temple. Secondly, the aim was to form as complete an image as possible of the sanctuary site and its associated finds in order to enhance the possibilities of comparison with the excavation data.

---

[11] After Burgers 1998.

Fig. 5.4. Research area around the sanctuary of S. Giovanni in Galdo indicating visibility (1: low, 5: high).

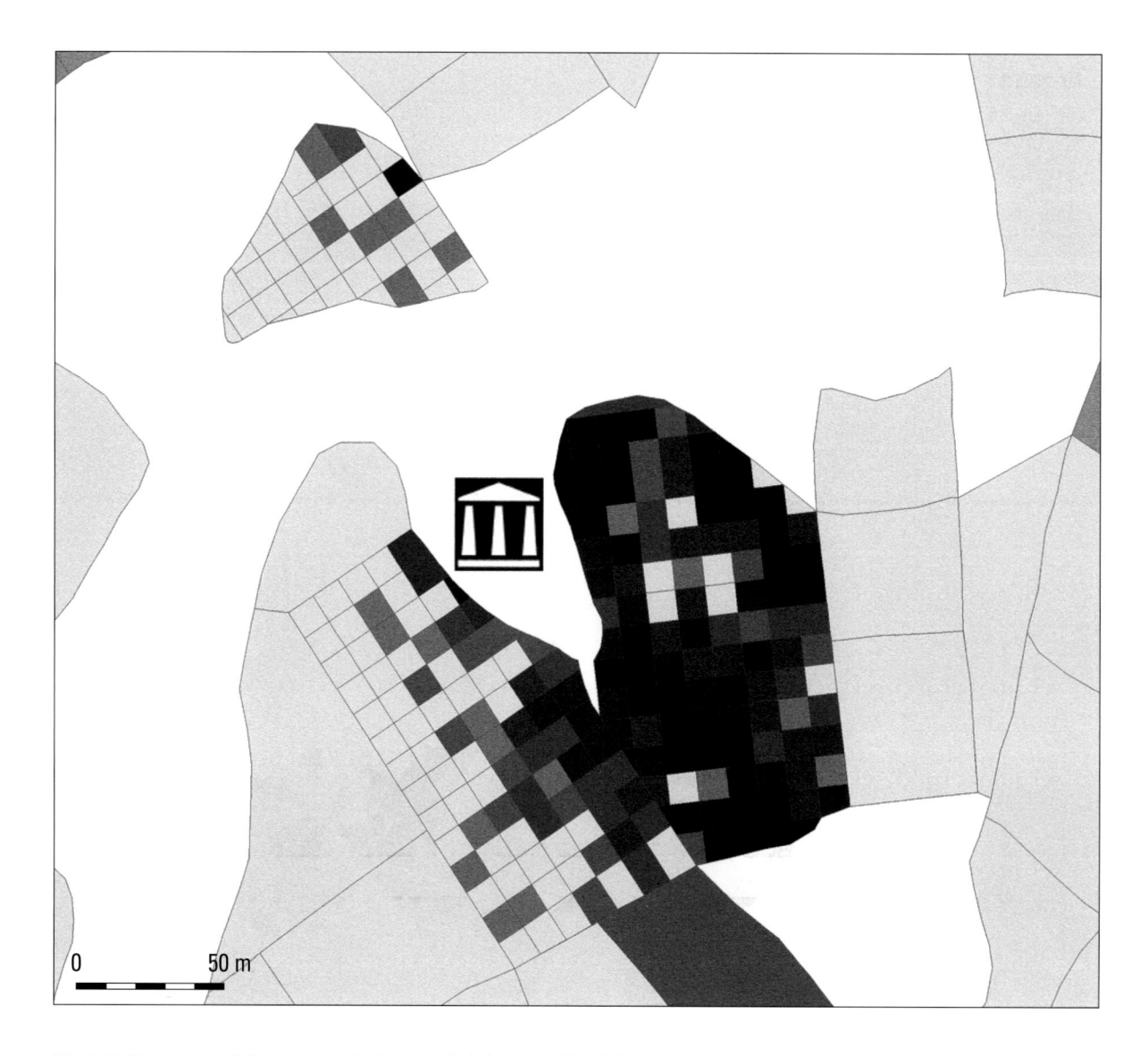

Fig. 5.5. Site survey of the sanctuary indicating find densities (detail from 5.6).

5.2.2 RESULTS

The contextualisation of the Samnite sanctuary of S. Giovanni in Galdo is of primary concern here and I will therefore focus on the results broadly concerning the Hellenistic (ca. fourth to first centuries BC) and Roman (imperial) periods. Reference will also be made to the situation in the Iron Age, here defined as ca. ninth-fifth centuries BC.[12] In general, the survey detected fairly high find densities and about 22 distinct sites that can be dated to the Iron Age, Hellenistic and Roman imperial periods have been recognised in the area of S. Giovanni in Galdo (figs. 5.6 and 5.7).

The following observations on the Hellenistic and Roman periods are based on finds retrieved from the entire research area. The black gloss ware is clearly distinguishable from Campanian or Latial produc-

[12] The data from the previous and later periods will be published in the final survey report. For this periodisation cf. Barker 1995, but here the more common (but neither neutral) periodisation 'Hellenistic' is adopted rather than 'Samnite'.

86

Fig. 5.6. Find densities of the Hellenistic and Roman periods in the area around the sanctuary of S. Giovanni in Galdo, quantities per ha.

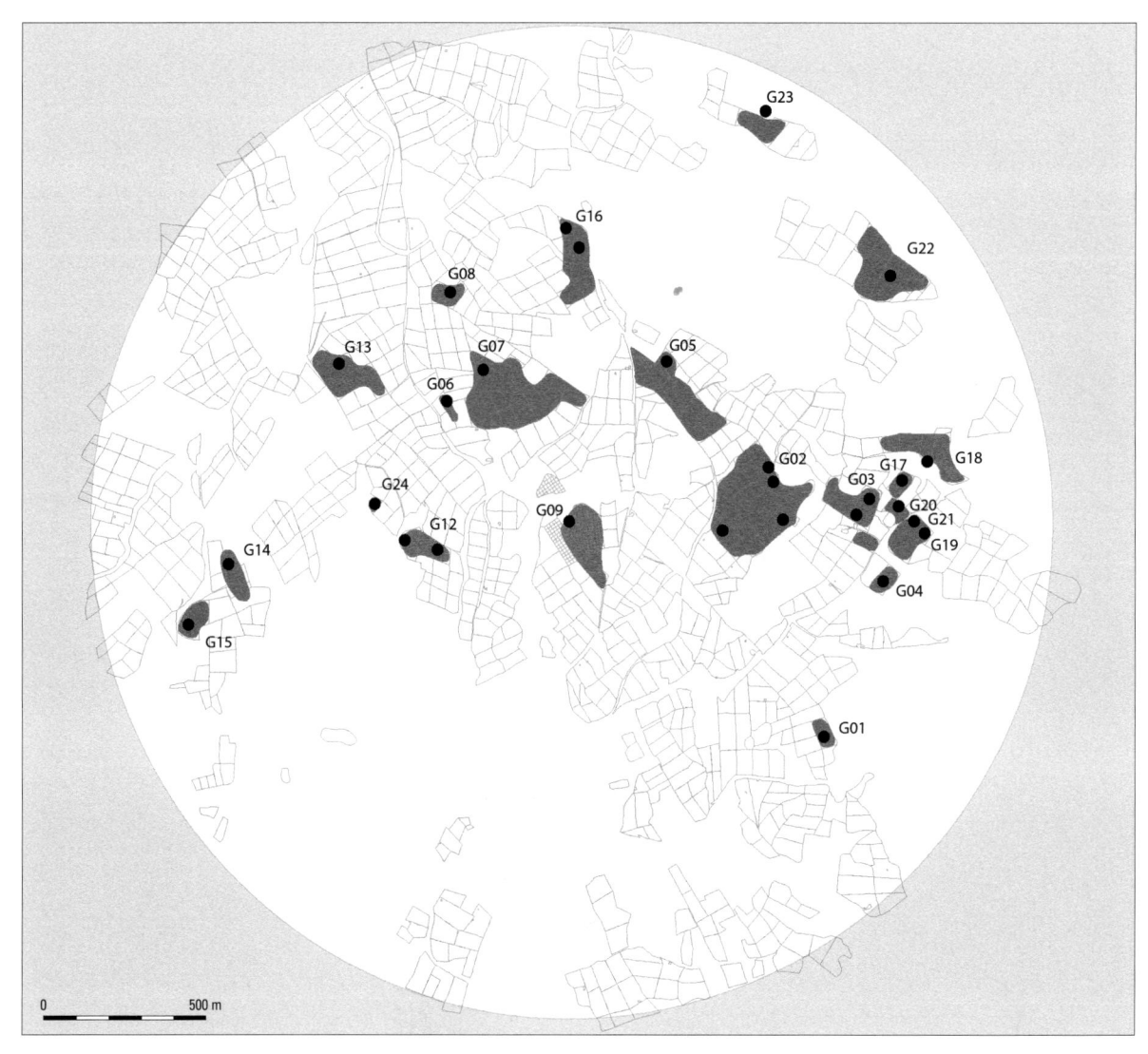

Fig. 5.7. Iron Age, Hellenistic and Roman imperial sites identified during the 2004 and 2005 surveys. The black dots represent probable subsoil archaeological remains from which the surface material presumably (at least in part) derives.

tion centres by its rather soft, often powdery fabric and pale or beige colour. The gloss is usually matt and black or brownish in colour. Although detailed fabric analysis in a regional perspective should be carried out, the repertoire of forms, which has parallels with other sites in the area,[13] suggests regional or local production. Only a few plain wares and sigillata were found and the latter point to a rather restricted repertoire. Few pieces of Italian sigillata were found, e.g. forms Ettlinger 10 and 34. As to the African red slip ceramics, especially Hayes forms 8, 9 and, to a lesser extent, 61 appear to have been well distributed.

The sanctuary site (G9) was clearly distinguishable as such (and yielded ca. 3200 finds) but without clearly defined concentrations within this site (fig. 5.8). Magnetometer prospection was carried out in the fields to the south and east of the sanctuary. No clear structures have been identified, which seems to support the hypothesis that the collected materials are related to the sanctuary itself. Here a small selection of the most common and diagnostic finds is illustrated (fig. 5.9). Amongst the finds are black gloss ceramics dating from

[13] Cf. *infra* on the excavation finds.

Fig. 5.8. The site of the sanctuary of S. Giovanni in Galdo as it appeared in the survey.

the third to first centuries BC (e.g. G9-10: Morel 2978c; G9-6: Morel 2652; G9-12: Morel 2984), including fragments of more particular forms such as unguentaria (G9-11). Also tiles (of the common type illustrated here for G9-49) and some Roman imperial wares (e.g. G9-3: Italian sigillata and G9-1: Hayes 8a) were collected. No ceramics predating the fourth century BC have been found in the sanctuary site.

As to the wider research area, to the east of the sanctuary Iron Age sites yielding large amounts of fine impasto have been recognised. These can be interpreted as a nucleation of settlement in the area in this period (fig. 5.10).[14] For the Hellenistic period, a fairly dense pattern of settlement was encountered

[14] G3, G5, G19-22. The quality and dimensions of the materials suggest that at least until recently some sites were well preserved.

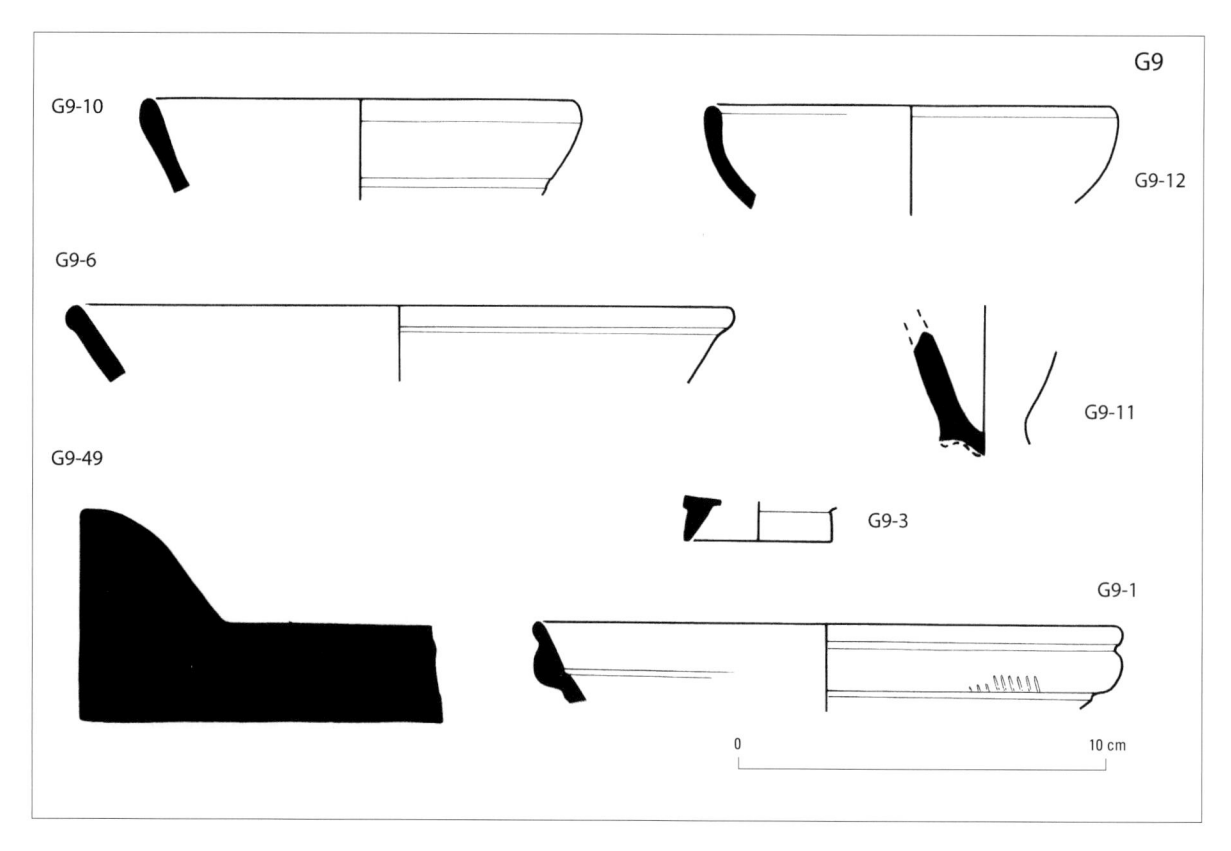

Fig. 5.9. Selection of finds from site G9 (sanctuary).

which covers a larger area than in the previous period. Within the sample area, 16 Hellenistic sites[15] were recognised. Many sites dating to this period are located to the east of the sanctuary (fig. 5.11) and several also yielded Iron Age materials (G3, G5, G19-G22). This surely suggests continuity. The so-called Ingiuno area (to the east of the sanctuary) appears also in this period most densely inhabited. This area is rich in natural springs and terraces and is delimited to the east and south by very steep slopes, descending in the east to the Vallone Visciglieto and in the south to the Torrente Fiumarello. In the centre of this panoramic plateau, at little more than 500 m from the sanctuary of S. Giovanni in Galdo, a considerably large concentration of archaeological material has been identified, consisting of large quantities of different coarse wares, tiles and some fine wares (site G2; fig. 5.12 and fig. 5.15 for the finds). The presence of woodland makes the precise dimensions of this site difficult to establish but it covers an area of at least 10 ha. Concentrated around this nucleus various smaller sites have been detected (G3, G17-21). These consist of limited concentrations of mostly tiles, coarse and plain wares. It seems possible to interpret the whole agglomeration as a village with various buildings with spaces in between. This image of various nuclei appears to be sustained by electric resistivity prospection that we carried out in a sample area (figs. 5.13 and 5.14).

The chronology of most of these sites (or nuclei belonging to one single 'site') ranges from the Iron Age well into the Roman period. Amongst the finds from the village, a selection of which is seen in fig. 5.15, are black gloss forms dating from the late fourth or rather third century BC (for example G2-8: Morel 2430; G2-9: Morel 7112 and G2-10: Morel 2770-2780) to the second and first centuries BC (for example G2-6: Morel 2252; G2-7: Morel 2286; G3-3 Morel 2974a). Coarse wares which are difficult to

---

[15] G1-5, G9, G12, G15-23.

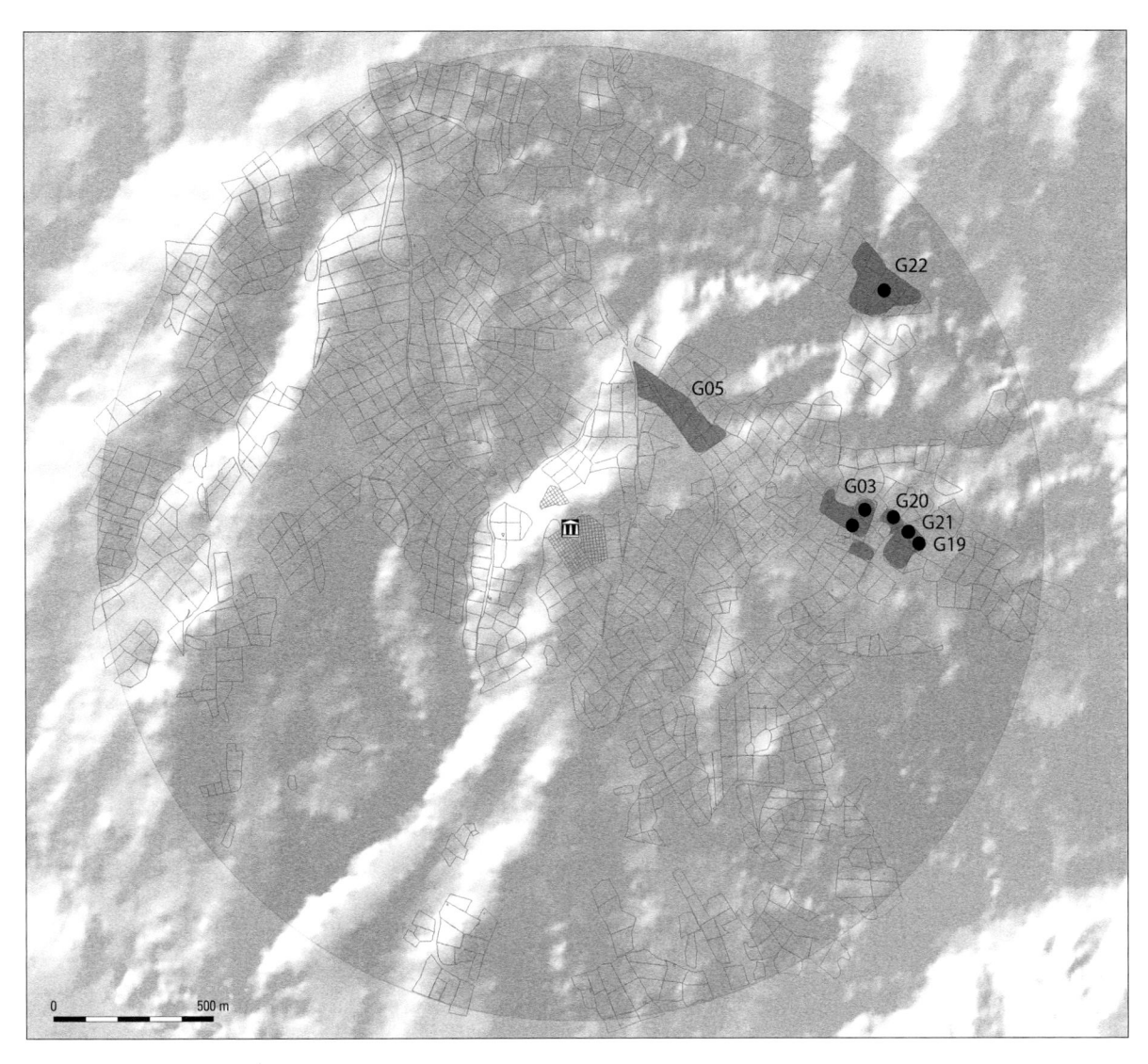

Fig. 5.10. Iron Age sites (the future sanctuary site is also indicated).

date (e.g. G2-19) and tiles (e.g. G2-54) make up the largest part of the finds. Whereas ceramics securely datable to the late Republican and early imperial period are generally scarce (cf. *infra*), imperial period occupation is attested by red slip wares (e.g. G3-2: Hayes 8b, of the second century AD and G2-1: Hayes 61a, of the fourth century AD). Not far and downhill from this site complex is site G22, which can be interpreted as a burial area, with finds from the Iron Age and Hellenistic periods.

Other Hellenistic sites are characterised by small, often relatively well definable nuclei of tiles, coarse wares and few fine wares (G1, G4-5, G12, G15-16 and probably G23). The dimensions of these various sites are largely comparable, and appear to represent small farms. Site G4, a typical example of such a small site, contained some black gloss sherds (e.g. G4-2), coarse wares (e.g. G4-4) and tiles (G4-10; see fig. 5.16). In spite of the limited extent of the surface scatter, resistivity prospection has revealed a quasi square feature of ca. 20 x 20 m (fig. 5.17).[16]

---

[16] The results will be published by Karel-Jan Kerckhaert.

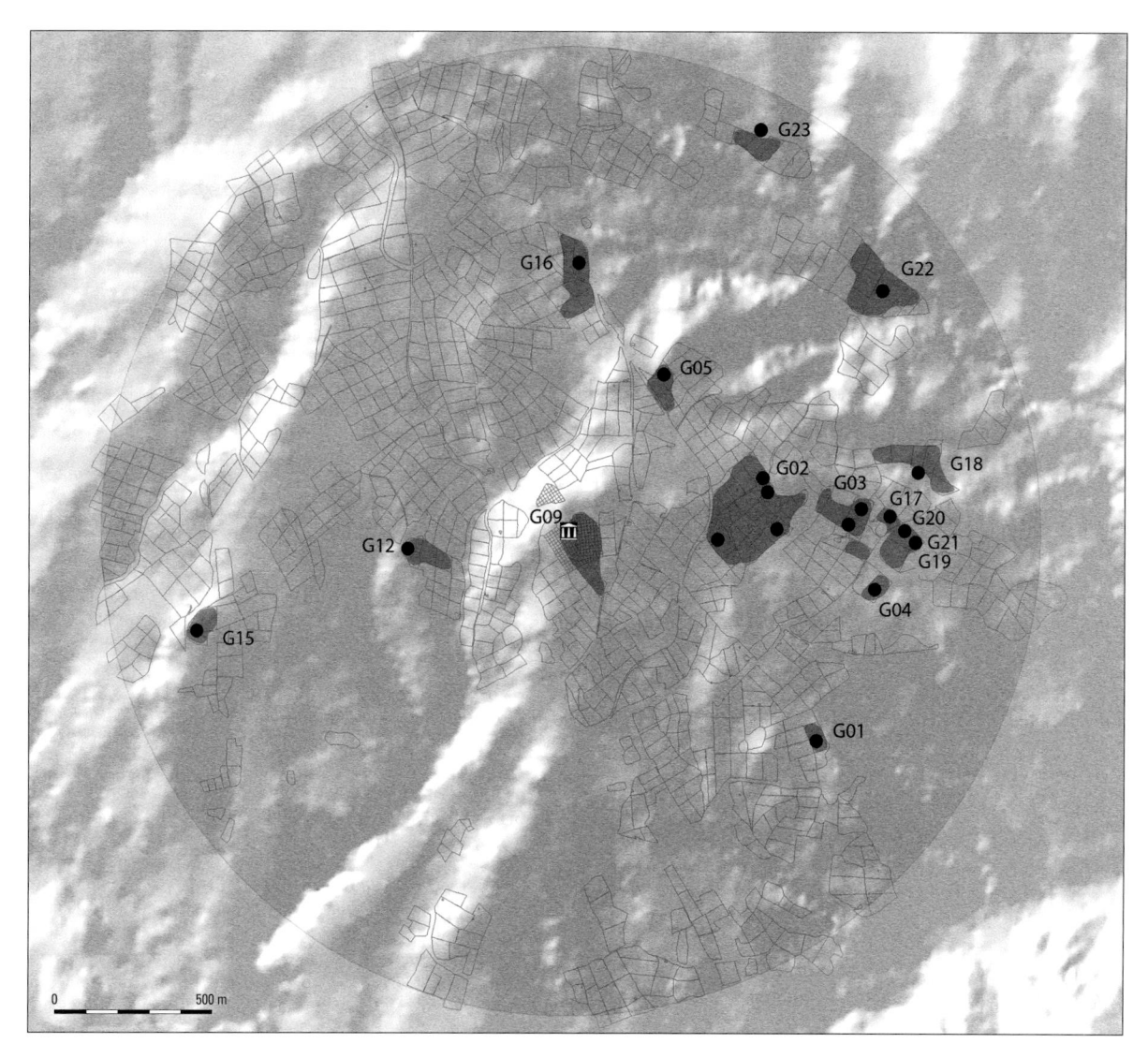

Fig. 5.11. Hellenistic sites.

The Roman period witnesses both change and continuity. A major problem affecting research is the absence of clearly datable ceramics for the period of the last century of the Republic and the early empire. The quantity of Italian sigillata collected thus far was very low but it remains unclear to what extent this is due to a historical 'crisis', archaeological visibility, or changed economic patterns without necessarily implying abandonment. In any case, the number of Roman sites is comparable to those dating to the Hellenistic period (about 13; fig. 5.18).[17] The location of some of these sites clearly differs from the Hellenistic period however. Many new sites appear in the previously uninhabited area to the northwest of the sanctuary, some of them showing remains of *opus spicatum* floors. Most conspicuously, a large *villa* of the imperial and late Roman period (G7) has been recognised to the north of the Colle Rimontato, with several building materials still visible on the surface and a vaulted well preserved *in situ*. The abundant ceramic materials at this site have direct parallels with the excavated *villa* of nearby

---

[17] G2-3, G6-9, G12-14, G18-20, G24.

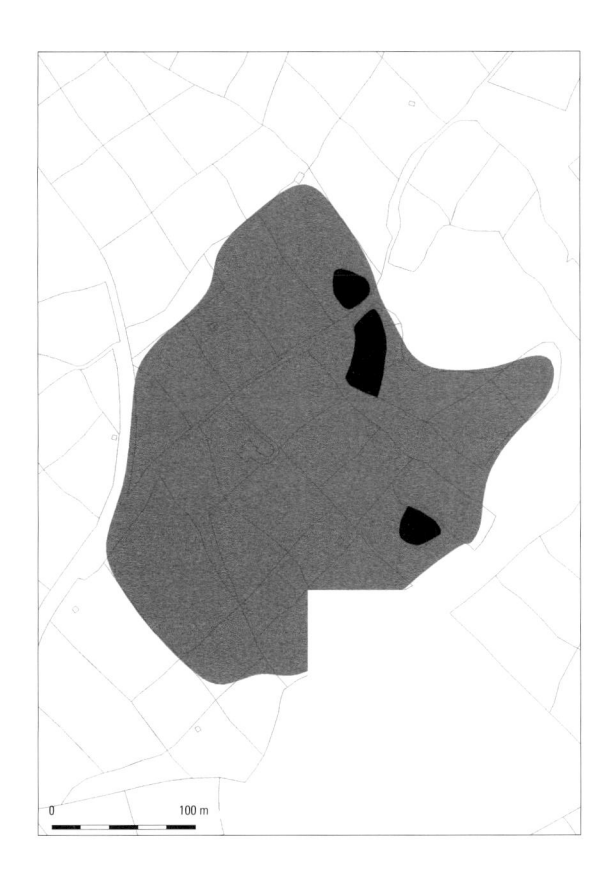

Fig. 5.12. Site G2, interpreted in conjunction with G3, G17-21 as a village. Higher surface find densities are indicated in black.

Fig. 5.13. Electric resistivity research at the site (photo J. Pelgrom).

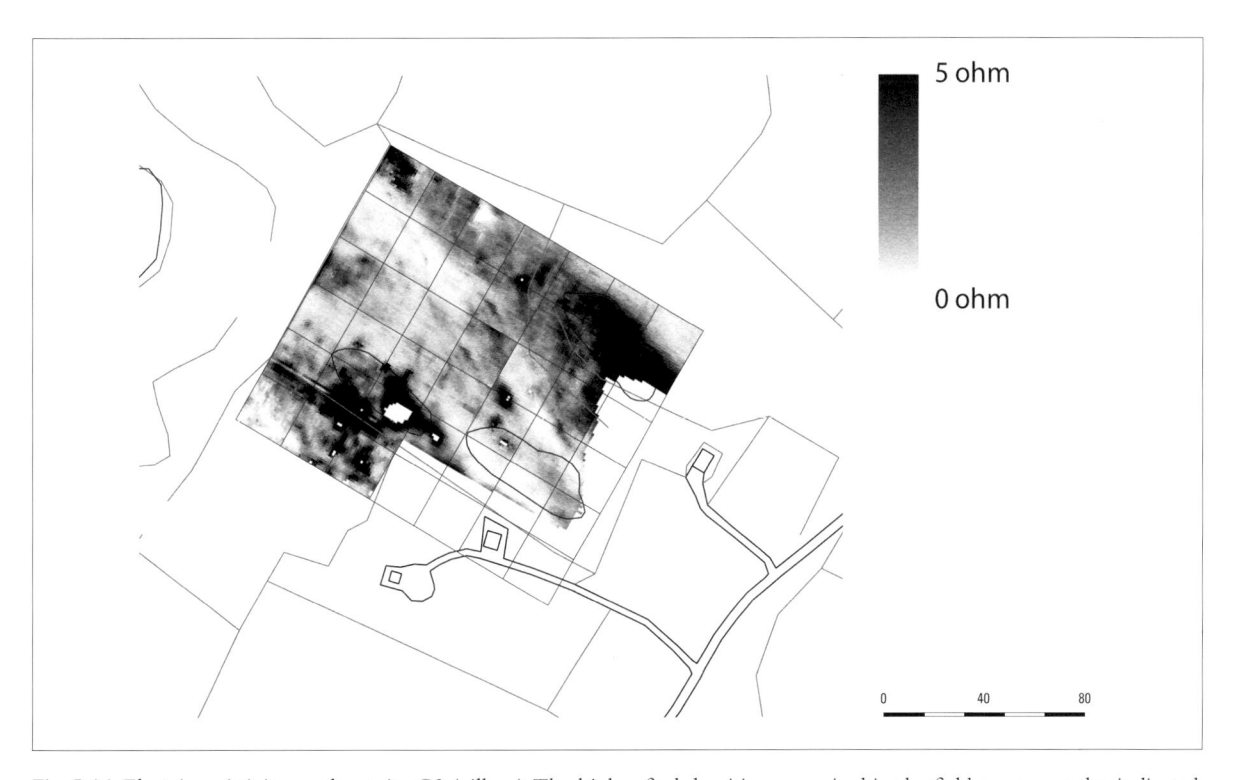

Fig. 5.14. Electric resistivity results at site G3 (village). The higher find densities recognised in the field survey are also indicated.

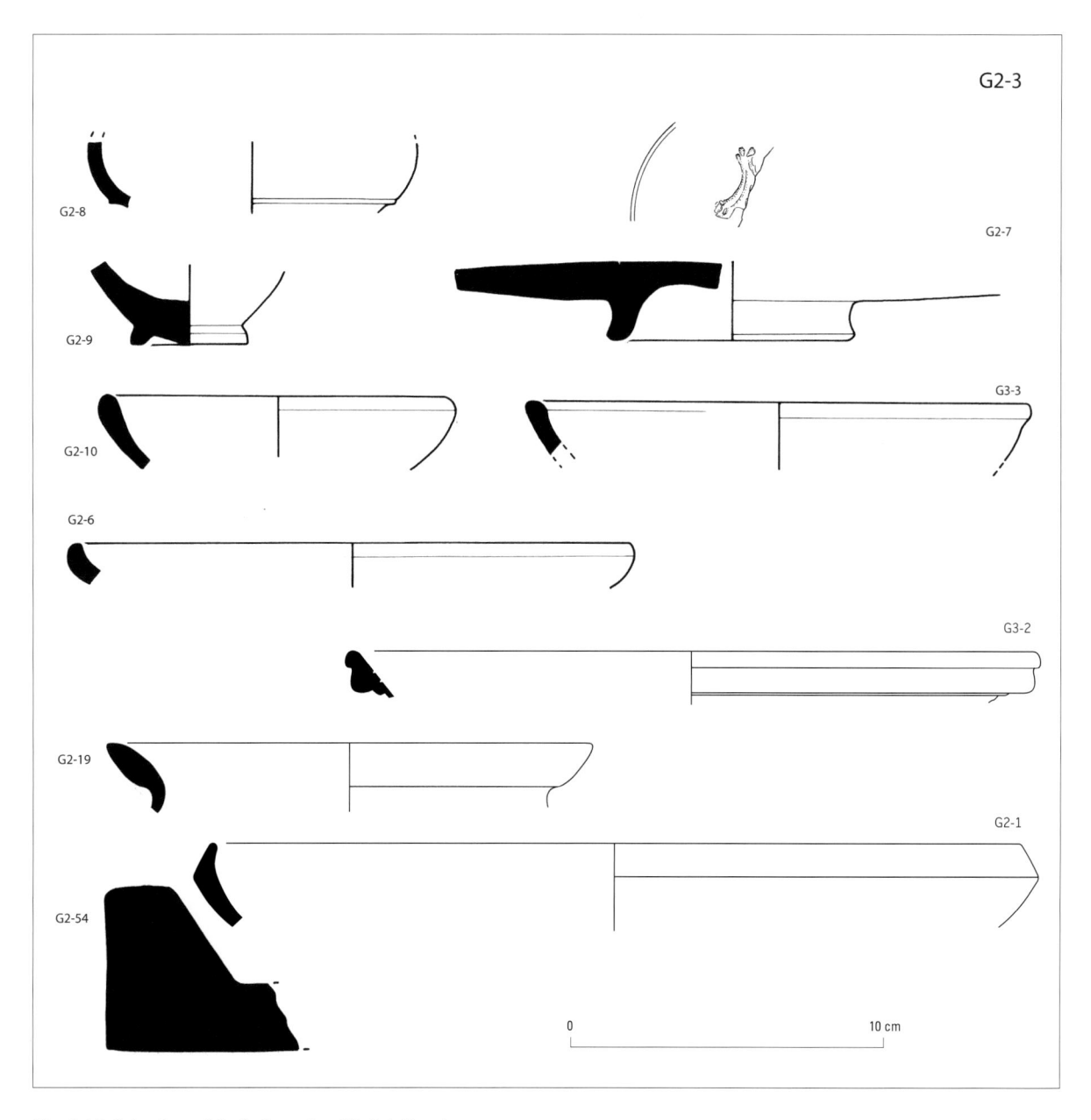

Fig. 5.15. Selection of finds from site G2-3 (village).

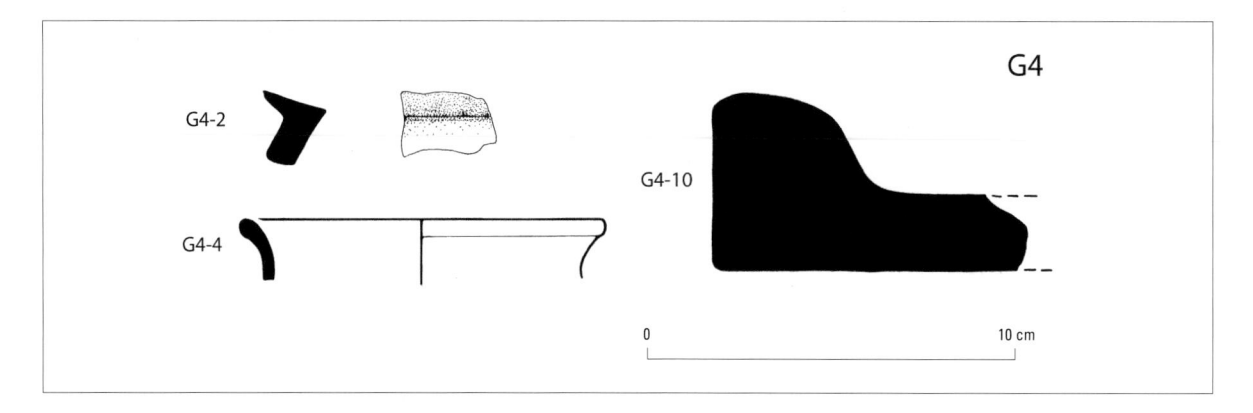

Fig. 5.16. Selection of finds from site G4 (Hellenistic farm).

94

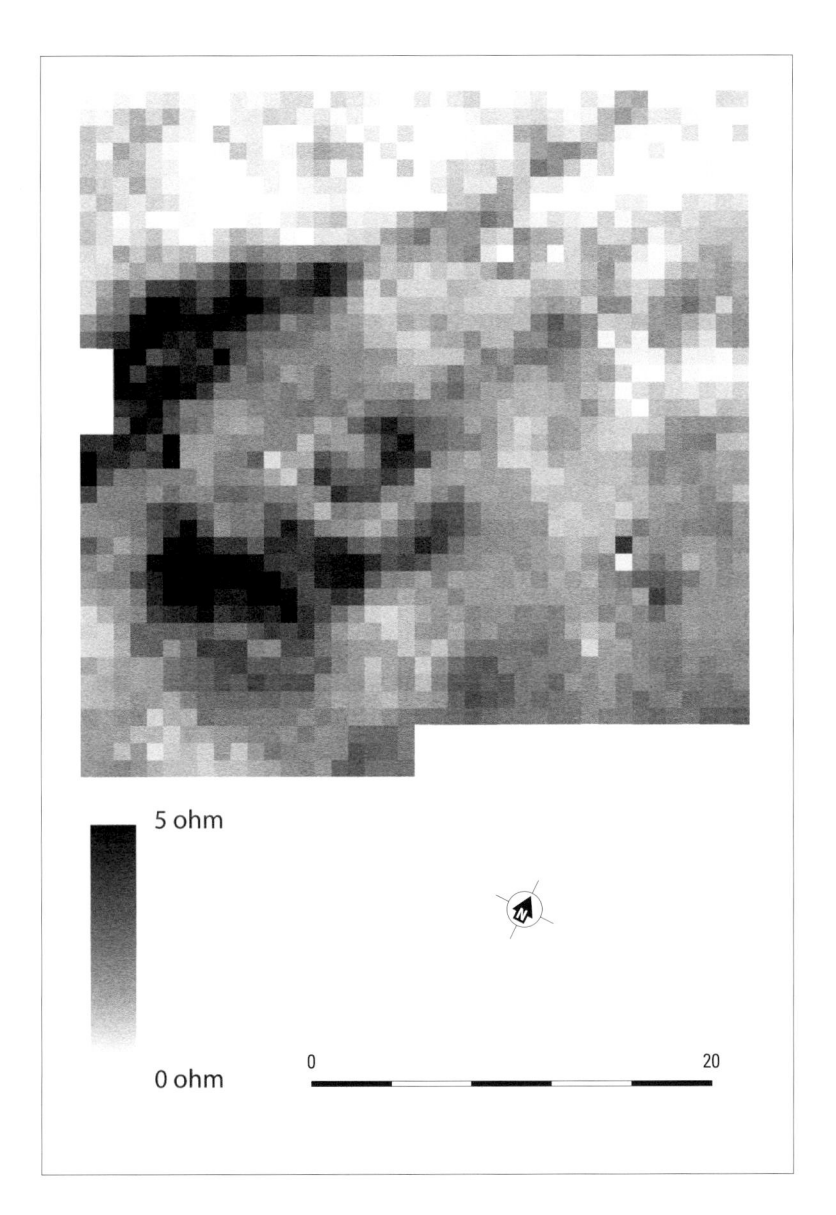

Fig. 5.17. Map showing site G4 (in black highest surface find density) and electric resistivity at site G4 showing a rectangular structure.

Matrice.[18] On the other hand, in some sites continuity with the Hellenistic period might be assumed (e.g. G2, G3, G9, G12, G18, G19, G20), namely, in some possible farm sites, the sanctuary site and the cluster of sites in the Ingiuno area that can be interpreted as a village. Interestingly, the dimensions of the sites in the Roman period are more heterogeneous than in the previous period, which might indicate a different and presumably more hierarchical use of the landscape.

[18] Lloyd/Rathbone 1984; Lloyd 1991b; Barker 1995, 224–226.

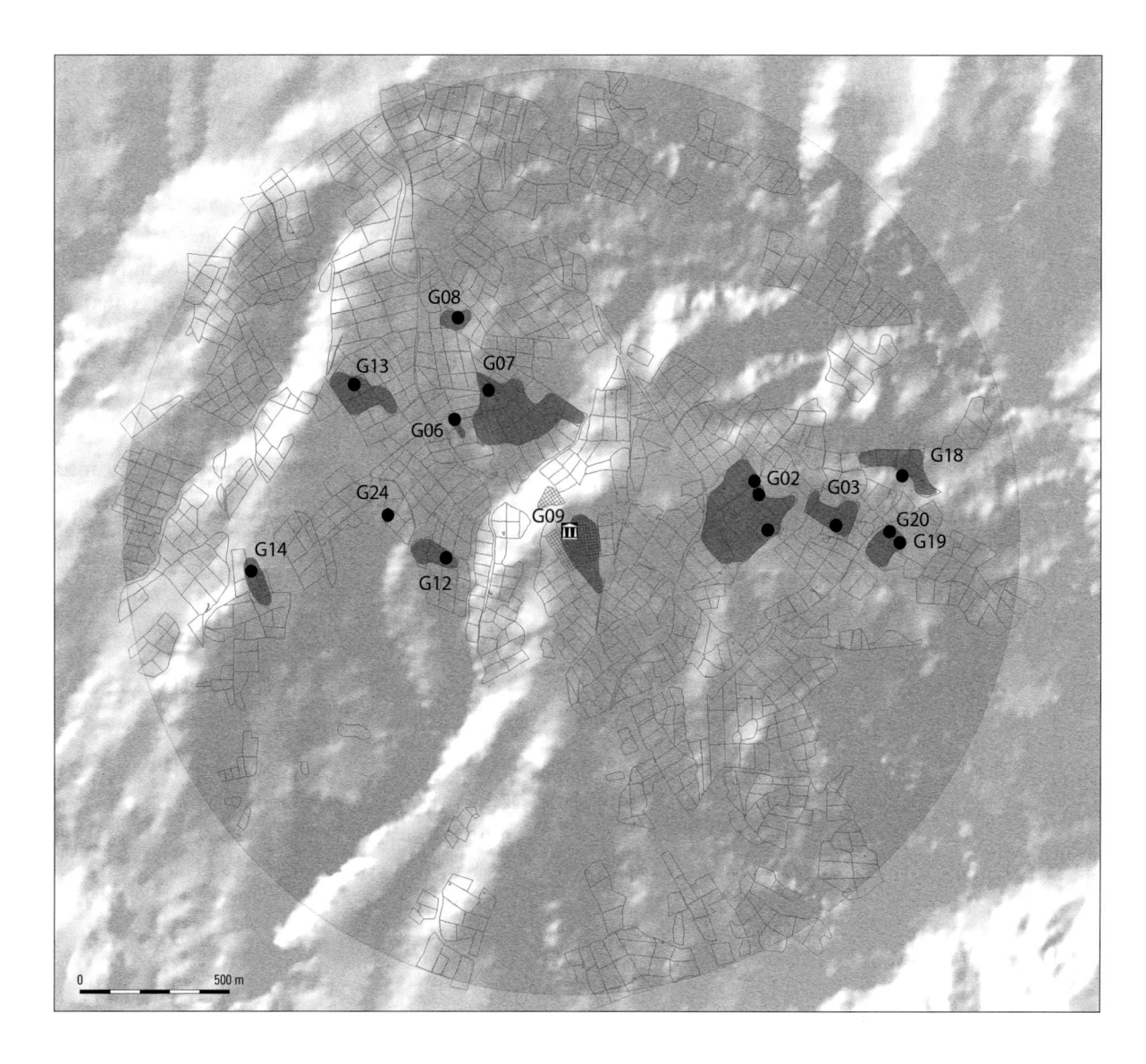

Fig. 5.18. Roman imperial sites.

5.3 THE EXCAVATION DATA (SOPRINTENDENZA PER I BENI ARCHEOLOGICI DEL MOLISE, 1974-1976)

Excavation data of the sanctuary were studied in order to establish the chronological range of the cult site and to relate the results of the survey to the development of the sanctuary itself. The 1970s rescue excavations have only been published summarily,[19] and precise documentation of the excavation is not available. The areas around the temple and the shrine itself were excavated first, whereas successive campaigns uncovered the two lateral porticoes, a large deposit of ceramics directly behind the temple and the front area of the precinct.[20] The ground plan and a section of the podium could thus be drawn (cf. Chapter 3, figs. 3.2 and 3.3)[21] and some of the architectural elements were restored. The beginnings

[19] Di Niro 1978a; Di Niro 1980.
[20] Di Niro 1980, 269.
[21] Di Niro 1980, 272-273 figs. 45-46.

of cult activity have been dated to the second century BC[22] or the end of the third – beginning of the second centuries BC.[23] Angela Di Niro from the *Soprintendenza per i Beni Archeologici del Molise*, who was responsible for the excavation, has kindly permitted a study of the unpublished materials and research was carried out by a small team in 2006.[24]

The majority of the material was found in the back chambers of the porticoes and in the space behind the precinct walls. Here the concentration of ceramics and other finds such as animal bones was so high that Di Niro interprets it as a deposit or dump of votive materials from the sanctuary.[25] The finds from the excavations of the sanctuary are stored by the *Soprintendenza* at Campobasso. Since no documentation of the excavation is yet available, any analysis of the finds with regard to the exact provenance within the excavation and especially quantification will remain conjectural, if not simply impossible. Since the present study is primarily concerned with establishing the chronological range and the general comparison of the finds with those from the survey, this limitation is not insurmountable.

The finds stored by the *Soprintendenza per i Beni Archeologici del Molise* can be roughly divided into three groups, one that has been studied and catalogued already by the Soprintendenza, contemporaneously with or shortly after the excavations, part of which has been drawn as well, a second group that has been catalogued but not studied or drawn, and a group that has not been studied at all. Both the finds and the documentation (*schede* and drawings) of the first group studied by the Soprintendenza were accessible for comparative use and have been checked and entered into a database. The last two groups of unstudied material were obviously of primary concern. These have been studied and consequently numbered and labelled according to a new system, in accordance with the database that was used for the 2004 and 2005 survey campaigns.[26] From these two groups, a total of 1326 items has been studied and entered into another (compatible) database. Type, fabric, colour, position of the fragment if applicable, diameter, provenance / stratigraphical information if indicated, and so on were noted, along with possible bibliographical references. A selection of the previously unstudied material is presented here as part of the general contextualisation of the sanctuary.

5.3.1 BLACK GLOSS

The black gloss pottery excavated from the sanctuary under study here numbers 258 items (about 30% of the total, and corresponding to approximately 180 individual forms) and is made of a fabric that is not very hard, often powdery, and mostly pale, greyish or beige in colour. The gloss is usually matt, lacking the bluish shine of Campanian wares, and black or brownish in colour. A comparatively restricted range of forms has been recognised, predominantly cups and dishes / plates in about equal quantities. Several pyxides were found as well as a few sherds from skyphoi. A fairly representative sample of the material encountered during the depot work is illustrated here. Besides the most common cups and plates, almost all differing forms are covered in this selection. Few specimens have exact parallels in Morel's typology

---

[22] Di Niro 1978a, 503, describes the black gloss finds as dating to the second and first centuries BC, followed by a "*quasi totale assenza di materiale*" until the second half of the first century AD.

[23] Di Niro 1980, 274.

[24] Anneke Dekker, Laura Hoff, Francesca Laera, Alma Reijling, Ilona Steijven, and Alessandra Zaccardi, in addition to the author.

[25] Di Niro 1978a, 502.

[26] The original administration was also preserved. E.g. SLP06_S145-T2: Sacred Landscape Project 2006, S(acco)145, T[=drawingselection] 1. When a *Soprintendenza* catalogue number was present, it was preserved and integrated e.g. SLP06_SG_75-107: Sacred Landscape Project 2006, and then the excavator's administration number SG75/107.

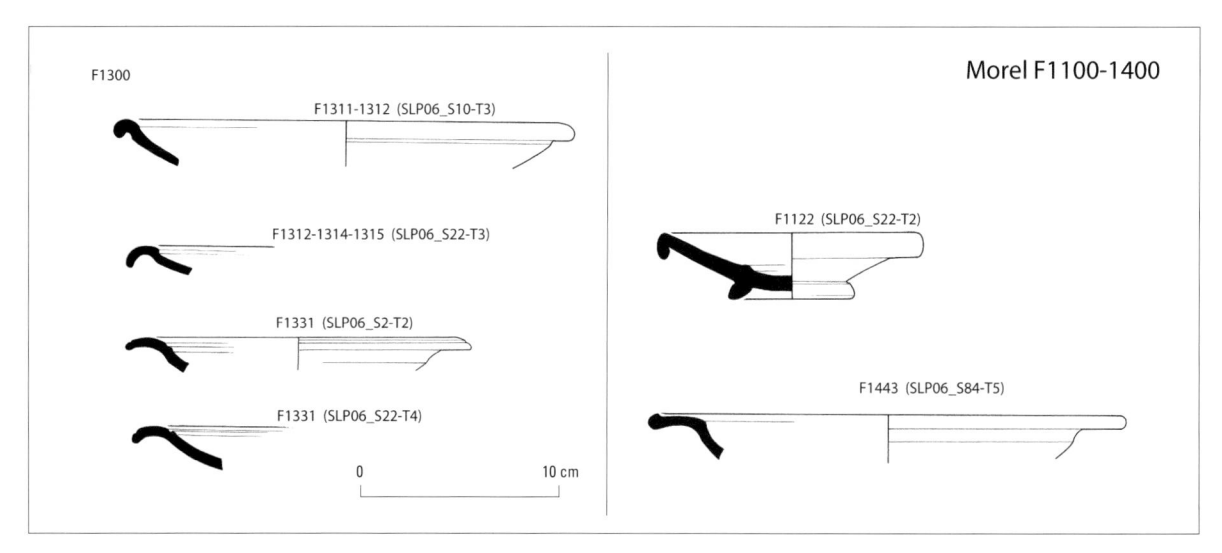

Fig. 5.19. Black gloss plates / dishes from the sanctuary excavations, Morel F1100-1400.

and local parallels, for example from Campochiaro,[27] Montevairano[28] and Capracotta,[29] are often far better, but these unfortunately lack an independent chronological base. Not surprisingly, some fine parallels can also be found in the more internal Campanian areas.[30] These characteristics suggest a regional or local production, although a detailed regional fabric analysis is required.[31] I present the forms according to Morel's typology.

Amongst the plates and dishes (fig. 5.19), Morel F1312-1315 are common, generically dated to the second century BC (cf. SLP06_S10-T3 and SLP06_S22-T3). Morel F1443 (SLP06_S84-T5) can also be dated to the (second half of) the second century BC. A relatively early form may be represented by F1331 (SLP06_S22-T4 and SLP06_S2-T2), still datable to the (second half of) third century BC. A somewhat less represented form in the context of S. Giovanni in Galdo is what appears to be a local variant of F1122 (SLP06_S22-T2). This shape is found in both Attic and Campana A workshops and consequently there is a huge difference between the dates (Attic: second half fourth century BC; Campana A: around 200 BC). Fairly well represented is a group of cups (fig. 5.20) that seem to be inspired by F2420-2424 (SLP06_S10-T1; SLP06_S1-T1[32]; SLP06_SG_75-100-898; SLP06_SG_75-311). These forms are generally dated to the late fourth or the beginning of the third centuries BC.[33] Good parallels have been found at the sanctuary of Campochiaro, scarico A, dated to the late fourth - beginnings of the third century BC[34] and the foundation layer of the south gate of Monte Vairano,[35] dated to the late fourth century BC. Other relatively early forms are F2783-2784 (SLP06_S10-T4; SLP06_S2-T6; SLP06_SG_75-103), mostly dated to the late fourth or first decennia of the third centuries BC.[36]

[27] *Campochiaro* 1982; Capini 1984.
[28] De Benedittis 1980.
[29] Rainini 1996.
[30] E.g. Pedroni 1986; Pedroni 1990.
[31] Only two sherds (SLP06_S90T1 and SLP06_S91T1) could possibly belong to Campana A but a regional origin cannot be excluded.
[32] It may, however, belong as well to F2534, dated to the second century BC.
[33] Cf. for the type, dated to the fourth century BC, in Campanian graves, Benassai 2004.
[34] *Campochiaro* 1982, 35-36, esp. no. 30. Cf. for the type also the specimen published by Di Niro in *Sannio* 1980 pl. 51 no. 2.
[35] De Benedittis 1980, 329, no. 5.
[36] Note that there are two production centres of F2784; in central Italy (Sabine / Latium / APE) at the beginning of the third century BC, and a Campanian A in the second century BC.

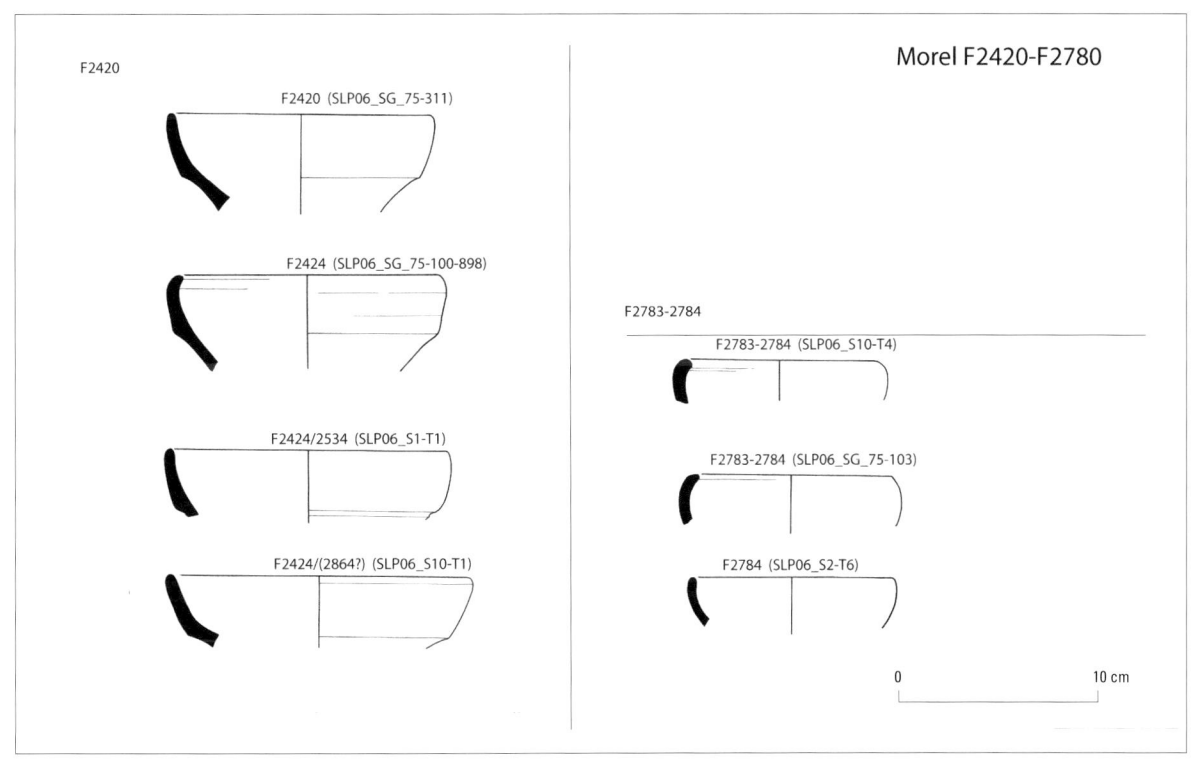

Fig. 5.20. Black gloss cups from the sanctuary excavations, Morel F2420 and F2780.

Later forms (fig. 5.21) are represented by F2610 (SLP06_SG_75-92)[37] and F2650 (SLP06_S22-T6), both of the second-first centuries BC (compare SLP06_S2-T9 – 2654 or 2653- and SLP06_S90-T2 -2654a2, first century BC). Another late cup might be represented by F2983 (SLP06_S90-T4), presumably datable to the beginning of the first century BC.

Only three skyphoi have been recognised, the specimen reproduced here in figure 5.22 (SLP06_S92-T1) does not fit easily into Morel's typology (generically, F4300), presumably due to its local or regional production. Its date may be quite early however, from the late fourth or beginnings of the third centuries BC.[38] Furthermore several pyxides generally dated to the third–first centuries BC, but mostly to the second and first centuries: F7513a1 (SLP06_S10-T6); F7511-7514 (SLP06_S22-T1[39]); F7544 (SLP06_S2-T1 and SLP06_S4-T4); F7530-7550 (SLP06_S5-T4) were found.

Other forms (fig. 5.23) include apode forms, F2150 (SLP06_S11-T4 -F2153 or 2154-; SLP06_S18-T1 and SLP06_S22-T7), and a goblet of the F7222 series (SLP06_S4-T6[40]), which could be dated to the third or second century BC. Only one clear stamped specimen was recognised in this sample (SLP06_S22-T9), and this may date to the third century BC.[41] A particular handle of the *anses bifides en double boudin* type, apparently relating to F3121, was also found (SLP06_SG_75-112-905).[42]

---

[37] It resembles F2621b too, dated earlier, that is, in the first half of the third century BC.

[38] Cf. e.g. Capini 1984, 29-32, nos. 67-68.

[39] 7512a1 comes closest, dated to the first half of the second century BC.

[40] Cf. Pedroni 1986, 699: probably local production from Cales, third to second centuries BC.

[41] Bernardini 1986, 198, nos. 26-27.

[42] Cf. also, Pedroni 1986, 55, 457-459, locally produced at Cales, and dated to the third to second centuries BC.

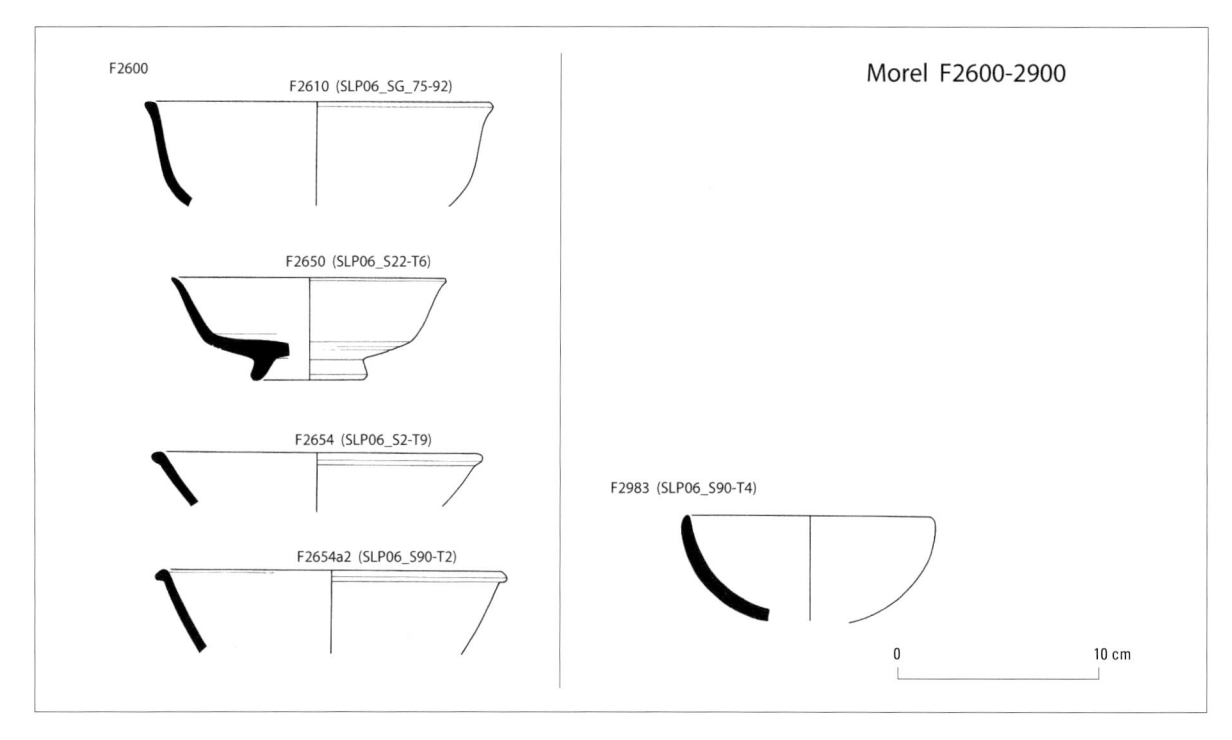

Fig. 5.21. Black gloss cups from the sanctuary excavations, Morel F2600-2900.

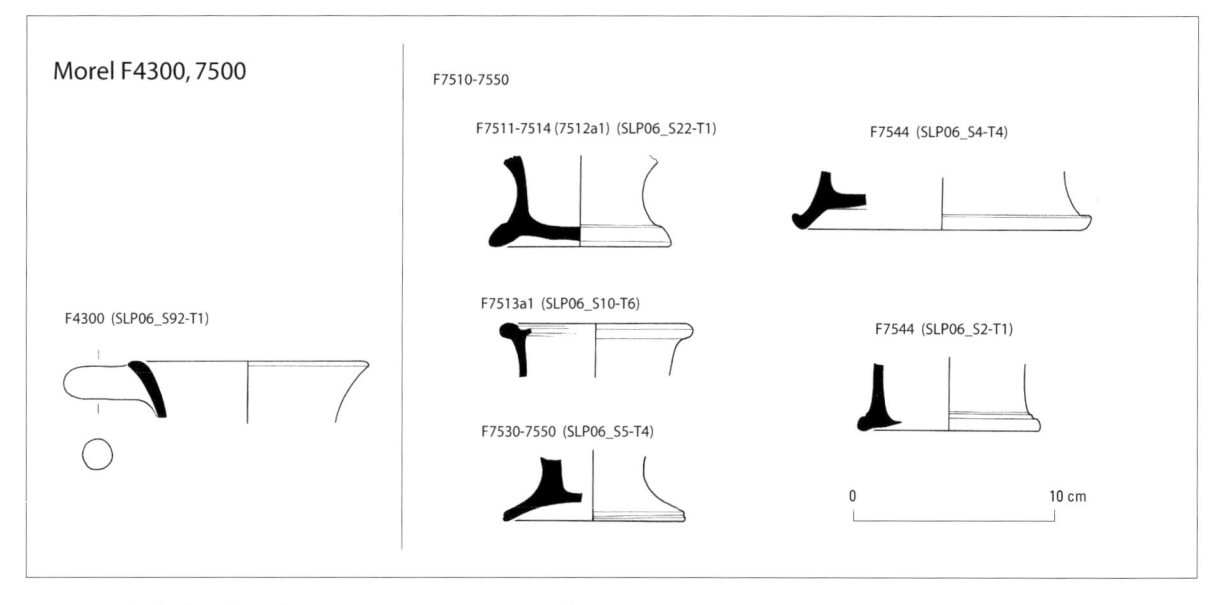

Fig. 5.22. Black gloss from the sanctuary excavations, Morel F4300, F7500.

5.3.2 ITALIAN TERRA SIGILLATA

The Italian sigillata forms (fig. 5.24) present amongst the excavation finds are not abundant (about 39 pieces corresponding to 18 whole forms). Recognisable forms are Ettlinger 8.1 (SLP06_S61-T1), Ettlinger 26.2 (SLP06_S67-T1), Ettlinger 29.1 (SLP06_S128-T4), Ettlinger 33.1 (SLP06_S33-T1), Ettlinger 34 (SLP06_S54-T1) and Ettlinger 37.1 (SLP06_S130-T2).[43] Whereas Ettlinger 8, 26 and 33

[43] Ettlinger *et al.* 1990.

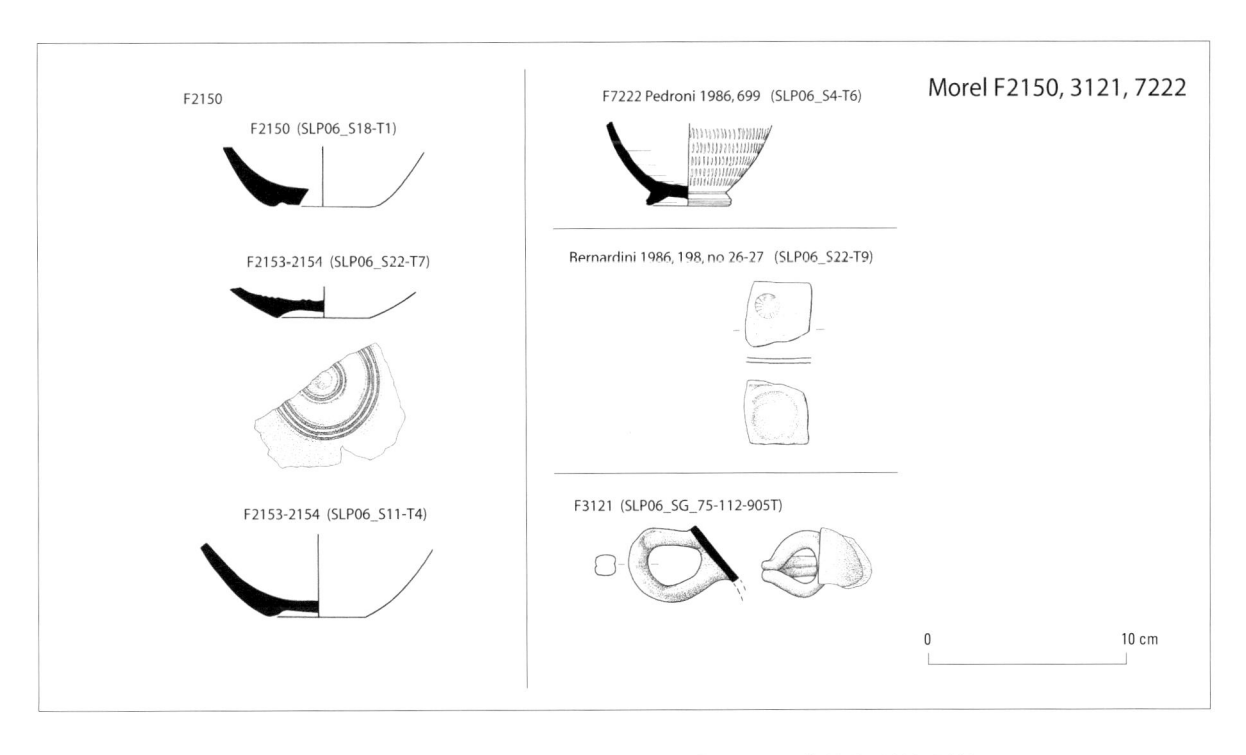

Fig. 5.23. Black gloss ceramics from the sanctuary excavations, various forms, Morel 2150, 3121, 7222.

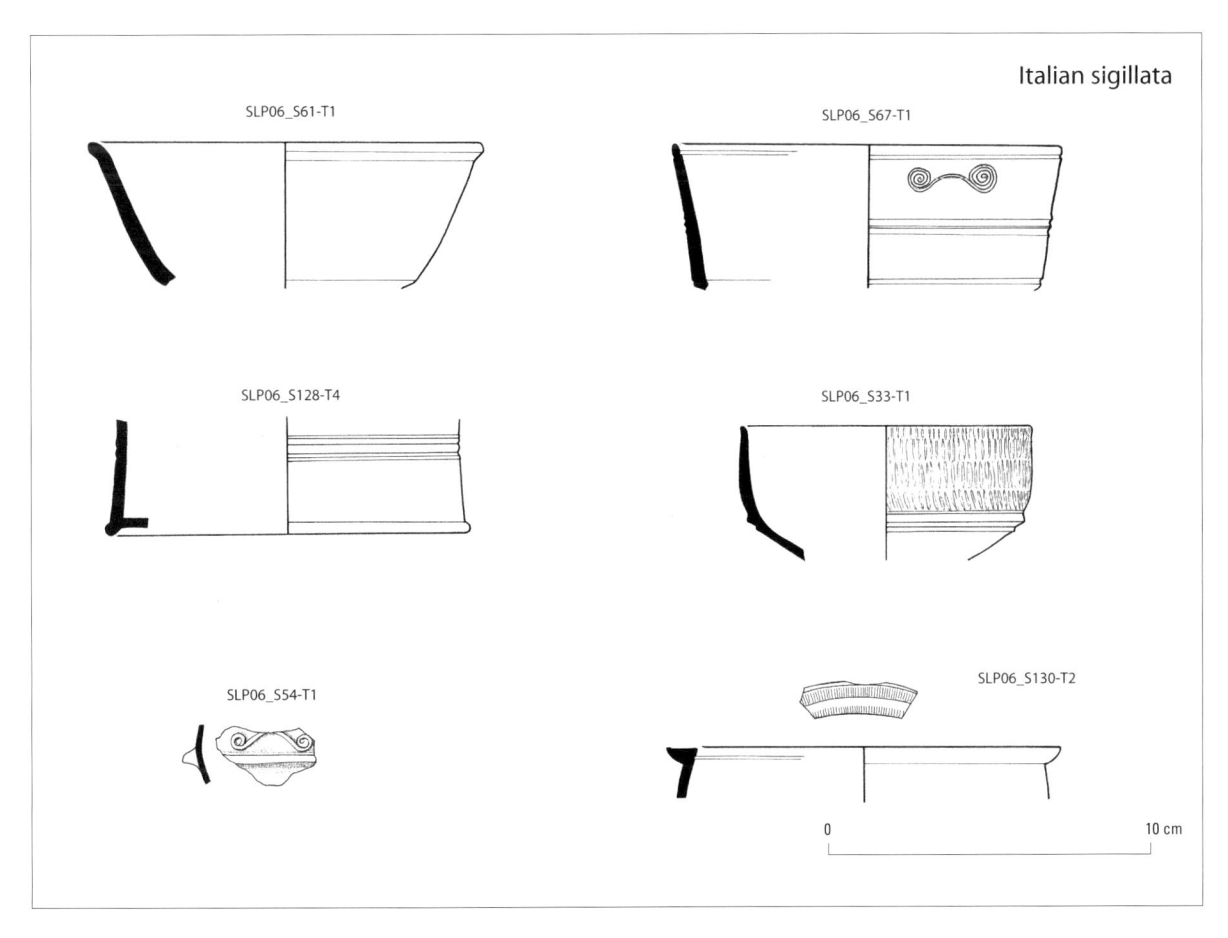

Fig. 5.24. Italian terra sigillata from the sanctuary excavations.

101

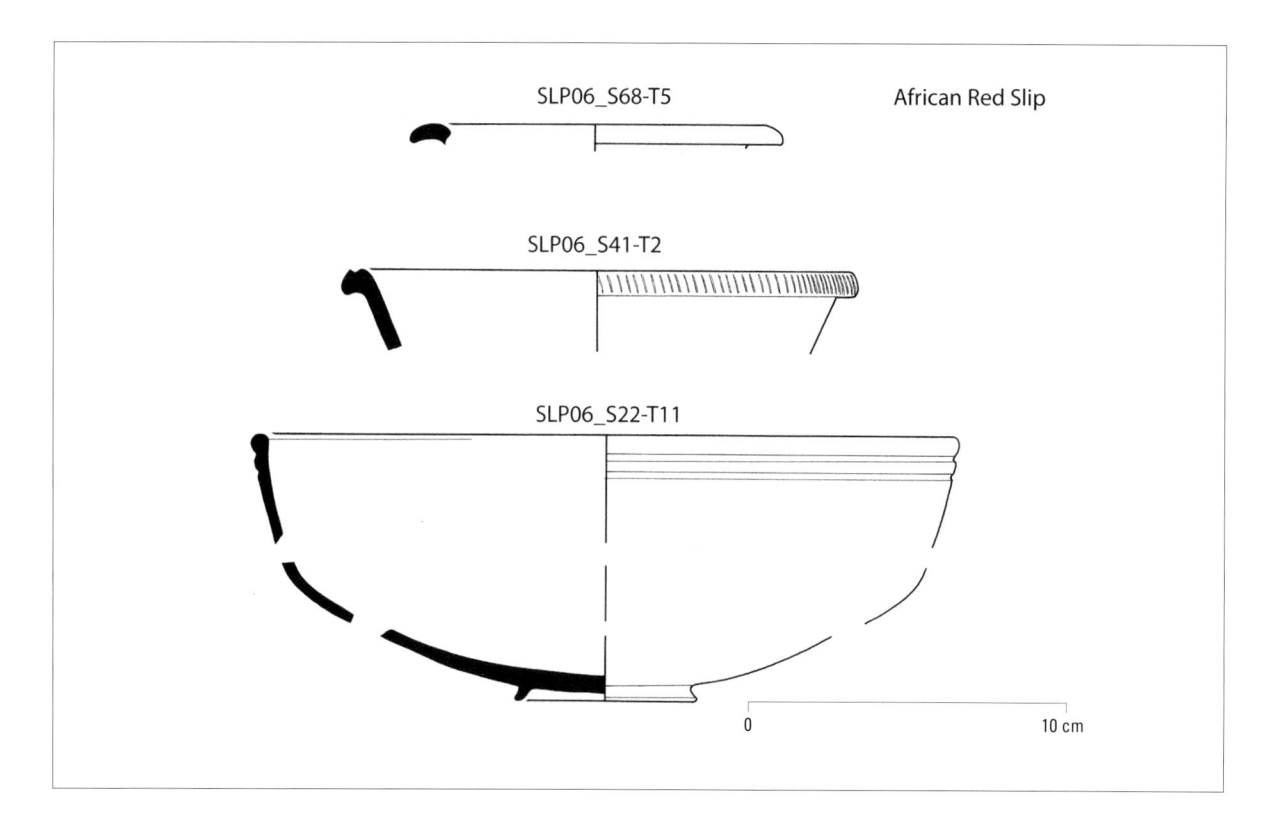

Fig. 5.25. African red slip wares from the sanctuary excavations.

generally date from the Augustan period to the first half of the first century AD, Ettlinger 29, 34 and 37 can be dated to the first century AD, especially from the middle of the century onwards.

5.3.3 AFRICAN RED SLIP

The African Red Slip (ARS) wares that were encountered in this study all relate to forms commonly dating to the second century AD (fig. 5.25). These comprise Hayes 3c (SLP06_S68-T5), dated to the mid-second century AD, and Hayes 5b (SLP06_S41-T2) which dates to the late first to early second century AD. The forms Hayes 9b (SLP06_S22-T11) and Hayes 8b (not illustrated, cf. fig. 5.15, G3-2), both dating to the second half of the second century (or even early third) AD[44] were most frequent.

5.3.4 OTHER FINDS

Many coarse wares were found, some of them decorated with incision lines or imprinting (cf. resp. SLP06_S26-T1 and SLP06_S12-T2). Although most forms recur, amongst other places, in the excavations at Capracotta (e.g. SLP06_S7-T2 and SLP06_S47-T1),[45] they are too generic to be dated on the basis of typology (fig. 5.26).

[44] Hayes 1972; Hayes 1980, 515.
[45] Rainini 1996.

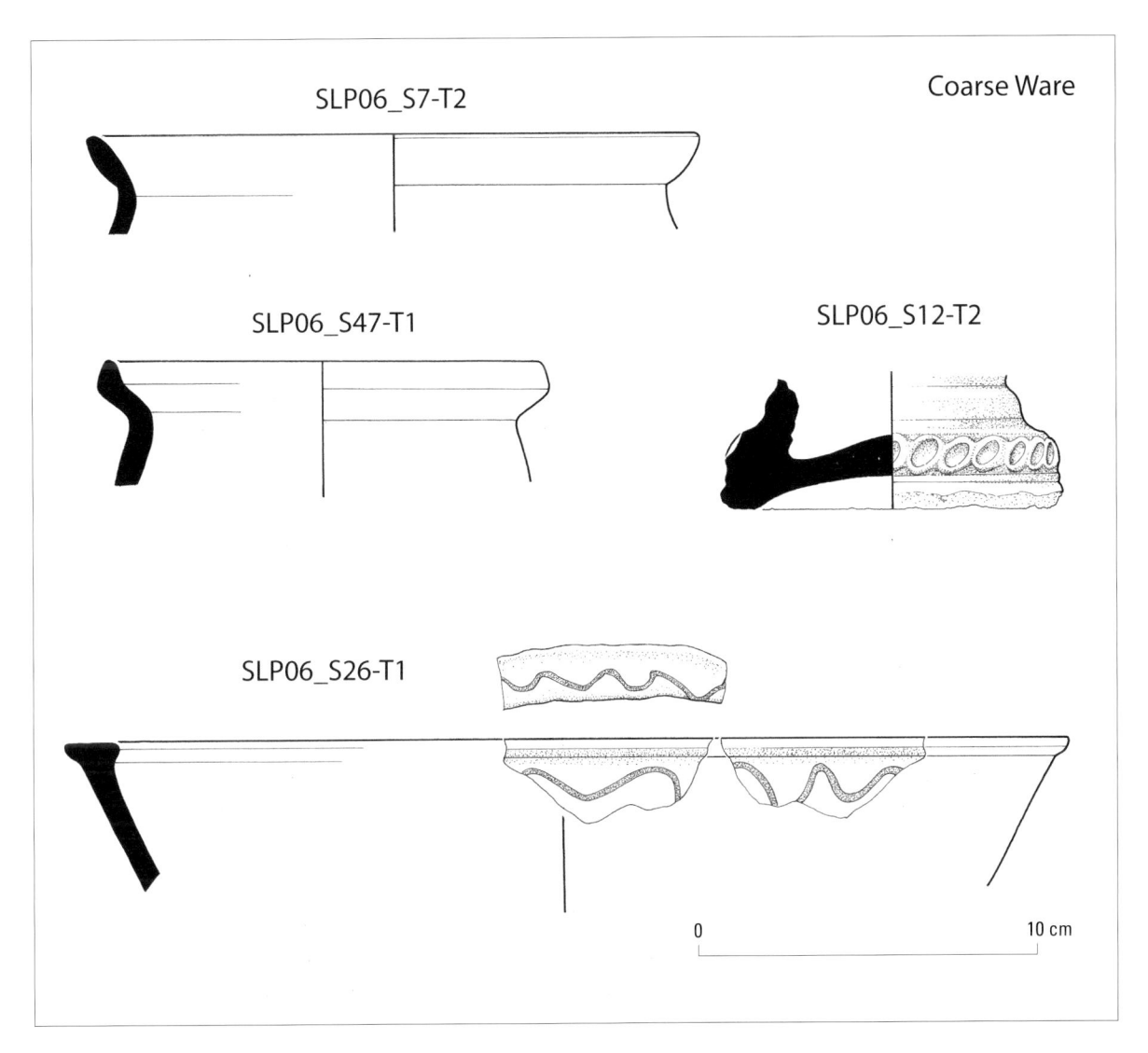

Fig. 5.26. Coarse wares from the sanctuary excavations.

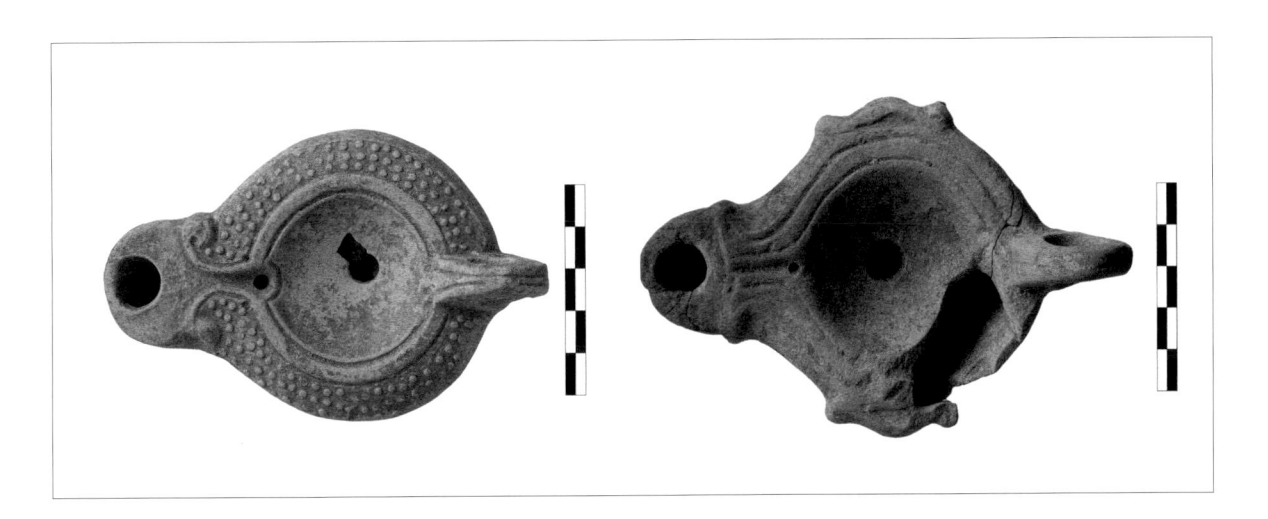

Fig. 5.27a and b. Lamps (SLP06_S55T1 and SLP06_SG74-283) from the sanctuary excavations (photo A. Dekker).

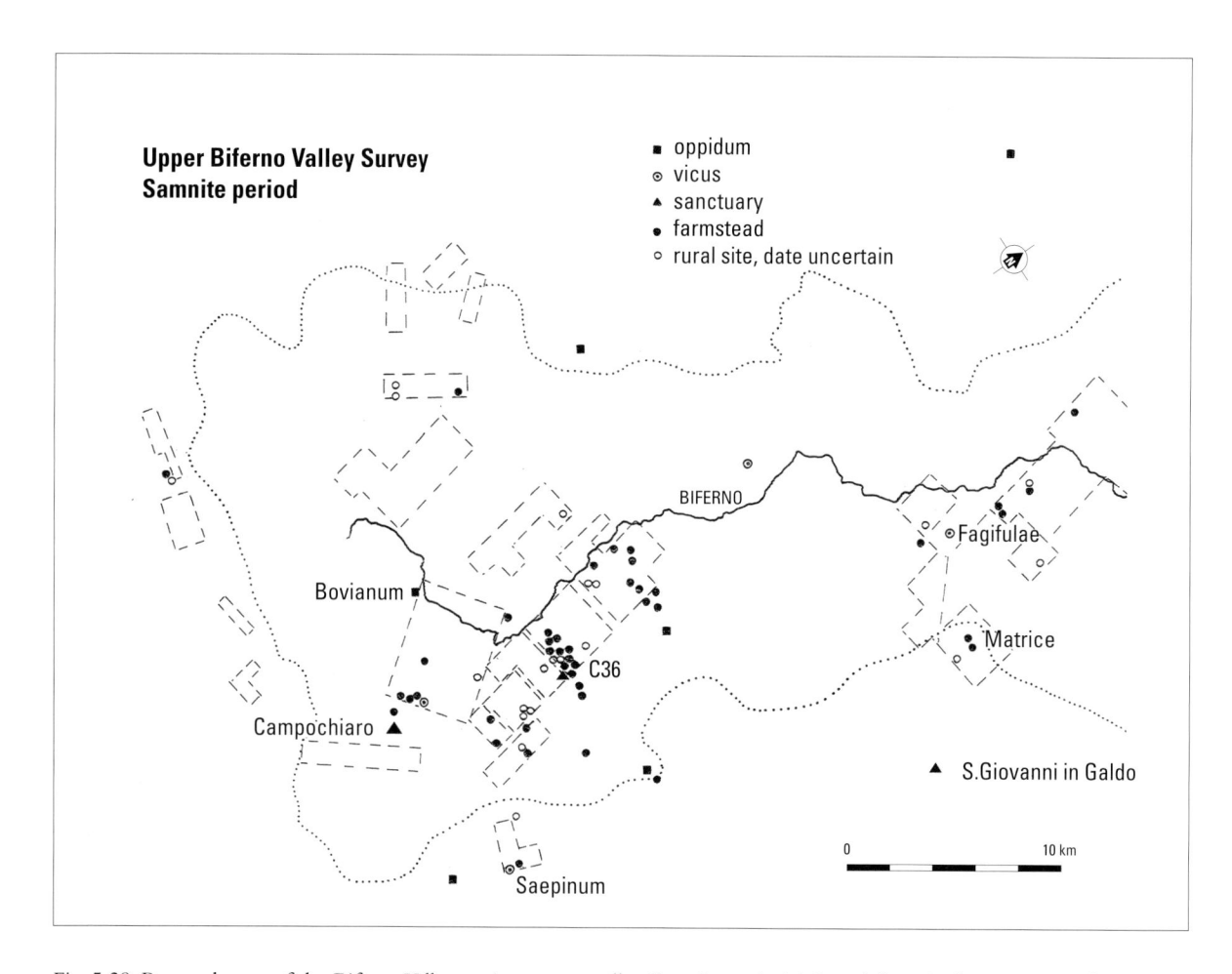

Fig. 5.28. Research area of the Biferno Valley project, upper valley, Samnite period (adapted from Barker 1995, 186 fig. 72).

Several lamps were also found (fig. 5.27), especially fragments and specimens dating to the first or second centuries AD (e.g. SLP06_S55T1: a '*Warzenlampe*', form Deneauve V D; here fig. 5.27a). Another type (SLP06_SG74-283), recognisable as Deneauve V G (fig. 5.27b), was also found in the sanctuary of Campochiaro and dates to the (first half of the) first century AD.[46]

5.4 CONCLUSION: A RURAL COMMUNITY AROUND THE SANCTUARY

The finds from the excavation of the sanctuary at S. Giovanni in Galdo indicate that the cult place was already frequented from the late fourth or early third century BC onwards. The finds also indicate a significant Roman phase of the sanctuary. This is best attested for the first and second centuries AD, later finds were not noted. Whether the sanctuary declined strongly after the Social War until the first half of the first century AD, as has been suggested,[47] is however difficult to say on the basis of the available data. Better dating of the late black gloss materials of the sanctuary, perhaps continuing well into the first cen-

---

[46] Deneauve 1969, 158-159; *Campochiaro* 1982, 73, no. 142.

[47] Di Niro 1978a, 503-504; Di Niro 1978a, 274, speaking of a "*mancanza pressochè totale di materiali databili alla seconda metà del I secolo a.C. e ai primi anni dell'impero*".

tury BC, could provide information in this regard (cf. also *infra* on the survey data). In addition, a change to ritual practices with a lower archaeological visibility cannot be excluded.

The 10 x 10 m site survey of the sanctuary yielded finds that can be related to the sanctuary itself and no significant differences in periodisation, forms or fabric were found with respect to the excavation data (except for the presence of tiles, which were not preserved by the excavators). The survey did not reveal distinct sites around the sanctuary and the magnetometric prospection did not reveal secondary structures.[48]

The field survey in the broader surroundings of the sanctuary did however record, as we have seen, a relatively high density of sites for both the Hellenistic and Roman periods. Most conspicuous was the discovery, at around 500 m from the sanctuary, of the site complex consisting of G2, G3 and G17-21, which seems to represent a village or at least an agglomeration covering a fairly large area of more than 10 ha. This site already existed in the Iron Age and continuity from this period onwards could be assumed (but in order to answer this question more satisfactorily our knowledge of the local chronology of the ceramics, especially impasto wares, should be enhanced). The situation is much clearer for the Hellenistic and Roman periods, which are our primary concern. Together with the nearby burial area downhill (G22) and several farms dispersed over the territory, an image of a rather 'complete' though spatially differentiated non-urban community arises. Although some sites also contain Iron Age finds, as a whole this settlement pattern seems to date to the (early) Hellenistic period. The village, already in use from the Iron Age onwards, presents a clear phase in the late fourth and early third centuries BC, which coincides with the first signs of cult activity on Colle Rimontato. Subsequently, in the course of the third and also second centuries BC, the landscape of S. Giovanni in Galdo appears to have been reorganised as is documented by the appearance of several small farm sites.

It therefore seems legitimate to conclude that the sanctuary of S. Giovanni in Galdo was not located in isolation, but within a thriving pattern of settlement that emerges in the archaeological record from the fourth to third centuries BC. On this basis, it seems reasonable to assume that the sanctuary was part of this very pattern. An observation that could support this hypothesis is that no finds belonging to the sanctuary could be positively identified as other than regionally produced and they do not differ from finds from the surrounding sites identified in the survey. The black gloss pottery definitely seems to relate to the same local or regional production in terms of form repertoire. The same repertoire is encountered in the excavation and in the survey data relating to the Roman period, with the exception that the sanctuary finds do not postdate the second century AD.

Interestingly, just like the excavation data from the sanctuary, the survey data from the entire research area present a 'gap' in the first century BC and early imperial period. This suggests that if the sanctuary was indeed subject to a strong decline in the first century BC, it cannot have been the result of selective abandonment or closure of the sanctuary within an otherwise unaffected settlement pattern. The idea of a general crisis resonates not only with Strabo (5.4.11; 6.1.2) but also with the results of the Biferno valley project, where a drop in sites of over 40% has been documented.[49] As noted however, bias due to the poor distribution of diagnostic finds for this period might distort the picture.[50]

The relatively high site density around the sanctuary encountered in the survey gives food for thought. The Biferno valley survey, for example, only recorded a fraction of the number of sites found at S. Giovanni in Galdo (in the neighbouring area of Matrice) in the Hellenistic period (see fig. 5.28). A similar situation is found in the Roman period.[51]

[48] With one possible exception, but further research (especially excavation) is necessary to establish the character of this possible site.

[49] Barker 1995, 224.

[50] Cf. Barker 1995, esp. 215 and in general e.g. the discussion in Patterson 2006a, 17-19, with bibliography.

[51] For the Roman period, cf. Barker 1995, 216, 237 figs. 80, 91.

This contrast could be explained by the differing experimental designs applied, viz. the intensity of the survey. However, although the research area around S. Giovanni in Galdo should be extended in order to be sure, it appears that human activity as a whole was concentrated in a limited area around the sanctuary, especially if one regards the fact that the area further south and east of the sanctuary is delimited by steep slopes. The further away one sampled from the sanctuary, the less material was encountered (cf. fig. 5.6). The sanctuary seems to have functioned as a pole of attraction, or the other way around – the sanctuary was inserted into a relatively densely inhabited area. Comparison with another area surveyed in the context of the Biferno valley project is suggestive and could perhaps scale down the bias effect of different survey strategies in this discussion. At site C36, Colle Sparanise, a small Samnite sanctuary has been recognised, probably of similar dimensions as the cult place of S. Giovanni in Galdo (see fig. 5.28).[52] Around the Colle Sparanise sanctuary, a dense cluster of sites was found – similar to the density encountered at S. Giovanni in Galdo – and has been interpreted by John Lloyd and Graeme Barker as a single substantial village rather than a cluster of farmsteads.[53] This parallel perhaps supports the interpretation of this type of sanctuaries as socio-religious centres for local communities, placed at the centre, rather than at the fringes of society.

In conclusion, the sanctuary of S. Giovanni in Galdo seems to have served a local community. It is probable that this accounts for the entire period of existence of the cult place – no major discrepancies between settlement pattern and sanctuary could be noted until the third century AD, when the sanctuary was apparently abandoned. This local embedding does not exclude a priori different functions, for instance as a territorial marker, but it could suggest that this was neither its original nor principal function (and it should be noted that there is no evidence whatsoever to suggest a territorial function). The same goes for the connection to the transhumance routes crossing the landscape. A connection cannot be excluded but the sanctuary finds do not offer any evidence in this respect. In any case, the mostly regionally produced ceramics do not differ from the finds in the domestic and burial sites identified in the survey. Crucially, it should be remembered that the very idea of the connection of rural sanctuaries with transhumance or ethnic borders has been prompted by the problems associated with isolated temples in an otherwise empty landscape (Chapter 4). This presumption of isolation, which also applied to the sanctuary of S. Giovanni in Galdo, is challenged by the discovery of a village and other sites in the direct environment of the cult place during the surveys. Indeed, it is in the context of a complete and dense, if perhaps locally oriented, community that the genesis, and later the monumentalisation, of the sanctuary of S. Giovanni in Galdo has to be understood. At the time of this monumentalisation, at the turn of the second century BC, the cult place had already been in existence for about two centuries. Questions regarding who financed and built the monumental temple cannot be answered with this experimental design – only epigraphic evidence could provide conclusive information.[54] But whether the monumentalisation just before the Social War was a centrally coordinated[55] or a local initiative, the intended audience seems to have been the local community of farmers and villagers reflected in the survey data.

---

[52] Barker 1995, 49-50 with fig. 24, 192, 223.

[53] Lloyd 1991a, 182: "in figure 1, the cluster of finds around the sanctuary site C36 is provisionally interpreted as an associated village or hamlet, and in figure 5 the cluster has been treated as a single site".

[54] Apart from some characters carved into ceramic materials, neither inscriptions nor brick stamps have been found. Cf. for the sanctuary Di Niro 1978b.

[55] As suggested, for example, by Coarelli/La Regina 1984, 296-297; cf. Chapter 3.

6 Roman Sacred landscapes? The *Pagus-Vicus* System Revised

"è proprio sicuro che l'unica chiave di lettura sia quella che vede nel pagus un sistema integrato in cui convivono oppida, vici e santuari?" (Letta 1997b, 313).

This cautious question posed in 1997 by Letta, himself one of the most influential advocates of the *pagus-vicus* system, indicates a growing discomfort with the system. It can now be answered in the negative. As I show in this chapter, there are strong reasons to abandon the traditional scheme. The consequences of the 'deconstruction' of the *pagus-vicus* system are manifold. First, its ubiquitous application to sanctuaries in virtually all areas of Italy lacking strong urban development should be abandoned. The model has been used more often than not in contexts lacking actual epigraphic evidence for a *vicus* or *pagus* (let alone both), and here the problem is limited to inappropriate terminology. This is for example the case for the sanctuary of S. Giovanni in Galdo, which in the past has been seen as functioning within a *pagus-vicus* system (cf. Chapter 5). Second, there are sanctuaries in central Italy which *do* yield epigraphic evidence for the involvement of a *vicus* or a *pagus*. In these cases, the implications of the problems with the *pagus-vicus* system entail much more than mere terminology, and ultimately have important consequences for ideas on the romanisation, religious and not, of Italy.[1]

The interpretation of the function and meaning of sanctuaries within the *pagus-vicus* system relies, by definition, on the acknowledgement of this very system as the most important structure in organising the territory. I have already discussed weaknesses in the attempts to interpret sanctuaries exclusively within the *pagus-vicus* system (Chapter 4). As I pointed out, the actual evidence for a relation between *vici* and *pagi* and sanctuaries is often tenuous. These weaknesses could be demonstrated 'internally', i.e. without discarding the whole framework of the *pagus-vicus* system. In the light of recent research however, it seems possible to go further and question the validity of the *pagus-vicus* system as such for describing Italic society.

A central element in the *pagus-vicus* system is the supposed hierarchy between *pagus* and *vicus* and it is this assumption that underlies modern conceptions of the differential functions of sanctuaries in Italic society. In this way, the presence of a *vicus* could be seen to necessarily imply the presence of a *pagus* and vice-versa.[2] Recently however, two different and important studies, that by Tarpin and that by Capogrossi Colognesi, have attacked this traditional understanding of the *pagus-vicus* system.[3] They show that positive evidence for the hierarchical relationship between *pagus* and *vicus* is thin, and that *vicus* and *pagus* should probably be seen as autonomous or complementary institutions. This implies that the hierarchical relationship between overarching *pagus* sanctuaries and minor *vicus* sanctuaries is untenable.

There is, however, a more fundamental challenge to the interpretation of sanctuaries related to *pagi* or *vici*, which concerns the origin and status of these institutions. The *pagus* is traditionally considered to be an ancient, typical Italic institution that continued to exist under Roman dominion. The standard account on the *vicus* is similar, depending as it is on the traditional interpretation of the *pagus*. However, there is good reason to question their Italic origin and pre-Roman character. Although Tarpin's and Capogrossi Colognesi's conclusions on this subject are not identical (or even compatible), they agree in questioning

---

[1] See also Stek in press.
[2] See Chapter 4.
[3] Tarpin 2002; Capogrossi Colognesi 2002. Cf. also Russo 2003.

the traditional view of the nature and development of both *pagus* and *vicus*. As will become clear after an evaluation of the evidence and the arguments put forward by these scholars, both *vicus* and *pagus* can best be understood as new *Roman*, rather than Italic institutions. This revision directly affects our understanding of the role of sanctuaries and religious structures related to *pagi* and *vici*, and I will argue that it is in this way that we may get insight into the commonly underplayed impact of Roman religion in the Italian countryside. In Chapter 7, I show how these new approaches affect the interpretation of Italic sanctuaries and, in the end, the 'romanisation' of Italy, but first I discuss the debate on *pagi* and *vici*.

6.1 THE PAGUS: "DIE URITALISCHE SIEDLUNGSFORM"?

It has been noted earlier that according to Salmon (1967) the *pagus* would represent an "immemorial Italic institution".[4] This notion is part of a long tradition, indeed in 1905 Ernst Kornemann described the *pagus* as "*die uritalische Siedlungsform*".[5] This idea is common in most modern scholarship on pre-Roman Italy, where *pagi* have been recognised in central Italy from the ca. seventh to the fifth century BC.[6] Moreover, this system would have persisted as a 'substrate' for the municipal system.[7] In this way, a paradigm has been formed which basically discerns continuity from a pre-Roman *pagus* to a Romano-Italic *pagus*. Capogrossi Colognesi has shown that the origins of this paradigm can be found in the work of Adolf Schulten and can be placed in a specific historiographic tradition in Germany at the end of the 19th century, which for politico-ideological reasons did not leave room for the structural existence of the village in Italy.[8] Since it is clear that the *pagus* played a role in Roman administration in the empire (there are, for example, *pagi* attested in various provinces, such as Roman Africa),[9] a model of diachronical evolution from a pre-Roman structure to a Roman one was created.[10]

The evidence for such an early date of origin and consequent evolution is poor. In the first place, we are dealing with a Latin term and therefore basically with Roman terminology, as has been carefully acknowledged by some scholars.[11] Yet this has not prevented modern scholarship from applying this Roman term to pre-Roman Italic society, implying that the Roman term translates or reflects a pre-

---

[4] Salmon 1967, 79.

[5] Kornemann 1905, 83.

[6] E.g. Torelli 1970-1971. Cf. Chapter 4.

[7] See discussion in Chapter 4.

[8] Schulten 1894, 656-671; Kornemann 1905, 78-84; Capogrossi Colognesi 2002, esp. 117-122.

[9] For which, see Teutsch 1962; Maurin 1995.

[10] Exceptions are Rudolph 1935, 50-51 and Frederiksen 1976, 344; the latter distinguishes two parallel types of *pagi*: "And while in some cases it is clear that these *pagi* of the Roman *census* were the old tribal *pagi* taken over and transformed into part of the new system, in other cases it seems certain that the *pagi* were new institutions." Frederiksen, moreover, concludes that during the late Republic *pagi* were "grouped together to form new *municipia* or were joined to old ones, or were created afresh wherever they did not exist". He thinks that this process was already under way in the late second century BC, but was only systematised under Augustus in his procedures for census taking (p. 352).

[11] E.g. Schulten 1894, 634 on the different application of the Roman term of *pagus* on various pre-existing situations: "*Damit ist nicht gesagt dass nicht etwa pagus ein einer grösseren Gruppe von Italikern gemeinsames Wort und ein gemeinsames Landtheilungselement sein könne. So lange aber das Wort in keiner der anderen italischen Sprachen nachgewiesen ist, kennen wir den pagus nur als den römischen Flurbezirk*". Laffi 1974, 336 cautiously says: "*ampie zone dell'Italia centro-meridionale ... si presentavano strutturate secondo un sistema di insediamenti che aveva nel pagus, o meglio in quello che i Romani chiameranno pagus, la sua fondamentale unità territoriale e amministrativa*," but propagates all the same the view that the *pagus-vicus* system is basically a pre-Roman feature, parallel to the Roman municipal system. The connection with the Greek *pagos* ("hill") by Dion. Hal. *Ant. Rom.* 4.15.2 is misinformed, although deriving from the same root *pag-* "fix" as pointed out by Page in the Loeb edition of 1939.

Roman entity.[12] Actually, the ancient authors never describe the allies or independent peoples of Italy as living in *pagi*.[13] Other arguments in favour of the pre-Roman character of the *pagus* have been put forth, the validity of which will be discussed here. Arguably, the presumed age-old pre-Roman origin of the *pagus* has been constructed along three main 'threads': the early *pagi* of the archaic *Urbs*, the changing status of Capua in the Republic, and the possibly 'traditional' names of some *pagi*.

6.1.1 ROME

Literary sources point to an ancient date of origin for *pagi* in the city of Rome.[14] Dionysius of Halicarnassus attributes the institution of the *pagus* in Rome to the mythical kings Numa and Servius Tullius.[15] The historicity of his account is notoriously hard to establish and in particular to what extent the Greek author described what he observed first-hand in the late first century BC and what could possibly refer to previous realities. As a matter of fact, in this passage Dionysius quotes some of his sources (4.15.1). The late third-second century BC authors Fabius Pictor and Cato and the somewhat obscure late second century BC writer Vennonius are named as sources for the division of Rome's territory into *tribus* (which were, according to Dionysius, subdivided into *pagi*).[16] It has been argued that many of the 'Servian' institutions (the *census* and the *tribus* division, which form the *terminus post quem* of the *pagus* division) reflect fourth century BC ideological constructions.[17] In Dionysius, the central role of the *pagi* is administrative, they are subordinate to the regulation of citizens and the collection of taxes and the festival of the *Paganalia* is portrayed as a consequence of this function.[18] The importance of *pagi* for taking the *census*, however, seems best documented from the Augustan age onwards.[19] Nonetheless, it might seem reasonable to conclude with Charlotte Schubert that, on the basis of Dionyius' sources, the connection between *pagus* and some form of territorial organisation must date to at least the second century BC.[20] In any case, the first epigraphic evidence from *pagi* in Rome is dated to the end of the second, early first centuries BC.[21]

---

[12] Cf. on the connection with the Oscan *touto*, e.g. Letta 1994; Letta 1997b, 313: "*si può riconoscere un nesso tra la touta italica … e il pagus attestato in queste aree in età romana?*".

[13] Tarpin 2002, 37.

[14] These *pagi* would, apparently, to some represent a later development of the "*pagus der Urzeit*"; Kornemann 1905, 82: "*Dem pagus der Urzeit stehen noch näher manche pagi bei den italischen Bergvölkern des Innern, wo sie noch nicht zu Flurbezirken von Städten, wie in Gegenden mit einer stärker fortgeschrittenen Entwicklung, z. B. in Latium, herabgesunken sind, sondern noch neben den Stadtgemeinden in einer gewissen Selbständigkeit sich erhalten haben.*"

[15] Dion Hal. *Ant. Rom.* 2.76.1, 4.14-15. The relevant texts are treated in the discussion on the installation of the *Paganalia*, Chapter 8.

[16] Dionysius cites Fabius Pictor, Vennonius and Cato for the new division in *tribus* (4.15.1) and Piso (4.15.5) for the installation of a city register which is paralleled with the function he ascribes to the *Paganalia*. However, he never refers directly to these sources writing on *pagi*. According to Frederiksen 1976, 345, "Dionysius seems here to be combining information taken from some antiquarian source with other items deriving from his own observation or contemporary knowledge". He continues, however: "Of course, the *pagi* had for centuries had religious functions."

[17] Humm 2001.

[18] Cf. the discussion in Chapter 8.

[19] Schubert 1996, 99-100.

[20] Schubert 1996, 100.

[21] *CIL* VI, 2219 and 2220.

6.1.2 CAPUA

An often cited argument in favour of the pre-Roman nature of the *pagus* concerns Capua. An inscription found in the area documents a decree of the *pagus Herculaneus*.[22] The inscription mentions magistrates of Jupiter Compagus and includes a consular date of 94 BC. According to the decree, the *magistri* are allowed to spend their money not, as was usual, on games, but on the restoration of a *porticus pagana*. As a reward the *magistri* are allowed to take their seats in the theatre at the games "as if they had given the games".

The *pagus* dates to the period before the Social War, a period in which Capua had no city rights. Capua, *civitas sine suffragio* since 338 BC,[23] had been punished by the Romans after their defection in the Hannibalic War. After its recapture in 211 BC senators were executed, people sold in slavery and Capua was deprived of its city status (Liv. 26.16). According to some authors, notably Ernst Kornemann and Jacques Heurgon, the epigraphically attested *pagus* would thus betray a 'relapse' of Capua to an ancient and pre-existing tribal *pagus* structure as a consequence of the Roman punishments.[24] However, as Martin Frederiksen has pointed out, the terminology of the inscription seems quite Roman, especially the consular dating. He concludes that this *pagus* may well be a result of "the Roman *census*, for we know that in 189 BC the Campani were included in the Roman *census* and subjected directly to the censors from Rome (Liv. 38.28.4)".[25] Indeed, the appearance of the *pagus Herculaneus* in this context seems to make much more sense in terms of Roman control rather than as the re-emergence of a putative tribal Italic institution in Campania which had been urbanised as early as the eighth century BC.[26]

6.1.3 PRE-ROMAN NAMES OF PAGI

Yet another argument that has often been put forth in favour of a pre-Roman origin of the *pagus* is the appearance of names of *pagi* that apparently originate in indigenous, pre-Roman contexts. For Schulten this was indeed decisive for recognising a pre-Roman origin for the *pagus*.[27] It is true that in some texts listing a number of *pagi*, the *tabulae alimentariae* of Beneventum in Hirpinic territory and of Veleia in

---

[22] *CIL* X, 3772. The inscription could belong to Capua, but also to Calatia: cf. Guadagno 1993, 409 n. 46.

[23] Liv. 8.14.10; Vell. Pat. 1.14.3.

[24] So e.g. Kornemann 1905, 81-82: "*Die unterste administrative Einheit ist auf italischem Boden in der vorstädtischen Zeit der pagus. Wenn später in der Epoche der Städte Rom einer italischen Gemeinde das Stadtrecht entzieht, wie z. B. Capua im hannibalischen Krieg, so treten die pagi wieder zu Tage und übernehmen ... die Pflichten der städtischen Verwaltung*"; Heurgon 1942, 117-118, speaking of "*les instincts plus profonds des populations*". Cf. discussion in Frederiksen 1976, 350-351 and Tarpin 2002, 40-43. Capogrossi Colognesi 2002, 162-163 demonstrates that Heurgon and Kornemann reflect a tradition presupposing some sort of inborn Italic propensity to revert to rurality, linked to the idea that all that is urban must be Roman.

[25] Frederiksen 1976, 351.

[26] Rudolph 1935, 51; Frederiksen 1976, 351; Frederiksen 1984, 266-268; Pobjoy 1998, esp. questioning the Oscan character of Capuan administration; Tarpin 2002, 40-43. Heurgon's argument indeed relies on the premise that there was a *pagus-vicus* system before the urbanisation of Capua, evidence for which is absent, or it should have been imported by the Samnites when they took Capua in 423 BC (Liv. 4.37.1). However, it is only generically said by Strabo (5.4.12) that the Samnites live *komedon*. As Capogrossi Colognesi 2002, 163 points out, this is to be translated with *vicatim*, not *pagatim* (cf. discussion *infra*). Heurgon therefore had to assume that a *vicus* implies the presence of a *pagus*...

[27] Schulten 1894, 632, on the fact that "*auch in den mittelitalischen Landschaften die römischen Inschriften pagi nennen. Diese Thatsache allein würde nun nichts beweisen, da die pagi mit der Anlage der römischen Colonien oder (seit 90) mit der Verwandlung der unterthänigen Orte in Municipien erst geschaffen sein könnten; aber entscheidend sind die Namen der pagi, welche uns die Alimentartafel von Veleia kennen lernt, und die zum guten Theile unrömisch sind*".

Liguria, pre-Roman names are present.[28] In particular, those from Veleia would prove the pre-Roman date of these *pagi*.[29] However, in these documents of Trajanic date only a very small number of *pagi* have such a name. In Beneventum only the *pagus Meflanus* seems to reflect a really non-Latin name.[30] In Veleia most *pagi* seem to bear gentilicial (*Domitius, Iulius, Valerius*, etc.) or theophoric names (*Apollinaris, Cerealis, Dianius, Venerius, Martius, Iunonius, Mercurialis*, etc.).[31] In the end, only three *pagi* seem to bear real indigenous names, *Eboreus, Moninas*, and *Luras*.[32]

Similarly, at Volcei, Ulubrae and Beneventum there are mostly localities and Latin gentilicial names and Roman theophoric names.[33] Whether there are many or not (and there are not, as we see), in principle pre-Roman *names* of *pagi* cannot attest to a pre-Roman *origin* because they might simply have been applied later to new institutions, which is in fact a rather common phenomenon in toponomy.[34] In conclusion, in Capogrossi's words: "*Quanto all'onomastica autoctona di certi pagi sembra abbastanza evidente che, in sé, un nome indigeno non possa attestare la preesistenza del pagus in quanto tale. A maggior ragione se immaginato come una precisa struttura costituente di una unità etnico-politica. Esso può semplicemente richiamare una preesistenza di popolazioni e di insediamenti, non anche la loro forma specifica.*"[35] What's in a name: in any case not the proof for a pre-Roman *pagus*.

6.2 THE PAGUS: A ROMAN INVENTION?

If Dionysius of Halicarnassus is to be trusted when he quotes his sources we may assume that the first *pagi* in the city of Rome have a second century BC *terminus ante quem*.[36] It is even harder to date the appearance of the *pagus* in the rest of Italy. Asides from the arguments just discussed, the traditional assumption of an early 'Sabellian' or 'Samnite' *pagus* rests on some indications given by the ancient authors. Literary sources are not very detailed due to a general lack of interest in the Italian countryside,[37] but ancient authors describe the settlement pattern of rural Italy as *vicatim* (most famously Livy 9.13.7), or as organised in *komai* or *komedon* according to the often quoted expression by Strabo 5.4.11 and 12.[38] However, *vicatim* (and *komedon*) cannot be equalled with *pagatim*. This would only be possible if one assumes a fixed hierarchical relation between *pagus* and *vicus* and this cannot be proven for central Italy.[39] So even if these early imperial definitions of territorial structures were applicable to earlier periods, this would attest to the existence of *vici*, not *pagi* in the Italian countryside.

As to the epigraphic evidence, there are few early mentions of *pagi*, besides the Capuan inscription from 94 BC. The only other examples of inscriptions mentioning a *pagus* in Italy dated before the Social

---

[28] *CIL* XI, 1147; *CIL* IX, 1455.

[29] Schulten 1894, 632-633; cf. *supra* n. 27.

[30] Veyne 1957, 92.

[31] *CIL* XI 1147; Veyne 1957, 91-93; Frederiksen 1976, 344. Only the *pagus Bagiennus* seems to take its name from the Celtic background but the first may refer to the city of Augusta Bagiennorum: Tarpin 2002, 38.

[32] Petracco Sicardi 1969, 215; cf. discussion in Tarpin 2002, 38.

[33] Frederiksen 1976, 344.

[34] Possibly, pre-Roman names are indicative in some way, but of what precisely is hard to say: Capogrossi Colognesi 2002, 180: "*al massimo qualche nome preromano di un pagus può aprirci qualche scorcio su realtà preromane*"; cf. also Tarpin 2002, 230 on a "*fond indigène encore vivace*" on which *pagi* were superposed.

[35] Capogrossi Colognesi 2002, 217.

[36] As does Schubert 1996, 100; cf. *supra*. In any case *CIL* VI, 2219 and 2220 attest to *pagi* at the end of the second / beginning of the first centuries BC (cf. e.g. Nonnis 2003, 40).

[37] Except in poetry: cf. esp. Chapter 8.

[38] But Strabo's point in 5.4.11 is precisely to indicate the way in which Roman intervention had altered the countryside, from wealth and urbanity to village-like structures! Capogrossi Colognesi 2002, 170.

[39] Capogrossi Colognesi 2002, 170. Cf. also *infra*.

War come from Ariminum (second half of the third century BC) and Cupra montana (second century BC).[40] In this context, Tarpin points out that Capua was under Roman control (cf. *supra*), Ariminum was a Latin colony and Cupra montana was located on *ager Romanus*. On the basis of the epigraphic evidence, he therefore concludes that it is difficult to consider the *pagus* as an Italic 'indigenous' structure.[41] After the Social War the *pagus* appears more often in Italy, which is by then wholly under Roman control. This cannot be explained merely as a result of an increase in the number of inscriptions. The conclusion seems, therefore, almost inescapable: the *pagus* is a corollary of Roman territorial control.[42] Although one may allow for some pre-Roman echoes in the Roman *pagi*, especially in the nomenclature,[43] convincing evidence for a pre-Roman origin or continuity into the Roman period is absent. It is, however, only from the reorganisation of the *census* by Augustus onwards that the *pagus* surfaces frequently in the official record. From then on references to *pagi* are often found in financial contexts.[44] Lands are now indicated by their location within certain *pagi* and the process of municipalisation seems to run synchronous with the division *per pagos*, even if the borders of the *pagi* do not always correspond with the municipal borders.[45]

In sum, the evidence suggests that the *pagus* was mainly devised as an instrument of Roman control in order to administrate people and property.[46] *Pagi* existed in Italy at least from the second half of the third century BC onwards (in the Latin colony of Ariminum), but their financial and administrative function can be clearly distinguished only from the time of the Augustan reforms onwards. The *pagus* was thus surely a rural structure in Italy (cf. also Chapter 4), but it depended on Roman and urban forms of government.[47]

6.3 THE PRE-ROMAN OR ROMAN VICUS

Traditionally, *vici* are considered to have formed an integral part of pre-Roman society, as single hamlets or clusters of hamlets located within the territorial district of the *pagus*. Three types of evidence have been evoked to demonstrate the pre-Roman origin and character of the *vicus*.[48] To begin with, inscriptions mentioning *vici* dating as early as the third century BC have been found in central Italy. While I refer to inscriptions in this section, a more detailed discussion is offered in Chapter 7. Second, the literary sources. These are, as opposed to references to the *pagus*, rather explicit, but at the same time enigmatic. The principal text is the damaged *lemma* by Festus (502, 508 L). The text seems to indicate that the *vicus* was the typical mode of settlement in the backward areas of the Marsi and Paeligni. This specific Italic location seems to point to the pre-Roman, Italic origin of the *vicus*. The third type of evidence, namely material remains, does not contribute to the debate.

---

[40] *CIL* I², 2897a and b; *CIL* IX, 5699. Cf. discussion in Chapter 7.
[41] Tarpin 2002, 39-40.
[42] Tarpin 2002, e.g. 40. Similarly Capogrossi Colognesi 2002.
[43] Cf. *supra* n. 34. There is a tendency to admit some pre-Roman reflections in the Roman *pagi*. Frederiksen 1984, 47 n. 22 states that the seven *pagi* of Nola "are probably Roman creations for administrative purposes, but probably reflect pre-existing settlement patterns to a certain extent". Capogrossi Colognesi 2002, 180 thinks that the pre-Roman names of *pagi* are in some way testimony of pre-Roman situations. Cf. Tarpin 2002, esp. 220-232 for the idea that marginal groups could express themselves "*à travers le pagus*" in the course of the process of statutory redefinition.
[44] Frederiksen 1976, 345-347; Capogrossi 2002, 198-203.
[45] Capogrossi Colognesi 2002, 203.
[46] Tarpin 2002, 190-193.
[47] Capogrossi Colognesi 2002, 227: "*appare abbastanza evidente la fisionomia del pagus come un sistema insediativo di carattere rurale in rapporto di subordinazione funzionale con l'assetto municipale romano.*"
[48] In addition to the ubiquitous but confusing interference with the *pagus* (according to the false logic *pagus* implies *vicus* and viceversa, cf. *infra*).

6.3.1 ARCHAEOLOGY

The presence of both pre-Roman and Roman village-like settlements or clusters of settlements – omnipresent in Italic archaeology – have induced researchers to generically term them *vici*, even in the absence of epigraphic or other evidence justifying such a specific identification. This has resulted in the situation that a clustered settlement that is not an *oppidum* is, in archaeological and ancient historical jargon, recognised as a *vicus*.[49] Obviously, archaeology is sometimes able to distinguish different types of settlement, with different sizes and perhaps functions, but is by definition not able to recognise the statutory or juridical status of such a settlement.[50] Once it is admitted that the term *vicus* relates to something more precise than, generically, 'village', archaeological evidence can neither prove nor falsify the existence of a *vicus* and is thus omitted from this discussion.

6.3.2 LITERARY SOURCES: FESTUS 502-508L

Festus' statement in his *de verborum significatu* on the Marsic and Paelignian *vici* presents an extremely difficult passage because it is fragmented and the topic is hotly debated in various studies.[51] I therefore point out some of the problems resulting from the interpretation of this text, in particular noting the consequences they could have for ideas on the origin of the *vicus*.

The text reads, in Lindsay's edition of 1913:

> (502 L) <vici> ... cipiunt ex agris, qui ibi villas non habent, ut Marsi aut Peligni. Sed ex vic[t]is partim habent rempublicam et ius dicitur, partim nihil eorum et tamen ibi nundinae aguntur negoti gerendi causa, et magistri vici, item magistri pagi quotannis fiunt. Altero, cum id genus aedificio<rum defi>nitur, quae continentia sunt his oppidis, quae ... itineribus regionibusque distributa inter se distant, nominibusque dissimilibus discriminis causa (508 L) sunt dispartita. Tertio, cum id genus aedificiorum definitur, quae in oppido privi in suo quisque loco proprio ita aedifica<n>t, ut in eo aedificio pervium sit, quo itinere habitatores ad suam quisque habitationem habeant accessum. Qui non dicuntur vicani, sicut hi, qui aut in oppidi vicis, aut hi, qui in agris sint vicani apellantur.

Apparently, three types of *vici* are envisaged, one rural, one (peri-)urban,[52] and one as a certain type of urban building. The first part on the 'rural *vicus*' is of most interest here. In Festus' passage there seems to be a division between land use oriented towards *villa*-type settlements and land use oriented towards *vicus*-type settlements, the last of which would be typical for the Marsi and Paeligni.

vici appellari incipiunt?
According to Mueller's integration (371), based on codex Vaticanus Latinus 3369,[53] we should read the beginning as <*vici appellari in*>*cipiunt*; in other words, "one starts calling *vici* the settlements in those areas which have no *villae*, such as amongst the Marsi and the Paeligni". With this chronological interpreta-

---

[49] This application is ubiquitous. Cf. e.g. the *CIL* volumes or the *Forma Italiae* series (e.g. Van Wonterghem 1984; De Felice 1994).

[50] Cf. the considerations in Capogrossi Colognesi 2002, 176-182 and in Tarpin 1999.

[51] See Letta 2005a; Todisco 2006. For an overview of the literary sources, cf. (besides Tarpin 2002 and Capogrossi Colognesi 2002) Curchin 1985.

[52] Cf. the emendation by Todisco 2006, 610: *quae continentia sunt his oppidis quae [eis finiuntur]*: "che si sviluppano in continuità a queste città che li assumono come confini"; cf. Letta 2005a, 93.

[53] Mueller 1839.

tion of >*cipiunt*, the conception of an ancient rural *vicus* as opposed to urban ones is confirmed.[54] Torelli, for instance, uses this interpretation of Festus in arguing for a watershed between landscapes organised according to the *villa*, and those according to the *pagus-vicus* system, which he calls the "world of non-cities" (cf. Chapter 1).[55]

Tarpin accepts Mueller's reading but not the traditional interpretation.[56] According to him, Festus' indication of the territories of the Marsi and Paeligni as the first regions where the *vicus* appeared could be nothing more than a general stereotype of these peoples as being culturally backward. The fact that *vici* would have appeared here first is no evidence for their indigenous origin. It may be in this area that the first *vici* were conceptualised as such because of special circumstances.[57] Furthermore, the opposition between a landscape with *villae* and a village landscape, which has been followed to an extent by modern scholars, can certainly not be accepted at face value and has proven to be over-simplistic. More specifically, the *vicus* appears quite often in combination with the *villa* and Varro's assertion that the *vicus* served as a provisioning centre for *villae* would point to an interdependency between *vicus* and *villa*.[58]

It is, however, possible to reconstruct the first line of the *lemma* differently. The codex Vaticanus Latinus 3369 does not form an independent tradition but is rather a tentative reconstruction of the mutilated principal Farnesian codex and Mueller's integration based on Vat.Lat. 3369 is therefore actually nothing more than an educated guess.[59] Alternatively, Elisabetta Todisco and Letta have (independently) recently proposed this reading, *[Vicus ter modis intelligetur. Uno, cum id genus aedificiorum definitur ad quae se re]cipiunt ex agris, qui ibi villas non habent* etc., which eliminates the 'chronological' value of *incipiunt* in favour of a verb of movement ("that type of buildings where those who have no villas congregate coming from the fields").[60] In this reading, the Marsi and Paeligni would still function as a mere example of backwardness but not necessarily indicate an ancient local (and indeed pre-Roman) origin. Both the interpretation of the traditional Muellerian text by Tarpin and the new reconstruction of the first phrase by Todisco and Letta would thus weaken the momentum of Festus as an argument for the pre-Roman character of the *vicus*.

Different integrations and subsequent interpretations: the place of the pagus *in Festus*
Since Festus mentions *magistri pagi* it has seemed plausible to some authors that somehow *pagi* originally formed part of Festus' *lemma* on *vici*. In his discussion of the relationship between *pagus* and *vicus*, Capogrossi Colognesi suggests that at the mutilated beginning of the *lemma pagi* were possibly mentioned as the unit containing the *villae*.[61] This reconstruction would imply a dichotomy between *pagus* and *vicus* landscapes, the first corresponding to a new Roman 'economic' land use based on the *villa*, the second to a more 'traditional' pattern of small villages economically based on, one supposes, mixed farming and pastoralism.

The notion that *vici* and *pagi* were possibly complementary has been examined by some authors who point to the regional diversity in the distribution of *pagi* and *vici*. Letta has underscored that the Marsi did not have *pagi* at all, whereas the Paelignian territory has not yielded even one *vicus*[62] and Tarpin has demonstrated an uneven distribution of *pagi* and *vici* for Germania.[63]

---

[54] Cf. Tarpin 2002, 55.
[55] Torelli 1995, 10: "The hill-fort fortified enclosures, the small farm scattered in the countryside ... , and the series of country sanctuaries perform the functions otherwise and elsewhere performed by the city. As a consequence, the rural villas for agricultural production are completely absent, as indeed is noted by the ancient sources [citing Festus]."
[56] Tarpin 2002, 53-54, 82.
[57] Tarpin 2002, 62, 82-83; cf. *infra*, and on these circumstances see Chapter 7.
[58] Varro, *Rust.* 1.16.4; Tarpin 2002, 55.
[59] Cf. Lindsay 1913, xi-xviii; Letta 2005a, esp. 81; Todisco 2006, 606 n. 4.
[60] Todisco 2006, 607-608; similarly Letta 2005a, 83.
[61] Capogrossi Colognesi 2002, 190.
[62] Letta 1993; cf. also Guadagno 1993.
[63] Tarpin 1993.

In a recent contribution to the debate, Letta has proposed yet another reading of Festus' *lemma*. His reconstruction results in a similar distinction, not between *pagi* and *vici* landscapes, but rather between landscapes made up of *pagi* and *vici* and landscapes exclusively provided with *vici*. As noted, Letta comes to a solution equivalent to Todisco's for the initial phrase of the *lemma*, but he is ready to reconstruct and re-order more of the remaining text. Letta emphasises the apparent distinction between two different types of rural *vici* in the *lemma*, one with and one without *respublica*. According to him, these would correspond respectively to *vici* with their own *magistri vici*, and those without their own *magistri*, consequently supervised by *magistri pagi*.[64] In sum, this would mean that some areas contained only *vici* and other areas *vici* within *pagi*.

The role of the *pagus*, and especially the contingent idea of 'dichotomised' landscapes suggested in different ways by Capogrossi Colognesi and Letta, must remain hypothetical as far as regards Festus' text. However, the important implication would be that whereas *pagi* relate to a new 'Roman' organisation, autonomous *vici* could indeed be seen as 'non-Roman' indigenous elements. In conclusion, the interpretation of the principal literary source offers different ideas on the character of the *vicus*. Beyond the distinction between an 'urban' and a 'rural' *vicus*, two alternative views could be elaborated, one that seeks to underscore the character of the *vicus* as a typical traditional Italic phenomenon and another that connects its invention to Roman times and influence. The elaboration of these different strands will now be outlined and evaluated.

6.3.3 THE VICUS AS AN 'ANTI-URBAN' AND NON-ROMAN INSTITUTION (CAPOGROSSI COLOGNESI)

Capogrossi Colognesi emphatically leaves open the possibility that the institution of the *pagus* formed an alternative settlement system with respect to the *vicus*, arguing that the presence of one would be at the cost of the other (which would also explain the scarcity of inscriptions mentioning both *pagus* and *vicus*).[65] This view enables the detachment of the origin of the *vicus* from that of the *pagus*. In this way, Capogrossi Colognesi raises the possibility that *vici* were actually pre-Roman in origin but consequently took on functions similar to those of the Roman *pagus* for administrative purposes. This idea has also been developed for other regions outside of Italy.

In his study on Roman Spain, Leonard Curchin argues that *vici* appeared in the "relatively unromanised zones of central, western and northwestern Iberia – none in Baetica or in eastern Spain – and that most of them bear non-Latin names", which according to him indicates that they were indigenous centres which may have existed since pre-Roman times.[66] Interestingly, according to Curchin, *pagi* were located "almost exclusively in the highly romanised province of Baetica", and always in areas where the agrarian space was regulated firmly, linked to the large-scale production of olive oil and the presence of colonies.[67] Moreover, *pagi* would bear, as opposed to the *vici*, largely Latin names (*Augustus*, *Suburbanus*), indicating at times the town to which the *pagus* was attributed and sometimes a topographical or functional indication, e.g. *pagus Carbulensis*

---

[64] Letta 2005a, 89: "*Si potrebbe pensare che la parte finale, con la menzione dei magistri vici e dei magistri pagi, intendesse riprendere la bipartizione iniziale tra vici con respublica e vici che ne sono privi, per precisare che, mentre i primi eleggevano ogni anno dei propri magistrati (magistri vici), gli altri, non avendone di propri, facevano capo ai magistri pagi, cioè ai magistri eletti dalla popolazione di un distretto rurale più ampio in cui era compreso il vicus.*" His translation of Festus' first *vicus* type would be (97-96): "*I vici possono intendersi in tre modi diversi. S'intendono nel primo modo quando così si definisce quel tipo di edifici in cui si ritirano di ritorno dai campi coloro che non hanno fattorie nei campi stessi, come i Marsi o i Peligni. Ma tra questi vici alcuni hanno proprie istituzioni e in essi si amministra la giustizia, altri non hanno nulla di tutto questo, tuttavia in essi si tengono giorni di mercato per esercitare il commercio, e come (negli uni) si eleggono ogni anno dei magistri del vicus, allo stesso modo (negli altri) si eleggono quelli del pagus.*"

[65] Capogrossi Colognesi 2002, e.g. 190; cf. Tarpin 1993.

[66] Generally: Curchin 1985; Curchin 1991, 124 (quote).

[67] Curchin 1991, 125.

(Carbula), *pagus rivi Larensis* (river Larensis), *pagus Marmorarius* (from an area with marble quarries).[68] Thus, according to Curchin, in Spain *pagi* would evidently be a creation of the Roman administration, whereas *vici* would "perpetuate pre-Roman villages".[69] This idea of dichotomisation between rural and perhaps more autonomous, indigenous *vici* versus Roman *pagi* would be confirmed by Curchin's observation that "*vici* are most often attested making religious dedications to indigenous gods, a function unrecorded for the *pagi*".[70]

Similarly, Capogrossi Colognesi sees the Italian *vici* as essentially non-Roman. The line of his argument unfolds along the general evolution of the village in the long term, from pre-Roman times to the medieval period. In the first place, Capogrossi Colognesi holds that the village was already important in the pre-Roman period. Subsequently, in the Roman period, the *vicus* would have constituted an 'alternative' to the city-based settlement pattern. He argues that since the Romans ultimately did not want to stimulate a village-like pattern of settlement, but rather an urban way of life, they did not organise the countryside according to *vici*, but according to the municipal system.[71] Aside from some *vici* that happened to be favoured by the new Roman pattern of settlement, for example along roads, *vici* would have been "*più tollerati che ulteriormente valorizzati*".[72] The structure of pre-existing villages would thus survive despite of, rather than thanks to, the Roman settlement organisation. It is in this way that the *vicus* appears to take on a slumbering existence during the Roman period, only to re-emerge in the medieval period, for it would be the "*duplice aspetto – il radicamento preromano e la sua estraneità o marginalità al modello 'urbanocentrico' romano*"[73] that explains the revival of the *vicus* exactly in the period that Roman control waned and hierarchical city-countryside relations deteriorated. This would also account for the apparently considerable level of self-government in *vici*.[74] The other way around, therefore, according to this logic the *pagus* was doomed to go under together with the municipal system on which it depended.[75]

6.3.4 THE VICUS AS A ROMAN, URBAN FEATURE (TARPIN)

A radically different approach to the *vicus* has been developed by Tarpin. This approach does not depart from the village as a structure, but rather from the institutional status of *vicus*. Apart from the problematic *lemma* by Festus, epigraphic evidence seems to be most authoritative with regard to this issue. In the territory of the Marsi, around the Fucine lake (*lacus Fucinus*) inscriptions mentioning *vici* can be dated as early as the end of the third century BC (for a detailed discussion see Chapter 7). At first this would seem a corroboration of Festus' text, or indeed an 'Italic' origin.

Tarpin however argues that as a basically Roman word,[76] the *vicus* was also a Roman institution.[77] The *vicus*-communities at the Fucine lake would not have been Marsic groups but rather groups of Latin or

---

[68] Curchin 1985, 338-342 (with previous bibliography).

[69] Curchin 1985, 342-343.

[70] Curchin 1985, 343. The religious role of *vici* and *pagi* will be discussed in detail in Chapters 7-9.

[71] Sometimes *vici* were upgraded to *municipia*; Capogrossi Colognesi 2002, 229.

[72] Capogrossi Colognesi 2002, 231.

[73] Capogrossi Colognesi 2002, 232; similarly, e.g., Volpe 1996, 146.

[74] Capogrossi Colognesi 2002, 228-230. The territorial role of *vici* is far less certain than that of *pagi* because it is not clear what their authority was over the surrounding countryside Cf. *Cod. Justin.* 6.25.9.1 for the category of *vici qui proprios fines habent*, cf. Tarpin 2002, 262-263.

[75] Capogrossi Colognesi 2002, 235.

[76] *Vicus* can etymologically be related to the form *wik or *weik, and stems from the same family as the Greek *oikos* and can be interpreted to have designated 'units of several families', between Latin *domus* and *gens* (Tarpin 2002, 11-14). It is in origin Indo-European but is not attested in the Osco-Umbran languages (contra Devoto; cf. Tarpin 2002, 10, 57), with the possible exception of a *vukes sestines* (Rix 2002, Um 31). Therefore, *vicus* seems.

[77] An additional argument is that *vicus* apparently designates a 'community' as well as the structure of a village (as becomes clear from dedications in the name of the *vicus*

Roman citizens.[78] The names, arguably of 'Sabellian' origin, are written down according to Latin norms and Tarpin also sees the appearance of magistracies such as *quaestor* as an indication of Roman administration, not as the local adaptation of Roman examples.[79] Tarpin connects the difference between the Paelignian and Marsic territories – the first yielding no *vici*, but *pagi*, the latter *vici*, but no *pagi* – to the different relationships these peoples had with the Romans. Whereas the Marsi would have been befriended and supplied troops for Rome in 225 BC, the Paeligni did not, and their community had been incorporated since 305 BC.[80]

In light of the date and location of the epigraphic evidence, a Roman origin of the *vicus* could well be defended. Moreover, Tarpin links the location of *vici*, often along roads and in the neighbourhood of colonies and therefore in Roman territory, to the identification of *vici* as groups of Roman or Latin citizens.[81] In other words, *vici* would constitute a general term for non-founded agglomerations of Roman citizens without proper jurisdiction.[82] This leads Tarpin to another tentative interpretation of Festus' *lemma* (in the Muellerian reading) arguing that the words *incipiunt appellari* could be understood as '*vici* are for the first time named as such in the territories of the Marsi and the Paeligni', whereas in other regions other names existed for the same or a similar institution (such as *forum* or *conciliabulum*). Tarpin observes that there are no *fora* and *conciliabula* attested in Marsic territory, which in his view proves the equivalence of the terms.[83] The specific situation of the Fucine area, lacking major roads, would explain the application of the 'urban' term *vicus* for a group of citizens instead of *forum* or *conciliabulum*, which would have instead been linked to viritane colonisation and road construction.[84]

According to Tarpin, the question is not so much one of traditional Italic patterns of settlement but rather one of Roman legal vocabulary. Rather than envisaging a development from rural to urban *vici*, Tarpin concludes that "*il est sans doute plus simple de retourner le discours traditionnel et de penser que l'on a dupliqué hors de Rome la structure fondamentale de la ville*".[85]

In conclusion, Tarpin sees *vici* as a corollary of Roman control and urban development. Importantly, he underlines the specific *urban* connotation the *vicus* had, as opposed to the 'rural' or non-urban *pagus*. The evidence for *vici* in the context of colonies can be seen to fit into this scheme. Supposing that the division of the city in colonies copied the division of the city of Rome, inscriptions mentioning *vici* found in colonies (for example in Ariminum and Cales) would refer to the urban centres of these colonies and not to villages in the territory.[86] Burgeoning from this urban situation, it is possible that over time the originally urban term was also applied more widely to groups of citizens outside the walls. The case of the *coloni Caedicianei*, who were located in a *vicus* outside Sinuessa, would illustrate the meaning of *vicus* as an indication of an agglomeration outside, but dependent on, the colony. As Tarpin puts it, "*un morceau de ville à la campagne*."[87]

– instead of the *vicani* - cf. e.g. Todisco 2004a). According to Tarpin 2002, 57) this meaning is at odds with the idea of an 'indigenous' Marsic *vicus*. In this view, the appearance of *vici* would indicate the falling apart of the Marsic community into different groups at time when other evidence seems to point to a growing tribal cohesion (exemplified by the communal coinage).

[78] Tarpin 2002, 57.
[79] Tarpin 2002, 57; *contra* Letta, cf. Chapter 7 for detailed discussion.
[80] Tarpin 2002, 59-61. Cf. Chapter 7.
[81] Tarpin 2002, esp. 83-86.
[82] Tarpin 2002, 72-81.
[83] Tarpin 2002, 82-83.
[84] Tarpin 2002, 85.
[85] Tarpin 2002, 83, 85 (quote).
[86] Torelli 1990; Tarpin 2002, 63; 243. This and other views are discussed in more detail in the section on the character of early colonial settlement in Chapter 7.
[87] Plin. *HN* 14.62 with *CIL* X, 4727 (= *CIL* I², 1578); Tarpin 2002, 243 (quote); 70-72.

6.3.5 EVALUATION I: THE VICUS AS A ROMAN, URBAN FEATURE

It is important to briefly evaluate the strengths and weaknesses of the views of Capogrossi Colognesi and Letta on the one hand and Tarpin on the other. As Tarpin shows, it seems fairly plausible that the term *vicus* was indeed applied within specifically Roman contexts, as opposed to indigenous pre-Roman contexts. While I am inclined to follow the main lines of his argument, his thesis has far-reaching implications for the interpretation of Roman influence in Italy in general, and, in this study, the role of sanctuaries in particular. Therefore, it is important to point out that not all arguments are equally strong or unambiguous. In fact, some of the evidence could be read differently.[88] Several arguments (especially the use of Latin, titles, onomastics) could be re-interpreted to reach different and contradictory conclusions.

The relationship between the Marsi and Romans, which according to Tarpin was good, is an example. The implication that *vici* were placed more on 'friendly' territory than otherwise is not self-evident. Colonies for instance were not exclusively placed in the territory of befriended groups either, and sometimes the opposite is true.[89] Moreover, the relationship between Marsi and Romans has been described as anything but friendly by other authors.[90] We may therefore have to account for different processes behind the installation of *vici* as well. Also the view that confiscated enemy territory (here that of the Paeligni) was more apt to be divided into *pagi* needs more elaboration. Ultimately, the character of pre-existing relationships between indigenous groups and Rome is perhaps too difficult to establish in these cases in order to use it as an independent argument in the present discussion.

Perhaps the most crucial point is the use of Latin onomastics and titles. Tarpin interprets the appearance of a *quaestor* as an indication of Roman presence. However, even if the debate on the origins of such titles is very complex, it is important to point out that an opposite argument could be, and has been, based on the same evidence, i.e. that these magistracies were local adaptations to Roman examples, or even just reflect the adoption of the Roman title without necessarily the corresponding functions, resulting in 'self-romanisation' at various levels.[91]

In conclusion, different perspectives lead to rather different interpretations of the same evidence. I believe these perspectives are ultimately determined by basic assumptions on the character of Roman control in Italy, and the view adopted on romanisation processes. Even if, like Tarpin, one argues for a Roman origin for the institution of the *vicus*, it is still questionable whether the *vicus*-structure was imposed 'from above', involving only Roman or Latin citizens or that this title was adopted or even sought after by the indigenous population that became enfranchised in the process.[92]

6.3.6 EVALUATION II: THE VICUS AS AN 'ANTI-URBAN' AND NON-ROMAN INSTITUTION

Let us consider the opposite view, which sees the *vicus* as a rural structure developing away from Roman influence. It may be clear that the picture that arises from the Spanish situation is (at least in some way)

---

[88] For example, it does not automatically follow that the apparent designation of a community with the word *vicus* runs counter to the formation or existence of a larger tribal community (Tarpin 2002, 57; cf. here n. 77): the existence of 'layered' group identities is a well-known phenomenon. Furthermore, there is no consensus on the status of the territory of Aveia as *civitas sine suffragio*, as Tarpin himself admits (Tarpin 2002, 58 n. 21) which would undermine the argument that the *vicus* was on Roman territory. On the appearance of the Roman goddess Victoria cf. Chapters 3 and esp. 7.

[89] Cf. e.g. Coarelli 1992.

[90] Letta 1972; cf. Tarpin 2002, 59-61.

[91] As in Letta/D'Amato 1975 no. 128 = *CIL* IX, 3849 (= *CIL* I², 388); see the discussion in Chapter 7.

[92] Cf. the remarks by Curchin 2005.

the exact opposite of what has been argued for the Marsic *vici*, whose appearance has been explained by the relatively early romanisation and friendly relationship with Rome. In the first place, it should be noted that it is not at all self-evident that the application or significance of the terms *vicus* and *pagus* were identical throughout the empire, as Curchin rightly stresses,[93] and indeed the contrary would seem to be true.

In any case, in Spain there could be circumstances which would soften the sharpness of the dichotomy between the rural pre-Roman *vicus* and urbanised Roman *pagus*. For instance, at least one *vicus* demonstrably directly depends on a larger town, Clunia[94] and although the etymology of the names may be largely indigenous, it would be equally possible to stress the 'Romanness' of many inscriptions. With regard to the venerated deities, for example, it is in the first place noticeable that more dedications by *vicani* are made to *Iuppiter Optimus Maximus* (four)[95] than to various local deities (three). This could of course be explained by presuming a process of *interpretatio* in which Jupiter disguises a native deity, but one could also argue for the undeniably Roman(-ised) aspect of such dedications.[96] Moreover, it should be stressed that also in Spain there is the familiar use of *vici* as urban subdivisions parallel to their use for rural villages, as the *vicus Forensis* and *vicus Hispanus* from Corduba prove.[97] In conclusion, the apparent contradiction between the indigenous Spanish rural *vicus* and the idea of the *vicus* as a Roman invention should perhaps not be overstated. This is especially true if one allows for the possibility that some pre-Roman centres were granted the legal status of *vicus* later on, or simply for the relatively large amount of 'indigenous' people included in new *vici*.

As to Capogrossi Colognesi's elegant *longue durée* explanation, it is more difficult to decide which arguments should be given precedence. Whereas his argument is well sustained, by emphasising the importance of the village structure in pre-Roman Italy as well as in late antiquity and Medieval times, one could wonder whether the explanation of the decline and re-emergence of the *vicus* and the contemporaneous rise and fall of the *pagus*, is not, as far as regards the *vicus*, more relevant to *structural* elements than to the names given to these structures. I therefore suggest that Capogrossi Colognesi's argument perhaps holds true for the role of the *village* as a structure of settlement in Italy, which however does not necessarily coincide with the institutional indication *vicus*.[98]

Both the interpretation of the *vicus* as a rural 'anti-urban' structure, and the opposite one, that of the *vicus* as a Roman administrative entity based on urban structures, have their merits since both give coherence to historical processes, albeit in different ways. Perhaps one could say that in Capogrossi Colognesi's account coherence in the development of the *vicus* is attained by viewing the historical development of the village (as a structure) over time. Tarpin on the other hand creates coherence on a different level, on that of terminology, in a historical development from *stadtrömischer vicus* to extensions of this onto the countryside, albeit always related to urban structures.

Once the interchangeability of the structure of the village and the term *vicus* is abandoned, the argument in favour of a Roman origin of the concept of *vicus* is most convincing. The administrative category of *vicus* appears to be strongly associated with Roman contexts and a village or conglomeration indicated as such depended therefore, in all likelihood, on a Roman system of administration.

[93] Curchin 1985, 328.

[94] Curchin 1985, 335; *ILER* 3492: *Dercinoassedenses, vicani Cluniensum*.

[95] Curchin 1985, 330-332; nos. 4, 6, 8, 14; no. 6 mentions only Jupiter, the other nos. (*Optimus*) *Maximus*. Cf. also, for Roman Gaul, Derks 1998, 188 on the collective dedications by *vici* or *vicani* which are "surprisingly often" addressed to the Capitoline gods and the imperial house.

[96] Curchin 1985, 335.

[97] Curchin 1985, 329-330: nos. A 1 and A 2.

[98] As a matter of fact, Capogrossi Colognesi often speaks of the role of the '*villaggio*' instead of that of the *vicus* proper. He is very aware of the limits of archaeology and the impossibility of the recognition of legal or hierarchical statuses other than in epigraphic sources (cf. Capogrossi Colognesi 2002, 176-182). However, his general argument (the supposed marginal role in Roman times and consequent re-emergence afterwards, as well as the presumed pre-Roman character of the *vicus* underscored at times) seems, at least sometimes, to conflate *vicus* and village.

It should be stressed, however, that if the status of *vicus* is documented for a village, this status does not preclude a pre-Roman origin of this village. Indeed, a legal status does not reveal all about the character and the social reality of the *vicus*. As I have stated, preconceptions concerning the Roman conquest and control underlie interpretations of the character of the *vicus*. Now, even if an entirely indigenous interpretation of the *vicus* may be ruled out, in my view there still remains a wide range of interpretations between local and 'Roman' aspects of the *vicus*. Are we dealing with a community of 'ex-pats', imported Roman (or Latin) citizens, or with an 'indigenous' village with (largely) 'indigenous' inhabitants upgraded to a specific status? And, above all, how does this relate to issues of cultural change in these locales? This question is discussed in more detail in Chapter 7, taking into account the religious role of the *vicus*.

In any event, it seems clear that if *vici* are explicitly mentioned in epigraphy, this does not refer to pre-Roman Italic structures but to a specific status within a *Roman* administrative system. This means that views of *vici* as a constitutive element of pre-Roman settlement organisation are erroneous. This revision applies to the model of the *pagus-vicus* system as a pre-Roman feature, as has become already clear from the conclusion that the *pagus* was a Roman instrument, but also to other variants[99] or conceptions, such as a model which envisages the Oscan *touto* to be constituted by *vici*.[100]

6.4 THE RELATIONSHIP BETWEEN PAGUS AND VICUS

The conclusions in the preceding sections have paved the way for the observations to be made here and can therefore remain brief. Since the publications of Tarpin and Capogrossi Colognesi in 2002, the general inappropriateness of the term *pagus-vicus* system (*sistema paganico-vicano*) has become clear.[101] However, the exact relationship between *pagus* and *vicus* remains obscure. It could be that it varied from place to place. Perhaps there was indeed a hierarchical connection between a tribal *pagus* and *vicus* north of Italy, at least from a Roman perspective, as indicated by Caesar for the Helvetii.[102] Inscriptions mentioning *pagus* and *vicus* together are however rare[103] and are completely absent in Samnium proper. It is possible that *pagus* and *vicus* actually constituted parallel or even 'competing' institutions. Capogrossi Colognesi would stress the independence of *pagus* and *vicus*. According to him, a *pagus* could include *vici*, but they also existed separately.[104] Tarpin on the other hand would even argue that the *vicus* is essentially an *urban* feature, whereas the *pagus* denotes *non*-urbanity, and that they are seldom found together for this reason.[105]

6.5 CONCLUSION: NEW PERSPECTIVES ON PAGUS AND VICUS

The pre-Roman origin of the *pagus* has been successfully deconstructed by the work of Capogrossi Colognesi and Tarpin. It is now clear that the *pagus* was essentially a territorial district forming part of a

---

[99] E.g. the *pagus-vicus-oppidum* system, promoted by Gualtieri 2004; and in this respect uncritically reviewed by the present author (Stek 2006).

[100] Cf. *supra* n. 12.

[101] For a critique see esp. Capogrossi Colognesi 2002, 182-186; Tarpin 2002, 4. Cf. also Grelle *et al.* 2004 (review of Capogrossi Colognesi 2002).

[102] The Helvetii were divided into four *pagi*; Caes. *B Gall.* 1.12.4-5.

[103] Amongst which near Rome *CIL* VI, 2221 which was found "*in fundo agri Romani*", mentioning *mag(istri) de duobus pageis et vicei sulpicei*, and *CIL* IX, 3521 on an aquaduct at Furfo, where *mag(istri) pagi* built something *de v.s.f.*, which could be an abbreviation for *de vici sententia faciundum*. See Capogrossi Colognesi 2002, 181 n. 51.

[104] Capogrossi Colognesi 2002, 252-253.

[105] Tarpin 2002, 244: "*L'élément déterminant de la nature des uici, ... , est le caractère urbain*"; whereas *pagi* and *pagani* would be defined negatively as "*extérieurs à quelque chose*".

Roman administrative system. The role and origin of the *vicus* is less clear and more open to debate but the term and its application point in the first place to Roman contexts. An origin in the city of Rome and its consequent application to designated 'pieces of city / clusters of citizens' in the conquered Italic countryside, as envisioned by Tarpin, seems most sensible. Tarpin would see both institutions of *pagus* and *vicus* as instruments of Roman control. While retaining some features of pre-Roman structures, and taking into account the presence of 'indigenous' people in the *vici*, he stresses that *pagi* and *vici* were not envisaged to secure continuity from the pre-Roman past. "*Leur rôle, bien au contraire, est de formaliser la possession du sol et l'intégration des individus dans un ensemble administratif et culturel fondé sur la suprématie de Rome.*"[106] Nonetheless, the character of the community indicated by the word *vicus* remains, within these legal boundaries, open to debate and probably varied across spatial and temporal contexts, and it is here that an interesting field of research lies open.

In the end, how does this discussion on *pagi* and *vici* inform our understanding of Republican Italy, and how should we imagine the make up of the Italian landscape visually? For the *vici*, one could tentatively imagine clusters of Roman or Latin citizens from Rome and other parts of Italy (especially as hamlets outside the urban centres of the colonies), as well as the installation of groups of indigenous people (perhaps enfranchised in the process) in new conglomerations, and finally pre-existing Italic villages that were granted a new, Roman, status. The *vicus*, indicating a legal status, is therefore distinct from the 'village' as a form of settlement, which seems to have been fairly ubiquitous in central-southern Italy. This means that the pre-Social War landscape of Italy would have been comprised of some towns, hill-forts and villages, some of which had a different status, indicated by the name *vicus*. If *vici* indeed had some territorial sovereignty, these borders were probably not readily 'visible' in the physical landscape.

Equally invisible,[107] but certainly there, were *pagi* that divided the countryside into administrative units, depending on the colonial or municipal centre. *Pagi* could comprise only land, some houses and perhaps sometimes a conglomeration indicated as *vicus* (but it is also possible that the *vicus* had its own territory apart from the *pagus*). It can be assumed that when it seemed practical the divisions of *pagi* followed already existing boundaries of the land, but when it did not there was no reason to follow the pre-Roman situation. Both *vici* and *pagi* were Roman instruments devised to administer people and property. Furthermore, the *pagi* and *vici* became the organisational units of religious activity. And even if *pagi* and the possible territories of *vici* were 'invisible' in the landscape, since they defined territories by imagined boundaries, there were means to construct these boundaries and make them indeed visible and 'tangible'. These means, in which religious ritual plays a key role, will be further investigated in Chapters 8 and 9. First, however, the consequences of this deconstruction of the *pagus-vicus* system for the interpretation of 'Italic' sanctuaries will be discussed in the next chapter.

---

[106] Tarpin 2002, 245.

[107] If one excludes, of course, the general territorial boundaries (field boundaries, roads, rivers) along which the *pagus* was most probably defined.

7   Cult and Colonisation: *Pagi, Vici* and Sanctuaries

How does the 'deconstruction' of the *pagus-vicus* system affect our understanding of rural sanctuaries in ancient Italy? In Chapter 4 I showed how the role of sanctuaries was derived from preconceptions on the settlement organisation of the Italic peoples. Following the basic notion of an ethnic or national group (*nomen*, *populus*, or *touto*) subdivided into *pagi* that in turn were made up of several *vici*, it was assumed that sanctuaries served these different organisational levels accordingly. Usually, a remarkable continuity of the system is presupposed. It is assumed (whether implicitly or explicitly) that this organisation originated in prehistoric times and represents some sort of typical, indigenous Italic feature which continued to exist in Roman times. It is from this perspective that the (presupposed) function of rural sanctuaries within this system is often quoted as 'proof' for the persistence of pre-Roman societal structures.[1] I discussed some problems with this model in Chapter 4, especially the available data for the identification of sanctuaries as belonging to a hierarchical structure of *vici* and *pagi*. It appeared that few to no inscriptions from cult places could possibly be interpreted as indicating such, and as has become clear in the preceding chapter, a fixed hierarchical relationship between *pagus* and *vicus* can probably in general be rejected.

This means that the common hierarchical view according to which Italic sanctuaries functioned on the different levels of *touto*, *pagus* and *vicus* can be dismissed. Of course, this is not to say that there was no hierarchical relation between Italic cult places, it is indeed well imaginable that Italic sanctuaries functioned on different levels within Italic society. Without firm epigraphical evidence however, this hierarchy cannot be related to Italic institutional structures, especially since it is wholly unclear to what extent the Roman institutions of *vicus* and *pagus* may have reflected previous territorial and administrative organisations. Consequently, attempts to reconstruct a possible hierarchical relationship should necessarily depart from archaeological and/or anthropological observations, as has been done in several studies for other areas.[2] It should be admitted however that such an approach, for instance taking into account the location within the settlement pattern and typological features of the cult places, is at most able to provide fairly general descriptive hierarchies with limited explanatory power.

More fundamentally however, in Chapter 6 it has become clear that according to recent research in the juridical-historical realm both *pagus* and *vicus* were probably Roman inventions, rather than 'fossils' of a pre-Roman reality. As a consequence, it is important to make a clear distinction between cult places in which the influence of a *pagus* or *vicus* is actually epigraphically attested, and those where this is not the case. This considerably narrows down the group of actual *pagus* and *vicus* sanctuaries. In the cases where relevant inscriptions are available however, there is no doubt that *pagi* and *vici* indeed exerted influence over sanctuaries – it is only the interpretation of these data with reference to a specific, 'Italic', hierarchical structure that can be dismissed.

---

[1]   E.g. Grossi 1980, 148 in his conclusion on the pre-Roman Marsic area: "*Si è così delineato un territorio dai confini ben precisi, organizzato con fortificazioni ("oppida"), villaggi ("vici") e santuari, e che solo con l'arrivo dei Romani sarà in parte ridotto, ma non sconvolto, nella sua unità più intima*" and Van Wonterghem 1984, 42.

[2]   Cf. Chapter 4. See e.g. on Etruria and Magna Graecia Edlund-Berry 1987 and Colonna 1985 and the hierarchical typologies for Lucania in Fracchia/Gualtieri 1989; Greco 2000; Horsnaes 2002.

Fig. 7.1. An inscription from S. Maria degli Angeli (*CIL* I², 1801) mentioning several *mag(istri) Mart(is)* who *ex pagi decr(eto)* saw to the erection of a *fornice(m) et parietes caementicios* (Degrassi 1986, pl. 87 fig. 1).

Therefore, I now wish to discuss new ways to interpret these sanctuaries. For if *vici* and *pagi* are indeed a Roman construct, what does this imply for the related cult places? Were the sanctuaries in which a *vicus* or a *pagus* was involved pre-Roman sacred places that took on a new function within a Roman administration of the land? Or were they instead new sanctuaries, following the new division of the land (and perhaps new inhabitants as well)? In order to try to answer these questions, which could in my view have important consequences for general ideas on Roman influence in the religious realm, it will be necessary to re-evaluate the epigraphic and archaeological evidence.

After giving an overview of the entire corpus of evidence, I focus on specific case-studies. First, the excavated sanctuary at Castel di Ieri near Superaequum will be presented as an example of a *pagus* sanctuary. Then the possible relationship between *vici*, *pagi* and Latin colonisation is reviewed. As a hypothetical example, I consider the case of the Latin colony of Ariminum (modern Rimini) in some detail, showing how links between the rural *pagi*, *vici* and the colonial centre may have been constructed.

Subsequently, attention is turned to the rural *vici* in the *ager Praetutianus*. In this area epigraphic evidence for *vici* can be complemented by archaeological data of related cult places and settlements. This evidence supports the idea that *vici* were a relatively new development in the area which was related to Roman intervention.

Finally, the area of the Marsi at the Fucine lake (*lacus Fucinus*) is discussed. The epigraphic evidence for this area is extraordinarily rich and invites reflection in some detail on the character of the *vici* and their cults attested here, especially since these *vici* were apparently located outside Roman territory. Previous studies, especially the important works on the subject by Letta, have emphasised the indigenous character of these *vici*.[3] Elaborating on the findings by Tarpin with regard to the Roman institutional character of the *vici*,[4] I will review the evidence in some detail and argue that the Fucine *vici* betray strong connections with Roman or Latin contexts on a political and cultural level. The cultural processes at work were, however, clearly more complex than a dichotomy between 'Italic' versus 'Roman' allows for. Rather than proposing that these *vici* were entirely 'Roman' enclaves, I shall argue that they should be seen as

[3] Starting with Letta 1972, see the bibliography.   [4] Tarpin 2002, esp. 56-57.

'new communities' within a new organisational structure, although as such certainly a result of Roman influence in the region. In this context, I will argue that cults had a crucial role to play in the cultural self-definition of these communities, which was oriented towards Rome.

7.1 PAGI AND VICI IN SANCTUARIES AND CULTS

"Die Zweckbestimmung ist zunächst eine sakrale" (Mommsen 1877 iii, 117 on the *pagus*)[5]

As has become clear in Chapter 4, the involvement of *pagi* in sanctuaries is less straightforward than has usually been assumed. For instance, the evidence for the supposedly typical examples of *pagus* sanctuaries at Fontecchio, S. Angelo in Cacumine and a possible cult place for Aternus is rather tenuous. But there are several instances of *pagi* involved in sanctuaries attested elsewhere. There is a large group of inscriptions commemorating the involvement of (magistrates belonging to) *pagi* in various building activities and these obviously also referred to sacred buildings. Sometimes they take the form of a decree made by a *pagus* (e.g., *ex pagi decreto*) which is for instance often found in Paelignian territory (see fig. 7.1).[6]

I have listed some thirty-odd inscriptions attesting *pagi* that (probably) refer to sanctuaries and/or cults within Italy. For the city of Rome, five inscriptions out of seven that mention activities related to a *pagus* are connected to a sanctuary or cult.[7] The earliest inscriptions are from the *pagus Ianicolensis* and date to the end of the second century or the beginning of the first century BC. Around two dozen inscriptions likely attest to a connection between *pagi* and a cult or sanctuary in the Italian regions outside Rome. This connection is usually some formal decision taken by the *pagus* and/or action undertaken by its officials. Most inscriptions record the building or restoration of (elements of) temples or are simply a dedication to the venerated deity (cf. *infra* on the characteristics of the venerated gods).[8]

---

[5] See the comment on this quote by Frederiksen 1976, 245: "and there is no need to cast doubt on this." Cf. also Salmon 1967, 80: "The *pagus* was a semi-independent country district, concerned with social, agricultural and especially religious matters." Cf. also Kornemann 1942b, 2319: "Er [der pagus] hat keine agrimensorische Bedeutung, sondern ursprünglich eigentlich nur oder wenigstens vor allem eine sakrale." Cf. Schulten 1894, 635.

[6] See the index by Tarpin 2002: five times attested (but referring to three different sites). A variant *l(ocus) d(atus) d(ecreto) p(agi)* seems to abound in France, whereas the expression *de pagi sententia* is attested both in central Italy (twice) and in Rome (twice); *ex pagi scitu* in central Italy (once) and Campania (once).

[7] *CIL* VI, 251 (= *CIL* VI, 30724) from the *via Appia* (27 AD); *CIL* VI, 2219 (= *CIL* I², 1000) and *CIL* VI, 2220 (= *CIL* I², 1001) (from S. Maria dell'Orto, the *pagus Ianicolensis*); *CIL* VI, 2221 (= *CIL* VI, 32452 = *CIL* I², 1002) (8 miles from Rome); *CIL* VI, 3823 (= *CIL* VI, 31577 = *CIL* I², 591) (gardens of Maecenas, near the 'arch of Gallienus', the so-called *S.C. de pago Montano*).

[8] Here a list is given of inscriptions commemorating the activity of a *pagus* or its officials within the religious realm. This list is not exhaustive but may represent the situation fairly well. For Rome, cf. preceding note, the rest of Italy proper has been included here (*Regiones* I–XI):

I: 1. *AE* 1989, 150 from Minturnae. Nonnis 2003, 46: "*I sec., metà circa*"; Tarpin 2002, I.A.13.21: "*deuxième moitié Ier siècle av. J.-C.*" (indirect: a *pagus Vescinus* supplemented the treasury of Mars for the construction of a theatre); 2. *CIL* X, 3772 (= *CIL* I², 682) from Capua / Calatia. *pagus Herculaneus*, 94 BC (cf. Chapter 6); 3. *CIL* X, 3783 (= *CIL* I², 686) from Bonaventura Natale (near Capua), 71 BC.

II: 4. *CIL* IX, 1618 from Beneventum (cf. Chapter 8 on the *lustratio pagi*).

IV: 5. *CIL* IX, 3523 from Castelvecchio Calvisio. Tarpin 2002, IV.16.22: "*fin de la République ou début Empire*"; 6. *CIL* I², 1801 from S. Maria degli Angeli (Pescosansonesco). Tarpin 2002, IV.11.22: "*République*"; 7. *CIL* I², 3269 from Carpineto della Nora. *ILLRP* 1271c: first century BC (cf. Chapter 8 on *thesauri*); 8. *Suppl.It.* n.s. V, Superaequum, no. 11. *AE* 1990, 234 from Gagliano

The date of the inscriptions is not always clear but the following can be said with some confidence. Two vessels with painted texts from Ariminum (so-called *pocula* or *pocola deorum*; cf. *infra*) can probably be related to some sort of sacred dedication, and therefore attest to *pagi* religiously active by the second half of the third century BC. A bronze *patera* from the second century BC found in Cupra montana, Picenum (*CIL* IX, 5699) with an enigmatic text (*V(ibius) Avilio(s) V(ibii) f(ilius) V(ibius) Alfieno(s) Po(blii) f(ilius) pagi veheia*) cannot, as it seems, be directly related to the religious realm[9] but anyhow indicates the presence of *pagi* elsewhere in this early period.[10] Besides this *patera* and the Ariminate *pocola*, the already mentioned inscription of Capua of 94 BC is the only document firmly dated to the period before the Social War. As noted in Chapter 6, the inscriptions on the vases from Ariminum dating to the second half of the third century BC were found in the centre of this Latin colony founded in 268 BC. The second century *patera* from Cupra montana was located in territory that apparently had held the status of *civitas sine suffragio* from 268 BC and had probably received the *optimum ius* by the time the *patera* was made.[11] Capua was still *sine suffragio* in 94 BC. In conclusion, there is no evidence for the presence of *pagi* that are involved in religious matters outside territory which was in some way under Roman control, which is of course in line with Tarpin's and Capogrossi's more general conclusions.

Almost half of the datable inscriptions belongs to the last century BC. Very few inscriptions are dated to the first century AD. This number does not increase significantly in the later imperial age (second to fourth centuries AD). Several undated inscriptions seem best placed in the imperial period because of formulas used, the objects of the dedications or the palaeography.

In conclusion, a considerable number of inscriptions set up by officials of a *pagus* or on a decree by a *pagus* document involvement in religious (building) activities. Mommsen was probably right in recognising the 'sacral' function of the *pagus* as essential, as noted in the quote at the beginning of this section.[12]

Aterno, loc. Ponte Vecchio. Buonocore (*Suppl.It.*): "*metà I sec. a. C. (ded[erunt/it]* indicates a dedication); 9. *CIL* I², 3254 if connected to *CIL* IX, 3312 (= *CIL* I², 1797) from Secinaro (for the connection, cf. Letta 1992, 115, n. 30, but note that during the construction of the fountain at S. Gregorio several funeral inscriptions were re-used pointing to other cults in these surroundings as well: Van Wonterghem 1984, 96-97). For the date: *CIL* I², 3254: "*metà I secolo a.C.*" (*Suppl.It.* n.s.V), and for *CIL* IX, 3312: "*metà I secolo a.C.*" (*Suppl.It.* n.s.V); 10. *CIL* IX, 3138 (= *CIL* I², 1793) from Prezza, church of S. Lucia. Tarpin 2002, IV.6.22: "*Ier siècle av. J.-C.*"; 11. *AE* 1914, 270 (= *CIL* I², 3255) between Castelvecchio Subequo and Secinaro. First century BC, (cf. discussion in Chapter 8).

V: 12. *CIL* IX, 5814 from Montorio al Vomano, not dated; 13. *CIL* IX, 5565 from Tolentinum: *tesseram paganicam*. Cf. discussion in Chapter 8. third-fourth centuries AD (Cancrini *et al.* 2001, 125-127).

VI: 14. *CIL* XI 5375 from Asisium (dedication to Jupiter Paganicus).

VII: 15. *CIL* XI, 3196 from Nepet, April 19 AD 18; 16. *CIL* XI, 3040 from Soriano nel Cimino, 4 BC; 17. *CIL* XI, 2921 (= *CIL* I², 1993) from Cellere, near Visentium, Tarpin 2002, VII.8.21: "*Ier siècle av. J.-C.*"

VIII: 18. *CIL* I², 2897a-b, two inscriptions on so-called *pocola* from Ariminum, third century BC. Cf. discussion *infra*; 19. *CIL* V, 762ab from Aquileia, second century AD. (Brusin 1991 no. 159 and 166).

X: 20. *CIL* V, 3249, from the environment of Verona; 21. *CIL* V, 3915, from Fumane, Val Policella; 22. *CIL* V, 3928, from Fumane, Val Policella; 23. *CIL* V, 4148, from Pedergnaga (between Cremona and Brescia), late Republican period (*InscrIt* X.5, 980 [Garzetti]); 24. *CIL* V, 4911, Inzin, Val Trompia; 25. *CIL* V, 4909, Bovegno, Val Trompia.

XI: 26. *CIL* V, 5112, from Bergomum.

[9] Therefore, it is not inserted in n. 8. Cf. Tarpin 2002, V.7.21, for bibliography.

[10] Cf. *infra* on the possible specific ritual role of *paterae* however.

[11] Humbert 1978, 349-354; cf. however Mouritsen 2007 for a general critique of the concept of the *civitas sine suffragio* as a provisional status which inevitably leads to the grant of *suffragium*, and especially the scarcity of evidence for the upgrading of *cives sine suffragio*.

[12] Whether it really was the "*Zweckbestimmung*" is more difficult to say, especially since this conception presupposes a neat distinction between the religious and other realms (cf. Chapter 10).

Indeed, this view is deeply rooted in modern scholarship.[13] As will be discussed in more detail in Chapter 8, the alleged Italic origin of the *pagus* has suggested that this religious aspect had an ancient and agricultural – indeed 'Italic' – character. However, since it has become clear that the *pagus* was a Roman, not an Italic institution, it follows that the religious aspects of the *pagus* should be re-examined, rather than mistaken a priori for forms of 'indigenous Italic' cult. Of course, it is not ruled out that Italic cults were involved, but Roman influence should not be excluded beforehand.

An overview of the deities that were worshipped in *pagus* contexts is revealing. Generally speaking, the involved deities cannot be defined as specifically 'indigenous Italic' gods:[14] Jupiter prominently features in many guises, e.g. *Victor*,[15] *Optimus Maximus*,[16] *Compagus*,[17] *Paganicus*[18]. Other cults include *Mars*,[19] *Juno* (*Regina*,[20] *Gaura*[21]), *Bona Dea*[22] (*Pagana*),[23] *Hercules Victor*,[24] *Minerva*,[25] *Laverna*,[26] *Ceres* ('*augusta mater agrorum*'),[27] *Nymphae*,[28] and the (*genius* of) the emperor.[29] Interestingly, the deity is often invoked as the tutelary god of the *pagus*, for example *Juppiter Paganicus*, *Juppiter Compagus*, *Bona Dea Pagana*, and the *Genii pagorum*.[30] If the dedication to Aternus could be securely connected to an inscription mentioning a *pagus*, which is now not the case, this would be an example of a local(ised) deity.[31]

No deity related to a *pagus* can be specifically associated with an 'Italic' context (in contrast to, for instance, Vesuna or Mefitis etc.). This general image does not change if only the Republican dedications are taken into consideration and therefore a bias by progressive Roman influence in the imperial period can be excluded. It is of course true that, although most gods venerated in the context of *pagi* do not appear to be specifically 'local' or 'Italic', it is not to be excluded either that these Latin names veil such 'original' deities. Not wanting to deny the possibility of indigenous substrates and complex processes of *interpretatio*, I have my doubts however, from a methodological point of view, about the often encountered idea of a Roman 'veneer' that would actually hide an 'intrinsic' indigenous continuity, not in the last place because it is impossible to prove or falsify.[32] What counts most here, in my view, is that knowledge of the Roman pantheon and the ability and willingness to accept Roman theonyms becomes manifest.

Also the relationship between *vici* and sanctuaries is often less straightforward than has been assumed in previous scholarship, but just as for the *pagi*, in many instances *vici* and its officials are nevertheless documented engaging in the management of sacred places and cults. In Rome, a large number of inscriptions attest to the involvement of *vici* in cults and cult places.[33] Most inscriptions are Augustan or later. The earliest datable (not necessarily 'religious') inscriptions relating to *vici* in Rome are a Sullan base

---

[13] A.o. Schulten, Kornemann, and Frederiksen, cf. *supra* n. 5.

[14] On the problem with recognising differences within a same, Indo-European, basic system, cf. Chapter 2.

[15] *CIL* I², 3269.

[16] *CIL* IX, 3523 if linked to *CIL* IX, 3519 (Letta 1992, 114 n. 26).

[17] *CIL* X, 3772.

[18] *CIL* XI, 5375.

[19] *AE* 1989, 150 (not directly attested; the construction of the theatre at Minturnae is financed *ex pecunia Martis* and by the *pagus Vescinus*).

[20] *CIL* XI, 2921 (= *CIL* I², 1993).

[21] *CIL* X, 3783 (= *CIL* I², 686).

[22] *CIL* IX, 3138 (= *CIL* I², 1793).

[23] *CIL* V, 762ab.

[24] *CIL* I², 3254; cf. the *pagus Herculaneus* of *CIL* X, 3772 (= *CIL* I², 682).

[25] *CIL* IX, 5814.

[26] *CIL* IX, 3138 (= *CIL* I², 1793).

[27] *CIL* XI, 3196.

[28] *CIL* V, 3915.

[29] *CIL* VI, 251 (= *CIL* VI, 30724). Possibly *Fides* could be added, cf. *infra*.

[30] *Genii pagorum*: *CIL* V, 3915; *CIL* V, 4911; *CIL* V, 4909.

[31] See Chapter 4. Indeed, despite a late Republican attestation of the deity in Vestine dialect (Ve. 227), Aternus is not necessarily an inherently 'Italic' name, it is a *local* toponym.

[32] See e.g. Letta 1992, 118-120 for an explicit plea for the mere 'superficial' and 'formal' romanisation of cults that would in reality and substance 'root' in Italic traditions.

[33] For the complete record of *vicus* inscriptions (85 in total), both religious and non-religious, for the city of Rome, see the catalogue in Tarpin 2002, 307-326.

from the Quirinal (83–80 BC)[34] and a column mentioning *magistri veici* dated to the central years of the first century BC.[35] The existence of a *vicus* already at the end of the third century BC in Rome is however attested by Plautus.[36] The earliest unequivocal evidence for involvement in the religious realm is the rebuilding of an *aediculam vici Salutaris* in 33 BC.[37]

As to Italy outside Rome, there are about a dozen inscriptions that can be connected to religious affairs.[38] Most datable inscriptions are from the Republican period. The so-called *pocola deorum* from the Latin colony of Ariminum mentioning *vici* and a dedication of a statue to Victoria on behalf of the *vecos Supinas* (*vicus Supinum*) in Marsic territory date to the second half of the third or the early second century BC.[39] A similar dedication of a statue, presumably to a deity, on behalf of the *vicus Petinus* might also date to the same period.[40] A dedication dated to the second century BC was made within the territory of the Aequicoli to the otherwise unknown god Nensinus, by decree of a *vicus*.[41] In Marsic territory again, another dedication was made by the *Aninus vecus* (*vicus Aninus*) to Valetudo in the early first century BC.[42] Several sacred activities involving a *vicus* are recorded for the first century BC, from central, central-southern (Pompeii) and northern Italy, and some for the imperial period.[43] The significance of the cults related to *vici* will be discussed in detail in the sections on Ariminum and the Fucine *vici*.

Whereas the diffusion of the *pagi* (even if based on a necessarily small sample) neatly coincided with Roman or Roman-controlled territory, this differs somewhat for the early appearance of the *vicus*. Of course, Cales in Campania, and Ariminum in Emilia Romagna, are both Latin colonies and the central-Italian *vici* in Trebula Mutuesca and Vestine and Aequicolan territory also fall within the area with (full or limited) Roman rights. However, the early dedications in Marsic territory are more problematic. The Marsi were not yet incorporated within the Roman *civitas* but held the status of *socii*. They would therefore contest the idea that *vici* represent Roman institutions, and this situation will be discussed in some detail in the last sections of this chapter.

---

[34] *CIL* VI, 1297 (= *CIL* I², 721).

[35] *CIL* VI, 1324 (= *CIL* I², 2514).

[36] Plaut. *Curc.* 482: *in Tusco vico ibi sunt homines qui ipsi sese venditant*.

[37] *CIL* VI, 31270.

[38] This list is not exhaustive but may represent the situation fairly well. Inscriptions relating to *vicani* have been omitted (cf. for these, Todisco 2001).
I: 1. *CIL* XIV, 4298 from Ostia, Bakker 1994, 119: "Late Augustan or Claudian." Cf. Chapter 9; 2. *AE* 1906, 79 from Frascati / Tusculum, Tarpin 2002, I.4.2. "*lettres du IIe siècle*"; 3. *AE* 1991, 389 from Bovillae; 4. *CIL* IV, 60 (= *CIL* I², 777) from Pompeii, 47–46 BC. Cf. Chapter 9.
IV: 5. *CIL* IX, 3513 (= *CIL* I², 756) *lex aedis Furfensis* from Furfo, 58 BC (cf. Chapter 4); 6. *CIL* IX, 3849 (= *CIL* I², 388) from the *vicus Supinum* (Trasacco), Tarpin 2002, IV.23.1 "*autour de 200 av. J.-C.*"; cf. *infra*; 7. *CIL* IX, 3813 (= *CIL* I², 391) from Castelluccio, Lecce dei Marsi, Tarpin 2002, IV.22.1: "*IIe siècle av. J.-C.*"; Letta 2001, 151: beginnings first century BC; 8. *AE* 1987, 321 from Vesce (Narsae), Tarpin 2002, IV.27.1: "*IIe siècle av. J.-C.*"; 9. Letta/D'Amato 1975 no. 188 = *CIL* I², 2874 from the *vicus Petinus* (near the Fucine lake), "*fin du IIIe siècle av. J.-C.*"
V: 10. *CIL* IX, 5052 (= *CIL* I², 765), from near Montorio al Vomano, 55 BC.
VI: 11. *CIL* XI, 4744 from S. Maria in Pantano, *vicus Martis Tudertium*.
VIII: 12. *CIL* I², 2899a-c from Ariminum, third century BC, three inscriptions on so-called *pocola* from Ariminum, third century BC. Cf. *infra* for discussion.
IX: 13. *InscrIt* IX-1, 59 from Bastita (Bastia).
X: 14. *CIL* V, 1829 from Iulium Carnicum, Zuglio, Tarpin 2002, X.2.1: "*deuxième quart du Ier siècle av. J.-C.*"; 15. *CIL* V, 1830 from Iulium Carnicum, Zuglio, Tarpin 2002, X.2.2: "*deuxième moitié du Ier siècle av. J.-C.*".

[39] *CIL* I², 2899a-c and *CIL* IX, 3849 (= *CIL* I², 388).

[40] Letta/D'Amato 1975 no. 188 = *CIL* I², 2874.

[41] *AE* 1987, 321.

[42] *CIL* IX, 3813 (= *CIL* I², 391).

[43] See *supra* n. 38.

[44] On the risk of the use of inscriptions mentioning restorations for an earlier phase, cf. Thomas/Witschel 1992

Although the precise relationship between *pagi*, *vici* and cult places remains mostly implicit in the epigraphy, it seems legitimate to suggest that these sanctuaries functioned as a sacral centre of the district or village, thereby at the same time stating the authority of the *pagus* or *vicus* by divine association. It could be surmised that, following the installation of a new *pagus* or *vicus*, sanctuaries were built *ex novo*, or that pre-existing sanctuaries were re-used. A combination of archaeological and epigraphic evidence would be required to test this assumption, but unfortunately very few inscriptions mentioning the involvement of *pagi* or *vici* can be related to clear and datable archaeological remains of a sanctuary. In most cases the inscription itself is the only attestation of the sacred place and inscriptions alone, both mentioning constructions *ex novo* and restorations, are (almost by definition)[44] not conclusive. In the following sections, I will discuss several cases in which more context is available in order to shed light on the character of cult places and cults related to *pagi* and *vici*.

7.2 PAGUS AND TEMPLE AT CASTEL DI IERI: CAPITOLINE ASPIRATIONS?

There is, to my knowledge, at present one striking exception to the noted absence of combined epigraphic and archaeological evidence for *pagi*: the sanctuary discovered in 1987 during the building of a house at località Madonna del Soccorso in the municipality of Castel di Ieri. Here, in the area of ancient Superaequum, the remains of a late Republican temple have been excavated under the direction of Adele Campanelli (fig. 7.2).[45]

The sanctuary site was already frequented before the late Republican monumental temple. This is attested by votives, amongst which are anatomical terracottas, and the remains of an older sanctuary.[46] The full-blown monumental phase of the temple is dated to the end of the second century BC. Its high podium measuring 15.12 x 19.8 m[47] was built in polygonal masonry lined with stone slabs and it was preceded by a flight of stairs. The cornice of the podium is of the *cyma recta* type, which has a good parallel in the sanctuary at Navelli (S. Maria in Cerulis) in Vestine territory, also dated to the second century BC.[48] The column bases also have the same profile.[49] The temple shows a three *cellae* plan. It had a deep pronaos, with four columns at the front and two central columns in the second row, in line with the dividing walls of the *cellae*. In the *cellae*, mosaic floors of white *tesserae* were laid with a band at the edges in black *tesserae*. In the central *cella*, a meander motif was placed at the centre, again in black *tesserae*. Moreover, the mosaic contained a text at the entrance. It mentions two or three individuals who were responsible for the building, *ex pagi decreto*.[50] The persons named are probably *magistri* who acted on a decree of the *pagus*. The text is dated palaeographically to the mid-first century BC.[51]

The monumental building project, begun at the end of the second century BC, was apparently only finished around the mid-first century BC by the *pagus*.[52] It is not certain whether two separate phases can be distinguished, or if we are rather dealing with the completion of one single project over a lon-

with Fagan 1996.

[45] Campanelli 2004.

[46] "*caratterizzato da uno zoccolo in pietra ed alzato in terra cruda*" (Campanelli 2004, 24).

[47] No height is given in Campanelli 2004.

[48] See Gros 2001 (1996), 147-149; cf. the related Latin inscription with archaic characters, *CIL* I², 3266.

[49] Campanelli 2004, 16-18.

[50] *C. [Vib]idius C.f. Ser(gia) Decr(ianus) L. P[eti]edius V. [f. / ae]de(m) fac(iendam) ex pag(i) de[cr(eto)] c(uraverunt) eid(em) q(ue) [p(robaverunt)]. AE* 2004, 489 = Buonocore 2004, 288-290 for the correction into two *magistri* rather than three, proposed in Buonocore 2002, 41, 45. The names recur in, amongst other places, Superaequum and Sulmo.

[51] Buonocore 2004, 288-290; (= *AE* 2004, 489).

[52] Campanelli 2004, 28.

[53] Cf. Buonocore 2004, 288 who mentions a "*prima fase di monumentalizzazione al II sec. a.C.*" and a "*seconda fase di rico-

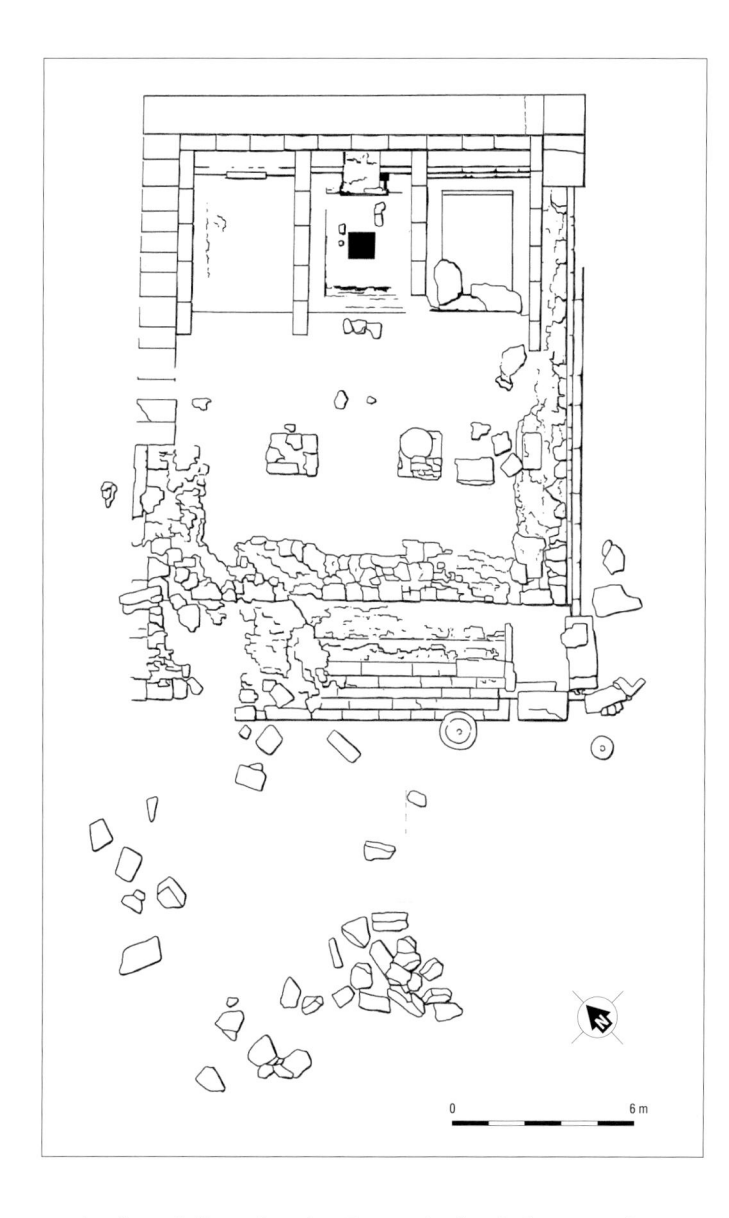

Fig. 7.2. Castel di Ieri, ground plan of the temple (adapted from Campanelli 2004, 18 fig. 7).

ger period of time.[53] The fact that the entrance to a space behind the central *cella* was blocked by the base of the cult statue at least suggests a change in plans.[54] Remains of a marble statue which was twice life-size have been found scattered over the temple area. This possible cult statue has, in light of the *aegis*, been identified as Minerva or as a particular type of Zeus/Jupiter.[55] Some remains could also perhaps point to a cult of Hercules, but the evidence does not seem to be compelling.[56] Various finds were retrieved, including coins and lamps. Some of the coins and fragments of Italian sigillata and thin-walled wares indicate that the temple continued to be used in the imperial period. Antefixes have been found of the type representing a winged Victoria, holding a wreath, and of a naked youth with a cloak.[57]

As a whole, the complex fits into the general Hellenistic-Italic architectural traditions typical of this period but there are also some distinctive details, such as the broad frontal stairs. In particular, influences from Latin and Roman contexts seem present. For example the column bases are very similar to those of the S. Pietro temple (dedicated to Apollo) in the Latin colony of Alba Fucens, as Campanelli points out. Even more striking is the ground plan. The three *cellae* with double colonnade in the pronaos, and indeed the frontal stairs, have suggestive parallels in the *Capitolia* of the colonies of Cosa and Luni, and also in the three *cellae* temple at Segni.[58]

struzione" after the Social War, whereas Campanelli 2004, 28 seems less sure, since she speaks of a "*impianto templare*" of the end of the second century but continues: "*Tuttavia il tempio ebbe la sua fase realizzativa, ricordata nella epigrafe dedicatoria, durante la metà del I secolo a.C. in concomitanza con gli eventi seguenti la guerra sociale, quando nell'area fu istituito il municipium di Superaequum, del cui territorio, entrò a far parte anche il pagus che aveva commissionato il nostro edificio.*"

[54] Campanelli 2004, 20, 27 for photographs.

[55] Minerva: Campanelli 2004; Zeus: pers. comm. Maria José Strazzulla.

[56] That is, "*un sedile in calcare locale decorato con finte rocce*" which could belong to a statue of a sitting Hercules (but note that Minerva is also depicted in this way), as well as a small archaic bronze statuette, Campanelli 2004, 22, 26.

[57] Campanelli 2004, 22, 28.

[58] Campanelli 2004, 27; see for '*Capitolium*-temples', Chapter 2.

[59] In Campanelli's words, "*uno straordinario esempio della volontà di autoromanizzazione delle élite locali che preferiscono*

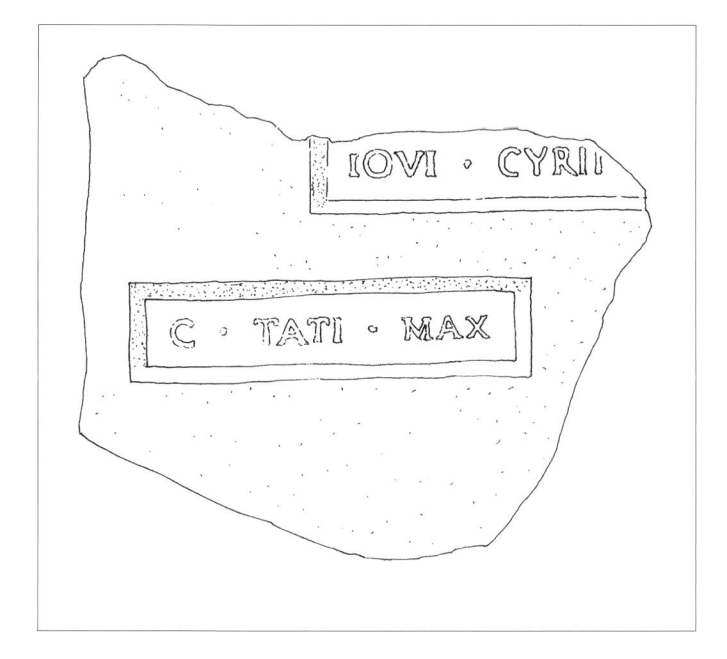

Fig. 7.3. Brick stamp mentioning Jupiter Curinus or Cyrinus (*CIL* IX, 3303a) found in proximity of the temple at Castel di Ieri (adapted from *CIL*).

This extraordinarily Roman aspect of the temple has been noted by the excavator, suggesting that it indicates a striking case of self-romanisation.[59] In this context, I would like to evaluate the possibility that this remarkably 'Roman' aspect of the temple was connected to the fact that a *pagus* was involved in its construction and thus try to provide a suitable explanation for the appearance of this particular complex in this place. It seems indeed possible to at least indirectly relate the late second century temple to the involvement of the *pagus*. The decree of the *pagus* can only be securely associated with the mid-first century completion, *or* reconstruction, of the temple. At that moment, the installation of the mosaic and the decree text in it were accompanied by the decoration of the walls with painted stucco, the terracotta decoration of the elevation and the placement of a large cult statue. However, the basic layout, including the three *cellae*, was already in existence and dates to the first phase, i.e. the late second century BC. One possible reconstruction of the course of events is therefore that around the mid-first century a *pagus* restored an already existing, *Capitolium*-like temple.[60] It follows that in this reconstruction, the 'Roman' layout of the temple cannot be related to the involvement of the *pagus*. The *pagus* would just have re-used a pre-existing three *cellae* temple.

Dating the installation of the *pagus* is thus important for establishing the relationship between the architectural design and the *pagus*. If it postdates the second century phase of the temple, it can evidently not have been responsible for its design. In theory, it is possible that the installation of the *pagus* coincided with the municipalisation of Superaequum which occurred after 49 BC.[61] However, 49 BC is only a *terminus post quem*.[62] Most authors agree that Superaequum only became *municipium* in the Augustan period, which would be in line with the few literary indications and the chronology of the archaeological remains.[63] The hypothesis of the installation of a *pagus* together with the installation of the *municipium* of

---

a scelte conservatrici di tipologie indigine ... l'enfatizzazione della loro istanza politica con una architettura di grande impegno" (Campanelli 2004, 27-28).

[60] This conception seems to follow from Buonocore's analysis: Buonocore 2004, 288-290.

[61] Castel di Ieri clearly falls within its municipal territory.

[62] On the basis of the presence of *IIviri* in Superaequum (*CIL* IX, 3307; 3309; 3310; 3313; *Suppl.It.* n.s.V, 111 no. 7): after this date the Caesarian reform seems to have replaced *IIIIviri* with *IIviri* in *municipia* founded from then onwards.

[63] Ovid. *Amor.* 2.16.1, probably dating to 4 BC, is the first, though indirect, proof of existence of the *municipium*. As to its earlier aspect, Strabo, citing Artemidoros of Ephesos of the late second century BC for this part of his text, for example omits Superaequum altogether, cf. Van Wonterghem 1984, 77; Coarelli/La Regina 1984, 117; Buonocore in *Suppl.It.* n.s.V, 92. Cf. also Buonocore 1990 for a *floruit* dated to the Augustan period.

Superaequum, which resulted in a rebuilding phase of the temple at Castel di Ieri, already in the middle of the first century BC would therefore press the evidence and is not necessarily attractive. In short, there is no reason to assume that the *pagus* involved in the construction activities of the temple around the middle of the first century BC was by then a recent institution in the area. Once it is accepted that the *pagus* was in existence already before the municipalisation of Superaequum, it follows that possibly the earlier construction phase of the temple, at the end of the second century BC, was begun by this *pagus*.[64] The presence of an early *pagus* in the area does not seem improbable since the area may have already been early under Roman control and part of it was annexed as early as 305 BC.[65] This would also explain the early latinisation of the area.[66]

In any case, an architectural complex with presumably quite 'Roman' connotations was installed on the site of an earlier sanctuary. The similarity to the second century *Capitolia* of colonies has already been noted. The scattered remains of a statue of Minerva (or Jupiter) found in around the central *cella*, lead Campanelli to suggest that the temple was dedicated to this goddess.[67] A fairly 'Roman' cult, perhaps in line with the architectural features.

However, this temple also presents (further) evidence for the cult of Jupiter. In an area not far from the temple, two brick stamps have been found at the end of the 19th century.[68] One reads *[io]vi quirin[o]*,[69] the other mentions *iovi cyrin[o]* and C. Tatius Maximus, apparently the producer of the bricks (see fig. 7.3).[70] Even before the 1987 discovery of the temple at località Madonna del Soccorso, these inscriptions have been interpreted as indicating a sanctuary of Jupiter in the area of Castel di Ieri.[71] As has been seen, the cult of Jupiter was particularly popular within *pagus* contexts (cf. the first century BC *Juppiter Victor decem paagorum* of Carpineto della Nora,[72] or the *Juppiter Compagus* of Capua in 94 BC).

Moreover, the temple has a clear three *cellae* plan. In this case the alternative interpretation as a central *cella* with *alae* can be excluded since all *cellae* are of equal size.[74] In this light, it seems tempting to interpret this three *cellae* temple, for which evidence of the cult of Minerva / Jupiter exists, as expressing a readiness to adopt the Capitoline model – even if we should allow for local adaptations and variations on the theme.[75] It should also be emphasised that the evidence on which grounds most 'established' *Capitolia* have been recognised as such is seldom any richer.[76]

It is to be regretted that Castel di Ieri appears to be the only case in which epigraphic and archaeological evidence can be integrated in order to furnish a more contextualised image of what cult places related to *pagi* looked like. At the same time, it is striking and perhaps somewhat disturbing that in the only case that this opportunity presents itself, the evidence breathes a rather 'Roman' or 'romanising'

---

[64] This seems to be the scenario envisioned by Campanelli: cf. n. 53.

[65] Diod. Sic. 20.90.3. Coarelli/La Regina 1984, 117, but cf. discussion in Humbert 1978, 227 esp. n. 80. Other *pagi* in this area are attested at least for the early imperial period: *CIL* IX, 3305 (*pagus Vecellanus*), 3311 (*pagus Boedinus*).

[66] Coarelli/La Regina 1984, 117.

[67] Campanelli 2004, 21-22.

[68] The temple is generally indicated as località Madonna del Soccorso; the stamp comes from the adjacent località Cese Piane: cf. the map in Van Wonterghem 1984, site 32.

[69] *CIL* IX, 3303b.

[70] *CIL* IX, 3303a.

[71] Van Wonterghem 1984, 107: "*Entrambi i frammenti sembrano provenire da un santuario di Giove, da situarsi probabilmente nei dintorni di Castel di Ieri*"; and cf. after the discovery, in 1987, Buonocore in *Suppl.It.* n.s.V, 97, who mentions the temple but does not discuss the implications. The stamps might date to the second century AD.

[72] *CIL* I², 3269. Cf. Chapter 8.

[73] *CIL* X, 3772. Cf. also the *Juppiter Paganicus* from Assisi (*CIL* XI, 5375).

[74] Cf. for *Capitolia* and temples with *alae*: Gros 2001 (1996), 136-140.

[75] On the epithet *Curinus*, cf. Van Wonterghem 1984, 107 with previous literature. For possible evidence for the cult of Hercules cf. n. 56. It should be pointed out that in fact in few *Capitolia* the 'ideal' type of Capitoline triad is attested.

[76] Cf. Barton 1982 and discussion in Chapter 2.

atmosphere. Indeed, what we may be seeing at Castel di Ieri, is a local expression of 'Romanness', the attempt of a local *pagus* community to keep up with Roman ideologies and values.

Even if there are, at least to my knowledge, no other clear architectural remains that can be linked to epigraphically attested *pagi* for the Republican period, there are additional indications of the religious contexts in which *pagi* exerted influence. This is not restricted to sanctuaries but extends to rituals which regard the *pagus* as an institution, as a group of people, and as a territorial entity. The clearest examples are the rituals related to the *pagi* of the Latin colony of Ariminum and the *lustratio pagi*. The *lustratio pagi* is discussed in Chapter 8 with reference to the *Paganalia*. The case of Ariminum, also involving *vici*, is discussed below in the context of Latin colonies.

7.3 COLONIES, PAGI AND VICI AND THE EXAMPLE OF ARIMINUM

It is worth briefly considering the link between *pagi*, *vici* and colonisation. Especially the discussion on *vici* is interesting, because these appear in both rural and urban contexts. A review of existing data and ideas on the relationship between *vici* and colonies could possibly advance our understanding of the character of *vici* in general, and in particular of the *vici* in the Praetutian and Marsic areas, examined in the subsequent sections. *Vici* are epigraphically attested in the Latin colonies of Ariminum and Cales. Usually it is assumed that these *vici* were urban subdivisions of the colony, but their location within the urban centre can be questioned. For the present study, it is important to evaluate the possibility that colonies or other centres controlled extra-urban *vici*, since this could shed light on religious aspects of the countryside and Roman influence outside urban structures.

7.3.1 ROMAN URBAN 'MIMIC':[77] THE ROMAN URBAN MODEL COPIED IN COLONIAL URBAN CENTRES?

The *vici* attested for Latin colonies sometimes bear suggestive names, such as a *vicus Esquilinus* in Cales and, for the imperial period, the *vicus Velabrus, Cermalus, Aventinus*, etc. in Ariminum. Roman toponyms were also copied in other colonies.[78] This has often been cited in support of the 'Gellian' view of colonies as small copies of Rome, i.e. that colonies from the moment of the foundation would have been *effigies parvae simulacraque populi Romani*.[79] The idea is that the colonies were divided in urban *vici* in a conscious imitation of Rome's topography, establishing an ideological link with the metropolis.[80] Ariminum and

---

[77] Cf. Bispham 2000b.

[78] Antiochia: *CIL* III, 6811-6812, 6835-6837, of Augustan date. In the Caesarian colony of Corinth sculptured bases have been found with inscriptions mentioning the different Roman hills (*Capitolinus mons* etc.) but no *vici*; cf. Meritt 1927, 452. Therefore, I do not see why the hills "*rende[no] inevitabile l'identificazione di questi simulacri con rappresentazioni simboliche dei vici della colonia cesariana*" (Coarelli 1995b, 176). Cf. Torelli 1988a, 66, also on the important role of Augustan or Julio-Claudian ideology. Cf. the evidence of Roman toponymy for Beneventum and Puteoli, dating to the imperial period. The Puteolan material seems to reflect an Augustan reorganisation of the colony: Bispham 2006, 90 n. 91.

[79] Gell. *NA* 16.13.9; e.g. Torelli 1990 esp. 53; Coarelli 1995b esp. 180: "*La definizione gelliana (e adrianea) delle colonie, come "effigies parvae simulacraque" di Roma non descrive dunque una realtà contemporanea, medio-imperiale ma – coerentemente con la cultura retrospettiva dello scrittore – la stessa struttura originaria delle colonie latine.*" Cf. Ando 2007, 431-432 for a reading of Gellius in its wider textual context.

[80] Cf. also Morel 1988, 60: "*vici [de Rimini], qui étaient les frères de ceux de Rome.*"

Cales are especially important for this discussion because here, as has been said, early inscriptions of *vici* have been documented on black gloss vases. In Ariminum, unnamed *vici* are thus documented in the third century BC, whereas in Cales, the earliest Latin colony (334 BC), an early black gloss vase has been found with a signature by the potter: *K(aeso) Serponio(s) Caleb(us) fece(t) veqo Esqelino C S*;[81] thus mentioning a *vicus Esquilinus*. Since another inscription from Cales mentions a *vicus Palatius*[82] it is suggested that Roman models were copied in a colonial context. Most importantly, this would have happened at an early date, since the *vicus Esquilinus* inscription can be dated to the third century BC.[83]

Adopting this approach, Coarelli strongly argues for the exportation and copying of an (idealised) Roman urban model.[84] According to him, the number of *vici* echoed the number of Roman urban divisions. Thus, the ancient colony of Norba had three *vici*, which would reflect the Romulean city with three regions. Colonies of the fourth century would have had five *vici*,[85] whereas in the third century seven *vici* would have been the norm. The proposed model is based on mimic, the Roman urban situation would have been directly copied or transposed to the urban divisions of Latin colonies.

If presented as above, the case for the copying of Roman topography from early times onwards might appear convincing but questions arise when it is examined in more detail. To begin with, there is little evidence for Coarelli's thesis distinguishing a direct relation between *Urbs* and colonial urban divisions, and his proposed development. In Ariminum, the Roman urban toponyms date to the imperial period. It is therefore not evident, as Coarelli suggests, that the division documented for the imperial period can be attributed to the moment of the foundation of the colony, in 268 BC.[86]

Moreover, no *vicus* is documented in Norba. The Norban *vici* are presupposed by recognising the topography of Rome in that of the colony by associating the cults of Norba – Juno Moneta, Diana, Juno Lucina – with the Roman Arx, Aventine and Esquiline respectively.[87] This point of departure is not really unbiased, but moreover, it does not prove in any way the existence of *vici*. The only unequivocal evidence for the possible copying of Roman toponymy in Latin colonies before the late Republican / imperial period remains the third century BC *vicus Esquilinus* from Cales.

In the end, the main question with regard to the copying of a Roman urban layout in colonies is then whether one accepts basic continuity from the Republican period to the better documented imperial period, or not. In the first scenario, the documentation for the Republican urban *vici* would just be a result of the scarcity of epigraphic data.[88] In the second scenario, the possibility of change in urban development and ideas of 'Romanness' and urbanity taking place from the mid-Republican to the late Republican and imperial period is left open.

I would like to further explore the second option, but first it is important to make two specifications with regard to the 'copying' of Roman urban toponymy. First, the use of Roman toponymy is best documented in the early imperial period, in which it also fits well ideologically. For example the toponyms

---

[81] The solution *C(ai) S(ervus)* or *c(um) s(uis)* (in *CIL* I², 416) is not sure, the letters may have been added later: see *ILLRP* 1217.

[82] *CIL* X, 4641.

[83] The dating of the cup is not unanimous, though: Coarelli 1995b, 177: "*ultimi decenni del IV secolo a.C.*"; Tarpin 2002: ca. 200 BC; Sanesi 1978, 76 and Guadagno 1993: first half third century BC.

[84] Coarelli 1995b; cf. Coarelli 1992 for a 'statist' conception of colonisation, assuming basic continuity from Archaic times onwards.

[85] Coarelli mentions Alba Fucens and Fregellae, citing Torelli 1991 for Alba Fucens. Torelli, however, does not mention the word *vicus* in this publication. No reference is given for Fregellae.

[86] Coarelli 1995b, 177; equally e.g. Ortalli 2000, 503: "*le iscrizioni vascolari attestano l'originaria ripartizione della città in vici, destinata ad essere riconfermata in età augustea.*"

[87] Proposed by Torelli 1988c, 134.

[88] Cf. Bispham 2006, 87, on the Calene *vicus Esquilinus*: "It must, I think, be admitted, that were our evidence for the middle Republic better, we would probably have similar examples from elsewhere."

of the Ariminate *vici* can be related to the Augustan re-colonisation.[89] Second, we should keep in mind the important observation by Bispham, that the colonial toponyms do *not* slavishly copy the Roman names of Roman urban divisions, but rather form a "re-application of placenames from Rome to colonial geography to produce new toponyms" and indeed that "our colonial toponyms are *Romanizing*, not Roman".[90] The process of naming should thus be seen as a creative process, rather than as a rigid transposition of some presupposed fixed 'urban system'. The implication is of course that the use of 'Roman' toponyms does not automatically mean that they were used for 'similar' – or indeed urban – realities.

7.3.2 THE POSSIBILITY OF EARLY RURAL ROMAN VICI NEAR LATIN COLONIES

Almost all reconstructions of *vici* in colonies are dominated by the idea that the Roman urban model was transposed to the *urban* division of the colony. However, since there is no firm evidence that the early colonial *vici* (i.e. in Cales and Ariminum) were indeed urban, the possibility that they were actually rural *vici* located outside the city walls should not be discarded a priori. In general, *vici* located in the countryside are attested at least from the end of the third century BC onwards.

The discussion can be related to the general make-up of early and mid-Republican colonies. First of all, the urban character of the colonial centre should not be exaggerated. It has been pointed out that the urban centres or *oppida* of colonies were rather small and perhaps did not need any further subdivision of the urban space in *vici*.[91] Evidence for densely populated urban areas in mid-Republican colonies is scarce. A well-known problem is that the urban centres of mid-Republican Latin colonies can not have physically accommodated within their walls the number of people which the ancient sources attribute to them.[92] Part of the population must have lived outside the urban centre. The idea that every single plot of assigned land would correspond to a single colonist's farm is also problematic. Field surveys in the territories of Latin colonies have revealed a rather uneven and nucleated pattern of settlement, rather than a regular pattern of dispersed sites.[93] Although at present there is no securely provenanced epigraphic evidence dating to the first phase of the colonies which can be related to such archaeologically attested nuclei, it is a distinct possibility that these nuclei reflect extra-urban *vici*.[94]

Many later rural *vici*, i.e. hamlets outside urban centres, are documented in inscriptions. No one would seriously consider relating these dedications, mostly in stone, found in the countryside to actions undertaken by urban *vici*.[95] Inversely, however, it is possible to question the presupposed *urban* status of some of the dedications of *vici* within the urban centres. One could well imagine that rural *vici* located somewhere in the territory of the urban centre brought dedications to the administrative or socio-political centre they depended on and this phenomenon is indeed documented.[96]

Moreover, what has proved to be the 'strongest' and sole contemporary evidence for the copying of Roman toponymy in *vici* in early colonial contexts, the *vicus Esquilinus* of Cales, is actually more compli-

---

[89] Already Mommsen suggested that the toponyms from Ariminum should be related to the installation of the *Colonia Augusta Ariminensis* (*CIL* XI p. 76), followed by Bispham 2006, 90 n. 91; cf. n. 78. (Sanesi 1978, 76 n. 15 raises the same possibility for Cales). Cf. Ando 2007 for 431-436 for triumviral and Augustan ideology in relation to colonies.

[90] Bispham 2006, 92. Colonial *vici* were thus not necessarily "*les frères de ceux de Rome*" (Morel 1988, 60, cf. *supra* n. 80), but rather, if anything, namesakes.

[91] Mingazzini 1958. Although one could object that such distinctions as *vici* could have served electoral purposes.

[92] Garnsey 1979.

[93] Pelgrom 2008.

[94] Cf. *infra* on the connection between the Marsic *vici* and Alba Fucens, and *vici* in the *ager Praetutianus* and Hatria.

[95] Cf. *infra* for discussion of localised names and archaeological remains of settlements related to inscriptions.

[96] In the *vicus Palatius* of Cales; cf. *infra*, also on *pagi* (and possibly rural *vici*) represented in the urban centre of Ariminum.

cated than it is often presented in discussions on colonisation in the 'Gellian view'. At first sight the presence of both a *vicus Palatius* and a *vicus Esquilinus* suggests a Roman type of urban organisation. However, the link between the two *vici* is not straightforward in view of the different dates and contexts in which the inscriptions were produced. Moreover, the urban location of both *vici* is contested.

Indeed, discussion is possible on the urban location of the *vicus Esquilinus*. The text (*K(aeso) Serponio(s) Caleb(us) fece(t) veqo Esqelino CS*) was applied in relief on a black gloss *patera* ('*Omphalosschale*') together with decoration of flying Erotes between floral motifs holding wreaths in their hands, and probably was intended to indicate the provenance of the potter and/or the place of production of the *patera*.[97] It is important to point out however that the original place of deposition is unknown,[98] it has even been suggested that the cup was actually produced on the Esquiline in Rome, where potters are known to have been active.[99] According to Paolino Mingazzini, this would explain the specification *Calebus*; indicating the potter's place of origin would only make sense 'abroad'.[100] However, if it is accepted that Kaeso Serponios worked at Cales,[101] it is still not certain that the text refers to an urban *vicus*.[102] Giuseppe Guadagno argues that the name does not so much reflect a Roman toponym but is rather applied because of the literal significance of the word. According to him, *esquilinus* would have been meant as an opposition to *inquilinus*; i.e. 'the *vicus* outside the city'.[103] This etymology might not convince everyone however[104] and perhaps we should admit that we simply do not know the location of the *vicus Esquilinus*, meaning that it can neither be cited as proof for an urban, nor for a rural *vicus*.

As to the *vicus Palatius*, Guadagno shows on the basis of a medieval source mentioning a location "*in vico qui Palaczu dicitur*" that it was probably extra-urban and located at the west end of the *ager Calenus*.[105] Interestingly, the inscription was found *within* the urban area of Cales.[106] The imperial inscription, engraved on a large marble slab, commemorates a congratulatory dedication of the *vicus* to the *patronus*

---

[97] Pagenstecher 1909, pl. 13.

[98] The vase ended up in the museum of Naples. Even if categorised under '*Calenische Reliefkeramik*' by Pagenstecher 1909 (where 'Calenisch' is used as a conventional term rather than as place of origin), it seems that the attribution of the find to the territory of Cales is based solely on the *Caleb(us)* text, which per se is not conclusive.

[99] Varro, *Ling*. 5.50. For other potters from Cales cf. Pagenstecher 1909, 147-149. K. Serponios is attested only once, while e.g. the potters L. Canoleios and the Gabinii are attested much better, often specifying *Calenos* or *Calebus*, but never mentioning *vici*.

[100] And thus also L. Canoleios and the Gabinii would have been working outside Cales according to Mingazzini 1958, 224-226.

[101] Sanesi 1978 for example rejects Mingazzini's idea, basing herself on the imperial *vicus Palatius* (which is however problematic, cf. *supra*) and the presence of kiln sites at Cales. Cf. n. 99: no other firmed vases from Kaeso Serponios have been found at Cales (cf. Pagenstecher 1909, who also states at p. 157 that Serponios' style was different ("*altertümlicher*") from the other Calene potters and that he "*keinen Nachfolger gefunden [hat]*"); a Calene production place is accepted by Pedroni 2001 109-110, who however does not offer further arguments (such as fabric analysis), but refers a.o. to Coarelli 1995b, thus closing the circle of reasoning (cf. Pedroni 1993, 226 proposing, on rather tenuous grounds – the location of a temple of Juno Lucina that is far from sure, and the association of this cult with the Esquiline in Rome – that the *vicus Esquilinus* might have been located at loc. Ponte delle Monache).

[102] Sanesi 1978, refuting Mingazzini's idea that the *patera* was made in Rome and arguing instead for a Calene production centre, thinks that the *vicus Esquilinus* might have been located outside the urban centre, but it is unclear on what grounds.

[103] Guadagno 1993, esp. 433-4

[104] Tarpin points out that a *vicus Esquilinus* thus understood seems to imply a *vicus Inquilinus* as well: Tarpin 2002: 84, n. 145, on the etymology cf. ibid. 87, n. 2. But it should be underscored that the co-existence of urban and extra-urban *vici* is not problematic per se.

[105] Guadagno 1993, 432.

[106] Guadagno 1993, 431 with n. 87. An extra-urban location had been suggested before, but on incorrect grounds.

of the city, L. Aufellius Rufus. The dedication was thus erected in the urban centre on which the extra-urban *vicus* apparently depended.[107] This is not only an eloquent document of the dependence of an extra-urban *vicus* on an urban centre, the fact that a *vicus* with a Roman urban toponym (*Palatius*) could be located *extra urbem* obviously weakens the 'urban mimic' thesis. This situation thus seems to support Bispham's warning that toponymy was used in a creative way (cf. *supra*) and it follows that urban names do not necessarily reflect an urban pattern.

But just how different was the colonial situation from Rome itself? The most widely accepted view envisages a development of urban Roman *vici* transposed to the urban centres of the colonies, in what would be a conscious imitation of the Roman urban topography. Moreover, in an elaboration of this scenario it is possible to see, in a secondary moment, the extension of this urban scheme into the territory of the colony, thus accounting for the rural *vici*. This 'Roman urban – colonial urban – rural development thesis' is the one adopted by Tarpin and fits well into the general 'Gellian' picture of colonies as small copies of Rome.

The alternative view, which is perhaps just as compatible with the evidence and the view of the *vicus* as a Roman development, is that the colonial *vici*, although clearly institutions adapted from Rome, were (also) located outside the colony's urban centre. This view might seem to run counter to the Gellian view of colonisation as it seems to presuppose the application of the same term (*vicus*) to a radically different pattern of settlement (rural) than that of Rome (urban). It might be argued however that this difference is to some extent only superficial, and may not have been understood that way in antiquity. If the *oppida* of the colonies did not contain intramural urban subdivisions, but rather controlled *vici* outside the colonial centre, this could perhaps correspond to ideas of Roman 'urbanity' as well, as the *vici* still depended on a political centre. Indeed, it should not be excluded that colonists could associate their own pattern of settlement with *an idea* of the layout of Rome itself, *e.g. Roma quadrata* or the Capitol were perhaps reflected in the colonial centre or *oppidum* and the Roman urban divisions were reflected in villages, *vici*, dispersed over the territory. This idea must for now of course remain hypothetical but could perhaps suggest some reconciliation between Roman ideological aspects of colonisation and the lack of archaeological evidence for urban development.

In sum, there is no conclusive evidence to ascertain the extra-urban *or* urban status of the early *vici* documented for Cales or Ariminum. Evidence for the 'imitation' of the topography of the city of Rome attested by Ariminate *vici* with the names *Aventinus, Germalus, Velabrus* (and, for that matter, the less direct *vici Dianensis* and *For(tunae)*) can be related to the Augustan re-colonisation and not to the original colonisation in 268 BC. The suggestive names of these *vici* therefore cannot be used to prove the urban status of the earlier *vici* of the colony. As with the Capitoline model, also in this case we should resist projecting later developments uncritically back to the mid-Republican period (cf. Chapter 2). I have explored the validity of an alternative 'rural' thesis for the early period. Arguably, such a view fits the evidence equally well but no decisive conclusions can as yet be drawn. In any case, the dichotomy between a 'rural' and an 'urban' thesis might be less severe if one regards the (idea of the) layout of the city of Rome itself in early times. Most important is however that the institution of the *vicus* and colonies were clearly closely related. This relationship could moreover be expressed through the performance of religious rituals. Such a ritual connection between urban centre, *vici* and territory (*pagi*) is best exemplified by the Latin colony of Ariminum, where black gloss cups mentioning both *vici* and *pagi* have been found in the urban centre. This phenomenon deserves some closer examination.

---

[107] Guadagno 1993, 432. The inscription can be dated to the second half of the first century AD.

7.3.3 A HYPOTHETICAL EXAMPLE: POCOLA DEORUM AND THE ARIMINATE VICI AND PAGI

The early *vici* of Ariminum are documented three times on fragments of black gloss ceramics.[108] *Pagi* are also mentioned on two other fragments. Not only the mention of *vici* and *pagi* as such is interesting, also the medium on which the texts were written provides precious information. By taking the objects themselves as a starting point, I will explore the possibility of reconstructing rituals connected to the *vici* and *pagi* of Ariminum.

The black gloss ceramics on which *vici* and *pagi* are written are generally identified as *pocola deorum*. This is the definition of a specific group of different black glazed forms presenting a theonym in the genitive and the word *pocolum* (= *poculum*) painted on it before firing (cf. figs. 7.4 and 7.5).[109]

These are mostly produced in Rome and its surroundings since some of the vases belong to the '*Atelier des Petites Estampilles*'. In general, they relate to 'Roman' or Latin contexts as is suggested by the use of the Latin language and the gods that are mentioned. Their geographical distribution is confined to the Latial and Etruscan areas and territories that were affected by Roman colonisation. The Latin colony of Ariminum would constitute a local production centre making its own *pocola* in the course of the third century BC after the deduction of the colony in 268 BC. However, imported *pocola* were also found.

Most *pocola* are dated to the third century BC.[110] *Pocola* have been found in different contexts, including funerary (esp. in Etruria) and domestic realms as well as cult places. This has led to various hypotheses regarding their function.[111] The now most commonly accepted interpretation is that the *pocola* were made and painted by order of the sanctuaries of the deities mentioned in the inscriptions.[112] The visitors of these sanctuaries bought the *pocola* there and could offer them instantly in the sanctuary or take them home as a souvenir, hence the different contexts in which they are found. The fact that the vase is actually indicated as *property* of the god, in the genitive, possibly points to its use for libation in both public and private contexts.[113]

The *pocolom* could have a rather 'personal' function, since it could be bought and dedicated, or taken home, by individual visitors. However, it was prefabricated, and no direct 'personalisation' of the cup seems to be intended as anyone passing by could buy a *pocolum*. For '*sovradipinta*' black gloss forms in general, it was also possible to order more specific texts. Sometimes the 'personal' aspect was emphasised by adding the name of the dedicant / commissioner that was then painted on the vase before firing.[114] This means that in such cases of 'specified' texts the party that ordered the text must have communicated with the potter / painter before production. Alternatively, the text was so generic and widely applicable that it could be mass produced. It is this last scenario that is envisaged for the standard *pocola* mentioning the name of the god, produced for a market of pilgrims or other visitors to the sanctuary.

The area of the Palazzo Battaglini in the urban centre of the colony of Ariminum has yielded various ceramic materials, amongst which vases defined explicitly as *poc[ola]* (one dedicated to Venus, another possibly to Diana, a third one unknown), and vases on which only the name of the god survives (Apollo, Hercules, Vulcanus) (see list *infra*). Five, or possibly six, vases from this group mention *pagi* (two) and *vici* (three; one inscription could relate to a *pagus* or a *vicus*, cf. *infra*) and these are also usually called *pocola* (see fig. 7.6).

---

[108] Perhaps four, cf. *infra*.

[109] Morel/Coarelli 1973; Cifarelli *et al.* 2002-2003, 280-296.

[110] Cf. the catalogue in Cifarelli *et al.* 2002-2003.

[111] They would have functioned in the ancestor cult, or rather as ex-voto's: see Cifarelli *et al.* 2002-2003, 285 for different contexts, 290-293 with bibliography on hypotheses regarding the function.

[112] Morel/Coarelli 1973, 57.

[113] Cifarelli *et al.* 2002-2003, 293.

[114] Alternatively, one could fire the vase a second time for 'fixing' the painted elements. Cf. discussion in Cifarelli *et al.* 2002-2003, 269-273. There is perhaps an example of a *pocolum* that was 'personalised' in such a way, found in Segni: Cifarelli *et al.* 2002-2003, esp. 268-273.

Fig. 7.4. *Pocolom Saeturni*, provenance unknown (*Roma* 1973, pl. VII, 29).

In light of the above, we should actually refrain from referring to the vases mentioning *pagi* and *vici* as *pocola*, first because they lack the *pocolum* text, the most significant identifying element but also because the function of the *pagi* and *vici* vases does not seem to be in accordance with that of the standard *pocola*. Is seems illogical to suppose that anyone passing by could or would buy a cup with the indication of the rather specific administrative entities of *pagus* or *vicus* on it, unless one was in some way related to these entities. This is in line with the context in which the *pagi* and *vici* inscriptions were found, namely public and/or sacral contexts, as opposed to funerary and domestic contexts.

Fig. 7.5. *Fortunai pocolo(m)*, possibly from Otranto (*CIL* I², 443).

In order to understand the character of the dedications involving the *pagi* and *vici* of Ariminum it is useful to briefly examine the possible interpretations of the texts themselves.

The texts are:[115]
1. *CIL* I², 2897a   *pagi. fid[ei, –elis* or *-idenatium?]*
2. *CIL* I², 2897b   *pa[gi?---]*
3. *CIL* I², 2899a   *veici [---]*
4. *CIL* I², 2899b   *veic[---]*
5. *CIL* I², 2899c   *[v]eic[i---]*
and possibly
6. *CIL* I², 2898   *]i. vesuini*

[115] One new '*poculum*' published by Minak 2006b and discussed by Braccesi 2006 could be reconstructed as *[v]ec(os) rai[* and thus constitute another *vicus* inscription (significantly with a proper name as it would seem), but Braccesi dismisses this reading in favour of a dedication to *Daeira*. Cf. n. 141.

139

I give also the texts of the *pocola* and vases on which a theonym might be read (see fig. 7.7):[116]

7. CIL I², 2885   *[Ven]erus. poclom*
8. CIL I², 2886   *?Dian]ai. pocol[om]*
9. CIL I², 2887   *[---] poc[olom]*
10. CIL I², 2894   *[Ap]ole[ni]*
11. CIL I², 2895   *Apol]eni*
12. CIL I², 2896a   *h(er)c(ules)* or *h(ercules) c(ustos) vel sim.*
13. CIL I², 2896b-f   *h(ercules)*
14. Minak a   *A]pollo* or *poclo*
15. Minak b   *Vu]lca[nus]*

Fig. 7.6. Some of the Ariminate *vici* and *pagi* inscriptions (Degrassi 1986, pl. 14, fig. 4).

The question is whether *vici* and *pagi* are nominative plural or genitive singular, which changes the meaning significantly. In the latter case, one is directed at an interpretation of the texts as dedications from distinctive *vici* and *pagi*, i.e. 'from *vicus* x' or 'from *pagus* y'. In this scenario, we will have to admit that in most cases the distinctive names of the *vici* and *pagi* are accidentally lost, apart perhaps from the *pagi Fid[*, which could also be reconstructed as a proper name of the *pagus* (e.g. *Fidenatium vel sim.*).[117] Another example of a 'specified' *vicus* or *pagus* could be formed by the *-]i vesuini* inscription in which the *–i* could perhaps be reconstructed as *[pag]i* or *[vic]i*. Perhaps, *vesuini* reflects a proper name of the *pagus* or *vicus*. It has even been suggested that it refers to the origin of the colonists, i.e. from the Vesuvian area.[118] In the genitive singular interpretation, the texts of *pagi* and *vici* appear to have been the result of a specific order to the potter / painter. This interpretation agrees well with the specific *vici* known from the imperial period (*Aventinus*, *Germalus* etc.). Reasoning from hindsight is risky but at least one *vicus* already had a proper name in the third century BC, the Calene *vicus Esquilinus*.

If the *pagi* and *vici* texts are nominative plural rather than genitive singular, this would mean that specific proper names of *pagi* and *vici* were absent. Annalisa Franchi De Bellis would thus interpret the texts rather as "*una dedica collettiva da parte dei pagi e dei vici riminesi*".[119] The letters *Fid[* should, according to Franchi De Bellis, be understood as an indication of the deity that was honoured, *pagi Fid[ei]* > 'the *pagi* to the goddess Fides'.[120] The text *-]i vesuini* would in her view not indicate the origin of the colonists from the Vesuvian area[121] but would rather be part of an onomastic formula in the genitive.[122] Not wanting to 'write history from square brackets', in the *vesuini*-case judgment is perhaps best suspended.

---

[116] Minak refers to Minak 2006b, 43, as yet unedited in the ususal corpora.
[117] Zuffa 1962, 99-103; Susini 1965, 150-151.
[118] Zuffa 1962, 102-103. Cf. discussion in Susini 1965, 146-147; *contra* Franchi De Bellis 1995.
[119] Franchi De Bellis 1995, 383; followed e.g. by Fontemaggi/Piolanti 2000.
[120] Franchi De Bellis 1995, 385.
[121] And neither a dedication to Vesuna: Zuffa 1962, 103; Susini 1965, 146-147.
[122] Franchi De Bellis 1995, 385.

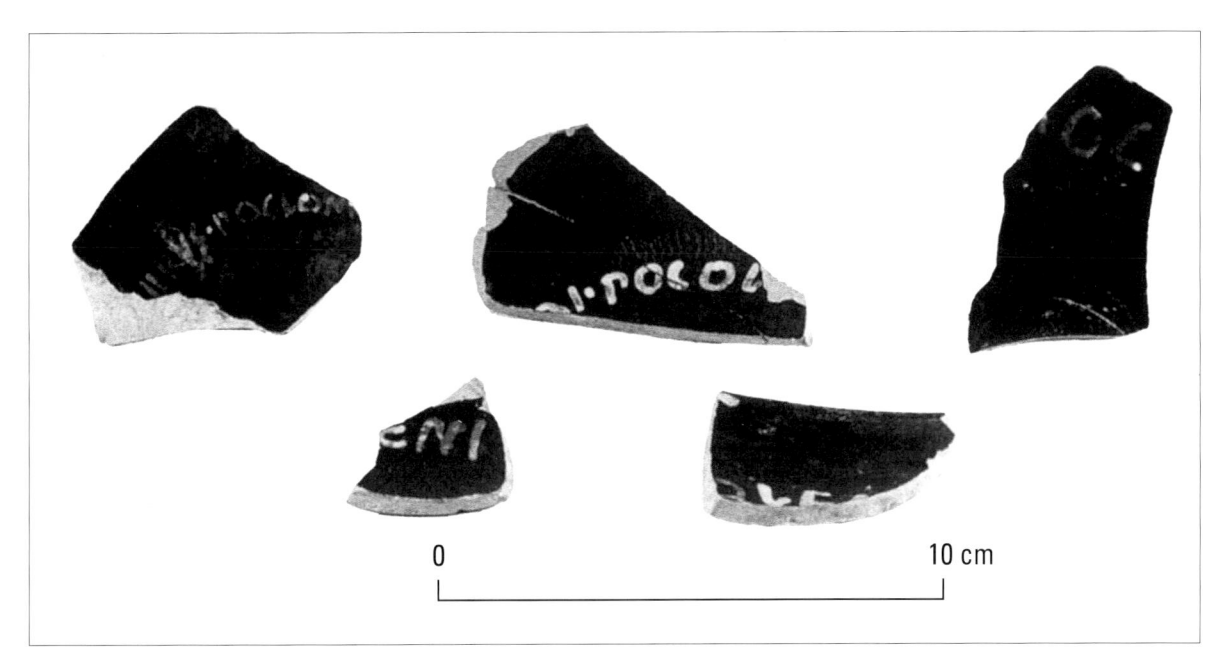

Fig. 7.7. Some of the Ariminate *pocola* (Degrassi 1986, pl. 14, fig. 5).

In any case, for both grammatic interpretations it is clear that representatives of different parts of (the territory of) the colony dedicated the objects in one central place in the urban centre, where apparently other more specific 'religious' dedications were also brought (the 'real' *pocola*, and the dedications to Apollo, Hercules and Vulcanus). This place could therefore, with some probability, be recognised as a cult place or at least as a politico-religious central place.[123] Essentially, it makes no difference whether it is defined as a 'cult place' or not. The point is that rituals involving socio-political entities were performed there.

Differently from the 'real' *pocola*, which were made for a generic audience, it seems probable that for the *vicus* and *pagus* cups an order was placed beforehand at the potter / painter. This will have been the case in both the interpretation as nominative plural and as genitive singular. The institutions of *pagus* and *vicus* are too specific for these cups to be produced unless following an explicit order or at least for some special occasion. Although in the nominative plural interpretation the *pagi* and *vici* are admittedly less specific, it is still hard to imagine that a potter / painter would prefabricate vases with *vici* and *pagi* texts just like that.

The differences between the grammatical interpretations consist in the emphasis put on the 'own' identity of specific *vici* and *pagi* (genitive singular plus proper distinctive names), or rather on their unity as a whole (nominative plural without specification). In both cases however a strong 'construction' of unity becomes apparent, since the *vici* and *pagi* were ritually united in the urban centre.

The *pagi* were beyond doubt located outside the city. As noted in Chapters 4 and 6, the *pagus* was an institution that was without exception located in the countryside. Therefore, the vases with *pagi* texts must reflect dedications *in* the urban centre by communities from *outside* the urban centre. The *vici* appearing on the same type of vases in the same context could reflect urban or rural *vici*, or a combination of both. The fact that other extra-urban communities (the *pagi*) were involved indicates that this specific dedicatory action in the central urban centre was at least not the privilege of urban entities.

If indeed some of these *vici* were extra-urban, this type of *vicus* would then be an agglomeration outside of, but dependent on the urban centre of the colony. Several sites have been recognised around

[123] The provenance of the finds is indicated as '*scavi di Palazzo Battaglini*', which is not specific, but a link between the different kinds of dedications can be, and without exception has been, surmised.

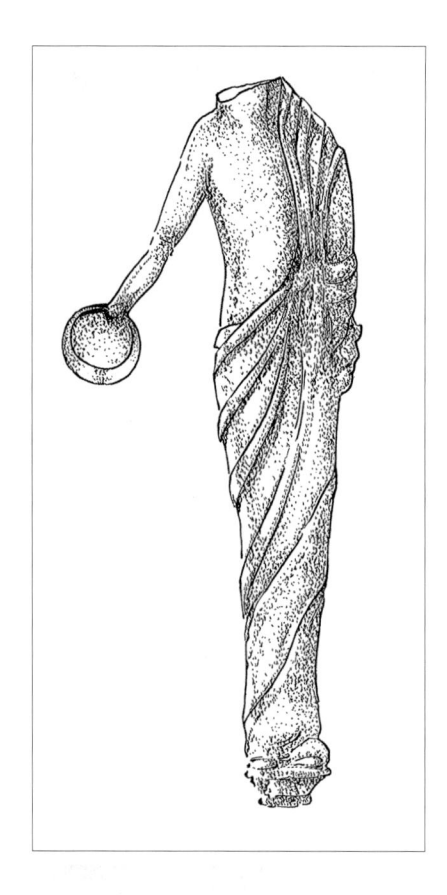

Fig. 7.8. Sacrificant in bronze with *patera* from votive deposit, Sarsina (adapted from Miari 2000a, 331, chart 101c).

Ariminum. None have yet yielded explicit epigraphic evidence for their possible status of *vicus*, although medieval sources locate a *vicus Popilius* at the site of S. Lorenzo in Strada.[124] Here, a sanctuary is attested by architectural terracottas dating between the second half of the second century BC and the first century BC. Other sites in the territory of the colony also point to the colonists' influence outside the urban centre.[125]

Be that as it may, what we can say with some certainty about Ariminum is that parts of the territory of the colony, *pagi* and (either rural or urban) *vici*, dedicated black gloss vessels in the urban centre, presumably in a sacral-political place. We could ask ourselves by what ritual action the vessels were offered and why they used these ordinary ceramics and not, for instance, stone stelae. It seems tempting to relate the form of the dedicated objects to their possible function. In general, *pocola deorum* are thought to have been used in libation rituals. Whereas *pocola deorum* are produced in varied open and closed forms such as cups, jugs, and plates,[126] the Ariminate vessels with *pagi* and *vici* inscriptions are exclusively open forms. The inscriptions were without exception applied on the inside of the vessel (cf. fig. 7.6).[127] Such forms, cups or *paterae*, are even more closely associated with libations and similar rituals, especially in the public realm.[128] In particular, *paterae* are known to

---

[124] Cf. Fontemaggi/Piolanti 1995, 538.

[125] Fontemaggi/Piolanti 1995, 557 with previous bibliography. Interesting with regard to other sites is the Covignano area, which was frequented from pre-Roman times onwards (cf. Cristofani 1995), but which also yielded a consistent corpus of Roman period materials. Fontemaggi and Piolanti date the "*maggiore sviluppo*" of the settlement in the early imperial period, but early black gloss pottery produced in Ariminum is also present (Fontemaggi/Piolanti 1995, esp. 542-545). Several cult places have been recognised in this area and they seem to have been reused or taken over and even monumentalised after the foundation of the colony. At least one monumental temple is attested by column drums later reused in a parish church and Italic-Corinthian capitals (belonging to a different building than the column drums: cf. Marini Calvani 2000). Two marble statues, one of Minerva with *aegis* and helmet, one possibly of Fortuna (cf. Marini Calvani 2000, 52) can be dated to the second half of the third century BC, that is directly after the foundation of Ariminum (Lippolis 2000).

[126] See the catalogues in Cifarelli *et al.* 2002-2003.

[127] See the catalogue in Cifarelli *et al.* 2002-2003. The precise forms of the cups cannot be found in the existing literature: unfortunately, a work from 1982 by C. Giovagnetti and O. Piolanti with a catalogue of all inscriptions and pottery, remains unpublished (cf. Franchi De Bellis 1995, 372). Cf. Riccioni 1965, 117-119, who defines all cups with *pagi* / *vici* texts (including the *pagi Fid[* inscription) as "*ciotola ad orlo rientrante*", just as most *pocola* with the names of deities (*Apollo* and *Jerus*). The piece with the *vesuini* text is described as a "*ciotola ad orlo pendente*", the forms of those with personal names differ sometimes as well. Cf. Franchi De Bellis 1995, 371: "*coppe, ciotole o patere.*"

[128] A dedication of a *pagus* from Cupra montana was also made on a *patera* but the character of this inscription is quite difficult to establish (*CIL* IX, 5699; cf. *supra*); cf. also the *vicus Esquilinus* from Cales, again recorded on a *patera*.

Fig. 7.9. Marble altar, Rome Palazzo dei Conservatori (inv.no. 3352), Augustan period (Fless 1995, pl. 45, fig. 1).

have been used for public libations, sacrifices (for sprinkling the animal, the serving of the *mola salsa*, the receiving of the blood), and as drinking vessels during ritual meals. Interestingly, they also figure in rituals with an explicit political component. In the time of Varro, the *patera* was used in the ritual installation of *magistri* because of its traditional value and the magistrates offered wine to the gods from a *patera*.[129] The

[129] Varro, *Ling.* 5.122: *Praeterea in poculis erant paterae, ab eo quod late patent ita dictae. Hisce etiam nunc in publico convivio antiquitatis retinendae causa, cum magistri fiunt, potio circumfertur, et in sacrificando deis hoc poculo magistratus dat deo vinum.*

dedication of the *patera* itself in a sanctuary is also attested in texts.[130] Their use in rituals is illustrated by the common type of small bronze statues of sacrificants holding a *patera* in one hand, here for example from a votive deposit of the second half of the third / beginning of the second century BC in Sarsina (cf. fig. 7.8).[131]

For what it is worth, *paterae* feature prominently in the iconography related to the activities of the *magistri vici* in the imperial period (fig. 7.9) and indeed the *Lares Compitales*, central to the *vicus* cult (cf. Chapter 9), are commonly depicted with *rhyton* and *patera* (cf. Chapter 9, fig. 9.8).[132] Admittedly, rituals involving *paterae* might have been rather general, but the above may provide an idea of the context in which the Ariminate vessels could have been used.

The entities that are indicated on the cups, *vici* and especially *pagi*, are basically territorial divisions. The form of the objects and the very dedication itself suggest a sacred rite of some sort. It could be asked what kind of rite would be appropriate in this context and I would suggest that the sacred rite expressing territoriality *par excellence* is the *lustratio*. During a *lustratio* the boundaries of a given space are ritually cleansed, redefined, and symbolically strengthened. At the same time, a certain *group* is defined.[133] Moreover, if the inscription reading *pagi Fid[* (*CIL* I², 2897a, here no. 1) indeed reflects a dedication to the goddess Fides on behalf of the Ariminate *pagi*, a parallel with the *Terminalia* would present itself since Fides is associated closely with the festival of boundaries.[134]

A temple to *Fides publica* or *Fides populi Romani* was built on the Capitol, close to the temple of Jupiter between 258 and 247 BC, suggesting that the goddess was of particular interest in Rome at that time.[135] Copies of treaties and decrees were exhibited in this temple.[136] This interest may moreover be reflected in a passage of Agathocles' *Perì Kyzíkou* of the third century BC, handed down by Festus. Here, Rhome, the granddaughter of Aeneas, is said to have dedicated the first temple to Fides on the Palatine.[137] This illustrates how strongly the goddess was connected to 'Rome' in the third century BC – the period in which the Ariminate *pagi* and *vici* performed their dedication.

It is not unimaginable that the Ariminate vases were deposited in the urban centre after having been carried around the boundaries of the *vici* (which could be both rural and urban) and *pagi* in question as a means of consolidating both territoriality and allegiance to the urban centre. Alternatively, the representatives of the *vici* and *pagi* dedicated the cups in the cult place on behalf of their communities but without a preceding *lustratio* of the territories. In both cases a centripetal procession could be surmised which 'materialised' the physical distance and at the same time the bond between centre and community.

Schematically, three different levels of ritual action can be hypothesised. First, the ritual enhancement of the boundaries of the rural and/or urban *vici* and the rural *pagi*. Second, the emphasing of the link

---

[130] Liv. 6.4.3; Plin. *HN* 12.42; cf. in general Von Schaewen 1940, 24-32; Siebert 1999, 40-44.

[131] Miari 2000a, with the '*schede*' on pp. 331-332. The statuettes were found at the NW corner of the forum.

[132] Cf. Hano 1986; see also Chapter 9 on the iconography of the *Lares Compitales*.

[133] Cf. Fless 2005, 54: "*Beide Rituale (scil. das Ritual des sulcus primigenius und die lustratio) dienen der Definition und Konstituierung eines Raumes oder einer Gruppe von Menschen, die sich in diesem Raum aufhält.*" For *vicus* in the sense of a community rather than a territorial entity, cf. *infra* on *CIL* IX, 3813 (= *CIL* I², 391); Letta 2001, 151.

[134] For the reading of *Fid[ei]* in *CIL* I², 2897a: Franchi De Bellis 1995, 385. I have doubts however as to the typical 'Sabine' nature of this goddess, Franchi De Bellis seems to connect this ethnic connotation (Varro, *Ling*. 5.74) to the origin of the colonists, but Fides was thought to be a very ancient Roman goddess, perhaps pre-dating Numa (Fest. 328 L.), for a date in the time of Numa: Liv. 1.21.4; Dion. Hal. *Ant. Rom*. 2.75.3; Plut. *Num*. 16.1.70.

[135] Cic. *Off*. 3.104. Cf. also Pisaurum (Cresci Marrone/Mennella 1984, 95) where a *cippus* was erected for *Fides* at the end of the third century BC. On the temple on the Capitol: Reusser 1993; on Fides: Piccaluga 1981; Freyburger 1986, esp. 229-317. Cf. also the *magistri* documented at Capua, who in 110 BC constructed a wall for Spes, Fides and Fortuna. *CIL* X, 3775 (= *CIL* I², 674).

[136] E.g. *CIL* I², 587 and *CIL* I², 589. Cf. Mommsen 1858.

[137] Fest. 328 L = *FGrH* 472 F5; cf. Aronen 1995.

between these *vicus*- and *pagus*-communities and the urban cult place, in the process also creating a link between the various dedicating *vici* and *pagi*. The third level would be represented by the possible wider ideological link with 'Romanness' or 'Latinity', expressed by the dedication in presumably the same place of the proper *pocola* and cups dedicated to gods. The presence of the god Apollo, named on two cups, is especially appropriate in rituals connected to the foundation of the colony, since he can be seen as the chief god for new founders in both Greek and Roman contexts.[138] It would perhaps go too far to recognise a 'Roman pantheon'[139] in the gods that are venerated, but there surely is a strong significance of the (cult) place for the colony as a new foundation, and in this creation Roman and/or Latin elements played an important role. By dedicating their vases in the same place that was thus associated with the foundation of the colony, the *vici* and *pagi* communities could emphasise the ideological construction of the colony and its territory. This place would have connected the diverse elements that were part of the colonial foundation to one another and perhaps also to Rome, or rather a more general idea of Romanness or Latinity.[140] Some *pocola* that were brought from other places in Italy and were deposited here could support this thesis.[141] In this respect, a locally produced black gloss cup impressed with a Roman *uncia* with a naval prow and the legend *Roma* is especially suggestive.[142]

In this discussion, the difference between rural and urban *vici* is of little importance. The rituals enhanced the bond between both rural units (the *pagi* and perhaps the *vici* – if it could be proven that they were rural) and urban units (urban *vici* – if it could be proven that they were urban) on the one hand and a central place on the other. This bond transcended the confines of both rural and urban units and was physically located outside their boundaries.

The religious role of the *pagus* and the *vicus* is discussed in more detail in Chapters 8 and 9 with reference to the two associated festivals, i.e. the *Paganalia* and the *Compitalia*. These festivals present important characteristics of the *lustratio* concept. It will become clear that the 'first level' of ritual action, which was focused above all on the *vicus* or *pagus* community itself, can be convincingly demonstrated in other contexts. Evidence for the sacred link between these communities and the urban centre (the 'second level') is generally less abundant but is at least securely attested in early Ariminum.

I will now discuss two areas that have securely documented rural *vici*, the *ager Praetutianus* and the Fucine area. After evaluating the evidence, I will return to the relationship between *vici* and colonisation.

---

[138] Susini 1965, 148; cf. Ortalli 2000, 503, according to whom the *pocola* were related to rituals associated with migration and foundation. Cf. the discussion on the early Latin dedications to Apollo in the Marsic area and the *ager Praetutianus*, n. 182. On Apollo and colonisation cf. e.g. Malkin 1986; Malkin 1998.

[139] Franchi De Bellis 1995, 371.

[140] Cf. *CIL* I², 40 (*c. manlio aci / cosol / pro poplo arimenesi*), which was dedicated in the sanctuary of Diana in Nemi, and *CIL* VI, 133 from Rome (*dianae sanctai ariminenses*), attesting to the religious and ideological connection of the Ariminates to Roman and Latin cult places of Diana (cf. Cicala 1995).

[141] Some of the *pocola* found in Ariminum can be distinguished by fabric and form to be of non-local origin including *CIL* I², 2885; *CIL* I², 2887 (Minak 2006b, esp. 43) just as the probable dedication to Vulcanus (Minak 2006a). If the diffusion of these *pocola* dedicated to gods can indeed be related to individual actions of the 'souvenir' type, this would document the connection between diverse Latin / Roman centres on a ritual level too. Francesca Minak argues that colonists took *pocola* from their home cities to the newly founded colony (Minak 2006a). All black gloss vases mentioning a *vicus* or *pagus* were, as it seems, locally produced. According to this logic, the reading *[v]ec(os) rai[* of the problematic new '*pocolum*', of local production, would not be impossible (published by Minak 2006b and discussed by Braccesi 2006, who ultimately prefers reading a dedication to *Daeira*). In this way, the patterns of import versus local production would echo the constructions of group feelings both on Latin and local levels.

[142] Zuffa 1962; cf. Morel 1988 esp. 60.

7.4 RURAL VICI AND SANCTUARIES IN THE AGER PRAETUTIANUS

In the *ager Praetutianus*, along the Adriatic coast, rural *vici* have been recognised and studied extensively. The link to sanctuaries is documented relatively well. This situation could be specific for the historical development and consequent patterns of settlement in this area. In itself this is not problematic because the example of the *ager Praetutianus* is in its own right relevant to the discussion of sanctuaries and the so-called *pagus-vicus* system. It is not inconceivable, however, that the relatively clear picture we have for the Praetutian area is due to the high intensity of research here, and that it in fact reflects a more common phenomenon.[143]

Rome conquered the area that they consequently called the *ager Praetutianus* in the early third century BC and it was assigned to *Regio V* (Picenum) under Augustus.[144] Before the conquest, people who apparently defined themselves as (some sort of) Sabines populated the area.[145] After the conquest by M.' Curius Dentatus in 290 BC and the foundation of the Latin colony of Hatria between 289 and 286 BC, the indigenous Praetutii probably received the *civitas sine suffragio* which was upgraded to the full citizenship in 241 BC.[146] The imposing sanctuary of Monte Giove (Cermignano), which would have been of central importance to (a section of) the Praetutii, was possibly taken over by the colonists.[147] Furthermore, the Roman colony of Castrum Novum was founded at the same time and a *conciliabulum*, where a *praefectura iure dicundo* was also installed, was located at Interamna Praetutiorum.

vici *and sanctuaries*

Several sites in this area represent sanctuaries directly related to settlements. Some of these settlements can be recognised as *vici* via epigraphic evidence. In her 1995 study, Maria Paola Guidobaldi dedicated a chapter to '*vici e santuari*', listing 17 sites, drawing conclusions on the organisation of the territory based on this dataset. I review and amend this dataset and then discuss her conclusions. The evidence for some sites that Guidobaldi interprets as sanctuaries relating to *vici*, does not allow this identification in my opinion. Nevertheless, they have been included here in order to furnish a better context.[148]

---

[143] Especially thanks to the publications by A. Staffa, G. Messineo, L. Franchi Dell'Orto in the Documenti dell'Abruzzo Teramano series. Moreover, Guidobaldi 1995 develops a specific interest in the link between colonisation, territory, and sanctuaries and *vici* in her excellent study on the colony of Hatria and the romanisation of the *ager Praetutianus*.

[144] Cf. Delplace 1993, esp. 11-34.

[145] On the formation of the *ethnos*, cf. Guidobaldi 1995, 48, 53-59, 177-179.

[146] Humbert 1978, 238-421, 378 n. 66 and 386-390; cf. however the general critique on the modern view of the *civitas sine suffragio* by Mouritsen 2007.

[147] Guidobaldi 1995, 50-52: an archaic Latin inscription mentions the *tribus* of the dedicants and another inscription found in the neighbourhood, dated 10 BC, commemorates a dedication to a *patronus* of the colony. Cf. Strazzulla 2006, 85-87 and in general on the Roman habit to incorporate important sanctuaries my Chapter 2.

[148] Only the sites with direct relevance to the subject have been included; Guidobaldi's Chapter '*vici e santuari*' also includes sites that are neither a Hellenistic sanctuary nor a *vicus* and sometimes the remains are too sparse to identify them as such. Therefore her sites 3 (archaic Latin inscription to Mania or nymph), 4 (some finds relating to a cult place), 5 (funeral inscription), 7 (remains of wall), 8 (archaic Latin inscription to Apollo), 12 (the 'ethnic' sanctuary of the Praetutii at Monte Giove, re-used or even usurped in Roman times, but not related to a *vicus*), 16 (altar), 17 (an apparently late dedication to Victoria) are not discussed here. The correspondence between the sites listed here and those of Guidobaldi is 1 ~ 1; 2 ~ 2; 3 ~ 6; 4 ~ 9; 5 ~10; 6 ~ 11; 7 ~ 13; 8 ~ 14; 9 ~ 15. Cf. also the recently excavated sanctuary at loc. Madonna della Cona, ca. 3 km from Interamna: Strazzulla 2006, 91, to be published by Vincenzo Torrieri.

1. Località Piano Vomano – Colle del Vento

The archaeological complex at Colle del Vento, examined by Luisa Franchi dell'Orto and Andrea Staffa, seems to consist of a hill-fort and a sanctuary, possibly combined with a settlement, dating to the period after the Roman conquest.[149] However, since there is no epigraphic (or toponymic) evidence to suggest that the status of this possible settlement was that of a *vicus*, Colle del Vento is omitted from the current discussion. Guidobaldi's interpretation of the site as a Roman territorial sanctuary beside which a *vicus* subsequently developed must remain hypothetical.

2. Località Case Lanciotti-Masseria Nisii (Comune di Montorio al Vomano)

In 1865 the ruins of a temple were found.[150] The double *cella* had a mosaic with an inscription, providing a consular date of 55 BC and the deity that was venerated, Hercules.[151] The musive inscription records three *magistri* who saw *d(e) v(ici) s(ententia)* to the construction of the temple and the painting of its walls.[152] Remains of a marble club were found in the *cella*.[153] Staffa suggests that some finds could indicate an earlier date for the cult place, associating it with second to early first century sanctuaries in Abruzzo and Molise.[154] Since a *magistra veneris* is also documented, Guidobaldi proposes a double cult of Hercules and Venus.[155] The *vicus* could be recognised in the area of present Montorio al Vomano, which is the only area in the environs of the sanctuary where "*elementi di una certa consistenza*" have been found.[156] This area is

[149] Polygonal walls enclose an area of ca. 1200 m², within which the foundations in *opus quadratum* of a temple of the Roman period have been recognised under the medieval remains of a church and a related settlement. Apart from explorations by Franchi dell'Orto and Staffa, no systematic excavation or survey has been undertaken and the site has been plundered. Although there seems to be no hard evidence for the presence of an ancient settlement, this seems to be at least presupposed (the title of the contribution of Franchi dell'Orto and Staffa reads *L'insediamento italico di Colle del Vento*) on the basis of the area enclosed; Franchi Dell'Orto/Staffa 1991, 173: "*A Colle del Vento abbiamo un'altura fortificata con al centro una struttura templare. L'area delimitata dal perimetro delle mura poligonali è di circa 1200 mq., una misura che ben si addice all'arx munita di un piccolo insediamento.*" The provenance of the ceramics within the complex published in Franchi Dell'Orto/Staffa 1991 is unfortunately unknown. Behind the walled enclosure on the hill-top is an area which yielded many ceramic materials, mostly medieval but also earlier, and this is where Franchi dell'Orto and Staffa think the ancient *vicus* was located (Franchi Dell'Orto/Staffa 1991, 174: some of the published ceramics also appear to have been found in this area). Whereas Dell'Orto and Staffa previously recognised a pre-Roman hill-fort in these remains, Guidobaldi points out that all materials can be dated after the beginning of the third century BC and may be related to Roman intervention. The location of the apparently new construction in the Roman period in relation to the construction of the *via Caecilia* at the beginning of the third century BC is suggestive (Guidobaldi 1995, 250).

[150] Staffa 1991, 202-204.

[151] *CIL* IX, 5052 (= *CIL* I², 765).

[152] One *magister*, Q. Ofillius Rufus son of Caius may have been family to a L. Ofillius Rufus, son of Lucius, in the Latin colony of Aesernia, who saw to the construction of a street there in about the same period (*CIL* IX, 2667): Staffa 1991, 203.

[153] Guidobaldi 1995, 250-253.

[154] Staffa 1991, 203.

[155] *CIL* IX, 5055. Note however that there are several instances of *magistri / ae* associated with certain deities that are active in sanctuaries of other deities, and it is not clear whether this has to imply a cult for the name-giving deities in those cult places as well. (cf. e.g. *CIL* IX, 3138: … *magistri laverneis murum caementicium / portam porticum / templum bonae deae* …).

[156] Staffa 1991, 200, 203, followed by Guidobaldi 1995, 250-253. However, nearer to the sanctuary, north and uphill, are the sites 36 and 38 (respectively Roseto and Rodiano-Campitello, Staffa 1991, 201) which yielded some late Republican and imperial material.

some 2 km further east along the river basin. Thus, although a *vicus* is attested by the inscription in the sanctuary, the *vicus* itself cannot be located with certainty.

3. Pagliaroli (Comune di Cortino)

At this site, the remains of a sanctuary of the second century BC have been found. Some elements of the rich architectural decoration seem to relate to the Latin colony of Hatria in style and production.[157] There is no epigraphic evidence to prove this connection, nor a connection to a *vicus*. A settlement is presupposed on the basis of other not further specified finds found in the area,[158] but for the analysis here of *vici* and sanctuaries, Pagliaroli should be left out.

4. Collina di S. Berardino

Votive material consisting of early black gloss and Italian sigillata was found at Collina di S. Berardino. According to Guidobaldi the sanctuary could represent "*uno dei primi atti di appropriazione del territorio da parte dei Romani insediatisi nell'agro pretuzio all'indomani della fulminea campagna di conquista di Manio Curio Dentato*". The link with a probable settlement, possibly with the status of *vicus*,[159] near Campovalano is not clear. Clearly, this evidence cannot be used in the present discussion.

5. *The* vicus Strament(arius) *or* Strament(icius)

In the *Comune* of Sant'Omero there is secure evidence for both a temple dedicated to Hercules and a *vicus*-settlement.[160] During the construction of a house next to the pre-Romanic church of S. Maria a Vico (!) in 1885 an inscription was found re-used as a tombstone and can now be seen walled into the church. The inscription, mentioning *cultores Herculis*, dates to the Trajanic period and is written in two columns, between which the club of Hercules is depicted.[161] The text sanctions the obligation to hold a yearly funerary banquet in memory of a certain Tiberius Claudius Himerius, son of Claudia Hedonia, in all probability members of the same college.[162] The phrase *in templo Herculis* documents the temple, whereas a *vicus Strament(arius)* or *Strament(icius)* is mentioned in the last part of the inscription. The settlement can be recognised in the rich archaeological material found in the area where the medieval church of S. Maria a Vico was later built, possibly directly on the foundations of the Hercules temple. The settlement seems to have flourished from the late Republican period well into the imperial period, although earlier ceramics could attest to continuity from prehistoric times.[163] Guidobaldi dates the formation of the settlement in the course of the second century BC.[164] In sum, at least in the imperial period a *vicus* with sanctuary is attested. Although the inscriptions do not allow for a secure Republican dating of the *vicus* (and sanctuary), the archaeological remains may support this date.

6. Contrada S. Rustico (Comune di Basciano)

In 1928 the remains of a temple were excavated, and research in the 1970s revealed both epigraphic and architectural evidence of this sanctuary, dated to the second century BC, and of a settlement that dates

---

[157] Guidobaldi 1995, 208-214, 257; Strazzulla 2006, 89-91.

[158] Guidobaldi 1995, 255. For the archaeological materials, Staffa 1991, sites 124, 234-239.

[159] On the basis of *CIL* IX, 5136, recording a dedication to Divus Julius, perhaps to be connected with the installation of statues to Caesar in the *municipia* and perhaps also *vici* of Italy: Guidobaldi 1995, 262.

[160] Staffa 1996, 283-285.

[161] The *cultores Herculis universi iurati per I(ovem) O(ptimum) M(aximum) Geniumque Imp(eratoris) / Caesaris Nervae Traiani Aug(usti) / Ger(manici)* stand in some way under the protection of Jupiter Optimus Maximus and the *Genius* of Trajan; cf. Delplace 1993, 243-244.

[162] Dessau, *ILS*, 7215.

[163] Staffa 1996, 283; site 117: 283-285; cf. Guidobaldi 1995, 263: "*tra il II secolo a.C. e il IV secolo d.C.*"

[164] Guidobaldi 1995, 264.

Fig. 7.10. Basciano, località S. Rustico. Settlement with temple (T) (adapted from Messineo 1986, 138 fig. 47).

slightly later, from the middle of the first century BC continuing into the late imperial period (figs. 7.10 and 7.11).

The temple was repaired in the imperial period but can be dated to the second century BC because of the symmetrical podium cornice which has parallels in S. Giovanni in Galdo, Fontecchio, Pietrabbondante A and the large temple at Schiavi d'Abruzzo. This date is confirmed by the architectural terracotta's.[165]

Underneath one of the buildings of the settlement (N3) apparently a votive deposit was found[166] together with black gloss ceramics dating to between the middle of the second and the middle of the first century BC,[167] thus providing the most important dating element of the structuration of the settlement complex as a whole, even if the link between the building and the deposit is not clear.[168] The oldest buildings seem to be S29 and S29a, which are made using the same technique as the temple.[169] The settlement

---

[165] Messineo 1986.

[166] Messineo/Pellegrino 1984.

[167] Messineo 1986, 149-154. Although Morel 2830 could be dated earlier (2831b is dated to the mid-third century BC, whereas the date of 2831a is uncertain: Morel 1981, 230).

[168] Messineo 1986, esp. 144, 149; Pellegrino/Messineo 1991.

[169] Messineo 1986, 144.

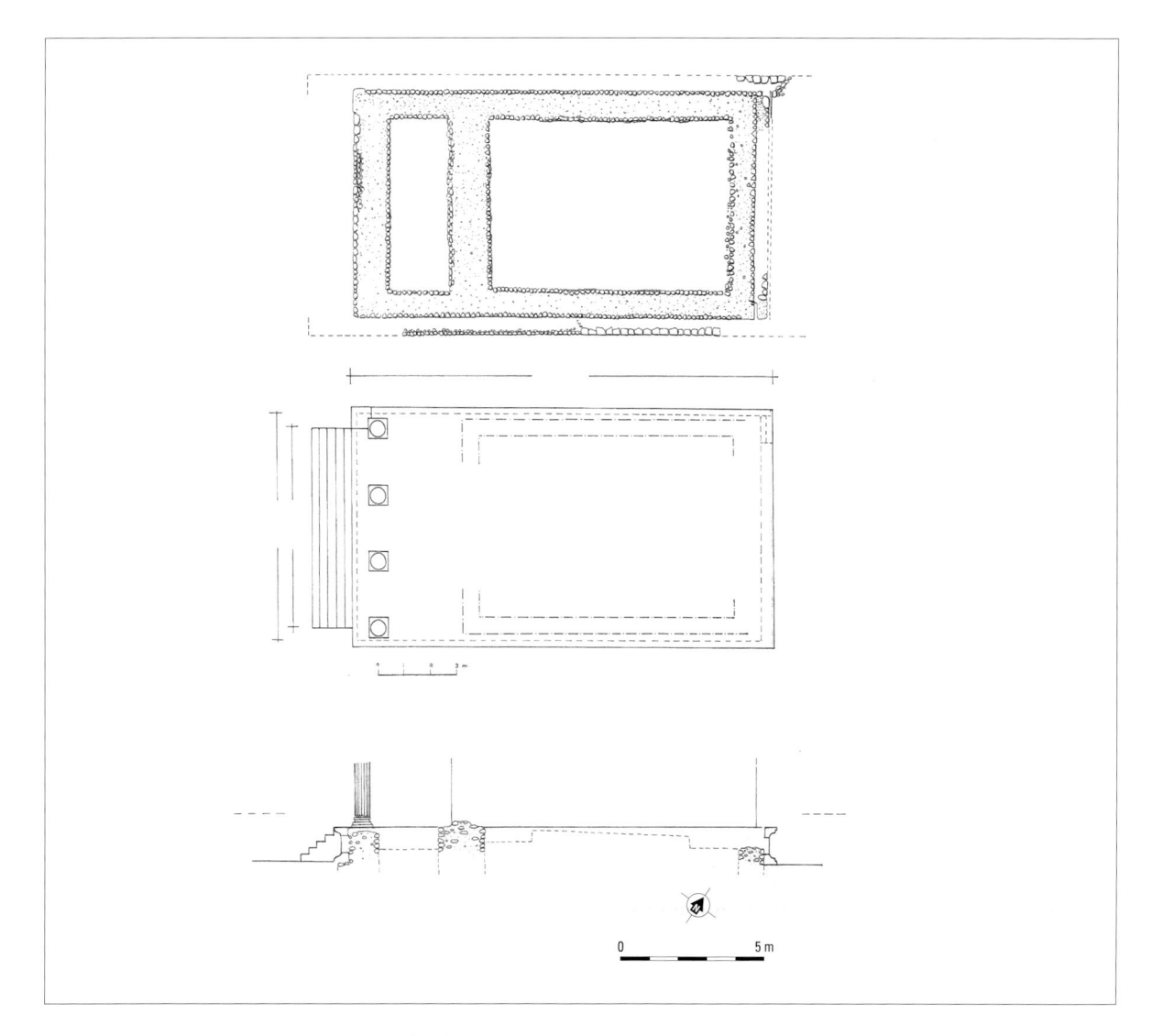

Fig. 7.11. Basciano, località S. Rustico. Temple, plan, reconstructed plan and reconstructed section (adapted from Messineo 1986, 160 figs. 82 and 83).

consists of two nuclei with an open space in between, possibly some sort of forum.[170] Contemporary tombs have been found which may have been related to the settlement.[171]

Two inscriptions commemorating construction works (an altar, walls, base, stairs) mention *magistri*[172] and another inscription with a dedication to Hercules reveals the venerated deity.[173] It thus seems clear that a temple to Hercules was installed here around the second half of the second century BC with a corresponding settlement. Although the *magistri* could have been *magistri vici* and thus indicate the status of *vicus* of the settlement, this is by no means certain.

---

[170] Messineo 1986, 147-148.

[171] Messineo 1986, 154-158. However, the link between settlement and burial area was not necessarily straightforward: the latter has tombs from the Archaic and the Roman periods, some of which presumably postdate the settlement.

[172] *CIL* IX, 5047 and *CIL* I², 3295. Generally, these are thought to be m*agistri vici* but there is no explicit evidence to suggest so.

[173] *CIL* I², 3294.

7. Cellino Vecchio, loc. Valviano, Case Carnevale (Comune di Cellino Attanasio)

An inscription dated to the second century BC mentions the construction by two *magistri* of *aras crepidine(m) colu(mnas)*, clearly a sanctuary.[174] Some black gloss ceramics were retrieved in the environs, and Guidobaldi proposes to recognise in this site "*un vicus retto da magistri, che nel corso del II secolo a.C. si fanno promotori della costruzione di altari, della crepidine e delle colonne di un edificio di culto*".[175] The interpretation of the settlement as a *vicus* is, just as it is for the site of S. Rustico, widely accepted.[176] This indeed seems possible but there is no conclusive proof since the word *vicus* is not mentioned in the inscription. The *magistreis* could therefore also be *magistri* of a *pagus* or yet another college under the protection of a deity (cf. *magistri herculis*, *martis* etc.).

8. Vico-Ornano (Comune di Colledara)

An early first-century BC inscription[177] walled into a church bears three names, interpreted by Guidobaldi as *magistri vici* and would according to her attest to the presence of a *vicus* in this area.[178] Two Roman columns with Doric capitals have been documented although only one drum survives. Apart from the suggestive modern toponym there is no hard proof that the settlement had the status of *vicus*.

9. Colle S. Giorgio (Comune di Castiglione Messer Raimondo)

A sanctuary is attested here by the remains of a podium and architectural terracottas. The material can be dated to the late Hellenistic period.[179] There is no epigraphic evidence and nothing is known about a possible related settlement.

In conclusion, only sites 2 and 5 can be securely used as examples of a *vicus* with a related sanctuary. Sites 6, 7 and 8 could have been related to a *vicus* but this cannot be established with certainty. In general, it is remarkable how a series of small settlements, almost all dating from the late Republican to imperial period, can be related to sanctuaries. How should we interpret these *vici* or non-specified settlements and related sanctuaries? In her study of the territory, Guidobaldi argues that the *vici* are to be understood as a continuation of a pre-Roman system and posits that the *pagus-vicus* system was in some way tolerated as an alternative 'indigenous' way of living.[180] As to the geographical dispersion of the sites in the area (cf. fig. 7.12), Guidobaldi argues that the territory of the colony of Hatria (established by Thiessen polygons) was free of *vici* and that in turn the concentration of *vici* is highest in the mountainous area around Interamna.[181]

The better arable area to the east however is free of *vici* which would point to the assignment of these areas to Roman colonists. This would be confirmed by the discovery of a dedication in archaic Latin to the colonial god Apollo in this area.[182] In short, the mountainous, internal areas would have been left to the indigenous Praetutii, whereas the Roman colonists took the plains and thus the better land.[183]

Guidobaldi thinks that the survival and even flourishing of some (pre-Roman) *vici* in Roman times in contrast to others can be related to individual agency and the "*carattere non univoco del processo di*

---

[174] *CIL* I², 1898.

[175] Guidobaldi 1995, 272.

[176] Cf. for example Menozzi 1998, 42; Grue 1998, 13; Staffa/Moscetta 1986, 194.

[177] *CIL* IX, 5048 (= *CIL* I², 1899).

[178] Guidobaldi 1995, 273.

[179] Iaculli 1993.

[180] Cf. Guidobaldi 1995, 178: "*l'organizzazione del territorio pretuzio al momento della conquista era essenzialmente di tipo paganico-vicano; come vedremo, essa sopravviverà in età romana quale alternativa indigena al modo di abitare cittadino introdotto dai Romani con le colonie.*"

[181] Guidobaldi 1995, 186.

[182] *CIL* I², 384. Cf. Susini 1965-66.

[183] Guidobaldi 1995, 187, 249.

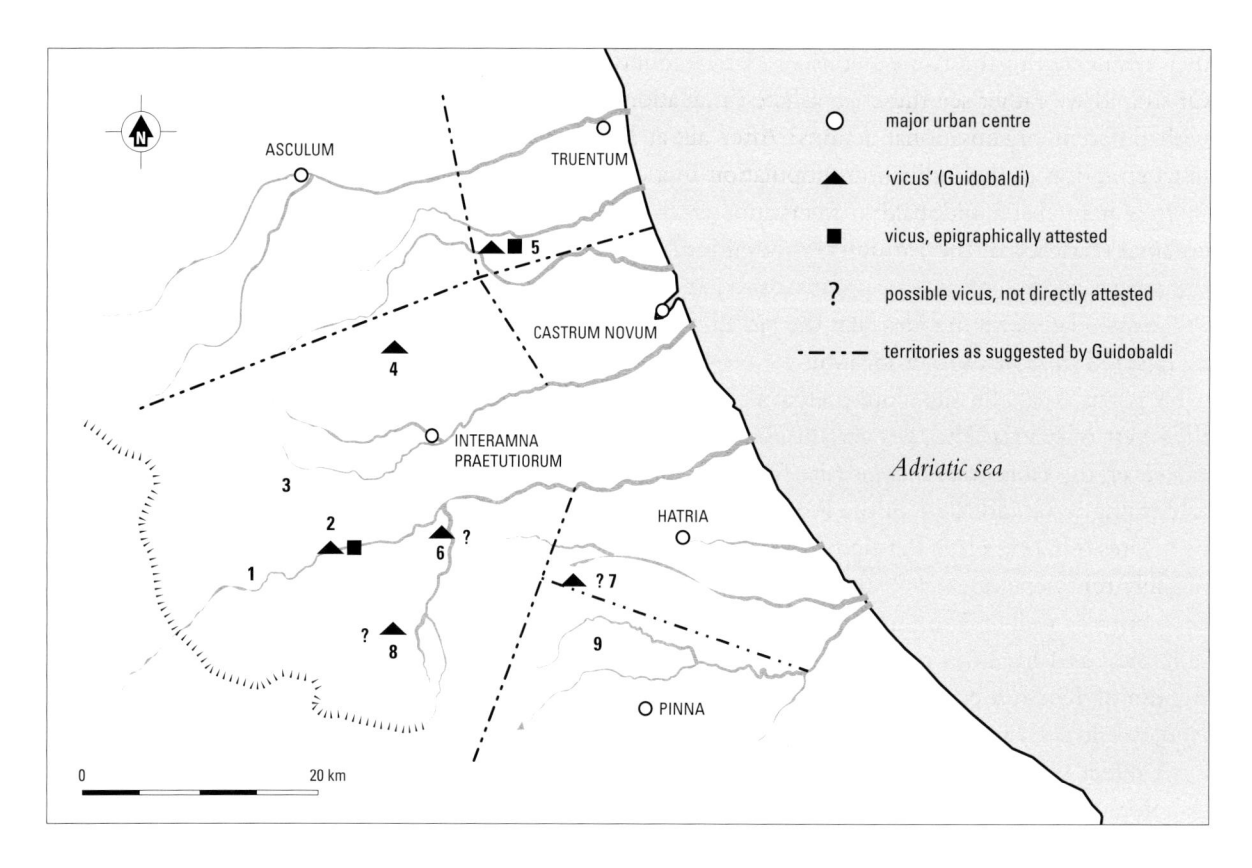

Fig. 7.12. *Vici* in the *ager Praetutianus* (adapted from Guidobaldi 1995, 248 fig. 5).

romanizzazione".[184] In this respect, she adopts a centre-periphery perspective, arguing that the sites near the centre of Interamna were most heavily hit by the Roman *viritim* assignations[185] whereas further away in the hinterland these sites could continue to flourish. Campovalano, where a Praetutian settlement ceased to exist in the course of the second century BC, would be an example of the first category.

This last settlement however was, as far as we know, not a *vicus* in the strict sense. The two securely attested *vici* in this area do not come across as pre-Roman settlements; on the contrary. An inscription dates site 2 (Località Case Lanciotti-Masseria Nisii) to 55 BC, although some remains could date to the second century BC at the earliest. The other site (5), the *vicus Stramentarius*, has yielded some pre-Roman materials but the formation of the settlement proper is dated to the second century BC. Even the inclusion of sites 6, 7, and 8 that could represent *vici* in spite of the lack of decisive evidence does not change the picture as these date also to a period after the Roman conquest, i.e. the second and early first centuries BC. The image of these *vici* as the remnants of pre-Roman settlement can thus be seriously questioned. It seems much more probable that the *vici* represent the outcome of processes that started after Roman interference.

Once the idea of *vici* as pre-Roman institutions is discarded, we should ask ourselves what these *vici* represented. Were they related to the colonisation of the *ager Praetutianus* and if so, in what way? Were

---

[184] Guidobaldi 1995, 247.

[185] Immediately after the Roman conquest, Interamna would have been made *conciliabulum*, "*un luogo di riunione dei Romani cives optimo iure, assegnatari di lotti individuali sulle terre confiscate ai Pretuzi*". The Praetutii would have received partial rights (*sine suffragio*) in change for the confiscations, but with the installation of the *tribus Velina* in 241 BC they had already received the *civitas optimo iure* (Guidobaldi 1995, 219; cf. Humbert 1978, 238-421, 378 n. 66, and 386-390).

they connected to the Latin colony of Hatria, founded 289–286 BC, and largely made up of colonists? Or should we rather see these *vici* as late installations (second to first centuries BC and later), associated with different organisational actions? After all, at least theoretically, one could also see the *vici* as the restructuration of the indigenous population in a different form (e.g. forced migration).[186]

It is here that Guidobaldi's observation with regard to the perceived location *outside* the Hatrian colonial territory of the *vici* deserves attention. As we have seen, it does not seem possible to consider this spatial configuration as a proof of the persistence of pre-Roman settlements because they were all of Roman date. Also the idea that the *vici* all depended juridically on the *praefectura* of Interamna[187] must be rejected in light of their location.

It is true that the sites interpreted as *vici* by Guidobaldi are largely located inland in the area further west of Hatria. The two certain *vici* lay outside the territory of Hatria as indicated by Guidobaldi. However, the *vicus Stramentarius* (site 5) seems to be located within the possible territories of Truentum (according to Guidobaldi), or the Roman colony (290–286 BC) of Castrum Novum (according to Toynbee). Sites 6 (Contrada S. Rustico) and 7 (Cellino Vecchio) where in both cases *magistri* were active, could possibly represent *vici*. Site 7 appears to have been located *within* the territory of Hatria and site 6 could have been as well.[188] The problem here is that the exact territory of Hatria in the Republican period is unknown and has been reconstructed on the basis of various indirect indications, or alternatively with the use of Thiessen polygons.[189] There are scholars who even argue that site 8, Vico-Ornano, possibly a *vicus*, was located in the territory of Hatria.[190]

A direct link between the *vici* (sites 2, 5 and perhaps 6, 7 and 8) and the *praefectura* at Interamna can therefore not be established at all sites, only site 2 certainly lies in Interamna's territory, and possibly site 6 and 8. I would argue that on the basis of this dataset it is not possible to determine a distinct pattern of settlement of *vici* surrounding the *praefectura* on which they would have depended as opposed to the territories occupied by the colonies. At the same time, it seems impossible to establish a direct link between *vici* and the colony of Hatria, apart perhaps from site 7 which could be a *vicus* in the second century BC, and to a lesser extent the uncertain *vici* of sites 6 and 8.

Therefore, we may conclude that the available data from the *ager Praetutianus* do not permit the association of *vici* with one particular and exclusive organisational structure. It is possible that the *vici* acted quite autonomously and had their own responsibilities and/or territorial authority on some administrative or juridical level, but were at the same time tied to one or more centres. The conclusion we *may* draw however with some confidence is that the *vici* of the *ager Praetutianus* represented new institutions, installed after the Roman conquest. Moreover, the distinction between *vici sensu stricto* and undefined

---

[186] Cf. M.G. Celuzza in Carandini *et al.* 2002, 108-110, for this suggestion for the territory of Cosa.

[187] Guidobaldi 1995, 247. On the Roman installation of Interamna cf. Humbert 1978, 239.

[188] Thus for example Strazzulla 2006, 89.

[189] The extension of the territory of the colony is established by Guidobaldi by using Thiessen polygons, which obviously leaves space for interpretation (cf. the remarks on Thiessen polygons in Chapter 4). On the basis of the map in Toynbee, site 6 would be located just over the edge of the colonial territory. The territories of colonies are mostly established by inferences from ancient descriptions and inscriptions with *tribus* indications. In the case of Hatria, Plinius states (*HN* 3.110) that the river Vomanus forms the north boundary. *CIL* IX, 5051 provening from Basciano, on the right bank of the river, mentions the hatrian *tribus Maecia*, but further upstream Interamna's territory would "*ohne Zweifel auf das rechte Ufer hinübergegriffen [haben], wie auch die heutige Diöcese*" (Beloch 1926, 555-556). However, Pliny seems to be mistaken on the southern boundary, which weakens his general credibility or accuracy. In any case, these are all fairly late sources and do not necessarily reflect the extension of the territory in the Republican period.

[190] Humbert 1978, 239 n. 131.

villages may help explain differences in the changing settlement pattern, for example the decline of some sites and the flourishing of others, i.e. the new *vici*.[191]

7.5 THE RURAL VICI NEAR THE FUCINE LAKE

In the Abruzzese mountains of central Italy there are other examples of rural *vici* documented as early as the end of the third and the second century BC. Although the archaeology is generally less rich than in the *ager Praetutianus*, the epigraphic record is especially revealing – or at least tantalising.

In modern Abruzzo, at the southern shores of the Fucine lake, rural *vici* demonstrate self-consciousness by their proper names, magistrates and cult places. The character of these *vici* is hinted at by the titles and names of their magistrates and by the identity of their gods. The *vici* are often termed 'Marsic' because of their alleged location within Marsic territory. Indeed, the Fucine *vici* are the only ones that (at least according to the traditional territorial reconstruction of Italy) lay outside Roman or Latin territory. In the following, I discuss the evidence for the *vicus Aninus, Petinus, Fistaniensis*, a potential *vicus* at Spineto and the *vicus Supinum*, and their possible relationship with the Latin colony of Alba Fucens which lies to the northwest of the lake (fig. 7.13).

The Aninus vecus *or* vicus Aninus

A *vicus Aninus* is recorded by an inscription found in the 19th century at Castelluccio, now part of the village of Lecce dei Marsi. The text reads *Aninus vecus / Valetudn[e] / donum / dant*.[192] The dedication to the goddess Valetudo seems to date to the second or beginnings of the first century BC.[193] The existence of the *vicus* under Tiberius is attested by a dedication to its inhabitants called *vicales Annini*.[194] An earlier dedication to Valetudo was also found.[195] This inscription, possibly on a *thesaurus* but now lost, was according to Mommsen written with '*litteris vetustissimis*', and may date at least as early as the second century BC.[196]

Adele Campanelli recognised the cult place of Valetudo in the sanctuary that she excavated near Lecce dei Marsi, along the river Tavana.[197] This is indeed the place where the Tiberian dedication to the *vicales Annini* was found but the dedications to Valetudo were retrieved in Lecce itself, in the quarter Castelluccio in a place corresponding to the remains of the *Sancti Martini in Agne* church which preserves the name of the *vicus*.[198] Limestone slabs, tuscanic capitals and column drums are documented here and Giuseppe

---

[191] It should be emphasised that although predating Tarpin's book, Guidobaldi's work in some respects paves the way for the deconstruction of the traditional view of the so-called *pagus-vicus* system. It may indeed seem that her data and interpretations fit much more comfortably within a 'Roman' perspective on *vici*: Guidobaldi tends to explain the installation of sanctuaries and villages in light of Roman influence, cf. e.g. Guidobaldi 1995, 249, 261, 276, and the perhaps somewhat uncomfortable combination, on p. 210, of colonial production of temple decoration related to indigenous *vici*: "*documenti archeologici … consentono infine di ritenere di produzione atriana almeno la decorazione accessoria dei templi che tra il II e la prima metà del I secolo a.C. sorgono nel territorio pretuzio al di fuori di veri e propri centri urbanizzati e spesso in rapporto con vici, la più vistosa sopravvivenza del tipo di popolamento indigeno.*"

[192] *CIL* IX, 3813 (= *CIL* I², 391) = Ve. 228 = Letta/D'Amato 1975 no. 111. An interesting element of the text is that *vecus* is the subject of the plural *dant*, which underscores the meaning of *vicus* as a designation of the community of inhabitants: Letta 2001, 151.

[193] Letta 2001, 151; according to Tarpin 2002, IV.22.1: "*IIe siècle av. J.-C.*"

[194] *AE* 1978, 286 = *AE* 1996, 513.

[195] *CIL* IX, 3812 (= *CIL* I², 390); Letta 2001, 151.

[196] On the basis of the apographs, cf. Letta 1997a, 332.

[197] Campanelli 1991.

[198] Grossi 1988, 120, 124 = no. 19 with n. 44 and no. 20.

Grossi locates the *vicus Aninus* in this place.[199] The cult place excavated by Campanelli might thus have been a rural cult place related to the *vicus Aninus* but was probably not dedicated to Valetudo, who was venerated in the *vicus* itself.[200] The *vicus* possibly took its name from the gens name Annius, i.e. 'the *vicus* of the *Annii*'.[201] This name is quite common and cannot attest to a Marsic origin of the family. Although the date is not certain, it seems reasonable to assume that the *vicus* already existed as such before the Social War.[202]

The vicus Petinus

A dedication of a statue dated to the late third century BC was "*trouvée en 1878 au lac Fucin*".[203] The inscription was made on a pierced bronze sheet, and was apparently meant to be attached to something, perhaps a base.[204] The dedication of a statue (*seino* > *signum*) documents a situation similar to that of the *vicus Supinum* (cf. *infra*).

The (reconstructed) text reads:

A: *[Pe(tro).Setmiu]s.Sep(i).f(ilius).et / [Petro? Ca]isius.Vet(us?) / [II.viri.fec]ront.veci / [Petini.ist?]ut.seino / [edndre.Co(n)s(e)nte(s).]fecront*

B: *Petro.Setm[ius.Sep(i).f(ilius).et.Pe?] / Cesieus.Vet(us?).II.[viri.fecront] / Veci.Petini.i[stut?.seinq(om)] / ednrde. Co(n)s(e)n[te(s).fecront]*[205]

The reconstruction of the text is not easy but according to Letta text A and text B (on the other side) were similar. Perhaps text B was not considered good enough by the epigrapher. According to Letta, the general meaning of the texts is quite clear and regards the erection of a statue to a deity by two magistrates from the *vicus Petinus*.[206] The two upright strokes (II) at the end of B line 2, where the sheet is broken, seem to refer to a number, rather than to an E of the praenomen of the patronymic formula (that would thus be located after the *tria nomina*).[207] Between the names of the (supposed) magistrates and the genitive *veci Petini* one would expect the title of the magistrates, the *II* would thus refer to the function the persons mentioned fulfilled, i.e. *II[viri]*. A parallel for these *duumviri* would, according to Letta, be represented by the *queistores* mentioned in a dedication from the *vicus Supinum* (cf. *infra*). These *queistores* would only be Latin in title, but not in function, whereas here in the *vicus Petinus* "*l'adeguamento ai modelli romani appare più completo*", perhaps due to a slightly later date of the inscription or different developments and local reactions to "*l'influsso romano*".[208] The *duumviri* attested here would thus have been local magistrates of the Marsic *vicus* inspired by Roman titles. The plausibility of this suggestion will be discussed below.[209]

---

[199] Grossi 1988, 120 n. 44, estimating a rather small area for the settlement, about one hectare. Apparently, however, on the basis of the location of necropoleis around it, which date to the late Republican / imperial period: "*Il vicus era di dimensioni modeste, circa un ettaro, dato che le necropoli sembrano circondarlo …*". For the location: "*Il vicus Aninus era posizionato sul sito dell'attuale quartiere di Castelluccio di Lecce dei Marsi fra i torrenti Tavana e S. Emma, alla base del colle di Cirmo.*" Grossi thinks that the *vicus Aninus* in the third and second centuries BC was linked to the hill-fort of Cirmo (where black gloss ceramics attest to Hellenistic presence), which he recognises as the "*Ocre di Cirmo (Ocri aninnas?)*" in map VI on p. 125, a suggestion to be treated with caution.

[200] Cf. Letta 1997a, 333 n. 41; for the rural sanctuary also Grossi 1988, 124 = no. 20.

[201] Letta/D'Amato 1975, 165.

[202] Cf. on the date of the inscription *supra* n. 193.

[203] Froehner cited in Letta/D'Amato 1975, 321.

[204] Letta/D'Amato 1975, 321-328.

[205] Letta/D'Amato 1975 no. 188 = *CIL* I², 2874 (on the assumption that side A and side B were similar).

[206] Letta/D'Amato 1975, 325.

[207] Pe- praenomen, Cesieus – nomen Vet(us?) –cognomen. This use is documented in Letta/D'Amato 1975 nos. 108 and 189. For E = patronymic formula: Degrassi in *ILLRP* 303.

[208] Letta/D'Amato 1975, 326.

[209] Letta/D'Amato 1975, 196, commenting on the *queistores* of the *vicus Supinum*, see the *duoviri* of the *vecus petinus* even as "*una conferma delle radici locali di questa magistratura (scil. dei queistores del vecos supinas)*".

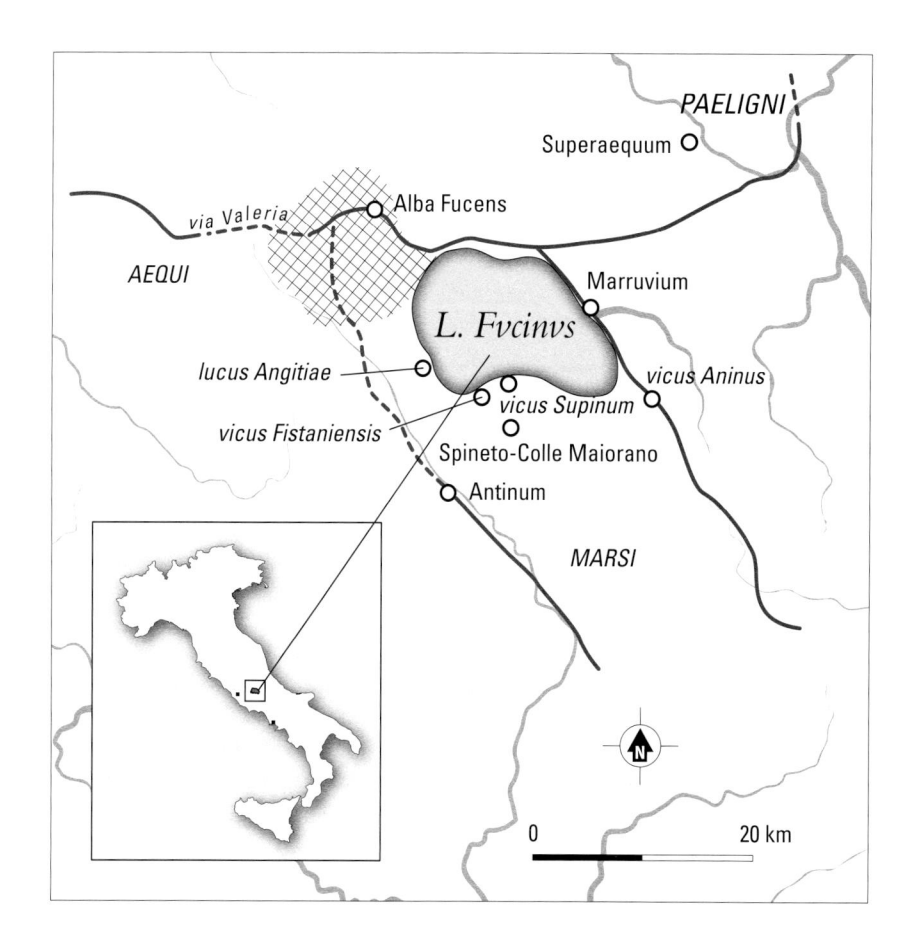

Fig. 7.13. Location of the *vici* south of the Fucine lake (the location of the *vicus Petinus* is unclear).

The name Setmius (= Septimius) is common but may come from Latium.[210] This is the first appearance of the name in the Marsic area. Later Septimii are recorded in the area at S. Benedetto,[211] in Marruvium,[212] and, thrice, in Alba Fucens.[213] Caisius or Ceisius is attested in only one other inscription in the area, found not far from Trasacco and possibly dating to the first half of the second century BC and mentioning a *liberta*.[214]

The name *Petinus* is difficult to explain, but may refer to a gentilician name (cf. *supra* on the *vicus Aninus*). Letta proposes to resolve *Consentes* for *Cosn* indicating the deities to which the statue was dedicated.[215] Because the precise find spot of the inscription is unknown, no archaeological remains can be related to it.

The vicus F(i)staniensis
A funerary inscription that is probably imperial in date was found at a location between Trasacco and Luco and it reads as follows: *d M s / C. Mario Placido lega / to vic i Fstanien / sis.Maria Fortu / nata.coniuci*

---

[210] Franchi De Bellis 1995, 382, on a T. Setmis who appears on a *pocolum* from Ariminum (377, no. 16). Letta/D'Amato 1975: "*equivalente di un latino Se(p)t(i)mius.*"

[211] *CIL* IX, 3748.

[212] Letta/D'Amato 1975, 33 no. 26.

[213] *CIL* IX, 3947, 4026, 4030.

[214] *CIL* IX, 3817 = Letta/D'Amato 1975, 328-330 no. 189, found near Trasacco ("*loc. Mole Secche, al confine con Collelongo*"). Cf. Letta/D'Amato 1975, 233 no. 139, for the form *Caesianus*.

[215] Letta/D'Amato 1975, 326.

incom / parabili cum quo vi / xit.annis.XXX.et C.Mari / us Placidus.patri pi / entissimo.b m.pi.r..[216] Letta locates the *vicus* at contrada Passarano at the border between the modern municipalities of Trasacco and Luco. Amongst other remains, this area yielded votive materials and black gloss wares, indicating that the area was frequented in the Hellenistic period.[217] As to the name *Fistaniensis* or *Estaniensis* (the reading is open to interpretation), this does not seem to refer to Marsic local toponymy or onomastics. An Estanius is known from Vestine Furfo,[218] i.e. probably another *vicus*, whereas a *Fistanus* appears in Interamna.[219] In spite of Hellenistic archaeological material, the inscriptions's late date precludes a secure conclusion on the Republican context.[220]

The 'vicus' of Spineto, Colle Mariano
Although there is no direct epigraphic evidence for a proper *vicus*, the archaeological remains and inscriptions found at Spineto, Colle Mariano, not far from the *vicus Supinum*, could be relevant.[221] Two and a half km SSW from Trasacco, a dedication to Hercules that can be dated to the end of the third or the beginning of the second century BC was found. It reads *C(aius) Atieius / T(iti) f(ilius) Hercol(e)*.[222] Grossi recognises a '*vicus*' and a sanctuary here on the basis of remains of the podium, column bases, black gloss ceramics dating to the third century and anatomical ex-votos.[223] Grossi argues that two other inscriptions found in the 19th century in the territory of Trasacco also belong to this sanctuary. One inscription mentions *mag(istri) He(rculis)* restoring elements of a theatre and organising *ludi scaenici*,[224] whereas another records *ma(gistri)* involved in the painting of a *scaenam*.[225] Yet another dedication to Hercules (*Herclo I[ovio?]*) was found on Colle S. Martino,[226] but according to Grossi both this and the other inscriptions should not be related to a possible sanctuary on that Colle but rather to the sanctuary at Spineto.[227]

The available epigraphic and archaeological evidence do not securely point to another *vicus*. However, if the early Latin inscription indeed originates from the same complex where black gloss ceramics and anatomical ex-votos were found, then it seems not improbable, in view of the later attested *magistri*, that this village also had the status of *vicus*.

---

[216] Letta/D'Amato 1975 no. 131 = *CIL* IX, 3856. (*b m.pi.r* is unclear, perhaps an error by the epigraphist for *b(ene) m(erenti) p(osu)<e=I>r(unt)*).

[217] Letta/D'Amato 1975, 220 n. 7; also an archaic bronze statuette was found. Cf. Grossi 1991, 215 n. 41 for "*resti pavimentali in cocciopesto decorato da tessere di calcare, numerosi frammenti di ceramica a vernice nera*". Grossi suggests that the *vicus* had an internal cult area that was perhaps dedicated to Hercules but it is unclear on what grounds. Cf. Grossi 1980, 136 for "*resti di un fondo di capanna*" and impasto ceramics.

[218] *CIL* IX, 3542.

[219] *CIL* I², 1905; cf. the origin of other similar names in the Sabine and Campanian areas in Letta/D'Amato 1975, 219.

[220] The fact that apparently a *legatus vici* is attested is confusing, since normally *legati* are documented only for colonies and *municipia* and this case has been explained as an exception: Letta/D'Amato 1975, 219 ("*forse in relazione ad eventi straordinari*").

[221] Grossi 1988, 113 with n. 26.

[222] Letta/D'Amato 1975 no. 137: loc. Colle Mariano or Maiorano (= *CIL* I², 2873b).

[223] Grossi 1988, 113 n. 26.

[224] *CIL* IX, 3857.

[225] Letta/D'Amato 1975 no. 143; according to Letta this must refer to the Republican period, not later than the mid-first century BC. For the relation to the '*vicus*' at Colle Mariano – Spineto, see also Letta 2001, 152.

[226] *T(itus) Vareci[o(s)] / Herclo / I[ovio(?)] / donom [ded(et?)] / [l]ube(n)s / mere[to]*: Letta/D'Amato 1975, 224-228 no. 135: Loc. La Mária, c.q. Colle S. Martino (= *CIL* I², 2873c).

[227] Grossi 1988, 113 n. 26 (rejecting Letta's [Letta/D'Amato 1975, 225] earlier proposal locating the sanctuary at the hilltop).

The vecos supinas *or* vicus Supinum *and its sanctuaries*
Near modern Trasacco, "*vicino al lago di Fucino*",[228] an inscription was found that records a dedication of a *seinom* > *signum* to Victoria by a *vecos Supinas*.[229] The text, inscribed in a parallelepipedal block with a height of 0.875 m reads: *vecos Sup(i)n[a(s) / Victorie seino(m) / dono dedet / lub(en)s mereto / queistores / Sa(lvius) Magio(s) St(ati) f(ilius) / Pac(ios) Anaiedio(s) St(ati) [f(ilius)*.[230] The characters date to the late third century BC or the beginning of the second century BC. The origin of the name of the *vicus* is not clear. It is possible that it developed either from a local toponym or from a *gens* name (for example Supni and Supnai are attested at Volterra) or the Latin word *supinus*.[231] The *vicus* has been convincingly recognised in the modern centre of Trasacco, where some ancient settlement remains, including a column drum and a capital, were found in front of the modern Municipio.[232]

Several cult places are attested for this *vicus*, located in or near the *vicus*, probably near the shore of the lake where the inscriptions were found.[233] Victoria seems to have occupied the most prominent place. A sanctuary for her is not only attested by the dedication of a statue but also by another inscription, probably dating to the second half of the second century BC. This inscription records the dedication of a *donum* to Victoria by one or two persons who may have been magistrates but may also have acted in their personal capacity (on this inscription cf. *infra*).[234] The cult of Victoria is the only one that can be related to the *vicus Supinum* with certainty because there is no mention of a *vicus* in the other inscriptions found in the territory of Trasacco. Nevertheless, the other cults remain relevant for the discussion.

Apollo is attested by a votive basis with an inscription that reads *C. Cisiedio(s) / Aplone / ded(et)* from loc. Madonella in the territory of Trasacco.[235] The inscription can be dated to the end of the third century BC on the basis of the characters. The dedication offers the first known appearance of the cult of Apollo in the Marsic area.

Other cults are also documented in the territory of Trasacco, not far from the *vicus Supinum*. A Latin inscription from loc. Pretaritta or Polaritti dating to the late third century BC lists three men who dedicate an altar to the deified lake, *Fucinus*.[236] (*St(atios) Staiedi(os). / V(ibios). Salviedi(os) / Pe(tro) Pagio(s) / Fougno / aram*). Possibly, this is a private dedication, rather than a formal public action. A cult related to the Fucinus is also attested for later periods.[237] Also from the environment of Trasacco, but possibly belonging to the '*vicus*' in the territory of Trasacco at Colle Mariano – Spineto are the (also early) dedications to Hercules (cf. *supra*).

Roman influence in the 'Marsic' vici
The appearance of this set of early Latin inscriptions at the Fucine lake is as striking as the interpretation is complicated. A precise understanding of the dedications is rendered difficult by a variety of circumstances. First, there are epigraphic and linguistic considerations which considerably affect the reading and interpretation of the inscriptions. Second, the link between the texts is difficult to establish, especially

---

[228] Rossi cited in Letta/D'Amato 1975, 192.

[229] Letta/D'Amato 1975 no. 128 = *CIL* IX, 3849 (= *CIL* I², 388). Cf. *supra* for a *seinom* (Letta/D'Amato 1975 no. 188 = *CIL* I², 2874), in a dedication from the *vicus Petinus* dating to the end of the third century BC.

[230] *CIL* IX, 3849 (= *CIL* I², 388). It reads *seinq(nom)* or *seino(m)*; see Letta 1979, 404-405, for the former but cf. Letta 2005b, 55-58, who now does not exclude *seino(m)*. For the dative in *–e* see the index in *CIL* I², on page 818, cf. also *CIL* I², 2631 from Veii. See for monophthongisation of *–ai / ae* now Adams 2007, 78-88.

[231] Letta/D'Amato 1975, 198-199 (Letta prefers a local toponym).

[232] Letta/D'Amato 1975, 205.

[233] Although in secondary context, reused in a stable. Letta/D'Amato 1975, 204-205.

[234] Letta/D'Amato 1975 no. 129 = *CIL* IX, 3848 (= *CIL* I², 387).

[235] Letta/D'Amato 1975 no. 129bis = *CIL* I², 2873a.

[236] Letta/D'Amato 1975 no. 134 = *CIL* IX, 3847 (= *CIL* I², 389).

[237] *CIL* IX, 3656; and *CIL*, IX 3887: *Onesimus Aug(usti) lib(ertus) / proc(urator) / fecit imaginibus et / Laribus cultoribus / Fucini*; cf. Letta 2001, 150 for the interpretation '… and for the *Lares* that protect the Fucinus'.

since the precise places of origin for most inscriptions are unknown, and we have to rely on often rather approximative testimonies. Following the first commentary on (part of) the group by Emilio Peruzzi,[238] Cesare Letta has edited and interpreted the texts in relation to historical and archaeological data, and together with additional topographical indications by, amongst others, Giuseppe Grossi it seems conceivable to outline some possible interpretations.[239]

Letta, who first published on the texts in the early 1970s, has also furnished more wide-reaching interpretations of the texts as a group. His contention that they would offer an indication of the 'precocious' romanisation of the Marsi is of particular importance. Over the years Letta has revised or adapted some of his original ideas. In general however, Letta's work is characterised by the notion that romanisation in the Marsic area, even if precocious, did not affect local Italic institutions at all levels and often did so only in name, not in substance. As to the cults documented by epigraphy, he argues that almost none can be linked to Roman influence and they instead either relate to indigenous Italic roots or direct Greek or Etruscan influence (esp. from Campania).[240]

Indeed there are often indications of Greek / Etruscan / Campanian influence rather than a direct 'Roman' role in the process. Moreover, a non-Roman emphasis in the scholarly debate is also justified in the context of the Romanocentric academic discourse which has dominated the writing of the history of ancient Italy. However, also in light of revisions subsequently made by the Abruzzese scholar himself, it is possible that in some instances possible 'direct' Roman influence has been downplayed.[241] Elaborating on the ideas put forward by Tarpin,[242] I therefore review questions of magistrature, onomastics and especially the cults.

Mimic or Roman magistrates? The queistores *of the* vicus Supinum
The magistrates named in the dedication to Victoria on behalf of the *vicus Supinum* (*CIL* IX, 3849 = I^2, 388) are in the nominative. According to Letta they are nevertheless to be understood as eponymous since no *faciundum curaverunt* or *locaverunt* follows their names.

Letta sees a parallel in a somewhat earlier inscription also found at Trasacco dating to the second half of the third century BC[243] in which the word *qestur* is followed by three names. Letta discerns an eponymous use of the two *q(ua)estur(es?)* that would refer to the two first names, *V(ibios) Salv[i(os)]* and *M(arcos) Paci(os)*. The last person, who is separated from the remainder of the text by a blank line, would have dedicated the object.[244] Another parallel would be the third century BC sheet from Antinum (Vetter 223) on which one or probably two[245] *meddices* are recorded dedicating to Vesuna. Here, a *cetur >censor* (or *quaestor* or even *centurio*) perhaps figures in the same eponymous sense (*pa.ui.pacuies.medis / vesune. dunom.ded / ca.cumnios cetur*).

---

[238] Peruzzi 1962.

[239] Letta/D'Amato 1975; Grossi 1988.

[240] Letta/D'Amato 1975 *passim*, Letta 2001, 145: "*A questa rapida e precoce romanizzazione culturale sul piano linguistico, onomastico, istituzionale e militare non sembra corrispondere un processo analogo sul piano religioso. Al contrario, la nutrita serie di dediche a varie divinità databili ad età anteriore alla Guerra Sociale tradisce la presenza di forti influenze greche, per le quali nella maggior parte dei casi si può escludere una mediazione romana.*"

[241] 'Direct' is used here as indicating the presence of new institutions and/or people connected to Latin / Roman colonisation / rule, in opposition to the idea of spontaneous 'self-romanisation' of indigenous Marsi.

[242] Tarpin 2002, 56-63.

[243] Letta 1979; *CIL* I^2, 2873d: *Q(ua)estur(es) / V(ibius) Salv[i(os)] / M(arcus) Paci(os) / Pe(tro) C(e)rvi(os)*.

[244] Letta 1979, 406-410.

[245] Cf. Letta 1997a and more general Letta 2005b, 48-54 with bibliography, in which Letta revises the 'Italic' aspects of the Caso Cantovios sheet from the sanctuary of Angitia at Luco (Ve. 228a = *CIL* I^2, 5), a dedication to the Dioscuri and Jupiter (Ve. 224), and the Antinum sheet in favour of a more Latin aspect.

This eponymous interpretation of the Supinate *queistores*, being a nominative, has important implications. Letta argues that it testifies to a 'survival of indigenous models in the first phases of romanisation' because in the Italic world *meddices* are used in an eponymous sense in the nominative. In other words, the *queistores* would be Roman in title but actually hide Italic institutions, perhaps indeed a college of *meddices*, as Letta suggests.[246]

In a later publication, Letta opts for a slightly different interpretation, but still emphasises the Marsic or Italic character of the magistrates. In his view, the Antinum sheet and the Supinum inscription would neatly reflect Marsic political organisation. Letta recognises in the *cetur* a magistrate on the level of the *nomen*. The *centurio* or **centuriator* (in the sense of *centuriare*, dividing the people in arms in *centuriae*) would have adopted his title from Roman models but in reality was the supreme magistrate of the Marsic federation.[247] This federation was made up, according to Letta, of *oppida* governed by *meddices* (the latter are also mentioned in the Antinum sheet).

One step lower in this reconstruction of a Marsic hierarchy are the *vici*. Subordinate to the *oppida*,[248] they had their own minor magistrates, the *queistores*, who are recorded at the *vicus Supinum*. The *vici*, although formally still under the jurisdiction of the *oppida*, would however demonstrate a search for some sort of autonomy. This would be indicated by the eponymous use of the *quaestores* and the very fact that they chose to imitate such a typical Roman institution.[249] In short, the *queistores* would have been magistrates of a local, Marsic political system who only borrowed their title from Rome, a case of "*mimesi culturale*" according to Letta.[250]

Although this proposal is ingeniously constructed, a different interpretation seems possible. The identification of the *cetur* mentioned in the Antinum sheet as a Marsic federal leader is not certain. The appearance of this function does not need to be interpreted as a Marsic military grade 'influenced' by Rome. It seems possible that the *cetur* himself was actually part of a Roman intervention, controlling in some way the Marsic community still ruled by *meddices*. This thesis is strengthened by the fact that the

---

[246] Letta/D'Amato 1975, 195 n. 7. The inscriptions of Antinum and Supinum would reveal "*una sopravvivenza di modelli indigeni nelle prime fasi della romanizzazione tra le guerre sannitiche e la Guerra Sociale: come ad Antinum l'eponimo è il censore (magistrato con denominazione forse romana), ma accanto ad esso figura ancora la magistratura italica del medis, così a Supinum vediamo dei queistores che, se sono romani nel nome, non sembrano esserlo nelle attribuzioni, giacché figurano non come semplici magistrati finanziari, ma come magistrati supremi ed eponimi.*" Letta/D'Amato 1975, 195, also referring to the Iguvine Tablets, where in the third century "*la moda romaneggiante*" would have led to calling *kvestur* a local eponymous leader (but in Letta 1979, 410 n. 29 this eponymous interpretation is discarded). Cf. also Letta/D'Amato 1975, 326: "*i queistores sembrano latini solo nel nome e nel carattere di collegialità uguale, ma non del tutto nelle attribuzioni.*" See Campanile 1995 for a college of *meddices* attested at Messina.

[247] Letta 2001, 144.

[248] Cf. esp. Grossi 1988; Grossi 1991 for this notion of interdependence.

[249] Letta 2001, 144-145. On 145: "*appare sintomatico di una volontà di assimilazione culturale al modello romano, il fatto che per i vici si adottasse una magistratura squisitamente romana, sia nel nome (che è incompatibile con la tradizione linguistica osco-umbra per la presenza della labiovelare qu-), sia nelle attribuzioni principalmente finanziarie.*"

[250] Letta 1979, 410: at Supinum would thus be proved "*l'esistenza, già verso la metà del III sec. a.C., di un collegio di magistrati supremi ed eponimi che ha preso a prestito il nome della magistratura ausiliaria romana dei questori, ha mutato cioè dalla cultura egemone un titolo, ma non le funzioni magistratuali corrispondenti. Un esempio evidente di mimesi culturale …*". For the view that the application of Roman titles is decisive in itself, see Tarpin 2002, 57: "*Le titre même de questeur ne peut renvoyer qu'à une institution romaine.*" This needs explanation however; the idea that Italic peoples adopted Roman magistratural titles in itself is generally accepted, cf. Chapter 1, and few will doubt that the *kvaíssturs* and *kenszurs* mentioned in Oscan epigraphy functioned at least in some cases in Italic political constellations.

name of the *cetur*, *Cominius*, is not found locally but does appear in Rome and Campania.[251] The *cetur* could thus have been mentioned in this dedication in the sense of "in the presence of *cetur* C. Cominius".[252]

Since the 'Marsic' inscriptions do not necessarily form a consistent group, this 'Roman' interpretation of the Antinum sheet would not necessarily mean that the *vicus Supinum* inscription has also to be read in a 'Roman' light. However, it would in any case mean that the *cetur* could not have had an eponymous function as he was not a magistrate. The other inscription from Trasacco with *qestur* > *q(ua)estur(es?)* (*CIL* I², 2873d) does not provide independent evidence for an eponymous use, and seems rather to have been interpreted as such in light of the Supinate inscription discussed here (the endings of both names and title are absent).

This means that the *queistores* of the *vicus Supinum* in their supposed eponymous function are alone in Marsic territory. As a matter of fact, an eponymous function in the nominative is not documented elsewhere in Latin, neither in the Marsic area nor elsewhere. Only the eponymous Oscan *meddices* of the Samnites Pentri would offer a parallel[253] but these are geographically, culturally and institutionally remote from the *vicus Supinum*. I would suggest that the idea that the eponymous *queistores* form an unequivocal 'indigenous element' or 'survival'[254] is thus significantly weakened.

Perhaps we should reconsider the possibility that a *curaverunt vel sim.* is omitted. The verb is also missing in the dedication to Fucinus found nearby and also dated to the late third century BC.[255] If this is true, the *queistores* could have had some role in the dedication in their task of controlling public money.[256] Alternatively, they could have been mentioned in the same sense as the *cetur* in Antinum may have been, 'the *queistores* saw to / were present at the dedication of a statue to Victoria by the *vicus Supinum*.'[257] Neither is it to be excluded that the *queistores* were not magistrates of the *vicus* but of another centre.[258]

It should be noted that the same case could be made for the *vicus Petinus* where *duumviri* are attested.[259] It is not necessary to explain these a priori as indigenous Marsic people aping the titles from the Roman system. Indeed, the name *Septimius* makes its first appearance in the Marsic area here and may originate in Latium.

The names of the inhabitants of the *vicus Supinum*, especially the *queistores* (even if their exact role is not fully understood), could also shed further light on the *vicus* and its context. Salvius is a praenomen that is common in central Italy, not specifically the Marsic region.[260] The praenomen Statius is quite generic in central Italy, especially in the Oscan areas, and for the Marsic area is best attested at Supinum itself, and once outside the *vicus* in nearby Collelongo.[261] The gentilician name *Magios* however seems

---

[251] Letta 1997a, 324-325, suggesting the possibility of a Roman temporary garrison, or a special mission, perhaps linked to the taking of a *census* and/or the levy. Apparently Letta rejected this idea later in favour of the Marsic federal leader thesis (Letta 2001, 144).

[252] Letta 1997a, 325.

[253] On tile stamps from Bovianum: La Regina 1989, 327-340.

[254] Letta/D'Amato 1975, 194 n. 3: "*a particolarità locale*" and some further, on p. 197 a "*sopravvivenza indigena*".

[255] Letta/D'Amato 1975 no. 134 = *CIL* IX, 3847 (= *CIL* I², 389) but it must be admitted that this is a different situation because in the Supinum inscription a verb is already present (*dedet*).

[256] Cf. Tarpin 2002, 57 n. 17.

[257] Cf. already Peruzzi 1962, 129: "… *è appunto per la solennità dell'occasione che questo titolo pubblico reca menzione dei questori.*"

[258] In the nearby Latin colony of Alba Fucens different *quaestores* are attested to in the imperial period. In general, it seems that the function (and number) of *quaestores* in Latin colonies was not standardised, Salmon 1969, 86.

[259] Cf. Guadagno 2005 for a similar deconstruction of *duumviri* in an Italic context.

[260] Cf. Letta/D'Amato 1975, no. 37 = *CIL* I², 3210 (S. Benedetto); cf. pp. 47-48, examples from Vestine, Marrucine, Paelignian and Umbrian areas, cf. also on the archaic abbreviation *Sa*.

[261] Marsic area: three times attested in Supinum (the other two: Letta/D'Amato 1975 no. 129 and 134 = *CIL* I², 2873a and *CIL* IX, 3847 = *CIL* I², 389) and once in Collelongo (funerary inscription): Letta/D'Amato 1975 no. 160.

to originate in Campania.[262] The other *queistor*, *Pac(ios) Anaiedio(s) St(ati) [f(ilius)* was, according to Letta, an indigenous Marsic person. The praenomen Pacius is common in central Italy but the gentilician *Anaiedio(s) > Annaedius* would be typically Marsic. However, the other attestation in Marsic territory is not certain[263] and the appearance of an *Annaedius* in the so-called *pagus Fificulanus* in the Vestine area cannot be used to stress the Marsic origin of the name.[264] In conclusion, at least one of the *queistores* may not have been of Marsic origin. Furthermore, a link between the *vicus* and Alba Fucens is documented by the appearance of the same names. In particular, the explicit mention of *Herennii Supinates* in or near the colony is striking and proves that there were direct contacts between the *vicus* and the colony.[265]

Cults

An important element that could help assess the character of the *vici* on the shores of the Fucine lake regards cults. Letta argues that almost all cults attested in the early epigraphy from the Fucine area can be linked to Campanian / Greek / Etruscan influences rather than direct Roman influence. In the dedication to Apollo, for instance, the syncopatic form *Aplone* instead of *Apolone*, which in Latin would have been normal, would indicate that the cult was adopted directly from the Greek / Etruscan sphere, especially Cuma, rather than from Rome. Letta indeed sees in this otherwise Latin inscription proof that the cult was not "*una recente innovazione (cultuale e linguistica) romana, ma al contrario è un tratto conservativo, una sopravvivenza di culti già radicati nell'uso e nella lingua locali da più generazioni*".[266] Equally, Letta argues that the cult of Hercules[267] can be accounted for by Greek-Etruscan, rather than Roman influence, because in one of the inscriptions the form *Herclo I(ovio?)* could only be explained by Etruscan influence.[268] Indeed, according to Letta, "*[q]uesto prova che la diffusione del culto di Ercole nella regione non fu dovuta a una mediazione culturale romana, ma si deve riportare, ... a contatti diretti stabiliti dalla transumanza con la Campania greco-etrusca*".[269] Even the local god Fucinus appears to have been, in a secondary moment, reformulated or interpreted in a Greek sense.[270]

An analysis of the validity of the linguistic arguments is outside the remit of this dicussion and therefore these observations are accepted as valid.[271] I limit myself to some more general remarks on the conclusions that have been drawn on the outcome of the linguistic evidence.

---

[262] Letta/D'Amato 1975, 200; Schulze 1933.

[263] An inscription from S. Benedetto, *[---]anna[edius?------]* could possibly be reconstructed this way (Letta/D'Amato 1975 no. 84).

[264] Even if this place was no *pagus* but perhaps rather a *vicus*... CIL IX, 3572 (Paganica): apart from the suggestive toponym, no *pagus* is attested here, a *vicus* is however mentioned in CIL IX, 3574, which may come from this area.

[265] CIL IX, 3906, for an overview of the *gens Herennia* in relation to Alba Fucens cf. Devijver/van Wonterghem 1981, cf. now Donderer 1994 for the interpretation as a '*Werbeschild*' for a stonecutters' workshop rather than a funerary or votive relief. Cf. also four other inscriptions in the territory of Alba (CIL IX, 3992-3994 and NSc 1911, 378) but also in Marruvium: CIL IX, 3717, 3728-3729, 3748). For other possibly Marsic families (Atiedii, Vettii, Pacuvii, Novii) attested in Alba, cf. Letta 1972, 102-103. It can well be imagined that local Marsic people were included in the colony (cf. in general Bradley 2006, 171-177). On the other hand, one has inversely to be careful with stating that 'indigenous' people were living in Latin colonies if the evidence for these families predominantly comes from (possible) *vici*. Indeed, it is not to be excluded that the analysis of onomastics and conclusions about their origins are in fact biased by the (often implicit) preconception that inscriptions found outside urban centres must relate to indigenous people.

[266] Letta/D'Amato 1975, 208. Letta suggests that Apollo was adopted amongst the Marsi "*non più tardi del IV sec. a.C., provenendo da Cuma*" (213).

[267] Perhaps relating rather to the unknown '*vicus*' at Spineto, Colle Mariano than to Supinum, cf. *supra*.

[268] Letta 2001, 152 :"*spiegabile solo con una mediazione etrusca*".

[269] Letta/D'Amato 1975, 226.

[270] Letta/D'Amato 1975, 222-224 no. 134; Letta 2001, 149-150.

[271] Cf. Crawford 1981 (reviewing a.o. Letta/D'Amato 1975), 158, who remarks on the idea of Greek influence rather than Roman, esp. for Apollo that "the arguments used are fragile in the extreme".

It is important to emphasise that the processes of cultural change in central Italy were complex and that Greek and Etruscan or more generally Campanian influences were undoubtedly important. However, this complexity should also take into account the role of the Roman conquest of, and presence in, this area. In other words, 'Roman' influence in the political, military or administrative sense need not always be 'Roman' in a cultural sense. Roman influence may have been characterised often by the moving of different elements and people in different regions, rather than by diffusing 'Roman culture', which is difficult to circumscribe, in particular in this early period (but cf. *infra*).[272] This means that the sudden appearance of new cults, even if 'originally' from other regions of Italy than Rome, could in some cases still have been related to 'Roman' influence.

For example, the *Aplone* dedication is the first attestation of the cult of Apollo in Marsic territory. Interestingly, Apollo was also venerated in Alba Fucens, in the temple of S. Pietro dating to the second century BC.[273] I think it is reasonable to argue that the cult of Apollo gained special importance in this area with the foundation of the colony of Alba Fucens in 303 BC. The cult of Apollo was firmly associated in Greek and Roman (or perhaps rather Mediterranean) thought with colonisation.[274] Moreover, the importance of the fact that the *Aplone* inscription is essentially in Latin should not be overlooked, even if the commissioner or the stone-cutter was not a native speaker of Latin and/or knew *Aplo* from elsewhere than Rome.[275] Thus, in this context, Apollo, surely not an exclusively Roman god, could have been all the same related to Roman influence in the area.

Moreover, a direct Roman connotation can be recognised in other cults in the Marsic area. Valetudo, to whom the *vicus Aninus* dedicated a sanctuary, has been regarded as a typical 'Italic' goddess by Letta.[276] It seems however more logical to link her to Roman ideologies in this period. Indeed, Giuseppina Prosperi Valenti has argued – independently from the *vicus* discussion – that Valetudo should be understood as a typical Roman goddess, in the same vein of 'divine virtues' or 'qualities' of third-century Rome.[277] Valetudo is also attested in Alba Fucens, albeit not in the Republican period.[278] Also the Dei Consentes can probably better be related to Roman influence.[279]

Central to this discussion is Victoria, to whom the *vicus Supinum* made official dedications. Indeed, Victoria is extraneous to the Osco-Umbran pantheon and only appears late in the second century BC or even at the beginning of the first century BC in the context of the Social War in central Italy. In Oscan, Victoria is first attested at Pietrabbondante (cf. Chapter 3).[280] In Rome, the cult of Victoria was already established at least from the early third century BC onwards, when L. Postumius Megellus dedicates a temple to her on the Palatine during the Samnite Wars, in 294 BC.[281]

---

[272] On the diffusion of material culture, cf. e.g. Freeman 1993 and here Chapter 1; on population movement Scheidel 2004.

[273] Mertens 1969, 13-22: a graffito, dated to AD 236, mentions the restoration of the temple of Apollo (cf. Guarducci 1953, 121).

[274] Cf. *supra* and following note.

[275] See the dedication to Apollo found in the *ager Praetutianus* in archaic Latin, dated to the third / second centuries BC, made by a *libertus* (*L. Opio C. l. / Apolene dono ded / mereto*; *CIL* I², 384), and interpreted as a Roman colonial cult by Guidobaldi 1995, 186-187, 260; see also the *pocola deorum* discussed *supra*.

[276] Letta 1997a.

[277] Prosperi Valenti 1998, esp. 61-75 on origins; according to whom, on p. 75, the goddess "*sia da annoverare tra le numerose divinità del pantheon strettamente romano*"

[278] *AE* 1988, 465 with Letta 1997a, 333.

[279] Even if adopting the Etruscan / Greek gods, the *name* and concept are very Roman: Long 1987, 235-243.

[280] Interestingly, by then, *Víkturraí* seems to assume a strong anti-Roman connotation. La Regina 1966, 275 points out that the diffusion of the cult could have been facilitated by the spread of Romano-Campanian coin-types of the third century BC.

[281] Liv. 10.33.9; cf. Hölscher 1967 for the special Roman character and the relationship with Nike.

Victoria can therefore best be understood as a 'Roman' introduction.[282] At the same time, her appearance should not be seen as the straightforward exportation of a fixed, pre-existing Roman cult. Rather, the manifestation of Victoria should be understood against the background of both contemporary developments in Italy and local concerns of the *vicus Supinum* on the shores of the Fucine lake. On the one hand, her rise may have been inspired by earlier deities who were associated with her, like Vica Pota.[283] According to Aldo Prosdocimi, this goddess takes her name from the same root as the word *vicus*.[284] Therefore, it cannot be excluded that Victoria – Vica Pota had a specific meaning for the institution of the *vicus*. Suggestive in this regard is that in the Republican *Fasti Antiates maiores* the festival of Vica Pota falls on January fifth, the last day of the *Compitalia*, the most important festival associated with the *vici* (cf. Chapter 9).[285]

On the other hand, the concept / deity of Victoria seems to have been a very specific outcome of socio-political processes in Rome itself at the end of the fourth and the third centuries BC, leading to the popularity and indeed invention of divine qualities in this period.[286] This can be compared to the cult of Salus (Safety), to whom a temple was also built in this period. The dictator C. Junius Bubulcus dedicated this temple on the Quirinal in 302 BC, returning in triumph just eight days after the defeat of the Aequi, who had revolted because the colony of Alba Fucens had been established within their borders in 303 BC.[287] Interestingly, the specific ideological value of both Victoria and Salus appears in a passage in Livy (26.33.8). After the recapture of Capua in 211 BC only two people were found who had supported the Roman case, a certain Cluvia Pacula had secretly supplied food to the starving prisoners and another woman, Vestia Oppia of Atella, had proved her loyalty by sacrificing daily to the Salus and Victoria *populi Romani*. The historicity of Livy's account is of course hard to evaluate but if it indeed relates to the end of the third century BC, this explicit statement about the ideological value of both goddesses would be contemporary with the Supinate dedication to Victoria.

Although an association with the possible 'tutelary deity' of the *vicus* Vica Pota should not be excluded,[288] I think that in conclusion the appearance of Victoria here should be primarily seen in the context of the new 'divine virtues' thriving in Rome at that time. In other words, just as Valetudo – 'Health' was venerated by the *vicus Aninus*, the Roman value of 'Victory' was venerated as a deity in the *vicus Supinum*.

To sum up, some of the supposedly 'indigenous' characteristics related to the Fucine inscriptions and especially the *vicus Supinum* can be questioned. The *queistores*, even if their precise role remains somewhat unclear, might be better understood as functionaries of a Roman / Latin political system rather than a Marsic federation. It seems unnecessary to understand their presence in the dedication to Victoria in an eponymous sense and this was the most important argument for their supposedly indigenous character. Relations between Alba Fucens and the *vicus Supinum* (and its environs) are documented by the recur-

---

[282] According to Luschi 1988 Victoria would actually hide a local Vacuna / Vesuna, through a process of *interpretatio*, but this suggestion can be discarded since no strong arguments are presented. Letta admits the Roman character of the deity, but explains the existence of "*il santuario marso di Victoria*" (Letta 1992, 115) as a result of the "*alto grado di romanizzazione raggiunto già in quest'epoca dai Marsi*"; the goddess would have been introduced in the wake of the Hannibalic War: Letta/D'Amato 1975, 204; cf. Letta 2005b, 54-55. If this is intended as a uniform process of 'romanisation' of the indigenous Marsi, one may disagree. This could also be a very local phenomenon, perhaps indeed restricted to the *vicus* itself (cf. discussion *infra*).

[283] Vica Pota: *vincendi atque potiundi*: Cic. *Leg.* 2.28; Carandini 1997, 207-211.

[284] Prosdocimi 1989, 491.

[285] *InscrIt* XIII.2, p. 2.

[286] See e.g. Hölscher 1967; Fears 1981a; in general Fears 1981b and now Clark 2007.

[287] Liv. 10.1.7-9. On the decoration by Fabius Pictor: Liv. 9.43.25; Dion. Hal. *Ant. Rom.*16.3.6; Val. Max. 8.14.6. The temple had been vowed during the Samnite Wars, Liv. 9.43.25.

[288] Cf. in general Hölscher 1967, 137, and esp. 179, estimating the influence of Vica Pota on Victoria as minimal.

rence of the same names in inscriptions. A link to Alba Fucens is perhaps also attested by the cults. The early Latin dedication to the god Apollo, associated with colonisation, may be understood in this way. Other gods venerated in the *vici*, such as Victoria and Valetudo, belong to 'Roman' ideological contexts.

This begs the question on the nature of the relationship between the Fucine *vici* and Roman colonisation of the area, and in particular the Latin colony of Alba Fucens. A direct relationship between colony and *vici* is apparently hard to sustain because the *vici* are conventionally located on Marsic, i.e. allied, territory which was only incorporated in the Roman citizen body after the Social War, and not on *ager Romanus* or within the territory of the Latin colony. It should be borne in mind, however, that the factual evidence for reconstructing the territory of the colony, especially to the south, should not be overrated.[289] Karl Julius Beloch, on whose efforts most scholars build, argues that the territory of Alba Fucens must have reached the Fucine lake because of its name *Fucens* and inscriptions mentioning the Alban *tribus Fabia* at Cese and south of Avezzano would indicate that it continued up to there.[290] An inscription found at *lucus Angitiae* would indicate that this was Marsic territory since the *tribus Sergia* is mentioned.[291] At least some inhabitants of the *vicus Supinum* were also inscribed in the *tribus Sergia*,[292] and it has been concluded that the *vici* were part of Marsic territory. However, this conclusion is less self-evident than it may appear. It should be noted that at best it indicates that the *vicus Supinum* was placed in the same *tribus* as the Marsic *and* Paelignian territories when the inhabitants of the Fucine area were divided in *tribus*, that is after the Social War.[293] In other words, it is difficult to imagine an 'ethnic' principle lying at the basis of this administrative distribution and thus it cannot be inversely used to establish the ethnicity or original affiliation of certain places in an earlier period.[294] Although I hesitate to make an affirmative statement in this regard, it follows that the original territory of the colony *might* have included the *vici* at the southern shores of the Fucine lake. In any case, their modern representation on maps within 'Marsic territory' does not reflect any factual juridical and historical evidence for the pre-Social War situation.

The vicus *as a 'new' community*
The old Latin inscriptions around the Fucine lake have often been seen as evidence for the early romanisation of the area. Indeed Letta discerns a "*processo inarrestabile di romanizzazione*" which could, according to him, be distinguished in the gradual changes documented in epigraphy. The Antinum inscription still

[289] The northern boundary is documented by inscribed stones explicitly mentioning the *Albensium fines*: CIL IX, 3929-3930, but these can probably be related to a new organisation of the territory in Hadrianic times, cf. Liberatore 2001, 187 with further references.

[290] Beloch 1926, 552. CIL IX, 3933 ("*alla Cese*"); CIL IX, 3922: funerary inscription, found "*ad viam consularem M p. ab Avezzano Lucum versus al sito Cerrito prope S. Mariam de Loreto*".

[291] CIL IX, 3894. On the use of *tribus* indications for establishing territories cf. Van Wonterghem 1984, 28-29 (with map of the Marsic / Paelignian area); the maps in Kiepert 1901 are based on the same principle, for which cf. Castagnoli 1958, 37.

[292] CIL IX, 3906 (= CIL I², 1814).

[293] Even the assertion that the *tribus* indication in e.g. CIL IX, 3906 relates to the *vicus Supinum* proper is unjustified, as Giuseppe Forni has noted, the *tribus* did not belong to a city but to the Roman citizens that were inscribed in it (Forni 1982). People belonging to different *tribus* could and did live in the same place and there are examples of different generations belonging to different *tribus*; see Buonocore 2003 with n. 22 (*AE* 1964, 15-33; CIL IX, 4967, with a father in the *Collina* and a son in the *Quirina*).

[294] Rather, the division could perhaps be seen as a practical and ad hoc act undertaken in the wake of political and/or military developments which sometimes coincided with 'ethnic groups'. The grouping together of the Paeligni and Marsi in the same *tribus* is seen by Mommsen as a punishment because this would restrict their electoral weight (Mommsen 1887, 105), but Taylor 1960, 113 thinks that the Romans respected (presumed) ethnic affiliations between Paeligni and Marsi.

retains Marsic language and onomastics and a *medis*, but also includes the Latin alphabet and the Roman name of *cetur* > *censor* (or **centuriator*).[295] An intermediate stage is seen in the inscription of the *vicus Petinus*, where the Latin onomastic system is applied but the language is still fundamentally Marsic.[296] Then, some 50 years later than the example of Antinum, Supinum would attest to the use of the Latin language and the Latin onomastic system as well as magistrates using Roman titles who would however have functioned in the way 'indigenous' magistrates did, rather than as Roman *quaestores*.[297]

There are, however, difficulties in this reconstruction of a Marsic politico-juridical system and its superficial and gradual romanisation. First, the inscriptions found around the Fucine lake do not *need* to form a homogeneous group representing a uniform political system. Second, the reconstruction of some parts is questionable. In particular, the interpretation of the *cetur* of the Antinum sheet as a Marsic federal leader can be challenged. Indeed, this person bearing a non-local name could perhaps better be understood as a Roman magistrate who controlled or supervised the Marsic community.

This would imply that the *cetur* was not used in an eponymous sense, which weakens the hypothesis that the *queistores* of the *vicus Supinum* were used as such. Indeed, it seems possible that the *queistores* fulfilled a similar role as the Roman *cetur* from Antinum and came from another (Roman or Latin) centre. Similarly, the possible *duumviri* of the *vicus Petinus* can just as well be related to direct Roman influence as to the adoption of Roman titles by indigenous Marsi for their own political system.

In general, the idea that Roman magisterial titles were adopted by 'indigenous' peoples without being part of the Roman political system suspiciously reflects an idea of 'self-romanisation' or 'emulation' in which Roman culture is seen as superior and therefore adopted straightforwardly by 'indigenous' populations (cf. Chapter 1). However, it does not seem logical that the Italic peoples adopted Roman titles as early as the third century BC if there were no political need to do so.

As noted in Chapter 6, Tarpin suggests that the institution of the *vicus* may have consisted of a small group of (Latin or Roman) citizens. In this respect the Marsic *vici* are especially problematic because they are located outside Roman / Latin territory, just south of the (perceived) territory of the Latin colony of Alba Fucens. Tarpin resolves the problem by arguing that there may have been a large portion of citizens there and by positing a far-reaching romanisation of the Marsi ("*romanisation rapide et intense*").[298] In this approach he follows Letta, who has emphasised the 'precocious romanisation' of the Marsic area.[299]

Additionally, Tarpin seeks to resolve the problem by stressing that there might have existed good political relations between Marsi and Romans, which runs counter to Letta's ideas.[300] Tarpin thus combines the early 'romanisation' (in the traditional sense) of indigenous Marsi with the placing of small groups of Latin or Roman citizens.[301] The two scenarios need not be interrelated however; political relations at the end of the fourth and beginning of the third centuries BC need not have been particularly strong and elites need not have been thoroughly 'romanised' before a community of Latin or Roman citizens could be installed.[302] There is evidence that Marsic cohesion in this period was quite strong, as is documented

---

[295] Letta/D'Amato 1975, 196-197. Following Salmon 1967, 90 with n. 3, that the *censor* is originally a Roman institution.

[296] Cf. Letta/D'Amato 1975, no. 188 = *CIL* I², 2874.

[297] Letta/D'Amato 1975, 196-197.

[298] Tarpin 2002, 62. Cf. also p. 57: "*les relations entre les élites marses et romaines semblent avoir été étroites et précoces.*"

[299] Cf. Letta 1972, 101, talking of "*la rapida e totale integrazione dei Marsi nel mondo romano*".

[300] Letta 1972, e.g. 77.

[301] Tarpin 2002, 62: "*Qu'il ait eu romanisation rapide et intense, ne serait-ce que des élites, ou implantation de petites communautés romaines n'a guère d'importance : ce qui compte est que l'élément indigène n'apparaît que peu dans le contexte des vici marses.*" I would say that, at least in the present discussion, this difference is highly important and interesting but it may be that the type of evidence needed to prove one option or the other is simply not available to us.

[302] Of course, this depends on the definition of the term 'romanised' (cf. Chapter 1), which seems to be used here as the adaptation to Roman customs at the expense of own cultural traditions.

for instance by their communal mint.[303] But this does not preclude a situation in which a small group of Latin or Roman citizens was installed, or installed itself, in an area otherwise inhabited by indigenous (but admittedly not too belligerent) Marsi. I would argue that Marsic resistance and Roman influence need not be mutually exclusive. Indeed, the opposite may have been true and this would reflect a common phenomenon in all historical periods (cf. e.g. Chapter 3).

In conclusion, what evidence do we have to establish the character of the *vici* around the Fucine lake? The magistrates found epigraphically indicate Roman models. In theory, this can be interpreted as indigenous and independent Marsi adopting Roman forms but perhaps is best seen as actions undertaken by Roman / Latin magistrates in or on behalf of these *vici*, or by indigenous people who operated within a Roman political system. The language used is Latin but at least some of the stone-cutters / commissioners did not master this language well, or were influenced by regional or local variations.[304] The names recurring on the Fucine inscriptions can only partly be connected to local families with some confidence. Some of the attested cults do not betray any 'direct' Roman influence and instead point to different regions in Italy, whereas others are clearly related to Roman concepts. How should one interpret this heterogeneous data set? Does it mean that Roman influence was minimal? Perhaps not: as I argued for the case of Apollo, the point is that the effect of 'Roman influence' could have simply consisted of a mix of different Italian traditions as a consequence of the re-ordering and administration of the population of the Italian peninsula.

In a situation like this, I think most weight should be given to the 'intentions' or 'aspirations' that become clear from the record. In other words, we should perhaps not look for failures in 'being Roman', such as grammatical 'errors', but rather consider the fact that the people of these *vici* were apparently willing to appear 'Roman'. Therefore, in this context I propose considering the *vici* as *new* Roman / Latin communities that were 'romanising', just as Rome itself was 'romanising' in this period.

These intentions clearly come to the fore in the cults, and Victoria is a good example in this respect. She was indeed quite 'Roman' with overtly political and military associations which are securely documented at the same time that the Supinate dedication was made. The installation of a cult to Victoria will have had heavy ideological connotations, especially in an area which was otherwise not yet *ager Romanus*.[305] In fact, the evidence does not preclude the possibility that the *vicus Supinum* was a new foundation with new inhabitants, whilst indigenous people may have been part of the newly installed *vicus*. If so, they may have functioned in the context of a *new* community, which had little relation to Marsic roots other than, perhaps, onomastics. This community, proudly boasting its own distinctive name, must of course not necessarily be defined as 'Roman' either, but the act of the installation of people from different regions of Italy perhaps including local people who consequently (try to) write Latin and worship Victoria, is directly related to Roman control and strategies of dominion. The *vicus Supinum* is therefore best understood as a *new*, rather than 'Roman' or 'Marsic' community, which appeared as a consequence of Roman imperial expansion. A similar case could be made for the *vicus Aninus* venerating Valetudo, a goddess for whom, despite the scarcity of the sources, a connection to the same ideological context as Victoria seems quite plausible.[306]

---

[303] La Regina 1970, 204.

[304] On these processes, cf. Adams 2007.

[305] Cf. Bispham 2000a, 10, on Victoria at Rome: "The worship of Victory becomes a key element in the religious identity of Rome; it shows Roman confidence, an appreciation of the fundamental changes being effected in the Italian peninsula by Roman arms."

[306] For example, Valetudo seems to be connected to Hygieia (*CIL* III, 7279, Athens: *Aesculapio et Valetudini*) and Salus (*RRC* no. 442), as well as Victoria (*RIC*, 1, no. 151): Weinstock 1955, 267.

If this 'romanising' interpretation of the 'Marsic' *vici* is correct, this would mean that Roman / Latin influence was not confined to (colonial) urban areas but also extended to rural areas, even outside the swathes of incorporated land and colonial territories usually presumed.[307]

An important result of this discussion on *vici*, in my opinion, is moreover that we need not regard the whole corpus of archaeological and epigraphic evidence as indicative of one broadly unitary development. Referring to the Marsic area, Letta posits a development in which 'early' or 'precocious' romanisation and Latinisation in the third century BC is followed by a '*rivendicazione*' of indigenous Marsic roots in the second century BC.[308] Even if Letta carefully allows for local variations, on the whole the entire epigraphical corpus is thus fitted into one model. However, if it is accepted that the *vici* represent rather isolated entities, possibly partly constituted by foreigners and probably incorporating some of the local population, but nonetheless 'Roman' in constitution and administrative structure, this part of the epigraphic corpus has to be seen apart from the evidence from the rest of the Marsic territory.

Instead of a unitary development, one could hypothesise separate or parallel developments. In this case an 'early romanisation' of some very small pockets on the shores of the Fucine lake could be envisaged, in contrast to 'indigenous' traditions elsewhere in the Marsic area. In this sense, the re-affirmation of 'Marsic identity' in the second century BC should be considered with caution since this inscription could belong to a different line of development.[309] It is perhaps to be regretted that in this view the 'really indigenous' developments in central Italy are even more difficult to grasp since in this new approach, a significant part of the epigraphic corpus is relegated to the 'Roman' or at least disproportionally 'hybrid' realm and thus stripped away from the 'Italic' record.

7.6 CONCLUSION: VICI, PAGI, SANCTUARIES AND 'NEW COMMUNITIES'

The consequences of the revision of the *pagus-vicus* system for the interpretation of sanctuaries in central Italy are substantial. The relationship between *pagus* and *vicus* was not hierarchical and thus ideas of a presumed hierarchy of sanctuaries based upon this relationship must be revised. Furthermore, the idea that every rural sanctuary must have belonged to a *vicus* or a *pagus* should be abandoned. Together with the idea that the installation of *pagi* and *vici* was related to Roman control, these points form the basis of my argument, enabling the following reassessments.

The direct relationship between the installation of *pagi* and *vici* and Roman control defies the common interpretation of sanctuaries related to a *pagus* or a *vicus* as pre- or non-Roman features. All inscriptions relating to cults or sanctuaries documenting a *pagus* or a *vicus* were found in contexts that were by then under Roman control, i.e. areas where the (partial) Roman or Latin right had been granted, with the possible exception of the 'Marsic' *vici*. This means that the cult places administrated by *pagi* and *vici* probably functioned in a (new) Roman reorganisation of the land and its people. Importantly, this

---

[307] Cf. in this context the remarks by Mouritsen 2007 on the *civitas sine suffragio* but actually questioning (p. 158) the whole "visual conceptualisation of Roman expansion", reflecting a combination of legal formalism and "a modern territorial concept of power".

[308] Letta 2005b, 53 on Ve. 225, dated to the end of the second or the beginning of the first century BC.

[309] Interestingly, the gods to whom the dedication is made seem to be fairly 'Roman' (cf. *CIL* XI, 6298 = *CIL* I², 375 for the *novensides* on *cippi* of *Pisaurum* [a *conventus* and subsequently a Roman colony of 184 BC] dating earlier than the Marsic inscription cf. Cresci Marrone/ Mennella 1984, 115-120; on the date cf. Coarelli 2000 and Harvey Jr. 2006). This different developmental line is of course not to be considered as isolated from other developments. Different 'lines' will on the contrary have influenced one another in a dynamic process.

institutional link to Roman control as such does not necessarily preclude that Italic people and Italic cults were involved.

However, it has been seen in this chapter that the cults associated with *pagi* and *vici* do not appear to be specifically or exclusively local or 'Italic' and they appear to conform to Roman standards. Only in very few cases is it possible to connect architectural and other archaeological remains of sanctuaries to epigraphically attested *pagi* or *vici*. More similar evidence could illuminate questions regarding the re-use or establishment *ex novo* of these cult places and the possibly divergent aspects of these sanctuaries in comparison to others that were not related to *vici* or *pagi*.

Such evidence does exist in the case of the temple at Castel di Ieri, which has been interpreted previously as an 'Italic' temple. In light of the above mentioned argument, however, I have proposed to reconstruct it as a 'Capitoline' temple associated with the influence of a *pagus*. We may thus see the temple as an expression of the commitment of the *pagus* community to Roman ideologies, which provides a suitable explanation for the striking 'Roman' features of the temple. No such clear architectural cases can be found for sanctuaries that functioned in a *vicus* context, although if it could be proven that Contrada S. Rustico (Basciano) in the *ager Praetutianus* did indeed have *vicus* status, this would be a case in point. On the other hand, the cultural context of *vici* and their cult places is generally easier to reconstruct than for the *pagi*. This is especially true for the Fucine area. Here, the evidence for the *vicus Supinum* reveals a Latin writing community that venerated the Roman goddess Victoria, just as the *vicus Aninus* worshipped Valetudo. Since there is no substantial evidence to suggest 'indigenous' cults or practices relating to *pagi* or *vici*, a correlation between sanctuaries associated with *vici* and *pagi* and Roman influence thus becomes manifest.

I have also tried to establish the nature of the relationship between *pagi*, *vici* and Roman control in the cases under study in more detail. As far as we can tell with the available evidence, these links do not seem to have been uniform. At the Latin colony of Ariminum, *vici* and *pagi* clearly depended in some way on their urban centre. This is already seen in the third century BC via the so-called *pocola*. In what was presumably an urban cult place, representatives of *pagi* and *vici* dedicated black gloss vessels. It is unclear (and in part depending on the reading of the inscriptions as genitive singular or nominative plural) to what extent these *vici* and *pagi* had their own distinctive identity and whether they wished to express this in the urban cult place.

Around the Fucine lake, the expression of an independent identity is documented in the rural *vici* in Marsic territory demonstrating proper names (*vicus Aninus, Supinum, Petinus* etc.). It could be argued that to these *vici*, apparently outside Roman or Latin territory, this own identity, expressed through a proper name, was especially important.[310] The relationship of the 'Marsic' *vici* with the colony of Alba Fucens was perhaps stronger than previously thought, although by no means unequivocal. The same goes for the *vici* in the *ager Praetutianus*, apparently not restricted to the territory of the colony of Hatria.[311] However, it also seems impossible to link the *vici* of the *ager Praetutianus* directly to the *praefectura* of Interamna, and thus to a different category of Roman control. Therefore, at present it does not seem possible to relate the institution of *vici* in these areas to one specific category of government or administration of the territory. A substantial problem in establishing such a relationship is that many of these categories are modern conceptualisations of a probably much more complex historical situation. Notwithstanding this caveat,

---

[310] Cf. Barth 1969, and my Chapters 1 and 3 on the 'construction of community'.

[311] It might be surmised that the people belonging to colonies sometimes lived in villages outside the urban centre and that these represent the *vici* that we find mentioned in inscriptions (cf. discussion *supra*). If such pockets of citizens, dependent on the colony could also be placed outside the direct 'territory' of the colony – inasmuch such a territory is reconstructable at all, cf. *supra* on Alba and Hatria – this would be a possible explanation for the Marsic *vici*. However, this must remain hypothetical.

following Tarpin it is perhaps appropriate to interpret *vici* as a convenient legal category that could be applied to different situations.[312]

It remains hard to establish the indigenous population's degree of involvement in the new *vici*. Contrary to previous arguments, it does not seem necessary to assume that the inhabitants of the *vici* were all of local origin. Although it is possible that pre-existing settlements were 'upgraded' to the status of *vicus*, a continuity in population cannot be automatically assumed. The onomastic evidence is poor or non-existent, except for the Marsic *vici*, where perhaps both local and 'foreign' people settled. Archaeology is unable to answer questions of ethnicity in this respect. We should bear in mind however, that a scenario of peoples merging and living happily together is not necessarily the most reasonable one. Relations between colonists and indigenous people need not have been peaceful. Livy notes that the Aequi revolted against the installation of Alba Fucens, and the Marsi against the colony of Carseoli, and in some cases genocide is mentioned.[313]

In general, the evidence for *vici* points to both 'Roman influence' and other influences either from local people or Italic people from other regions. Instead of, in reaction to previous scholarship, conceptualising *vici* as entirely 'Roman' elements, we could perhaps think of them as communities of mixed origins. Conveniently, we could designate these *vici* as 'new communities' and the same possibly also applies for *pagi*. At least in some cases, these 'new communities' clearly aspired to adopt a Roman ideology. It is in this sense that the Capitoline aspirations of a Paelignian *pagus* could be explained, just as the appearance of the 'divine qualities' Victoria and Valetudo on the shores of the Fucine lake. To my mind, this apparent willingness to construct a Roman ideology is most crucial to the discussion. This willingness can be explained by the need of the newly established groups to form a cohesive community, for which common ground was sought and found within the political and institutional frameworks that lay at the origins of their very existence. Moreover, an oppositional process in which the new groups sought to reinforce their allegiance to the Roman powers in reaction to the outer environment is not unimaginable.

Thus in Ariminum the new communities ritually enhanced their bond with the urban administrative centre. Special festivals and rituals seem to have existed in order to celebrate and define their own territorial boundaries and institutional character. Perhaps, also these communities sacrificed for a divine quality, that of Fides. The importance of specific rituals and festivals for *pagus* and *vicus* communities cannot be underestimated, and will therefore be further explored in the next two chapters on the festivals most closely associated with the *pagus* and the *vicus*, respectively the *Paganalia* and the *Compitalia*.

---

[312] Tarpin 2002. Tarpin actually emphasises the specificity of the term but argues that it could be correctly used in different (legal) situations.

[313] Liv. 10.1.7; 10.3.2. Cf. Bradley 2006, 171-177.

8 Roman Ritual in the Italian Countryside? The *Paganalia* and the *Lustratio Pagi*

Notwithstanding the difficulties with the *pagus-vicus* system outlined above, it is clear that both *pagus* and *vicus* were at some point important for the organisation of the territory. To summarise, the main problems with the *pagus-vicus* system are 1) the presumed pre-Roman date and 'Italic' nature of both institutions in Italy outside Rome, which are difficult to support; and 2) the presumed hierarchical relationship between *pagus* and *vicus*, viz. the idea that a *pagus* contained one or more *vici*. Be that as it may, epigraphic and literary sources indicate clearly that both *vicus* and *pagus* performed specific functions at least in some contexts and periods. Amongst these functions the religious aspect is particularly conspicuous.

In the following chapters I discuss the main religious activities that were performed in or overseen by *pagi* and *vici*. I argue that the religious dimension of both *vicus* and *pagus* was of considerable importance, not in pre-Roman times, when *pagi* and *vici* were not in existence, but under Roman rule. *Vicus* and *pagus* seem to have had a strong religious role in specific 'Roman' contexts: i.e. in Rome, in parts of Italy after their incorporation by Rome during the Republican period and presumably in large parts of Italy after the Social War. Indeed, I think this religious dimension was fundamental for the creation and definition of the new communities that found themselves in the Italian landscape as a result of colonisation and/or the reorganisation of the territory and its population.

Modern scholarship on Roman religion often highlights the romantic aspect of the 'rustic' rituals associated with the rural *vicus* and the *pagus*. Most important of these were the religious festival of the *pagi*, the *Paganalia*, and that of the *vici*, the *Compitalia*. Although these festivals are usually portrayed as bucolic, agricultural rituals of olden days, I will question this view. I argue that available evidence points us in a different direction and that the festivals were related to Roman administrative control. In this way, the rituals connected to the *vicus* and the *pagus* appear as important elements for the definition of the newly formed groups and at the same time as vehicles for the formation and control of Roman Italy.

8.1 PAGUS AND PAGANALIA: BETWEEN RUSTICITY AND ADMINISTRATIVE CONTROL

pagus agat festum: pagum lustrate, coloni (Ov. *Fast.* 1.669)

Elements of rustic cult abound in Augustan literature, poetry, and art, such as the wall painting from Boscotrecase illustrated below (fig. 8.1). Both *vicus* and *pagus* are often explicitly linked to it. The *pagus* is frequently used to situate a cultic scene by association in a 'rural' context. This rustic image of *pagus* religion is widely accepted in modern scholarship. For example Horace's Ode 3.18, in which a *pagus* seems to constitute the background for the celebration of a festival in honour of Faunus, has provoked lyrical reactions by modern scholars because it would give us insight into 'true country religion'.

Fig. 8.1. Wall-painting with 'sacro-idyllic' landscape from Boscotrecase, Red Room, North wall (after Von Blanckenhagen/Alexander 1990, pl. 24).

Faune, Nympharum fugientum amator,
per meos finis et aprica rura
lenis incedas abeasque parvis
aequus alumnis,
si tener pleno cadit haedus anno
larga nec desunt Veneris sodali
vina craterae, vetus ara multo
fumat odore.
ludit herboso pecus omne campo
cum tibi nonae redeunt Decembres,
festus in pratis vacat otioso
cum bove pagus,
inter audacis lupus errat agnos,
spargit agrestis tibi silva frondes,
gaudet invisam pepulisse fossor
ter pede terram

'Faunus, lustful pursuer of the fleeing Nymphs, come gently onto my land with its sunny acres, and as you depart look kindly on my little nurslings, seeing that a tender kid is sacrificed to you at the end of the year, plenty of wine is available for the mixing bowl (Venus' companion), and the old altar smokes with lots of incense. The whole flock gambols in the grassy meadow when your day comes round on the fifth of December. The village in festive mood is on holiday in the fields along with the oxen, which are also resting. The wolf wanders among the lambs, and they feel no fear. The forest sheds its woodland leaves in your honour. The digger enjoys beating with his feet in triple time his old enemy, the earth.'
(translation Loeb)

According to William Warde Fowler, "no picture could be choicer or neater than this ... We are for a moment let into the heart and mind of ancient Italy, as they showed themselves on a winter holiday".[1] Even more poetically, Howard Scullard writes on the poem (as usual closely following Fowler):

> "Here we have the essence of true Roman country religion: the appeal to the vague and possibly dangerous spirit that guards the flocks to be present, but not to linger too long; the smoking altar of earth; the simple offering of wine and kid; the gambolling sheep; the quiet relaxation after the year's toil, and the dance on the

---

[1] Fowler 1925, 257.

hated land which had demanded so much labour. Horace knew the conventions of pastoral poetry, but here he is surely depicting what he himself had seen and perhaps shared in. This annual festival was held in the pagi and not in Rome, so that it is not registered in the calendars, but it is included here [scil. in Roman festivals] because it must have played a significant part in the lives of many Romans, especially in early days."[2]

As discussed in Chapter 6, the rural *pagus* has often been seen as a typically Italic institution, existing from time immemorial. The religious role of the *pagus* has also been emphasised in modern literature, if not taken for granted. The above cited examples[3] attest to a general attitude to religion associated with the *pagus* which is essentially one of rusticity and rurality.[4] The rusticity of this religious aspect of the *pagus* is implicitly or explicitly equated with the presumed ancient or 'timeless' character of the *pagus*. In this way, rural contexts and its religious aspects are associated with 'Italic', age-old and immutable traditions, without however adducing hard proof for this general idea.

The image of the foremost religious aspect of the *pagus*, the festival of the *Paganalia* evoked by modern interpreters of ancient texts, also seems to fit well into this rustic, agricultural ideal. However, a brief reassessment of the sources shows that this scenario is more complex than usually assumed and the main source even reveals a fairly different story. Indeed, both the incentive behind the creation of the festival and the actions undertaken during the festival appear to have been quite pragmatic as they were related to the Roman administrative system.

8.1.1 PAGANALIA, SEMENTIVAE, AND LUSTRATIO PAGI

Only few references to the *Paganalia* are known to us. Modern scholarship has attempted to supplement knowledge about the festival by equating the *Paganalia* to other rituals and festivals, especially the *lustratio pagi* and the *Sementivae*. This rather confusing amalgamation of evidence has consequently been used to identify the character of the *Paganalia*. Therefore, it is useful to briefly examine the relationship between *Paganalia*, *Sementivae* and *lustratio pagi*.

The discussion is prompted by a description of the winter festival of the *Sementivae* in Ovid's *Fasti* (1.657-696). Ovid recalls a *lustratio pagi* in line 1.699. Some have equated it with the *Paganalia*. In particular, the triple repetition of *pagus, pagum, paganis* has suggested to many that Ovid is referring to the *Paganalia*, in turn leading to the assumption that *Paganalia* can be equated with *Sementivae*.[5] Particularly popular has been the suggestion that the *Sementivae* represented the official 'state' festival whereas the *Paganalia* would represent its rural equivalent.[6]

---

[2] Scullard 1981, 201.

[3] Of course Horace comes from the Italic region Lucania but it should be remembered that it is in the same Odes (3.2.13) that the famous line *dulce et decorum est pro patria mori* appears. On the ambiguous relationship of Roman poets and writers with regard to their background, see Gasser 1999. Cf. also Yntema 2009 on Ennius.

[4] Cf. Todisco 2004a for the image of *vici* and pagi in the sources. On 'rusticising' trends with regard to religion in Roman society in general, see Dorcey 1992 and North 1995.

[5] E.g. Scullard 1981, 68; Fowler 1925, 294, n. 3: "But the distinction is perhaps only of place; or if of time also, yet not of object and meaning." Cf. also following note.

[6] E.g. Fowler 1925 who assumes that the *Sementivae* were celebrated under the "less technical" name of the *Paganalia* in "the country" (294, cf. also preceding note), and Bailey 1932, 147. Further references in Delatte 1937, 104-105. Recently, the argument has been restated by Baudy 1998, 186-187, who sees the *Paganalia* as "*ein eigenständiges ländliches Äquivalent [zum staatsrömischen Aussaatfest]*" (however not citing the previous and similar conclusions by e.g. Fowler and Bailey, nor the criticisms by Delatte).

Others, including Georg Wissowa, are inclined to view the *Paganalia* and the *lustratio pagi* as two equal and separate entities.[7] However, a *lustratio* seems to have been a common element, not an equivalent, of certain festivals.[8] In fact, it does not seem improbable that Ovid compared and blended details from different festivals, which is in line with the representation of religious rites in a Callimachean tradition.[9] It is thus possible to dismiss the idea that Ovid's *lustratio pagi* relates to the *Paganalia* proper whilst retaining the possibility that a *lustratio* was held during the *Paganalia*.[10] Ultimately, this non-exclusive relationship seems to be proven by the fact that a *lustratio pagi* is known epigraphically for June 5, another for May or March 11 but not winter, which would be the period of the *Sementivae*.[11]

Another short passage has also been cited in support of the connection between *Paganalia* and *Sementivae*. Varro speaks of the *Paganicae* after having discussed the *Sementivae* and considers both festivals as agricultural feasts.[12] Most scholars have understood *Paganicae* as a synonym for *Paganalia*. However, the possibility that *Paganicae* does not relate to the *Paganalia*, but rather to another ritual or festival held in the *pagus* from which it takes its name, should perhaps be considered, especially since Varro uses the word *Paganalia* two lines earlier (in an apparently unrelated context).[13] In any case Varro does not equate the *Sementivae* and the *Paganicae* but instead compares them on the basis of the connection with agriculture and their status as *feriae conceptivae*.[14]

Now that the relationship between *Paganalia*, other festivals and the *lustratio pagi* has been defined more precisely, it becomes possible to evaluate the actual evidence for the character of the *Paganalia* proper. For if the *Paganalia* and the *Sementivae feriae* are not identical, it follows that references to the latter cannot be used to clarify the character of the former.[15] And when these references are indeed dismissed, it seems legitimate to question the typically *agricultural* character of the *Paganalia* that has been accepted almost unanimously in studies on the *Paganalia*.[16]

---

[7] Ov. *Fast.* 1.669 would refer to the *lustratio*. Rohde 1942, 2294: "... die lustratio pagi, die als besonderes Fest neben den P.[aganalia] anzumerken ist"; Wissowa 1912, 143 and 439 n. 7 ("*Erwähnt von Varro, Ling. 6.26 unter dem Namen paganicae (feriae) ... Sie sind ein agrarisches Fest ... verschieden sowohl von den Feriae Sementivae, mit denen sie oft zusammengeworfen werden, wie von der lustratio pagi.*" The elegy on a rustic festival from Tib. 2.1 which inspired Ovid's lines does not mention the *Paganalia* either. Cf. Maltby 2002, 359: "Many of the individual details crop up again in Ovid's description of the January festival of the *Paganalia* or the *Feriae Sementivae* (*Fast.*1.657ff.). But the fact that Ovid was imitating T[ibullus] does not prove that T[ibullus] was describing the *Paganalia*." Cf. on Tibullus' elegy, Baudy 1998, 127-147.

[8] And other occasions: cf. *infra*.

[9] See Green 2004, 309; Miller 1991, 117 with n. 23.

[10] Delatte 1937, 104-107.

[11] *CIL* IX, 1618: on occasion of the birthday of a benefactor (Baudy 1998, 187 explains this as an exception: "*Demnach konnte anscheinend der winterliche Ritus – unter geänderten Vorzeichen – im Sommer wiederholt werden*") and *CIL* IX, 5565.

[12] Varro, *Ling*. 6.26. According to him, the *Paganicae* were *agriculturae causa susceptae*; i.e. their date would be established according to the agricultural calendar.

[13] Baudy 1998, 187 argues in defence of the equation *Paganicae* = *Paganalia* that in this context (*Ling*. 6.26) an intended (*feriae*) *Paganicae*, in consonance with the *feriae Sementivae*, would explain the difference. Varro, *Ling*. 6.24: *Dies Septimontium nominatus ab his septem montibus, in quis sita Urbs est; feriae non populi, sed montanorum modo, ut Paganalibus, qui sunt alicuius pagi*. Varro, *Ling*. 6.26: *Sementivae Feriae dies is, qui a pontificibus dictus, appellatus a semente, quod sationis causa susceptae. Paganicae eiusdem agriculturae causa susceptae, ut haberent in agris omnis pagus, unde Paganicae dictae.*

[14] Cf. also Macrob. *Sat*. 1.16.6, where the *Sementivae* and *Paganalia* are listed apart from one another. Cf. Miller 1991, 117 n. 23 on the comparative character of the statements in Varro and Ovid.

[15] Cf. Wissowa 1912, 143 and 439 n. 7; Delatte 1937, 104-105. Cf. Fraschetti 1990, 159 with n. 59.

[16] Although Delatte points out with clarity that Dionysius is the main source, he still recognises an agricultural aspect to the *Paganalia*: "... *aux yeux de Denys ... les Paganalia sont une fête de la vie agricole*" (Delatte 1937, 106). Cf. Baudy 1998, esp. 188-189 and 190: "*Die Paganalia hatten also nicht nur eine agrarische, sondern zugleich eine wichtige soziale Bedeutung,*" consequently stating that Dionysius did not consider the former but was only interested in

Ovid's text stages a general *lustratio pagi* in the context of the *Sementivae* and Macrobius states that the *Paganalia* were *feriae conceptivae* (i.e. a mobile feast and not part of the *feriae stativae*, the fixed public calendar), listing the festival together with the *Latinae*, *Sementivae* and the *Compitalia*.[17] Even if it were true that many agricultural festivals were *feriae conceptivae*, it would be wrong to turn the argument around and state that the *Paganalia* were an agricultural festival because they are *feriae conceptivae*. Clearly, the *feriae Latinae* in honour of *Juppiter Latiaris*, announced on the mons Albanus by the new consuls, cannot be considered agricultural and neither can, as I will argue in the next chapter, the *Compitalia*.

The only text possibly explicitly linking the festival to agriculture seems to be Varro, who states that the date of the *Paganicae* was established according to the agricultural calendar.[18] However, one should be careful in identifying the *Paganicae* with the *Paganalia* and we should therefore refrain from reading too much into this passage. The only pertinent texts that securely relate to the *Paganalia* proper do not give the slightest hint of an agricultural function or character of the festival.

8.1.2 THE PAGANALIA ACCORDING TO DIONYSIUS OF HALICARNASSUS

In his *Roman Antiquities* (4.14-15), Dionysius of Halicarnassus provides the only detailed narrative of the festival of the *Paganalia* available to us. He informs us that the *Paganalia*, just as the *Compitalia* discussed in the next chapter, were instigated by king Servius Tullius (trad. 578 to 535 BC) while creating the new *tribus* division of Rome.[19] Dionysius tells us that Servius Tullius extended the division of the city proper to four instead of three urban *tribus* and divided the countryside in an unknown number of rural *tribus*.

the latter. Tarpin 2002 treats Dionysius' account in detail, but his study is not concerned with the character of the festival in general and in light of the other sources.

[17] Macrob. *Sat.* 1.16.6: *conceptivae sunt quae quotannis a magistratibus vel sacerdotibus concipiuntur in dies vel certos vel etiam incertos, ut sunt Latinae Sementivae Paganalia Compitalia.*

[18] Varro, *Ling.* 6.26.

[19] In 2.76.1, Dionysius attributes the installation of *pagi* to king Numa. In this passage an administrative function is also made clear. It is discussed in more detail in the passage on Servius, where the relationship with the *tribus* and the *Paganalia* is also discussed.

[20] Cf. Thomsen 1980, 251-252, who dismisses the idea that Servius installed the *pagi* and *Paganalia*, arguing that these were much older.

[21] Loeb translation of Dion. Hal. *Ant. Rom.* 4.15 (see for 4.14 Chapter 9): "Tullius also divided the country as a whole into twenty-six parts, according to Fabius, who calls these divisions tribes also and, adding the four city tribes to them, says that there were thirty tribes in all under Tullius. But according to Vennonius he divided the country into thirty-one parts, so that with the four city tribes the number was rounded out to the thirty-five tribes that exist down to our day. However, Cato, who is more worthy of credence than either of these authors, does not specify the number of the parts into which the country was divided. After Tullius, therefore, had divided the country into a certain number of parts, whatever that number was, he built places of refuge upon such lofty eminences as could afford ample security for the husbandmen, and called them by a Greek name, *pagi* or "hills". Thither all the inhabitants fled from the fields whenever a raid was made by enemies, and generally passed the night there. These places also had their governors (*archontes*), whose duty it was to know not only the names of all the husbandmen who belonged to the same district but also the lands which afforded them their livelihood. And whenever there was occasion to summon the countrymen to take arms or to collect the taxes that were assessed against each of them, these governors assembled the men together and collected the money. And in order that the number of these husbandmen might not be hard to ascertain, but might be easy to compute and be known at once, he ordered them to erect altars to the gods who presided over and were guardians of the district, and directed them to assemble every year and honour these gods with public sacrifices. This occasion also he made one of the most solemn festivals, calling it the *Paganalia*; and he drew up laws concerning these sacrifices, which the Romans still observe. Towards the expense of this sacrifice and of this assemblage he ordered all those of the same district to contribute each of them a certain

Pagi would have constituted the subdivisions of these rural tribes. All *pagi* would have had altars (βωμούς) for the celebration of the *Paganalia*. His description contains little historicity[20] but may echo a historical situation in some way and is of importance for the understanding of the religious role of the *pagus*.[21] Some general important features in Dionysius' account can be pointed out. From the outset, Dionysius connects the installation of the *Paganalia* to the administrative division of Rome and its peri-urban area. Indeed, this passage (4.14-15) is part of a description of Servius' *res gestae*, which culminates in the installation of the *census* (4.16).

Related to the numbering procedures described by Dionysius, there seems to be a hierarchy in the sequence of actions. First a division is made, both of the urban and the rural area, and then magistrates are appointed to ascertain the number of inhabitants, and their land property. This, as is explicitly stated, serves the military levy and the taxation. The festivals of the *Compitalia* (4.14) and the *Paganalia* (4.15) were only subsequently created to *facilitate* the counting procedure.[22] With regard to the *Paganalia*, Dionysius states that in order to easily establish the number of inhabitants of the *pagi* ("…but might be easy to compute and be known at once"), these were ordered to erect altars upon which yearly sacrifices were to be made. This yearly festival was consequently established under the name of *Paganalia*.

Dionysius then proceeds to explain how the counting was facilitated by the creation of the festival, every man, woman and child had to offer a different type of coin. In this way, "those who presided over the sacrifices" could establish the population numbers distinguished by sex and age.[23] In the structure of his general narrative, Dionysius of Halicarnassus establishes a dichotomy between the urban and the rural population since he first considers in 4.14 the rituals of the *Compitalia*, also instigated by Servius Tullius, in relation to the division of the city of Rome in four *tribus*. The next section, cited here (4.15), is explicitly devoted to the countryside directly outside the city (τήν χώραν ἅπασαν) and it is in this context that the *Paganalia* are discussed. In this way, a distinction between urban and non-urban is made, because the *Compitalia* would perform functions for the urban tribes and the *Paganalia* accordingly for the rural tribes.[24]

piece of money, the men paying one kind, the women another and the children a third kind. When these pieces of money were counted by those who presided over the sacrifices, the number of people, distinguished by their sex and age, became known. And wishing also, as Lucius Piso writes in the first book of his *Annals*, to know the number of the inhabitants of the city, and of all who were born and died and arrived at the age of manhood, he prescribed the piece of money which their relations were to pay for each into the treasury of Ilithyia (called by the Romans Juno Lucina) for those who were born, into that of the Venus of the Grove (called by them Libitina) for those who died, and into the treasury of Juventas for those who were arriving at manhood. By means of these pieces of money he would know every year both the number of all the inhabitants and which of them were of military age. After he had made these regulations, he ordered all the Romans to register their names and give in a monetary valuation of their property, at the same time taking the oath required by law that they had given in a true valuation in good faith; they were also to set down the names of their fathers, with their own age and the names of their wives and children, and every man was to declare in what tribe of the city or in what district of the country he lived. If any failed to give in their valuation, the penalty he established was that their property should be forfeited and they themselves whipped and sold for slaves. This law continued in force amongst the Romans for a long time. [4.16.] After all had given in their valuations, Tullius took the registers and determining both the number of the citizens and the size of their estates, introduced the wisest of all measures, and one which has been the source of the greatest advantages to the Romans, as the results have shown…[the *census*]."

[22] Cf. Delatte 1937, 103. The *Compitalia* and Dion. Hal. *Ant. Rom.* 4.14 are discussed in Chapter 9.

[23] Cf. however Thomsen 1980, 210-211 according to whom Dionysius' description of the offering of different coins "bears the stamp of legend".

[24] Another example of this distinction is the idea that the festivals were not listed in the Roman calendar: cf. Fowler 1925, 16 who argues that all rites which did not concern the state as a whole but only parts of it, such as *pagi*, could not be included in the state calendar. One of the central ideas in modern scholarship derived from, amongst other things, Dionysius' description, is that the

8.1.3 RUSTIC IMAGES OF ADMINISTRATIVE CONTROL

Citing Dionysius' text together with the Odes by Horace and other bucolic descriptions, modern scholarship on Roman religion often views *pagus* rituals and the *Paganalia* in idealised rustic terms.[25] Similarly, the conflation of evidence for what are actually distinct rituals and festivals has favoured an agricultural interpretation. These traditions have formed an image of the *Paganalia* festival as an agricultural, rustic feast of vetust origins. Reading the relevant lines of Dionysius of Halicarnassus in their broader context however, the conclusion must inevitably be that, at least from Dionysius' point of view, the *Paganalia* were basically a ritualisation of the administration of the rural population on behalf of the Roman state.[26] Modern scholarship has long recognised this administrative aspect in Rome and the creation of *pagi* and their relationship to the 'Servian reform' of the *tribus* have received considerable attention.[27] However, the consequences of this specific administrative character of the religious festivals of both *Paganalia* and, as we will see, *Compitalia*, for the rural *pagi* and *vici* in the rest of Italy are yet to be evaluated.

8.2 LUSTRATIO PAGI AND PAGANALIA IN ITALY OUTSIDE ROME

The presumed origin and character of the festival in archaic Rome remains difficult to determine and is outside the scope of this discussion. In any case, it seems highly unlikely that the *Paganalia* and *Compitalia* existed in Italy outside the archaic city-state of Rome before the installation of *pagi* and *vici* outside Rome. If the festivals were also being performed in the 'Italic' countryside, could it be that they had a similar administrative incentive, or at least aspect, to them, as described in Dionysius for the *chora* of Rome? The evidence being meagre, the following discussion asks more questions than its answers. Yet, it is hoped that this will stimulate further discussion.

In the first place, we should acknowledge that there is no direct (epigraphic) evidence that the *Paganalia* proper were indeed celebrated in the Italian countryside (and neither is there for Rome itself).[28]

Paganalia in Rome are to be understood as the festival of the *pagani* as opposed to that of the *montani*, whose festival in turn would have been the *Septimontium*. In this way, both *Paganalia* and *Septimontium* would be state festivals for complementary parts of society, the urban population as opposed to the rural population (implicated also by Fest. L 284; cf. Varro, *Ling.* 6.24), e.g. Rohde 1942. Cf. Capogrossi Colognesi 2002, 43-49, 228 n. 9. This distinction may also exist in the function of the *census* since the procedure is different for the rural and the urban tribes Interestingly, Tarpin suggests that at least in Dionysius' description the urban *census* was more directed at the military levy, whereas the rural *census*, organised in *pagi*, seems to have been primarily oriented on taxation: Tarpin 2002, 187-188 and esp. 193-211.

[25] Or Dionysius is even omitted altogether; e.g. Scullard 1981, 68.

[26] This observation, of course, does not favour an 'instrumentalist' view of the festival, or religion in general. This administrative function could have been deeply embedded in 'religious' behaviour. Cf. Pieri 1968, 28 who argues: "*Cette méthode de dénombrement par le truchement d'offrandes apportées à un culte ou au cours d'une fête religieuse ... trouve peut-être son explication dans la croyance assez répandue chez les peuples anciens que le dénombrement d'une population était une opération impie et fort dangereuse qui nécessitait par là-même une cérémonie de purification.*"

[27] On the *stadtrömische pagi* and their relation to the Servian reforms and/or *census* cf. e.g. Last 1945, 38-42; Pieri 1968, 23-34; Thomsen 1980 (who thinks the *Paganalia* existed much earlier, 251-252); Fraschetti 1990, 148-160; Gabba 1991, 181-185; Humm 2001; Schubert 1996, 99-100, who thinks that the *census* function is Augustan, but states: "*Die religiösen Funktionen der pagi sind unbestritten und weisen auf ein hohes Alter dieser Einrichtung hin*" (99). Cf. Chapter 6.

[28] If the solution *paganic[is]* in *CIL* V, 4148 (from Pedergnaga, Brescia, of the late Republican period) is dismissed as a reference to the *Paganicae (feriae)*. Discussion in Todisco 2004b, 189-196. On the connection between the *lustratio pagi*, attested epigraphically in various places in Italy, and the *Paganalia* cf. *infra*.

Therefore, all arguments are by necessity more or less derivative. I think, however, that there is reason to suppose that the *Paganalia* were celebrated in *pagi* in areas in central Italy. It is true that Dionysius' account relates to the mythical regal period but he does describe, at least in part, a later or contemporary situation[29] and also explicitly states (4.15.3) that the laws, according to which the *Paganalia* are to be performed, are still observed in his time, i.e. early imperial Rome. Since *pagi* are by definition located outside urban areas, and the *Paganalia* are also located in the countryside by Varro (*Ling.* 6.24; in opposition to the urban *Septimontium*), it is certain that the festival was celebrated in the later *pagi* in 'a' countryside. Even if the evidence does not specify the location of the celebration within Italy (or rather, precisely *because* it does not), it seems implausible to me that the celebration of the *Paganalia* was confined to the old peri-urban *pagi* of Rome,[30] and I think it would be counter-productive to refrain from the conclusion that the *Paganalia* were celebrated in the *pagi* of Italy, wherever they were installed.

8.2.1 THE LOCATION OF THE FESTIVAL

The next question thus concerns the location of the celebration of the *Paganalia*. What we can say, on the basis of Dionysius' narrative, is that for inhabitants of the *pagi*, the *Paganalia* seem to have consisted of the coming together of people (σύνοδον; 4.15.4), the payment of apposite coins (νόμισμα; 4.15.4), and a communal sacrifice (θυσίαις κοιναῖς; 4.15.3).[31] With regard to the location of these rituals, it is often suggested that the festival took place at the central sanctuary of the *pagus*.[32] This may seem self-evident but the location is nowhere explicitly indicated nor is it qualified as a sanctuary since Dionysius only talks of "altars" (βωμούς; 4.15.3) for each *pagus*.[33] The description in Dolabella (L 302.1) of an intriguing rural sanctuary with four open sides would, according to Louis Delatte, refer to such a *pagus* sanctuary but this seems unfounded because there is no reference to the *Paganalia* or to a *pagus* (cf. also the discussion on *compitum* sanctuaries in Chapter 9).[34]

Perhaps it is not too far-fetched to suppose that the sanctuaries where *magistri pagi* were active, or where the influence of *pagi* is otherwise attested (*de pagi sententia vel sim.*), indeed formed the appropriate places for some of the rituals connected to the *Paganalia*, but this is not documented.

8.2.2 LUSTRATIO PAGI

It has been suggested that a *lustratio pagi* could be part of the *Paganalia*, even if Dionysius does not directly mention it in his description.[35] At any rate, the very existence of the *lustratio pagi* is highly important

---

[29] There are various anachronisms; cf. Schubert 1996, 99-100.

[30] On these *pagi* (the *pagus Succusanus*, *pagus Montanus*, and those of the Aventine, Janiculum, and ss. Quattro Coronati ('*pagus Caelemontanus*'), all apparently one time outside the city borders), see Fraschetti 1990, 148-160.

[31] Fraschetti 1990, 160 suggests moreover that the *ludi* mentioned in *CIL* VI, 30888 = *CIL* I², 984 (first century BC) might have been part of the *Paganalia* as well, and, referring to *CIL* VI, 2219 = *CIL* I², 1000 (around 100 BC) "*non è improbabile che, sempre nel corso dei Paganalia, i pagani del Gianicolo banchettassero insieme, utilizzando anche a questo scopo la culina fatta approntare da un loro magister*" (ibid.).

[32] E.g. Rohde 1942, 2294: "*Dass die Feier der P.[aganalia] an dem sakralen Zentrum des Pagus stattfand, dass wohl ebenfalls mit Pagus bezeichnet wurde, geht aus Dion. Hal. deutlich hervor.*"

[33] Unless they are to be understood as a *pars pro toto* of course.

[34] Delatte 1937, 109-110; cf. Wissowa 1901b, 793, who considers this a *compitum*; both theories are regarded suspiciously by Rohde 1942, 2294.

[35] Cf. Dion. Hal. *Ant. Rom.* 2.76.1 on the installation of *pagi* by Numa, where the magistrates of the *pagi* make their rounds in order to establish the condition of the fields.

Fig. 8.2. An inscription perhaps mentioning an *iter paganicam* found between Castelvecchio Subequo and Secinaro (*CIL* I², 3255) (Degrassi 1986, pl. 84, fig. 5).

because it attests to the ritual definition of territory and territoriality.[36] At the same time, the group of people living within it was defined. Importantly, we are certain that the *lustratio pagi* was performed in the *pagi* of Italy. Siculus Flaccus, who was a land surveyor active in the second century AD, comments on the importance of the *lustratio pagi* in his *de condicionibus agrorum* (9-10). He even asserts that the extent of the territory of the *pagus* could be deduced from the area that was covered by this ritual. According to Siculus, the *lustratio* would be performed by the *magistri pagorum*.[37]

Lustrationes pagi are also attested epigraphically in *pagi* in 'Italic' areas.[38] However, their connection to the *Paganalia* remains unclear since *lustrationes* could also be performed on other occasions, as attested by *CIL* IX, 1618 from Beneventum.

Some scholars recognise a *lustratio pagi* in a problematic inscription found between Castelvecchio Subequo and Secinaro in Paelignian territory (fig. 8.2). The inscription, dated to the first century BC,[39] mentions three *magistri pagi* who *iter / paganicam fac(iunda/um) / ex p(agi) s(citu) c(uraverunt) eidemq(ue) p(robaverunt)*.[40] The discussion has centered on the interpretation of *iter* and *paganicam* and their relation-

---

[36] See Baudy 1998 on the role of the *lustratio*. Cf. esp. p. 96-99 for '*römische Umgangsriten*' as '*symbolische Reviermarkierung*'.

[37] Grom. Lat. L 164.64. *magistri pagorum quod pagos lustrare soliti sint, uti trahamus quatenus lustrarent*. It does not seem possible to establish whether the *archontes*, organisers of the *Paganalia*, mentioned by Dionysius (4.15.3) can be equated with *magistri* or rather *praefecti pagi* (nonetheless: Delatte 1937, 106; cf. on the titles Tarpin 2002, 188, 196-197 and in general on the officials of the *pagus* 285-290).

[38] For the sources, cf. Wissowa 1912, 143 n. 2; Böhm 1927, 2032-2033; Latte 1960, 41 n. 2.

[39] La Regina 1967-68, 433.

[40] *AE* 1914, 270 = *CIL* I², 3255.

ship. Some read *iter paganicam*, i.e. some sort of road of the *pagus* or in the direction of a *Paganica*, others are inclined to integrate *iter(um)* as referring to the office-holding *magistri* and think *paganicam* is an adjective to an omitted substantive (*lustrationem, ara, aedes, vel sim.*).[41] Depending on the accepted reading, a link with rituals connected to the *pagus* is not to be excluded but a proper *lustratio pagi* or the celebration of the *Paganalia* is not attested.

An example of a true *lustratio* is documented in Picene territory via a small perforated bronze tablet (13.5 x 13 cm) found in the area of Tolentinum.[42] The text, which can be dated to the third century AD, reads: *tesseram paga/nicam L(ucius) Vera/tius Felicissi/mus patronus / paganis pagi / Tolentine(n)s(is) hos/tias lustr(um) et tesser(as) / aer(eas) ex voto l(ibens) d(onum) d(edit) / V Id(us) Ma(rtia, -ia)s felicit(er)*, which could be translated as "*tessera* of the *pagus*. Lucius Veratius Felicissimus, patron, offered to the inhabitants of the *pagus* of Tolentinum the sacrificial animals, the lustration, and the bronze *tesserae*, as a result of a vow, with pleasure. 11 March / May, auspiciously."[43] Although there has been discussion on the object of dedication, it is now accepted that the inscription refers to a *lustratio pagi* during which sacrificial animals were led around the *pagus*.[44] The form and size of the *tessera* resembles a *tessera frumentaria* and therefore this *tessera paganica* was probably used in a personal capacity rather than as a commemorative *tabula*. These *tesserae* were probably used as tokens to indicate the membership of the *pagus*. In the context of the festivities of the *pagus Tolentinensis*, it might therefore seem that Veratius not only paid for the animals and the *lustratio* but also for the admission tickets of the *pagani* to the celebration.[45]

8.2.3 THE PAYMENT FOR THE RITUALS AND THESAURI

Another element which might shed light on the rituals and practices of the members of the *pagus* is an inscribed *thesaurus* that has been found at Carpineto della Nora, in the Vestine area (fig. 8.3). The conserved calcareous block (h. 44 x l. 86 x w. 60 cm) is hollowed out in order to contain the coins that were

---

[41] The editor, Persichetti 1914, 131, read *iter Paganicam* (*scil. versus*), i.e. a road leading to Paganica, a modern place name in the area which according to him was identical in antiquity (followed by La Regina 1967-68, 376). Latte 1960, 42 n. 2. however recognised a *lustratio pagi*, reading *paganicam* (*scil. lustrationem*), and *iter* as *iter(um)*, i.e. 'again, a second time' and relating to the *lustratio*. In other words, the *magistri* would have cared for the *lustratio pagi* [that was held] again. Latte's reading is refuted by van Wonterghem, who favours an interpretation of *iter paganicam* as road and according to him indicated a 'tratturo', which would explain the use of the word *iter* rather than *via vel sim.* (Van Wonterghem 1984, 98-99). Buonocore on the other hand interprets *iter* as *iter(um)*, but according to him this would relate to the office held 'again' by the three *magistri* and he proposes to amend a forgotten object *paganicam* (*aedem vel sim.*). Thus, three *magistri pagi* who were in office for the second time would have cared for the construction of an *ara paganica*, *aedes paganica*, *aedicula paganica* or *porticus paganica* (in *Suppl. It.* n.s. V, 116; Buonocore 1993, 52 = Buonocore 2002, 34). In turn, Letta thinks that the *magistri* constructed an *iter paganicum*: "*cioè una strada che attraversava tutto il territorio del pagus, collegando i vari vici tra loro e col santuario comune*"; Letta 1993, 37. In fact, both solutions, *iter* or *iterum*, require the acceptance of grammatical inconsistencies, i.e. *iter paganicam* instead of correctly *paganicum* on the one hand (Letta 1993, 37 explains the female *paganicam* instead of neutrum *paganicum* with a mental association with *viam*) or the omission of a substantive where *paganicam* relates to (Buonocore 1993, 52 = Buonocore 2002, 34 suggests that *paganica* is perhaps an otherwise unknown substantive). An additional problem is that the integration *iter(um)* would implicate a recurrence of the board of three *magistri pagi*, which seems improbable to Letta 1993, 37. Todisco 2004b, 186-189 suggests that the *magistri* saw to the construction of both a road and an object defined *paganicam* (*aedes vel sim.*).

[42] *CIL* IX, 5565.

[43] Following Cancrini *et al.* 2001, 123-125.

[44] Cancrini *et al.* 2001, 123-125 with previous literature, e.g. Scheid 1990, 449.

[45] Cancrini *et al.* 2001, 125; cf. Virlouvet 1995, 344 n. 96.

Fig. 8.3. A *thesaurus* from Carpineto della Nora (*CIL* I², 3269) (Degrassi 1986, pl. 89, fig. 3).

to be thrown into the *thesaurus*. The inscription dates to the first century BC and mentions four people who restored the object and dedicated it to *Juppiter Victor decem paagorum*.[46]

The appearance of *thesauri* in Italy is a relatively late phenomenon that only seems to start at the beginning of the second century BC.[47] Most Italian *thesauri* date to the end of the second and the first centuries BC.[48] The inscriptions sometimes only bear the names of the instigators, as in Carpineto and Ferentillo,[49] but in other cases the titles reveal actions undertaken by *duoviri*, such as in Luna,[50] *praetores* in Anagnia,[51] and *magistri*, such as in Hatria (fig. 8.4).[52]

[46] *CIL* I², 3269; *ILLRP* 1271c. La Regina has interpreted the apparent meeting of different *pagi* in one sanctuary as part of a structuration process, a "*normale processo sinecistico*", whereas the 'final stage' of *municipium* was never reached here (La Regina 1967-68, 414; cf. also the description of the sanctuary of Hercules Curinus as the "*santuario tutelare del sinecismo*": Coarelli/La Regina 1984, 132). The notion of an evolutionary development from single *pagi* to *municipium* can now however be dismissed, cf. Chapter 6.

[47] Kaminski 1991, 106.

[48] On Italian *thesauri*: Degrassi 1967; Ciampoltrini 1993; Catalli/Scheid 1994; Nonnis 1994-1995; Crawford 2003b; Letta 2004.

[49] Ferentillo (first half first century BC): *CIL* XI, 4988. According to La Regina 1967-68, 414 the people mentioned in the Carpineto *thesaurus* are "*dei semplici magistri Iovis Victoris, addetti all'amministrazione del culto*" and not *magistri pagi*. Letta 1993, 43 n. 44 dismisses this idea and proposes individuals acting on their own behalf.

[50] *CIL* XI, 1343, cf. Ciampoltrini 1993, dating it to the end of the second or rather the beginning of the first century BC.

[51] *CIL* I², 2536, dated to the second half of the second century BC. Cf. Nonnis 1994-1995, 160.

[52] *CIL* I², 3293, dated to the second century BC by Torelli 2005, 355, but see Nonnis 2003, 48 for a first century BC date.

Fig. 8.4. A *thesaurus* from Hatria (*CIL* I², 3293) reading *P(ublius) Au[f]ilius P(ubli) f(ilius) / C(aius) Magius M(arci) f(ilius) / magist(ri)* (Degrassi 1986, pl. 98, fig. 2).

In the territory of Pausulae, a *municipium* in the Picene area,[53] a *thesaurus* was found together with ca. 5000 Republican silver *denarii*. The inscription, a dedication to Apollo, can be dated to the second half of the second century BC.[54]

I think that the second century BC date of introduction, the Latin language used, and the magistrates and the gods involved (Jupiter Victor, Apollo, Fortuna,[55] Minerva,[56] Vesta,[57] Hercules[58] and possibly

[53] The inscription comes from località S. Lucia, between S. Claudio al Chienti and Morrovalle.
[54] *CIL* IX, 5805; Gasperini 1983, 16; cf. Kaminski 1991, 165-167 and Crawford 2003b, 78-79.
[55] *CIL* XIV, 2854 from Praeneste and *CIL* XI, 6307 from Pisaurum.
[56] *AE* 1985, 266 from Sora (79-40 BC).
[57] *AE* 1904, 210 from Beneventum (second century BC).
[58] La Torre 1989a, 140, from the sanctuary of Hercules Curinus near Sulmona.

Venus[59]) suggest that these *thesauri* are a new phenomenon in the Italic areas and related in some way to Roman / Latin influence. The geographical distribution of the *thesauri* seems to sustain this impression:[60] Fregellae (second century BC),[61] Beneventum (second century BC), Hatria (second-first centuries BC) and Luna (end second century BC) are colonies.[62] The Hernician city Anagnia was under Roman control since 306 BC[63] whereas the *thesaurus* can be dated to the second half of the second century BC. Also the Picene area, where the second-century BC *thesaurus* dedicated to Apollo was found, was by then long incorporated by Rome.[64] The same goes for a second-century BC *thesaurus* found in Arpinum, which was under Roman control since 305 BC.[65] If a block with a dedication to Valetudo, dating as early as the second century BC from the *vicus Aninus* was indeed a *thesaurus*, this would be another example (for a discussion on the Roman connotations of Valetudo and the *vicus Aninus* see Chapter 7).[66]

The exceptions to this connection with Roman or Latin influence are few, and the evidence remains somewhat tenuous. A *thesaurus* found in the sanctuary of Hercules Curinus at Sulmona could possibly be an example of a *thesaurus* in allied territory, but only if it dates from before the municipalisation of Sulmo, which does not seem probable.[67] A *thesaurus* is, however, mentioned in line 29 on side B of the late second-century BC treaty between Abella and Nola, otherwise written in the Oscan language.[68] Another possible *thesaurus* in an 'indigenous' context is a block revealed in a second- or first-century BC sanctuary at Pescosansonesco in the Vestine area.[69] The rectangular calcareous block presents an iron ring on top, and an inscription in the Vestine or a Vestine-Latin language which reads: *T. Vetis C. f.t.cule t. p.* Letta suggests that the block was the lid of a *thesaurus* and reconstructs *t(hesaurum) p(osuit)*.[70] However, both the identification of the object and the interpretation of the text do not appear to be compelling, as Letta himself admits.

---

[59] In Anagni, since *p(ecunia) Venerus* has been used, cf. Nonnis 1994-1995, 164.

[60] *Thesauri* appear in some Latial sanctuaries but these are quite late. Cf. Praeneste: *CIL* XIV, 2854 (Caligula) (but cf. criticism by Crawford 2003b, 76); Lanuvium (*CIL* XIV, 4177) (end first century BC).

[61] Lippolis 1986, 32, from the sanctuary of Aesculapius. Cf. for a *thesaurus* in the city: Coarelli 1981a, 41.

[62] The Latin colony of Sora (303 BC) could be included but this *thesaurus* is dated to the first half of the first century BC (Catalli/Scheid 1994).

[63] Humbert 1978, 214. The city was possibly made *praefectura* in that year.

[64] In the third century BC. Humbert 1978, 237-244. An inscribed *thesaurus* comes from the Umbrian town Amelia, which may have retained allied status until the Social War (Bradley 2000, 120-122), but the *thesaurus* is dated to the first century BC; the same goes for the first-century *thesaurus* from Ferentillo. The *thesaurus* of Pettino near Amiternum (*CIL* IX, 4325 = *CIL* I², 1856) is not dated but appears in *ILLRP*, no. 532. At Collepietro, near Superaequum, a *thesaurus* was found with coins, including one reading *Diovis / stipe* (*CIL* I², 2484). The lid of a possible *thesaurus* was found in a votive deposit at S. Pietro in Cantoni: Matteini Chiari 2000, 284.

[65] For the *thesaurus* Sogliano 1896, 370, according to whom the *thesaurus* had "*l'aspetto di un enorme uovo*" and Hülsen 1907, 237 n. 1 with fig. 1. on p. 239. Apparently a Roman *praefectura* was installed in 305 BC, it became *municipium* in 90 BC.

[66] *CIL* IX 3812 (= *CIL* I², 390; cf. *CIL* IX, 3813), now lost. Catalli/Scheid 1994, no. 12, marked 'uncertain' by Crawford 2003b, 79.

[67] Cf. Coarelli/La Regina 1984, 127-129 and La Torre 1989a (on the *thesaurus*: 140 and 143 fig. 55). An earlier incorporation of the entire area is however not excluded. On the status of the Paeligni see Coarelli/La Regina 1984, 113: in 305 BC part of their territory was apparently annexed by Rome (Diod. Sic. 20.90.3), probably the area around Superaequum. See also Chapter 7.

[68] Ve. 1. According to La Regina 2000, post-Gracchan.

[69] The status of this area is not clear in all respects but it was conquered already in 290 BC (Humbert 1978, 226-233). The *thesaurus* of Carpineto della Nora, only ca. 10 km distant from Pescosansonesco, also belongs to this territory.

[70] Letta 2004.

There remains the question of what this apparent correspondence between Roman political influence and the appearance of *thesauri* means. Torelli connects their appearance in time and place to the "*definitiva ellenizzazione delle architetture religiose e profane di Roma e dei socii italici*",[71] which may indeed seem attractive since the phenomenon is well known in earlier Greek contexts. At the same time it is somehow strange that the earliest Italian *thesauri* seem to be restricted to areas where Roman political influence was strong, whereas the hellenisation of Italy does not seem to have been directly linked to Roman influence. Perhaps another suggestion of Torelli, that the phenomenon may have been linked to the "*sostanziale monetizzazione del regime delle offerte*"[72] in the second half of the second century BC, could be better related to Roman influence but it is still striking that the evidence is restricted to particular areas of central Italy.

In any case, the appearance of a *thesaurus* in a sanctuary to 'Jupiter Victor of the ten *pagi*' taps into a new fashion or changed rituals which seem in one way or another related to Roman influence, and the same goes for the possible *thesaurus* of the *vicus Aninus* dedicated to Valetudo. Generally, these *thesauri* would have served as receptacles for contributions by participants of the cult, which were to be used, amongst other things, to finance the festivals and associated *ludi*. This calls to mind the above quoted assertion of Dionysius (4.15.4) that for the funding of the activities during the *Paganalia* all inhabitants of the *pagus* had to throw in their apposite νόμισμα ("Towards the expense of this sacrifice and of this assemblage he ordered all those of the same district to contribute each of them a certain piece of money, the men paying one kind, the women another and the children a third kind"). Whether the second suggestion by Dionysius that "when these pieces of money were counted by those who presided over the sacrifices, the number of people, distinguished by their sex and age, became known" is also true, remains impossible to prove.

8.3 CONCLUSION: THE RITUAL DEFINITION OF NEW COMMUNITIES

To sum up, we have seen that in modern literature on ancient religion the *pagus* is often evoked as a locale of rusticity and rurality. This is partly justified by a similar attitude in early imperial poetry, where the countryside is exalted as part of Augustan ideology. Along the same lines, the most important religious festival associated with the *pagus*, the *Paganalia*, has been conceptualised as an agricultural feast of great antiquity. Yet, this image is not backed up by the evidence. The sources tell us little else other than that the *Paganalia* involved a specific group located in the countryside and that the festival was designed for administrative purposes.

Part of the *Paganalia* was probably a *lustratio* of the *pagus*. Such a *lustratio* was however not exclusively performed on the occasion of the *Paganalia*. During the *lustrationes* the inhabitants of the *pagus* made a circumambulation around their territory and thereby ritually enhanced its borders. At the same time the group that was included within this territory was being redefined by this ritual. The *lustratio* will have had an important integrative function for the community. By re-emphasising or ritually constructing the community, previous relations and boundaries were erased and the new community established and augmented its authority by divine legitimisation. This process of group formation also becomes apparent in the archaeological and epigraphic record in the form of *tesserae paganicae* which express the affiliation of individuals to the *pagus* and the communal sanctuaries installed *ex pagi decreto vel sim.*, where the inhabitants of the *pagus* probably also paid their contributions to the festivities as part of changed ritual practices which are related to Roman influence.

---

[71] Torelli 2005, 355.

[72] Ibid.

Fig. 8.5. Wall-painting with 'sacro-idyllic' landscape within decorative scheme from the villa of Agrippa Postumus at Boscotrecase, Red Room, North wall (after Von Blanckenhagen/Alexander 1990, pl. 21).

I think it should not be excluded that these group formation processes, and perhaps related administrative purposes, informed the main rituals celebrated in the countryside *pagi*, although these aspects are concealed behind general references to rusticity by early imperial poetry and modern interpretation. Indeed, we should try to put images of rustic and frugal cult into perspective. An analogy can perhaps be found in the 'sacro-idyllic' landscape shown at the beginning of this chapter (fig. 8.1). This image has to be understood within a new, very Roman decorative scheme belonging to a villa of the last decade BC, the ensemble being typical for the Augustan age (fig. 8.5). In a similar way, the rustic images of *pagus* cult activity in Augustan poetry could be imagined as being enclosed in a Roman framework.

9 Roman Ritual in the Italian Countryside? The *Compitalia* and the Shrines of the Lares Compitales

"The separation between city cult and family or farm cult should not be exaggerated" (Beard *et al.* 1998, 50).

What the *Paganalia* were to the *pagi*, the *Compitalia* were to the *vici* of Rome. The festival is the clearest religious aspect connected to the institution of the *vicus* and therefore will be discussed in some detail. The religious festival of the *Compitalia* or 'crossroads festival'[1] was celebrated in both city and countryside. Even if clearly a Roman festival and best known from urban contexts, it is usually assumed that it originated as a rural cult which was later incorporated in the city, where it became the principal festival of the *vici* or urban quarters. Arguably, this idea of a rural origin resonates with the idea of the *pagus-vicus* system as an 'immemorial' Italic institution (see Chapter 6). In this chapter, it will be argued that like the *Paganalia*, the spread of the *Compitalia*, a Roman urban festival with administrative aspects, might have been in the opposite direction, i.e. outside Rome alongside Roman influence. Moreover, it is argued that the festival was important for the definition and enhancement of groups participating in it. Although the precise relationship between the rural *vici* of Italy and the *Compitalia* is difficult to establish, there is clear evidence that the *Compitalia* were indeed celebrated in the countryside. I will tentatively suggest that in some cases ancient Italic sanctuaries were re-used for celebrating the Roman rite of the *Compitalia*, by now functioning within a Roman administrative and religious system.[2]

9.1 THE COMPITALIA: A PARADOXICAL PICTURE

At the end of his letter to Atticus (2.3), Cicero (probably writing from his country house) refers to the political situation in Rome and his role within it, noting: *sed haec ambulationibus Compitaliciis reservemus. Tu pridie Compitalia memento. Balineum calfieri iubebo. Et Pomponiam Terentia rogat; matrem adiungemus* ('But this point must be reserved for our strolls at the *Compitalia*. Do you remember the day before the festival? I will order the bath to be heated, and Terentia is going to invite Pomponia. We will make your mother one of the party').[3] In this way, Cicero informs us about how he imagines spending the *Compitalia* or crossroads festival, writing as it seems in December of the year 60 BC. The impression that arises, on a private level, is that of a relaxed holiday with time for family and friends alike.

At the same time, the moveable feast of the *Compitalia* constituted the most important religious festival associated with the *vici* or wards of Rome. According to Dionysius of Halicarnassus, writing in the Augustan period, the festival was installed together with the urban *vici* as a means of administrative control in order to be able to count the inhabitants of Rome. Other evidence confirms this public or civic character of the festival. The *Compitalia* were relevant to both what we would call the 'private' and 'public' domain.

---

[1] From *compitum* = 'crossroads', cf. *infra*.

[2] The main content of this chapter has been published in a slightly different form in Stek 2008.

[3] 2.3.5, translation Loeb (D.R. Shackleton Bailey).

Another paradoxical aspect concerns the location of the *Compitalia*. The festival is often associated with the urban plebs and therefore placed in an urban setting. On the other hand, passages by Roman authors refer to a rustic setting of the *Compitalia*. Modern historiography has subsequently translated this situation in various ways. Most popular is the view of the *Compitalia* as a festival of agricultural or rural origin which was only later incorporated in the city. However, not much attention has been paid to the celebration of the *Compitalia* in the countryside and, more problematically, it is not known where the festival was celebrated in the countryside.

The aim of this chapter is to delineate an historical development of the *Compitalia* and to shed light on its rural cult places by reviewing these apparent oppositions of public vs. private and urban vs. rural. After briefly introducing the *Compitalia*, I will focus on three main areas.

First, the character of the community that participated in the cult will be discussed. Often, the *Compitalia* are seen as "very much a family-affair".[4] On the other hand there seems to be a strong civic or public aspect to the festival. I therefore discuss the relevant textual evidence and argue that this 'double' image of public and private also emerges from the archaeological record. I suggest that it is precisely this all-embracing quality of the *Compitalia*, cutting through these distinctions and including all inhabitants, that distinguishes it from other festivals.

Second, the location of the celebration of the *Compitalia* as indicated in literature and epigraphy will be considered. The situation for both city and countryside will be surveyed, thereby discussing the *Compitalia*'s presumed rural origin. It is shown that the evidence for a development from an agricultural, rural cult to an urban Roman cult is meagre. Most likely, the spread of the *Compitalia* followed a different trajectory and were exported from Rome to other areas influenced or inhabited by Romans at least as early as the second half of the second century BC.

Third, the argument on the location of the *Compitalia* will be examined within the context of cult places, taking into account what constituted a *compitum* shrine and where such a shrine was located. Several urban *compitum* shrines have been unearthed and their different architectural forms will be discussed briefly. The rural cult places where the *Compitalia* were celebrated in the countryside have never been identified. I suggest that the problematic description in a scholion on Persius has distracted scholarly research on the shrines of the *Lares Compitales* from the question of where the *Compitalia* were actually celebrated. Tentatively, I argue that ancient rural sanctuaries built by 'Italic' peoples were suitable sacred places to be re-used later within a Roman religious, social and political system. There is evidence to suggest that some of the resumed or continued religious activities in ancient 'Italic' sanctuaries related to the *Compitalia*.

9.1.1 THE FESTIVAL OF THE COMPITALIA

The *Compitalia* consisted of sacrifices at *compita* (crossroads and by extension the shrines placed there; from *competere* or 'coming together' cf. *infra*) and games, the *ludi Compitalicii*. Certainly, meals were part of the festival[5] and, as noted above, Cicero muses on strolls.[6] Like the *Paganalia*, the *Compitalia* were part of the *feriae conceptivae*, that is the festivals which had no fixed date but were to be established anew each year. At least in the late Republic, they were announced eight days beforehand, in December, by the *praetor*.[7] Normally, the *Compitalia* were celebrated some days after the *Saturnalia* (17 December), probably most often at the very end of December or the beginning of January.[8]

---

[4] Scullard 1981, 60.

[5] Cf. the alternative etymology from '*conpotando, id est simul bibendo*' in schol. Pers. 4.28.

[6] Cic. *Att.* 2.3.4. I thank Dr. L. B. van der Meer for the suggestion (pers. comm.) that *ambulatio* possibly refers to the *lustratio*.

[7] Gell. *NA* 10.24.3.

[8] Dion. Hal. *Ant. Rom.* 4.14.4. Known dates include: December 31, 67 BC, January 1, 58 BC, January 2, 50 BC (Asc. p. 65 C; Cic. *Pis.* 8; Cic. *Att.* 7.7.3).

As to the cult personnel, *magistri* who were allowed to wear the *toga praetexta* presided over the *Compitalia*.[9] With reference to the rustic environment, Cato (*Agr.* 5.3) informs us about the modus operandi at the ideal *villa*, namely that the bailiff (*vilicus*) of the agricultural enterprise could assume the presiding role over the activities on behalf of his master.[10]

In the literary tradition, the origin of the *Compitalia* is connected to the creation of the four urban regions by king Servius Tullius (cf. *infra*). Historically on some firmer ground, it appears that colleges of *magistri* that organised the *Compitalia* in Rome became a focus of popular political activity around the middle of the last century BC. Fear of 'subversive' political activities and riots of the *collegia* that were mainly made up of freedmen and slaves explains the suppression of the *collegia* and the connected *ludi Compitalicii* in 64 BC by the Senate.[11] The consequent attempts, not always successful, to re-establish them attest to the political struggles of this period.

It was exactly this political connotation, and association with the plebs, that made the cult at the *compita* of each *vicus* an attractive focus of attention for Augustus.[12] Between 12 and 7 BC Augustus restructured the city into fourteen urban regions and an unknown number of *vici*.[13] A number of 265 *vici* becomes clear from the *census* of 73 AD.[14] The objects of veneration were two *Lares* who are now associated with the *Genius Augusti*.[15]

In this way, the *compita* were effectively used to disseminate the emperor cult to the general populace over a wide area. It is often assumed that Augustus deliberately revived and promoted the *Compitalia* in order to literally bring the emperor cult (in the form of the *Genius*) amongst the people by absorbing

---

[9] Cic. *Pis.* 8; Liv. 34.7.2; Asc. p. 7. C. There has been much discussion on the date and character of the *magistri vici*; cf. Flambard 1977, Flambard 1981; Fraschetti 1990; Tarpin 1999; Tarpin 2002; Bert Lott 2004. On the date: it is clear that at least from the middle of the first century BC on *magistri vici* did exist (*contra* Fraschetti): cf. *CIL* IV, 60 which lists magistrates for a Pompeian *vicus* for 47-46 BC, and *CIL* VI, 1324 (= *CIL* I², 2514), a column from Rome, datable to around the 50s BC, that mentions *magistri veici* (Tarpin 2002, 133-134, also for other examples). Liv. 34.7.2 mentions *magistri vicorum* for 195 BC. Cf. also Bert Lott 2004, esp. 41-44 who argues that *magistri vici* were already in action by the time of the second Punic War. On their character: the image that arises of the *magister vici* is not one of splendour. Juvenal (10.103) calls him a *pannosus aedilis*, an aedile in tatters. The office came to be mostly associated with the lower classes of society (Liv. 34.7.2: *infimum genus* for 195 BC), which has also been seen as a way to emphasise the essentially popular character of the main festival they organised. Flambard 1981, 157, estimates that three-quarter of the *magistri* known to us through inscriptions were slaves or freedmen and therefore sees the *Compitalia* as a specific 'slave-festival', or as a "*propédeutique civique*" (166, cf. Dion. Hal. *Ant. Rom.* 4.14), a learning school for slaves and freedmen to learn to behave like real Roman citizens (followed by Jongman 1988, 297-298; cf. Bömer 1957, esp. 32-56). It seems however that, at least during the *Compitalia*, *magistri vici* held "not just semi- or unofficial positions, but rather positions recognised as part of the civic and religious administration of the city": Bert Lott 2004, 43. Although late Republican and early imperial evidence indicates that personnel was recruited from the lower echelons of society, it appears that within this range, they occupied a relatively elevated position, as is revealed for example by the costs of being in office (cf. Patterson 2006a, 252-263).

[10] *CIL* V, 7739 from Liguria seems to confirm this privilege, here a *vilicus* dedicates a *comp(itum)* [*et*] *aram* to the Lares.

[11] Cf. on the subject: Flambard 1977, 1981; Fraschetti 1990, 204-273; Bert Lott 2004, esp. 54-55, who concludes that the *ludi* were curtailed but not the *Compitalia* ("a public ritual of the state religion") themselves.

[12] Cf. e.g. Alföldi 1973; Fraschetti 1990, 204-273.

[13] Suet. *Aug.* 30.

[14] Plin. *HN* 3.66. Cf. also the *maxima ter centum totam delubra per urbem* installed by Augustus according to Verg. *Aen.* 8.716, explained by Servius ad loc. as *compita*, but the word *maxima* is perhaps not appropriate for this interpretation. Cf. Tarpin 2002, 124, n. 89.

[15] For altars and *aediculae*: Alföldi 1973, 31-36; Hano 1986.

him, as it were, between the ancestors.[16] In the same vein, Augustus rededicated the old temple of the *Lares in summa Sacra Via*.[17] The Augustan reform is important here because all evidence dating after 12-7 BC may have been influenced by it.

Having introduced the *Compitalia*, a festival with possibly archaic origins which was organised by *magistri* (*vici*) and centred upon *compita*, the cult places of the *vici*, I will now discuss some specific elements of the ritual and the festival.

9.2 PRIVATE AND PUBLIC: AN INTEGRATIVE CULT

For any analysis of its social and political significance, it is of central importance to ask to which group in society the *Compitalia* catered. Delineating the 'community of cult' is also pivotal for the question in what type of cult places the *Compitalia* could be celebrated. Although some sources direct us towards a view of the *Compitalia* as a largely family-oriented festival, other evidence suggests a wider audience. Sometimes, these different locales have been interpreted as indicative of a distinction between a public and a private cult.

9.2.1 'PRIVATE': A FAMILY AFFAIR?

Let us first briefly review the argument for the *Compitalia* as a family cult. At least in later times it seems that the *Lares Compitales* were assimilated with deified souls of the dead, or gods of the underworld, as Festus says.[18] Some scholars argue that this aspect of veneration of the dead should be linked to an ancestor cult.[19] In this way, the *Compitalia* would come close to a cult that is centred on the family. Other arguments have also been brought to the fore to sustain the thesis that the *Compitalia* were essentially a family occasion, for example the presence of altars to the *Lares* and mural paintings documenting scenes associated with the *Compitalia* inside some houses on Delos may at first sight corroborate such an interpretation (but cf. *infra*).

Drawing broad comparisons ("as our New Year's day follows Christmas, so a short time after the Saturnalia the Romans enjoyed a second period of feasting and goodwill"), Scullard emphasises that the

---

[16] Cf. Beard *et al*. 1998, 185; Gradel 2002, esp. 116-130. The issue is complex; the *Lares* are seen by some as the spirits of the dead. In this view, the revival of the *Lares*-cult at the *compita* associated with the emperor would therefore reflect the dissemination of the private cult of the house of Augustus over the *vici* of the city. Cf. *infra*.

[17] *Res Gestae* 19.2. cf. Ziolkowski 1992, 97-98.

[18] Fest. p. 108 L. *laneae effigies compitalibus noctu dabantur in compita, quod Lares, quorum is erat dies festus, animae putabantur esse hominum redactae in numerum deorum*; p. 273 L: *pilae et effigies viriles et muliebres ex lana Compitalibus suspendebantur in compitis quod hunc diem festum esse deorum inferorum quos vocant Lares putarent quibus tot pilae quot capita servorum tot effigies quot essent liberi ponebantur ut vivis parcerent et essent his pilis et simulacris contenti*. Cf. Macrob. *Sat*. 1.7.34-35, describing the hanging of dolls from the *compita* during the festival. There has been much discussion on the credibility of the interpretation of the dolls (and the *Lares* in general) as indicating an ancestor cult (as Festus suggests) or even as a substitute for human sacrifices: Macrobius (as cited) mentions the practice of human sacrifice, apparently instigated by Tarquinius Superbus after a response of an oracle, which was subsequently abolished by – significantly – the founder of the Republic, Iunius Brutus, who replaced the real heads for 'dummies'.

[19] The discussion on the origin of the *Lares*, protective deities of the fields (Wissowa) or rather linked to the dead / ancestors (Samter), started with Wissowa 1897, Wissowa 1902, 166-177 and Samter 1901, 105-123; Samter 1907; Laing 1921; Tabeling 1932. See now Scheid 1990, 587-598; Coarelli 1983, 265-282.

Compitalia "still remained very much a family affair".[20] In order to lend weight to his argument, Scullard points out that Cicero did not want to disturb Pompey at his Alban *villa* during the *Compitalia*. Cicero indeed declares that he wanted to arrive one day later because he did not want to intrude in family affairs (*ne molestus familiae veniam*).[21]

This argument might not be valid. First, reference is made here to a social group that in all probability did not define itself primarily through neighbourhood connections, as is in fact already pointed out by Pompey's leisure in his villa in the country during the *Compitalia*. Second, Cicero is known to have been extremely attentive not to disturb his hosts. For example, he was ridiculed for his preference to use *deversoria*, his own small inns, where he rested during his travel to his *villae*, instead of staying with elite friends in the countryside, as was common practice according to the custom of capitalising personal *hospitia*.[22] Cicero insisted, in almost literally the same words, that he would rather avoid disturbing his hosts "*ne semper hospiti molestus sim*".[23] Leaving this last, rather anecdotal, argument aside, we may however conclude that the evidence for a 'familial' aspect, although present, is not very strong, and in any case this aspect did not have an exclusive character. There are indications that the principal group involved in the *Compitalia* was a somewhat larger unit.

9.2.2 'PUBLIC': THE ORIGIN OF THE COMPITALIA ACCORDING TO DIONYSIUS OF HALICARNASSUS

Indeed, there is evidence that the *Compitalia* had a public character. The fact that a *praetor* announced the festival emphasises its public and civic relevance.[24] However, the most important source for the apparently 'public' character of the *Compitalia* is Dionysius of Halicarnassus, who notes that the *Compitalia* were closely bound with the administration of inhabitants in the city. King Servius Tullius (trad. 578-535 BC) is evoked as the instigator of the festival that resulted as a consequence of the division of the city into four regions.[25]

> "And he ordered that the citizens inhabiting each of the four regions should, like persons living in villages, neither take up another abode nor be enrolled elsewhere; and the levies of troops, the collection of taxes for military purposes, and the other services which every citizen was bound to offer to the commonwealth, he no longer based upon the three national tribes, as aforetime, but upon the four local tribes established by himself. And over each region he appointed commanders, like heads of tribes or villages, whom he ordered to know what house each man lived in. After this he commanded that there should be erected in every street (στενωπούς) by the inhabitants of the neighbourhood chapels (καλιάδας) to heroes whose statues stood in front of the houses (ἥρωσι προνωπίοις), and he made a law that sacrifices should be performed to them every year, each family contributing a honey-cake … This festival the Romans still continued to celebrate even in my day in the most solemn and sumptuous manner a few days after the Saturnalia, calling it the Compitalia, after the streets (στενωπῶν); for compita is their name for streets."

---

[20] Scullard 1981, 59, 60.

[21] It seems certain that the villa of Pompey, not Cicero's own villa, is intended, as e.g. Latte 1960, 91-92 assumes (to strengthen a similar argument, that the city-based owners did not interfere with the ritual on their own estates, which were instead presided over by their *vilici*).

[22] For *deversoria*: Cic. *Att.* 10.5.3, 11.5.2, 14.8.1; ridicule: Cic. *Fam.* 12.20. Cf. Pfeilschifter 2006, 134 n. 69.

[23] Cic. *Fam.* 7.23.3.

[24] Gell. *NA* 10.24.3.

[25] Dion. Hal. *Ant. Rom.* 4.14.2-4, translation adapted from Loeb; for the connection with slaves also present in Dionysius' account cf. *supra* n. 9.

Fig. 9.1a. Painted *compitum* with hanging dolls from altar, Pompeii, (Via dell'Abbondanza, SW corner of Ins. IX, 11) (Spinazzola 1953, 178 fig. 216).

Analogous to the discussion of the *Paganalia*, the sequence Dionysius employs is worthy of attention. King Servius begins with the establishment of four regions (or tribes) in which people are obliged to enlist for the military levy and the collection of taxes. Then the king proceeds by establishing 'commanders' who administered the whereabouts of the population. Only after this does Servius turn to the religious component of his reform, namely the erection of shrines in every street and the institution of a yearly ritual, the *Compitalia*. According to Dionysius therefore – and this is of central importance – the *Compitalia* were devised as a means to establish cohesion between different people who formed part of the same administrative units.

At the same time the *Compitalia* appear as a means to count the inhabitants of each district. This can be seen in Festus' account, in which he described how during the night before the *Compitalia* woollen dolls were suspended from the *compita*. Each member of the *compitum* community had to be represented, the free men and women by male and female woollen dolls (*effigies*) and woollen balls (*pilae*) for slaves.[26] Leaving aside questions on the rather obscure origins of this rite,[27] the significance of the rite as a possible means to register the number of inhabitants is clear. For just as in the *Paganalia*, where according to Dionysius people could be recognised by the donation of different coins, the *pilae* and *effigies* (as well as the cakes) of the *Compitalia* could also serve as an indication of the number of people living in each unit. The presence of a similar rite in the two festivals, which are both linked to the administration of the Roman population, can be no coincidence.[28]

[26] Fest. p. 108 L, p. 273 L; Macrob. *Sat.* 1.17.35 (cf. *supra* n. 18 for text). Cf. esp. Radke 1983.

[27] Cf. *supra* n. 19.

[28] Cf. Delatte 1937; Holland 1937, 439; Dumézil 1961; Flambard 1981.

Fig. 9.1b. Detail of 9.1a. (Spinazzola 1953, 179 fig. 217).

This possible administrative aspect mentioned by Festus and Macrobius can perhaps be discerned in the material record.[29] In Pompeii, representations of dolls hanging from the altars are indeed documented (figs. 9.1a and b).[30] On stylistic grounds Thomas Fröhlich assigns none of these particular paintings to before the Augustan period.[31] However, one painting showing dolls is dated to the early Augustan period, around 20 BC.[32] If Fröhlich's date is correct, it would attest to the practice of hanging dolls prior to the Augustan reforms, otherwise only known from fairly late writers.[33]

[29] Spinazzola 1953, 179-180, figs. 215-218 for dolls. In fig. 218 the thread from which the doll is hanging can be seen. It should be noted that the rite could as well be related to the offering of the dolls to the *Lares* by girls reaching adulthood: Pseudoacronis Schol. on Hor. *Sat.* 1.5.65-66 (cf. also the three *asses* offered by a nubile woman, *infra* n. 41). The intimate link between rites of passage and *Compitalia* is also clear in a fragment from Varro's *Menippeae* (Varro, *Sat. Men.* fr. 463 Buech. = Non. Marc. p. 538) from which can be deduced that apart from balls and/or dolls, hair nets (*reticula*) and breast bands (*stróphia*) were also offered and these are the same gifts offered by maidens before the wedding to the Lares, Venus, and Fortuna Virgo (Samter 1907, 379-380; cf. Torelli 1984, 97).

[30] On two façade paintings: Fröhlich 1991, F29 and F66; domestic shrines: Helbig 1868, 56, 60. Fröhlich 1991, 34: genius altars: L1, L37, L82, L83; snake altars: L24, L26, L29, L61, L81, L94, L98.

[31] Fröhlich 1991, 68-109. But cf. Tybout 1996, 362-364 for the problems with dating.

[32] L29, late second style, dated to the around 20 BC (Fröhlich 1991, 70-72). The first phase of F66 is similarly dated, but the paintings on which the dolls appear are from later phases (Fröhlich 1991, 337).

[33] Festus (late second century AD; the possible influence of earlier sources [Varro?] cannot be proved) and Macrobius (late fourth / fifth centuries AD). It should be stressed that it is in no way clear that this practice goes indeed back to archaic times, as often seems to be assumed, apparently on the grounds that it appears as a very ancient custom, also present in other Indo-European cultures (cf. Dumézil 1961). Delos can apparently not help to stretch the chronology back to before 69 BC. To my knowledge, this type of depiction of an altar with schematic dolls does not appear on the painted altars from Delos (based on a cursory examination of the illustrations in Bulard 1926a, Bruneau 1970, Bezerra de Meneses/Sarian 1973, and Hasenohr 2003. On the altar depicted on wall Γ/1 [Bezerra de Meneses/Sarian 1973, figs. 21-22] is a stroke, but this does not seem to represent a doll). However, this absence of evidence cannot conversely attest to the absence of an administrative aspect of the *Compitalia* in this period and could be explained by the particular political status of Delos.

Whether or not the origin of this festival may be traced as far back as the time of Servius Tullius is a question to which no satisfactory answer can be expected,[34] but the point to be made here is that religious rituals could play an explicit role in consolidating administrative control. Dionysius understood the installation of a cult and festival rather straightforwardly as a deliberate means to integrate people.

9.2.3 VICUS AND COMPITUM

Certainly, the *Compitalia* brought people from a defined neighbourhood together. The *Compitalia* are generally considered to be the most important festival celebrated in the *vici* and were organised *vicatim*. The connection with the *vicus* becomes clear from the associations in texts and the context of the relevant passages and is stated explicitly by Asconius when he assigns a role to *magistri vicorum* in the organisation of the *ludi Compitalicii*.[35] The passage by Pliny the Elder commenting on the division of the city sustains this connection: *ipsa dividitur in regiones XIIII, compita Larum CCLXV*.[36] Apparently, *compita* could be used as a metaphor or rather as a *pars pro toto* for the urban *vici*. At Pompeii a *collegium* of *magistri vici et compiti* is documented by a text painted on a tufa block and dated to 47 and 46 BC.[37] This juxtaposition seems to indicate that the tasks of a *magister vici* included, or could include, the maintenance of the *compitum*.[38] In Dionysius' account, the ambiguity of the terms also becomes clear and he states that 'κομπίτους γὰρ τοὺς στενωποὺς καλοῦσι'; 'for they call στενωποὺς *compita*'; στενωπός is the normal Greek translation of Latin *vicus*.[39]

9.2.4 'PRIVATE' AND 'PUBLIC' IN CITY AND COUNTRYSIDE

Thus, for the city the connection between the organisation of the festival and the urban *vicus* is clear and it was the *magistri* of these territorial districts who organised and presided over the event. It would

[34] It may seem rather arbitrary from a historical point of view, even if ideologically, and therefore historiographically, it indeed makes sense: many administrative institutions are ascribed to this king who was himself believed to be the son of a *Lar* (Plin. *HN* 36.204). The strong connection between the institutions of Servius Tullius and the counting of citizens is thus clear and has long been acknowledged, e.g. Flambard 1981, 156; Tarpin 2002, 106-111; *contra* Bert Lott 2004, 36, who limits himself to the statement that the "meaning of this enigmatic ceremony [*scil.* hanging dolls] is unclear". Fraschetti 1990, 208 also does not think that a form of *census* is intended, pointing to other ways of counting inhabitants mentioned in Dion. Hal. *Ant. Rom.* 4.15, e.g. the offering of coins for newborns to Juno Lucina, for dead to Libitina, for youth becoming men to Juventas. Dionysius mentions these methods in a certain order (first *Compitalia*, then *Paganalia*, then Lucina-Libitina-Juventas) leading up to "the wisest of all measures", the first *census*, which suggests some kind of connection. Cf. Chapter 8.

[35] Asc. p. 7 C. Cf. *supra* n. 9. For the problems with different readings on the basis of the different interpunctuation that can be applied, cf. Fraschetti 1990, 228.

[36] Plin *HN* 3.66.

[37] *CIL* IV, 60; cf. *CIL* VI, 14180 for Augustan Rome.

[38] The explicit mention of both elements could, however, attest to the situation that these functions were not exactly synonymous or interchangeable, but perhaps the commissioners of the text (in all probability the *magistri* themselves) wanted to boast about as many aspects of their function as possible, therefore including a facet of their profession that was actually taken for granted.

[39] Mason 1974, 85. Hasenohr 2003, 193 thinks that the confusion is due to the co-existence of the Lares' epiteths *Compitales* and *Viales* and that their cult was sometimes celebrated in the streets and sometimes at the crossroads.

Figs. 9.2a and b. Delos, painted altar indicating a sacrifice *ritu romano* (Bulard 1926b, pls. XVII and XXIV).

be peculiar to assume that a 'family' cult was supervised by (semi)-officials,[40] if not expressly to forge a connection between the (members of the) family and a larger entity. Therefore, without rejecting the 'familial' aspect, which is undeniably present, it is perhaps better to understand the organisation of the *Compitalia* as an attempt to integrate family and society and to strengthen the ties between private and civic life, already intertwined so deeply.[41]

The situation in the countryside may at first seem different. In the villa envisaged by Cato, the *vilicus* took care of the extended household, of which the bailiff himself was part. Here then, it seems that the *Compitalia* indeed involved the household, or extended family, and not a larger group. Leaving the problems and degree of credibility of 'the Catonian villa' for what they are, there are other reasons to doubt the 'family' character of the *Compitalia* at the *villae*. In the first place one could be inclined, at least from the late Republican period onwards, to regard the community of a large villa, both in population size, dimensions and maybe also in structural character as a small *village* rather than what one normally associ-

---

[40] This would indeed be possible, of course, if one accepts the function of the *collegia* as a kind of mock-officials, or as a '*propédeutique civique*' in order to give slaves something similar to the 'real world', thereby reinforcing the existing power structures. I do not think this vision can be upheld however, in light of the undeniable public and administrative aspects. cf. *infra* n. 69.

[41] Other rites performed at the *compitum* than the *Compitalia* proper underline this function. Varro *apud* Non. 531 M mentions the custom for a bride to offer three *asses*, one to give the bridegroom, one to offer *in foco larium familiarum* and one in *conpito vicinale*. Cf. the observations by Piccaluga 1961, 90: "*l'offerta fatta in occasione di un matrimonio univa in un tutto unico e le divinità legate alla casa e al focolare, e quelle venerate al crocivia.*"

195

ates with the word villa. It is possible that this community was physically more or less self-contained and that therefore further inclusion or integration with other civic structures was simply not feasible.[42] In order to examine the question of public vs private further with archaeological examples, we turn now to the island of Delos.

Delos

The best material evidence with regard to the *Compitalia* in the Republican period is not to be found in Italy but on Delos. From the third century BC onward this commercial centre, part of the Cyclades, was frequented by Romans and other people from Italy[43] and especially flourished after 166 BC, when it was declared a free harbour and put under the administration of Athens. Notwithstanding its location outside of Italy, the *Compitalia* are best understood in this context of a community of merchants from Italy.

Wall-paintings in and on houses and chapels show sacrificial scenes and other aspects of the cult, and inscriptions in Greek mention the existence of a college of *kompetaliastai*.[44] At the so-called *agora des compétaliastes*, a temple was probably dedicated to the *Lares Compitales*.[45] The people that feature in these inscriptions are slaves and freedmen, mostly from the Eastern Mediterranean. The people who are depicted are clearly Italians since they wear togas (white and sometimes the purple-banded *praetexta*) and *calcei* at their feet. Moreover, they sacrifice *ritu romano* with veiled head (figs. 9.2a and b). The most plausible interpretation is therefore that the Greek and eastern slaves and freedmen of the inscriptions were servants in Italian families.[46]

Because the paintings are located both in and outside the houses, the connection between the archaeological evidence and the epigraphic attestation of the *Compitalia* is not straightforward. Typical for the debate on the *Compitalia*, the paintings were first interpreted as a domestic cult of the *Lares Familiares*[47] because the *Compitalia* were expected to take place at crossroads. Later this attribution was revised and the festival depicted at the doors was identified as the *Compitalia* and its entirely public character was emphasised.[48]

Recently, Claire Hasenohr has opted for a more sophisticated solution and concludes that the *Compitalia* on Delos were celebrated both on a 'private' level at the shrines near and in houses and on a more 'official' level at the temple of the *Lares* in the agora.[49] At this temple, the *kompetaliastai* would have made an official, communal sacrifice on behalf of the Italian community during the *Compitalia*. This double celebration could be explained by the particular socio-political conditions on Delos where the *Compitalia* would have become a means of self-affirmation for the Italian community.[50] The expatriate Romans and other Italians used the *Compitalia* in order to secure or re-affirm social relations and it is possible that this community's construction by ritual was even more pronounced in this alien context.[51]

[42] Cf. further in this chapter on Cato.
[43] In the context of Delos, the term 'Italians' will be used to indicate both 'Romans' and other peoples provenant from Italy.
[44] The inscriptions are normally found on bases of statues and include dedications to the *theoi*, perhaps to be identified with the *Lares Compitales*: *Inscriptions de Délos* 1760-1766, 1768-1771. Other deities such as Heracles, Zeus Eleutherios, Dionysos, Pistis, and Roma are also mentioned.
[45] Hasenohr 2001.
[46] Bruneau 1970, 617-620.
[47] Bulard 1926b.
[48] Bruneau 1970, 589-620; esp. 603, 613 on the non-domestic character.
[49] Hasenohr 2003, 170, 214.
[50] Hasenohr 2003, 214-218.
[51] Cf., e.g. Cohen 1985, for anthropological examples; see Chapter 1.

Italy

There is evidence to suggest that this 'double' nature of the *Compitalia* does not apply to Delos alone. In Pompeii a distinction between domestic *lararia* and the shrines outside the houses (and especially on the crossroads) has suggested a separation between the domestic cult of the *Lares Familiares* and the public cult of the *Lares Compitales* linked with the administrative organisation of the city.[52] In light of the Delian evidence however, Hasenohr questions this neat distinction. There are rather many altars, often in the same street, to be maintained by the *magistri* and sometimes they seem to be directly related to the more important Pompeian *domus*. She suggests that at least some of the shrines outside the houses were built by the inhabitants of these houses, rather than by the city administration.[53]

The literary sources indicate a varied location of the cult. Whereas Festus states that the dolls were suspended from the *compita*, Macrobius locates them 'at every door'.[54] As a matter of fact, one passage of Cato may be directly related to this diversification of location. In prescribing the responsibilities and duties of the *vilicus*, the bailiff, Cato states that he *rem divinam nisi compitalibus in compito aut in foco ne faciat*.[55] Most often, this is interpreted to mean that "the *vilicus* must generally not partake in religious rituals, if not (*nisi*) at the crossroads during the *Compitalia*, or at the domestic hearth."[56]

However, if we agree that both *in compito* and *in foco* refer to *compitalibus*, which seems possible to me,[57] in this passage both aspects of the same cult, that of the family hearth and of the *compitum* community, are present. A possible translation would then be that "the *vilicus* must not partake in religious rituals, if not during the *Compitalia*, [which he can perform] at the crossroads or at the domestic hearth."[58] Then, the 'twofold' character of the *Compitalia* could not be summarised better; partly to be celebrated at the domestic hearth, partly at the local *compitum*, where the congregated community was somewhat larger, probably consisting of more family units together.

9.2.5 'PUBLIC' AND 'PRIVATE', OR INTEGRATION OF BOTH?

In conclusion, it is tempting to suppose that the *Compitalia* were celebrated in Italy in similarly diverse locales as documented for Delos. Still, one has to remain cautious with the division in and distinction of 'public' or 'official' and 'private' or 'domestic' locales, which might seem to suggest the existence of two parallel but isolated worlds. I would therefore hesitate to define the diversity of the contexts in which

---

[52] For *lararia* cf. Fröhlich 1991 with Tybout 1996; for *Compitalia* and administrative aspects *CIL* IV, 60; *CIL* I², 2984; Van Andringa 2000, 73-75.

[53] Hasenohr 2003, 192.

[54] Fest. p. 108 L; Macrob. *Sat.* 1.7.35, cf. Dion. Hal. *Ant. Rom.* 4.14.3: προνωπίοις. According to Hasenohr, this would indicate that the Lares were not only venerated at the crossroads as *Lares Compitales*, but also in the streets (as *Lares Viales*) and on the walls of the houses (she avoids to attach a name to these last *Lares*) (Hasenohr 2003, 194). In this way, crossroads, streets and houses are all present. It is perhaps not necessary to see the location of the *Lares* in such a structured way (cf. *infra*), but the main line of reasoning is convincing. Hasenohr uses the Italian evidence for both Delos and Italy (esp. Pompeii), but also emphasises the specificity of Delos.

[55] Cato *Agr.* 5.3.

[56] Loeb [1934] gives: "He must perform no religious rites, except on the occasion of the *Compitalia* at the crossroads, or before the hearth."

[57] Maybe better than understanding *in compito* as referring alone to *compitalibus* and *in foco* instead referring directly back to *rem divinam*. *In compito* would not add any further information to *compitalibus* if not used in some way to distinguish it from *in foco*: apparently this did not speak for itself and a specification had to be made. I thank Dr. V. Hunink for advice on this issue.

[58] Thus also the translation by Goujard 1975, 15: "*qu'il ne fasse pas de sacrifice, sinon lors de la fête des carrefours, au carrefour ou au foyer, sans ordre du maître.*"

the *Compitalia* were apparently celebrated as 'double'.[59] It is important to note that in no literary source on the *Compitalia* is a distinction between location (*in compito, in foco, in compitis, in foribus*) explicitly equated with public versus private contexts. Ultimately, the matter is far too problematic to decide to which degree liturgical paintings in the atrium of a *domus* or altars against the façade are to be considered private and to what extent a *collegium* or club of freedmen and slaves, certainly of the same houses, can be regarded as 'public' or 'official', with the risk of projecting modern ideas of public and private upon probably different ancient realities.[60]

This is not to say that we have to leave the subject in aporia. Let us shift focus from the question of public and private to what actually seems to have happened, i.e. a festival being celebrated both in the open air, at open places, on the corners, in the streets and inside houses. The same rituals were performed both at a temple at the agora[61] and in front of the houses.

What appears is a clear image of a ritual of *integration*, the ramification of the same rituals in diverse contexts engineers the integration of these contexts in one festival and it seems that this constitutes the major aspect of the *Compitalia*. The practice of hanging dolls and balls to represent every inhabitant on the *compita* and doors ties in with this integrative function. These objects could serve as an indication of the number of people living in each unit, and, as Dionysius informs us, this was the very purpose of the *Compitalia*. Again, the formation of a community becomes clear from this practice, a community that transcends, or more correctly includes, the level of the family.[62]

If the peculiarity of the Delian *Compitalia* lies not so much in their presence in different social contexts, it may be in another aspect because it is striking that a festival bound up intrinsically with the administrative division in *vici*, as becomes clear from the Italian evidence, is present in a context that evidently lacked such an administration. The decision of the Italians to take the festival with them to Delos was therefore in all probability a voluntary one. Apparently the festival was popular enough amongst and 'internalised' in many of the Italians by the time they moved to Delos. Moreover, this phenomenon is documented strikingly early in the archaeological record, which shows that the *Compitalia* were already celebrated by the third quarter of the second century BC.[63]

---

[59] Bakker 1994 includes the *compita* (just as *mithraea*) in his work on private religion in Ostia, defining 'private' as restricted versus 'public' = unrestricted, the cult at the *compitum* being restricted to the neighbourhood (cf. also review by R. Laurence, *ClR* 48, 2 [1998], 444-445). However, the definition of the *compita* could maybe better be 'compartimentalised' *vel sim.*, since every citizen ended up at a *compitum* at some place.

[60] Inasmuch as a division in public and private is tenable at all in this context, this should not neatly coincide with spatial divisions.

[61] For Pompeii, the so-called *Tempio dei Lari pubblici* (VII 9.3) in the forum would have represented a similar situation, but this identification is actually based on no evidence (cf. Fröhlich 1991, 37). The identification is from Mau 1896, esp. 299-301; also rejected by e.g. Coarelli *et al.* 1997, 163-165.

[62] Cf. the observations by Piccaluga 1961, esp. 89-90 on the Lares. A very direct statement on the all-embracing aspect of the *Compitalia* is made in Festus, if we accept the identification of the *Laralia* with the *Compitalia*, as Wissowa suggests (Wissowa 1912, 149): (Fest. 253 L) *popularia sacra sunt, ut ait Labeo, quae omnes cives faciunt, nec certis familiis attributa sunt: Fornacalia, Parilia, Laralia, Porca praecidanea.*

[63] The liturgical paintings were regularly renewed and on the basis of technical research Bruneau has calculated that in the house opposite the Maison de la Colline, the first painting may originate from around 120 BC (Bruneau 1970, 619-620) and not much later, at least at the end of the second century BC, a *collegium* of *kompetaliastai* was in action (615). Although the literary sources indicate a relatively early date, in Italy most archaeological evidence does not. Sources: Naevius, third century BC; Cato, first half second century BC, also Lucilius (6.252-253 Warmington, second century BC) probably refers to the *Compitalia* when speaking of "that slaves festival which cannot be expressed in hexameters": Palmer 1976, 167-168. For what it is worth, Livy (4.30.10) mentions *vicis sacellisque* for 428 BC which, if not an anachronism, may reflect an early connection between *vici* and religious shrines. Cf. Bert Lott 2004, 39-41 for discussion, cf. also *infra*.

These considerations leave us with two options for a conclusion. If we believe Dionysius, the *Compitalia*, part and parcel of the administrative organisation of the city of Rome from their early beginnings (possibly in the archaic period or the fourth century BC) had by then been rooted so firmly in the annual cycle of festivals that they were celebrated independently from their administrative function. If, on the other hand, we hold that Dionysius' account merely reflects the reality at the time he was writing, and that his statement on the antiquity of the institution is just an example of the (unintentional) invention of tradition, one has to suppose that the *Compitalia* were originally just a popular festival that only later (perhaps in the first century BC, under Caesar, and surely under Augustus)[64] acquired its administrative aspect (possibly together with its 'tradition').[65]

In conclusion, the often expressed argument that the *Compitalia* were largely a family feast, might miss the point. Neither is it necessary to regard them exclusively as an official cult, extraneous to domestic cult.[66] The Delian evidence testifies to the celebration of the *Compitalia* in both contexts, as Hasenohr has made clear. The evidence from Italy and the Catonian passage may indicate that the Delian situation was not exceptional in this respect. At least in Rome and in Pompeii the *Compitalia* were associated with administrative and/or political concerns. However, it is not clear if this politico-administrative connection was present from the very beginning, as Dionysius would have it, or was added at a later point in time. The evidence does not lead us further back than Caesar.[67] Whereas its politico-administrative dimension for this period remains obscure, it is certain that the *Compitalia* were already part of Romano-Italic society in the second century BC. The festival could by then be used to consolidate and 'construct' the Romano-Italic community.[68] The *Compitalia* were essentially an integrative cult, inclusive rather than exclusive in character, being an official festival.[69]

---

[64] Fraschetti 1990, 206-207 proves, on the basis that the *Lares Augusti* and new *ludi* do not yet feature, that Dionysius describes the *Compitalia* from before the Augustan reform. Cf. on vici in Rome Bert Lott 2004 and now Wallace-Hadrill 2008, 259-312.

[65] The Servian tradition may originate with the early annalists, who may have presented him as the first *popularis*: Alföldi 1973, 19.

[66] E.g. Bruneau 1970, 603 on the paintings outside the Delian houses: "*elles commémorent la célébration des Compitalia qu'organisaient des individus de naissance grecque, mais affranchis ou esclaves des Roomaioi établis dans l'île. Les peintures des autels n'ont donc rien à voir avec la religion domestique des Romains ou des Italiens,*" with emphasis on the ethnic differences but also implying a strong private and public distinction.

[67] For Rome, Dion. Hal. *Ant. Rom.* 4.14; for Pompeii *CIL* IV, 60 (the attestation of *magistri vici et compiti* is in itself no evidence for the administration of people, cf. however Jongman 1988, 295-310; with Mouritsen 1990).

[68] Indeed, as Hasenohr 2003, 218 states a "*moyen d'affirmation de la puissance de la communauté italienne de Délos*".

[69] Linderski 1968, 107 (cf. the remarks in Linderski 1995, 645-647); Bert Lott 2004; *contra* Gradel 2002, 128-130. Without wanting to play down the 'servile' aspect of the *Compitalia*, especially emphasised by Bömer, Flambard and others (followed by Jongman 1988; cf. also Tybout 1996, 366-370), who seem to understand the integrative function of the *Compitalia* especially in the sense that lower status groups were accommodated by allowing them to mimic civic structures (Flambard 1981, 166 speaks of a "*propédeutique civique*", Jongman 1988, 297 of a "pseudo *cursus honorum*"), I would like to emphasise here that ultimately all inhabitants, i.e. slaves, freedmen and citizens, were included, as is testified by the woollen dolls for free persons, balls for slaves. The fact that the *praetor* announced the festival is especially significant: cf. Fraschetti 1990, 204. Cf. *supra* n. 9.

9.3 THE DEVELOPMENT OF THE COMPITALIA: FROM THE COUNTRYSIDE TO THE CITY OR VICE VERSA?

"*Das Fest trägt einen ländlichen Character,*" Wissowa stated in 1901.[70] In both ancient and modern texts on the *Compitalia*, a contradictory image arises with regard to the locale of the *Compitalia*. On the one hand, rustic elements are emphasised, whereas on the other an urban setting is attested by both the rioting in the 60s and 50s BC and the association with the urban plebs, as well as the association with the administrative division of the city. In order to make sense of this situation, presumably in combination with the assumption that the *Compitalia* rituals are of very ancient origin,[71] modern research has tended to conceptualise a particular development of the festival. This development would have encompassed the implementation or adaptation of a rural festival celebrated by agricultural communities in an urban context. Along these lines Scullard states, "thus the state, as so often, developed its urban counterpart of what had originally been a country festival."[72] Timothy Potter follows this idea and seems to envisage the introduction of the *Compitalia* in the city in a rather straightforward manner as a result of migration, "It [*scil.* the *Compitalia*] was in origin an agricultural ceremony to propitiate the *lar*, or spirit that presided over each farm, and it is striking to see how the traditions of the countryside became incorporated into the life of the towns, to which so many rural folk migrated."[73]

Although this view of the development of the *Compitalia* is often present in studies on the subject, for instance in the most recent exhaustive treatment of the Roman *vici* and their rituals,[74] actual evidence for such a development from rural to urban is absent. It should be stressed that nowhere is explicit mention made of the *Compitalia* as an exclusively rustic cult. Festivals that are indeed clearly connected with the countryside are the festivals of the *Robigalia* (in order to protect the crops from blight), the *Fordicidia* (the sacrifice of a pregnant cow to *Tellus*), the *Cerealia* and *Vinalia*. The *Ambarvalia* (lustration of the fields) and the *Sementivae* (the sowing of the seed) seem to have catered even more exclusively to the countryside. In my view however, the *Compitalia* do not belong in this group.[75]

---

[70] Wissowa 1901a, 791.

[71] Scullard 1981, 58: "Their [*scil.* Compitalia] history spans a thousand years, from primitive agricultural beginnings, through 'the solemn and sumptuous' celebrations which Dionysius witnessed in Augustan Rome, and on to the late Empire"; Wissowa 1897, 1872: "*seit unvordenklicher Zeit.*" Cf. also Flambard 1981, 146, who sees the "*cérémonie immémoriale*" of the *Argei* as the predecessor of the *Compitalia*, since Varro (*Ling.* 5.45-54) states that the *sacraria Argeorum* were connected to the division of the city, just as the *Compitalia* were later. Latte argues that the festival was older than the institution of the praetorship (Latte 1960, 91 n. 1).

[72] Scullard 1981, 59 (= Fowler 1925, 294).

[73] Potter 1987, 173.

[74] Bert Lott 2004, 38, "it is unclear when the probably earlier agricultural *Compitalia* was first adapted to an urban setting and focused on neighborhoods rather than farms, but it must have been early in Roman history," and further on *vici*, "Indeed the replication of rural districts in imagined subdivisions of the urban space with local voluntary associations like the *vici* in Rome is a common phenomenon in societies making the transition from a non-urban to an urban existence," but cf. Tarpin 2002 and *infra*. Similar ideas on the development from agricultural to urban in e.g. Gradel 2002, 124; Fröhlich 1991, 26; Orr 1978, 1565-1566; Alföldi 1973, 19; Bailey 1932, *passim*, e.g. 107, 147, 172. Cf. also Pisani Sartorio 1988, 23 who states, unclear on what grounds, that: "*I Lares Compitales erano legati particolarmente alla sfera agricola, i Lares Viales alla sfera pastorale e ai boschi.*"

[75] *Contra* Beard et al. 1998, 50 who list as "quite specifically rural festivals" *Ambarvalia, Sementivae* and *Compitalia* (strangely, because specifying that they were celebrated "both in Rome and in the countryside") together because they would be "outside the civic structure of the city", being *feriae conceptivae* (not at a fixed date). Most mobile festivals have indeed an agricultural character ("*quasi tutte*" Dumézil 1974 [1977]), 480), but this circumstance cannot *vice versa* serve as a proof. It is true that the *Compitalia* could assume the character of a yearly celebration at the end of the agricultural season,

Of course there are instances of a rustic setting of the *Compitalia* (for example Cato's villa), which confirm that the *Compitalia* were also celebrated outside the city. However, they do not prove an anteriority of supposedly 'rural *Compitalia*' with respect to a later urban variant.[76]

The archaeological evidence cannot prove a transition from rural to urban either. *Compitum* shrines have been exclusively found in urban contexts in Rome, Delos, Pompeii and Ostia, the earliest dating to the second century BC.[77] The identification of one extra-urban *compitum* at Tor de' Cenci that would date as early as the seventh century BC is not convincing since this interpretation relies on the sole fact that ritual remains (especially animal bones) and burials were found in connection with a crossroads.[78] I do not deny that such places could have had religious and/or ritual importance also in earlier times, but the existence of a *compitum* with the associated *Compitalia* is not attested here.

according to a scholion at Persius (4.28; cf. *infra* n. 120 for text) the *Compitalia* were celebrated *finita agricoltura*, but this (rather late) assertion obviously does not attest to the *origin* of the *Compitalia* as an agricultural festival. On the problems with clear-cut definitions of festivals, cf. in general Beard *et al.* 1998, 47.

[76] Commenting quite explicitly on the link between city and countryside is the scholion on Persius 4.28: *vel compita sunt non solum in urbe loca, sed etiam viae publicae ac diverticulae aliquorum confinium* ..., which, if anything, seems to attest to the urban setting as the more 'natural' one rather than the rural setting, although in the context the agricultural aspect is highlighted. An overview of the principal literary sources: 1) Cato *Agr.* 57.1; Plin. *HN* 19.114; Prop. 4.1.23; Festus p. 108 L, 273 L; Auson. *De feriis Romanis*, 17-18 do not specify. Equally, Varro, *Ling.* 6.25 does not specify if the roads are outside the city, but one may suppose it. Suet. *Aug.* 31 mentions the *Compitalia* together with the *Lupercalia* and the *Ludi saeculares*, all restored by the princeps, but a specification of the locale is absent. 2) For an urban context: Dion. Hal. *Ant. Rom.* 4.14; the references by Cicero on Clodius relate to a deeply urban-plebeian context, cf. Flambard 1977; Flambard 1981. The statement by Aulus Gellius (*NA* 10.24.3) that the *Compitalia* were announced by the *praetor* locates them in the city. Ovid. *Fast.* 5.145-146 and Macrob. *Sat.* 1.7.34 refer to the city. If the *maxima ter centum totam delubra per urbem* installed by Augustus according to Verg. *Aen.* 8.716 do relate to *compita* (but cf. *supra* n. 14) this is another case in point. 3) For a non-urban (which is not the same as rural) setting: Pers. 4.26-30, with the scholion ad loc. (cf. *infra* n. 120). Dolabella apparently also refers to a rural setting, but it is unclear if this text refers to a *compitum*: cf. *infra* n. 121. Cic. *Leg.* 2.19 contrasts the *Larum sedes in agris* with the urban *delubra*, and Wissowa 1901b, 793 thinks that with the first the *sacella* at the *compita* are meant (cf. Cic. *Leg.* 2.27). Maybe not surprisingly Verg. *G.* 2.382 refers to a rural context. The description by Philargyrius on this passage of the *compita* can be related to the countryside because it is specified that *pagani agrestes* go there (Philarg. Verg. G. 2.382). Cf. Hor. *Epist.* 1.1.49-51. Macrob. *Sat.* 1.16.6: mentions the *Compitalia* as one group together with the 'rural' festivals of the *Sementivae* and the *Paganalia*, being all *feriae conceptivae*. Bert Lott 2004, 33 n. 34, sees two passages of Cicero as referring to "the rural *Compitalia*" once for 59 BC at a *villa* in Antium (*Att.* 2.3), and once for 50 BC at a *villa* of Pompey (*Att.* 7.7.3). But these *villae* relate clearly more to an urban way of life with rich urban people enjoying their *otium* than to countryside religion. Augustine relates that the shameful cult of Liber was celebrated at the *compita* in the countryside, but the festival significantly includes the city as the worshippers move from the rural shrines into the city: *De civ. D.* 7.21.

[77] For a clear overview of Rome, Pompeii and Ostia see Bakker 1994, 118-133; for Pompeii, cf. Van Andringa 2000.

[78] Bedini 1990 apparently tries to connect the burials with the interpretation of the *Lares* as the *Manes* of the dead (Samter's interpretation: cf. *supra* n. 19): "presso di essi era infatti usanza seppellire i morti dei vici confinanti, rappresentando il Compitum un luogo di confine, una 'soglia critica' come il limite fra i due mondi dei vivi e dei morti" (122).

The earliest archaeological evidence for the *Compitalia* relates to an urban setting[79] and this urban connotation is secured for the last century of the Republic and emphasised by Augustus.[80] However, the *Compitalia* were not an exclusively *stadtrömisches* festival, since there is clear evidence that they were also celebrated in the countryside. At the same time it should be emphasised that all evidence relating to the *Compitalia* from outside the city of Rome is without exception located in spatial and temporal contexts which are either Roman or strongly influenced by Rome. Cato's passage, for example, cannot be related to traditional Italic countryside ritual, rather he refers to a specific Roman situation in the countryside, the villa. Many aspects of the *Compitalia* are actually best attested for 'romanised' Campania[81] and for Delos, equally under strong Roman influence.[82] Thus, the *Compitalia* were also celebrated outside the city of Rome and in areas with a large Italic component of the population, but influenced strongly, at least politically and apparently culturally, by Rome.

To sum up, on the basis of direct archaeological or textual evidence it is impossible to argue that the *Compitalia* evolved from a rural to an urban cult.[83] There is, in my view, no reason to exclude the possibility that the festival of the *Compitalia* was initially related to the Roman urban structure and was only later transposed to other areas. No evidence whatsoever can be related to pre-Roman or non-Roman Italic contexts. To be precise, this does not exclude the possibility that the *Compitalia* indeed had old agricultural roots before being incorporated in the city of Rome (perhaps during the urbanisation process itself), but I would suggest that the subsequent spread over Italy and beyond started from Rome.

From the moment that the *Compitalia* were intrinsically associated with the institution of the *vicus*, one could propose that the development of the *Compitalia* was parallel to that of the *vicus*.[84] As noted in Chapter 6, the development of the *vicus* was essentially an urban Roman one and the subsequent spread of this Roman institution in the Roman territory therefore also depended on the urban Roman model.[85] What is the significance of the *Compitalia* and their administrative aspect? Could it be possible that the

---

[79] At Delos. It does not seem possible to distinguish whether the location of the scene described by Naevius is rural or urban; Naevius ap. Festus 230 M.

[80] Cf. Phillips III 1988, who thinks that it was especially in the rural areas that the festival persisted in late Roman times, "In its rural guise it would of course find favour with the pagans who still populated the countryside. In its urban manifestation of *genius*-worship of a pagan emperor it would irritate Christians" (384). Bakker 1994, 195 thinks that from the period of the Soldier emperors onwards the cult declined.

[81] Johnson 1933, esp. 118-123; Van Andringa 2000.

[82] Bruneau 1970, 586-589. On the Delian *rhoomaioi* and *italikoi* cf. e.g. Brunt 1971, 205-214; and esp. Adams 2002; Mavrojannis 1995 sees a very strong Roman influence on Delos (and even assumes the presence of *vici* there, without presenting any evidence however).

[83] The discussion on the character and origin of the *Lares* is of course intimately related to this question, as Wissowa and others would like to interpret them as protection gods of the fields (cf. *supra*). But I believe it is more correct to separate this discussion from the evaluation of the contexts of the festival of the *Compitalia* involving the *Lares Compitales*. Some myths link the *Lares Compitales* directly to the city of Rome, such as Ovid. *Fast*. 2.610-616 (nymph Lara, daughter of Tiber, mother of *Lares Compitales*).

[84] See Laurence 1994 and Van Andringa 2000 viz. the introduction of the *vici* and *Compitalia* as following the installation of the Roman colony at Pompeii. The institution of the *Compitalia*, including the dedication of altars, accompanied the division of the city of Pompeii in *vici* with the founding of the Roman colony by Sulla (Laurence 1994, 39; Van Andringa 2000, 72-73, states "*De toute évidence, les fêtes compitalices organisées dans la cité vesuvienne étaient calquées sur le modèle romain. Les cultes de carrefour furent vraisemblablement institués lors de l'établissement de la colonie, initiant alors une réorganisation de l'espace urbain*"). Put simply, this would mean that the *vicus*-division and the *Compitalia* were exported from Rome to other cities. I see no reason to think that this was different in other areas, and especially, in non-urban contexts.

[85] Tarpin 2002. On the 'urbanity' of early *vici* cf. the discussion in Chapter 7.

Compitalia were not so much a harmless agricultural festival of the olden days but were rather exported along with a new Roman administration of the conquered territories?

9.4 THE COMPITUM SHRINES: FORM AND LOCATION IN CITY AND COUNTRYSIDE

It is time to take a look at the sacred place and its possible architectural elaboration. First the evidence for the actual physical location of the *compita* will be surveyed and subsequently their different physical aspects.

9.4.1 CROSSROADS AND SHRINES

Some evidence regarding the location of the *compitum* has already been presented in the preceding analysis of the context of the *Compitalia*. It has become clear that the shrines where the festival was held were located both in the city of Rome and in the rest of Italy, and sometimes clearly outside urban structures. Usually, one speaks of the *Compitalia* as the festival of the 'crossroads'. The actual location however, is not unequivocal. The *OLD* gives as the meaning of *compitum* "a place where three or more roads meet" (cf. fig. 9.3). In almost every standard study on Roman religion the idea recurs that 'the Romans' believed every crossroads to be charged with spiritual energy and this seems to derive from this specific understanding of *compitum*.[86]

A more precise definition of *compitum* refines this 'crossroads' meaning noting that it constitutes the place where different territories (*partes*) meet, which means that the shrines should not by definition be located at (a conjunction of) roads.[87] In any case, they were located at a central point and they served as a meeting place for local inhabitants. This was the case in the cities but this basic principle will not have been different in the countryside. For example, Cicero tells us that the farmers and their dependants met at shrines *in fundi villaeque conspectu*.[88] It becomes clear that people of the land aggregated (*rustici celebrabant*[89]; *ubi pagani agrestes bucina convocati solent inire concilia*[90]) at these shrines, which emphasises their communal function. I believe it is difficult to arrive at a more precise identification of the places where the *Compitalia* were celebrated in the countryside on the basis of the cited sources.[91] Therefore, I will first discuss the much richer evidence of the urban contexts and the physical forms the *compitum* shrines could assume there. In light of the conclusions on the urban contexts, we will return to the problem of the countryside shrines.

---

[86] Cf. schol. Pers. 4.28: *Compita sunt loca in quadriviis...*

[87] Philarg. on Verg. G. 2.382: *compita, ut Trebatio placet, locus ex pluribus partibus in se vel in easdem partes ex se vias atque itinera dirigens, sive is cum ara sive sine ara, sive sub tecto sive sub di(v)o sit.*

[88] Cic. *Leg.* 2.27, cf. supra n. 76.

[89] schol. Pers. 4.28.

[90] Philarg. on Verg. G. 2.382. Fowler (1925, 279, n. 2), "no doubt discussion about agricultural matters."

[91] According to Wissowa 1901b, 793, *CIL* VI, 29784 (*Via quae ducit / per agrum / Nonianum / a m(illiario) XX devertic(ulo) / sinistrosus / per compitum / secus piscinam / in fundo / Decimiano / Thalamiano / iunctis debetur / ita uti hodie / in uso est*) would prove that the *compitum* is "*ein Heiligtum des ländlichen pagus*". Apart from the somewhat confusing introduction of a *pagus* in this context, which is not mentioned, this inscription (found '*sub Aventino*') does to my mind only indicate that there is a *compitum* somewhere, without saying anything about its "audience", although presumably being situated in a rural setting.

Fig. 9.3. A Pompeian painting showing a *compitum* with shrines (Casa della Fontana Piccola) (Dar.-Sag. II, 1429 fig. 1887).

The location of compita in the city
Many *compitum* shrines located in urban contexts have been identified, but they were not always, as the modern *vulgata* would have it, located at crossroads. The *compita* found in Rome were located in streets and squares, the only certain *compitum* of Ostia stands on a square and in Delos shrines were located both in streets outside of houses and on a square.[92] *Compita* at Pompeii[93] are located in streets and crossroads.[94] Whereas at Rome the *compitum* would constitute the cult centre for each *vicus*, this situation may have been different in Pompeii because the number of altars there is too high and it has been suggested that the altars formed the boundary markers of the *vicus*.[95] It is sometimes argued that before the Augustan reform the number of *compitum* shrines was much larger and that Augustus reduced their number in order to avoid the uprisings associated with their personnel in the mid-first century BC.[96] This could mean that the equalling of *vicus* with *compitum* by Pliny might represent the centralisation of the cult under Augustus.[97]

---

[92] Dondin-Payre 1987; Pisani Sartorio 1988; Bakker 1994, esp. 128, 196-197; Hasenohr 2003.

[93] Laurence 1994; Van Andringa 2000.

[94] A surmised shrine of the *Lares* on the forum can be dismissed however, cf. *supra* n. 61.

[95] Laurence 1994, 41. Bakker 1994, 197: "Apparently the *compita* were here, [*scil.* at Pompeii] contrary to Rome, as numerous as in the Republican period and still meant for the *geitones*. Consequently the relation between the shrines and the *vici* was different from that in Rome: the Pompeian *vici* could have more than one shrine." Van Andringa seems to think that the shrines included a larger entity than the *vicus* (*regiones*?): "*De toute évidence, et le constat est au moins valable pour l'époque impériale, les sanctuaires de carrefour délimitent et définissent des circonscriptions administratives plus larges, englobant le réseau des vici*" (2000, 75).

[96] E.g. Bakker 1994, 196: "If the number of shrines was smaller, the amount of officials was smaller, and thus control easier," and Laurence 1994, cf. also preceding note.

[97] This does, of course, not undermine the existing connection, which must not be 1:1, between *compitum* and *vicus*. Laurence 1994, 42 detects this process also in Pompeii, "the identity of the inhabitants of each *vicus* became concentrated upon the centralised shrine of the *Lares Augusti* rather than the altars of the *Lares Compitales* that marked the boundaries of the pre-Augustan *vici* of their ancestors." It should be noted however that for Rome there is no evidence that there were more *compitum* shrines in one *vicus* before 73 AD.

Architecture

Apart from its indicating a location, the word *compitum* could also mean the sacred structure sometimes present at this location.[98] Whereas some ancient written sources are rather enigmatic with respect to the physical appearance of the *compitum* shrines, archaeology offers a rather familiar image. The archaeological remains that can be securely identified as *compita* (by inscriptions and/or images of *Compitalia*-rites) all point to rather 'normal' shrines. Interestingly, there is a plethora of different forms of these *compitum* shrines. In Pompeii most shrines that can be interpreted as a *compitum* consist of painted façades and/or masonry altars.[99] Delos also presents altars and/or paintings[100] and there is one central *compitum shrine* on the *agora des compétaliastes* which had the features of a small round temple.[101]

In Rome some *compitum* shrines have been unearthed.[102] One likely *compitum* shrine has been identified in Via di S. Martino ai Monti.[103] It presents two phases, the most recent of which is dated by an inscription to the Augustan period.[104] The scarce remains of the pre-Augustan phase, not dated more precisely, consisted of a square structure of travertine blocks, possibly an altar. The Augustan phase presents a podium of tufa blocks lined with marble slabs and a flight of marble steps. Behind the podium was a large base with another, inscribed, base or *cippus* on top. Although not much is known, the absence of evidence of a superstructure could suggest an open-air (*sub divo*) shrine.

The *compitum Acilium*, identified by an inscription from 5 BC mentioning *mag(istri) vici compiti Acili*, was found during the construction of the Via dei Fori Imperiali (figs. 9.4 and 9.5).[105] Its architectural form is known quite well: a podium (2.80 x 2.38 x 1.40 m) lined with travertine slabs was accessible by a flight of four steps. On the rear part of the podium was a *cella*, in front two columns supported a roof.[106] In short, the features of this *compitum* shrine are very much those of a small temple, although no altar was found in front of it.

An inscription mentioning the reconstruction of an *aedicula reg(ionis) VIII Vico Vestae* from AD 233 has been connected to a structure built against the *Atrium Vestae* on the forum.[107] The structure consists of a podium with two columns supporting a superstructure, indeed an *aedicula* or 'small temple'.[108] During the excavations led by Andrea Carandini on the Palatine, near the crossroads of the *clivus Palatinus* and

---

[98] One could suspect that structures could sometimes, by extension, also be called *compitum* by association because of their function and/or appearance, even if they lacked a 'formal' location at a *compitum* = crossroads / border point, but this is impossible to prove.

[99] Bakker 1994, 198; cf. overview of the Pompeian evidence 125-127.

[100] Hasenohr 2003.

[101] Hasenohr 2001; *contra* Mavrojannis 1995.

[102] For an overview of the Pompeian, Ostian and Roman evidence see Bakker 1994, 124-132, which is used here together with information in the relevant entries of *LTUR*, Dondin-Payre 1987, Pisani Sartorio 1988, Van Andringa 2000. Pisani Sartorio (esp. 31-32) identifies several mostly small rectangular structures on the *Forma Urbis Romae* as *compita*. Although sometimes suggestive, I do not consider these here since their status as *compitum* cannot be proved and they cannot add much to our architectural knowledge.

[103] Gatti 1888.

[104] Dated 10 BC, recording the erection of a statue to Mercurius, which can be related to the distribution of statues *vicatim* by Augustus: Suet. *Aug*. 57; this forms the basis for the identification as a *compitum*.

[105] *AE* 1964, 74. Dondin-Payre 1987; Coarelli 1983, 39-40, fig. 8 for location.

[106] Bakker 1994, 125.

[107] *CIL* VI, 30960. Lanciani 1882, 229-231; Coarelli 1983, 265-270.

[108] Another *compitum* shrine with a similar rectangular plan has been noticed near the temples of Mater Matuta and Fortuna, at the *vicus Iugarius*, but almost nothing has been published: Coarelli 1988a, 244; for location, cf. 235 fig. 48.

Fig. 9.4. The *compitum Acilium* (Colini 1961-1962, 152 fig. 7).

the *sacra via* some remains of *opus caementicium* have been identified as a *compitum* shrine[109] similar to the *compitum Acilium*.[110] It has been dated to the mid-first century BC.[111]

In Ostia inscriptions attest to the existence of *compitum* shrines[112] but the only architectural remains which can be securely related to a *compitum* shrine consist of the marble altar at the Piazza dei Lari.[113] The round altar was dedicated to the *Lares Vicin*[*ales*] by a *magister* or *magistri*.[114] Directly south of the altar is a basin, north of the altar is a building with several entrances (some closed off in later periods). Jan Theo Bakker thinks this building behind the altar is connected to the altar (fig. 9.6) and that the ensemble would form a *compitum* shrine or building, relating the entrances to the somewhat enigmatic qualifications in ancient authors of *compita* as '*pervia*' or '*pertusa*'.[115] In this respect, Bakker follows Laura Holland in her interpretation of Persius' story of a miser who, celebrating the *Compitalia*, *iugum pertusa*

---

[109] M.L. Gualandi in: Carandini/Papi 2005, 125-126.

[110] Although one should bear in mind that its beautiful full-colour reconstruction drawings rely on the *compitum Acilium* rather than on the remains actually found. Only a rectangular structure in *opus caementicium*, and another small piece of this *opus* in front of it was found; no trace of the roof or the columns has been found, not even the original height of the podium.

[111] On the basis of a rather direct association with the textual sources on the repression of the *collegia*, the construction of the compitum is ascribed to Clodius himself (!). In any case, the structure was destroyed some time between the time of Caesar and 7 BC. M.L. Gualandi in: Carandini/Papi 2005, 126.

[112] For the Ostian evidence: Bakker 1994, 118-124, 243-250.

[113] The structure on the Bivio del Castrum, at a major crossroads, cannot be connected firmly to the relevant inscriptions: Bakker 1994, 121-122.

[114] *CIL* XIV, 4298.

[115] Pers. 4.28: *quandoque iugum pertusa ad compita figit*. Cf. Calp. *Ecl.* 4.126: *pervia compita*.

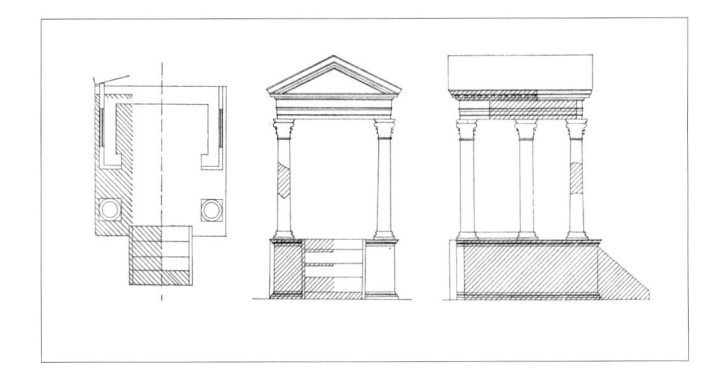

Fig. 9.5. The *compitum Acilium* (adapted from Colini 1961-1962, 155 fig. 12).

ad compita figit. The scholiast on Persius explains that it was the custom that farmers fixed broken yokes to the *compitum* as a sign of completed agricultural labour or because the instrument was considered sacred.[116] Holland points out that a yoke does not break easily and that here the *iugum* refers to a sacred structure that was fixed in the ground, perhaps two uprights and a crossbeam, forming some sort of symbolic sacred gate.[117] Bakker thinks that the structure north of the altar on the Piazza dei Lari at Ostia "with its many wide entrances, is actually to be understood as consisting of six gates, and that it belongs to the class of the *pervia compita*".[118] This would correspond to the description of the scholiast on Persius, who emphasises that *compita* could be accessible from all four sides[119] and that they were *quasi turres*; 'almost towers'.[120]

In this context, also a suggestive description by Dolabella, presented as part of an explanation on how to establish boundaries within his general guidelines for land surveyors, has often been related to *compita*:

> "Boundaries relating to shrines ought to be examined in the following way. If the shrine is positioned where four boundaries meet and establishes the boundary for four properties, look for four altars; moreover the shrine has four entrances so that anyone can enter through his own land to conduct a sacrifice... Now, if the shrine is between three properties, it has three entrances, if between two, then it has two entrances."[121]

In a manuscript dating to the late ninth century AD (Gud. lat. 105) an illustration of this quadrilateral sanctuary is given (fig. 9.7). This illustration cannot be dated with certainty. The Gudianus manuscript is a copy of a copy of an early 9th century illustrated manuscript (Pal. lat. 1564). Although it seems plausible that some illustrations to the gromatic texts served a didactic purpose and may date to the period of the writers collected in the *Corpus Agrimensorum Romanorum*, it is impossible to determine the date of the illustrations with any precision. In any case, they will probably have been altered in the process of copying.[122]

---

[116] schol. Pers. 4.28; cf. *infra* n. 120 for text.

[117] Holland 1937.

[118] Bakker 1994, 200.

[119] Cf. e.g. Lee/Barr 1987, 125.

[120] schol. Pers. 4.28: *Qui quotiens diem festum aratro fixo in compitis celebrat, timens seriolam vini aperire, acetum potat. Compita sunt loca in quadriviis, quasi turres, ubi sacrificia finita agricultura rustici celebrant. Merito pertusa, quia per omnes quattuor partes pateant, vel vetusta. Aut compita proprie a conpotando, id est simul bibendo, pertusa autem, quia pervius transitus est viris et feminis. Vel compita sunt non solum in urbe loca, sed etiam viae publicae ac diverticulae aliquorum confinium, ubi aediculae consecrantur patentes, ideo pertusa ad compita; in his fracta iuga ab agricolis ponuntur velut emeriti et elaborati operis indicium, sive quod omne instrumentum existiment sacrum. Vel compita dicuntur, ad quae plura itinera competunt. Quamvis rei divinae operatur: Nec sic tamen ab avaritia discedit: timetque dolium aperire diu servatum.*

[121] L 302.1: *Fines templares sic quaeri debent; ut si in quadrifinio est positus et quattuor possessionibus finem faciet. Quattuor aras quaeris, et aedes quattuor ingressus habet ideo ut ad sacrificium quisquis per agrum suum intraret. Quod si desertum fuerit templum, aras sic quaeris. Longe a templo quaeris pedibus XV, et invenis velut fundamenta aliqua. Quod se inter tres, tria ingressa habet: inter duos dua ingressa habet templum.*

[122] Cf. the discussion in Campbell 2000, xxi-xxvi.

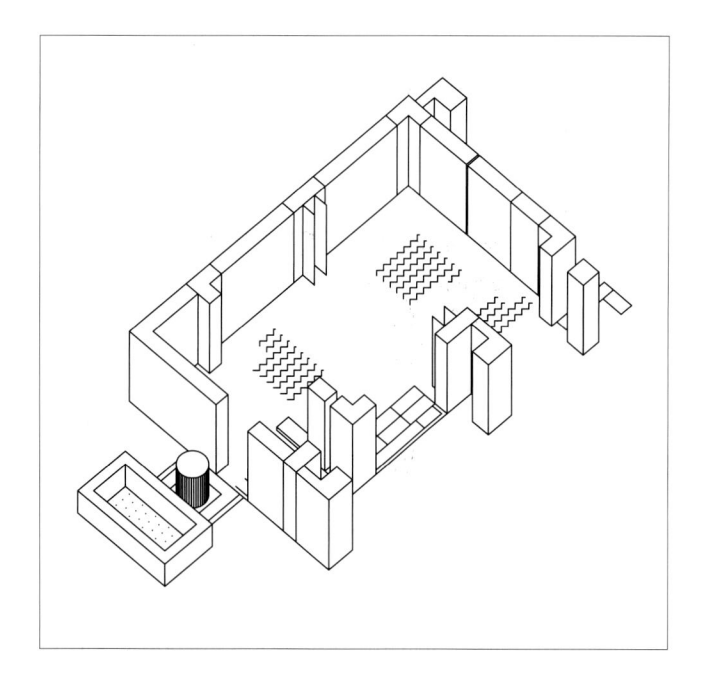

Fig. 9.6. A '*compitum pervium*' at Ostia? (Bakker 1994, 119 fig. 17).

Wissowa argued that Dolabella's text describes a *compitum*, "*An diesen Compitalsacella wird alljährlich die Festfeier der Compitalia abgehalten, aber auch sonst bilden sie für die umwohnenden Landleute den sacralen Mittelpunkt.*" However, nowhere in Dolabella's text is it explicitly stated that a *compitum* is meant, rather it is surprising that the word is not mentioned.[123] Perhaps with the exception of Ostia, a structure fitting the descriptions of Persius' scholiast and Dolabella has never been attested archaeologically. Moreover, one has to be careful not to read too much into the scholion on Persius. The word *pertusa* used by Persius could also have been used to indicate the 'shabbiness' of the structure, *pertusa* in the sense of 'rotten' or 'perforated'. This is Walter Kissel's interpretation, who states that the interpretation of the scholiast of *pertusa* ('*quia per omnes quattuor partes pateant*') is "*weder sprachlich noch sachlich akzeptabel: Für pertundere bzw. pertusus lässt sich nirgendwo die wertneutrale Bedeutung "offen" nachweisen ... Richtiger wird man pertusa daher in seiner gängigen Bedeutung "durchlöchert" fassen ... und auf den ruinösen Zustand des sacellum beziehen.*"[124] Actually, the scholiast also gives this option, "*pertusa*; because it is open on all four sides or because it is old", *vel vetusta*.[125] The interpretation of *pertusa* as indicating the shabbiness rather than the architecture of the structure would also fit quite well in the context of Persius' satirical description of a miser.[126] Thus, while the explicit explanation of 'open on all four sides' can be dismissed, the Calpurnian *compita pervia* remain.[127] Calpurnius does not unequivocally describe the *shrines* however, he could have used *compitum* here in the sense of 'crossroads'[128] and if indeed a shrine is intended, *pervia* could just indicate an association with the *location* of the shrine. Maybe it is best here, in the absence of conclusive archaeological and textual evidence, to dismiss the *pervia compita* as a category of cult places.

Indeed, from other literary evidence, it becomes clear that the discrepancy between the shrines attested in archaeology and texts need not be so problematic. In both inscriptions and texts it appears that a *compitum* could be called *sacellum*, a freestanding altar with an enclosure (*saeptum*)[129] or *aedicula*. An *aedicula* is literally a 'small temple' but can also designate other sacred structures, such as a chapel containing a statue.[130]

---

[123] Samter 1907, 369-371; cf. Laing 1921, 135; Böhm 1925, 808.

[124] Kissel 1990, 537, who also thinks (in n. 113) that *pertusa* is a conscious *imitatio* of the Calpurnian *pervia*. The interpretation in Holland 1937 is qualified as "*völlig verfehlt*": 538, n. 114.

[125] Kissel 1990, 537, n. 111, see n. 120 for text. The scholia on Persius are hard to date but the earliest manuscript dates to the 11th century; cf. Zetzel 2005.

[126] Cf. Harvey 1981, 116 (on lines 29-32), "The wretched picture contrasts with the traditional lavishness of the *Compitalia*."

[127] Calp. *Ecl.* 4.126.

[128] Cf. the translation by Amat 1991, 42: "*à la croisée des grands chemins*"; similarly Schröder 1991, 190.

[129] Cf. Gell. *NA* 7.12.5.

[130] Cf. Menichetti 2005.

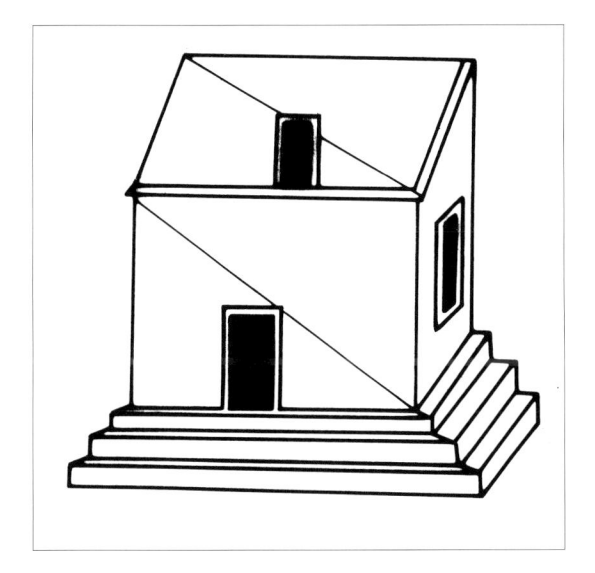

Fig. 9.7. Illustration of Dolabella's text in the Gudianus manuscript (adapted from Campbell 2000, 310 fig. 200).

The variety of architectural forms apparent from the archaeological evidence finds direct confirmation in the description of *compita* by Philargyrius on Vergil's *Georgics* 2.382: *compita ... sive is cum ara sive sine ara, sive sub tecto sive sub di(v)o sit*, 'be it with or without (permanent) altar, with or without roof.' It is this freedom in the choice of what structure or place to use to celebrate the *Compitalia* that I would like to stress here, for above all, both archaeological and literary sources suggest that the *compitum* shrine had no uniform architectural form. The physical appearance *did not matter* very much as long as the place could fulfil its ritual functions. This observation is important for the ensuing discussion.

The absence of compita in the countryside
From both the literary and the epigraphic evidence it has become clear that the *Compitalia* were also celebrated in the Italian countryside and that there were indeed *compitum* shrines.[131] However, none has been found across Italy.[132]

In one of the few studies on agricultural cults in the countryside, Claudia Lega notes this discrepancy between the literary sources mentioning various rural and agricultural cults and the lack of archaeological evidence.[133] In a situation like this, two options are usually put forward. The first is that archaeology has not yet provided, or is in general unable to provide, positive evidence for the rural or agricultural cults. The other is that the textual sources are wrong. Without doubt, the most logical conclusion in this case is to blame the poor state of archaeological knowledge or even its fundamental inability to furnish this evidence. Thus, according to Lega, these rites are just archaeologically invisible because probably "*si svolgessero su un altare provvisorio innalzato presso i campi e [che] le offerte fossero unicamente doni in natura. Questo spiegherebbe la perdita totale delle testimonianze archeologiche. Gli stessi compita, dove, come si è detto, gli abitanti delle zone agricole circostanti si recavano a celebrare la fine del raccolto, dovevano essere per la maggior parte strutture in materiale deperibile o piccole costruzioni andate completamente distrutte*" (added emphasis).[134]

It is indeed perfectly possible that the absence of archaeological evidence indicates that these cults did not leave traces. Maybe it is fairer to say that there might still be some archaeological remains, but that until now nothing has been found. That not even one rural *compitum* shrine has been found should then be explained as coincidental. Still, it is somewhat surprising that a rite that was apparently celebrated by the whole population of Roman Italy did not leave any material trace.

---

[131] Cf. *supra* esp. n. 76 for literary sources, *infra* for inscriptions.

[132] Rejecting the identification of a structure at Tor de' Cenci as a *compitum*, cf. *supra* n. 78.

[133] Lega 1995, 124.

[134] Lega 1995, 124. Cf. also Kissel 1990, 537, who thinks they were mostly made of wood.

Fig. 9.8. *Lar Compitalis* from the Lucanian sanctuary of Torre di Satriano (courtesy of the Archivio Fotografico della Scuola di Specializzazione in Archeologia di Matera).

This is odd, especially because inscriptions from Italy record elements that clearly do not belong to perishable constructions, apart from the rather explicit inscription mentioning *compitum ex saxo fecere*,[135] an inscription dated 1 BC from Verona mentions the rebuilding of a *compitum* with a *tectum*, *parietes*, *valvas* and *limen*.[136] An inscription from Picenum records the building of a *crepidinem circum cumpitum tectum pertextum*, a podium or sidewalk (*crepido*) around a *compitum* and the roof of the *compitum* from the end of the second century or the beginning of the first century BC.[137] From Beneventum comes an inscription recording the building of a *porticum cum apparatorio et compitum*.[138] At least the first two seem to suggest the form of a small temple. Although it is impossible to be sure about the urban or extra-urban location of these examples (perhaps the *compitum* from Picenum was extra-urban but this is uncertain, whereas the *compitum* from Beneventum was, because of its link with a *lustratio* of a *pagus*, certainly extra-urban), it shows at least that *compitum* shrines in different areas of Italy were not inferior to those in Rome as regards architectural elaboration. Just to put things in perspective, most 'normal' temples in Italy do not yield any, let alone more elaborate inscriptions than the ones just cited.

However, there may be another explanation that questions whether we are looking for the right model, or rather, for the right structures. The (literary) discussion on the scholion on Persius with its fascinating '*turres*' and multiple entrances and the consequent quest to retrieve this structure archaeologically may have attracted too much attention, without leaving room for other possibilities.

There is of course a danger in reasoning from silence, but we could ask ourselves what places were most eligible for the celebration of the *Compitalia* or, as Philargyrius states, the places *ubi pagani agrestes bucina convocati solent inire concilia*; the places 'where the rural population, called together by a horn, used to meet'.[139] Once one is not looking for a tower-like structure with multiple entrances, but accepts that virtually all known bigger *compitum* shrines bore close resemblance to, or simply were, small temples, another option comes into view. Although as yet no conclusive evidence can be presented, I would make

[135] *CIL* V, 844 from Aquileia. Kissel 1990 sees the stone construction conversely as a "*besonders hervorzuhebende Ausnahme*" (537), proving that normally they were not made of durable materials, but cf. the other inscriptions I mention here. The fact that diverse inscriptions mention a rebuilding of *compita* (537, n. 112) proves nothing, most temple complexes have been rebuilt but were not therefore previously made of perishable materials.

[136] *CIL* V, 3257.

[137] *CIL* I², 3078; Cancrini *et al*. 2001, 154-156.

[138] *CIL* IX, 1618.

[139] Phil. Verg. G. 2.382.

the cautious suggestion that the *Compitalia* could have been, in part, celebrated at the 'Italic' sanctuaries dispersed over the Italian countryside.

This type of sanctuary, often of modest dimensions, was the meeting place of old for the rural population. One could imagine that at least some of the pre-existing sanctuaries could have been adapted to serve this new purpose for the community, together with smaller altars or shrines of which virtually no trace has been left. It is also possible that new sanctuaries were erected; we should not exclude that some sanctuaries that have been regarded as 'Italic' are actually new constructions within the new Roman organisation of the landscape, as has been discussed in Chapter 7.

Perhaps strengthening the suggestion of re-use is the fact that in some 'Italic' temples evidence for a later *Lares*-cult has been found. In the Italic sanctuary at Torre di Satriano which flourished in the fourth to third centuries BC in Lucanian territory, a statuette of a *Lar* and the introduction of oil lamps in the sanctuary have been connected to a cult of the *Lares* in Roman times.[140] The oil lamps would be explained by the fact that the *Lares* cult was held *noctu*, as Festus states. The statuette, dated to the second or third quarter of the first century AD, indeed follows the iconography of a *Lar Compitalis*, dancing and with a *rhyton* in one hand, a *patera* in the other (fig. 9.8).[141] Suggestive in this regard is that also in many other 'Italic' sanctuaries oil lamps of especially the Roman period have been found.[142]

Also in Samnium proper, at the cult place of Pietracupa in the area of Castropignano, a small statuette of a *Lar Compitalis* has been found.[143] This cult place was in use at least from the fourth century BC onwards and presents all the characteristics of a typical Samnite sanctuary comparable to, for instance, that of S. Giovanni in Galdo, Colle Rimontato. It seems therefore plausible that this sanctuary assumed a new function in the Roman period.

Although archaeological research has tended to neglect the later phases of Italic sanctuaries (which are often overlooked or only summarily published), a very large number of these sanctuaries were also frequented in the Roman period. This has been seen in the present study in the case of S. Giovanni in Galdo, where a substantial Roman phase is documented (see Chapter 5). The character of this use in Roman times is however poorly understood. If the suggestion is right that the 'rural' *Compitalia* were celebrated here at least in some cases, this would constitute a tangible example of the ways in which the old cult places could assume new functions under changed social and political circumstances.[144] This could contribute to the complex discussion on continuity and change between pre-Roman and Roman times, for instance the shift to oil lamps in the Roman period attests to different cult practices, whereas continuity could be seen in the place of worship.

In the cases just mentioned there are no further indications for the possible *vicus* status of the communities visiting these sanctuaries in Roman times. Nevertheless, and although there is as yet no hard evidence, it seems to me quite plausible that especially cult places related to rural *vici* (such as those discussed in Chapter 7) were appropriate locations for (part of) the rituals associated with the rural *Compitalia*. In Chapter 8, it was shown that it is probable that the *Paganalia* were instigated together with

---

[140] S. De Vincenzo in: Osanna/Sica 2005, 452-457. *Lararia* have been found in the temple of Venus at Pompeii (wall paintings in the foundation rooms of the terraces). Cf. the contributions by Emmanuele Curti and Antonella Lepone on the "*giornata di studi sul tempio di Venere a Pompei*", D.A.I. Rom, 4-5-2006, which will be published.

[141] S. De Vincenzo in: Osanna/Sica 2005, 198-199, 452.

[142] E.g. as well at Campochiaro, *Campochiaro* 1982, 72-75, and at San Giovanni in Galdo, cf. Chapter 5. But this could of course, as the scale of the phenomenon may suggest, reflect a more general change in ritual or refer to other rites held *noctu*.

[143] Sardella 2008, 174.

[144] An inscription from Atina perhaps commemorating a dedication to the typical Italic goddess Mefitis and the *Lares* would be especially interesting as an illustration of the complexity of the processes at work: *CIL* X, 5048; Calisti 2006, 267.

the installation of *pagi*. Similarly, it could be suggested that the *Compitalia* were celebrated in the Roman rural *vici* in the Italian countryside. One could imagine how in this way a Roman rite served to define and enhance the small new 'Roman' *vicus* community, a situation which may not have been so different from that documented for Delos.

9.5 CONCLUSION: ROMAN INSTITUTIONS AND RITUAL IN THE ITALIAN COUNTRYSIDE

The *Compitalia* were the most important festival associated with the *vici*. Dionysius of Halicarnassus says that the festival was installed together with the *vici* in the regal period, as a means of administration and control of the urban population. It has often been regarded as a family or slave festival but actually involved all inhabitants of the *vicus*, and in the city of Rome the festival was announced by the *praetor*. This suggests a function that both exceeds and includes the private or personal sphere. The archaeological evidence supports this all-encapsulating characteristic of the festival, liturgical paintings and shrines related to the *Compitalia* are found in both domestic (houses) and public (temples on squares) contexts.

Evidence for the hypothesis that the *Compitalia* festival had agricultural or rural origins and was only later incorporated in or transferred to the city is meagre. Of course, it is possible that the Roman urban cult originated as a Roman agricultural ritual but this must then have occurred in a period beyond our vision. From the moment that we are able to recognise the *Compitalia* as such, its development seems to have taken the opposite direction, i.e. from the city of Rome outwards to other cities, and the countryside. The *Compitalia* seem indeed to be strongly associated with urban contexts, where they first appear in our record. Interestingly, their appearance is quite early and contemporary literary passages indicate that the *Compitalia* existed in Rome at least by the third century BC. The archaeological and epigraphic evidence, especially from Delos but also from Picenum, shows that it is possible to identify the *Compitalia* being celebrated at least by the second half of the second century BC outside Rome. It is well possible therefore that the *Compitalia* were disseminated along with Roman control, perhaps in accordance with the institution of the *vicus*. This reading is in some way in line with Dionysius' account.

In the urban centres of Rome, Pompeii, Ostia and Delos diverse *compita* (i.e. *compitum* shrines) have been identified. The literary evidence on the physical aspect of *compitum* shrines is equally diverse. Leaving out the discussion on the *compita pervia*, enigmatic buildings with multiple entrances probably based on a wrong understanding of Persius by his scholiast, it can be concluded from both archaeology and literary sources that almost every sacred structure would do for the celebration of the *Compitalia*. The more elaborate *compitum* shrines, such as those excavated in Rome and some attested epigraphically elsewhere, actually looked like small temples.

Despite the fact that the *Compitalia* were also clearly celebrated outside urban structures, *compitum* shrines have never been found in the countryside. It is possible that this is due to a lack of archaeological research or poor visibility, if it is assumed that these structures were constructed of perishable materials. However, there is evidence to suggest that some pre-existing 'Italic' sanctuaries served as the structures where the Roman festival of the *Compitalia* was celebrated. In particular, sanctuaries that epigraphically demonstrate an intimate link with one or more rural *vici* could be possible candidates, which would explain the references to the rural *Compitalia* and its Roman urban origin at the same time.

10 Conclusions

Cult places played a central role in the widespread political, social and cultural changes in central-southern Italy in the last four centuries BC. It has been seen that Italic sanctuaries were evoked by Roman historians as loci for resistance or ideological battle during the various wars resulting in the conquest of Italy. The Samnites swore secret oaths against Roman power and Rome summoned the tutelary deities of enemy cities. Once Italy was conquered, Roman attention shifted to other areas and we hear little or nothing about what happened subsequently to Italic sanctuaries and religion. The literary information we do have, from the early imperial period onwards, relates to a by then 'pacified' peninsula. In particular in the Augustan period, Italian countryside religion is represented as rustic, pure and timeless. But what happened in the period between the conquest and nostalgic romanticism?

The changing religious landscape of central-southern Italy in the crucial period of the last four centuries BC is poorly understood. What we do know is that monumental temples lay dotted over the scarcely urbanised Italic landscapes. They are the result of a frenetic building activity in the religious realm in the third and second centuries BC which is unparalleled by contemporaneous developments in civic or domestic architecture. The question of how sanctuaries and cults relate to changes in society following the Roman conquest has been central to this study. Previous studies on sanctuaries and their relationship to cultural and political developments have usually focused on the architecture and decoration of single sites. This is a useful approach in its own right but does not take into account the full scale of specific social and political contexts within which the cult places functioned in antiquity. In addition, the interpretation of cultural models and elements (in modern scholarship defined as e.g. 'Roman', 'Latial', 'Hellenistic') depends on the specific ideological climate present in the ancient communities that built them. When addressing questions on larger socio-political developments, the 'landscape', in the broadest sense of the word, surrounding a sanctuary is arguably more revealing than its physical appearance alone. A contextual approach has therefore been applied in this study in an attempt to understand better the interaction between sanctuaries and patterns of settlement and institutional structures. With this central aim of contextualisation, various methods including historiographical and epigraphic research as well as archaeological field research have been applied, thus yielding different perspectives. In this way, ideological, spatial, and institutional contexts have been tentatively reconstructed and I have tried to demonstrate how important these contexts are for our ideas about cult places and the society they were part of. In these concluding remarks I shall summarise the main results and try to draw together the threads of the preceding approaches and arguments.

ROME AND ITALY: IDEAS ON CULTURAL CHANGE AND RELIGIOUS ROMANISATION

The issue of sanctuaries and society in the Republican period is connected to the general debate on the character of Roman control and supremacy over Italy (Chapter 1). Related ideas on cultural change are usually studied under the heading of 'romanisation'. In the 19th century the idea took root that, from the third century BC onwards, Italy and Rome underwent a process of gradual cultural convergence under Roman guidance. Over time, Italic peoples would have increasingly assimilated themselves in language, customs and political institutions to Roman standards. This view relies to an extent on idealist and teleological notions, the historiographical roots of which have been traced by Henrik Mouritsen. The mechanism of cultural change which is usually presupposed in this 'idealist' approach is that of 'self-romanisation', according to which Italic peoples would have voluntarily adopted Roman culture out of a wish to become Roman. This concept has been challenged from the 1990s onwards in Anglo-Saxon studies, pointing out the complexity of the interpretation of 'Roman' material culture and the underlying frame of thought which takes the superiority of Roman culture for granted. Crucial points to learn from these critiques are that the adoption of Roman culture should not be seen as a self-evident natural process and that the meaning attributed to cultural elements by the ancient audience is not stable but depends on the overall context. At the same time however, this trend in studies inspired by postcolonial theory has often underestimated Roman impact and strategies and has tended to overemphasise 'native' agency. In general, different models of romanisation processes can be shown to have determined to a large extent the interpretation (and selection) of our dataset. In this light, I have in this study refrained from defining or adopting an overarching theoretical model of 'romanisation' at the outset and instead tried to investigate single historical cases in some detail. This bottom-up approach leaves room for the whole scale of possible developments currently available in models and theories, from resistance to emulation strategies.

The debate on Roman influence in the religious realm in Italy has different disciplinary backgrounds in mainland Europe's linguistic and religion studies (Chapter 2). In these traditions, 'Italic religion' and Roman religion have been studied either separately or as basically one and the same system. Studies into aspects of what has been called 'religious romanisation' are therefore relatively recent in date. One trend in the debate with strong parallels to the general romanisation discussion has put emphasis on the spread of Roman religious models in Italy such as *Capitolium*-temples and anatomical votive terracottas. This spread is conceived of in two ways, first as documenting 'Romans or Latins abroad' reproducing Roman religious models (especially in the case of colonial contexts). Second, these models would have been copied by the Italic allies, inspired by the 'superiority' of Roman religious culture. For instance, the spread in Italy of anatomical votives has been seen as a direct result of the pre-eminence of Roman culture and a similar case has been made for *Capitolium*-style temples. However, evidence for this spread of Roman religious models as a consequence of their 'superiority' is problematic. Recent studies have questioned the 'Roman' character of anatomical votives, and *Capitolia* are actually less well attested for the early phases of colonies than is often assumed. And although at least from the second century BC onwards *Capitolia* will – in Roman contexts – indeed have expressed allegiance to the Roman model, the significance of the adoption of the model outside Roman contexts is hard to establish and will have varied from place to place (cf. *infra*).

With regard to direct Roman intervention in religious affairs outside Roman territory, Rome is usually thought to have adopted a *laissez-faire* policy. The *senatusconsultum de Bacchanalibus* of 186 BC could be an exception to this rule if it extended to areas outside *ager Romanus*, which remains unclear. Be that as it may, the primary Roman concern seems to have been the possible political dimension of the cult organisation, not the cult itself. Direct Roman intervention has also been recognised in the destruction or closing down of other cult places. However, this aspect has been overemphasised in modern research and no coherent policy of the kind can be discerned in the Republican period.

According to conventional understanding, the real Roman impact would have consisted of an emphasis on urban development, rather than on countryside cult places. This shift of attention would have led to the gradual abandonment of the latter. In cases that non-urban cult places continued, they would have remained largely unaffected by Roman influence. Generally, non-urban cult places are thus seen as traditional elements of the Italian landscape, only remotely touched by historical developments. These considerations on romanisation and its religious dimensions formed the background to the subsequent chapters.

THE IDEOLOGICAL CONTEXT: MATERIAL CULTURE AND MEANING IN SAMNITE SANCTUARIES

The importance of the ideological context is shown in a case study on Samnite sanctuaries (Chapter 3). Here, the limits of an isolated architecture-oriented perspective are pointed out by demonstrating the problematic link between cultural models or elements and ideology.

At the sanctuary of Pietrabbondante, in the heartland of ancient Pentrian Samnium, a monumental temple-theatre complex, Temple B, was erected at the end of the second century BC. Modern scholars recognise Roman influence in the architectural model. The combination of theatre and temple would recall the *comitium-curia* scheme, whereas the three *cellae* of the temple would mimic the Capitoline model. However, at the time of the building of the complex there were growing tensions between Rome and the Samnites which would ultimately result in the Social War (91-88 BC). Weaponry and Oscan inscriptions found at the sanctuary demonstrate that it since long functioned as an important focus of Samnite military and political power. In particular, the explicit mention of *safinim* in an inscription found in the sanctuary, designating it as belonging to the ethnic group of the Samnites, is suggestive. The rich contextual evidence for the case of Pietrabbondante makes clear that in this period a common symbolic language was available to both Roman and Samnite communities, which could be used actively and creatively for different purposes. This symbolic language can be discerned clearly in coinage: a Samnite coin struck in the period of the Social War represents the Samnite bull goring the Roman she-wolf (Chapter 3, fig. 3.4). Arguably, architectural models were used in a similar way in antiquity, that is through active appropriation to fit local ends. 'Traditional' elements have been recognised in the ground plan of the sanctuary, which might recall the Livian description (10.38) of the *locus consaeptus* where Samnite elite soldiers swore their oath before the battle at Aquilonia in 293 BC. Whether this 'traditionalising' interpretation holds true or not, in any case a particular and original complex was constructed, which was moreover echoed in the contemporaneous smaller sanctuary of S. Giovanni in Galdo, Colle Rimontato.

In conclusion, although at Pietrabbondante elements that appear (to us moderns) as 'Latin' or 'Roman' were adopted, this cannot simply be interpreted as the acceptance of Roman rule or the wish to 'become Roman'. Rather, it can be seen as the choosing of 'building materials' for the construction of a Samnite Pentrian identity at the end of the second century BC. Despite the general reservations one could have about the facile adoption of similar terms, I think that in this case it is legitimate to speak of 'cultural resistance'. Yet it is important not to equate this with cultural continuity. Indeed, there *was* cultural change but without loss of local distinctiveness.

THE SPATIAL CONTEXT: THEORIES ON THE AUDIENCES OF SANCTUARIES

Knowledge of the socio-economic and political context within which sanctuaries came into being and functioned is crucial for their understanding. By studying the spatial setting and function of sanctuaries within larger socio-economic and political structures, the groups of people that saw and visited the cult places might be established. This is not only important for a better understanding of the general socio-political role of cult places, but also for the intended impact of the monumentalisation of cult places. In many discussions on architecture and meaning, such as the one in Chapter 3, the intended audience remains a moot point.

Previous research has put forward some general ideas on the role of sanctuaries in Italic society but explicit attempts to establish a relationship between sanctuaries and patterns of settlement or institutional structures are less numerous. I have distinguished three main approaches in the existing literature (Chapter 4). Firstly, transhumance economy has been linked to Italic sanctuaries of the Apennine and Samnite areas. Cult places would have been located as staging posts along the *tratturi* intersecting the Apennines, providing shelter for herdsmen and offering a safe place for trade. Wealth accumulated by transhumance would have been employed for the monumentalisation of the sanctuaries. The popularity of Hercules, as patron deity of herdsmen and trade, in the Apennine areas has been interpreted as evidence supporting this theory. However, the link between sanctuaries and *tratturi* is less clear than has been suggested and an association of the cult of Hercules with trade is actually best documented for urban contexts, not for rural Italic sanctuaries. Alternatively, Italic sanctuaries and their associated cults have been interpreted as boundary markers of ethnic groups. Since ethnic groups are by their very nature fluid and elusive, and supporting evidence is absent, this approach is impossible to test. The model of territorial shrines derives from Greek (and to a lesser extent Tyrrhenian) contexts, with presumably very different spatial and hierarchical structures. Without hard evidence, it is perhaps better not to apply this model to the inland Italic situation. A third model which does take into account the specific Italic context is the so-called *pagus-vicus* system. In this system, *pagi* (territorial districts) and villages (*vici*) would together make up the Italic *touto* or *nomen*. A related hierarchy of sanctuaries belonging to respectively *touto*, *pagi* and *vici* has been particularly popular in modern studies.

It is important to point out that all three models have virtually no evidential basis in archaeology or historical sources. In particular, the first two models rely heavily on preconceptions about Italic economy and spatial organisation. Arguably, the formation of these models has been influenced by the visual impression of the archaeological landscapes of central Italy, which until recently was basically one of 'emptiness'. Only the most visible remains, i.e. those of hill-forts and sanctuaries, have traditionally attracted attention, whereas minor and dispersed rural settlements are seriously underrepresented or simply absent in this image. At least to some degree, the apparent 'isolation' of monumental sanctuaries might have suggested that larger economic or political structures (transhumance; frontiers of ethnic tribes) determined the presence of sanctuaries. For the *pagus-vicus* system – in fact emphasising rural settlement – the discussion is different because its roots lie in modern interpretations of ancient literary traditions rather than in economic and geopolitical models.

THE SPATIAL CONTEXT: PROBLEM-ORIENTED FIELD SURVEY AROUND A SAMNITE SANCTUARY

Since evidence for the spatial context of Italic sanctuaries is mostly absent, and at the same time its influence on interpretation is significant, a research approach for dealing with this issue has been developed and tested on the Samnite sanctuary of S. Giovanni in Galdo, Colle Rimontato (Chapter 5). This small temple, monumentalised around the end of the second century BC and reflecting the ground plan of Temple B at Pietrabbondante, was until recently located in an 'empty' landscape as the settlement pattern in this area was almost completely unknown. The small temple had previously been interpreted in light of transhumance, or alternatively as part of a *pagus-vicus* system, but has above all been seen as a prime example of an isolated and rural Italic sanctuary.

Research has consisted of intensive off-site field survey in an area with a radius of ca. 1.5 km around the sanctuary. It has been combined with a study of the finds from the excavation of the sanctuary carried out by the *Soprintendenza per i Beni Archeologici del Molise* in the 1970s. The survey revealed a nucleated settlement pattern to the east of the sanctuary in the Iron Age. For the Hellenistic period, a particularly high density of sites in the area around the sanctuary has been documented, amongst which several farms and a burial area. Most importantly, at about 500 m from the temple, a major site which can be interpreted as a village was found. Inhabited from the Iron Age onwards, it was enlarged in the Hellenistic period, when it covered an area of at least 10 ha, and it continued well into the Roman period.

As for the sanctuary, the excavation finds as well as the survey data indicate that the beginnings of the cult place can be dated to the end of the fourth or early third century BC. Many finds dating to the imperial period document its use in this period. The complex of village, farms, burial area and sanctuary might reflect a rather 'complete' Samnite community already established in the early Hellenistic period.

This community formed the audience for a traditionalising yet fashionable monumental sanctuary that echoed the central political sanctuary at Pietrabbondante, constructed just before the Social War broke out. In the absence of epigraphic evidence, we can only speculate as to the identity of the initiators of the monumentalisation project. Whether it was 'state intervention' aimed at winning the hearts of the local population for the Samnite cause, or rather a local initiative, aimed at joining in with this development, remains a tantalising question. Even if the monumentalisation of the sanctuary may relate to larger societal structures or developments, the function of the cult place can be understood within the local community of farmers and villagers that the survey has revealed.

Moreover, the site density recorded in the field survey for the Hellenistic and Roman periods is considerable and attests to anything but an 'empty' landscape. This high density of sites in the research area must not reflect an overall high site density in this part of Samnium. Perhaps it can indeed be related to the presence of the cult place, as a comparison with a sanctuary recorded in the Biferno Valley survey, equally located within a dense pattern of settlement, could indicate. This suggests that these 'rural' sanctuaries were not located at the periphery but rather at the centre of society.

THE INSTITUTIONAL CONTEXT: SANCTUARIES AND THE SO-CALLED PAGUS-VICUS SYSTEM

The study of cult places within settlement organisation was followed by the analysis of a particularly popular model of Italic society, the *pagus-vicus* system. This term is traditionally used to indicate a pattern of settlement characterised by dispersed farms and villages. As conventional understanding has it, this would have been an ancient and specifically Italic system. Moreover, sanctuaries would have been directly related to the different hierarchical levels of *touto*, *pagus* and *vicus* that are discerned in this model. However, this view has proved to be fundamentally problematic. Recent studies in the legal and institutional realm by Luigi Capogrossi Colognesi and Michel Tarpin have attacked the basis of the system (Chapter 6). Rather than representing "*die uritalische Siedlungsform*",[1] the *pagus* was in all probability a Roman administrative division of the land. The opinions on the *vicus* are more diverse. Whereas Capogrossi Colognesi maintains that the *vicus* represents an ancient Italic reality, Tarpin has convincingly argued to the contrary. According to him, the *vicus* was a Roman legal or administrative category. In sum, *pagi* might be 'Roman' territorial divisions, and *vici* small 'Roman' villages – 'Roman' here meaning 'the result of Roman intervention'. Moreover, the presumed hierarchical relationship between *pagus* and *vicus* can be dismissed.

Because sanctuaries have generally been seen as functional elements within the *pagus-vicus* system, these reconsiderations significantly impact on ideas on Italic rural sanctuaries. In my view, the implications are twofold.

First, the general hierarchical view of Italic sanctuaries as functioning within the *pagus-vicus* system should be abandoned. As noted in chapter 4, in many cases this conclusion was reached in the absence of epigraphic documentation of *pagi* or *vici*. In these instances, this misinformed, and misleading, terminology can easily be replaced with less determinative terms such as 'dispersed settlement organisation' or 'village-farm pattern of settlement'. Of course, it is possible that Italic sanctuaries functioned on different levels within such a 'dispersed settlement organisation'. However, in the absence of explicit epigraphic

---

[1] Kornemann 1905, 83.

evidence, attempts to reconstruct possible hierarchical configurations should depart from archaeological or anthropological observations, rather than from preconceived views of Italic institutional structures. This would lead almost by definition to more general descriptive typological or functional hierarchies, such as those based on location analysis.

Second, for those sanctuaries which indeed can be related to *vici* or *pagi* (a relationship only recognisable by explicit epigraphic evidence), the consequences are more serious. These sanctuaries cannot be seen as part of a pre-Roman, Italic reality or a direct continuation thereof. On the contrary, they seem to have functioned within a new Roman institutional context. At least institutionally, we may therefore posit that such sanctuaries betray change, rather than continuity. In this way, the revision of *pagus* and *vicus* from an institutional perspective may also have significant implications for ideas on the cultural 'romanisation' of Italy. These implications have until now barely been discussed. Therefore, I explored aspects of these cultural implications in relation to sanctuaries and cults (Chapters 7 to 9). One of the crucial questions concerns the identity of the inhabitants of *pagi* and *vici*. The fact that the institutions they happened to be part of were the result of Roman intervention does not automatically imply that they were also 'Roman' in a cultural sense. I have argued that the available evidence nonetheless points to Roman or 'romanising' aspirations on the part of these specific rural communities. Significantly, this process is especially seen in the religious realm. In this way, the discussion on *pagi* and *vici* leads us to the recognition of, and explanation for, Roman religious influence in the countryside.

To this end, the epigraphic evidence for the involvement of *pagi* and *vici* in sanctuaries in Italy has been surveyed and four cases with the best contextual evidence have been examined in more detail (Chapter 7). The traditional assumption that *pagi* and *vici* were Italic, pre-Roman structures has to an extent determined the interpretation of the related cults and sanctuaries, indeed stressing their 'pre-Roman' or 'Italic' character. Upon closer examination however, for several cases the factual arguments turn out to be weak. Even if there would surely be no point in overstating the possible 'Roman' elements in reaction to the old paradigm, I believe there are striking aspects that suggest allegiance to Roman religious ideas and models.

For instance, the recently excavated sanctuary at Castel di Ieri in the central Apennines, dating to the end of the second century BC, was (re-)constructed *ex pagi decreto*. It presents strikingly romanising aspects, which I believe could well be explained by the involvement of this *pagus*. The cult place strongly resonates with the 'Capitoline' model, which may be understood as an expression of adherence to Roman ideologies by this *pagus* community.

A second case explores the connection of *pagi* and *vici* to Latin colonies. The possibility that extra-urban *vici* depended on colonial urban centres is examined. Although there is no conclusive evidence for the location of colonial *vici* outside the urban centre from the foundation of the colony onwards (but neither for the opposite argument, that they were exclusively urban), such extra-urban *vici* at least existed in later periods, and this might provide a point of departure for understanding non-urban aspects of mid-Republican colonisation. The strong relationship of *pagi*, *vici* and the colonial centre is documented in the Latin colony of Ariminum (Rimini), where black gloss vases with inscriptions mentioning *pagi* and *vici* have been found. Tentatively, I have reconstructed a ritual designed to enhance cohesion between the different communities belonging to the colony, both within and outside the city walls. Arguably, *pagi* and *vici* communities expressed allegiance to Rome by dedicating to the divine virtue of Fides in a cult place which also seems associated with other Roman gods.

The third case examines the *vici* and sanctuaries found in the *ager Praetutianus* on the Adriatic coast. *Vici* and related sanctuaries appear to be a relatively late phenomenon, from the second century BC onwards and thus postdating the Roman conquest. The differentiation between *vici stricto sensu* and other villages also allows revising the general picture of decline in the settlement evolution in this area.

The fourth case regards the *vici* documented along the Fucine Lake in Marsic territory. These *vici* are amongst the most complex and interesting ones because of their early date (third to second centuries

BC) and rich epigraphic evidence for cults. The *vici* and their cults have usually been interpreted as 'indigenous' Marsic elements. This argument cannot be supported but it would be equally incautious to regard them instead as entirely 'Roman' enclaves. Closer examination points to a more complex reality in which possibly both native people and foreigners functioned within a new Roman institution. It is argued that these 'new communities' were oriented on 'Roman' ideological models and constructed their own 'Romanness' by writing in Latin and, especially, venerating gods like Victoria and Valetudo, which were popular ideological concepts in this period in the city of Rome. The institutional embedding as well as the search for common ground among the inhabitants of these new communities can account for these processes, which perhaps also had an oppositional character with respect to the surrounding indigenous groups. In sum, in these institutionally Roman contexts of *pagus* and *vicus*, religion was central to the construction of community.

ROMAN RITUALS IN THE ITALIAN COUNTRYSIDE? THE PAGANALIA AND THE COMPITALIA

Pagus and *vicus* communities moreover celebrated their own festivals, respectively the *Paganalia* and the *Compitalia* (Chapters 8 and 9). The *pagus* features in early imperial poetry as the ideal rustic locale for religion. This rusticity evokes an ancient or 'immemorial' image and modern authors have accepted and perhaps even amplified this image. On closer analysis, however, the evidence for the most prominent religious aspect of the *pagus*, the festival of the *Paganalia*, reveals quite a different reality. An agricultural association is actually poorly attested and, for what it is worth, Dionysius of Halicarnassus (*Ant. Rom.* 4.14-15) plainly connects the festival to the taxation of the inhabitants of the *pagus*. On firmer ground, both epigraphy and literary sources document the *lustratio pagi*, a circumambulation by the inhabitants of the *pagus* around their territory. The possible impact of the installation of the Roman *pagi* in the Italian countryside comes into focus: the ritual act would have erased or 'overwritten' pre-existing divisions and boundaries from the landscape. At the same time, the 'new community' constituting the *pagus* ritually confirmed and legitimised its position and territory.

The festival of the *Compitalia* or 'crossroads festival' is best known from its association with the urban plebs and social unrest in late Republican Rome, leading to the suppression of the organising *collegia* and the restructuring of the festival under Augustus. The festival is usually thought to have originated as a rural cult of great antiquity ("*seit unvordenklicher Zeit*")[2] which was later incorporated in or transferred to the city, where it became the principal festival of the *vici* or urban quarters of Rome. There is clear evidence for the celebration of the *Compitalia* in the countryside but I have argued that the development of the festival was the other way around, spreading from Rome to the countryside. Evidence from Delos and Picenum suggests that this spread predated the Social War and was already underway in the second century BC. Like the *Paganalia*, the *Compitalia* had a strong integrative potential, defining the community of the *vicus* by performing communal rituals.

There is discussion on the cult places of the *Lares Compitales* in the countryside; the remains of *compitum* shrines have been found in, but never outside, urban contexts. Dismissing an erudite yet quite implausible tradition in modern research on the special appearance of rural *compitum* shrines (based on Dolabella L 302.1 and a scholion on Persius 4.28), I have suggested that ancient Italic sanctuaries were reused for the purpose. The presence of statuettes of *Lares Compitales* of the Roman period in some Italic cult places could support this idea. In that case, the ritual may have again contributed to the creation of a new reality and community of cult, yet under the guise of continuity.

---

[2] Wissowa 1897, 1872.

CONCLUSION

The arguments presented in this study have above all pointed out the importance of religion and cult places for the affirmation of different groups in central-southern Italy in the last centuries BC. This process was not limited to Italic groups but also applies to colonies and other new 'Roman' communities installed in the Italian landscape. In this last section, I would like to discuss this main conclusion within the framework of cultural change in Italy ('romanisation') and its more specific religious aspect ('religious romanisation').

As noted in Chapter 1, in the 'traditional' view of romanisation a linear and gradual development of cultural convergence is envisaged. Clearly, the evidence presented in this study tends to undermine any notion of a general and gradual development towards unity. Rather, it points at a competitive atmosphere which is moreover strongly geographically differentiated. To recognise differentiation in romanisation processes is of course not new but it is often thought of in *regional* terms. The recognition of the Roman institutions of *pagi* and *vici* could to some extent complicate this regional approach and suggests an even more pronounced and fragmented differentiation, especially for central Italy. As the *vici* at the Fucine lake seem to indicate, differentiation could be very *local* in nature. This means that generating a history of Italy in regional terms can lead to a biased picture in some cases. This effect of differentiation has been demonstrated for the *ager Praetutianus* when discussing settlement developments but it also applies to the area of the Marsi. Indeed, the Marsi are usually thought to have been 'precociously' romanised. However, once the evidence relating to the *vici* on the shores of the Fucine Lake is put aside, 'the Marsi' appear much less romanised. By increasing the analytical resolution, much sharper variation within regions, and indeed the existence of different communities, can come to light.

An important theme in this study regards the categories of rural and urban. An overly rigid distinction between the two has proved to be highly problematic. This is indicated by the intricate relationship between the two, which is also seen on a religious level, as has been argued for instance for Ariminum. Here, rural communities are ritually bound to the urban centre. Arguably, one of the most interesting outcomes is that Roman (religious) influence was not limited to towns, as is usually thought, but also applied to specific rural communities in the countryside, i.e. *pagi* and *vici*. This also provides a convenient and in my view much more persuasive explanation for the mechanisms through which Roman ideologies and culture could spread through Italy. This is especially interesting since the traditional models, presupposing a rather abstract 'irradiation' starting from Roman urban centres and/or simplistic or colonialist notions of emulation ('self-romanisation'), have recently been shown to be inadequate. Just the physical proximity of Roman and Italic people, no longer separated by an imaginary dichotomy between Roman–urban and native–non-urban societies, would make close cultural contact and reciprocal influence a much more likely scenario especially if indeed, as it seems, local people were also part of these new communities.

The 'traditional' view of a linear and gradual convergence is thus complicated by differentiation. However, the arguments put forward in this study do not comply with some important notions of the postcolonial critique of the traditional view either. The tendency to minimise Roman impact, often present in postcolonial studies, is not sustained by the arguments presented in this study. In my view, Roman influence was considerable in the processes under discussion. It has already been noted that Roman religious influence can be discerned in the countryside but more importantly, processes witnessed in 'Italic' contexts cannot be seen in isolation from Roman impact either.

Temple B at Pietrabbondante is a clear example. No intrinsic 'Roman' meaning can be attached to the cultural models adopted in this temple complex. However, this 'Samnite' phenomenon should not be disconnected from Roman impact altogether because the *necessity* to affirm Samnite sentiments was prompted by changes that were at least *to an extent* brought about by Roman dominion. To what extent is surely open to debate, but as the famous coin with the Samnite bull molesting the Roman she-wolf suggests, Rome was certainly on Samnite minds.

Dynamic processes of religious self-affirmation are documented for various 'Roman' and 'Italic' communities and a connection or interplay on some level may be assumed. In the second century BC evidence for religious expressions of communal pride abounds, for example in Samnium, and in Roman contexts *Capitolia* become prominent from the second century BC onwards. The first evidence for cults related to *pagi* and *vici* dates to the late third and second centuries BC. I do not suggest a direct relation or 'confrontational' interaction between these phenomena, although I would not exclude it either. Nonetheless, it appears that the expression of communal identities through religious aspects is especially important in this period and it is tempting to relate this to a general climate of change, competition, and search for new self-definitions.

The fundamental contribution by the revisionist critique inspired by postcolonial thought is the 'deconstruction' of metanarratives in historiography (Chapter 1). Revisionists have warned against writing history from hindsight. However, the deconstruction of traditional frameworks does not automatically imply that we should abandon also the 'traditional' recognition of Roman impact and influence; that would result in throwing away the proverbial baby with the bathwater. Yet, it is important to acknowledge that this undeniable Roman influence was never self-evident and we should continuously ask how and why cultural change occurred, and along which lines. Arguably, the 'deconstruction' of modern frameworks has cleared the way for the recognition of the role of 'construction' in antiquity.

Indeed, the key to understanding the processes under consideration seems to be the constructive character of communities. It is here that religion takes first place, in the establishment or redefining of new groups that were formed as a consequence of the Roman conquest. Throughout this study, the constructive aspect of the processes under way has been demonstrated. This is particularly seen in Samnium. If the Samnite temples were perhaps traditionalising in some senses, they were in no way immutable fossils of ancient times and fashionable models were adopted and remoulded in creative ways to fit specific contemporary needs. This phenomenon should therefore certainly not be seen as attesting 'continuity' or lingering traditions, but as a new construct designed for a specific moment in time. Cult places became the focus for the affirmation of a *new* community – even if this community tried to present itself as traditional as possible.

Interestingly, a similar process might be recognised in 'Roman' contexts. The 'Romanness' in the 'new communities' of *pagi* and *vici* was not inherent to the institutions themselves, rather it was consciously forged. The clearest example is the *vicus Supinum*, possibly made up, at least in part, by Marsic locals, who put their public dedication to *Victoria* in Latin. The relation between *pagi*, *vici* and urban centre that was symbolically affirmed by dedicating cups in the colony of Ariminum is another case. The rituals of the *Compitalia* and the *Paganalia*, with their explicit preoccupation with the defining of both territory and included community, also stress this point.

These conclusions on the constructive aspect of these cultural processes tap into ideas on continuity. The importance of the 'moment' and the relative unimportance of 'real' tradition has been stressed for the Samnite case. Another, more tangible argument in this direction regards the Roman phases of Italic sanctuaries. A chronological continuity in the archaeological material is often implicitly equated with continuity of practice. This is also connected to modern ideas on the persistence and immutable character of (especially countryside) religion and cult places, often betraying romantic notions. Although such a scenario of persisting traditions is possible, radical changes, both in ritual and the community involved, should not be excluded a priori either. As shown for the rituals and festivals connected to *pagi* and *vici*, notions of 'timelessness' and great antiquity are to a large extent based upon Augustan and later sources and should be critically regarded.

The constructive aspect of religion and religious rituals emphasised above should not be mistaken for liberty of action and choice. The character of the Roman religious influence which I have tentatively discerned in the Italian countryside, especially in the festivals of the *Compitalia* and the *Paganalia*, seems primarily defined as a consequence of administrative organisation, thus providing the framework within which specific religious practices are fitted. Arguably, it is precisely in this realm of administrative organisation that we might be able to recognise 'Roman religion' at work. The 'embeddedness' of religion in ancient society is well known, yet we should face the full scale of its consequences. It not only means that notions of proselytism are anachronistic (cf. Chapter 2), but also that 'religious toleration' had its limits within this same 'embeddedness'. Being part of a community, or administrative institution, plainly meant joining in its rituals and was probably not a matter of choice. Views of sanctuaries and cults as facultative and separate domains, primarily pertinent to personal religious experience, are more likely to reflect modern attitudes than ancient reality. Ultimately, these observations might again emphasise the importance of the ideological, spatial, and institutional contexts within which cult places functioned.

Abbreviations

Classical sources

Aen.	*Aeneid*
Agr.	*De agricultura*
Ant. Rom.	*Antiquitates Romanae*
Att.	*Epistulae ad Atticum*
Aug.	*Divus Augustus*
B Gall.	*Bellum Gallicum*
Cod. Justin.	*Codex Justinianus*
Curc.	*Curculio*
De civ. D.	*De civitate Dei*
Ecl.	*Eclogues*
Ep.	*Epistulae* (Pliny)
Epist.	*Epistulae* (Horace)
Fam.	*Epistulae ad familiares*
Fast.	*Fasti*
G.	*Georgics*
HN	*Naturalis historia*
Leg. agr.	*De lege agraria*
Leg.	*De legibus*
Ling.	*De lingua latina*
NA	*Noctes Atticae*
Num.	*Numa*
Off.	*De officiis*
Pall.	*De Pallio*
Pis.	*In Pisonem*
Pun.	*Punica*
Rust.	*De re rustica*
Sat.	*Saturnalia* (Macrobius)
Sat.	*Satirae* (Horace)
Sat. Men.	*Saturae Menippeae*
Tib.	*Tiberius*

Journals, series and reference works

AdI	*Annali dell'Istituto di Corrispondenza Archeologica*
AE	*Année Epigraphique*
AJA	*American Journal of Archaeology*
AncSoc	*Ancient Society*
AnnPerugia	*Annali della Facoltà di lettere e filosofia, Università degli Studi di Perugia. Studi Classici*
AnnPisa	*Annali della Scuola normale superiore di Pisa*

ANRW	*Aufstieg und Niedergang der römischen Welt*
AntCl	*L'Antiquité classique*
ArchCl	*Archeologia Classica*
ArchRel	*Archiv für Religionswissenschaft*
BA	*Bollettino di archeologia*
BAR Brit. Ser.	British Archaeological Reports, British Series
BAR Int. Ser.	British Archaeological Reports, International Series
BCH	*Bulletin de correspondance hellénique*
BCom	*Bullettino della Commissione archeologica comunale di Roma*
BEFAR	Bibliothèque des Écoles Françaises d'Athènes et de Rome
BStorArt	*Bollettino della Unione storia ed arte*
BullArchNap	*Bullettino archeologico napolitano*
CAH	*Cambridge Ancient History*
CahGlotz	*Cahiers du Centre Gustav-Glotz*
CEFR	Collection de l'École française de Rome
CIL	*Corpus Inscriptionum Latinarum*
ClMediaev	*Classica et mediaevalia*
ClPhil	*Classical Philology*
ClR	*The Classical Review*
CRAI	*Comptes rendus des séances de l'Académie des Inscriptions et Belles-Lettres*
CuadPrehistA	*Cuadernos de Prehistoria y Arqueología de la Universidad autónoma de Madrid*
Dar.-Sag.	Daremberg, C./E.Saglio, 1873-1914: *Dictionnaire des antiquités grecques et romaines d'après les textes et les monuments*, Paris.
Dessau, ILS	Dessau, H., 1892-1916: *Inscriptiones Latinae Selectae*, Berlin.
DialA	*Dialoghi di archeologia*
EAA	*Enciclopedia dell'arte antica classica e orientale*
FGrH	Jacoby, F., 1926-1957: Die Fragmente der griechischen Historiker, Berlin.
GaR	*Greece and Rome*
HarvStClPhil	*Harvard Studies in Classical Philology*
ILER	*Inscripciones latinas de la España romana*
ILLRP	*Inscriptiones Latinae liberae rei publicae*
InscrIt	*Inscriptiones Italiae*
JdI	*Jahrbuch des deutschen archäologischen Instituts*
JRA	*Journal of Roman Archaeology*
JRS	*Journal of Roman Studies*
LCL	Loeb Classical Library
LTUR	*Lexicon Topographicum Urbis Romae*
MEFRA	*Mélanges de l'Ecole française de Rome, Antiquité*
MemAccLinc	*Atti dell'Accademia nazionale dei Lincei. Classe di scienze morali, storiche e filologiche, Memorie*
MemPontAcc	*Atti della Pontificia accademia romana di archeologia, Memorie*
MonAnt	*Monumenti Antichi*
MünstBeitr	*Münstersche Beiträge zur antiken Handelsgeschichte*
NSc	*Notizie degli scavi di antichità*
OCT	Oxford Classical Texts
OLD	Oxford Latin Dictionary
PBSR	*Papers of the British School at Rome*
Pocc.	Poccetti, P., 1979: *Nuovi documenti italici*, Pisa.

PP	*La parola del passato*
ProcCambrPhilSoc	*Proceedings of the Cambridge Philological Society*
QuadChieti	*Quaderni dell'Istituto di archeologia e storia antica, Università di Chieti*
QuadTopAnt	*Quaderni dell'Istituto di topografia antica dell'Università di Roma*
RCulClMedioev	*Rivista di cultura classica e medioevale*
RE	*Paulys Realencyclopädie der classischen Altertumswissenschaft*
REA	*Revue des études anciennes*
REL	*Revue des études latines*
RendPontAc	*Atti della Pontificia accademia romana di archeologia, Rendiconti*
RhM	*Rheinisches Museum für Philologie*
RIC	*The Roman Imperial Coinage*
RM	*Mitteilungen des deutschen archäologischen Instituts, römische Abteilung*
RNum	*Revue numismatique*
Roscher, ML	Roscher, W.H., 1897-1902: *Ausführliches Lexikon der griechischen und römischen Mythologie*, Leipzig.
RRC	*Roman Republican Coinage*
RStPomp	*Rivista di Studi Pompeiani*
Sa.	Samnite inscriptions in Rix, H., 2002: *Sabellische Texte. Die Texte des Oskischen, Umbrischen und Südpikenischen*, Heidelberg (Handbuch der italischen Dialekte 5).
ScAnt	*Scienze dell'Antichità*
StAnt	*Studi di Antichità*
StClOr	*Studi classici e orientali*
StEtr	*Studi etruschi*
StMatStorRel	*Studi e materiali di storia delle religioni*
StRomagn	*Studi Romagnoli*
Suppl.It.	*Supplementa Italica*
ThesCRA	*Thesaurus Cultus et Rituum Antiquorum*
TMA	*Tijdschrift voor Mediterrane Archeologie*
TransactAmPhilAss	*Transactions of the American Philological Association*
Ve.	Vetter, E., 1953: *Handbuch der italischen Dialekte*, Heidelberg.
VisRel	*Visible Religion*
WorldA	*World Archaeology*
WürzbJb	*Würzburger Jahrbücher für die Altertumswissenschaft*

Bibliography

Classical Sources

Augustinus, *De civitate Dei*, libri 4-7, ed. W.M. Green, 1963, London/Cambridge Mass. (LCL 412).
Asconius, *Orationum Ciceronis quinque enarratio*, ed. A.C. Clark, 1907, London.
Ausonius, *De feriis Romanis*, ed. H.G. Evelyn-White, 1968, London/Cambridge Mass. (LCL 96).
Caesar, *De bello Gallico*, ed. H.J. Edwards, 1970, London/Cambridge Mass. (LCL 72).
Calpurnius Siculus, *Eclogae*, ed. D. Korzeniewski, 1971, Darmstadt (Texte zur Forschung 1).
Cato, *De agricultura*, ed. R. Goujard, 1975, Paris (Collection Budé).
Cicero, *De lege agraria*, ed. J.H. Freese, 1967, London/Cambridge Mass. (LCL 240).
Cicero, *De legibus*, ed. C. Walker Keyes, 1970, London/Cambridge Mass. (LCL 213).
Cicero, *De officiis*, ed. W. Miller, 1968, London/Cambridge Mass. (LCL 30).
Cicero, *Epistulae ad Atticum*, ed. D.R. Shackleton Bailey (4 vols), 1999, London/Cambridge Mass. (LCL 7, 8, 97, 491).
Cicero, *Epistulae ad familiares*, ed. D.R. Shackleton Bailey (3 vols), 2001, London/Cambridge Mass. (LCL 205, 216, 230).
Cicero, *In Pisonem*, ed. N.H. Watts, 1972, London/Cambridge Mass. (LCL 252).
Diodorus Siculus, *Bibliotheca historica*, libri 19.66-20, ed. R.M. Geer, 1954, London/Cambridge Mass. (LCL 390).
Dionysius of Halicarnassus, *Antiquitates Romanae*, ed. E. Carey (7 vols), 1937-1950, London/Cambridge Mass. (LCL 319, 347, 357, 364, 372, 378, 388).
Dolabella, ed. F. Blume/K. Lachmann, A. Rudorf (2 vols), 1848-1852, Berlin.
Festus, *De verborum significatu*, ed. W.M. Lindsay, 1913, Leipzig (Bibliotheca scriptorum graecorum et romanorum teubneriana).
Gellius, *Noctes Atticae*, ed. J.C. Rolfe (3 vols), 1927-1928, London/Cambridge Mass. (LCL 195, 200, 212).
Horatius, *Carmina*, ed. N. Rudd, 2004, London/Cambridge Mass. (LCL 33).
Horatius, *Satirae, Epistulae*, ed. H. Rushton Fairclough, 1929, London/Cambridge Mass. (LCL 194).
Juvenalis, *Satirae*, ed. J.D. Duff, 1925, Cambridge.
Livius, *Ab urbe condita*, libri 1-10, ed. B.O. Foster (4 vols), 1919-1926, London/Cambridge Mass. (LCL 114, 133, 172, 191).
Livius, *Ab urbe condita*, libri 26-30, ed. F.G. Moore (2 vols), 1949-1950, London/Cambridge Mass. (LCL 367, 381).
Livius, *Ab urbe condita*, libri 31-42, ed. E.T. Sage (4 vols), 1949-1950, London/Cambridge Mass. (LCL 295, 301, 313, 332).
Lucilius, ed. E.H. Warmington, 1938, London (LCL 329).
Macrobius, *Saturnalia*, ed. P.V. Davies 1969, New York (Records of civilization. Sources and studies 79).
Ovidius, *Fasti*, ed. J.G. Frazer/G.P. Goold, 1989, London/Cambridge Mass. (LCL 253).
Ovidius, *Heroides. Amores*, ed. G. Showerman/G.P. Goold, 1977, London/Cambridge Mass. (LCL 41).
Persius, *Saturae*, ed. S.M. Braund, 2004, London/Cambridge Mass. (LCL 91).
Plautus, *Curculio*, ed. P. Nixon, 1918, London/Cambridge Mass. (LCL 61).
Plinius, *Epistulae*, ed. B. Radice (2 vols), 1968, London/Cambridge Mass. (LCL 55, 59).
Plinius, *Naturalis historia*, libri 3-19, ed. H. Rackham (4 vols), 1942-1950, London/Cambridge Mass. (LCL 352, 353, 370, 371).

Plinius, *Naturalis historia*, libri 36-37, ed. D.E. Eichholz, 1962, London/Cambridge Mass. (LCL 419).

Plutarchus, *Vitae*, ed. B. Perrin, 1958, London/Cambridge Mass. (LCL 46).

Polybius, *The histories*, libri 1-8, ed. W.R. Paton (3 vols), 1922-1923, London/Cambridge Mass. (LCL 128, 137, 138).

Propertius, *Elegiae*, ed. G.P. Goold, 1990, London/Cambridge Mass. (LCL 18).

Silius Italicus, *Punica*, libri 9-17, ed. J.D. Duff, 1934, London/Cambridge Mass. (LCL 278).

Strabo, *Geographica*, ed. H.L. Jones (8 vols), 1917-1949, London/Cambridge Mass. (LCL 49, 50, 182, 211, 223, 196, 241, 267).

Suetonius, *Vitae Caesarum*, ed. J.C. Rolfe, 1960, London/Cambridge Mass. (LCL 31).

Tertullianus, *De Pallio*, ed. M. Turcan, 2007, Paris.

Tibullus, *Carmina*, ed. F.W. Cornish/J.P. Postgate/J.W. Mackail/G.P. Goold, 1988, London/Cambridge Mass. (LCL 6).

Valerius Maximus, libri 6-9, ed. D.R. Shackleton Bailey, 2000, London/Cambridge Mass. (LCL 493).

Varro, *De lingua latina*, ed. R.G. Kent (2 vols), 1958, London/Cambridge Mass. (LCL 333, 334).

Varro, *De re rustica*, ed. W.D. Hooper/H.B. Ash, 1967, London/Cambridge Mass. (LCL 283).

Varro, *Saturae Menippeae*, ed. F. Buecheler, 1963, Berlin.

Velleius Paterculus, *Historia Romana*, ed. F.W. Shipley, 1924, London/Cambridge Mass. (LCL 152).

Vergilius, *Aeneis*, ed. H. Rushton Fairclough/G.P. Goold, (2 vols), 1999-2000, London/Cambridge Mass. (LCL 63, 64).

Vergilius, *Eclogae, Georgica*, ed. H. Rushton Fairclough/G.P. Goold, 1999, London/Cambridge Mass. (LCL 63).

Modern sources

Aberson, M., 1994: *Temples votifs et butin de guerre dans la Rome republicaine*, Rome (Bibliotheca Helvetica Romana 26).

Adamik, T., 2003: Temple regulations from Furfo (CIL I^2 756), in H. Solin/M. Leiwo/H. Halla-aho (eds), *Latin vulgaire, latin tardif VI. Actes du VIe Colloque international sur le latin vulgaire et tardif, Helsinki, 29 août-2 septembre 2000*, Hildesheim/Zürich/New-York, 77-82.

Adams, J.N., 2002: Bilingualism at Delos, in J.N. Adams/M. Janse/S. Swain (eds), *Bilingualism in Ancient Society. Language Contact and the Written Word*, Oxford, 103-127.

Adams, J.N., 2003: *Bilingualism and the Latin language*, Cambridge.

Adams, J.N., 2007: *The regional diversification of Latin 200 BC - AD 600*, Cambridge.

Alcock, S.E., 1993: *Graecia capta. The landscapes of Roman Greece*, Cambridge.

Alcock, S.E./R. Osborne (eds), 1994: *Placing the gods. Sanctuaries and sacred space in ancient Greece*, Oxford/New York.

Alcock, S.E./R. Osborne (eds), 2007: *Classical Archaeology*, Malden (Blackwell studies in global archaeology 10).

Alföldi, A., 1973: *Die zwei Lorbeerbäume des Augustus*, Bonn (Antiquitas. Abhandlungen zur Vor- und Frühgeschichte, zur klassischen und provinzial-römischen Archäologie und zur Geschichte des Altertums 14).

Almagro Gorbea, M., 1982: *El santuario de Juno en Gabii*, Roma (Bibliotheca Italica. Monografías de la Escuela de Historia y Arqueologá en Roma 17).

Amat, J., 1991: *Bucoliques. Calpurnius Siculus. Éloge de Pison / Pseudo-Calpurnius*, Paris (Collection des universités de France).

Ampolo, C., 1993: Boschi sacri e culti federali. L'esempio del Lazio, in O. De Cazanove/J. Scheid (eds), *Les bois sacrés. Actes du colloque international, Naples 23 - 25 novembre 1989*, Naples (Collection du Centre Jean Bérard 10), 159-167.

Ando, C., 2007: Exporting Roman religion, in J. Rüpke (ed.), *A companion to Roman religion*, Malden (Blackwell companions to the Ancient World), 429-445.

Aronen, J., 1995: s.v. Fides, templum, in E. M. Steinby (ed.), *LTUR*, Roma, 252.

Badian, E., 1958: *Foreign clientelae (264-70 B.C.)*, Oxford.

Bailey, C., 1932: *Phases in the religion of ancient Rome*, Berkeley.

Bakker, J.Th., 1994: *Living and working with the gods. Studies of evidence for private religion and its material environment in Ostia (100 B.C. -500 A.D.)*, Amsterdam.

Barbanera, M., 1998: *L'archeologia degli Italiani. Storia, metodi e orientamenti dell'archeologia classica in Italia*, Roma (Nuova biblioteca di cultura).

Barker, G., 1989: Animals, ritual and power in ancient Samnium, in P. Meniel (ed.), Animal et pratiques religieuses. Les manifestations matérielles. Actes du colloque international de Compiègne, 11-13 novembre 1988, Paris (Anthropozoologica. Numéro spécial 3), 111-117.

Barker, G., 1995: *A Mediterranean valley. Landscape archaeology and Annales history in the Biferno Valley*, London/New York.

Barker, G./J. Lloyd (eds), 1991: *Roman landscapes. Archaeological survey in the Mediterranean region*, London (Archaeological monographs of the British School at Rome 2).

Barth, F., 1969: *Ethnic groups and boundaries. The social organization of cultural difference*, London.

Barton, I.M., 1982: Capitoline temples in Italy and the provinces (especially Africa), in *ANRW*, II, 12, 1, Berlin, 259-333.

Basanoff, V., 1945: *Evocatio*, Paris.

Baudy, D., 1998: *Römische Umgangsriten. Eine ethologische Untersuchung der Funktion von Wiederholung für religiöses Verhalten*, Berlin/New York Religionsgeschichtliche Versuche und Vorarbeiten 43).

Beard, M./J. North/S. Price, 1998: *Religions of Rome*, Cambridge.

Bedini, A., 1990: Un compitum di origine protostorica a Tor de' Cenci, *Archeologia laziale* 10, 121-133.

Beloch, K.J., 1926: *Römische Geschichte bis zum Beginn der punischen Kriege*, Berlin/Leipzig.

Bénabou, M., 1976: *La résistance africaine à la romanisation*, Paris (Textes à l'appui).

Benassai, R., 2004: S. Prisco la necropoli Capuana di IV e III sec. a. C., in L. Quilici/S. Quilici Gigli (eds), *Carta archeologica e ricerche in Campania, 2. Comuni di Brezza, Capua, San Prisco*, Roma (Atlante tematico di topografia antica 15, 2), 73-229.

Bendlin, A., 2000: Looking beyond the civic compromise. Religious pluralism in late Republican Rome, in E. Bispham/C. Smith (eds), *Religion in archaic and republican Rome and Italy. Evidence and experience*, Edinburgh, 115-135.

Bernard, H., 1908: *Le sénatus consulte des Baccanales*, Paris.

Bernardini, P., 1986: *Museo Nazionale Romano. Le ceramiche, la ceramica a vernice nera del Tevere*, Roma.

Bert Lott, J., 2004: *The neighborhoods of Augustan Rome*, Cambridge.

Bezerra de Meneses, U./H. Sarian, 1973: Nouvelles peintures liturgiques de Délos, in *Etudes déliennes publiées à l'occasion du centième anniversaire du début des fouilles de l'Ecole française d'Athènes à Délos*, Athènes (BCH Supplément 1), 77-109.

Bianchi, U., 1950: Disegno storico del culto capitolino nell'Italia romana e nelle provincie dell'Impero, *MemAccLinc* 2, 349-415.

Bispham, E., 2000a: Introduction, in E. Bispham/C. Smith (eds), *Religion in archaic and republican Rome and Italy. Evidence and experience*, Edinburgh, 1-18.

Bispham, E., 2000b: Mimic? A case study in early Roman colonisation, in E. Herring/K. Lomas (eds), *The emergence of state identities in Italy in the first millennium BC*, London (Accordia specialist studies on Italy 8), 157-186.

Bispham, E., 2006: *Coloniam Deducere*. How Roman was Roman Colonization during the Middle Republic?, in G. J. Bradley/J.-P. Wilson (eds), *Greek and Roman Colonisation. Origins, Ideologies and Interactions*, Swansea, 73-160.

Bispham, E., 2007: *From Asculum to Actium. The Municipalization of Italy from the Social War to Augustus*, Oxford (Oxford classical monographs).

Blomart, A., 1997: Die "evocatio" und der Transfer fremder Götter von der Peripherie nach Rom, in H. Cancik/J. Rüpke (eds), *Römische Reichsreligion und Provinzialreligion*, Tübingen, 99-111.

Böhm, F., 1925: s.v. Lares, *RE* XXII, 806-833.

Böhm, F., 1927: s.v. Lustratio, *RE* XIII, 2029-2039.

Bömer, F., 1957: *Untersuchungen über die Religion der Sklaven in Griechenland und Rom*, Mainz/Wiesbaden (Abhandlungen der Geistes- und Sozialwissenschaftlichen Klasse. Akademie der Wissenschaften und der Literatur).

Bonifacio, R., 2000: Il santuario sannitico di Casalbore e il suo materiale votivo, in *Studi sull'Italia dei Sanniti*, Milano, 33-35.

Bottini, A., 1994: Culti e religiosità degli Italici, in P. G. Guzzo/S. Moscati/G. Susini (eds), *Antiche genti d'Italia. Rimini 20 marzo - 28 agosto 1994*, Roma, 77-81.

Braccesi, L., 2006: In margine ai *pocola*. Una nuova testimonianza, 2, in *Ariminum. Storia e archeologia*, Roma (Adrias 2), 47-50.

Bradley, G.J., 1997: Archaic sanctuaries in Umbria, *CahGlotz* 8, 111-129.

Bradley, G.J., 2000: *Ancient Umbria. State, culture, and identity in central Italy from the Iron Age to the Augustan era*, Oxford.

Bradley, G.J., 2002: The Romanisation of Italy [Long review of Mouritsen 1998], *JRA* 15, 401-406.

Bradley, G.J., 2005: Aspects of the cult of Hercules in Central Italy in L. Rawlings/H. Bowden (eds), *Herakles and Hercules. Exploring a Graeco-Roman divinity*, Swansea, 129-151.

Bradley, G.J., 2006: Colonization and identity in Republican Italy, in G. J. Bradley/J.-P. Wilson (eds), *Greek and Roman Colonisation. Origins, Ideologies and Interactions*, Swansea, 161-187.

Bradley, G.J., 2007: Romanization. The end of the peoples of Italy?, in G. J. Bradley/E. Isayev/C. Riva (eds), *Ancient Italy. Regions without Boundaries*, Exeter, 295-322.

Bradley, G.J./J.-P. Wilson (eds), 2006: *Greek and Roman Colonisation. Origins, Ideologies and Interactions*, Swansea.

Briquel, D., 2003: Le « Fanum Voltumnae ». Remarques sur le culte fédéral des cités étrusques, in A. Motte/C. M. Ternes (eds), *Dieux, fêtes, sacré dans la Grèce et la Rome antiques. Actes du colloque tenu à Luxembourg du 24 au 26 octobre 1999*, Turnhout (Homo Religiosus, Série II, 2), 133-159.

Briscoe, J., 2003: A. Postumius Albinus, Polybius and Livy's account of the Bacchanalia, in *Hommages à Carl Deroux, 4. Archéologie et histoire de l'art. Religion*, Bruxelles (Collection Latomus 277), 302-308.

Briscoe, J., 2008: *A commentary on Livy. Books 38-40*, Oxford.

Brown, F.E., 1980: *Cosa. The making of a Roman town*, Ann Arbor (Jerome lectures 13).

Brown, F.E./E.H. Richardson/L. Richardon Jr., 1960: *Cosa II. the temples of the Arx*, Rome (Memoirs of the American Academy in Rome 26).

Brown, M.F., 1996: On resisting resistance, *American Anthropologist* 98, 729-735.

Bruneau, P., 1970: *Recherches sur les cultes de Délos à l'époque hellénistique et à l'époque impériale*, Paris (BEFAR 217).

Brunt, P.A., 1965: Italian aims at the time of the Social War, *JRS* 55, 90-109.

Brunt, P.A., 1971: *Italian manpower 225 B.C.-A.D. 14*, London.

Brusin, J.B., 1991: *Inscriptiones Aquileiae I*, Udine.

Bulard, M., 1926a: *Description des revêtements peints à sujets religieux*, Paris (Exploration archéologique de Délos 9).

Bulard, M., 1926b: *La religion domestique dans la colonie italienne de Délos d'après les peintures murales et les autels historiés*, Paris (BEFAR 131).

Buonocore, M., 1990: Riflessioni sul processo di municipalizzazione di Superaequum, *Bullettino della Deputazione abruzzese di storia patria* 80, 51-56.

Buonocore, M., 1993: Problemi di amministrazione paganico-vicana nell'Italia repubblicana del I secolo a.C., in A. Calbi/A. Donati/G. Poma (eds), *L'epigrafia del villaggio. Atti del Colloquio Borghesi, Forlì 27-30 settembre 1990*, Faenza (Epigrafia e antichità 12), 49-59.

Buonocore, M., 2002: Roma e l'Italia centrale dopo la guerra sociale. Amministrazione, territorio e comunità, in M. Buonocore (ed.), *L'Abruzzo e il Molise in età romana tra storia ed epigrafia*, L'Aquila (Studi e testi. Deputazione abruzzese di storia patria 21), 29-45.

Buonocore, M., 2003: La tribù predominante fra i cittadini di *Trebula Mutuesca*, *Epigraphica* 65, 47-61.

Buonocore, M., 2004: Novità epigrafiche dall'Abruzzo, in M. G. Angeli Bertinelli/A. Donati (eds), *Epigrafia di confine. Confine dell'epigrafia*, Faenza (Epigrafia e antichità 21), 281-320.

Burgers, G.J., 1998: *Constructing Messapian Landscapes. Settlement Dynamics, Social Organization and Culture Contact in the Margins of Graeco-Roman Italy*, Amsterdam (Dutch monographs on ancient history and archaeology 18).

Burgers, G.J., 2002: The aims of the RPC project, in P. Attema/G. J. Burgers/E. v. Joolen 5, *New developments in Italian landscape archaeology. Theory and methodology of field survey, land evaluation and landscape perception. Pottery production and distribution. Proceedings of a three-day conference held at the University of Groningen, April 13-15, 2000*, Oxford (BAR Int. Ser. 1091), 7-12.

Burgers, G.J./P. Attema/M. van Leusen, 1998: Walking the Murge. Interim report of the Ostuni field survey (Apulia, southern Italy), *StAnt* 11, 257-282.

Burgers, G.J./J.P. Crielaard, 2007: Greek colonists and indigenous populations at L'Amastuola, southern Italy, *BABESCH* 82, 77-114.

Burnett, A., 1998: The coinage of the Social War, in U. Wartenberg/R. Witschonke (eds), *Coins of Macedonia and Rome. Essays in honour of Charles Hersh*, London, 165-172.

Cagiano De Azevedo, M., 1940: I "Capitolia" dell'impero romano, *MemPontAcc* 1-76.

Caliò, L.M., 2003: La scuola architettonica di Rodi e l'ellenismo italico, in L. Quilici/S. Quilici Gigli (eds), *Santuari e luoghi di culto nell'Italia antica*, Roma (Atlante tematico di topografia antica 12), 53-74.

Calisti, F., 2006: *Mefitis. Dalle madri alla madre. Un tema religioso italico e la sua interpretazione romana e cristiana*, Roma.

Campana, A., 1987: *La monetazione degli insorti italici durante la guerra sociale (91-87 a.C.)*, Soliera.

Campanelli, A., 1991: Il santuario italico-romano di Lecce dei Marsi, in *Il Fucino e le aree limitrofe nell'antichità (Avezzano 10-11 novembre 1989)*, Roma, 325-330.

Campanelli, A., 2004: Il tempio italico, in A. Campanelli (ed.), *Il tempio italico di Castel di Ieri. Architettura e religione dell'antica area superaequana*, Raiano (AQ), 15-31.

Campanelli, A./A. Faustoferri (eds), 1997: *I luoghi degli dei. Sacro e natura nell'Abruzzo italico. Mostra Chieti 16 maggio - 18 agosto 1997*, Pescara.

Campanile, E., 1991: Note sulle divinità degli Italici meridionali e centrali, *StClOr* 41, 279-297.

Campanile, E., 1995: L'iscrizione Vetter 196 e una ipotesi sulla genesi del meddicato duplice a Messina, *Athenaeum* 83, 463-462.

Campbell, J.B., 2000: *The writings of the Roman land surveyors. Introduction, text, translation and commentary*, London (JRS Monograph 9).

Campochiaro 1982: *Campochiaro. Potenzialità di intervento sui beni culturali*, Matrice.

Cancik-Lindemaier, H., 1996: Der Diskurs Religion im Senatsbeschluss über die Bacchanalia von 186 v.Chr. und bei Livius (Buch XXXIX), in H. Cancik (ed.), *Geschichte, Tradition, Reflexion, 2. Griechische und römische Religion. Festschrift für Martin Hengel zum 70. Geburtstag*, Tübingen, 77-96.

Cancik, H., 1985-1986: Rome as Sacred Landscape. Varro and the End of Republican Religion in Rome, *VisRel* 4-5, 250-265.

Cancik, H., 2008: Römische Religion. Eine Skizze, in H. Cancik-Lindemaier (ed.), *Römische Religion im Kontext. Kulturelle Bedingungen religiöser Diskurse*, Tübingen (Gesammelte Aufsätze 1), 3-61.

Cancrini, F./C. Delplace/S.M. Marengo, 2001: *L'evergetismo nella regio V (Picenum)*, Tivoli (Picus. Supplementi 8).

Capini, S., 1984: La ceramica ellenistica dallo scarico A del santuario di Ercole Campochiaro, *Conoscenze* 1, 9-57.

Capini, S., 1991a: Il santuario di Ercole a Campochiaro, in S. Capini/A. Di Niro (eds), *Samnium. Archeologia del Molise,* Roma, 115-119.

Capini, S., 1991b: Il santuario di Pietrabbondante, in S. Capini/A. Di Niro (eds), *Samnium. Archeologia del Molise,* Roma, 113-114.

Capini, S., 1996: Su alcuni luoghi di culto nel Sannio Pentro, in L. Del Tutto Palma (ed.), *La tavola di Agnone nel contesto italico. Convegno di studio, Agnone 13 - 15 aprile 1994,* Isernia, 63-68.

Capini, S., 2000: Una dedica ad Ercole dal santuario di Campochiaro, in *Studi sull'Italia dei Sanniti,* Milano, 230-231.

Capini, S., 2003: Il santuario di Ercole a Campochiaro, in L. Quilici/S. Quilici Gigli (eds), *Santuari e luoghi di culto nell'Italia antica,* Roma (Atlante tematico di topografia antica 12), 233-250.

Capini, S./A. Di Niro (eds), 1991: *Samnium. Archeologia del Molise,* Roma.

Capogrossi Colognesi, L., 2002: *Persistenza e innovazione nelle strutture territoriali dell'Italia romana,* Napoli.

Cappelletti, M., 1991: La fase romana del santuario di Campochiaro, in S. Capini/A. Di Niro (eds), *Samnium. Archeologia del Molise,* Roma, 237-239.

Caputo, P., 2000: Su un frammento di pittura funeraria di Cuma, in *Studi sull'Italia dei Sanniti,* Milano, 74-77.

Carafa, P., 1998: Le frontiere degli dei. Osservazioni sui santuari di confine nella Campania antica, in M. Pearce/M. Tosi (eds), *Papers from the EAA Third Annual Meeting at Ravenna 1997, 1. Pre- and protohistory,* Oxford 211-222.

Carandini, A., 1997: *La nascita di Roma. Dèi, Lari, eroi e uomini all'alba di una civiltà,* Torino (Biblioteca di cultura storica 219).

Carandini, A./F. Cambi/M.G. Celuzza/E.W.B. Fentress (eds), 2002: *Paesaggi d'Etruria. Valle dell'Albegna, Valle d'Oro, Valle del Chiarone, Valle del Tafone,* Roma.

Carandini, A./E. Papi, 2005: Palatium e Sacra Via II. L'età tardo-repubblicana e la prima età imperiale (fine III secolo a.C. - 64 d.C.), *BA* 3-327.

Carter, J.C., 1994: Sanctuaries in the Chora of Metaponto, in S. E. Alcock/R. Osborne (eds), *Placing the gods. Sanctuaries and sacred space in ancient Greece,* Oxford/New York, 161-198.

Carter, J.C., 2006: *Discovering the Greek countryside at Metaponto,* Ann Arbor (Jerome lectures 23).

Càssola, F., 1970-71: Romani e Italici in Oriente, *DialA* 4-5, 305-322.

Castagnoli, F., 1958: *Le ricerche sui resti della centuriazione,* Roma.

Catalli, F./J. Scheid, 1994: Le *thesaurus* de Sora, *RNum* 36, 55-65.

Cecconi, G.A., 2006: Romanizzazione, diversità culturale, politicamente corretto, *MEFRA* 118, 81-94.

Champion, T.C., 1989: *Centre and periphery. Comparative studies in archaeology,* London (One world archaeology 11).

Ciampoltrini, G., 1993: Un *thesaurus* di Luni (CIL XI, 1343), *Athenaeum* 81, 642-644.

Cianfarani, V., 1960: *Santuari nel Sannio,* Chieti.

Cianfarani, V./L. Franchi Dell'Orto/A. La Regina (eds), 1978: *Culture adriatiche di Abruzzo e di Molise,* Roma.

Cicala, V., 1995: Diana ariminense. Tracce di religiosità politica, in A. Calbi/G. C. Susini (eds), *Pro poplo arimenese. Atti del convegno internazionale "Rimini antica. Una respublica fra terra e mare". Rimini, ottobre 1993,* Faenza (Epigrafia e antichità 14), 355-365.

Cifarelli, F.M., 2003: *Il tempio di Giunone Moneta sull'acropoli di Segni. Storia, topografia e decorazione architettonica,* Roma (Studi su Segni antica 1).

Cifarelli, F.M./L. Ambrosini/D. Nonnis, 2002-2003: Nuovi dati su Segni medio-repubblicana. A proposito du un nuovo pocolom dall'acropoli, *RendPontAc* 75, 245-325.

Clark, A.J., 2007: *Divine qualities. Cult and community in Republican Rome,* Oxford (Oxford classical monographs).

Coarelli, F., 1980: *Roma,* Roma (Guide archeologiche Laterza. L'Italia 6).

Coarelli, F., 1981a: *Fregellae. La storia e gli scavi*, Roma (Città del Lazio Antico).

Coarelli, F., 1981b: *L'area sacra di Largo Argentina*, Roma (Studi e materiali dei musei e monumenti comunali di Roma. Ripartizione 10, Antichità belle arti e problemi di cultura).

Coarelli, F., 1983: *Il foro romano. Periodo arcaico*, Roma (Lectiones planetariae).

Coarelli, F., 1987: *I santuari del Lazio in età repubblicana*, Roma (Studi NIS archeologia 7).

Coarelli, F., 1988a: *Il foro boario. Dalle origini alla fine della repubblica*, Roma (Lectiones planetariae).

Coarelli, F., 1988b: I santuari, il fiume, gli empori, in A. Schiavone (ed.), *Storia di Roma, 1. Roma in Italia*, Torino, 127-151.

Coarelli, F., 1989: *Minturnae*, Roma (Studi e ricerche sul Lazio antico).

Coarelli, F., 1992: Colonizzazione e municipalizzazione. Tempi e modi, *DialA* 10, 21-30.

Coarelli, F., 1995a: Venus Iovia, Venus Libitina? Il santuario del fondo Patturelli a Capua, in *Studi in memoria di Ettore Lepore, 1. L'incidenza dell'antico. Atti del convegno internazionale (Anacapri 24 - 28 marzo 1991)*, Napoli, 371-387.

Coarelli, F., 1995b: I vici di Ariminum, *Caesarodunum* 29, 175-180.

Coarelli, F., 1996: Legio linteata. L'iniziazione militare nel Sannio, in L. Del Tutto Palma (ed.), *La tavola di Agnone nel contesto italico. Convegno di studio, Agnone 13 - 15 aprile 1994*, Isernia, 3-16.

Coarelli, F., 1997: *Il Campo Marzio. Dalle origini alla fine della Repubblica*, Roma.

Coarelli, F., 2000: Il Lucus Pisaurensis e la romanizzazione dell'ager Gallicus, in C. Bruun (ed.), *The Roman Middle Republic. Politics, religion, and historiography, c. 400 - 133 B.C. Papers from a conference at the Institutum Romanum Finlandiae, September 11 - 12, 1998*, Rome (Acta Instituti Romani Finlandiae 23), 195-205.

Coarelli, F., 2001a: Il Foro Triangolare. Decorazione e funzione, in P. G. Guzzo (ed.), *Pompei. Scienza e società. 250° anniversario degli scavi di Pompei. Convegno internazionale, Napoli 25 - 27 novembre 1998*, Milano, 97-107.

Coarelli, F., 2001b: Il rescritto di Spello e il santuario etnico degli Umbri, in *Umbria cristiana. Dalla diffusione del culto al culto dei santi. Secoli IV - X. Atti del XV Congresso internazionale di studi sull'alto medioevo, Spoleto 23 - 28 ottobre 2000*, Spoleto, 39-51.

Coarelli, F./A. La Regina, 1984: *Abruzzo Molise*, Roma (Guide archeologiche Laterza. L'Italia 9).

Coarelli, F./E. La Rocca/M. de Vos/A. de Vos, 1997: *Pompeji. Archäologischer Führer*, Augsburg.

Cohen, A.P., 1985: *The symbolic construction of community*, London.

Colini, A.M., 1961-1962: *Compitum Acili*, BCom 78, 147-157.

Colonna, G., 1962: Saepinum. Ricerche di topografia sannitica e medievale, *ArchCl* 14, 80- 107.

Colonna, G., (ed.) 1985: *Santuari d'Etruria*, Milano.

Colonna, G., 1988: Il lessico istituzionale etrusco e la formazione della città, specialmente in Emilia Romagna, in *La formazione della città preromana in Emilia Romagna. Atti del convegno di studi, Bologna - Marzabotto 7-8 dicembre 1985*, Bologna (Studi e documenti di archeologia 3), 15-36.

Colonna, G., 1991: Acqua Acetosa Laurentina, l'ager Romanus antiquus e i santuari del I miglio, *ScAnt* 5, 209-232.

Colonna, G., 1996: Alla ricerca della metropoli dei Sanniti, in *Identità e civiltà dei Sabini. Atti del XVIII Convegno di studi etruschi ed italici, Rieti - Magliano Sabina 30 maggio - 3 giugno 1993*, Firenze, 107-130.

Colonna, G., 2004: I santuari di Veio. Ricerche e scavi su Piano di Comunità, in H. Patterson (ed.), *Bridging the Tiber. Approaches to regional archaeology in the middle Tiber valley*, London (Archaeological monographs of the British School at Rome 13), 205-221.

Comella, A.M., 1981: Complessi votivi in Italia in epoca medio- e tardo-repubblicana, *MEFRA* 93, 717-803.

Comella, A.M., 1982-1983: Riflessi del culto di Asclepio nella religiosità popolare etrusco-laziale e campana di epoca medio e tardo-repubblicana, *AnnPerugia* 20, 215-244.

Conta Haller, G., 1978: *Ricerche su alcuni centri fortificati in opera poligonale in area campano-sannitica, valle del Volturno, territorio tra Liri e Volturno*, Napoli.

Cooley, A.E., 2006: Beyond Rome and Latium. Roman religion in the age of Augustus, in C. E. Schultz/P. B. Harvey (eds), *Religion in republican Italy,* Cambridge (Yale classical studies 33), 228-252.

Corbier, M., 1991: La transhumance entre le Samnium et l'Apulie. Continuités entre l'époque républicaine et l'époque impériale, in *La romanisation du Samnium aux IIe et Ier siècles av. J.C. Actes du colloque, Naples 4-5 novembre 1988,* Naples (Bibliothèque de l'Institut Français de Naples. Série II, 9), 149-176.

Cornell, T.J., 1989: The conquest of Italy, in F.W. Walbank (ed.), *CAH 7.2* (2nd ed.), Cambridge, 351–419.

Cornell, T.J., 2004: Deconstructing the Samnite wars. An essay in historiography, in H. Jones (ed.), *Samnium. Settlement and cultural change. The proceedings of the Third E. Togo Salmon Conference on Roman Studies,* Providence R.I. (Archeologica transatlantica 22), 115-131.

Costabile, F., 1984: *Istituzioni e forme costituzionali nelle città del Bruzio in età romana. Civitatis foederatae, coloniae e municipia in Italia meridionale attraverso i documenti epigrafici,* Napoli (Pubblicazioni della facoltà di giurisprudenza di Catanzaro 2).

Crawford, M.H., 1981: Italy and Rome (review article), *JRS* 71, 153-160.

Crawford, M.H., 1985: *Coinage and money under the Roman republic. Italy and the Mediterranean economy,* London (The library of numismatics).

Crawford, M.H., 1995: La storia della colonizzazione romana secondo i romani, in A. Storchi Marino (ed.), *L'incidenza dell'antico. Studi in memoria di Ettore Lepore,* Napoli, 187-192.

Crawford, M.H., (ed.) 1996: *Roman statutes,* London (Bulletin of the Institute of Classical Studies supplement 64).

Crawford, M.H., 2003a: Land and people in Republican Italy, in D. Braund/C. Gill (eds), *Myth, history and culture in republican Rome. Studies in honour of T.P. Wiseman,* Exeter, 56-72.

Crawford, M.H., 2003b: Thesauri, hoards and votive deposits, in O. De Cazanove/J. Scheid (eds), *Sanctuaires et sources dans l'antiquité. Les sources documentaires et leurs limites dans la description des lieux de culte. Actes de la table ronde organisée par le Collège de France, l'UMR 8585 Centre Gustave-Glotz, l'Ecole française de Rome et le Centre Jean Bérard, Naples, 30 novembre 2001,* Naples (Collection du Centre Jean Bérard 22), 69-84.

Crawford, M.H., 2005: Transhumance in Italy. Its history and its historians, in W.V. Harris/E. Lo Cascio (eds), *Noctes Campanae. Studi di storia antica e archeologia dell'Italia preromana e romana in memoria di Martin W. Frederiksen,* Napoli (Itala tellus 1), 159-179.

Crawford, M.H., 2006: Pietrabbondante. Coinage, epigraphy and cult, *Orizzonti* 7, 81-84.

Cresci Marrone, G./G. Mennella, 1984: *Pisaurum* I, Pisa (Biblioteca di studi antichi).

Cristofani, M., 1995: Genti e forme di popolamento in età preromana, in A. Calbi/G. C. Susini (eds), *Pro poplo arimenese. Atti del convegno internazionale "Rimini antica. Una respublica fra terra e mare". Rimini, ottobre 1993,* Faenza (Epigrafia e antichità 14), 145-181.

Curchin, L.A., 1985: Vici and pagi in Roman Spain, *REA* 87, 327-343.

Curchin, L.A., 1991: *Roman Spain. Conquest and Assimilation,* London/New York.

Curchin, L.A., 2005: Review of Tarpin 2002, *Klio* 87, 528-529.

Curti, E., 2000: From Concordia to the Quirinal. Notes on religion and politics in mid-Republican-hellenistic Rome, in E. Bispham/C. Smith (eds), *Religion in archaic and republican Rome and Italy. Evidence and experience,* Edinburgh, 77-91.

Curti, E., 2001: Toynbee's legacy. Discussing aspects of the Romanization of Italy, in S. J. Keay/N. Terrenato (eds), *Italy and the west. Comparative issues in Romanization,* Oxford, 17-26.

Curti, E./E. Dench/J.R. Patterson, 1996: The archaeology of central and southern Roman Italy. Recent trends and approaches, *JRS* 86, 170-189.

D'Agostino, B., 1991: The Italian perspective on theoretical archaeology, in I. Hodder (ed.), *Archaeological theory in Europe,* Cambridge, 52-64.

D'Ercole, V., 2000: I 'paesaggi di potere' dell'Abruzzo protostorico, in G. Camassa/A. De Guio/F. Veronese (eds), *Paesaggi di potere. Problemi e prospettive. Atti del Seminario, Udine 16-17 maggio 1996,* Roma (Quaderni di Eutopia 2), 121-152.

D'Ercole, V./V. Orfanelli/P. Riccitelli, 1997: L'Abruzzo meridionale in età sannitica, in A. Campanelli/A. Faustoferri (eds), *I luoghi degli dei. Sacro e natura nell'Abruzzo italico. Mostra Chieti 16 maggio - 18 agosto 1997*, Pescara, 21-24.

D'Ercole, M.C., 2002: Importuosa Italiae Litora. La côte adriatique entre le Biferno et l'Ofanto. Le paysage et les échanges à l'époque archaïque, Naples (Études Centre Jean Bérard 6).

Dahlheim, W., 1968: *Struktur und Entwicklung des römischen Völkerrechtes im 3 und 2. Jahrhundert v. Chr.*, München (Vestigia 8).

De Benedittis, G., 1977: *Bovianum ed il suo territorio. Primi appunti di topografia storica*, Salerno (Documenti di antichità italiche e romane 7).

De Benedittis, G., 1980: L'oppidum di Monte Vairano ovvero Aquilonia, in *Sannio. Pentri e Frentani dal VI al I sec. a.C. Isernia, catalogo della mostra*, Roma, 321-341.

De Benedittis, G., 1990a: Alcune riflessioni sull'abitato italico di Monte Vairano, in M. Salvatore (ed.), Basilicata. L'espansionismo romano nel sud-est d'Italia. Il quadro archeologico. Atti del convegno, Venosa 23 - 25 aprile 1987, Venosa, 253-255.

De Benedittis, G., 1990b: Monte Vairano. Tratturi, economia e viabilità, Conoscenze 6, 13-27.

De Benedittis, G., 1991: Monte Vairano, in *La romanisation du Samnium aux IIe et Ier siècles av. J.C. Actes du colloque, Naples 4-5 novembre 1988,* Naples (Bibliothèque de l'Institut Français de Naples. Série II, 9), 47-55.

De Benedittis, G., 2004: Bovianum, Aesernia, Monte Vairano. Considerazioni sull'evoluzione dell'insediamento nel Sannio Pentro, in H. Jones (ed.), *Samnium. Settlement and cultural change. The proceedings of the Third E. Togo Salmon Conference on Roman Studies,* Providence R.I. (Archeologica transatlantica 22), 23-33.

De Cazanove, O., 2000a: Bacanal ou citerne? A propos des salles souterraines de la domus II à Bolsena et de leur interprétation comme lieu de culte dionysiaque, *AntCl* 69, 237-253.

De Cazanove, O., 2000b: I destinatari dell'iscrizione di Tiriolo e la questione del campo d'applicazione del senatoconsulto De Bacchanalibus, *Athenaeum* 88, 59-69.

De Cazanove, O., 2000c: Some thoughts on the 'religious romanization' of Italy before the Social War, in E. Bispham/C. Smith (eds), *Religion in archaic and republican Rome and Italy. Evidence and experience,* Edinburgh, 71-76.

De Cazanove, O., 2001: Itinéraires et étapes de l'avancée romaine entre Samnium, Daunie, Lucanie et Etrurie, in D. Briquel/J. P. Thuillier (eds), *Le censeur et les Samnites. Sur Tite-Live, livre IX,* Paris (Études de littérature ancienne 11), 147-192.

De Cazanove, O., 2007: Pre-Roman Italy, before and under the Romans, in J. Rüpke (ed.), *A companion to Roman religion,* Malden (Blackwell companions to the Ancient World), 43-57.

De Felice, E., 1994: *Larinum,* Firenze (Forma Italiae 36).

De Franciscis, A., 1956: *Templum Dianae Tifatinae,* Caserta (Archivio storico di terra di lavoro 1).

De Juliis, E., 1994: Le genti adriatiche, in *Antiche genti d'Italia. Rimini 20 marzo - 28 agosto 1994,* Roma, 41-45.

De Petra, G./P. Calore, 1900: Interpromium et Ceii, *Atti della Reale Accademia di archeologia, lettere e belle arti* 15, 19-25.

de Polignac, F., 1984: La naissance de la cité grecque. Cultes, espace et société VIIIe-VIIe siècles avant J.-C., Paris (Textes à l'appui).

de Polignac, F., 1994: Mediation, competition, and sovereignty. The evolution of rural sanctuaries in Geometric Greece, in S. E. Alcock/R. Osborne (eds), *Placing the gods. Sanctuaries and sacred space in ancient Greece,* Oxford/New York, 3-18.

de Ruyt, C., 1983: *Macellum. Marché alimentaire des Romains,* Louvain-la-Neuve (Publications d'histoire de l'art et d'archéologie de l'Université catholique de Louvain 35).

Degrassi, A., 1967: Epigraphica 3, *MemAccLinc* 13, 43-46.

Degrassi, A., 1986: *CIL I Pars 2. Fasc. 4. Addenda tertia 2. Tabulae 2,* Berlin.

Delatte, L., 1937: Recherches sur quelques fêtes mobiles du calendrier romain, *AntCl* 6, 93-117.

Delplace, C., 1993: *La romanisation du Picenum. L'exemple d'Urbs Salvia,* Rome (CEFR 177).

Dench, E., 1995: *From barbarians to new men. Greek, Roman, and modern perceptions of peoples of the central Apennines,* Oxford (Oxford Classical Monographs).

Dench, E., 1997: Sacred springs to the Social War. Myths of origins and questions of identity in the central Apennines, in T. J. Cornell/K. Lomas (eds), *Gender and ethnicity in ancient Italy,* London (Accordia specialist studies on Italy 6), 43-51.

Dench, E., 2004: Samnites in English. The legacy of E. Togo Salmon in the English-speaking world, in H. Jones (ed.), *Samnium. Settlement and cultural change. The proceedings of the Third E. Togo Salmon Conference on Roman Studies,* Providence R.I. (Archeologica transatlantica 22), 7-22.

Dench, E., 2005: *Romulus' Asylum. Roman identities from the age of Alexander to the age of Hadrian,* Oxford.

Deneauve, J., 1969: *Lampes de Carthage,* Paris.

Derks, T., 1998: *Gods, temples and ritual practices. The transformation of religious ideas and values in Roman Gaul,* Amsterdam (Amsterdam archaeological studies 2).

Desideri, P., 1991: La romanizzazione dell'Impero, in A. Schiavone (ed.), *Storia di Roma 2.2. I principi e il mondo,* Torino, 577-626.

Devijver, H./F. van Wonterghem, 1981: Die Inschriften von Alba Fucens und die *gens Herennia, AntCl* 50, 242-257.

Di Niro, A., 1977: *Il culto di Ercole tra i Sanniti Pentri e Frentani. Nuove testimonianze,* Salerno (Documenti di Antichità italiche e romane 9).

Di Niro, A., 1978a: S. Giovanni in Galdo, in V. Cianfarani/L. Franchi Dell'Orto/A. La Regina (eds), *Culture adriatiche di Abruzzo e di Molise,* Roma, 500-504.

Di Niro, A., 1978b: S. Giovanni in Galdo (CB), *StEtr* 46, 444-455.

Di Niro, A., 1980: Il santuario di S. Giovanni in Galdo, in *Sannio. Pentri e Frentani dal VI al I sec. a.C. Isernia, catalogo della mostra,* Roma, 269-281.

Di Niro, A./P.P. Petrone, 1993: Insediamenti di epoca sannitica nel territorio circostante la valle del torrente Tappino (Campobasso, Molise), *PBSR* 61, 7-49.

Donderer, M., 1994: Weder Votiv- noch Grabrelief, sondern Werbeschild eines Steinmetzateliers, *Epigraphica* 56, 41-52.

Dondin-Payre, M., 1987: Topographie et propagande gentilice. Le compitum Acilium et l'origine des Acilii Glabriones, in *L'Urbs. Espace urbain et histoire (Ier siècle av. J.-C. -IIIe siècle ap. J.-C.),* Rome (CEFR 98), 87-109.

Dorcey, P.F., 1992: *The cult of Silvanus. A study in Roman folk religion,* Leiden (Columbia studies in the classical tradition 20).

Dumézil, G., 1961: Quaestiones indo-italicae 8-10, *Latomus* 20, 264-265.

Dumézil, G., 1974 (1977): *La religione romana arcaica,* Roma.

Dyson, S.L., 1992: *Community and society in Roman Italy,* Baltimore (Ancient society and history).

Dyson, S.L., 2003: *The Roman countryside,* London (Duckworth debates in archaeology).

Edlund-Berry, I.E.M., 1987: *The gods and the place. Location and function of sanctuaries in the countryside of Etruria and Magna Graecia (700-400 B.C.),* Stockholm (Skrifter utgivna av Svenska Institutet i Rom 43).

Elia, O./G. Pugliese Carratelli, 1975: Il santuario dionisiaco di S. Abbondio a Pompei, in *Orfismo in Magna Grecia. Atti del 14. Convegno di studi sulla Magna Grecia, Taranto, 6-10 ottobre 1974,* Napoli (Convegno di studi sulla Magna Grecia 14), 139-153.

Elia, O./G. Pugliese Carratelli, 1979: Il santuario dionisiaco di Pompei, *PP* 34, 442-481.

Ettlinger, E. *et al.,* 1990: *Conspectus formarum terrae sigillatae Italico modo confectae,* Bonn (Materialien zur römisch-germanischen Keramik 10).

Fabbricotti, E., 1982-83: Il santuario di Atessa, *QuadChieti* 3, 85-119.
Fabbricotti, E., 1997: Il santuario di Atessa, in A. Campanelli/A. Faustoferri (eds), *I luoghi degli dei. Sacro e natura nell'Abruzzo italico. Mostra Chieti 16 maggio - 18 agosto 1997,* Pescara, 75-76.
Fagan, G.G., 1996: The reliability of Roman rebuilding inscriptions, *PBSR* 64, 81-93.
Faustoferri, A., 2003: Prima dei Sanniti. Le necropoli dell'Abruzzo meridionale, *MEFRA* 115, 85-107.
Fears, J.R., 1981a: The theology of victory at Rome. Approaches and problems, in *ANRW,* II, 17, 2, Berlin, 736-826.
Fears, J.R., 1981b: The cult of virtues and Roman imperial ideology, in *ANRW,* II, 17, 2, Berlin, 827-948.
Feeney, D., 1998: *Literature and religion at Rome. Cultures, contexts, and beliefs,* Cambridge (Roman literature and its contexts).
Felletti Maj, B.M., 1977: *La tradizione italica nell'arte romana,* Roma (Archaeologica 3).
Fenelli, M., 1975: Contributo per lo studio del votivo anatomico. I votivi anatomici di Lavinio, *ArchCl* 27, 206-252.
Fentress, E.W.B., (ed.) 2000a: *Romanization and the city. Creation, transformations and failures,* Portsmouth (JRA Supplementary series 38).
Fentress, E.W.B., 2000b: Frank Brown, Cosa, and the idea of a Roman city, in E. W. B. Fentress (ed.), *Romanization and the city. Creation, transformations and failures,* Portsmouth (JRA Supplementary series 38), 11-24.
Ferri, G., 2006: L'evocatio romana. I problemi, *StMatStorRel* 30, 205-244.
Fincham, G., 2002: *Landscapes of imperialism. Roman and native interaction in the East Anglian Fenland,* Oxford (BAR Brit. ser. 338).
Flambard, J.-M., 1977: Clodius, les collèges, la plèbe et les esclaves. Recherches sur la politique populaire au milieu du 1er siècle, *MEFRA* 89, 115-156.
Flambard, J.-M., 1981: Collegia Compitalicia. Phénomène associatif, cadres territoriaux et cadres civiques dans le monde romain à l'époque républicaine, *Ktema* 6, 143-166.
Fless, F., 1995: *Opferdiener und Kultmusiker auf stadtrömischen historischen Reliefs. Untersuchungen zur Ikonographie, Funktion und Benennung,* Mainz.
Fless, F., 2005: s.v. Römische Prozessionen, *ThesCRA* I, 33-58.
Flower, H.I., 2000: Fabula de Bacchanalibus. The Bacchanalian cult of the second century BC and Roman drama, in G. Manuwald (ed.), *Identität und Alterität in der frührömischen Tragödie,* Würzburg (Identitäten und Alteritäten 3. Altertumswissenschaftliche Reihe 1), 23-35.
Flower, H.I., (ed.) 2004: *The Cambridge companion to the Roman republic,* Cambridge.
Fontemaggi, A./O. Piolanti, 1995: Il popolamento nel territorio di Ariminum. Testimonianze archeologiche, in A. Calbi/G. C. Susini (eds), *Pro poplo arimenese. Atti del convegno internazionale "Rimini antica. Una respublica fra terra e mare". Rimini, ottobre 1993,* Faenza (Epigrafia e antichità 14), 531-561.
Fontemaggi, A./O. Piolanti, 2000: Scheda 180, in M. Marini Calvani/R. Curina/E. Lippolis (eds), *Aemilia. La cultura romana in Emilia Romagna dal III secolo a.C. all età costantiniana,* Venezia, 510-511.
Forni, G., 1982: Umbri antichi iscritti in tribù romane, *Bollettino Dep. Storia Patria per l'Umbria* 79, 21-23.
Fowler, W.W., 1925: *The Roman festivals of the period of the Republic. An introduction to the study of the religion of the Romans,* London.
Fracchia, H.M./M. Gualtieri, 1989: The social context of cult practices in pre-Roman Lucania, *AJA* 93, 217-232.
Fraenkel, E., 1932: Senatus consultum de Baccanalibus, *Hermes* 67, 369-396.
Franchi De Bellis, A., 1995: I "pocola" riminesi, in A. Calbi/G. C. Susini (eds), *Pro poplo arimenese. Atti del convegno internazionale "Rimini antica. Una respublica fra terra e mare". Rimini, ottobre 1993,* Faenza (Epigrafia e antichità 14), 367-391.
Franchi Dell'Orto, L./A.R. Staffa, 1991: L'insediamento italico di Colle del Vento, in *La valle dell'alto Vomano ed i Monti della Laga,* Pescara (Documenti dell'Abruzzo teramano 3), 167-174.

Frankfurter, D., 1998: *Religion in Roman Egypt. Assimilation and resistance,* Princeton (Mythos. The Princeton Bollingen series in world mythology).

Fraschetti, A., 1990: *Roma e il principe,* Roma/Bari.

Frateantonio, C., 2003: *Religiöse Autonomie der Stadt im Imperium Romanum. Öffentliche Religionen im Kontext römischer Rechts- und Verwaltungspraxis,* Tübingen (Studien und Texte zu Antike und Christentum 19).

Frederiksen, M.W., 1968: Review of Salmon 1967, *JRS* 58, 224-229.

Frederiksen, M.W., 1976: Changes in the patterns of settlement, in P. Zanker (ed.), *Hellenismus in Mittelitalien. Kolloquium in Göttingen vom 5. bis 9. Juni 1974,* Göttingen, 341-354.

Frederiksen, M.W., 1984: *Campania,* London.

Freeman, P.W.M., 1993: 'Romanisation' and Roman material culture [Long review of Millett 1990a], *JRA* 6, 438-445.

Freeman, P.W.M., 2007: *The best training-ground for archaeologists. Francis Haverfield and the invention of Romano-British archaeology,* Oxford.

Freyburger, G., 1986: *Fides. Etude sémantique et religieuse depuis les origines jusqu'à l'époque augustéenne,* Paris (Collection d'études anciennes).

Fröhlich, T., 1991: *Lararien- und Fassadenbilder in den Vesuvstädten. Untersuchungen zur volkstümlichen pompejanischen Malerei,* Mainz (Mitteilungen des Deutschen Archaeologischen Instituts. Römische Abteilung. Ergänzungsheft 32).

Gabba, E., 1972: Urbanizzazione e rinnovamenti urbanistici nell'Italia centro-meridionale del I sec. a.C., *StClOr* 21, 73-112.

Gabba, E., 1975: Mercati e fiere nell'Italia romana, *StClOr* 24, 141-166.

Gabba, E., 1976: *Republican Rome, the army, and the allies,* Berkeley.

Gabba, E., 1991: *Dionysius and the history of archaic Rome,* Berkeley (Sather classical lectures 56).

Gabba, E., 1994a: *Italia romana,* Como (Biblioteca di Athenaeum 25).

Gabba, E., 1994b: Rome and Italy. The Social War, in *CAH 9.2 (2nd ed.),* Cambridge, 104-128.

Gabba, E./M. Pasquinucci (eds), 1979: *Strutture agrarie e allevamento transumante nell'Italia romana (III-I sec. a.C.),* Pisa (Biblioteca di studi antichi 18).

Gaggiotti, M., 1983: Tre casi regionali italici. Il Sannio Pentro, in M. Cébeillac-Gervasoni (ed.), *Les bourgeoisies municipales italiennes aux 2e et 1er siècles av. J.C. Centre Jean Bérard, Institut français de Naples, 7-10 décembre 1981,* Paris 137-144.

Gallini, C., 1973: Che cosa intendere per ellenizzazione. Problemi di metodo, *DialA* 7, 175-191.

Galsterer, H., 1976: *Herrschaft und Verwaltung im republikanischen Italien. Die Beziehungen Roms zu den italischen Gemeinden vom Latinerfrieden 338 v. Chr bis zum Bundesgenossenkrieg 91 v. Chr.,* München (Münchener Beiträge zur Papyrusforschung und antiken Rechtsgeschichte 68).

Gargola, D.J., 1995: *Lands, laws, and gods. Magistrates & ceremony in the regulation of public lands in Republican Rome,* Chapel Hill (Studies in the history of Greece & Rome).

Garnsey, P.D.A., 1979: Where did Italian peasants live?, *ProcCambrPhilSoc* 25, 1-25.

Gasperini, L., 1983: Spigolature epigrafiche marchigiane, *Picus* 3, 7-21.

Gasser, F., 1999: Germana patria. Die Geburtsheimat in den Werken römischer Autoren der späten Republik und der frühen Kaiserzeit, Stuttgart (Beiträge zur Altertumskunde 118).

Gatti, G., 1888: Di un sacello compitale dell'antichissima regione Esquilina, *BCom* 16, 221-232.

Gentili, M.D., 2005: Riflessioni sul fenomeno storico dei depositi votivi di tipo etrusco-laziale-campano, in A. M. Comella/S. Mele (eds), *Depositi votivi e culti dell'Italia antica dall'età arcaica a quella tardo-repubblicana,* Bari (Bibliotheca archaeologica 16), 367-378.

Glinister, F., 2006a: Reconsidering "religious Romanization", in C. E. Schultz/P. B. Harvey (eds), *Religion in republican Italy,* Cambridge (Yale classical studies 33), 10-33.

Glinister, F., 2006b: Women, colonisation and cult in hellenistic central Italy, *ArchRel* 8, 89-104.

Goujard, R., 1975: *De l'agriculture. Caton,* Paris (Collection Budé).

Gradel, I., 2002: *Emperor worship and Roman religion,* Oxford (Oxford classical monographs).

Graves-Brown, P./S. Jones/C. Gamble, 1996: *Cultural identity and archaeology. The construction of European communities,* London.

Greco, E., 2000: Santuari indigeni e formazione del territorio in Lucania, in S.Verger (ed.), *Rites et espaces en pays celte et méditerranéen. Etude comparée à partir du sanctuaire d'Acy-Romance (Ardennes, France),* Rome (CEFR 276), 223-229.

Green, S.J., 2004: *Ovid, Fasti I. A commentary,* Leiden (Mnemosyne. Supplements 251).

Grelle, F./E. Lo Cascio/M. Silvestrini, 2004: A proposito di L. Capogrossi Colognesi, Persistenza e innovazione nelle strutture territoriali dell'Italia romana, Napoli 2002, *Epigrafia e territorio. Politica e società. Temi di antichità romane* 7, 297-322.

Gros, P., 2001 (1996): *L'architettura romana. Dagli inizi del III secolo a.C. alla fine dell'alto impero. I monumenti pubblici,* Milano (Biblioteca di archeologia 30).

Gros, P./M. Torelli (eds), 1988: *Storia dell'urbanistica. Il mondo romano,* Bari/Roma.

Grossi, G., 1980: L'assetto storico-urbanistico del territorio del Fucino nel periodo italico (VII-III sec.a.C.), in W. Ciancusi/U. Irti/G. Grossi (eds), *Profili di archeologia marsicana,* Avezzano, 119-185.

Grossi, G., 1988: Topografia antica del territorio del Parco Nazionale d'Abruzzo (III sec.a.C.-VI sec.d.C.), in *Il territorio del Parco nazionale d'Abruzzo nell'antichità. Atti del I Convegno nazionale di archeologia. Villetta Barrea, 1-2-3 maggio, 1987,* Civitella Alfedena, 111-135.

Grossi, G., 1991: Topografia antica della Marsica (Aequi-Marsi e Volsci). Quindici anni di ricerche, 1974-1989, in *Il Fucino e le aree limitrofe nell'antichità (Avezzano 10-11 novembre 1989),* Roma, 199-237.

Grue, F., 1998: Ricognizioni nell'Ager Hatrianus. Storia, insediamenti ed economia di un territorio. Età romana. Storia ed economia del territorio, *MünstBeitr* 17, 12-19.

Gruen, E.S., 1990: *Studies in Greek culture and Roman policy,* Leiden (Cincinnati classical studies. New series 7).

Guadagno, G., 1993: *Pagi* e *vici* della Campania, in A. Calbi/A. Donati/G. Poma (eds), *L'epigrafia del villaggio. Atti del Colloquio Borghesi, Forlì 27-30 settembre 1990,* Faenza (Epigrafia e antichità 12), 407-444.

Guadagno, G., 2005: La "precoce romanizzazione" delle aree italiche in età preromana. Luoghi comuni, in D. Caiazza (ed.), *Italica ars. Studi in onore di Giovanni Colonna per il premio i Sanniti,* Piedimonte Matese, 399-411.

Gualtieri, M., 2000: Una lex osca da Roccagloriosa (SA). Il contesto storico-archeologico, *Ostraka* 9, 247-253.

Gualtieri, M., 2004: Between Samnites and Lucanians. New archaeological and epigraphic evidence for settlement organization, in H. Jones (ed.), *Samnium. Settlement and cultural change. The proceedings of the Third E. Togo Salmon Conference on Roman Studies,* Providence R.I. (Archeologica transatlantica 22), 35-50.

Gualtieri, M./H. Fracchia, 1990: *Roccagloriosa I. L'abitato. Scavo e ricognizione topografica (1976-1986),* Napoli (Bibliothèque de l'Institut français de Naples. Sér. II, 8. Publications du Centre Jean Bérard 8).

Gualtieri, M./H. Fracchia, 2001: *Roccagloriosa II. L'oppidum Lucano e il territorio,* Napoli (Collection du Centre Jean Bérard 20).

Guarducci, M., 1953: Alba Fucens. Graffiti nell'antico tempio sul colle di S. Pietro, *NSc* 7, 117-125.

Guarducci, M., 1981: Graffiti parietali nel santuario di Ercole Curino presso Sulmona, in L. Gasperini (ed.), *Scritti sul mondo antico in memoria di Fulvio Grosso,* Roma, 225-240.

Guidobaldi, M.P., 1995: *La romanizzazione dell'ager Praetutianus (secoli III-I a.C.),* Napoli (Auctus 3).

Guidobaldi, M.P., 2005: Materiali di tipo "etrusco-campano" in un santuario marrucino. L'esempio della Grotta del Colle di Rapino, in A. M. Comella/S. Mele (eds), *Depositi votivi e culti dell'Italia antica dall'età arcaica a quella tardo-repubblicana,* Bari (Bibliotheca archaeologica 16), 391-398.

Gustafsson, G., 2000: *Evocatio deorum. Historical and mythical interpretations of ritualised conquests in the expansion of ancient Rome,* Uppsala (Historia religionum 16).

Guzzo, P.G., 1987: Schema per la categoria interpretativa del "santuario di frontiera", *ScAnt* 1, 373-379.

Guzzo, P.G., 2003: Sul mito di Sibari, *BABESCH* 78, 221-223.

Hall, J.M., 2002: *Hellenicity. Between ethnicity and culture*, Chicago/London.

Hano, M., 1986: A l'origine du culte imperial. Les autels des Lares Augusti. Recherches sur les thèmes iconographiques et leur signification, in *ANRW*, II, 16, 3, Berlin, 2333-2381.

Hanson, J.A., 1959: *Roman theater-temples*, Princeton (Princeton Monograph in art and archaeology 33).

Hanson, W.S., 1997: Forces of change and methods of control, in D. J. Mattingly (ed.), *Dialogues in Roman imperialism. Power, discourse, and discrepant experience in the Roman empire*, Portsmouth (JRA Supplementary series 23), 67-80.

Harvey Jr., P.B., 2006: Religion and memory of Pisaurum, in C. E. Schultz/P. B. Harvey (eds), *Religion in republican Italy*, Cambridge (Yale classical studies 33), 117-136.

Harvey, R.A., 1981: *A commentary on Persius*, Leiden (Mnemosyne. Supplements 64).

Hasenohr, C., 2001: Les monuments des collèges italiens sur l'agora des Compétaliastes à Délos, in J.-Y. Marc/J.-C. Moretti (eds), *Constructions publiques et programmes édilitaires en Grèce entre le IIe siècle av. J.C. et le Ier siècle ap. J.C. Actes du colloque organisé par l'Ecole française d'Athènes et le CNRS, Athènes 14 - 17 mai 1995*, Paris (BCH Supplément 39), 329-348.

Hasenohr, C., 2003: Les *Compitalia* à Délos, *BCH* 127, 167-249.

Hatzfeld, J., 1912: Les Italiens résidant à Délos mentionnés dans les inscriptions de l'île, *BCH* 36, 5-218.

Hatzfeld, J., 1919: *Les trafiquants italiens dans l'Orient hellénique*, Paris (BEFAR 115).

Häussler, R., 1998: Motivations and ideologies of Romanization, in C. Forcey/J. J. Hawthorne/R. Witcher (eds), *TRAC 97. Proceedings of the Seventh Annual Theoretical Roman Archaeology Conference, University of Nottingham, April 1997*, Oxford, 11-19.

Häussler, R., 2005: Dynamik der Romanisierung der Religion. Zur Kultkontinuität in der Narbonensis, in W. Spickermann/K. Matijevi/H. H. Steenken (eds), *Rom, Germanien und das Reich. Festschrift zu Ehren von Rainer Wiegels anlässlich seines 65. Geburtstages*, Sankt Katharinen (Pharos 18), 340-369.

Häussler, R./A.C. King (eds), 2007: *Continuity and innovation in religion in the Roman West*, Portsmouth (JRA Supplementary series 67).

Haverfield, F.J., 1912: *The Romanization of Roman Britain*, Oxford.

Hayes, J.W., 1972: *Late Roman pottery*, London.

Hayes, J.W., 1980: *A supplement to late Roman pottery*, London.

Helbig, 1868: *Wandgemälde der vom Vesuv verschütteten Städte Campaniens*, Leipzig.

Henig, M., 1984: *Religion in Roman Britain*, London.

Heurgon, J., 1942: *Recherches sur l'histoire, la religion et la civilisation de Capoue préromaine des origines à la deuxième guerre punique*, Paris.

Hingley, R., 1996: The 'legacy' of Rome. The rise, the decline and fall of the theory of Romanization, in J. Webster/N. J. Cooper (eds), *Roman imperialism. Post-colonial perspectives. Proceedings of a Symposium held at Leicester University in November 1994*, Leicester (Leicester archaeological monographs 3), 35-48.

Hingley, R., 2000: *Roman officers and English gentlemen. The imperial origins of Roman archaeology*, London.

Hingley, R., 2005: *Globalizing Roman culture. Unity, diversity and empire*, London.

Hobsbawm, E.J.E./T.O. Ranger (eds), 1983: *The invention of tradition*, Cambridge (Past and present publications).

Hodder, I./C. Orton, 1976: *Spatial analysis in archaeology*, Cambridge (New studies in archaeology 1).

Holland, L.A., 1937: The shrine of the *Lares Compitales*, *TransactAmPhilAss* 68, 428-441.

Hölscher, T., 1967: *Victoria Romana. Archäologische Untersuchungen zur Geschichte und Wesensart der römischen Siegesgöttin von den Anfängen bis zum Ende des 3. Jhs. n.Chr.*, Mainz.

Horden, P./N. Purcell, 2000: *The corrupting sea. A study of Mediterranean history*, Oxford.

Horsnaes, H.W., 2002: Lucanian sanctuaries and cultural interaction, in P. Attema/G. J. Burgers/E. v. Joolen (eds), *New developments in Italian landscape archaeology. Theory and methodology of field survey, land evaluation and landscape perception. Pottery production and distribution. Proceedings of a three-day conference held at the University of Groningen, April 13-15, 2000,* Oxford (BAR Int. Ser. 1091), 229-234.

Hülsen, C., 1907: Der Hain der Furrina am Janiculum, *RM* 22, 225-254.

Humbert, M., 1978: *Municipium et civitas sine suffragio. L'organisation de la conquête jusqu'à la guerre sociale,* Rome (CEFR 36).

Humm, M., 2001: Servius Tullius et la censure. Élaboration d'un modèle institutionnel, in M. Coudry/T. Späth (eds), *L'invention des grands hommes de la Rome antique. Die Konstruktion der grossen Männer Altroms,* Paris (Études d'archéologie et d'histoire ancienne), 221-247.

Iaculli, G., 1993: *Il tempio italico di Colle S. Giorgio (Castiglione Messer Raimondo),* Penne.

Johnson, J., 1933: *Excavations at Minturnae. II. Inscriptions. Part 1. Republican magistri,* Philadelphia.

Johnson, J., 1935: *Excavations at Minturnae I. Monuments of the Republican Forum* Philadelphia.

Jolivet, V./F. Marchand, 2003: L'affaire du Bacanal. Nouvelles réflexions sur le sanctuaire bachique du Poggio Moscini à Bolsena, in L. Quilici/S. Quilici Gigli (eds), *Santuari e luoghi di culto nell'Italia antica,* Roma (Atlante tematico di topografia antica 12), 35-51.

Jones, H., (ed.) 2004: *Samnium. Settlement and cultural change. The proceedings of the Third E. Togo Salmon Conference on Roman Studies,* Providence R.I. (Archeologica transatlantica 22).

Jones, S., 1997: *The archaeology of ethnicity. Constructing identities in the past and present,* London.

Jongman, W.M., 1988: *The economy and society of Pompeii,* Amsterdam.

Jost, M., 1985: *Sanctuaires et cultes d'Arcadie,* Paris (Études péloponnésiennes 9).

Kahrstedt, U., 1959: Ager publicus und Selbstverwaltung in Lukanien und Bruttium, *Historia* 8, 174-206.

Kaminski, G., 1991: Thesauros. Untersuchungen zum antiken Opferstock, *JdI* 106, 63-181.

Keaveney, A., 1987: *Rome and the unification of Italy,* London.

Keay, S.J., 1988: *Roman Spain,* London.

Keay, S.J./N. Terrenato (eds), 2001: *Italy and the West. Comparative issues in Romanization,* Oxford.

Keil, J., 1934: Das sogenannte Senatus consultum de Bacchanalibus, *Hermes* 68, 306-312.

Kent, J.P.C., 1978: *Roman coins,* London.

Kiene, A., 1845: *Der römische Bundesgenossenkrieg,* Leipzig.

Kiepert, H., 1901: *Formae orbis antiqui,* Berlin.

Kissel, W., 1990: *Aulus Persius Flaccus. Satiren,* Heidelberg (Wissenschaftliche Kommentare zu griechischen und lateinischen Schriftstellern).

Kleibrink, M., 2001: The search for Sybaris. An evaluation of historical and archaeological evidence, *BABESCH* 76, 33-70.

Kornemann, E., 1905: Polis und Urbs, *Klio* 5, 72-92.

Kornemann, E., 1942a: s.v. Oppidum, *RE* XVIII, 708-725.

Kornemann, E., 1942b: s.v. Pagus, *RE* XVIII, 2318-2339.

Krause, W., 1936: Zum Aufbau der Bacchanal-Inschrift, *Hermes* 71, 214-220.

La Penna, S., 1997a: Il santuario italico di Quadri, in A. Campanelli/A. Faustoferri (eds), *I luoghi degli dei. Sacro e natura nell'Abruzzo italico. Mostra Chieti 16 maggio - 18 agosto 1997,* Pescara, 68-69.

La Penna, S., 1997b: Il santuario italico di Schiavi d'Abruzzo, in A. Campanelli/A. Faustoferri (eds), *I luoghi degli dei. Sacro e natura nell'Abruzzo italico. Mostra Chieti 16 maggio - 18 agosto 1997,* Pescara, 81-88.

La Penna, S., 1997c: Stipe votiva di Schiavi, in A. Campanelli/A. Faustoferri (eds), *I luoghi degli dei. Sacro e natura nell'Abruzzo italico. Mostra Chieti 16 maggio - 18 agosto 1997,* Pescara, 117-126.

La Penna, S., (ed.) 2006: *Schiavi d'Abruzzo. Le aree sacre,* Sulmona.

La Regina, A., 1966: Le iscrizioni osche di Pietrabbondante e la questione di Bovianum vetus, *RhM* 109, 260-286.

La Regina, A., 1967-68: Ricerche sugli insediamenti vestini, *MemAccLinc* 13, 363-446.

La Regina, A., 1970: Note sulla formazione dei centri urbani in area sabellica, in *La città etrusca e italica preromana,* Bologna, 191-207.

La Regina, A., 1970-1971: Contributo dell'archeologia alla storia sociale. Territori sabellici e sannitici, *DialA* 4-5, 443-459.

La Regina, A., 1976: Il Sannio, in P. Zanker (ed.), *Hellenismus in Mittelitalien. Kolloquium in Göttingen vom 5. bis 9. Juni 1974,* Göttingen 219-244.

La Regina, A., 1980: Dalle guerre sannitiche alla romanizzazione, in *Sannio. Pentri e Frentani dal VI al I sec. a.C. Isernia, catalogo della mostra,* Roma, 29-42.

La Regina, A., 1984: Aspetti istituzionali del mondo sannitico, in *Sannio. Pentri e Frentani dal VI al I sec. a.C. Atti del convegno, Isernia 10-11 novembre 1980,* Campobasso, 17-25.

La Regina, A., 1989: I Sanniti, in G. Pugliese Carratelli (ed.), *Italia omnium terrarum parens,* Milano, 301-432.

La Regina, A., 1991: Abitati indigeni in area sabellica, in J. Mertens/R. Lambrechts (eds), *Comunità indigene e problemi della romanizzazione nell'Italia centro-meridionale, IV-III secolo a.C.,* Bruxelles, 147-155.

La Regina, A., 2000: Il trattato tra Abella e Nola per l'uso comune del santuario di Ercole e di un fondo adiacente, in *Studi sull'Italia dei Sanniti,* Milano, 214-222.

La Torre, G.F., 1989a: Il santuario di Ercole Curino, in *Dalla villa di Ovidio al santuario di Ercole Curino,* Sulmona, 115-150.

La Torre, G.F., 1989b: Una dedica all'Aterno divinizzato dal territorio di Interpromium, *Epigraphica* 51, 129-139.

Lackner, E.M., in press: Arx und Capitolinischer Kult in den Latinischen- und Bürgerkolonien Italiens als Spiegel römischer Religionspolitik, in M. Jehne (ed.), *Religiöse Vielfalt und soziale Integration. Die Bedeutung der Religion für die kulturelle Identität und die politische Stabilität im republikanischen Italien.*

Laffi, U., 1974: Problemi dell'organizzazione paganico-vicana nelle aree abruzzesi e molisane, *Athenaeum* 52, 336-339.

Laffi, U., 1978: La lex aedis Furfensis, in *La cultura italica. Atti del convegno della società italiana di glottologia, Pisa 19 e 20 dicembre 1977,* Pisa (Orientamenti linguistici 5), 121-144.

Laing, G., 1921: The origin of the cult of the Lares, *ClPhil* 16, 124-140.

Lambrechts, R., 1970: *Les inscriptions avec le mot "tular" et le bornage étrusques,* Florence.

Lanciani, R., 1882: *NSc* 216-240.

Last, H., 1945: The Servian reforms, *JRS* 35, 30-48.

Latte, K., 1960: *Römische Religionsgeschichte,* München (Handbuch der Altertumswissenschaft 5, 4).

Laurence, R., 1994: *Roman Pompeii. Space and society,* London.

Lauter, H., 1976: Die hellenistischen Theater der Samniten und Latiner in ihrer Beziehung zur Theaterarchitektur der Griechen, in P. Zanker (ed.), *Hellenismus in Mittelitalien. Kolloquium in Göttingen vom 5. bis 9. Juni 1974,* Göttingen, 413-422.

Lee, G./W. Barr, 1987: *The Satires of Persius,* Liverpool (Latin and Greek texts 4).

Le Gall, J., 1976: Evocatio, in *Mélanges offerts à Jacques Heurgon. L'Italie préromaine et la Rome républicaine,* Rome (CEFR 27), 519-524.

Lega, C., 1995: Topografia dei culti delle divinità protettrici dell'agricoltura e del lavoro dei campi nel suburbio di Roma, in L. Quilici/S. Quilici Gigli (eds), *Agricoltura e commerci nell'Italia antica,* Roma (Atlante tematico di topografia antica 1), 115-125.

Lejeune, M.L., 1972: Sur l'aspect fédéral du sanctuaire samnite de Calcatello, *REL* 50, 94-111.

Lejeune, M.L., 1990: *Méfitis, d'après les dédicaces lucaniennes de Rossano di Vaglio,* Louvain-la-Neuve (Bibliothèque des cahiers de l'Institut de linguistique de Louvain 51).

Leone, R., 1998: *Luoghi di culto extraurbani d'età arcaica in Magna Grecia,* Firenze (Studi e materiali di archeologia 11).

Letta, C., 1972: *I Marsi e il Fucino nell'antichità,* Milano (Centro studi e documentazione sull'Italia romana. Monografie a supplemento degli Atti 3).

Letta, C., 1979: Una nuova coppia di questori eponimi (*qestur*) da Supinum, *Athenaeum* 57, 404-410.

Letta, C., 1988: Oppida, vici e pagi in area marsa. L'influenza dell'ambiente naturale sulla continuità delle forme di insediamento, in M. Sordi (ed.), *Geografia e storiografia nel mondo classico,* Milano, 217-233.

Letta, C., 1991: Aspetti della romanizzazione in area marsa. Il centro di Amplero, in J. Mertens/R. Lambrechts (eds), *Comunità indigene e problemi della romanizzazione nell'Italia centro-meridionale, IV-III secolo a.C.,* Bruxelles, 157-175.

Letta, C., 1992: I santuari rurali nell'Italia centro-appenninica. Valori religiosi e funzione aggregativa, *MEFRA* 104, 109-124.

Letta, C., 1993: L'epigrafia pubblica di *vici* e *pagi* nella Regio IV. Imitazione del modello urbano e peculiarità del villaggio, in A. Calbi/A. Donati/G. Poma (eds), *L'epigrafia del villaggio. Atti del Colloquio Borghesi, Forlì 27-30 settembre 1990,* Faenza (Epigrafia e antichità 12), 33-48.

Letta, C., 1994: Dall'"*oppidum*" al "*nomen*". I diversi livelli dell'aggregazione politica nel mondo osco-umbro, in L. Aigner Foresti/A. Barzanò/C. Bearzot (eds), *Federazioni e federalismo nell'Europa antica. Bergamo, 21 - 25 settembre 1992. Alle radici della casa comune europea, 1,* Milano, 387-405.

Letta, C., 1997a: I culti di Vesuna e di Valetudo tra Umbria e Marsica, in G. Bonamente/F. Coarelli (eds), *Assisi e gli Umbri nell'antichità,* Assisi, 317-339.

Letta, C., 1997b: Review of *Insediamenti fortificati in area centro-italica,* Pescara 1995, *Athenaeum* 85, 309-313.

Letta, C., 2001: Un lago e il suo popolo, in A. Campanelli (ed.), *Il tesoro del lago. L'archeologia del Fucino e la collezione Torlonia,* Pescara, 139-155.

Letta, C., 2004: Un thesaurus nel santuario oracolare? Osservazioni sull'iscrizione vestina di Monte Queglia a Pescosansonesco (PE), in *Archaeologica Pisana. Scritti per Orlanda Pancrazzi,* Pisa, 237-243.

Letta, C., 2005a: Vicus rurale e vicus urbano nella definizione di Festo (PP.502 E 508 L.), *RCulClMedioev* 47, 81-96.

Letta, C., 2005b: I Marsi dal III sec. a. C. all'alto impero nella collezione Graziani di Alvito (FR), in H. Solin (ed.), *Le epigrafi della Valle di Comino,* Abbazia di Casamari (FR), 47-62.

Letta, C./S. D'Amato, 1975: *Epigrafia della regione dei Marsi,* Milano (Centro studi e documentazione sull'Italia romana. Monografie a supplemento degli Atti 7).

Levene, D.S., 1993: *Religion in Livy,* Leiden (Mnemosyne. Supplements 127).

Levick, B.M., 1967: *Roman colonies in Southern Asia Minor,* Oxford.

Liberatore, D., 2001: Alba Fucens, in A. Campanelli (ed.), *Il tesoro del lago. L'archeologia del Fucino e la collezione Torlonia,* Pescara, 186-210.

Linderski, J., 1968: Der Senat und die Vereine, in M. N. Andreev/J. Irmscher/E. Pólay/W. Warkallo (eds), *Gesellschaft und Recht im griechisch-römischen Altertum,* Berlin (Schriften der Sektion für Altertumswissenschaft. Deutsche Akademie der Wissenschaften zu Berlin 52), 94-132.

Linderski, J., 1995: *Roman questions,* Stuttgart.

Linke, B., 2000: "Religio" und "res publica". Religiöser Glaube und gesellschaftliches Handeln im republikanischen Rom, in B. Linke/M. Stemmler (eds), *Mos maiorum. Untersuchungen zu den Formen der Identitätsstiftung und Stabilisierung in der römischen Republik,* Stuttgart (Historia. Einzelschriften 141), 269-298.

Lindsay, W.M., 1913: *Sexti Pompei Festi de verborum significatu quae supersunt cum Pauli epitome,* Leipzig.

Lippolis, E., 1986: L'architettura, in F. Coarelli (ed.), *Fregellae, 2. Il santuario di Esculapio,* Roma, 29-41.

Lippolis, E., 2000: Cultura figurativa. La scultura "colta" tra età repubblicana e dinastia antonina, in M. Marini Calvani/R. Curina/E. Lippolis (eds), *Aemilia. La cultura romana in Emilia Romagna dal III secolo a.C. all'età costantiniana,* Venezia, 250-278.

Lloyd, J.A., 1991a: Farming the highlands. Samnium and Arcadia in the Hellenistic and early Roman Imperial periods, in G. Barker/J. Lloyd (eds), *Roman landscapes. Archaeological survey in the Mediterranean region,* London (Archaeological monographs of the British School at Rome 2), 180-193.

Lloyd, J.A., 1991b: The Roman villa at S. Maria della Strada, Matrice, in S. Capini/A. di Niro (eds), *Samnium. Archeologia del Molise,* Roma, 261-262.

Lloyd, J.A./N. Christie/G. Lock, 1997: From the mountain to the plain. Landscape evolution in the Abruzzo. An interim report on the Sangro Valley Project, 1994-95, *PBSR* 65, 1-57.

Lloyd, J.A./D.W. Rathbone, 1984: La villa romana a Matrice, *Conoscenze* 1, 216-219.

Lomas, K., 1996: *Roman Italy, 338 B.C. - A.D. 200. A sourcebook,* London.

Lomas, K., 2004: Italy during the Roman republic, 338 - 31 B.C., in H. I. Flower (ed.), *The Cambridge companion to the Roman republic,* Cambridge, 199-224.

Long, C.R., 1987: *The Twelve Gods of Greece and Rome,* Leiden (Études préliminaires aux religions orientales dans l'Empire romain 107).

Luschi, L., 1988: Un caso di continuità di culto dall'epoca preromana al medioevo. Vacuna e Angitia, in *Il territorio del Parco Nazionale d'Abruzzo nell'Antichità,* Civita Alfedena, 197-201.

MacDonald, A.H., 1944: Rome and the Italian Confederation (200-186 B.C.), *JRS* 34, 11-33.

Malkin, I., 1986: Apollo Archegetes and Sicily, *AnnPisa* 16, 959-972.

Malkin, I., 1987: *Religion and colonization in ancient Greece,* Leiden (Studies in Greek and Roman religion 3).

Malkin, I., 1998: *The returns of Odysseus,* Berkeley.

Malone, C./S. Stoddart, 1994: *Territory, time and state. The archaeological development of the Gubbio basin,* Cambridge.

Maltby, R., 2002: *Tibullus. Elegies. Text, introduction and commentary,* Cambridge (Arca 41).

Mancini, M.C., 1998: I riflessi economici e sociali della transumanza nell'Italia centro-meridionale adriatica, *MünstBeitr* 17, 20-28.

Mariani, L., 1901: Aufidena. Ricerche storiche e archeologiche nel Sannio settentrionale, *MonAnt* 10, 225-638.

Marinatos, N./R. Hägg (eds), 1995: *Greek sanctuaries. New approaches,* London.

Marini Calvani, M., 2000: Uomini e dei. Religione e politica sul colle di Covignano, in A. Fontemaggi/O. Piolanti (eds), *Rimini divina. Religioni e devozione nell'evo antico,* Rimini, 49-53.

Martina, M., 1998: Sul cosiddetto *Senatusconsultum de Bacchanalibus, Athenaeum* 86, 85-110.

Mason, H.J., 1974: *Greek terms for Roman institutions. A lexicon and analysis,* Toronto (American studies in papyrology 13).

Massa-Pairault, F.-H., (ed.) 1990: *Crise et transformation des sociétés archaïques de l'Italie antique au Ve siècle av. J.C. Actes de la table ronde, Rome 19-21 novembre 1987,* Rome (CEFR 137).

Matteini Chiari, M., 1994: Sepino. Lo scavo del tempio in località San Pietro, *Conoscenze* 7, 23-29.

Matteini Chiari, M., 1997: s.v. Sepino, *EAA* II Supplemento 1971-1994, 216-220.

Matteini Chiari, M., 2000: Il santuario italico di San Pietro di Cantoni di Sepino, in *Studi sull'Italia dei Sanniti,* Milano, 280-291.

Matteini Chiari, M., (ed.) 2004: *La Dea, il Santo, una Terra. Materiali dallo scavo di San Pietro di Cantoni di Sepino, catalogo della mostra,* Roma.

Mattingly, D.J., 1997: Dialogues of power and experience in the Roman empire, in D. J. Mattingly (ed.), *Dialogues in Roman imperialism. Power, discourse, and discrepant experience in the Roman empire,* Portsmouth (JRA Supplementary series 23), 7-24.

Mattingly, D.J., 2002: Vulgar and weak 'Romanization', or time for a paradigm shift? [Long review of Keay and Terrenato 2001], *JRA* 15, 536-540.

Mattiocco, E., 1981: *Centri fortificati preromani nella Conca di Sulmona. In appendice il centro fortificato del Colle delle Fate di Ornella Zanco,* Chieti.

Mau, A., 1896: Der staedtische Larentempel in Pompeji, *RM* 11, 285-301.

Maurin, L., 1995: Pagus Mercurialis Veteranorum Medelitanorum. Implantations vétéranes dans la vallée de l'oued Miliane. Le dossier épigraphique, *MEFRA* 107, 97-135.

Mavrojannis, T., 1995: L'*aedicula* dei *Lares Compitales* nel *Compitum* degli *Hermaistai* a Delo, *BCH* 119, 89-123.

McInerny, J., 2006: Sacred land and the margins of the community, in R. M. Rosen/I. Sluiter (eds), *City, countryside, and the spatial organization of value in classical antiquity*, Leiden (Mnemosyne. Supplements 279), 33-59.

Menichetti, M., 2005: s.v. Aedicula (romano-repubblicana), *ThesCRA* IV, 162-164.

Menozzi, O., 1998: Ricognizioni nell'Ager Hatrianus. Storia, insediamenti ed economia di un territorio I, La ricerca. Metodologia, finalità e lettura dei dati. Viabilità e quadro degli insediamenti, *MünstBeitr* 17, 33-45.

Meritt, B.D., 1927: Excavations at Corinth, 1927, *AJA* 31, 450-461.

Mertens, J., 1969: Deux temples italiques à Alba Fucens, in J. Mertens (ed.), *Alba Fucens II*, Bruxelles, Rome, 7-22.

Messineo, G., 1986: Il vicus di S. Rustico, in *La valle del medio e basso Vomano, II*, Roma (Documenti dell'Abruzzo teramano 2), 136-167.

Messineo, G./A. Pellegrino, 1984: Ellenismo in Abruzzo. La stipe di Basciano, in *Alessandria e il mondo ellenistico-romano. Studi in onore di A. Adriani, III*, Roma, 695-710.

Metzler, J./M. Millet/N. Roymans/J. Slofstra (eds), 1995: *Integration in the Early Roman West. The role of culture and ideology*, Luxembourg (Dossiers d'archéologie du Musée National d'Histoire et d'Art 4).

Miari, M., 2000a: I culti in epoca preromana. Persistenza e continuità, in M. Marini Calvani/R. Curina/E. Lippolis (eds), *Aemilia. La cultura romana in Emilia Romagna dal III secolo a.C. all'età costantiniana*, Venezia, 320-322.

Miari, M., 2000b: *Stipi votive dell'Etruria padana*, Roma (Corpus delle stipi votive in Italia 11).

Miller, J.F., 1991: *Ovid's Elegiac Festivals*, Frankfurt a. M. (Studien zur klassischen Philologie 55).

Millett, M., 1990a: *The Romanization of Britain. An essay in archaeological interpretation*, Cambridge.

Millett, M., 1990b: Romanization. Historical issues and archaeological interpretation, in T. Blagg/M. Millett (eds), *The early Roman empire in the West*, Oxford, 35-41.

Minak, F., 2006a: Addendum sui *pocola*, in *Ariminum. Storia e archeologia*, Roma (Adrias 2), 239-240.

Minak, F., 2006b: In margine ai *pocola*. Una nuova testimonianza, 1 in *Ariminum. Storia e archeologia*, Roma (Adrias 2), 41-46.

Mingazzini, P., 1938: Il santuario della dea Marica alle foci del Garigliano *MonAnt* 32, 693-981.

Mingazzini, P., 1958: Tre brevi note di ceramica ellenistica, *ArchCl* 10, 218-226.

Modes, 1983: *Modes de contacts et processus de transformation dans les sociétés anciennes. Actes du colloque de Cortone (24-30 mai 1981) organisé par la Scuola normale superiore et l'École française de Rome avec la collaboration du Centre de recherches d'histoire ancienne de l'Université de Besançon*, Rome (CEFR 67).

Mommsen, T., 1858: Sui modi usati dai Romani nel conservare e pubblicare le leggi e i senatusconsulti, *AdI* 198-205.

Mommsen, T., 1877: *Römisches Staatsrecht*, Leipzig.

Mommsen, T., 1887: Die römische Tribuseintheilung nach dem marsischen Krieg, *Hermes* 22, 101-106.

Mommsen, T., 1899: *Römisches Strafrecht*, Leipzig.

Mommsen, T., (1976) 1854-1855: *Römische Geschichte*, München.

Moormann, E.M., in prep.: *Divine interiors. Mural paintings in Greek and Roman sanctuaries*.

Morel, J.-P., 1976: Le sanctuaire de Vastogirardi (Molise) et les influences hellénistiques en Italie centrale, in P. Zanker (ed.), *Hellenismus in Mittelitalien. Kolloquium in Göttingen vom 5. bis 9. Juni 1974*, Göttingen 255-262.

Morel, J.-P., 1981: *Céramique campanienne. Les formes*, Rome (BEFAR 244).

Morel, J.-P., 1984: Gli scavi del santuario di Vastogirardi, in *Sannio. Pentri e Frentani dal VI al I sec. a.C. Atti del convegno, Isernia 10-11 novembre 1980*, Campobasso, 35-41.

Morel, J.-P., 1988: Artisanat et colonisation dans l'Italie romaine aux IVe et IIIe siècles av. J.-C., *DialA* 6, 49-63.

Morel, J.-P./F. Coarelli, 1973: Pocola, in *Roma medio repubblicana. Aspetti culturali di Roma e del Lazio nei secoli IV e III a.C.*, Roma, 57-66.

Mouritsen, H., 1990: A note on Pompeian epigraphy and social structure, *ClMediaev* 61, 131-149.

Mouritsen, H., 1998: *Italian unification. A study in ancient and modern historiography*, London (Bulletin of the Institute of Classical Studies. Supplement 70).

Mouritsen, H., 2004: Pits and politics. Interpreting colonial fora in Republican Italy, *PBSR* 72, 37-67.

Mouritsen, H., 2006: Hindsight and historiography. Writing the history of pre-Roman Italy, in M. Jehne/R. Pfeilschifter (eds), *Herrschaft ohne Integration? Rom und Italien in republikanischer Zeit*, Frankfurt a. M. (Studien zur Alten Geschichte 4), 23-37.

Mouritsen, H., 2007: The *civitas sine suffragio*. Ancient concepts and modern ideology, *Historia* 56, 141-158.

Mueller, K.O., 1839: *Sextus Pompeius Festus. De verborum significatione quae supersunt cum Pauli Epitome*, Leipzig.

Naerebout, F.G., 2007: The temple at Ras el-Soda. Is it an Isis temple? Is it Greek, Roman, Egyptian, or neither? And so what?, in L. Bricault/M. J. Versluys/P. G. P. Meyboom (eds), *Nile into Tiber. Egypt in the Roman world. Proceedings of the IIIrd International Conference of Isis Studies, Faculty of Archaeology, Leiden University, May 11-14, 2005*, Leiden (Religions in the Graeco-Roman world 159), 506-554.

Nielsen, I., 2002: *Cultic theatres and ritual drama. A study in regional development and religious interchange between East and West in Antiquity*, Aarhus (Aarhus studies in Mediterranean antiquity 4).

Nippel, W., 1997: Orgien, Ritualmorde und Verschwörung? Die Bacchanalien-Prozesse des Jahres 186 v.Chr., in U. Manthe/J. von Ungern-Sternberg (eds), *Grosse Prozesse der römischen Antike*, München, 65-73.

Nonnis, D., 1994-1995: Un "thesaurus" iscritto d'età repubblicana da Anagni, *RendPontAc* 67, 153-165.

Nonnis, D., 2003: Dotazioni funzionali e di arredo in luoghi di culto dell'Italia repubblicana. L'apporto della documentazione epigrafica, in O. De Cazanove/J. Scheid (eds), *Sanctuaires et sources dans l'antiquité. Les sources documentaires et leurs limites dans la description des lieux de culte. Actes de la table ronde*, Naples (Collection du Centre Jean Bérard 22), 25-54.

North, J.A., 1979: Religious Toleration in Republican Rome, *ProcCambrPhilSoc* 205, 85-103.

North, J.A., 1995: Religion and rusticity, in: T.J. Cornell/K. Lomas (eds), *Urban society in Roman Italy*, London, 135-150.

Oakley, S.P., 1995: *The hill-forts of the Samnites*, London (Archaeological monographs of the British School at Rome 10).

Orlin, E.M., 1997: *Temples, religion and politics in the Roman Republic*, Leiden (Mnemosyne. Supplements 164).

Orr, D.G., 1978: Roman domestic religion. The evidence of the household shrines, in *ANRW*, II 16.2, Berlin, 1557-1591.

Ortalli, J., 2000: Rimini. La città, in M. Marini Calvani/R. Curina/E. Lippolis (eds), *Aemilia. La cultura romana in Emilia Romagna dal III secolo a.C. all età costantiniana*, Venezia, 501-506.

Osanna, M./M.M. Sica, 2005: *Torre di Satriano I. Il santuario lucano*, Venosa (Quaderni archeologici. Deputazione di storia patria per la Lucania).

Osborne, R./B. Cunliffe, 2005: *Mediterranean urbanization 800-600 BC*, Oxford (Proceedings of the British Academy 126).

Pagano, M., 2005: Osservazioni sulla storia del complesso di Santa Maria delle Monache e sulla topografia antica di Isernia, *ConocenzSemest* 1, 69-78.

Pagano, M./A. Ceccarelli/A. D'Andrea, 2005: La ripresa delle esplorazioni e degli scavi nel santuario italico di Vastogirardi (IS), in D. Caiazza (ed.), *Italica ars. Studi in onore di Giovanni Colonna per il premio i Sanniti*, Piedimonte Matese, 451-505.

Pagenstecher, R., 1909: *Die kalenische Reliefkeramik*, Berlin (Jahrbuch des Kaiserlichen Deutschen Archäologischen Instituts. Ergänzungsheft 8).

Pailler, J.M., 1986: *Bacchanalia. La répression de 186 av. J.C. à Rome et en Italie. Vestiges, images, tradition*, Rome (BEFAR 270).

Palmer, R.E.A., 1976: A poem of all season. AE 1928.108, *Phoenix* 30, 159-173.

Paoletti, M., 1988: L'insediamento di Amplero (Collelongo e Ortucchio) dall'età preromana al tardoantico. Sintesi delle ricerche, in *Il territorio del Parco nazionale d'Abruzzo nell'antichità. Atti del I Convegno nazionale di archeologia, Villetta Barrea 1-3 maggio 1987,* Civitella Alfedena, 209-249.

Pasquinucci, M., 1996: Il Sannio Pentro. Territorio ed economia, in L. Del Tutto Palma (ed.), *La tavola di Agnone nel contesto italico. Convegno di studio, Agnone 13 - 15 aprile 1994,* Firenze, 17-26.

Patterson, J.R., 2006a: *Landscapes and cities. Rural settlement and civic transformation in early imperial Italy,* Oxford.

Patterson, J.R., 2006b: Rome and Italy, in N. Rosenstein/R. Morstein-Marx (eds), *A companion to the Roman Republic,* Malden (Blackwell companions to the ancient world), 606-624.

Pedroni, L., 1986: *Ceramica a vernice nera da Cales,* Napoli.

Pedroni, L., 1990: *Ceramica a vernice nera da Cales 2,* Napoli.

Pedroni, L., 1993: Problemi di topografia e urbanistica calena, *Samnium* 66, 208-230.

Pedroni, L., 2001: *Ceramica calena a vernice nera. Produzione e diffusione,* Città di Castello.

Pelgrom, J., 2004: Sacrale plaatsen en culturele identiteit in Romeins Lucanië, *TMA* 32, 21-28.

Pelgrom, J., 2008: Settlement Organization and Land Distribution in Latin Colonies before the Second Punic War, in L. de Ligt/S. J. Northwood (eds), *People, Land and Politics. Demographic Developments and the Transformation of Roman Italy 300 BC-AD 14,* Leiden (Mnemosyne. Supplements 303), 317-356.

Pellegrino, A./G. Messineo, 1991: Note sul vicus di S. Rustico di Basciano (Teramo), *Miscellanea Greca e Romana* 16, 269-286.

Persichetti, N., 1914: Dell'antico nome del villaggio di Paganica nei Vestini, *RM* 29, 127-139.

Peruzzi, E., 1962: Testi latini arcaici dei Marsi, *Maia* 14, 117-140.

Petracco Sicardi, G., 1969: Problemi di topografia veleiate, in *Atti del III Convegno di studi veleiati, Piacenza, Veleia, Parma 31-5 - 2-6 1967,* Milano, 207-218.

Petrocelli, E., (ed.) 1999: *La civiltà della transumanza. Storia, cultura e valorizzazione dei tratturi e del mondo pastorale in Abruzzo, Molise, Puglia, Campania e Basilicata,* Isernia.

Pfeilschifter, R., 2006: How is the empire? Roms Wissen um Italien im dritten und zweiten Jahrhundert v.Chr., in M. Jehne/R. Pfeilschifter (eds), *Herrschaft ohne Integration? Rom und Italien in republikanischer Zeit,* Frankfurt a. M. (Studien zur Alten Geschichte 4), 111-137.

Phillips III, C.R., 1988: The compitalia and the 'carmen contra paganos', *Historia* 37, 383-384.

Piccaluga, G., 1961: Penates e Lares, *StMatStorRel* 32, 81-97.

Piccaluga, G., 1974: *Terminus. I segni di confine nella religione romana,* Roma (Quaderni di studi e materiali di storia delle religioni 9).

Piccaluga, G., 1981: Fides nella religione romana di età imperiale, in *ANRW,* II, 17, 2., Berlin, 703-735.

Pieri, G., 1968: *L'histoire du cens jusqu'à la fin de la république romaine,* Paris (Publications de l'Institut de droit romain de l'Université de Paris 25).

Pippidi, D.M., (ed.) 1976: *Assimilation et résistance à la culture gréco-romaine dans le monde ancien. Travaux du VI-e Congrès International d'Études Classiques (Madrid, 4 au 10 septembre 1974),* Paris.

Pisani Sartorio, G., 1988: Compita Larum. Edicole sacre nei crocicchi di Roma antica, *BStorArt* 31, 23-34.

Pobjoy, M., 1998: The decree of the Pagus Herculaneus and the Romanisation of Oscan Capua, *Arctos* 32, 175-195.

Pobjoy, M., 2000: The first Italia, in E. Herring/K. Lomas (eds), *The emergence of state identities in Italy in the first millennium B.C.,* London, 187-211.

Polinskaya, I., 2003: Liminality as metaphor. Initiation and the frontiers of ancient Athens, in D. B. Dodd/C. A. Faraone (eds), *Initiation in ancient Greek rituals and narratives. New critical perspectives,* London, 85-106.

Porzio Gernia, M.L., 2004: *Offerta rituale e mondo divino. Contributo all'interpretazione delle tavole di Gubbio,* Alessandria.

Potter, T.W., 1987: *Roman Italy*, London.

Poultney, J.W., 1959: *The bronze tables of Iguvium*, Baltimore (Philological monographs of the American Philological Association 18).

Prosdocimi, A.L., 1984: *Le tavole Iguvine*, Firenze (Lingue e iscrizioni dell'Italia antica 4).

Prosdocimi, A.L., 1989: Le religioni degli Italici, in G. Pugliese Carratelli (ed.), *Italia omnium terrarum parens*, Milano, 477-545.

Prosperi Valenti, G., 1998: *Valetudo. Origine ed aspetti del culto nel mondo romano*, Roma (Studi pubblicati dall'istituto italiano per la storia antica 67).

Radke, G., 1983: Wollgebilde an den Compitalia, *WürzbJb* 9, 173-178.

Rainini, I., 1985: *Il santuario di Mefite in Valle d'Ansanto*, Roma (Archaeologica 60).

Rainini, I., 1996: *Capracotta. L'abitato sannitico di Fonte del Romito*, Roma.

Rainini, I., 2000: Modelli, forme e strutture insediative del mondo sannitico, in *Studi sull'Italia dei Sanniti*, Milano, 238-254.

Renfrew, A.C., 1975: Trade as action at a distance. Questions of integration and communication, in J. Sabloff/C. C. Lamberg-Karlovsly (eds), *Ancient civilization and trade*, Albuquerque (School of American research. Advanced seminar series), 3-59.

Renfrew, A.C., 1985: *The archaeology of cult. The sanctuary at Phylakopi*, Athens/London (Supplementary volume of the the British School of Archaeology at Athens 18).

Reusser, C., 1993: *Der Fidestempel auf dem Kapitol in Rom und seine Ausstattung. Ein Beitrag zu den Ausgrabungen an der Via del Mare und um das Kapitol 1926-1943*, Roma (Bullettino della Commissione Archeologica Comunale di Roma. Supplementi 2).

Riccioni, G., 1965: Ceramiche rinvenute nell'area del palazzo ex Battaglini, in *Arte e civiltà romana nell'Italia settentrionale. Dalla repubblica alla tetrarchia. Catalogo Bologna, Palazzo del'Archiginnasio, 20 settembre - 22 novembre 1964*, Bologna, 111-121.

Rix, H., 2002: *Sabellische Texte. Die Texte des Oskischen, Umbrischen und Südpikenischen*, Heidelberg (Handbuch der italischen Dialekte 5).

Rizzi, V., 1855: Nuove scoperte sannitiche, *BullArchNap*, serie 2 3, 130-139.

Rohde, G., 1942: s.v. Paganalia, *RE* XVIII-1, 2293-2295.

Roma 1973: *Roma medio repubblicana. Aspetti culturali di Roma e del Lazio nei secoli IV e III a.C.*, Roma.

Romanisation 1991: *La romanisation du Samnium aux IIe et Ier siècles av. J.C. Actes du colloque, Naples 4-5 novembre 1988*, Naples (Bibliothèque de l'Institut Français de Naples. Série II, 9).

Rosenberger, V., 2005: Prodigien aus Italien. Geographische Verteilung und religiöse Kommunikation, *CahGlotz* 16, 235-257.

Rouveret, A., 1986: Tite-Live, Histoire romaine IX,40. La description des armes samnites ou les pièges de la symétrie, in A.-M. Adam/A. Rouveret (eds), *Guerre et sociétés en Italie aux Ve et IVe siècles avant J.-C.*, Paris, 91-120.

Roymans, N., 1995: Romanization, cultural identity and the ethnic discussion, in J. Metzler/M. Millet/N. Roymans/J. Slofstra (eds), *Integration in the Early Roman West. The role of culture and ideology*, Luxembourg (Dossiers d'archéologie du Musée National d'Histoire et d'Art 4), 47-65.

Roymans, N. (ed.), 1996: *From the sword to the plough. Three studies on the earliest romanisation of Northern Gaul*, Amsterdam (Amsterdam Archaeological Series 1).

Rudolph, H., 1935: *Stadt und Staat im Römischen Italien. Untersuchungen über die Entwicklung des Munizipalwesens in der republikanischen Zeit*, Leipzig.

Rüpke, J., 1990: *Domi militiae. Die religiöse Konstruktion des Krieges in Rom*, Stuttgart.

Rüpke, J., 1995: *Kalender und Öffentlichkeit. Die Geschichte der Repräsentation und religiösen Qualifikation von Zeit in Rom*, Berlin (Religionsgeschichtliche Versuche und Vorarbeiten 40).

Rüpke, J., 2007: Roman religion- religions of Rome, in J. Rüpke (ed.), *A companion to Roman religion*, Malden ((Blackwell companions to the Ancient World), 1-9.

Russo, F., 2003: Il sistema insediativo sannitico nelle fonti letterarie, *RCulClMedioev* 45, 277-304.

Sabattini, A., 1977: Sulla transumanza in Varrone, *Athenaeum* 55, 199-203.

Salmon, E.T., 1967: *Samnium and the Samnites*, Cambridge.

Salmon, E.T., 1969: *Roman colonization under the Republic*, London (Aspects of Greek and Roman Life).

Salmon, E.T., 1982: *The making of Roman Italy*, London (Aspects of Greek and Roman life).

Samter, E., 1901: *Familienfeste der Griechen und Römer*, Berlin.

Samter, E., 1907: Der Ursprung des Larenkultes, *Archiv für Religionswissenschaft* 10, 368-392.

Sanesi, L., 1978: Sulla firma di un ceramista caleno e sulla questione dei *vici*, *PP* 39, 74–77.

Sannio 1980: *Sannio. Pentri e Frentani dal VI al I sec. a.C. Isernia, catalogo della mostra*, Roma.

Sannio 1984: *Sannio. Pentri e Frentani dal VI al I sec. a.C. Atti del convegno, Isernia 10-11 novembre 1980*, Campobasso.

Sanniti 2000: *Studi sull'Italia dei Sanniti*, Milano.

Sardella, B., 2008: Esperienze di survey. Castropignano, in G. De Benedittis (ed.), *Molise. Esperienze di survey. Riccia, Oratino, Castropignano*, Isernia, 122-211.

Schachter, A., (ed.) 1992: *Le sanctuaire grec. Huit exposés suivis de discussions*, Vandœuvres–Genève (Entretiens sur l'antiquité classique 37).

Scheid, J., 1985a: Numa et Jupiter ou les dieux citoyens de Rome, *Archive des sciences sociales des religions* 59, 41-53.

Scheid, J., 1985b: *Religion et piété à Rome*, Paris (Textes à l'appui).

Scheid, J., 1987: Les sanctuaires de confins dans la Rome antique. Réalité et permanence d'une représentation idéale de l'espace romain, in *L'Urbs. Espace urbain et histoire. Ier siècle av. J.C. - IIIe siècle ap. J.C. Actes du colloque international, Rome, 8 - 12 mai 1985*, Rome (CEFR 96), 583-595.

Scheid, J., 1990: *Romulus et ses frères. Le collège des Frères Arvales, modèle du culte public dans la Rome des empereurs*, Rome (BEFAR 275).

Scheid, J., 1997: Comment identifier un lieu de culte?, *CahGlotz* 8, 51-59.

Scheid, J., 1999: Aspects religieux de la municipalisation. Quelques réflexions générales, in M. Dondin-Payre/M.-T. Raepsaet-Charlier (eds), *Cités, municipes, colonies. Les processus de municipalisation en Gaule et en Germanie sous le Haut-Empire romain*, Paris (Histoire ancienne et médiévale 53), 381-423.

Scheid, J., 2006a: Oral tradition and written tradition in the formation of sacred law in Rome, in C. Ando/J. Rüpke/S. Blake (eds), *Religion and law in classical and Christian Rome*, Stuttgart (Potsdamer Altertumswissenschaftliche Beiträge 15), 14-33.

Scheid, J., 2006b: Rome et les grands lieux de culte d'Italie, in A. Vigourt/X. Loriot/A. Bérenger-Badel/B. Klein (eds), *Pouvoir et religion dans le monde romain*, Paris, 75-86.

Scheidel, W., 2004: Human mobility in Roman Italy, I. The free population, *JRS* 94, 1-26.

Schiavi 2001: *Schiavi d'Abruzzo. "Verso la cima del monte". I templi italici, l'ambiente e il territorio, l'archeologia e la storia*, Sulmona.

Schröder, B., 1991: *Carmina non quae nemorale resultent. Ein Kommentar zur 4. Ekloge des Calpurnius Siculus*, Frankfurt a.M. (Studien zur klassischen Philologie 61).

Schubert, C., 1996: *Land und Raum in der römischen Republik. Die Kunst des Teilens*, Darmstadt.

Schulten, A., 1894: Die Landgemeinden im römischen Reiche, *Philologus* 53, 629-686.

Schulze, W., 1933: *Zur Geschichte lateinischer Eigennamen*, Berlin (Abhandlungen der Königlichen Gesellschaft der Wissenschaften zu Göttingen. Philologisch-historische Klasse. Neue Folge 5, 5).

Scott, J.C., 1990: *Domination and the arts of resistance. Hidden transcripts*, New Haven.

Scullard, H.H., 1981: *Festivals and ceremonies of the Roman republic*, London (Aspects of Greek and Roman life).

Siebert, A.V., 1999: *Instrumenta sacra. Untersuchungen zu römischen Opfer-, Kult- und Priestergeräten*, Berlin (Religionsgeschichtliche Versuche und Vorarbeiten 44).

Sirago, V.A., 2000: *Il sannio romano. Caratteri e persistenze di una civiltà negata*, Napoli (Citra & ultra 2).

Sisani, S., 2001a: Aquilonia. Una nuova ipotesi di identificazione, *Eutopia* 1-2, 131-147.
Sisani, S., 2001b: *Tuta Ikuvina. Sviluppo e ideologia della forma urbana a Gubbio*, Roma.
Sisani, S., 2002: British Umbria. Quasi una recensione ad uno studio recente, *Eutopia* 2, 123-139.
Sisani, S., 2007: *Fenomenologia della conquista. La romanizzazione dell'Umbria tra il IV sec. a.C. e la guerra sociale*, Roma (Quaderni di Eutopia 7).
Sogliano, A., 1896: Arpino. Stipe di monete repubblicane di bronzo, *NSc* 370-371.
Sordi, M., 1969: *Roma e i Sanniti nel IV secolo a.C.*, Rocca San Casciano (Saggi di antichità).
Sordi, M., (ed.) 1984: *I santuari e la guerra nel mondo classico*, Milano (Contributi dell'Istituto di storia antica 10).
Spadea, R., 1977: Nuove ricerche sul territorio dell'ager Teuranus, *Klearchos* 19, 123-159.
Spadea, R., 1988: I Brettii e l'ager Teuranus, in P. Poccetti (ed.), *Per un'identità culturale dei Brettii*, Napoli, 201-208.
Spinazzola, V., 1953: *Pompei alla luce degli scavi nuovi di Via dell'Abbondanza (anni 1910-1923)*, Roma.
Staffa, A.R., 1991: Contributo per una ricostruzione del quadro insediativo dall'età romana al medioevo, in *La valle dell'alto Vomano ed i Monti della Laga*, Pescara (Documenti dell'Abruzzo teramano 3), 189-267.
Staffa, A.R., 1996: Contributo per una ricostruzione del quadro insediativo dall'età romana al medioevo, in *Le valli della Vibrata e del Salinello*, Pescara, 252-331.
Staffa, A.R./M.P. Moscetta, 1986: Contributo per una carta archeologica della media e bassa Valle Del Vomano, in *La valle del medio e basso Vomano, II*, Roma (Documenti dell'Abruzzo teramano 2), 167-223.
Stazio, A./S. Ceccoli/J.-L. Amselle (eds), 1999: *Confini e frontiera nella grecità d'Occidente. Atti del trentasettesimo convegno di studi sulla Magna Grecia, Taranto 3-6 ottobre 1997*, Taranto (Convegno di studi sulla Magna Grecia 37).
Stek, T.D., 2004: Rome en Samnium. Een dialoog, *TMA* 32, 29-36.
Stek, T.D., 2005a: Sacred landscape and the construction of identity. Samnium and the Roman world, in C. Briault/J. Green/A. Kaldelis/A. Stellatou (eds), *SOMA 2003. Symposium on Mediterranean archaeology (Conference Proceedings, London 21- 23 February 2003)*, London (BAR Int. Ser. 1391), 147-150.
Stek, T.D., 2005b: Sacrale landschappen en survey. Opzet voor een interpretatie van het romaniseringsproces in Midden-Italië, in E. van Rossenberg/J. Hendriks/A. Bright/D. Smal (eds), *SOJAbundel2002/2003*, Leiden/Amsterdam, 177-184.
Stek, T.D., 2006: Settlement and cultural change in central-southern Italy [Long review of Jones 2004], *JRA* 19, 401-406.
Stek, T.D., 2008: A Roman cult in the Italian countryside? The *Compitalia* and the shrines of the *Lares Compitales*, *BABESCH* 83, 111-132.
Stek, T.D., in press: 'Italic' or 'Roman' sanctuaries and the so-called *pagus-vicus* system. Questions of cult and continuity, in M. Jehne (ed.), *Religiöse Vielfalt und soziale Integration. Die Bedeutung der Religion für die kulturelle Identität und die politische Stabilität im republikanischen Italien*.
Stek, T.D./J. Pelgrom, 2005: Samnite sanctuaries surveyed. Preliminary report of the sacred landscape project 2004, *BABESCH* 80, 65-71.
Strazzulla, M.J., 1971: *Il santuario sannitico di Pietrabbondante*, Roma (Documenti di antichità italiche e romane 1).
Strazzulla, M.J., 1981: Le terrecotte architettoniche. Le produzioni dal IV al I sec. a.C., in A. Giardina/A. Schiavone (eds), *Società romana e produzione schiavistica, 2. Merci, mercati e scambi nel Mediterraneo*, Bari, 187-207.
Strazzulla, M.J., 2006: I santuari, in P. de Felice/V. Torrieri (eds), *Museo Civico archeologico F. Savini (Teramo). Catalogo*, Teramo, 85-98.
Susini, G.C., 1965: Aspects de la romanisation de la Gaule Cispadane. Chute et survivance des Celtes, *CRAI* 1965, 143-163.

Susini, G.C., 1965-66: Coloni romani dal Piceno al Po, *Studia Picena* 33-34, 82-143.

Sydenham, E.A., 1952: *The coinage of the Roman republic*, London.

Tabeling, E., 1932: *Mater Larum. Zum Wesen der Laren-religion*, Frankfurt a.M. (Frankfurter Studien zur Religion und Kultur der Antike 1).

Tagliamonte, G., 1994: *I figli di Marte. Ricerche di storia sociale su mobilità, mercenari e mercenariato italici in Magna Grecia e Sicilia*, Roma (Tyrrhenica 3).

Tagliamonte, G., 1997: *I Sanniti. Caudini, Irpini, Pentri, Carricini, Frentani*, Milano (Biblioteca di archeologia 25).

Tagliamonte, G., 2002-2003: Dediche di armi nei santuari sannitici, *CuadPrehistA* 28-29, 95-125.

Tagliamonte, G., 2004: Horsemen and Dioskouroi worship in Samnite sanctuaries, in H. Jones (ed.), *Samnium. Settlement and cultural change. The proceedings of the Third E. Togo Salmon Conference on Roman Studies*, Providence R.I. (Archeologica transatlantica 22), 103-114.

Tagliamonte, G., 2006: Et vetera spolia hostium detrahunt templis porticibusque. Annotazioni sul riuso delle armi dedicate nell'Italia antica, *Pallas* 70, 265-287.

Tagliamonte, G., 2007: Considerazioni sull'architettura santuariale di età tardo-repubblicana tra Campania e Sannio, in L. Quilici/S. Quilici Gigli (eds), *Architettura pubblica e privata nell'Italia antica*, Roma (Atlante tematico di topografia antica 16), 53-68.

Takács, S.A., 2000: Politics and religion in the Bacchanalian affair of 186 B.C.E., *HarvStClPhil* 100, 301-310.

Tarpin, M., 1993: Inscriptions des vici et des pagi dans les Trois Gaules et les Germanies in A. Calbi/A. Donati/G. Poma (eds), *L'epigrafia del villaggio. Atti del Colloquio Borghesi, Forlì 27-30 settembre 1990*, Faenza (Epigrafia e antichità 12), 217-236.

Tarpin, M., 1999: Colonia, municipium, vicus. Institutionen und Stadtformen, in N. Hanel/C. Schucany (eds), *Colonia, municipium, vicus. Struktur und Entwicklung städtischer Siedlungen in Noricum, Rätien und Obergermanien. Beiträge der Arbeitsgemeinschaft "Römische Archäologie" bei der Tagung des West- und Süddeutschen Verbandes für Altertumsforschung in Wien, 21.-23.5.1997*, Oxford (BAR Int. Ser. 783), 1-10.

Tarpin, M., 2002: *Vici et pagi dans l'Occident romain*, Rome (CEFR 299).

Taylor, L.R., 1960: *The voting districts of the Roman republic*, Rome (Papers and monographs of the American Academy in Rome 20).

Terrenato, N., 1998a: The Romanization of Italy. Global acculturation or cultural bricolage?, in C. Forcey/J.J. Hawthorne/R. Witcher (eds), *TRAC 97. Proceedings of the Seventh Annual Theoretical Roman Archaeology Conference, University of Nottingham, April 1997*, Oxford 20-27.

Terrenato, N., 1998b: Tam firmum municipium. The Romanization of Volaterrae and its cultural implications, *JRS* 88, 94-114.

Terrenato, N., 2001: A tale of three cities. The Romanization of northern coastal Etruria, in S.J. Keay/N. Terrenato (eds), *Italy and the West. Comparative issues in Romanization*, Oxford 54-67.

Terrenato, N., 2005: "Start the revolution without me". Recent debates in Italian classical archaeology, in P. Attema/A. Nijboer/A. Zifferero (eds), *Papers in Italian archaeology, 6. Communities and settlements from the neolithic to the early medieval period. Proceedings of the 6th Conference of Italian archaeology held at the University of Groningen, Groningen Institute of Archaeology, April 15-17, 2003*, Oxford (BAR Int. Ser. 125), 39-43.

Terzani, C., 1991: La colonia latina di Aesernia, in S. Capini/A. Di Niro (eds), *Samnium. Archeologia del Molise*, Roma, 111-112.

Terzani, C., 1996: L'ambiente latino. Isernia, in L. Del Tutto Palma (ed.), *La tavola di Agnone nel contesto italico. Convegno di studio, Agnone 13 - 15 aprile 1994*, Isernia, 3-16.

Teutsch, L., 1962: *Das Städtewesen in Nordafrika in der Zeit von C. Gracchus bis zum Tode des Kaisers Augustus*, Berlin.

Thomas, E./C. Witschel, 1992: Constructing reconstruction. Claim and reality of Roman rebuilding inscriptions from the Latin West, *PBSR* 60, 135-177.

Thomsen, R., 1980: *King Servius Tullius. A historical synthesis,* Copenhagen (Humanitas 5).

Tocco, G., 2000: Frammento di legge in lingua osca su tavola bronzea, in *Studi sull'Italia dei Sanniti,* Milano, 224-229.

Todd, M., 1985: Forum and Capitolium in the Early Empire, in F. Grew/B. Hobley (eds), *Roman urban topography in Britain and the Western empire. Proceedings of the Third Conference on Urban Archaeology, London 1985,* London, 56-66.

Todisco, E., 2001: I vicani cultori degli dei, *Epigrafia e territorio. Politica e società. Temi di antichità romane* 6, 137-147.

Todisco, E., 2004a: La percezione delle realtà rurali nell'*Italia* romana. I *vici* e i *pagi, Epigrafia e territorio. Politica e società. Temi di antichità romane* 7, 161-184.

Todisco, E., 2004b: Testimonianze sui paganici?, *Epigrafia e territorio. Politica e società. Temi di antichità romane* 7, 185-209.

Todisco, E., 2006: Sulla glossa "vici" nel "De verborum significatu" di Festo. La struttura del testo, in L. Capogrossi Colognesi/E. Gabba (eds), *Gli statuti municipali,* Pavia (Pubblicazioni del CEDANT 2), 605-614.

Torelli, M., 1968: Il donario di M. Fulvio Flacco nell'area di S. Omobono, *QuadTopAnt* 5, 71-76.

Torelli, M., 1970-1971: Contributo dell'archeologia alla storia sociale. L'Etruria e l'Apulia, *DialA* 4-5, 431-442.

Torelli, M., 1973: Le stipi votive, in *Roma medio repubblicana. Aspetti culturali di Roma e del Lazio nei secoli IV e III a.C.,* Roma, 138-139.

Torelli, M., 1977: Greci e indigeni in Magna Grecia. Ideologia religiosa e rapporti di classe, *Studi Storici* 18, 45-61.

Torelli, M., 1982: Veio, la città, l'arx e il culto di Giunone Regina, in H. Blanck (ed.), *Miscellanea archaeologica Tobias Dohrn dedicata,* Roma, 117-128.

Torelli, M., 1983: Edilizia pubblica in Italia centrale tra guerra sociale ed età augustea. Ideologia e classi sociali, in M. Cébeillac-Gervasoni (ed.), *Les bourgeoisies municipales italiennes aux IIe et Ier siècles av. J.C. Centre Jean Bérard, Institut français de Naples, 7-10 décembre 1981,* Paris (Bibliothèque de l'Institut français de Naples. Sér. II, 6), 241-250.

Torelli, M., 1984: *Lavinio e Roma. Riti iniziatici e matrimonio tra archeologia e storia,* Roma (Lectiones Planetariae).

Torelli, M., 1988a: Aspetti ideologici della colonizzazione romana più antica, *DialA* 6, 65-72.

Torelli, M., 1988b: Le popolazioni dell'Italia antica. Società e forme del potere, in A. Schiavone (ed.), *Storia di Roma, 1. Roma in Italia,* Torino, 53-74.

Torelli, M., 1988c: L'età regia e repubblicana, in P. Gros/M. Torelli (eds), *Storia dell'urbanistica. Il mondo romano,* Bari/Roma, 3-164.

Torelli, M., 1990: Il modello urbano e l'immagine della città in S. Settis (ed.), *Civiltà dei Romani. La città, il territorio, l'impero,* Milano, 43-64.

Torelli, M., 1991: Il 'diribitorium' di Alba Fucens e il 'campus' eroico di Herdonia, in J. Mertens/R. Lambrechts (eds), *Comunità indigene e problemi della romanizzazione nell'Italia centro-meridionale, IV-III secolo a.C.,* Bruxelles, Rome, 39-63.

Torelli, M., 1992: Aspetti materiali e ideologici della romanizzazione della Daunia, *DialA* 10, 47-64.

Torelli, M., 1993a: Fictiles fabulae. Rappresentazione e romanizzazione nei cicli figurati fittili repubblicani, *Ostraka* 2, 269-299.

Torelli, M., 1993b: Gli aromi e il sale. Afrodite ed Eracle nell'emporia arcaica dell'Italia, in A. Mastrocinque (ed.), *Ercole in occidente,* Trento (Labirinti 2), 91-117.

Torelli, M., 1995: *Studies in the romanization of Italy,* Edmonton.

Torelli, M., 1996: La romanizzazione del Sannio, in L. Del Tutto Palma (ed.), *La tavola di Agnone nel contesto italico. Convegno di studio, Agnone 13 - 15 aprile 1994,* Firenze, 27-44.

Torelli, M., 1999: *Tota Italia. Essays in the cultural formation of Roman Italy,* Oxford.

Torelli, M., 2005: s.v. Thesaurus, *ThesCRA* IV, 354-356.

Torelli, M./L. Lachenal (eds), 1992: *Da Leukania a Lucania. La Lucania centro-orientale fra Pirro e i Giulio-Claudii,* Venosa.

Turfa, J.M., 2004: s.v. Anatomical votives, *ThesCRA* I 359-368

Tybout, R.A., 1996: Domestic Shrines and 'Popular Painting'. Style and Social Context [Long review of Fröhlich 1991], *JRA* 9, 358–374.

Untermann, J., 2000: *Wörterbuch des Oskisch-Umbrischen,* Heidelberg (Handbuch der italischen Dialekte 3).

Uytterhoeven, I., 1998-99: The forum of Aesernia. A development sketch, *AncSoc* 29, 241-266.

Valente, F., 1982: *Origine e crescita di una città,* Campobasso.

Valenza Mele, N., 1996: Una nuova tomba dipinta a Cuma e la "legio linteata", in *L'incidenza dell'antico. Studi in memoria di Ettore Lepore,* Napoli, 325-360.

Vallet, G., 1968: La cité et son territoire dans les colonies grecques d'Occident, in *La città e il suo territorio. Atti del Settimo convegno di studi sulla Magna Grecia, Taranto 8-12 ottobre 1967,* Napoli (Convegno di studi sulla Magna Grecia 7), 67-141.

Van Andringa, W., 2000: Autels de carrefour, organisation vicinale et rapports de voisinage à Pompéi, *RStPomp* 11, 47-86.

Van Andringa, W., 2002: *La religion en Gaule romaine. Piété et politique (Ier-IIIe siècle apr. J.-C.),* Paris (Collection des Hespérides).

Van Dommelen, P., 1998: *On colonial grounds. A comparative study of colonialism and rural settlement in first millennium B.C. West Central Sardinia,* Leiden (Archeological studies Leiden University 2).

Van Dommelen, P., 2001: Cultural imaginings. Punic tradition and local identity in Roman Republican Sardinia, in S.J. Keay/N. Terrenato (eds), *Italy and the west. Comparative issues in Romanization,* Oxford, 68-84.

Van Dommelen, P./N. Terrenato (eds), 2007: *Articulating local cultures. Power and identity under the expanding Roman Republic,* Portsmouth (JRA Supplementary series 63).

Van Leusen, P.M., 2002: *Pattern to process. Methodological investigations into the formation and interpretation of large-scale patterns in archaeological landscapes,* PhD thesis, University of Groningen, Groningen.

Van Wonterghem, F., 1984: *Superaequum, Corfinium, Sulmo,* Firenze (Forma Italiae Regio IV, 1).

Van Wonterghem, F., 1999: Il culto di Ercole e la pastorizia nell'Italia centrale, in E. Petrocelli (ed.), *La civiltà della transumanza. Storia, cultura e valorizzazione dei tratturi e del mondo pastorale in Abruzzo, Molise, Puglia, Campania e Basilicata,* Isernia, 413-428.

Veronese, F., 2000: Poleis, santuari e 'paesaggi di potere' nella Sicilia greca di età arcaica, in G. Camassa/A. De Guio/F. Veronese (eds), *Paesaggi di potere. Problemi e prospettive. Atti del Seminario, Udine 16-17 maggio 1996,* Roma (Quaderni di Eutopia 2), 239-283.

Vetter, E., 1953: *Handbuch der italischen Dialekte,* Heidelberg.

Veyne, P., 1957: La table des Ligures Baebiani et l'institution alimentaire de Trajan, *MEFRA* 69, 81-135.

Virlouvet, C., 1995: *Tessera frumentaria. Les procédures de la distribution du blé public à Rome,* Rome (BEFAR 286).

Volpe, G., 1996: *Contadini, pastori e mercanti nell'Apulia tardoantica,* Bari (Munera 6).

Vomano, 1986: *La valle del medio e basso Vomano, II,* Roma (Documenti dell'Abruzzo teramano 2).

Vomano, 1991: *La valle dell'alto Vomano ed i Monti della Laga,* Pescara (Documenti dell'Abruzzo teramano 3).

Von Blanckenhagen, P.H./C. Alexander, 1990: *The Augustan villa at Boscotrecase,* Mainz (Sonderschriften. Deutsches Archäologisches Institut Rom 8).

Von Schaewen, R., 1940: *Römische Opfergeräte, ihre Verwendung im Kultus und in der Kunst,* Berlin.

Walbank, F.W., 1972: Nationality as a factor in Roman history, *HarvStClPhil* 76, 145-168.

Wallace-Hadrill, A., 2008: *Rome's cultural revolution,* Cambridge.

Walsh, P.G., 1996: Making a drama out of a crisis. Livy on the Bacchanalia, *GaR* 43, 188-203.

Ward-Perkins, J., 1961: *Veii. The historical topography of the ancient city,* London.

Warmington, E.H., 1938: *Remains of old Latin 3,* London (LCL 329).

Webster, J., 1995: Interpretatio. Roman word power and the Celtic gods, *Britannia* 26, 153-161.

Webster, J., 1996-97: Necessary comparisons. A post-colonial approach to religious syncretism in the Roman provinces, *WorldA* 28, 324-338.

Webster, J., 2001: Creolizing the Roman provinces, *AJA* 105, 209-225.

Weinstock, S., 1955: s. v. Valetudo, *RE* VIII, 264-270.

Whittaker, C.R., (ed.) 1988: *Pastoral economies in classical antiquity,* Cambridge (Cambridge philological society. Supplementary volumes 14).

Whittaker, C.R., 1997: Imperialism and culture. The Roman initiative, in D. J. Mattingly (ed.), *Dialogues in Roman imperialism. Power, discourse, and discrepant experience in the Roman empire,* Portsmouth (JRA Supplementary series 23), 143-163.

William Rasmussen, S., 2003: *Public portents in republican Rome,* Rome (Analecta Romana Instituti Danici. Supplementum).

Williams, J.H.C., 2001: Roman intentions and Romanization. Republican northern Italy, c. 200 - 100 BC., in S. J. Keay/N. Terrenato (eds), *Italy and the West. Comparative issues in Romanization,* Oxford, 91-101.

Wissowa, G., 1897: s.v. Lares, *Roscher, ML* II², 1868-1897.

Wissowa, G., 1901a: s.v. Compitalia, *RE* IV, 791-792.

Wissowa, G., 1901b: s.v. Compitum, *RE* IV, 792-794.

Wissowa, G., 1902: *Religion und Kultus der Römer,* München (Handbuch der klassischen Altertums-Wissenschaft 5, 4).

Wissowa, G., 1912: *Religion und Kultus der Römer,* 2, München (Handbuch der klassischen Altertums-Wissenschaft 5, 4).

Woolf, G., 1996-97: Beyond Romans and natives, *WorldA* 28, 339-350.

Woolf, G., 1997: Polis-religion and its alternatives in the Roman provinces, in H. Cancik/J. Rüpke (eds), *Römische Reichsreligion und Provinzialreligion,* Tübingen, 71-84.

Yntema, D.G., 2006: The birth of a Roman southern Italy. A case study. Ancient written sources and archaeological evidence on the early Roman phase in the Salento district, southern Italy (3rd - 1st century B.C.), *BABESCH* 81, 91-133.

Yntema, D.G., 2009: Material culture and plural identity in early Roman southern Italy, in T. Derks/N. Roymans (eds), *Ethnic constructs in antiquity. The role of power and tradition,* Amsterdam (Amsterdam archaeological studies 13), 145-166.

Zaccardi, A., 2007: Il santuario di S. Giovanni in Galdo. Nuove proposte interpretative e ipotesi ricostruttive, *Conoscenze* 2, 63-96.

Zanker, P., (ed.) 1976: *Hellenismus in Mittelitalien. Kolloquium in Göttingen vom 5. bis 9. Juni 1974,* Göttingen.

Zetzel, J.E.G., 2005: *Marginal scholarship and textual deviance. The Commentum Cornuti and the early scholia on Persius,* London (Bulletin of the Institute of Classical Studies supplement 84).

Zevi, F., 1995: I santuari federali del Lazio. Qualche appunto, *Eutopia* 4, 123-142.

Zifferero, A., 1995: Economia, divinità e frontiera. Sul ruolo di alcuni santuari di confine in etruria meridionale, *Ostraka* 4, 333-350.

Zifferero, A., 1998: I santuari come indicatori di frontiera nell'Italia tirrenica preromana, in M. Pearce/M. Tosi (eds), *Papers from the EAA Third Annual Meeting at Ravenna 1997, 1. Pre- and protohistory,* Oxford (BAR Int. Ser. 717), 223-232.

Zifferero, A., 2002: The Geography of the Ritual Landscape in Complex Societies, in P. Attema/G. J. Burgers/E. van Joolen (eds), *New developments in Italian landscape archaeology. Theory and methodology of field survey, land evaluation and landscape perception. Pottery production and distribution. Proceedings of a three-day conference held at the University of Groningen, April 13-15, 2000,* Oxford (BAR Int. Ser. 1091), 246-265.

Ziolkowski, A., 1992: *The temples of Mid-Republican Rome and their historical and topographical context,* Rome (Saggi di storia antica 4).

Zuffa, M., 1962: Nuove scoperte di archeologia e storia riminese, *StRomagn* 13, 85-132.

Index

The following index lists places, peoples, deities, individuals and major subjects and themes in the text. Rural cult places are listed by the localities and municipalities with which they are usually indicated, in case of ambiguity both are listed separately. Names occurring in inscriptions but not further discussed are not included. Individuals are listed by *nomen*, though major authors are cited by their common English name. Ancient authors are listed only for passages where they or their work are discussed at some length.

A

Abella 57, 65, 183
Abruzzi 55
Abruzzo 32, 35, 56, 60, 61, 62, 64, 71, 81, 154
acculturation 9, 12
Aeneas 29, 50, 144
Aequi 60, 164, 170
Aequicoli 71, 72, 128
Aesculapius 24, 27, 30, 183
Aesernia, Isernia 40, 42, 49, 53, 147
ager Calenus 136
  - see also Cales
ager Praetutianus 22, 124, 135, 145-154
  - see also Praetutii
ager Romanus 19, 21, 112, 165, 167, 214
ager Teuranus 19, 20
  - see also Tiriolo
agora des compétaliastes 196, 205
  - see also Delos
agriculture (importance for Italic society) 37
  - supposed agricultural roots of *Compitalia* 188, 200-203, 212
  - supposed agricultural roots of *Paganalia* 171-177, 184, 219
  - see also economy
alae 41, 49, 132
  - see also *Capitolium*
Alba Fucens 33, 55, 57, 71, 130, 134, 135, 154, 156, 161-166, 169, 170
Alfedena (Curino) 38
allies 3, 11, 12, 13, 19, 20, 47, 50, 109, 214

  - Roman religious influence on 5, 18-34, 214-215, 220-221
  - see also citizenship, Social War
Amaredius, C. 71
Ambarvalia 200
Amelia 183
Amiternum 75, 183
Amplero 38
anachronism
  - in views on ancient colonisation 15, 25, 26, 133-137
  - in views on ancient religion 18, 222
  - see also romanisation, teleological approaches towards
Anagnia 181, 183
Anaiedio(s) *see* Annaedius
anatomical exvotos (Etrusco-Latial-Campanian votives) 23-25, 27, 28, 34, 129, 157, 214
Angitia 32, 159
Aninus vecus see vicus Aninus
Annaedius 158, 162
antefixes 130
Antinum 159, 160, 161, 165, 166
Antiochia 133
Antium 201
Antrosano 71
Aphrodite Nikèphoros 46
Apicius, (C)apicius 82
Apollo 130, 140, 141, 145, 146, 151, 158, 162 , 165, 167, 182, 183
Apulia 55
Aquileia 126, 210
Aquilonia 1, 40, 51, 215

architecture (architectural models)
  - as indicative of 'cultural influence' 25-28, 48-51, 129-133, 214, 215, 218
  - as indicative of traditionalism 51, 52, 215
  - see also 'style', *Capitolium*
Argive Heraion 59
Argos 59
Ari 63
Ariminum 22, 23, 112, 117, 124, 126, 128, 133-135, 138-145, 156, 169, 170, 218, 220, 221
Arpinum 183
Asia Minor 26
Asisium, Assisi 126, 132
'Atelier des Petites Estampilles' 138
Atessa 43, 63
Athens 167, 196
Atina 211
Aufellius Rufus, L. 137
Aufenginum 70, 72
auguraculum 22
Augusta Bagiennorum 111
Augustan art and poetry (representation in) 2, 37, 171-173, 177, 184, 185, 213, 219, 221
Augustus (Octavian) 26, 30, 32, 33, 108, 112, 146, 189, 190, 199, 201, 202, 204, 205, 219
Aurunci 46
autoromanizzazione 12, 131
  - see also self-romanisation
Aveia 118
Avezzano 165

257

B
Bacchanalia, Bacchanal 19-21, 28, 33, 214
Bacchus 19
Bantia 13
Barisciano 73
Basciano 148, 149, 150, 153, 169
Basento 60
Bastita 128
belief (limits of personal expressions of) 222
bellum civile 12
bellum sociale see Social War
Beneventum 110, 111, 179, 182, 183, 210
Bergomum 126
Biferno Valley Project 36, 80, 81, 104-106, 217
bilingualism (as a model) 14
black gloss ceramics 22, 23, 31, 86, 88, 90, 91, 97-100, 104, 105, 134, 136, 137, 138, 142, 145, 148, 149, 151, 155, 157, 169, 218
Boiano 56
- *see also* Bovianum
Bona Dea 127
Bonaventura Natale 125
Bovegno 126
Bovianum 28, 29, 38, 76, 161
- *see also* Boiano
Bovillae 128
Bradano 60
Brescia 126, 177
Brettii 10, 20
Britain, romanisation of 12
Bruttium 19
Bucchianico 63
bull (Samnite bull) 47, 50, 215, 220
Buxentum 21

C
Caere 60
Caesar 26, 120, 148, 199, 206
Caisius 156
Calatia 110, 125
Cales 99, 117, 128, 133, 134-137, 142
Caligula 183
Calpurnius 208
Campani 10, 110
Campochiaro 28, 29, 43, 47, 55, 56, 70, 71, 75, 98, 104, 211
Campovalano 148, 152
Canoleios, L. 136
Capena 31, 65
Capitolium, Capitolia 5, 22-28, 34, 35, 40, 49, 130-132, 214, 221
Capracotta 39, 98, 102
Capua 1, 4, 26, 29, 35, 109, 110, 112, 125, 126, 132, 144, 164
Capys 1, 29
Carbula 116
Carpineto della Nora 125, 132, 180, 181, 183
Carricini 36, 60, 63
Carseoli 24, 170
Carthage 26, 30, 32
Carvilius Maximus, Sp. 1
Casalbore 27, 49
Case Carnevale 151
Case Lanciotti-Masseria Nisii 147, 152
Castel di Ieri 124, 129-133, 169, 218
- loc. Madonna del Soccorso 129, 132
- loc. Cese Piane 132
Castelluccio 128, 154, 155
Castelvecchio Calvisio 125
Castelvecchio Subequo 32, 126, 179
Castiglione Messer Raimondo 151
Castropignano 211
Castrum Novum 146, 153
Cato 109, 175, 189, 195, 197
- *see also* villa
Caudine Forks 30
Ceisius *see* Caisius
Cellere 126
Cellino Attanasio 151
Cellino Vecchio 151, 153, 161
census 108-110, 112, 176, 177, 189, 194
centre-periphery model 11
★centuriator 160 166
centurio 159 160
Cercemaggiore 39
Cerealia 200
Ceres 127
Cermignano 146
Cese 165
cetur 159, 160, 161, 166
chora 60, 61, 177
- *see also* colonisation, Greek
Cicero 25, 187, 188, 191, 203
Cirmo 155
citizenship 3, 12, 18, 19, 146
- and religion 18, 19
- as primary goal of the *socii* in the Social War 3, 11, 12
civilising mission 9, 13
- *see also* colonialism, nationalism, romanisation
civitas 67, 70, 77, 128
civitas sine suffragio 110, 118, 126, 146, 168
Claudius Himerius, Tib. 148
clientela model 11
- *see also* romanisation
Clitumnus 33
Clodius Pulcher, P. 201, 206
Clunia 119

Cluvia Pacula 164
coarse ware ceramics 90, 91, 102, 103
coinage 66, 117, 163, 176, 178, 180, 183, 192, 194
- coins deposited in cult places 43, 80, 82, 130, *see also thesauri*
- ideological messages on 47, 50, 215, 220
Colledara 151
Collelongo 38, 156, 161
Colle Mariano 157, 158, 162
Collepietro 183
Colle Rimontato 6, 43, 51, 79-83, 92, 105, 211
- *see also* S. Giovanni in Galdo
Colle S. Giorgio 151
Colle S. Martino 157
Colle Sparanise 47, 106
Colle del Vento 147
Collina di S. Berardino 148
colonialism 9, 14
- *see also* postcolonialism
colonisation Roman/Latin:
- religious aspects of 21-28, *see also* anatomical votives, *Capitolium, pocola deorum*
- relative urbanity of 26, 133-135
- relation to *vici* and *pagi* 7, 133-145, 152-154, 165, 169, 218, 221, *see also* Alba Fucens, Ariminum, *vici, pagi*
- indigenous peoples and colonists, difficulties in distinguishing 162, 170
Greek:
- relation to extra-urban sanctuaries 58-60
- *see also* Magna Graecia
Cominium Tuticum 46, 48
Cominius 161
comitium-curia complex 48-50, 215
community, symbolic construction of
- importance of religion for 14, 47, 52, 144, 179
- specific rituals related to: *see* Ariminum, *Compitalia, Paganalia, pocola deorum, lustratio*
Compitalia 7, 171, 175, 176, 177, 187-212, 219, 221
compitum 178, 187, 188, 189, 190, 191, 194, 195, 197, 198, 201, 203-210, 212, 219
compitum Acilium 205-207
conciliabulum 19, 20, 117
congeries armorum 39
Consentes, Dei *see* Dei Consentes
continuity of cult places
- attested after the Social War 28, 29, 31-33, 74-76
- possibly hiding different phenomena 211, 219, 221
Contrada S. Rustico 148, 153, 169
conventus 168
Corduba 119
Corfinium 50, 57
Corinth 133
Corpus agrimensorum romanorum 207

Cortino 148
Corvaro 24
Cosa 23, 130, 153
Covignano 142
Crecchio 63
creolisation 14
crisis, of the Italic peoples (as a prerogative for romanisation) 10, 17
Croton 29
cult statues, deportation of 30, 31
cultural bricolage 14
cultural identity 25
- *see also* ethnicity, community
cultural unification 9-16, 37, 220
Cuma 162
Cupa (Gildone) 81-83
Cupra maritima 32
Cupra montana 112, 126, 142
Curino 38
Curius Dentatus, M'. 31, 146

D
Daeira 139, 145
Dei Consentes 163
Delos 44, 45, 48, 190, 193, 195, 196, 197, 201, 202, 204, 205, 212, 219
deversoria 191
Diana 134, 138, 140
- Tifatina 1, 29, 33, 35
- Aventine 22, 134
- Nemi 145
Didyma 59
Dionysius of Halicarnassus
- reliability of 109, 199
- on the *Paganalia* 175-178, 184
- on the *Compitalia* 191-194, 199
Divus Julius 148
Dolabella 178, 207-209
dolls, hanging of 190, 192-194, 198
- *see also compitum, Compitalia*
duumvir
155, 161, 166
- *see also* magisterial titles, institutional structure of Italic peoples

E
economy
- of Samnium 37
- economic functions of sanctuaries 33, 55-58, 65, *see also lex aedis Furfensis*
- profits from Roman empire 44-45
- *see also* market functions of cult places, *negotiatores*
effigies 190, 192
- *see also pilae*
Emilia Romagna 128
emulation 10, 13, 49, 51, 214, 220
- *see also* self-romanisation, *autoromanizzazione*
Erotes 136
ethnicity, construction of 41, 46-48, 215

- ethnic boundaries marked by cult places 62-65, 77, 216
Etruria 24, 54, 58, 60, 64, 65, 69, 123, 138
European Union 36
evocatio 30-32

F
Fabius Pictor 109
Faesulae 26
Fagnano Alto 70
Falerii 30, 31
fanum Fortunae 32
fanum Voltumnae 28, 30, 32, 46, 70
farms
- in survey area 91, 94, 95, 105, 216, 217
- as part of Italic settlement pattern 6, 38, 39, 66, 68, 77, 217
- as part of colonial settlement pattern 135
- *see also* villa
Fasti Antiates maiores 164
federal state organisation of Samnite society *see* state organisation of Samnite society
Ferentillo 181, 183
feriae conceptivae, feriae stativae 174, 175, 188, 200, 201
feriae Latinae 175
Feronia
- Civita di Bagno 61 -*see also lucus Feroniae*
festivals
- importance of for communities 14, 170
- *see also Compitalia, Paganalia* and generally under festival names
Festus 18, 113-117, 190, 192, 193
Fiamignano 71
Fides
127, 140, 144, 170, 218
- temple on the Capitol 144
field survey
- indispensability of 63
- as methodology 80-84
foideratei, foederati 20, 21
Fontecchio 70, 72, 125, 149
Fordicidia 200
Fortuna
142, 144, 182, 193, 205
forum
- colonial evidence for 25
- sanctuaries taking over function of 69
- *pecuarium* 55, 57
France 125
Frascati 128
Fregellae 50, 134, 183
Frentani 35, 36, 60, 63
Fucinus, see lacus Fucinus
- deity 158, 161, 162

Fulvius Flaccus, Q. 1, 29
Fumane 126
Furci 63
Furfo 70, 73, 120, 128, 157
- *see also lex aedis Furfensis*

G
Gabii 48, 49
Gabinii 136
Gagliano Aterno 125
Gallienus, arch of 125
Garigliano 46
Gaul 119
Gauls 30
Gellius, Aulus 22, 23, 201
genius 127, 193, 202
gens competition 1, 45
Germania 114
Gildone, loc. Cupa 81-83
GPS (Global Positioning System), used in survey 84
graves
- found in survey area 91, 105, 106
- relation to cult places 62, 63
- *see also* necropoleis
Greek colonisation *see* colonisation, *see also* Magna Graecia
group formation, group identity *see* community, ethnicity
Gubbio 64
Gudianus Latinus 207, 209

H
Hannibal 29, 40
Hatria 135, 146, 148, 151, 153, 169, 181, 182, 183
hellenisation 15, 16, 25, 27, 52, 184
- as a substitute for direct Roman influence 15, 16, 25
Helvetii 120
Heraklesschalen 23
Hera Lacinia 29
Hercules 23, 32, 55-57, 65, 71, 73, 76, 127, 130, 132, 138, 140, 141, 147, 148, 150, 157, 158, 216
- Curinus 32, 56, 71, 75, 76, 181-183
- Jovius (?) 157, 162
- Salarius 55
- Victor 127
Herennii Supinates 162
hierarchy
- between *pagus* and *vicus* 7, 67, 74, 107, 111, 120, 217
- in sanctuaries 70, 74, 77, 107, 123, 168, 216, 218
hill-forts 35, 38, 39, 53, 66, 67, 69, 80, 121
- *see also oppidum*
Hirpini 46
Hispellum 32
Histonium 63
historiography 1, 3, 30, 188, 221

259

Horace 171-173
hospitium 191
hybridisation 14
Hygieia 167

I
idealism 9-12, 15, 16, 214
Iguvine Tablets 64, 160
impasto ceramics 89, 105, 157
imperialism, Roman (ideas on) 9-16
Indo-European theory 17
inscriptions, indispensability of in determining institutional status 13, 121, 218
institutional structure of Italic peoples 38, 46-48, 65-74, 107-121, 159-168
- see also *touto*, *pagus-vicus* system, *quaestor*, magisterial titles
Interamna Praetutiorum 146, 151-153, 157, 169
interpretatio 119, 127, 164
interpretive archaeology 4, 9
- see also postprocessual archaeology
Inzin 126
Isaura Vetus 30
isolation of sanctuaries 79-104, 216, 217
Iuvanum 63
iuventutes 72
Italia 19, 47
Italica 50
Iulium Carnicum 128

J
Junius Bubulcus, C. 1, 164
Juno
- Caelestis 30
- Curitis 30
- Gaura 127
- Lucina 134, 136, 176, 194
- Moneta 134
- Regina 2, 30, 31, 127
- Sospita 33
Jupiter
- Compagus 110, 127, 132
- Curinus 131, 132
- Latiaris 175
- Liber 71, 73
- Optimus Maximus 119, 127, 148
- Paganicus 126, 127, 132
- Quirinus 70, 72, 76
- Stator 71
- Trebulanus 71, 74
- Victor *decem pagorum* 73, 75, 76, 127, 132, 181, 184
Juventas 176, 194

K
komedon 66, 110, 111
- see also *vicatim*, *pagatim*
kompetaliastai 196, 198
- see also *Compitalia*, Delos
Kos 45, 48

L
lacus Fucinus, Fucine lake 116, 117, 124, 128, 154, 155, 156, 158, 162, 164-170, 218, 220
La Mária 157
lamps (found in S. Giovanni in Galdo) 103, 104
- change in ritual 211
language
- use of Latin 12, 13, 138, 167, 182
- Italic languages and dialects 116, 127, 166, 183
Lanuvium 33
Lara 202
Laralia 198
Lares
- Compitales 144, 187, 188, 190, 196, 197, 200, 202, 204, 219
- Familiares 196, 197
- Viales 194, 197, 200
- Vicinales 206
Larinum 57, 79
Latial influences 6, 48-51, 156, 161, 213
Latinus 50, 113, 114
Latium 24, 45, 48, 50, 58, 98, 109, 156, 161
Laverna 217
Lavinium 33
Lecce dei Marsi 128, 154, 155
legio linteata 1, 40, 51
levy 161, 176, 177, 192
lex aedis Furfensis 71-73, 128
lex Osca Bantina 13
lex Ursonensis 26
libation 138, 142
Liber 71, 73, 201
Libitina 176, 194
Liguria 111, 189
Lindos 45
Liternum 26
Livy (on Samnites) 1, 36, 37, 40, 51, 66, 111
- the role of religion in 30
Locri 29
locus consaeptus 1, 40, 51, 215
longue durée 6, 82, 119
Lucani 46
Lucania 38, 69, 81, 123, 173, 211
Luceria 22, 24, 57
Luco dei Marsi 156, 157, 159
lucus Angitiae 32, 33, 165
lucus Feroniae 29, 31-33, 65
ludi Compitalicii 188, 189, 194, 199
ludi Saeculares 201
Luna 26, 130, 131, 181, 183
Lupercalia 201
lustratio 144, 145, 174, 188, 200
- *pagi* 125, 133, 144, 145, 171, 173-175, 177-180, 184, 210, 219
luxuria 37

M
Madonna della Cona 146
Maecenas 125
Magios 161
magisterial titles 159-167
- see also *duumvir*, *cetur*, *quaestor*, *magistri pagi/vici*
magistri pagi 110, 113-115, 129, 178-180
magistri vici 72, 113, 115, 128, 144, 150, 151, 153, 157, 189, 190, 194, 197, 199, 206
Magna Graecia 54, 59, 63, 65, 69, 123
Marica 46
market function of cult places 33, 55-58, 65, 68, 76
- see also economy
marriage 193
Marrucini 27
Marruvium 156, 162
Mars 125, 127
Marsi 60, 71, 74, 112-118, 124, 128, 154, 155, 159, 162, 164-167, 170, 220
material culture (problems of interpretation) 13, 14, 25-28, 39-52, 213-215, 220
Matrice 39, 95, 105
meddix 45, 66, 159, 160, 161
Mefitis 46, 55, 127, 211
Messina 160
Metapontum 59-61
métissage 14
migration 15, 145, 153, 200
Miletus 59
mimic (copying of Roman toponyms) 133-135, 137
Minerva 30, 127, 130, 132, 142, 182
- Capta 30
Minturnae 26, 125, 127
mola salsa 143
Molise 6, 13, 35, 36, 79, 80, 82, 97, 147, 216
moneterisation 184, see also coinage
Mons Albanus 175
Mons Tifata 29, 33
Monte Cavo 33
Monte Giove 32, 146
Monte Morrone 56
Monte Pallano 38
Monte Saraceno 53
Monte Vairano 38, 98
Montorio al Vomano 126, 128, 147
monumentalisation 2, 44-52, 76, 77, 79, 106, 215, 216, 217
mosaic 44, 129, 131, 147
municipalisation 5, 18, 32, 56, 68, 74-77, 112, 131, 132, 183
municipalia sacra 18

N
Narbo 22
Narsae 128

nationalism 3, 12
Navelli 129
necropoleis 60-62, 69
   - in survey area 6, 82
   - relation to cult places 63
   - *see also* graves
negotiation, as a model 16
   - *see also* romanisation
negotiatores 44, 45
Nensinus 128
Nepet 126
New Archaeology 9
   - *see also* processual archaeology
Nike 163
   - *see also* Victoria
Nola 65
nomen 20, 41, 46, 67, 70, 74, 123, 160, 216
   - *see also touto, populus*
Norba 134
Norbanus 33
Novensides 168
Numa 60, 109, 144, 175, 178
Nursia 24
Nymphae 127

O
oath
   - between allies in the Social War 50
   - Samnite oath at Aquilonia 1, 50, 81, 213, 215
Ofillius Rufus, L. 147
Omphalosschale 136
oppidum 22, 26, 38, 67, 69, 70, 107, 113, 120, 123, 135, 137, 160
   - *see also* hill-forts
Orsogna 63
Ostia 128, 198, 201, 204, 206-208, 212
   - Piazza dei Lari 206, 207
   - Bivio del Castrum 206
Otranto 139
Ovid 173-175

P
Pacius 162
Paccius, Ovius 1
Paeligni 60, 63, 112-114, 117, 118, 165, 183
Paestum 24
Paganalia 7, 109, 133, 145, 170, 171-185, 187, 192, 194, 201, 219, 221
Paganica 73, 162, 180
Paganicae 174, 175, 177
pagatim 110, 111
   - *see also vicatim, komedon*
Pagliaroli 148
pagus
   - Roman character of 111, 112
   - *Apollinaris* 111
   - *Augustus* 115
   - *Bagiennus* 111
   - *Boedinus* 132

   - '*Caelemontanus*' 178
   - *Carbulensis* 116
   - *Cerealis* 111
   - *Dianius* 111
   - *Domitius* 111
   - *Eboreus* 111
   - Frentanus 73
   - *Herculaneus* 110, 125, 127
   - *Ianicolensis* 125
   - *Iulius* 111
   - *Iunonius* 111
   - *Luras* 111
   - *Marmorarius* 116
   - *Martius* 111
   - *Meflanus* 111
   - *Mercurialis* 111
   - *Moninas* 111
   - *Montanus* 178
   - *rivi Larensis* 116
   - *Suburbanus* 115
   - *Tolentinensis* 180
   - *Valerius* 111
   - *Vecellanus* 132
   - *Venerius* 111
   - *Vescinus* 125, 127
pagus-vicus system
   - the model 65-68
   - related to cult places 68-77
   - deconstruction 107-121
   - *see also* institutional structure of Italic peoples
Palatinus Latinus 1564 207
Palombaro 63
Papirius Cursor, T. 1
Passarano 157
pastoralism, *see also* transhumance 37, 55, 114
patera
   - *pagus* inscription 126
   - role in sacrifices 142-145
   - attribute of *Lares Compitales* 144, 211
Pausulae 182
PDA (Personal Digital Assistant), used in survey 84
Pedergnaga 126, 177
Peltuinum 70
Pentri, Pentrian Samnium 1, 6, 25, 35-52, 60, 63, 70, 74, 76, 79, 161, 215
perceptions of Italic peoples 37, 58
Persius (and scholion on) 188, 201, 206-208, 210, 212, 219
personal experience 222
Pescara 72
Pescosansonesco 125, 183
Pettino 183
Philargyrius 209, 210
Piano Vomano 147
Picenum (Picene area) 22, 32, 48, 126, 146, 154, 180, 182, 183, 210, 212, 219

Pietrabbondante
   - sanctuary 1, 6, 25, 28, 29, 32, 39, 40-53, 65, 69, 70, 71, 79-82, 215-217, 220
   - loc. Troccola 53
Pietracupa 211
pilae 190, 192
   - *see also effigies*
Pisaurum 24, 144, 168, 182
Plestia 24
Po basin 60
pocola deorum 22, 126, 128, 138-145, 163
podium 22, 40-44, 48, 49, 70, 82, 96, 129, 149, 151, 157, 205, 206, 210
Polaritti 158
polis 58, 59, 64, 65
   - *see also* colonisation, Magna Graecia
polygonal walls 38, 42, 129, 147
pomerium 22, 26, 60
Pompadeius Silo, Q. 50
Pompeii 20, 26, 48, 55, 192, 193, 194, 197, 198, 199, 201, 202, 204, 205, 211, 212
   - S. Abbondio 20, *see also Bacchanalia*
Pompey 191, 201
populus 46, 66, 67, 70, 123
   - *see also touto, nomen*
portico 42, 43, 51, 96, 97
postcolonialism 3, 5, 13, 15, 34, 48, 214, 220, 221
postprocessual archeology 9, 16, 54
   - *see also* interpretive archaeology
Postumius Albinus, Sp. 30
Postumius Megellus, L. 163
praefectura 20, 33, 40, 146, 153, 169, 183
Praeneste 30, 182, 183
Praetutii 60, 146, 151, 152
praetor 20, 188, 191, 199, 201, 212
Pretaritta 158
Prezza 74, 126
processions 14, 59, 64, 79, 144
   - *see also* festivals
processual archaeology 9, 14
Proserpina 29
public-private, character of *Compitalia* 190-199
Puteoli 133

Q
Quadri 43, 71, 74
quaestor, '*queistores*' 117, 118, 155, 158-166
   - *see also vicus Supinum*, institutional structure of Italic peoples
Quirinus 1, 70, 72, 76
   - *see also* Jupiter Quirinus

R
Rapino 63, 70
religious intervention 18-21, 28-31

religious toleration 17-19
- limits of 222
resistance 1, 6, 13, 14, 28, 35, 36, 47, 48, 52, 167, 213-215
- *see also* romanisation
respublica
- the *pagus-vicus* system as persisting under Roman rule 68
- the autonomy of *vici* 115
Rhome 144
Rhomos 29
rhyton 144, 211
ritu romano 195, 196
Robigalia 200
Rocca d'Oratino 38
Roccagloriosa 38
Rodiano-Campitello 147
romanisation
- in a historical perspective 3, 4, 9-16
- diversity in response 4, 13, 14
- local approach to 4, 13-16, 214
- teleological approaches towards 10, 11, 213, 214
- provoking resistance 13
- of the countryside 32-34, 220
- local differentiation 220
- *see also* self-romanisation
Romanitas 12, 13, 34
Roman material culture 9, 13, 14, 214
- *see also* material culture
Romanness 13, 16, 22, 25, 27, 40, 46, 119, 133, 134, 145, 219, 221
- *see also Romanitas*
Romanocentrism 3, 11, 12, 16, 36, 159
Roman strategies, undervaluation of 3, 5, 14, 15, 214, 220
Rome
- as the cultural and political centre of Italy 9-16
- romanisation of rome 15, 16, 164, 167
Topography:
- *Atrium Vestae* 205
- Aventine 22, 134, 178
- *campus Martius* 64
- Capitol 137, 144
- *clivus Palatinus* 205
- Palatine 144, 163, 205
- Quirinal 1, 128, 164
- *Sacra via* 190, 206
- Via dei Fori Imperiali 205
- Via di S. Martino ai Monti 205
Roseto 147
Rossano di Vaglio 46, 69
rural (definition) 79
- *see also* urban-rural dichotomy, urbanity
rusticity 2, 171-173, 177, 184, 185, 188, 189, 200, 201, 213, 219
- *see also* Augustan art and poetry

S
Sabelli 11, 37, 75
Sabines 37, 47, 65, 146
sacrifice 1, 29, 47, 53, 65, 68, 143, 172, 175, 176, 178, 184, 188, 190, 191, 195-197, 200, 207
sacro-idyllic landscapes 172, 185
- *see also* rusticity, Augustan art and poetry
Saepinum (Terravecchia) 38, 57, 76
safinim 40, 41, 46, 53, 215
Sagittario 56
Salona 22
Salus 1, 164, 167
Samnites 1, 6, 10, 11, 13, 16, 22, 25, 28, 29, 35-42, 44-56, 58, 62, 66-71, 74, 75, 79, 81, 86, 104, 106, 111, 163, 164, 211, 215-217, 220, 221
- *see also* Carricini, Pentri, Frentani, Samnium etc.
'Samnite league' 46, 69
- *see also touto*
Samnite Wars 35-37, 39, 40, 42, 163, 164
Samnium 4, 6, 25, 32, 35-39, 42, 45, 50, 52, 54, 67, 74, 75, 79, 80, 120, 211, 215, 217, 221
S. Agata in Campo Macrano 32
S. Angelo in Cacumine 71, 72
S. Benedetto 156, 161, 162
S. Buono 63
S. Giovanni in Galdo 6, 29, 39, 42-45, 51, 52, 55, 70, 71, 79-82, 84-90, 98, 104-107, 149, 211, 215, 216
S. Gregorio 126
S. Lorenzo in Strada 142
S. Maria degli Angeli 124
S. Maria dell'Orto 125
S. Maria in Pantano 128
S. Maria a Vico 148
S. Martino di Picenze 73
S. Pietro in Cantoni 43, 183
S. Rustico 148-151, 153, 169
Sant'Omero 148
Sarno 48
Sarsina 142, 144
Saturnalia 188, 190, 191
Scafa 72
Schiavi d'Abruzzo 27, 29, 43, 57, 70, 71, 149
Secinaro 74, 126, 179
Segni 130, 138
self-romanisation 5, 10-16, 19, 52, 118, 131, 159, 166, 214, 220
- *see also* emulation, *autoromanizzazione*, romanisation
Sementivae 173-175, 200, 201
senatusconsultum de Bacchanalibus, see Bacchanalia
Septimius 156, 161
Septimontium 174, 177, 178

Serponios, K. 134, 163
Servius Tullius 109, 175, 176, 189, 191, 194
Setmius *see* Septimius
Siculus Flaccus 179
signinum, opus 44
Sinuessa 117
Sipontum 21
Social War 3, 5, 11-13, 18, 19, 28, 29, 32, 33, 35, 41, 42, 47-50, 52, 56, 67, 68, 76, 77, 104, 106, 110-112, 121, 171, 183, 215, 217, 219
- *see also* citizenship
socii see allies
Sora 182, 183
'*sovradipinta*' 138
- *see also pocola deorum*
Spain 26, 115, 116, 119
spicatum, opus 92
Spineto 154, 157, 158, 162
Spoletium 33
spolia hostium 39
Staatis L. Klar, G. 41
Staii (gens Staia) 40, 44
state organisation of Samnite society 46
- *see also touto, nomen*
state religion 18, 19, 189, 191-194
statuettes 82, 130, 144, 157
- as indicators of cult places 56, 62, 63
- of *Lares Compitales* 211, 219
Strabo 10, 111
'style' (architectural) 25, 35, 48-51
sulcus primigenius 22, 26, 29, 144
Sulla 26, 33, 71, 72, 202
Sulmo 32, 56, 71, 75, 76, 129, 182, 183
Superaequum 32, 76, 124, 125, 129, 130-132, 183
survey methodology *see* field survey

T
Tabula Alimentaria 110
Tabula Peutingeriana 55, 56
Tarquinia 60
Tavana 154, 155
taxation 176, 177, 219
Teanum Apulum 57
Teate 63
telamones 42
Tellus 200
Terminalia 60, 144
terra sigillata 88, 89, 92, 100, 101, 130, 148
Terravecchia 38
territoriality 60, 62, 144, 179
theatres 157
- temple-theatre complex 40, 41, 48, 215
- *see also comitium-curia* complex

thesauri 44, 154, 180-184
- *see also* coinage, monetarisation
Thiessen polygons 62, 63, 151, 153
- problems in use 63, 153
Tiber 202
Tiberius 26, 154
Timpone della Motta 63
Tiriolo 19, 20
Tivoli 48, 55
Tolentinum 126, 180
Tollo 63
Tor de' Cenci 201, 209
Torre di Satriano 210, 211
touto 46, 66, 67, 69, 70, 74, 77, 109, 120, 123, 216, 217
- *see also nomen, populus,* institutional structure of Italic peoples
Touxion 46
- *see also* Cominium
traditionalism 51, 52, 215, 217, 221
Trajan 22, 148
transhumance 6, 37, 45, 55-58, 65, 76, 77, 79, 106, 215, 216
- *see also tratturi*
Trasacco 71, 74, 128, 156-159, 161
- *see also vicus* Supinum
tratturi 55-58, 76, 79, 180, 216
- *see also* transhumance
Trebula Mutuesca 24, 128
tribus
- division of Rome 109, 175-177
- used for establishing territories 153, 165
  - *Collina* 165
  - *Fabia* 165
  - *Maecia* 153
  - *Quirina* 165
  - *Sergia* 165
  - *Velina* 152
Truentum 153
Tufillo 63
tumulus graves 61, 63
- *see also* graves, necropoleis
Tusculum 128

U
Ulubrae 111
Umbria 58
urbanity, *urbanitas* 22, 25, 27, 33, 34, 111, 120, 134, 137, 202
- *see* urban-rural dichotomy
urban-rural dichotomy 7, 34, 120, 121, 214, 218, 220
- *see also* colonisation
Urso 26

V
Vacri 63
Vacuna 164
Val d'Ansanto 46
Valetudo 74, 128, 154, 155, 163-165, 167, 169, 170, 183, 184, 219

Val Policella 126
Val Trompia 126
Valviano 151
Vastogirardi 29, 43, 45, 70, 71
Vaticanus Latinus 3369, codex 113, 114
vecos Supnas see vicus Supinum
Veii 2, 30, 31, 158
Veleia 110, 111
Venafrum 40
Vennonius 109, 175
Venus 138, 140, 147, 172, 176, 183, 193, 211
Veratius Felicissimus, L. 180
Verona 126, 210
Verres, C. 29
ver sacrum 47
Vertumnus 30
Vesce 128
Vespasian 33
Vesta 182
Vestia Oppia 164
Vestini, Vestine area 60, 70, 75, 76, 127-129, 157, 161, 162, 180, 183
Vesuna 127, 140, 159, 164
via Appia 125
- *Caecilia* 147
- *Laurentina* 60
Vibo Valentia 19, 20
vicales Annini 154
vicani 74, 113, 117, 119, 128
Vica Pota 164
vicatim 66, 110, 111, 194, 205
- *see also komedon, pagatim*
Vico-Ornano 151, 153
Victoria
- general 130, 146, 163, 164, 167
- as a Roman ideological model 163-165, 167-170, 219, 221
- near the Fucine Lake 71, 74, 118, 128, 158, 159, 161, 163-165, 167, 170, 219, 221
- temple on the Palatine 163
- in Pietrabbondante 46, 50, 163
- *see also* Víkturraí
vicus
- *Aninus* 74, 128, 154-156, 163, 164, 167, 169, 183, 184
- *Aventinus* 133, 137, 140
- *Esquilinus* 133-136, 140, 142
- *Fistaniensis* 154, 156, 157
- *Forensis* 119
- *Furfensis* 71, 73
- *Germalus* 137, 140
- *Hispanus* 119
- *Iugarius* 205
- *Martis Tudertium* 128
- *Palatius* 134, 135, 136, 137
- *Petinus* 128, 154-156, 158, 161, 166, 169
- *Popilius* 142
- *Salutaris* 128
- *Stramentarius* (or *Stramenticius*) 148, 152, 153
- *Supinum* 46, 71, 74, 128, 154-167, 169, 221
- *Tuscus* 128 - *Velabrus* 133, 137
- *Vestae* 205
Víkturraí 46, 49, 50, 163
- *see also* Victoria
villa
- in relation to *vicus* and *pagus* 113, 114
- found in survey area 92, 95
- 'Catonian' 195, 196, 201
- celebration of *Compitalia* 189, 191, 195, 196, 201-203
village
- part of traditional Italic settlement patterns 6, 38, 39, 66-68, 77, 108, 114, 116, 121, 216, 217
- found in survey area 90, 91, 93-95, 105, 106, 216, 217
- relationship to the institutional category of *vicus* 113, 119
- related to Roman colonisation 117, 137, 169
- *see also vicus*
Vinalia 200
Visentium 126
víteliú 41, 47
- *see also* bull, Samnite
- *see also* Italia
Volcei 111
Volsinii 20, 30
Volterra 158
Vomano 79, 153
votives 5, 23, 24, 27, 31, 34, 39, 54, 60, 97, 129, 144, 148, 149, 157, 158, 162, 183, 214
- *see also* anatomical exvotos
Vulcanus 138, 140, 141, 145

W
war booty 1, 39
warfare
- and sanctuaries 29-33
- *see also* war booty
weapons (found in sanctuaries) 1, 39, 42, 46, 53, 215
wolf (Roman she-wolf) 47, 50, 215, 220
world-system theory 9